John Adams
A LIFE

*

John Ferling

AN OWL BOOK

Henry Holt and Company
New York

Henry Holt and Company, Inc.
Publishers since 1866
115 West 18th Street
New York, New York 10011

Henry Holt® is a registered
trademark of Henry Holt and Company, Inc.

Copyright © 1992 by The University of Tennessee Press
All rights reserved.
Published in Canada by Fitzhenry & Whiteside Ltd.,
195 Allstate Parkway, Markham, Ontario L3R 4T8.

Library of Congress Cataloging-in-Publication Data
Ferling, John E.
John Adams: a life / John Ferling.—
1st Owl Book ed.
p.   cm.
Originally published: Knoxville: University of
Tennessee Press, 1992.
"An Owl book"—T.p. verso.
Includes bibliographical references and index.
1. Adams, John, 1735–1826.   2. Presidents—United
States—Biography.   I. Title.
[E322.F47   1996]   96-11723
973.4'4'092—dc20   CIP
[B]

ISBN: 0-8050-4576-7

Henry Holt books are available for special promotions
and premiums. For details contact: Director, Special Markets.

First published in hardcover in 1992 by
The University of Tennessee Press.

First Owl Book Edition—1996

Printed in the United States of America
All first editions are printed on acid-free paper.∞

1   3   5   7   9   10   8   6   4   2

Frontispiece: John Adams in 1783, aged forty-eight. Oil on
canvas by John Singleton Copley. Courtesy: Harvard University
Portrait Collection. Bequest of Ward Nicholas Boylston, 1828.

Contents

*

PART ONE
Love of Fame

*

PART TWO
An Epocha in History

*

*

*

Preface

I FIRST ENCOUNTERED JOHN ADAMS, I think, when as an undergraduate I was assigned to read a few pages of his diary. I did not find him endearing. He appeared obsessive, neurotic, unhappy, and, worst of all, humorless.

Probably because of the impression I had formed, I rather successfully avoided Adams for the next twenty or so years, until research for a book on America's early wars obliged me to reacquaint myself with him. I had wondered how Adams, who never served in the military, coped emotionally with the French and Indian War, which had erupted when he was in his prime, and with the War of Independence, which as a member of Congress he had helped bring about. This time I found Adams very different. He seemed to be more human—and full of contradictions. Still troubled, he also seemed to be meditative, insightful, and provocative, though at times didactic. He was sometimes churlish, but in private and with friends he could be engagingly witty. He was terribly self-centered, but in his relationship with his wife and children his shortcomings were tempered by a deep, abiding love.

The research on early American warfare also led me to George Washington, who, like Adams, was a terribly complex individual. A biography of Washington followed, but throughout my work on him I knew that someday I would come back to Adams. There were simply too many questions to be answered, questions about his public conduct and his private life.

I confess that at the outset of my work on Washington and Adams I was intrigued with each man but liked neither. My feelings changed as each work progressed. Toward Washington, I felt profound admiration blossom. Toward Adams, I felt esteem and affinity burgeon, although those feelings were tempered by repugnance for the way he often treated his family.

It was my good fortune to come to know both men, especially Adams, the less Olympian of the two, a man of more common attributes who struggled mightily for every achievement and whose integrity and unyielding commitment to principle are often unknown virtues today.

This study could not have been completed without the assistance of many others. Considerable financial support was provided by the Learning Resources Committee of West Georgia College. Albert S. Hanser and James T. Gay generously cooperated by providing teaching schedules that afforded time for research and writing. Dean Richard Dangle of West Georgia College made available funds for a trip to comb through papers whose existence I discovered only at the last minute. Elmira Eidson, who efficiently manages the history department of which I am a member, helped in countless ways.

I am indebted to numerous people who provided kind assistance in the course of my research. Long days and nights away from home were made more pleasant by the amenable aid I received from the librarians and historians in several libraries. I am grateful for the many courtesies extended at the American Antiquarian Society, the Boston Public Library, the Houghton Library of Harvard University, the Library of Congress, the New-York Historical Society, the New York Public Library, the National Archives, and the Pennsylvania Historical Society. I am particularly indebted to Peter Drummey, Virginia Smith, and numerous others at the Massachusetts Historical Society who patiently answered my questions, assisted in my searches, and suggested helpful avenues to pursue.

Several librarians at the Irvine Sullivan Ingram Library of West Georgia College provided invaluable assistance, especially Nancy Farmer and Deborah Novak who cheerfully—I think—responded to what must have seemed my unending requests for materials through interlibrary loan.

Edith B. Gelles, Gregg L. Lint, and James Kirby Martin read the manuscript at various stages and offered many valuable suggestions for improvement.

I am indebted to Cynthia Maude-Gembler and Tana McDonald who believed in this undertaking and helped with its completion. And I am grateful to Lee Campbell Sioles and Jean Tyrone, without whose assistance a very different book would have appeared.

I owe a special debt to Ara Dostourian, who opened his home to me during several research trips to New England.

Finally, to Carol, who has always shared and supported my love of scholarship, whatever the burden or the pain.

*

Introduction

LIFE, FOR MOST AMERICANS, did not change significantly between 1735, the year of John Adams's birth, and 1826, the year of his death. Although the two dates were separated by nearly a century, most people continued to live and work on farms. Daily life had a rhythm, a tempo set by nature, which governed the practice of agriculture. In New England, men, often accompanied by their sons, trudged to the fields in March to inaugurate the season with ditching. Then came plowing, planting, mowing, weeding, and harvesting, until the annual cycle ended with the slaughter of livestock in mid-autumn. The wives and daughters also had economic responsibilities within the family, the same chores, in fact, that their European ancestors had performed centuries before: they tended the poultry, milked the cows and made butter and cheese, grew vegetables in summer, gathered fruit in early fall, assisted with the butchery of the stock, sewed, spun, washed, cleaned, cooked, and cared for the children.

Labor was manual, and the tools with which the farm families of 1826 worked were similar to those used by their predecessors four generations earlier. Men struggled with plows made of ash, wielded metal axes, hoes, scythes, and crosscut saws, and swung a heavy cradle to harvest grain under a hot September sun. Women cooked in a vast open fireplace, sewed and made candles without the assistance of machinery, and on the ritual Monday washday still plunged their arms into near-boiling water to scrub the clothes.

In both periods most people married in early spring or late fall, so the newlyweds would have some time to themselves before the demands of the farm encroached; most frequently, the children—five or six living children per family on average—were born in late winter or early spring and customarily arrived at about thirty-month intervals. Few people received more than two or three years of formal education. Unless a new frontier beckoned, few people traveled beyond the immediate area of their birth, and most people got about by walking, on horseback, or in a horse-drawn conveyance. A vaccination against smallpox was developed in the eighteenth century, but few other advances in medical science were made and both eras demonstrated a terrible similarity in mortality statistics. About one person in six died in the first year of life, and another one in ten perished before adulthood. People lived in fear of maundering epidemics, and no illness, not even a common cold, could be treated with indifference. In 1826 most people lived in small, sparsely furnished, drafty, and uninsulated habitations of one to three rooms; if they attempted to read or sew after dark, they still relied on a flickering candle. People in both eras used chamber pots and outdoor privies. They bathed once a week. Mostly they wore clothing made at home, save for shoes and men's work garments fashioned by skilled artisans. Even their diets remained much the same. Corn and pork, often made into a dull and tasteless stew or potage, together with bread, cheese, and dried beef (washed down with beer, cider, coffee, or tea) constituted the daily fare, month after month, year after year.[1]

Nevertheless, if a sameness characterized daily existence, change—considerable change—had occurred. At the time of John Adams's birth, the European settlers in eastern North America dwelled in the colonies of Great Britain. Settlement had not moved far inland; Winchester, Virginia, located in the lovely Shenandoah Valley in 1731, was perhaps Anglo-America's most western outpost in 1735. Ninety years later, independence had long since been achieved. The United States had supplanted the colonies, and its domain extended beyond the Mississippi River into a region that Britain had not yet claimed in 1735. Two great revolutions had occurred in this span of nearly a century. The American Revolution and the French Revolution changed the way people thought. The age of deference first had given way to the age of republicanism. By 1826 new winds still were blowing. A new hero was emerging in America that year, Andrew Jackson, who reflected the nation's embrace of democracy, by which he meant majoritarian rule.

John Adams's long life had spanned an exciting time, an age in which he played an important political and intellectual role. He vividly remembered England's last colonial wars with France for control of North America, and until middle age he remained a loyal citizen of the British empire. He witnessed the colonists' earliest protests against British rule and eventually played an active role in the popular defiance of British law. In fact, his early writings helped to shape the intellectual content of the protest movement. He served in Congress; indeed, no one played a greater role in making American independence a reality. He spent nearly a decade abroad as an American envoy, during which time he played a vital role in negotiating the treaty that brought peace following the long War of Independence. Later, he held the highest office in the land under the newly ratified Constitution of 1787, and as president he courageously chose to pursue a course he thought best for the nation, though it was fraught with personal political dangers.

Yet, despite his accomplishments, John Adams continues to be one of the least understood of the Founding Fathers. According to conventional wisdom, the contributions that he made to his age are less significant than those of the other great leaders of Revolutionary America, George Washington, Benjamin Franklin, Thomas Jefferson, and perhaps even Samuel Adams and Alexander Hamilton. To some he has even been a comic figure, a man full of puff and pomposity, a vain, posturing sort who took on a ridiculous cast when he sought to play a role for which he was ill suited. He has always been seen as honest and dedicated, but to the general public, even today, he remains little more than a "boiled shirt" or a "priggish" bore, as two popular publications recently described him.[2]

Three major biographers have coped with Adams in this century. Writing soon after World War I, Gilbert Chinard found Adams to be "stanch, honest, stubborn and somewhat narrow," and he made his subject into the Clemenceau of his time, the "most realistic statesman of his generation in America," a fierce patriot whose achievements outpaced those of Jefferson.[3] Thirty years later, in another era of conservatism and at the height of the Cold War, Page Smith, in a long narrative biography, championed Adams as a guide and preceptor to mid-twentieth century America. This Founding Father, Smith said, had been a bulwark against the "heralds of the new age," the radicals such as Thomas Paine and the Jacobins whose promise of progress threatened to take human-kind down a road filled with violence and anarchy and despair.[4] More recently, Peter Shaw has sought to remediate the deficiencies in those earlier works through a psychointellectual biography.[5] Shaw sought to deduce Adams's motives by understanding his mind and personality. He discovered a man perpetually at war with himself. Adams's life was reduced to a quest to satisfy his intense ambitions and to come to grips with his passion for fame, a battle that he lost, for ultimately his struggle resulted only in his being seen as vain and pompous, thus diminishing his importance.

In some respects, Adams was his own worst enemy. He left behind mountains of writings, much of it his private musings. During his retirement, he not only devoted abundant time to his correspondence but also nursed a deep bitterness because of his defeat in the presidential election of 1800. He sent out letter after captious letter, railing at those who had betrayed him and seeking to comprehend and explain other men's success and his failure.

Adams was not the only leader rent from his wife by the call of duty, but he was away from Abigail for extraordinarily long stretches. Much of the time between early 1775 and August 1785, they lived apart, and during these protracted separations he often wrote the most candid letters to her, confiding in her as he could in no other. He told her of his frustrations, anger, joy, envy, infirmities, aspirations, and despair. And for years he kept a diary, a journal in which he recorded his innermost thoughts, excoriating himself for his short-comings, debating with himself over his hopes and his means of fulfilling his dreams, wrestling with the dilemmas he faced.

No other revolutionary figure left behind anything remotely akin to that preserved by Adams and his heirs. Washington, Franklin, and Jefferson, like

Adams, bequeathed voluminous files of correspondence to historians. But Washington's writings were so carefully guarded that the reader can almost feel him taking pains to choose each word lest he reveal his inner self; Franklin and Jefferson were less reserved, but each appeared—both in person and in their correspondence—to be a more private person than Adams, less willing to permit scrutiny of their thoughts and feelings. Whatever Washington might have written to his wife during the long, lonely, often dark periods of separation, was lost forever when Martha burned his letters after he died. Jefferson's wife was dead by the time duty took him from Monticello for long stretches, and Franklin simply wrote home infrequently and then quite discreetly. Nor does Washington's diary or the memoranda made by Jefferson, those which came to be known as the "Anas," even remotely divulge either man's intrinsic side; Washington's diary, in fact, often consists of little more than a compendium of daily temperatures and a record of visitors to Mount Vernon.

What can be seen of Adams, therefore, is exceptional. As a consequence, the tendency of historians has been to see him as an exception. Among other things, his private writings made clear his pettiness, his ambition, his vanity, his enmities. The temptation has existed, therefore, to portray him as more petty, more ambitious, more vain, and more malicious than others.

Adams's political thought also has plagued his reputation. His last major contributions to political theory were out of step with the direction in which American thought would proceed in the generations following his retirement. Not only did this taint Adams, but some historians who have been his most ardent defenders during this century have sometimes sought to use his writings in the cause of reaction, often misinterpreting what Adams in fact sought to say two hundred years ago.

This biography is not meant to be an apologia for John Adams. He often displayed unattractive qualities, including calculation, excessive ambition, rage, jealousy, and vanity. He was ill suited for some of the public roles he played. His habitual absences from his wife were deplorable, his virtual abandonment of some of his children during the long war years was unconscionable. Adams was well aware of his "Deficiences," as he put it, and in many letters he spoke of his dark, unsavory attributes.[6] But like most humans, John Adams was a man of many personae. This biography seeks to discover the total person, to understand him in the context of his time and to compare him to other major American leaders of his era, and to assess his successes and failures, both as public figure and private individual.

Adams lived in times that were strikingly different from our own. In his days a journey from Boston to Philadelphia consumed nearly two weeks, transit from America to Europe often required forty to fifty days. He read by candlelight and wrote with a quill, was reduced to breathless excitement upon viewing an experimental attempt to make electricity, once was beside himself with wonder at the novel view he beheld from a height equivalent to four or five stories, occasionally took his turn as a citizen walking the Boston fire watch throughout long, cold New England nights, watched his daughter undergo surgery before the discovery of anesthesia, and not only lost an infant child but saw friends and relatives die from diseases such as diphtheria, influenza, smallpox, and yellow fever.

Nevertheless, John Adams's dilemmas were timeless. Could he succeed in his career without resorting to wickedness? Could a political leader be truly independent and genuinely serve the public? Could the demands of his work and public responsibilities be reconciled with the needs and interests of his family? Did he seek public office for his own ends or those of society? How should he respond to acts of treachery committed by his compatriots? Could he make political decisions that were personally harmful but necessary for the greater good?

Adams once said that he would like to write a history of his times. If he ever undertook such a project, he said, he would approach it "with an Hand as severe as Tacitus" as he objectively sought to "draw the Portrait of every character that has figured in the business." That was what he expected from historians who might scrutinize his behavior. "The faithfull Historian," he wrote, "delineates Characters truly, let the Censure fall where it will."[7] And, he might have added, the scrupulous historian also must forthrightly record the memorable achievements and the benignant virtues.

PART ONE

*

Love of Fame

CHAPTER I

*

Vanity Is My Cardinal Vice

A T ONE TIME TREES HAD STOOD as far as one could see. Oak, elm, maple, and a score of other varieties had marched through the valleys and up the slopes of the nearby Blue Hills, their silent trek interrupted only by occasional blue-green ponds and the rivers that coursed and eddied toward the neighboring coast. Then the English settlers had come. Sturdy farmers mostly, these men and women of the Puritan exodus came to hew a community out of the woodlands.

A century later, in 1735, the village of Braintree, Massachusetts, an old settlement by American standards, stood on what had been that forest floor, its corners even yet remorselessly nipping at the wilderness. White clapboard farmhouses dotted the landscape, each structure looking more or less like its neighbor. Fields, stripped now of all timber, splayed out behind the houses, each home to reluctant summer crops of corn and wheat. Barns and sheds and outbuildings—some whitewashed, a few painted, most simply left to weather, all beacons to the austere struggle with nature that faced the residents—were sprinkled about the homesteads. Cattle and oxen, and here and there a horse or two, mutely grazed over a fallow section, their meanderings inhibited by rude wooden fences or low walls fashioned from the region's ubiquitous rock and stone. Fast by each house lay a small tilled area, the garden plot, the annual source of the inviting array of vegetables that made up the New Englander's diet.

There was no downtown in Braintree, but without doubt the Congregational Church adjacent to the village green was the center of town, geographically as well as spiritually and socially. Its white spire visible from every cove and field within the community, the church, like a magnet, lured every able inhabitant to worship twice on Sunday and once in midweek. But the church's influence stretched beyond the devotionals. It lapped into the affairs of the grief-stricken, sanctioned the joyous moments of birth and marriage, sculpted even the social and political awareness of the villagers.

The power of the church was but one manifestation of the premodern, almost medieval, aspect of life in early eighteenth-century America. This still was a time when New Englanders thought in terms of a stratified society. In Braintree or any other hamlet, ordinary folk stepped aside when the elite walked past, heralding their social betters with the doff of a hat. Church pews, as well as slaves, were purchased as advertisements of their owners' rank. Even though most adult white males met the sex and property qualifications for voting, the most distinguished men habitually were chosen to hold office. Women were second-class citizens, disenfranchised, not permitted to be assertive in public, facing little choice in life but the demanding regimen of unremitting daily toil and the apparently ceaseless bearing of children.

Most of Braintree's residents were farmers, but some did not farm at all or, at best, were part-time husbandmen. Some were professional people, others ran taverns, and still others—the propertyless—picked away at odd jobs. Second to yeomen, though, were skilled artisans, craftsmen who supplied the town's needs and who prospered as the cultivators flourished. Even in a small village such as this, carpenters and blacksmiths were essential. There was a need, too, for a miller and a tailor; and a gunsmith, a tanner, a cooper, and a seamstress also could find enough business to make a living. So could a cordwainer, or shoemaker.

Deacon John Adams was both a farmer and a cordwainer. From mid-March to autumn, his little farm of about fifty acres occupied his attention, as he battled both the indifferent soil of New England and the vicissitudes of its weather to grow wheat and corn, oats and barley. When the lowering fall skies signaled an end to the growing season, he turned to making shoes, working at a low bench in a tiny room off the kitchen. The Deacon was a respected man in Braintree, although neither he nor any of the Adamses had ever been part of the truly elite within the community. But he had lived here all his life, and, while he was not formally educated, he was evidently looked upon as an intelligent and sober man. Over the years he served as a tithingman, tax collector, and militia officer; on nine occasions he was elected to the town's board of selectmen and served fourteen terms as a deacon in his church. Much later his son remembered that no public business was transacted in Braintree without the consent of Deacon John Adams.[1]

In the fall of 1735, the Deacon was nervous and excited. At the age of forty-four he was about to become a father for the first time. Curiously, in an age when most men married while still in their early twenties, he had wed only recently. During the previous autumn, he had married Susanna Boylston of Muddy River, or Brookline, a woman twenty years his junior.

Just as the first crocus and daffodil were heaving through the late winter snow, Deacon Adams learned that Susanna was carrying their child. Both continued their routines through the spring and summer, though anticipation, excitement, and an unspoken apprehension were their daily companions. Finally, fall arrived. Abruptly, the morning air again became crisp and nippy, and it was late in the forenoon when the autumn fog burned away to unmask the gaudy red and yellow hills around Braintree. For the Adamses, expectancy had turned to suspense and then to anxiety by the time the moment arrived. When the long-awaited day came, Susanna was assisted by a midwife; for the Deacon there was nothing to do but wait and absent-mindedly tinker at his bench. Then suddenly it was over. A baby's piercing cries filled the house. The news was good. Mother and son were fine. The boy would be named for his father— John Adams. It was October 19, 1735.

Young John Adams grew up in the kind of orthodox farmhouse familiar to every New England hamlet, a squarish, frame structure with two bedrooms upstairs and two more rooms—kitchen and living room—downstairs. A huge fireplace, open on both sides, divided the rooms on each floor. An "add-on," two tiny rooms that languished beneath a low, steep roof, seemed to grow out of the rear of the house. This lean-to, called a "leanter" in the Yankee dialect, was dark and dreary, terribly cold in the winter, close and stifling in the dead of summer. These two rooms were set aside for John and his younger brothers, Peter Boylston, born in 1738, and Elihu, who arrived six years later.[2]

In most ways life in the Adams household must have resembled that of other families. The house was commonplace enough. There were three children, just slightly below the average. Both parents worked diligently, the Deacon toiling inside and out year-round, while Susanna managed the house, tended the garden, and taught each son to read when he reached age five. As was true of most families in Braintree, Deacon Adams and his wife sought to live by Puritan tenets handed down from Massachusetts' past. Regular church attendance was mandated. Work was important and hard work would be rewarded. John recalled that his parents had made him aware of the evils of both excessive leisure and sexual promiscuity; they "held every Species of Libertinage in . . . Contempt and horror," he recollected, and painted "pictures of disgrace, or baseness and of Ruin" that would result from licentious behavior. But John and Susanna were not narrow-minded tyrants. John remembered their "parental Kindness," and until he was about six years of age he enjoyed a childhood much like that of other lads in Braintree.[3]

On windy spring days John struggled to launch the kite he and his brothers had fashioned. He and his friends wrestled and shot marbles, and when the long, bitter winters plummeted onto New England, he searched out a frozen pond where he could skate, oblivious, as only children can be, to the numbing winds and tortuous temperatures. He seemed addicted to the outdoors. More than anything else, John liked to hunt and fish and swim. He patrolled the region about Braintree until he was familiar with every eddy and hill. He often trekked through waist-high brush, hoping to scare out a rabbit, or he plunged deep into the woods, hiding in an alcove near an abundance of oaks, waiting silently for a squirrel to appear, straining to hear a rasping bark or the muted scratching of a forager. On murky, chilly days in late autumn he liked nothing better than crouching in tall marsh grass to await a flock of migrating ducks or geese. Three creeks sluiced through Braintree, and John knew each intimately. He fished from the banks of these streams, and on lazy summer afternoons he and his companions swam in their placid waters.[4]

Each family is unique, however. Young John was raised in a household presided over by two strong-willed parents. Once he grew old enough to notice such things, he concluded that his parents bickered to an unusual degree. "Reason" prevailed in the homes of most of his friends, he thought, but "Passion" ruled within the Adams family. He thought his mother usually won the battles, too. She "fretts, squibs, scolds, rages, raves" until she has her way, he wrote. But his father was a strong, intrusive presence as well, just as John would be with his own sons. John later spoke of being "overawed" by the Deacon. Perhaps what he meant was that his father, well-known and esteemed within Braintree, made it clear early on that he expected even greater accomplishments of his son.[5]

In eighteenth-century farm villages children were prized, among other reasons, for the additional labor they provided. Beginning with their ninth or tenth birthday, youngsters were expected to assist their parents. Young girls began to cook and sew, to spin and weave, to tend the garden and care for the younger children. The little boys went into the fields with their fathers, performing light tasks at first, then after two or three years, they too were engaged fully in farm work. That was the fate of the younger Adams boys, Peter Boylston and Elihu.

Deacon Adams had nothing like this in mind for John, however. Even before their marriage, he and Susanna had decided that their first son would receive a good education. There was to be formal instruction, capped by schooling at Harvard College. John's grandparents had followed that course, though it was his uncle, not his father, who had attended college.

Young John's formal education began when he was about six years old. First, he attended a "Dame School," an academy for boys and girls, conducted in the teacher's house. The students spent hour upon hour reading and reciting the admonitions and platitudes of *The New England Primer,* a handy little combination hornbook, primer, and catechism. "He who ne'er learns his ABC, forever will a blockhead be," the text warned. And it advised that "In Adam's fall, we sinned all."

It was not long before John was transferred to Braintree's Latin School, a more demanding institution conducted by Joseph Cleverly, a young man in his late twenties who had graduated from Harvard College eight or nine years before.[6] Students who enrolled in a Latin academy instead of in the more traditional common, or public, school were earmarked for a lengthy spate of instruction—up to a dozen years—presumably culminating in a college education. The Latin School experience normally lasted six to eight years, or until both the Latin master and college officials deemed the student adequately prepared for a higher education. Classes usually were conducted in the master's chambers, and these sessions often consisted of a stiflingly redundant pattern of reading and reciting. Latin, of course, was at the heart of the curricula. The young scholars gradually moved from a study of the rules of grammar to an examination of a Latin textbook, then to a consideration of the classics, beginning with Cicero. Greek was a part of the curricula too, a strange language with a dissimilar alphabet, syntax, and system of grammar; ultimately, students were expected to competently translate it into both Latin and English. Although rhetoric and logic were thought of as part of the classical curricula, they received less attention. The study of rhetoric was designed to teach the pupil to write and speak with elegance, while logic was thought to provide an understanding of rational thought; both were cardinal assets for clergymen and lawyers, the professions that most of these students were expected to choose. Arithmetic was about the only other subject a Latin student encountered in any depth, though he might also receive the very slightest exposure to higher mathematics, navigation, geography, and astronomy.[7]

Adams's account of his youth differs from the formulaic success story so popular in American history. In his account he was not driven to succeed. Indeed, he resisted doing what was necessary to elevate himself. Success came only because of the wisdom of his father, who ultimately insisted that he complete his education.

In fact, little is known of young John's early education. In his *Autobiography,* written sixty years later, he devoted only two brief paragraphs to this part of his schooling. Clearly, however, he did not remember fondly his first experiences in school. He depicted himself as a poor student. He was truant repeatedly, often sneaking away in midmorning to hunt or fish; he spent many hours shivering in the damp cold while awaiting a deer or watching carefully for approaching geese, but "I cared not," he wrote later, "if I could but get away from school." When he was in school, he daydreamed. It could not be helped, he said; classes were boring, his schoolmaster was rancorous and hateful, and the atmosphere was cheerless.[8]

Adams remembered that his yearning to quit school produced years of contention with his father. Once, he recalled, he told his father that he had no desire to complete his education, to go on to college. He longed only to be a farmer, he said.

"A Farmer!" the Deacon cried. "Well I will show you what it is to be a Farmer."

Early the following morning, father and son descended into the marsh in pursuit of thatch. All day, under a hot sun, the two struggled through knee-

deep mud, stooping and cutting and lifting, and finally tying together bundles
of thatching. Only when the sun began to set and the black water numbed their
feet did the Deacon call an end to the day's work. Bone-tired, John trudged
home behind his father. When they reached the house, the elder Adams asked
his son how liked farming now.

"I like it very well Sir," he replied wearily.

"Ay but I dont like it so well," the Deacon stormed. "[Y]ou shall go to
school. You will comply with my desires." It was a mandate Adams remembered hearing frequently.

But the Deacon did find a new teacher for his son. Joseph Marsh, the son of
his former pastor, became John's new master. The student responded to the
change, or so Adams later recalled. Beyond the reach of Cleverly, whom he
depicted as lazy, indifferent, and malevolent, young John's work improved.
Within eighteen months his teacher judged him ready to apply for admission
to Harvard College.[9]

One can only guess at the veracity of Adams's tale, but much of it rings true.
He was hardly the first young boy to prefer the excitement of the outdoors to
school; he must have missed the bounteous hills and forests about Braintree
where he had frolicked and where, undoubtedly, many of his old companions
continued to hunt and fish while he languished in a stuffy classroom. Nor can it
be doubted that as a young boy he longed to farm. His father, a natural role
model, was a farmer; his younger brothers were destined to be farmers and
probably had completed their schooling and were working with their father
while John toiled with his studies. His world was a world of farmers, a time
when the majority of males in Braintree earned their livelihood from the earth.

Yet, Adams's memory of his early education is more than a story of youthful
boredom and frustration. He depicted these years as among his least happy
time, a period that stuck in his mind throughout his life as having been
particularly joyless and contentious. His long bout with Master Cleverly left
an unpleasant pall. Strong-willed and obstinate like his father, there must have
been many unwelcome confrontations with the Deacon as well. Mostly, however, Adams must have found this to be an anxious time because of the heavy
burden he carried. He was the son chosen for schooling, and he was expected
to excell. Like any child, he must have wondered whether he was adequate to
his assignment. Years later he remembered quite vividly how he had feared
being "sett down for a fool" if he failed to achieve what was expected of him.[10]

Adams recalled having displayed no more enthusiasm over attending college than he had exhibited for his preparatory schooling. He feared that he
would fail the admission examination at Harvard, which consisted of an interview and a grilling by the president and several faculty members—an experience that would have frightened any boy of fifteen, as John was in spring 1751.
Master Marsh tried to hearten the youngster with assurances that he would
pass the test, but John's misgivings were so great that he recollected the

journey to Cambridge as "very melancholly" and stressful, so much so that he even contemplated wheeling his horse about and returning home. Only the certainty of his father's disappointment and outrage, he said, kept him going. To his surprise the faculty treated him kindly and he passed the examination. Accepted by the college, he was almost light-headed as he galloped home, for he knew his father would be "well pleased and . . . very happy."[11]

Harvard was an enclave of learning at a time when few people (about one-half of one percent of all males, and no females) attended college. It was nestled among stately elms and oaks, the Charles River gurgling past on one side and rustic Cambridge lying remote on another flank. Harvard's freshmen customarily were adolescent boys of only fourteen or fifteen. Almost all hailed from New England; in fact, most, like John, came from the eastern shore of Massachusetts. These young scholars were drawn almost exclusively from the middle and upper social classes, and many were the sons of Harvard graduates.

Those lads who enrolled at Harvard in the mid-eighteenth century entered an academic environment whose roots were tethered not only to a much earlier age but also to the aristocratic tradition of European higher education. The curriculum included the classical fare to which these boys had been introduced in their Latin schools, so that during their four-year stay in Cambridge their familiarity with Latin and Greek, rhetoric and logic, was to be honed and deepened. Yet, change was occurring in education, as in many aspects of life, as the eighteenth century progressed. In the generation before John enrolled the curriculum had been broadened to add emphasis to the natural sciences, natural philosophy, and moral philosophy. In addition the tutorial system of the previous century, a practice by which one professor shepherded an entire class through its four years of college, had given way to the specialized professorship. In each area of the curriculum, students now were more likely to encounter a scholar with a particular expertise. A generally more liberal environment also characterized academic endeavors at Harvard, and some faculty now even encouraged their students to examine critically the various theological systems.

What had not changed was the exacting regimen demanded of the young students at Harvard. Most mornings saw the boys tumble from their spartan rooms even before sunrise. Prayers and breakfast at six commenced the day, followed by classes and study from eight until five, with only a brief break for lunch. Prayers followed the completion of the day's classes, a light supper was served at seven, and study probably continued late into the night. Scholars they might have been, but they were also rambunctious youths. Upperclassmen hazed freshmen, and it was a rare student who was immune from sophomoric high jinks. Under cover of darkness, students sometimes torched the faculty's outhouses or ensconced "borrowed" livestock in the college chapel. The faculty and administration struck back by punishing the younger students with fines and even floggings.[12]

Despite his initial reservations, John found his college years pleasant. When he discovered that he was a capable student, his earlier timidity subsided and school ceased to be the burden it once had been. He later spoke of these times as being "gay, gorgeous," a period that "invigorated my Body, and exhilerated my soul." The change was so sudden and dramatic that he could not explain it. His newfound "Love of Books and . . . fondness for Study" was a "Curiosity," he admitted. No less surprising was his declining interest in sports and hunting, and even in girls. Adams's progress as a student was due in part to maturation and to his changed environment; surrounded by young men who soon would enter the professional world and taught by men who were the antithesis of the husbandmen he had known in Braintree, Adams's horizons expanded. No doubt he discovered too that his scholastic achievements brought rewards. He said that his father applauded the "relaxation of my Zeal for my Fowling Piece" in preference to books, a sign that his relationship with his father had become less contentious.[13]

When his senior year arrived with a stunning swiftness, Adams, like many other collegians, still had not decided on a career. As late as the time of his birth, the clergy was the favored calling among Harvard's students; by the time he enrolled, change was occurring. As the secular winds of the eighteenth-century Enlightenment began to blow across New England, more students were attracted to careers in law or medicine than to the church. Only an occasional student selected some other course, perhaps a career in business, teaching, or even farming.[14]

Deacon Adams had always presumed his son would enter the clergy, but it was not a calling that appealed to John. While clergymen remained esteemed members of Massachusetts society, John did not hold the profession in high regard. The recurrent ecclesiastical squabbles that seemed to erupt as inevitably as summer brushfires led him to look upon preachers as dogmatic and bigoted sorts eternally engaged in meaningless disputations. He equated the calling with banality and inefficacy, and he spoke of ministers as being "effeminate" and "unmanly." Adams understood, moreover, that his temperament was ill-suited for the pulpit. He was too churlish and caustic, too stubborn and impatient, too opinionated and egotistical to counsel the troubled; he wanted his time for reading and study, not for calling on parishioners who were ill or behind in their tithes. Adams treasured his independence and he sought a profession that would permit him considerable latitude. The church did not offer that luxury. There were too many rules to observe and too many people to please, a fact brought home to him even as he grappled with his choices. His father, together with several compatriots, acted to remove Braintree's Congregational pastor, a man who—according to town gossips—lost his wife to another man because "he did not use her well" and whose behavior was "too gay and light."[15]

As the end of his senior year neared, John increasingly contemplated a legal career. It was not a choice that his father prized. The Deacon, reflecting the old Puritan distaste for barristers, looked upon lawyers as self-serving and treacherous; they were inclined to "sacrifice all, to their own Advancement," even to betray the well-being of the community and the nation if private interest dictated, he advised his son. But John knew that such an outlook was antiquated; in the more cosmopolitan centers, at Boston and Harvard, for instance, the legal profession had grown in respectability. Men from the leading families in New England—the Otises, Sewalls, Olivers, and Pynchons—now were drawn to this calling.

John thought it important that some of his fellow students and members of the Harvard faculty urged him to study law. They pointed out, he remembered, that he had a flair for public speaking, and in all likelihood, they must have gently sought to persuade him that his personality was better suited for the bar than the pulpit. Of course, he had his own reasons for contemplating the law. He knew that a good law practice would enable him to live comfortably if not luxuriously. He knew as well that the law would leave him time for himself, for reading, writing, or thinking. Yet, these were not the amenities of the profession he found most intriguing. As his twentieth birthday loomed, John understood, perhaps for the first time, that it was recognition and esteem that he sought most. He filled his diary with references to his yearning to achieve "Honour or Reputation"; he sought something that would permit him to gain "more defference from [his] fellows," he said. By age twenty-one he had begun to speculate on what was required to become "a great Man," and in the privacy of his own thoughts he confessed that he longed for the day when his achievements would be esteemed as great. John Adams no longer wished merely to be known, he longed to be remembered. At about this time, he told a friend that he sought to avoid the fate of "the common Herd of Mankind, who are to be born and eat and sleep and die, and be forgotten." Although he could hardly anticipate such an occurrence, he added, "I am not ashamed to own that a Prospect of an Immortality in the Memories of all the Worthy, to [the] End of Time would be a high Gratification to my Wishes." To establish a law practice, he concluded, offered the best hope of realizing his ends. While he knew that it was an attorney's lot to spend much time "pleading dry and difficult cases," he also knew that lawyers practiced in and presided over important courts, that through their counsel to influential businessmen they exercised considerable power, and that more lawyers had begun to enter public life, even to hold seats in the provincial assembly. Moreover, the legal profession offered a means by which a young man born to a humble family could rise. This was a calling, therefore, that not only drew the elite to its ranks but also increased the likelihood of the New England elite being drawn from those ranks.[16]

Still, John was haunted by doubts. He was reluctant to disappoint his parents, who had sacrificed to provide his education. He feared too that he might never become anything but a petty lawyer, confined to a small office in a small village, spending his days "raking amidst the rubbish of Writs, indight-ments, Pleas, ejectments, enfiefed, illatebration and a 1000 other lignum Vitae words which have neither harmony nor meaning." But most troubling to Adams were his reasons for wishing to be a lawyer. While he admitted his lust for recognition and fame, he simultaneously denounced himself for daring to be ambitious. These pursuits conflicted with his sense of Puritan ethics. He excoriated himself for his self-serving thoughts—it was mere "trumpery," he admitted—and told himself that he must seek instead a calling that would result in the promotion of the "happiness of [his] fellow men." Unable to decide, he accepted an offer that came just after he spoke at graduation exer-cises; he would become the Latin master at the Worcester grammar school, about fifty miles west of Boston. But Adams looked upon teaching as a tempo-rary assignment, something to do only until he decided whether to study for the clergy or the law; if he chose the latter course, he would pay for the studies himself from the salary he earned as a teacher.[17]

Adams was quickly disenchanted with his new life. After the intellectual stimulation of Harvard College, not to mention the comradeship of campus life, Worcester seemed dreary. The village resembled most other towns in the province but with a population of about fifteen hundred, it was larger. Still, to John's way of thinking, Worcester was isolated and utterly lacking in social opportunities. To make matters worse he soon came to regard teaching as a "school of affliction," a daily drudgery of squiring "a large number of little runtlings, just capable of lisping A.B.C. and troubling the Master." Like so many other teachers, he too developed an aversion to his pupils, whom he regarded as dull and stupid, uninspired and uninspiring.[18]

The drabness of his lifestyle was mitigated only by the friendliness of Worcester's social leaders. John frequently was invited to dinner, or for an evening's chat over tea and cake. He spent many long winter evenings about the hearth, discussing and debating the great issues of the day, especially the thorny theological problems that troubled these villagers.[19]

By the end of his first year as a schoolmaster, John still had not begun to study law. In fact, he seemed to be caught up in a morass of inactivity. Try as he might to drive himself to read and to continue his studies in preparation for his legal apprenticeship, he made little headway. Early in 1756 he resolved to make better use of his time, but it was to no avail. All his resolutions were of "a very thin and vapory Consistence," he lamented. He was in the grip of a "senseless Torpitude." He lazed about. He daydreamed. "[S]loth and negli-gence," he raged at himself, "will be the ruin of my schemes."[20]

Young Adams's indecision continued until it closed in upon him. Preaching still held little appeal for him. He toyed with the idea of becoming a physician, though he thought practicing medicine meant unremitting work for little pay and scant recognition. The law, he continued to believe, afforded the most alluring possibilities, including "an Avenue to the more important offices of the state." Yet, he hesitated. Not only was he loath to displease his father, but he too harbored many of the Deacon's and rural Braintree's suspicions of attorneys. He wondered if lawyers inevitably provoked more problems than they solved. Was the lawyer a parasite? Did an attorney have to enrich himself by impoverishing others? John wrestled with these issues. He also struggled with his motives for pursuing the law. He admitted to his diary that he was compelled in this direction because he sought fame. "Vanity I am sensible, is my cardinal Vice and cardinal Folly," he wrote. Was that dangerous? Was ambition an evil thing? Did the quest for material reward amount to profligacy? Would his yearnings lead him down the road to "weaknesses and Fopperies." As a lawyer, could he make any contribution to society?[21]

On the eve of his second year as a teacher, John realized that he could no longer postpone his decision. He did not wish to teach for more than another year or two; he was eager to resolve his dilemma and get on with his life. But that made the decision no easier. Anguished and under heavy stress, he was tortured by self-doubt. He questioned his abilities. Could he speak with eloquence to a jury? Could he even master his legal studies? "I am dull, and inactive, and . . . all the Spirits I can muster, are insufficient to rouse me," he excoriated himself. "My Brains seem constantly in . . . great confusion, and wild disorder. . . . I have never any bright, refulgent Ideas."[22]

He vacillated to the very end. First, he decided to study for the pulpit, then a bit later he abruptly opted for the law. In late summer 1756, just a few weeks short of his twenty-first birthday, he contracted with James Putnam, only twenty-eight years old himself, but Worcester's leading attorney, to begin an apprenticeship. He was to study under Putnam for two years, and during that period he was to move in with his mentor and his family, paying his tutor one hundred dollars in addition to monthly room and board.[23]

It was done, although he continued to be haunted by lingering doubts. "Necessity drove me to this Determination, but my inclination I think was to preach," he wrote in his diary on the day he signed on with Putnam. That was clearly not the case, and Adams knew it. In fact, in his very next sentence he noted that a career in the clergy "would not do."[24]

Adams had known what he wanted to do at least since his senior year in college, twenty-four months before he reached his decision. It had taken that long for him to convince himself of the rectitude of his choice. And even then, as he moved his belongings to his new home, he sought to assure himself that he would never act meanly or unjustly while practicing the law. "I set out with firm Resolutions," he remarked. "The Practice of the Law, I am sure," he told himself, "does not dissolve the obligations of morality or of Religion."[25]

CHAPTER 2

*

Shall I Creep or Fly?

ADAMS'S DIARY ENTRIES MAKE IT CLEAR that his
last two years in Worcester, the years that he studied under Putnam,
were terribly unpleasant. He blamed his unhappiness on the "lonely unsociable" life-style he was compelled to lead because of his heavy work load; teaching by day and studying by night was a "dreary ramble" that left no time for
relaxation, he said. In fact, Adams had a fairly busy social life, but, save for a
rare evening with one or two indifferent acquaintances from his college years,
he rarely had the opportunity to socialize with anyone his own age. He neither
courted any of the young ladies of Worcester nor met many of the young men.
However, several local luminaries took to Adams. He was a frequent guest in
the home of one or another of the Chandlers, the leading family in pre-Revolutionary Worcester; he was often invited to dine with the family of Timothy
Paine, a member of the Massachusetts assembly; and Nahum Willard, a prosperous physician who had rented him a room before he moved in with the
Putnams, also seemed to enjoy his company. On those evenings, Adams and
his older hosts adjourned to a parlor following dinner, where they smoked
(John had used tobacco since he was eight years old), drank tea or beer, and
argued vociferously, usually about politics or theology. But, in the real sense of
the word, Adams had no friends.[1]

In truth, as Adams said, most of his time was taken up by his studies. His
method of preparation for the bar was typical for the time. An occasional young
colonist traveled to England to study formally in the Inn at Court in London,
but few could afford such an indulgence; and as there were no law schools in
America, most students signed on to apprentice under a licensed lawyer, a
practice still pursued in Abraham Lincoln's time nearly a century later. In most
instances the training began with reading. The master assigned books from his
library, then quizzed the student. Soon the student accompanied the master to
court, first merely to observe, then gradually to prepare briefs in some of the
teacher's cases. When the master felt the student was ready to proceed on his
own, usually after about two years, he wrote a letter of certification that was
often tantamount to an admission to the bar.[2]

Putnam was a busy man with a young, growing family. He was not much older than Adams, and he had been in practice for less than a decade. At best, therefore, he was a competent teacher. Adams once complained that Putnam could have devoted more time to him and, in particular, might have provided him with tips to save him much time and grief once he had his own practice.[3] Nevertheless, theirs was not a rancorous relationship and Adams's later writings contained none of the bitterness that he directed toward Master Cleverly. In fact, once his legal studies began in earnest, Adams appears to have overcome quickly his earlier reservations about practicing law, in part, no doubt, because he found Putnam to be kind and honest. While he was lonely and undoubtedly missed the affable, sometimes raucous companionships of the college dormitory, he seemed to have enjoyed a waning of the stress that had been his companion for two years as he sought to make a career decision. He must have found, as he had earlier at Harvard, that he was fully capable of handling his studies and must have been delighted to be making progress at last toward the calling of his choosing.

What caused the greatest problems for Adams during his final years in Worcester was not his law study but indecision and misgivings over what role he should play in a war that commenced in 1756. The long struggle between France and Great Britain for dominion in North America, a contest that had resulted in three wars since 1689, erupted anew that year in a conflict often called the French and Indian War. Massachusetts immediately raised an army, as it had during almost every generation since the founding of the province.

Few young men in Adams's circumstances enlisted in the volunteer army. Most who bore arms were either urban laborers or the landless sons of farmers, both of whom were enticed by the cash and land bounties offered for service. But Adams, it appears, desperately wished to serve. "I longed more ardently to be a Soldier than I ever did to be a Lawyer," he later told his wife. Moreover, for having failed to join the army, Adams appears, quite unreasonably, to have borne a sense of guilt. Many years later he continued to be troubled by whether his conduct during this war had been that of a "coward."[4]

What can account for Adams's unusual behavior? For one thing, the citizen-soldier was venerated in colonial Massachusetts. Articulate spokesmen for society repeatedly glorified the alleged virtues of warriors. Soldiers were the subject of heroic narratives and poetic elegies, monuments were erected to these heroes, and hamlets were named in their honor. Adams, like any awestruck, unknown young man, longed to cut a figure that would earn him renown and glory. In addition, several generations of Adamses, including Deacon Adams, had soldiered during one crisis or another. Young John Adams was quite aware that he was the first member of his family who "*degenerated* from the virtues of the house so far as not to have been an officer in the militia."[5]

There was still another factor. During all his life Adams's writings included references to "effeminate" and "manly" behavior. While it was not uncommon for men in the eighteenth century to think along such lines, Adams appears to have devoted unusual consideration to the matter, suggesting that he was not entirely comfortable with his masculinity. Tension in his outlook may have stemmed from the fact that in a predominately agrarian society he did not work with his hands; indeed, in cataloguing his distaste for the clerical profession, he had specifically equated the calling with comfort and muliebrity. By contrast, for a man such as George Washington, who toiled as a surveyor, managed a farm, and served as a soldier before his twenty-first birthday, concern with issues of manliness was virtually nonexistent in his writings. Adams, however, often reflected on his appearance and he frequently judged others according to their "manly" mannerisms. Surely, he was keenly aware that his society depicted soldiering as an act of "true manliness and grandeur," a concept that Adams accepted. He spoke frequently of sharpening "the true *martial* qualities" in his character, and later, during the Revolution, he suggested that no man could seek a more lofty goal than to live according to the "great, manly, warlike virtues." Not surprisingly, he was daunted when he met several British officers who briefly bivouaced near Worcester, and he undoubtedly shared the feelings of a friend who admitted that he felt inferior when he was in the presence of "soldiers with their Guns upon their shoulders."[6]

Adams partially resolved his dilemma by agreeing to carry a military dispatch from Worcester to Newport, Rhode Island. It was a long, arduous journey, but the nearest enemy soldier was hundreds of miles away, so he was in no particular danger. Nevertheless, his writings suggest that he made himself believe that the assignment was so strenuous that it nearly ruined his health. As he matured, though, he came to understand that the learned contribute to society just as soldiers do, albeit without the acclaim lavished upon warriors. Later, he fondly quoted Ovid's declaration of his superiority to soldiers: "I am outstanding in intellect. My mind is superior to my hand. All my force is in my mind."[7]

In August 1758, two years after he began, Adams completed his study under Putnam. Several of the older men who had befriended him urged him to remain in Worcester, and as an inducement they offered him the post of town registrar, a sinecure that would see him through while his law practice was getting started. Adams declined; he did not wish to compete with Putnam, he said. Besides, his father had invited him to return home. Not only could he save money by living at home, but he could practice in Braintree, where no formally trained attorney had yet opened shop. The most important factor in his decision, however, was that Braintree was located in the Boston judicial district. Adams had long ago decided that it was not enough to be a lawyer. He wished to be a well-known lawyer, and he knew that his chance for recognition was greater in Boston than in a remote village such as Worcester.[8]

Adams's first task was to be admitted to practice in Boston. Putnam provided him with a list of the city's four most eminent lawyers: Jeremiah Gridley, Oxenbridge Thacher, Benjamin Prat, and James Otis, Jr. Early that fall young Adams set off for the provincial capital, hoping to meet each man. However scant, any support that he might receive from these esteemed gentlemen would give him an edge in the pernicious competition for survival among the city's legion of struggling, unknown lawyers.

After four years at Harvard College, Adams was no stranger to Boston, and he probably took for granted the features of the city that most struck visitors. Newcomers from the rural hinterlands were awed by the population density in the city, where more than fifteen thousand people were crowded into an area of about two by three miles. Most lived in small, drab residences, each house close to its neighbor and looking out upon an unpaved street. Boston thoroughfares always caught the attention of guests: the streets seemed to be the handiwork of a tipsy, or at least befuddled, urban architect. They meandered, they crisscrossed, and all too often they stopped abruptly, for no good reason.

Those dark, quiet streets that led nowhere belied the intense vitality that surged from the very viscera of the city. At the waterfront on the east and south sides of the city, dozens of vessels lay at anchor, their tall masts hovering above the long, busy warehouses along the shoreline. Workers scurried about the docks or shuffled between the shops and the harbor, pushing carts laden with commodities from throughout America, the Caribbean, England, and western Europe. The clangor and blat of labor and trade filled the air. Here and there stood large buildings, each one more ornate and imposing than any in a small farming village, structures resonating the cold, distant urban aura. And in and out of those edifices filed prominent men: wealthy and esteemed merchants, public officials, and lawyers. John Adams yearned to be one of them someday soon.

Adams first visited old Jeremiah Gridley, dean of the city's bar. He had taught many of Boston's best attorneys, and once he had been nominated for attorney-general of the province, only to be turned down by the governor. He welcomed John to his office and administered a lengthy examination. John performed so spectacularly that Gridley was persuaded not only to serve as his sponsor but also to make available his extensive library for the young man's use. Indeed, Gridley acted like a kindly father toward Adams, to whom he proferred two pieces of advice: do not marry early in life, and enter practice out of a love for the law, not from a quest for wealth.

Adams next called on Oxenbridge Thacher, younger than Gridley but reserved and difficult to talk with. Thacher was a bookish sort who had turned to the law only after failing as a clergyman; he was more interested in the philosophical aspects of jurisprudence than in its practice. Like Adams he valued the free time that a law practice afforded for his own pursuits. Thacher in fact did not even quiz John on the law. He asked him questions about metaphysics, a subject about which neither man knew the least thing, Adams later remembered. The interview went well, however, and Thacher, while less effusive than Gridley, promised John his support.

John's session with Benjamin Prat was less favorable. Prat, a one-legged man wracked by constant pelvic pain (he had lost his limb in a fall from a horse), permitted Adams only a minute of his time, then curtly refused his support. But Prat's action was not the result of any shortcoming exhibited by Adams; Putnam had failed to write a letter of recommendation for John.

Although Adams could not have foreseen such a development, James Otis, Jr., the fourth distinguished Boston lawyer upon whom he called, was destined to exert a powerful influence upon him. Indeed, Otis became something of a hero for Adams, a role model upon whom he fashioned his behavior and professional style during his early struggle to launch a career. Otis came from quite a different background than Adams. Members of his prominent family from Barnstable on Cape Cod had attended Harvard College since early in the century; through wealth derived from a thriving retail and mercantile endeavor, the Otises owned slaves and lived in a large house whose basement was always carefully stocked with a pipe of Madeira and the best claret available. James Otis, Jr., ten years older than John, had completed his studies at Harvard in 1743. A bright, sensitive, introspective youth, he had longed to spend his life studying the classics; his father, an intrusive and overbearing man, had other ideas. James was compelled to study the law, learning the trade from Gridley, a family friend. When James completed his studies he wished to practice in Boston, but his father made him practice first in Plymouth, where any errors of youth and inexperience would cause minimal damage. Young Otis was permitted to move to Boston in 1750. From the beginning he occupied an exalted position among the city's attorneys, a status derived largely from his father's prominence in the Massachusetts assembly for the previous five years, but a status solidified through his marriage to a Boston heiress. In no time, his clients included the greatest merchants in the city, including the Hancocks.

Despite his initial reservations about practicing law, Otis grew to relish his calling. He discovered that the courtroom was like a theater. With a sixth sense for understanding the thoughts of others, he found that he could manipulate a jury just as a skilled actor could manage an audience. He soon learned, too, that by combining his understanding of the classics with his naturally glib, flamboyant, and loquacious manner, he not only could succeed as a lawyer but also could win the plaudits he had never garnered at home as the son of a hard, even jealous, father. Typically, when young Adams called on him, Otis performed, using John as an audience. He welcomed the younger man not as a student but as a brother, and rather than quiz him on the law, Otis simply pattered on, treating his supplicant to a protracted discourse on Latin and Greek prosody.[9]

With the interviews behind him, John embarked on the toughest competition of his life. He appraised the other aspiring lawyers in his district, young men like Ned and Samuel Quincy and Robert Treat Paine. A bit older and far more sure of himself, Paine, in Adams's estimation, seemed a step ahead of him at the outset. The Quincys, like so many others, had family ties that seemed to give them a crucial advantage over John. To his diary, in fact, Adams complained that he had no books for his library and no friends to pave his way. "[I]t is my Destiny to dig Treasures with my own fingers. No Body will lend me or sell me a Pick axe," he moaned. He believed too that his rivals were treacherous and sought to harm him. Paine and the Quincy boys, he charged, spread the rumor that he was "a Numbskull and a Blunder Buss."[10]

Adams realized immediately that he if was to make a living from the law he could ill afford to leave any stone unturned. He mapped out a regimen of additional study, a course of reading designed to span seven long years, each step meticulously laid out on a highway from one classic tract to another. He would master every facet of the law until he, like Otis, could dazzle any jury and could surpass all his competitors. It was a fine idea, but John soon rebelled against the regimentation required. For years, first under Master Marsh in Braintree, then at Harvard, and finally as an apprentice under Putnam, he had held to a schedule of pensive, absorbing study. Now he wanted more free time, an opportunity to savor Boston, and the freedom to be part of a society of people his own age, something he had not enjoyed for three years.

Adams joined an ever-widening circle of young men and women who gathered often to play cards, to listen to one of the musically inclined play the violin or flute, or just to idle away a dreary winter evening in conversation. Often invited was Pastor Anthony Wibard, called to Braintree's North Precinct Church during John's junior year at Harvard, but most of the young men were struggling young lawyers. Robert Treat Paine was in the group, although John looked upon him more as a competitor than a confidant. A couple of years older, also a Harvard graduate, and a veteran of the French and Indian War, Paine seemed to delight in hectoring Adams. He discovered John's weak spots and directed his acerbic wit and brash and caustic barbs at those chinks in Adams's armor. John was driven to distraction by his antagonist, and though Paine seems to have been genuinely popular and rather likable, Adams railed in his diary that Bob Paine was a shallow and childish materialist. Adams in fact had many acquaintances but few friends. He was closest to Zabdiel Adams, his cousin, nineteen to John's twenty-three in 1758, and to Richard Cranch, a decade older, a mature immigrant from England who farmed, made and repaired watches, and operated a small glass manufactory in

Braintree. But Adams yearned in vain for recognition from his peers. He filled his diary with lamentations of his disconsolate and lonely existence, crying that he had "no . . . Companions for Pleasure either in Walking, riding, drinking, husling, or any thing else."[11]

This was a difficult time for Adams. Every beginning lawyer struggled to establish his business. It would have been unusual moreover, for a young attorney not to have been anxious at the prospect of appearing before an older magistrate or competing against a veteran adversary. Adams had much to do in order to prepare himself, but there were many distractions. Instead of studying as he should, he daydreamed, gossiped with neighbors, and helped his father with the farm chores. He excoriated himself for sleeping late or staying out far into the night. He idled while "100 of the best Books lie on the shelves." In addition, he feared that his pursuits were "unmanly Pleasures." "I have smoked, chatted, trifled, loitered away this whole day almost," he raged more than once. "I'le be curst," he added, "if any young fellow can study, in this town." Nor did he lament only his habits. He regarded himself as pretentious, and he must have been seen by his acquaintances in a similar light, for even he acknowledged that he adopted an affected manner of speaking and acting in hope of deceiving others into believing him wise beyond his years. Like many young practitioners, Adams feared from the start that he might not be "Cunning enough to cope" with his rivals. When he lost his first case because he prepared a defective writ—he waited with dread for Robert Paine to "pick up this Story to laugh at"—fresh doubts were sown. He was "very anxious," he said, that he might never become a lawyer of renown.[12]

Social pressures added to the burden of launching a legal practice. Adams, probably for the first time, was in a position to go courting. Shy and uncomfortable in the presence of women, and as his writings throughout his life indicate, troubled by feelings of guilt and constraint in sexual matters, this was a particularly painful period for him. He had no more than returned to Braintree than he was "over head and ears" in love with an unidentified young woman. By January, however, that mysterious lass was forgotten, and another girl became the focal point of his life. Hannah Quincy, the daughter of Col. Josiah Quincy of Germantown, was a coquettish, unattached young woman of twenty-two who captivated Adams. He visited her often that winter, infatuated with her enigmatic, magical airs, her beauty, intelligence, and tenderness, and even with her coy, gentle ridicule of his pompous behavior. She was taken by him as well, and the couple often talked about marriage but always in an oblique manner. He told her about the long struggle he faced in establishing his practice; she replied that she could live with poverty. He told her he could not marry for four or five years; she preferred a lengthy engagement, she responded. Each dropped hints that they longed to wed. But dawdling John could not ask the question and Hannah, eager to have a family, began seeing another man, Bela Lincoln, a Hingham physician who had attended college with Adams. Soon Hannah and Bela were engaged. When they married the following year, Adams sank into a deep despondency over his loss. For more than a year, he could not even drink tea—not a beverage easily forsworn by an eighteenth-century New Englander—because it provoked painful reminders of the good times he and Hannah had shared; no matter what he did, he saw "that face, those eyes, that shape, that familiar friendly look." And like many another rejected suitor, he worried whether her behavior was yet another confirmation of his unfitness. Fearing too that others would presume she had repudiated him, he spread the story that he had broken off their relationship because "she repelled me."[13]

Nothing seemed to go smoothly for young Adams. During 1759 and 1760 it appeared that his law practice would never take hold. "I feel vexed, fretted, chafed, the Thought of no Business mortifies, stings me," he moaned. But he knew the lack of business would be temporary. He could not know, however, whether he would win renown as a lawyer, and recognition was what he impatiently hungered for. Throughout this period, he repeatedly confided to his diary his "strong Desire of Distinction," his dread of remaining "unknown." He was "aspiring and ambitious," he said. "Oh Madness, Pride," he wrote, excoriating himself for seeking repute, while in the next breath he lamented: "I shall never shine."[14]

When he told acquaintances, such as Robert Treat Paine and Samuel Quincy, of his yearning for notability, they only laughed. Chastened but undeterred, he searched for the means that would bring him notoriety. He closely observed politicians and other lawyers, believing he "could get more by studying [them] . . . than . . . by reading Justinian and all his voluminous" commentaries. He endeavored to mimic Otis and Putnam. In court he imitated the latter's sneer, his contemptuous look, his guileful air. He still sought to camouflage his real personality through pretense. He fell into the "Habit of affecting Wit and Humour, of shrugging [his] Shoulders, and moving [and] distorting the Muscles of [his] face." He searched continually for other avenues to recognition. "I have been stupid" in having failed to meet the right people, he thought. He should visit the leading teachers, physicians, and businessmen in Braintree, not taking up so much of their time that they would be angered but just enough to "get their good Word." He knew that this would be an uphill battle. His personality was unsuited for banter. He was too reserved with too "too stiff a face and air." A man with this disposition could never backslap and converse with the local inhabitants "on the common Tittletattle of the Town." How then could he talk with "Men of figure, Character [and] fortune?" He had no idea. Perhaps the best alternative would be to "look out for a Cause to Speak to." He might speak out with a "Boldness, Forwardness [that] will draw attention." This was Adams's dilemma. One course to possible acclaim offered only years of painful study. The other course—the way of contrivance and action—held out the possibility of more rapid success. What should it be, he wondered. "A bold Push, a resolute attempt, a determined Enterprize, or a slow, silent, imperceptible creeping. Shall I creep or fly?"[15]

Adams chose to fly. Two years after opening his practice he admitted that he had "executed none of [his] Plans of study." He chose instead to search for a cause. He found it in the temperance issue. He campaigned to reduce the number of inns in Braintree, and he succeeded. Early in 1761 the Braintree Board of Selectmen voted to reduce the number of licensed inns to just three. Then he turned to those given to what he called "Petty fogging." In the absence of a formal bar association to set high standards for licensing a practice, virtually anyone could represent a client. Those who lacked professional training were called "pettyfoggers"; they caused more problems than they solved and, in the process, blackened the reputation even of trained lawyers. Adams had little initial success in this crusade, although he surely must have gained the admiration of other barristers who harbored the same adverse opinions toward these interlopers.[16]

About this time, his diary shows, his caseload began to increase, most of his clients seeking help with problems arising from inheritance. In the fall of 1760 he scored his first victory before a jury, and it left him lightheaded. "The story of Yesterday's Tryal spreads. They say I was saucy," he wrote, basking in the glow of his achievement. Subsequent successes increased his confidence. References to his wretched condition and his inadequacies grew less frequent, then disappeared altogether. Where once he had excoriated himself for every shortcoming, now, after a setback, he told his diary: "I was too incautious, and unartful in my Proceeding, but Practice makes perfect." By early the following year, he noticed that he had grown "more expert, less diffident. I feel my own strength," he reported. He began to notice the "respectful face[s]" of his peers; he was pleased to see that the pettifoggers looked upon him with some fear. Soon, well-established attorneys—men like Jonathan Sewall, whose uncle was the chief justice of Massachusetts, and Peter Oliver, a member of the provincial council—took note of him. However, the first considerable payoff for his efforts came in November 1761 when he was admitted to practice before the superior court in his province. Not only was his reputation enhanced but he could now take cases that would previously have been denied him.[17]

The one really dark moment for Adams in this period occurred with the death of his father in late May 1761. At the age of seventy-one, the Deacon had fallen victim to an influenza epidemic that swept across Braintree that spring. For a time thereafter, John was despondent and introverted, even engaging in the critical self-scrutiny that he had largely abandoned as his practice stabilized. Eventually, he felt better, evidently happier, in fact, than he had been in years. His career was progressing nicely, and now he was a freeholder, having inherited one-third of his father's estate. Among other things, John Adams was for the first time able to hold local office.[18]

Adams's growing success stemmed from many sources. The child of ambitious parents who had demanded achievements of their son, Adams from age twelve or thirteen had seen little alternative but to work assiduously to better himself. Coming of age in an environment of lingering Puritanism was also crucial to his development. Deep seeds were planted in him: introspection, earnestness, and seriousness would be components of his personality all his life. From Puritanism too came the notion that his achievements would be handsomely rewarded. In his struggling first months of practice when he cried out in his diary that he expected to "have some Boon . . . fame, fortune, or something" in return for his deprivation, it was the legacy of Puritanism speaking.[19]

In addition, he learned from Master Marsh and at Harvard as well that hard work bore fruit. He lived by a self-imposed discipline, a trait that remained with him all his life. In these years, despite his admission that he did not strictly adhere to his self-assigned regimen, he did read and study. "I have read Gilberts 1st Section, of feuds, this evening but am not master of it," he recorded in his diary on October 5, 1758. The following day, his entry read: "am now reading over again Gilberts section of feudal tenures." And he read it again the next day, and the next, and the day after that. "Read in Gilberts Tenures. I must and will make that Book familiar to me," he exclaimed on October 9. On the tenth he could say with pride: "I read him slowly, but I gain Ideas and Knowledge as I go along." "This small volume will take me a fortnight, but I will master it," he wrote on the twelfth, and he kept at it until he thoroughly knew Gilbert.[20]

Finally, Adams was a keen observer of others. Although loath to admit it, he feared that a man's persona might be more crucial to his success than the talents he displayed. He wanted to believe that "Figure, and shew, may indeed attract the Eyes, and Admiration of the Vulgar, but are little very little regarded by wise Men." After a year of struggling in the thicket of competition in the Boston and Suffolk County courts, he was no longer so certain. Sometimes, there was more to be learned from watching the powerful at town meetings and on muster day than from cloistering oneself in a room with a book, he said; a good imitation of the successful "may serve good Ends in Life, may procure Respect," he ruefully admitted.[21]

Thus began a pattern that became habit. All his life Adams closely scrutinized successful men, seeking to learn their secrets. Later, men such as Benjamin Franklin and George Washington fascinated him, not just because he was perplexed by their achievements but because of what he might gather from an understanding of their methods. During these early years, he watched Gridley and Otis, Sewall and Oliver, for any clues they might provide to assist the furtherance of his ambitions. But he understood that he could neither change his personality nor adapt to a demeanor with which he was uncomfortable. He realized, too, that he was not a very good actor. In James Otis and

Oxenbridge Thacher, however, Adams found a sterling attribute that he sought to emulate. Each man was an outstanding orator. All the men that he esteemed were talented, but Thatcher and Otis were set apart from the others by their eloquence, their oratorical skills. Thacher was a man of "amiable manners" who spoke with "a very easy and musical Eloquence" that "made him very popular." Adams could not match that style, but in Otis he appears to have found his model. If his writings offer a guide, Otis must have spoken with felicity and force, expressing himself in a manner at once elegant and trenchant yet again witty and satirical, passionate and sublime. Adams once equated an Otis speech to "a flame of fire" fueled by considerable research, filled with numerous allusions to classical antiquity, and delivered in "a torrent of impetuous eloquence." Adams was closer to Otis, who was half again his age, than to Thacher. Otis, Adams thought, was "more like a Brother than a father" and saw him as the most "manly and Commanding Character of his age at the bar." Moreover, he discovered that Otis's oratorical skills had "secured him a commanding popularity." Adams had no stomach for dissembling, but in Otis and his oratory he found a way toward the renown he craved.[22]

At first glance, young John Adams's obsession with recognition seems odd. In contrast to the great mass of his contemporaries, his yearning was exceptional. Yet when Adams is compared to other high achievers of his generation, his behavior appears more normal. Young Washington sought recognition just as fervently, and he impatiently pursued a commission in the British army during the French and Indian War as the most rapid means of procuring attention. The youthful Thomas Jefferson dreamed of someday sitting on the King's Council in Virginia, while Alexander Hamilton, born too late to soldier in the war in the 1750s, announced: "I contemn the grovling and condition of a Clerk or the like, to which my Fortune, &c., contemns me." He wished for war, through which he could be catapulted into notoriety; his hero was James Wolfe, the British general who died in the assault on Quebec in 1759. Benjamin Franklin, who grew up earlier in Boston, exhibited the same industriousness and ambition that Adams would evince. He mapped out an extensive regimen of self-improvement, as did Adams, and found his role models in Jesus and Socrates. Adams, and many others who would subsequently play an important role in the affairs of early America, were the sort of men that historian Douglass Adair aptly describes as "passionately selfish and self-interested," men who shared a common attribute, a love of fame.[23]

How can one account for John Adams's passionate search for glory and renown? The principal figure in his formative years was his father. Whatever the Deacon may have been, Adams looked upon him as a man of "Industry and Enterprize," the "honestest Man I ever knew," a man who rose above the level attained by his own father through his "Wisdom, Piety, Benevolence and Charity." In contrast with other men of similar backgrounds, John never discovered "his Superiour." After a youthful rebellion against his strong-willed father, John spent the rest of his life attempting to satisfy the Deacon's ambitious dreams for him, yet endeavoring to fulfill those hopes without offending his father through self-serving or treacherous acts. And this would produce the central tension throughout Adams's life. He was driven by a "Passion for superiority," he once said, while he yearned to "subdue every unworthy Passion and treat all men as I wish to be treated by all."[24]

Sometime in 1759, John met Abigail Smith, daughter of the Reverend William Smith of nearby Weymouth. Abigail did not immediately sweep John off his feet. Still trying in vain to shake his lingering affection for Hannah Quincy, John compared every aspect of the two—who were second cousins—and Abigail finished a distant second. She was a wit, John thought, but she lacked Hannah's tenderness and flirtatious manner, and she was not as open or frank. It was an unfair comparison, of course; Abigail was barely fifteen, while Hannah was a mature young woman in her early twenties. Moreover, John was still in the thrall of Hannah, and no other young lady would have held much appeal for him then. Their relationship was complicated, moreover, by Adams's feelings toward Abigail's father, whom he saw as a "crafty, designing" sort given to an ostentatious display of wealth.[25] After one or two evenings together, probably in Abigail's home, the two did not see one another again for two years.

Two years later the two were reintroduced, probably by Richard Cranch, Adams's farmer-clockmaker friend who was courting Mary Smith, Abigail's older sister. This time, things were quite different. Adams was twenty-seven and more mature. Hannah was in the past as well, and with his growing success as a lawyer he was a far more confident young man than he had been in 1759. Abigail had changed, too. Having just turned seventeen, she must have borne little resemblance to the young girl Adams had met previously.

Abigail was one of four children in the Smith family, a clan that lived comfortably, supported by the revenue from two farms, the Reverend Smith's clerical salary, and the labor of four slaves. Abigail was a bright young woman, with more than a bit of native intelligence and with more tutoring than females usually received, even those of her station. Mary and her mother initially had overseen her training, but it had been an unsystematic endeavor designed largely to assure that Abigail was merely literate. The arrival of Cranch changed everything. Beginning when Abigail was about eleven, he served as a surrogate college professor, introducing this remarkably talented and in-quisitive young lady to Shakespeare, John Milton, and Alexander Pope, as well as to her personal favorite, James Thompson, author of *The Seasons*. Despite her progress, however, she was not sent to a female finishing school. Chronic illness had plagued her childhood and though the maladies were always minor, her overprotective and rather domineering mother presumed that Abigail's constitution was too weak to withstand the strains of being far from home.[26]

Abigail had never seriously been courted by anyone before John surfaced; however, she made up for lost time when he entered her life. By spring 1763 the two found it difficult to be apart, and languid John, while not quite proposing, had begun to drop hints that he wished to marry. When they could be alone they talked of everything, and they petted and caressed until the wee hours. By August he longed passionately for "her fair Complexion, her Crimson Blushes and her million Charms and Graces." Her only faults, he once told her, were her shyness and timidity, her inability to sing (Abigail admitted to singing like the "screech of a peacock"), and her pigeon-toed walk, a gait quite the opposite of a "stately strutt," as he put it. Otherwise, she was "bright and luminous." That fall Abigail, now nineteen, accompanied John on his legal circuit, a monthlong trek from one county courthouse to another. The two planned to marry, though John hoped to postpone matters just a little longer. But there was no question of his love for her. She was "a constant feast" to him, a "Prudent, modest, delicate, soft, sensible, obliging, active" young lady. Yet he remembered Gridley's advice about deferring marriage, and he was not certain that he could meet the financial demands of a growing family. More than anything, though, he found important personal decisions difficult to make.

But this was a decision that Abigail helped him reach. After a year's courtship, she began to nudge him gently. For a time he demurred, then he relented, agreeing to marry in October 1764. The date was pushed back a bit so that John could be inoculated against smallpox as his job required considerable travel and, hence, repeated exposure to the ever-present danger of the disease.[27]

Sooner or later, virtually every adult in this era experienced the terror of an epidemic. Abigail once watched helplessly as diphtheria invaded Weymouth, killing dozens of children, including eleven in one week, and John of course had witnessed the death of his father and seventeen others from the same neighborhood in the recent influenza scourge in Braintree. But an inoculation existed for smallpox, and by the 1760s variolation had become so commonplace that even the poor were usually treated once an epidemic had begun. Many affluent citizens, on the other hand, took the inoculation as children or young adults, for experiments earlier in the century in both Boston and London had demonstrated that, through such a procedure, the scourge of smallpox might be prevented. Through inoculation, a healthy person was deliberately infected with a mild case of smallpox; thereafter, that individual was forever immune to the disease. Inoculation was a relatively safe procedure, although those who submitted to it faced an emotional and, on occasion, a physical ordeal. Variolation was preceded by a weeklong administration of purgatives and cathartics, and following the inoculation the patient still was confronted with not only six weeks of rest but also a protracted diet of milk, bread, pudding, and rice. Days of discomfort might follow the immunization, and even when the patient felt well again, rest in quarantine was required for about five more weeks. Some patients, moreover, emerged with a badly pockmarked face, disfigured by the loathsome pustules that signified the disease.[28]

John began his tribulations at home on a Sunday in April. Abigail was beside herself with anxiety, although one of her uncles had cheered her with the news that John's physician had never lost a patient during this procedure. John faced the ordeal with serenity; he had wrestled with the matter for months, but once he decided this was the wisest course he made peace with himself. He retreated to his room with his brother Peter Boylston, who also was to be inoculated. For a week they stayed indoors, sticking to their meager preparatory diet, taking mercury tablets, and smoking ipecacuanha, an exotic plant that possessed emetic, diaphoretic, and purgative properties. After a week he and eight others—including Abigail's brother William, her uncle Cotton Tufts, a physician, and two of Hannah Quincy's brothers—checked into a Boston hospital, where they finally were inoculated. The procedure took only a moment. The physician simply inserted an infected thread inside a tiny incision in John's left arm. Three of the patients fell quite ill within twenty-four hours, but John was fine until the sixth day, and even then he experienced nothing worse than a period of chills and hot flashes followed by a generally feeble and listless sensation. He developed few pustules and was left with no permanent scars. Once past the critical point he simply had to endure a month of convalescence, isolated in the hospital lest he transmit the disease to others. He lulled away the time by reading, playing cards, and talking with his fellow shut-ins, and by writing to Abigail (though he cautioned her to first disinfect each letter by immersing it in heavy smoke). He also read and reread the letters she sent to him, missives at first filled with apprehension, then admitting a loneliness so great that she longed to come to the hospital if only to see him through a window.[29]

When he was discharged from the infirmary in May, John celebrated with a meal of two and one-half dozen oysters, washed down by Malaga, a strong, sweet dessert wine. And, of course, he and Abigail were reunited after a painful separation of more than forty days. They saw one another frequently that summer. They planned the details of their wedding and engaged in the kind of talk that has always preoccupied lovesick young couples. It was a happy and busy time. Abigail visited friends and cousins in Newtown and Mystic as often as she could, for she knew that pregnancies and small children soon would leave her little time or strength for travel. She hurried into Boston occasionally, too, shopping for her wedding gown as well as for furnishings for their new home, a small farm next door to the house in which John had been born, property that he had inherited from his father. Between the calls of the legal circuit, John tended to the mending of his newly acquired estate, draining a swamp, building and repairing fences, clearing brush, and personally planting a large vegetable garden. Then, too, there were the summer evenings when John, the day's work completed, rode down to Weymouth. It was a fine season, a happy time when it was exhilarating to sit outside on a warm night, enveloped by a gentle estival breeze, listening to the songs of the crickets and the tree frogs, talking of this and that, and wondering how marriage would change one's life.[30]

Both grew anxious as the wedding day approached. Abigail had a spell of migraine headaches and insomnia, maladies that for her were unusual only in their increased frequency. Nor did John feel well, perhaps as a result of the strain and apprehension that mounted as the date of the wedding drew near. But finally the day arrived, October 25, 1764.[31]

Friends and relatives poured into Weymouth. The ceremony, performed at Abigail's home by her father, was short and painless. A long reception followed, an occasion when typically the men gathered in one room to drink, smoke, and swap stories—frequently ribald wedding-night tales—while the ladies adjourned to another portion of the house to gossip and advise the bride. Somehow John and Abigail, each anxious and weak and self-conscious, and longing to be alone, made it through the day. At last they were truly united. John was twenty-nine and his bride, twenty.

John Adams was happier that winter than he had been in years. So too was Abigail, who happily discovered that her husband's severe manner—at times almost forbiddingly haughty and arrogant—was just a front, an affectation behind which lurked a gentle and tender man. The couple set up housekeeping in a century-old saltbox, a small, unpainted cottage facing the main road of Braintree and occupying the lot next door to the house in which John had been raised. The downstairs consisted of a spacious kitchen, a seldom-utilized parlor, John's study, and cramped quarters for Judah, the family's servant. Four bedrooms made up the second floor, although two were tiny cubicles squeezed beneath the eaves. The house squatted on the foreside of John's little farm, a plot of only forty infecund acres, a rather unrelenting tract that at least surrendered firewood and tolerated livestock, apple trees, a summer garden, and a hen house.[32]

That first winter John and Abigail sometimes walked together or spent hours in the crisp New England air sleighing over freshly fallen snow. Often they just sat in front of a roaring fire on dark, bitterly cold evenings, talking and loving and getting accustomed to living together. By Christmas, Abigail knew she was pregnant, a circumstance that drew the two even closer as they expressed their joys and fears at the prospect of childbearing and parenthood. John's happiness at his domestic serenity was matched by the contentment he felt over the progress of his career.

John Adams's Braintree, Massachusetts, birthplace (*right*) and residence (*left*) following his marriage in 1764. Painting by Frankenstein. *Courtesy: U.S. Department of the Interior, National Park Service, Adams National Historic Site, Quincy, Massachusetts.*

Early in the winter Jeremiah Gridley sent John a cryptic note requesting that the young man stop by his office. John hurried off, perplexed and concerned. But Gridley merely asked him to consider joining Sodalitas, a group of four barristers who met frequently to share their study of the law. John immediately accepted, flattered by this sign of recognition. Beginning in January 1765 the men met each Thursday evening to discuss a previously designated section of a legal classic, and after airing some of his views before these critics, Adams scratched them onto paper and saw them published in a Boston newspaper.[33]

Adams's willingness to expose himself to the barbs of others was an indication of his growing self-confidence. Indeed, this was his second venture into publishing. In the spring and summer of 1763 he had published seven essays in Boston newspapers, treatises that included his initial plunge into the murky waters of political theory. These first discourses were prompted by a spirited newspaper debate over local political issues, pitting Lt. Gov. Thomas Hutchinson and John's old friend Jonathan Sewall against James Otis. While these men and the factions gathered about them debated important issues, such as the naming of a new agent to represent Massachusetts in London, Adams recognized that at bottom this was a contest between ambitious men for greater power. His essays, therefore, ridiculed both parties. He wrote anonymously, signing each article "Humphrey Ploughjogger," a rube who was heedless of the rules of grammar and spelling. "I Arnt book larnt enuff, to rite so polytly, as the great gentlefolks," he declared. However, he proceeded to lampoon the "grate men [who] dus nothin but quaril with anuther and put peces in the nues paper against one anuther." His principal point, made in jest, was that if all the dangers the two sides warned of came true, they would "all be made slaves on." It was a quip that could still draw a laugh in 1763. Twenty years later, Adams dismissed these articles as "fugitive pieces . . . not worth mentioning," although he recollected with some pride that his Ploughjogger essays had "excited more merriment than all my other writings together."

Adams wrote several other essays in 1763 that were published in the *Boston Gazette* under the signature "U." These pieces were quite serious, even scholarly. They were inspired by Adams's defense of Gen. William Brattle, a member of the provincial council. In June, Brattle and John Murray, a legislator from Rutland, engaged in fisticuffs in the streets of Boston. Brattle ultimately retained Adams as his attorney and brought suit for trespass against Murray. The case led Adams to dilate on human nature, then to ponder how government might be fashioned to control the dark side of man's drives, especially his propensity to lust after power, an issue to which he repeatedly turned in his writings. Adams offered a commonplace solution. He championed the staple of English Whig theory, the notion that only a government balanced between monarchy, aristocracy, and democracy could restrain men in their inevitable pursuit of "wanton Pleasures" or safeguard the great majority from those in power who if unchecked would give vent to their "capricious Will." No other choice existed, he wrote, for as every man was liable to "vanity, excessive ambition and venality," it followed that no man could be trusted to be *"infallible* or *impeccable* in government."[34]

Adams's bustling schedule of study and court appearances frequently separated him from his wife, even during these apprehensive months of her pregnancy. Childbearing, whatever the joys, was an anxious time for every woman in the eighteenth century. By modern standards the mortality rate both for mothers and infants was staggering, a grievous state brought about largely by an inadequate knowledge of combating infection. Given Abigail's history of chronic illness, the couple feared that pregnancy would place her in unusually perilous straits. As the anticipated arrival date grew near, Abigail—with John on the road tending to his legal chores—went to her parent's home. She arrived at their door just in time, for on a hot Sabbath morning in July she gave birth to a baby girl. That same day, Abigail's father, Reverend Smith, baptized the infant. She was named after her mother, but everyone would call her Nabby.[35]

At the first opportunity Adams scurried to Weymouth, where he was relieved to find both his wife and daughter in good health. He remained with them as long as he could, pitching in to help with some of the chores necessitated by Nabby's arrival. Abigail, in fact, would nurse her baby for a year, the customary procedure in the more affluent households of that day. Not until Nabby was twelve months old would her mother's milk be supplemented by cornmeal and water, and weeks more would pass before she was introduced to mashed fruit and vegetables. Only much later, perhaps in her third year, would Nabby first taste meat.[36] Abigail and her husband were drawn even closer in these months, bonded in that special way that only the birth of a first child can occasion. Everything seemed to be going quite well, Adams thought. His law practice was growing, his talent as an attorney had not gone unnoticed, and his domestic good fortune seemed limitless.

Suddenly, however, his serenity was shattered. Massachusetts was plunged into great turmoil over the Stamp Act, legislation enacted by Parliament. Riots ensued and the courts closed their doors. Some talked as though the crisis could even mean war between the colonists and Great Britain. Men were compelled to choose sides: loyalty to the parent state or open defiance of British law.

John was dismayed, frightened that the emergency might destroy all that he had labored to build, and he reacted to the tumultuous events in the most personal terms, outraged that a law passed in a faraway city by a distant government could so easily jeopardize his future. He was not a statesman, and his response was unstatesmanlike. The Stamp Act crisis "is very unfortunate for me," he lamented in his diary, for "[I am] just getting into my

Geers, just getting under Sail." He had struggled with poverty and toiled to get ahead with very little assistance from anyone. He had been groping in "dark Obscurity, till of late, and had just become known, and gained a small . . . Reputation." He wrote, "This execrable Project was set on foot for *my* Ruin."[37]

What Adams feared was indeed about to occur. The world of this uncelebrated young provincial was on the verge of changing, but in a way that he could never have imagined in 1765.

CHAPTER 3

*

To Thine Own Self
Be True

READERS OF THE *Boston Gazette* opened their little newspaper
in the fall of 1765 to discover that "Humphrey Ploughjogger" had
paid another visit to their pages, his first in more than a year. The Stamp Act
was on his mind. This Yankee hayseed found the tax deplorable for all the
conventional reasons. Not only was it unconstitutional but it would impover-
ish a good many sturdy yeomen. Yet this rustic commentator struck a somewhat different chord: whereas many of the protest leaders depicted the duty as
a threat to the unsullied innocence of America, Ploughjogger saw in colonial
resistance a means by which the old-time virtues that once prevailed in New
England might be restored.

Intruding into his attack on the tax was a visceral assault on the signs of
decadence that he perceived in Boston. Hardly sounding like the rude bump-
kin he pretended to be, Ploughjogger charged that the marketplace had become so saturated with cheap liquor that "folks drink toddy and flip instead of
cyder." Young people, he complained, had abandoned the modest apparel of
their parents. Now "all the young men buy them blue surtouts, with fine
yellow buttons, and boughten broad cloth jackets and breeches—and our
young women wear callicoes, chinces and laces, and other nicknacks to make
them fine," he moaned. These habits were symptomatic of a growing indi-
vidualism, of a tendency to ignore communal values in favor of a hedonistic
self-indulgence, he implied. It was better to wear homespun, or even the "hide
of [a] fat Ox . . . with the hair on" it. The world of the fathers was slipping
away, but here, now, was an opportunity for redemption, a chance for these
"naughty jacks and trollops" to "leave off such vanity." Members of this generation—which had descended from a "Race of Heroes," as Adams put it in
another piece in January—could disabuse themselves of their insatiable "Lust
[after] Gain and Power," and show "themselves worthy of their Ancestors"
through a reassertion of the "highest Reverence for Virtue."[1] To oppose this

unjust act, he seemed to say, was to hark back to New England's ancestral
spirit of resistance to evil and at the same time cast off the vices of the modern
world, reawakening the refulgent virtues of yesteryear.

Over the past few years a new British imperial policy had begun to unfold,
though Adams and most other colonists had paid scant attention. In part, it
was Britain's very success that forced it to consider a new policy. Great Britain
had won the French and Indian War in 1763, securing Canada and all territory
east of the Mississippi River as bounty from its late foes. With the acquisition of
this vast domain Great Britain possessed an empire larger than any seen in the
western world since the collapse of Rome more than a thousand years earlier.
But the British empire had been gained at a staggering cost in blood and
money. In a bit longer than half a century Britain had fought four wars for
America, episodic armed conflicts that plunged the nation into an astonishing
indebtedness. By 1765 the British empire groaned beneath an almost unimaginable debt of £137 million.

Yet, it was not just the deficit that concerned statesmen in Whitehall. For
years London had been plagued by the fear that the Americans secretly wished
to be independent, and the conduct of many colonists in the final intercolonial
war only intensified those suspicions. Some colonies had refused to supply
their quotas of troops, most had provided inadequate financial assistance, and a
few even had persisted in trading with the enemy while their English and
American brethren died on American battlefields. Things had turned out well
enough, too well perhaps, for the victory only added to London's mistrust.
Now the ministry feared that the removal of the threat of Franco-Spanish
encirclement of its seaboard colonies might have disposed of the necessity for
these provinces to rely on London for protection.[2]

To that concern was added still another. According to the ancient precepts
of mercantilism, colonies existed for the benefit of the parent state, and almost
from the beginning of America's settlement, Britain's rulers—when permitted
the luxury of peace—had tinkered with their kingdom, endeavoring to make it
run as the learned treatises declared it should. They meddled with crop production, sought to regulate manufacturing, tampered with trade, scrutinized
the currency, and pried into the operations of the provincial governments. Yet
British hegemony over America's mainland colonies had never seemed weaker
than it did at the conclusion of the French and Indian War. One antidote, it was
said, might be the creation of a titled nobility in America, and there was talk
too of establishing an Anglican bishopric for the colonies. But most proposals
aimed at somehow centralizing Britain's control, whether that meant parliamentary taxation of the colonists, royalization of all the provinces, or, as an ex-
governor of Pennsylvania and Massachusetts suggested, merging the separate
colonies into one "GRAND MARITIME PROVINCE." Most of these

proposals never were attempted, but their very suggestion revealed the altered mood in high ruling circles.[3]

Serious discussion about reforming the management of the British empire went back fifteen years, but it fell to George Grenville to head the postwar ministry and to devise and implement a policy. Out of the partisanship and expediency of day-to-day politics, a new three-pronged colonial policy was born. In order to avoid levying additional taxes at home Grenville's ministry first hoped to tighten the execution of the existing trade laws by collecting the custom duties that earlier, distracted administrations had permitted to go unacquired. Next, again hoping to forbear new levies at home, the government wished to raise a revenue in America by taxing the colonists. Finally, the ministry sought judicious management of the newly acquired territories.

While a resolutely nonpolitical John Adams was distracted by his impending marriage and his struggle to establish his legal practice, the news of Grenville's initial measures reached the colonies. The Revenue Act of 1764— the colonists persisted in calling it the Sugar Act—was the ministry's initial levy. London sought income by lowering the duty on foreign sugar imported into America; to assure its collection the measure not only strengthened the customs service, it created alongside existing provincial admiralty courts, a supercourt, the Court of Vice Admiralty for all America, a tribunal with both appellate and original jurisdiction that was to try—without benefit of jury and before a Crown-appointed magistrate—all suspected violators of British mercantile legislation.[4]

The Sugar Act provoked some opposition in the colonies, mostly in the form of pamphlets humbly dilating upon the measure. Adams's benefactor, James Otis, wrote the best of the lot, a somewhat confused treatise that nevertheless clearly conveyed the argument that the rights of the unrepresented Americans were violated by a parliamentary tax. Almost fifty years later an elderly John Adams recalled that Otis's writings and actions had profoundly influenced his thinking at the time. In fact, however, at the moment the Sugar Act became law, young Adams was writing: "For many Years past, I have not felt more serenely. . . . My Heart is at ease. Business of every kind, I have banished from my Thoughts."[5] His thoughts were not untypical, for the few voices raised against the Sugar Act failed to rally public opinion into any substantive protest movement.

The Stamp Act of 1765, which placed duties on nearly all publicly issued documents and licenses, was another matter, however. Grenville had anticipated some colonial opposition, but he failed to foresee the magnitude of the American protest that occurred. Soon America was ablaze with demonstrations and riots. More pamphlets churned off the colonists' presses, less adumbrative than those of the Sugar Act tempest, however, and an economic boycott of the commodities of the parent state was instituted. Of greater significance—though the fact was only dimly perceived in London—the crisis caused many in the colonies to rethink ingrained attitudes, including both the nature of the British government and its relationship to America.[6]

The impact of the Stamp Act on Massachusetts cannot be overestimated. This British act not only solidified significant political changes that had already commenced, but it also transformed the constitutional and ideological outlook of many within the colony.

At the outset of the decade Massachusetts was politically divided into factions loosely called the Court party and the Country party. The Court party was strongest in maritime towns and those inland villages with close economic ties to the commercial east coast, but the key figure in the party was the royal governor; in fact, it was his ability to distribute lucrative jobs to his dutiful adherents that held the party together. The opposition party traditionally garnered its strength from the less commercially active, more inward-looking towns situated in regions that remained committed to an agrarian economy and way of life. For as long as anyone could remember, the domination of the Court party had been almost absolute, especially in administrative and judicicial matters, as well as in the Council, the upper house of the provincial assembly. But toward the end of 1760 a realignment of political forces began in Massachusetts.

Personalities played a role in the reordering of factions. When Gov. Francis Bernard named Thomas Hutchinson to be chief justice of the superior court late in 1760, his decision provoked deep rifts within the Court party. Hutchinson already sat on the council, served as magistrate of two lower courts, and held the lieutenant governorship. That was too much power for one man, many concluded. Furthermore, Hutchinson was bereft of formal legal training. His appointment aroused bitterness among attorneys who had worked diligently to bring professionalism to the practice of the law. Finally, contemporaries believed that Hutchinson's selection provoked the powerful Otis family, which believed that its patriarch, Col. James Otis, Sr., deserved the appointment as a reward for years of faithful service. Whether from principal or pique, it was at this moment that the Otis brigade, always loyal members of the Court party, switched its allegiance to the Country party.

At this same moment the government of Massachusetts became embroiled in a furious battle with many of Boston's leading merchants, an encounter that furthered the burgeoning political shift. For years it had been an open secret that many merchants smuggled into the colony items that were taxable or prohibited altogether by Britain's commercial laws. With the outbreak of the French and Indian War in 1756, however, the Massachusetts Superior Court not only issued writs of assistance, virtual blanket search warrants, to customs officers engaged in patrolling Boston's waterfront, but it had more systematically sought to prosecute trade violations. At the time, James Otis, Jr., had been the king's advocate general of the Vice Admiralty Court in Boston; Otis, thus, had been the Crown's principal prosecutor of Massachusetts businessmen accused of illegal trade. But when he switched parties, Otis, together with Oxenbridge Thacher, was retained by several Boston merchants in an action to prevent Judge Hutchinson from issuing new writs; Jeremiah Gridley, once Otis's mentor, and, like Otis and Thacher, a benefactor of young John Adams, defended the government. Otis proved to be the most important presence in the courtroom, for he based his opposition to the writs on a constitutional principle; perhaps the most eloquent lawyer in Massachusetts, Otis took the position that Parliament lacked the authority to issue general search warrants. Eventually the battle spilled out of the courtroom and became a struggle between the Court party, which had no choice but to support the Crown, and the metamorphic Country party.

The Court party won the court battle, but it lost the war that followed. Hutchinson ultimately issued the writs of assistance, but many of Boston's merchants soon switched their allegiance to the opposition faction. Hard times that set in after 1763 furthered the growth of the Country party. After the French and Indian War, Boston fell victim to an economic depression occasioned by the withdrawal of the British armed forces, the cessation of wartime contracts, and record British imports that flooded the colonial market. The poor economy meant belt-tightening for most merchants, bankruptcy for some. The Sugar Act and Stamp Act only exacerbated the plight of those who survived. For many insecure, desperate merchants the suddenly revitalized party of Otis and Thacher offered the best vehicle through which to resist a provincial administration bent on enforcing Whitehall's measures. By 1763 the Country party controlled Boston's delegation to the assembly—Otis and Thacher occupied two of the delegation's four seats—and by the time of the Stamp Act two years later, the party dominated the legislature.[7]

Even so, the Country party was largely ineffective in the crisis of 1765. To a large degree the party had been built on the personalities of its two leaders. But Thacher died during the summer of 1765, a victim of smallpox, while Otis, already beginning to display the unmistakable signs of mental instability, was too often confused and ineffectual. His behavior was characterized by bewildering equivocations. The colony's leading foe of the Sugar Act, Otis first defended the Stamp Act, then attacked it, then denounced as treasonous virtually all opposition to the duties. The upshot of his "distracted" behavior, as John Adams labeled his conduct, as well as Thacher's untimely demise, was that the Country party was rendered temporarily leaderless.[8] Incapable of resolute action, therefore, the Massachusetts Assembly in 1765 did little more than urge the convocation of an intercolonial congress to consider the Stamp Act.

Outside the languid assembly, however, Massachusetts radicals were not without leaders. The principal figure in this netherworld in 1765 was Samuel Adams. Despite a comfortable childhood and a degree from Harvard College,

Sam Adams's most noteworthy aspect in forty-three years was his singular lack of achievement. He had dribbled away his inheritance, then he had failed in several business ventures. He eked out a living as a petty official, first as a tax assessor, then as a tax collector. But by the mid-1760s he was deeply in debt and his family was reduced to dwelling in a ramshackle house, his children to wearing secondhand clothes provided by relatives and friends. The Anglo-American crisis that erupted that year changed everything.

Samuel Adams always had been fascinated by political power, but there was far more to him than a mere lust after office. Still a youngster when the Great Awakening, a religious revival, had swept through the northeast provinces in the early 1740s, he had been transformed by the experience. He had come to cherish the old Puritan virtues of his ancestors and had grown wary of change, lest that Puritan rectitude be destroyed. Long before anyone thought of the Stamp Act, Samuel Adams fretted over the threats of change to the old Puritan nucleated communities, with their ideals of consensual harmony and public good. Adams saw his mission as the preservation of ancestral probity, not the adoption of a new revolutionary code. His message was an exhortation to virtuous behavior. He worried about "luxury," a term in his lexicon that encapsulated what today might more generally be thought of as "change" or "progress" or, better yet, "modernization." "Luxury," he thought, inevitably led society toward sloth and cowardice and self-indulgence. For a man who believed that change was to be resisted, the Stamp Act unavoidably became symptomatic of everything that he feared. The legislation threatened to enfeeble the colonists' self-mastery and, in turn, to imperil the old value system. Moreover, resistance to the act could be a cathartic experience, one that required spartan, frugal, virtuous behavior by the colonists, and that could restore the old values. Samuel Adams, John thought, was "a wedge of steel," vibrant, tough, durable, resolute. He was not, like his cousin John, a legalistic sort. Indeed, according to John, he had only a shallow understanding of constitutional matters. But, John added, Samuel had "the most thorough Understanding of Liberty, and . . . the Temper and Character of the People."[9]

It was this understanding that enabled Samuel Adams to mold a significant political transformation during the Stamp Act crisis. Moving into the void left by Thacher's demise and Otis's instability, Samuel Adams took control and "out of doors," outside the legislative hall, he fashioned the Popular, or Whig, party, as it would be called thereafter. It was a masterstroke. He succeeded in forging a link between Boston, the epicenter of the province's resistance movement, and the towns of Massachusetts. It was his genius to recognize that utterly disparate elements in rural and urban Massachusetts shared a fear of change, allowing him to mold an alliance from among such dissimilar factions. His coalition consisted of urban merchants who had prospered under the old colonial policy; skilled artisans and unskilled laborers who toiled in the metropolis; farmers in the interior towns, some of whom fretted over the diminishing quality of life in small agricultural villages; those laden with guilt at their own avaricious conduct in the ever-expanding economic milieu; and those virtual utopianists who cherished the real or imagined ethical imperatives of an earlier age, people like Samuel Adams himself, who consciously or unconsciously were haunted by the failure of their colony to realize its mission and who groaned under the burden of sensing that their society had fallen from grace.[10] For at least some of these people the Stamp Act produced a rebirth, a secular awakening that was to be even more powerful than the religious upheaval through which an earlier generation had sought to grapple with many of these same problems.

Samuel Adams organized his disparate contacts, preached to the downtrodden, coaxed the affluent, goaded, guided, and taught. He was tireless. In his single-minded pursuit of a goal, a foe once remarked, he "eats little, drinks little, sleeps little, thinks much." As often is the case with a great leader, there was some charismatic aspect in his makeup, some quality that prompted men to follow his lead. Perhaps it was his face, ruggedly handsome and dominated by penetrating eyes, although the most striking aspect of his appearance was a countenance that radiated determination and vigor and self-assurance. And, he was a refined man. John Adams thought him a gentleman of "genteel Erudition [and] obliging, engaging Manners." Abigail thought him a man of "good breeding" to whom affectation was a stranger. His only fault, thought John, was that his love of politics led him to neglect his family, although Abigail thought Samuel and his wife made a "charming pair," a couple who exuded "the tenderest affection towards each other."[11]

Samuel Adams did not act alone in arousing Boston to action. His principal followers were skilled artisans and small businessmen rather than wealthy merchants, and his goals required a large army. For this he turned to the unskilled workers, a class that took its orders from other leaders, from men such as William Molineux, owner of a hardware store, a businessman with a penchant for amalgamating and activating workers (he later was dubbed the "first leader of dirty matters"), and Ebenezer Mackintosh, a cordwainer and sealer (that is, an inspector of leather goods) who divided his spare time between organizing brigades of fire fighters in the South End and marshaling them into action when public protest was required.

There is much disagreement among historians over the motives of the crowds that took to the streets in the summer of 1765, though there can be little doubt that for the city's roustabouts and leather-apron men who joined in the protest, there was much about which to complain. If prosperity can trickle downhill, hard times have a way of surging downward, the misery becoming more widespread and burdensome as it seeps into the lower economic orders. Boston's working classes were caught in a devilish squeeze, the victims of the postwar depression on the one hand, prey to rising prices on the other. By the mid-1760s one in three males was too poor to own any taxable property, and access to the middle class seemed to be steadily diminishing. Life at the bottom of society often meant inadequate housing, a sparse and monotonous diet, an insufficient supply of firewood and apparel, and a dearth of those appurtenances and opportunities that can brighten one's existence. Before the summer of 1765 ended, the workers had publicly vented their frustrations.[12]

On the morning of August 14, Samuel Adams brought his first crowd into the streets. It listened to speeches, then hanged effigies of Andrew Oliver, the province's stamp collector, and Lord Bute, King George III's mentor and a man widely suspected of being the real power behind the Grenville ministry. The demonstration could not have been more orderly. That evening Adams and his confederates organized a second rally, to which all residents of Boston—except the city's black inhabitants—were invited. This crowd, composed largely of unskilled laborers, soon got out of hand, tearing down a building owned by Oliver and about to set to work on his mansion when its organizers reestablished control. Two weeks later the mob struck again. This time Hutchinson was the target. His house was looted and demolished; when the sun rose the following morning, all that remained of this once handsome mansion was the frame. By that time, moreover, a badly shaken Andrew Oliver had resigned as stamp collector.[13]

By then, too, something else had been achieved. The upheaval had produced a metamorphosis in the constitutional and ideological outlook of many citizens. No one was more aware of the dramatic changes than John Adams. Just before Christmas 1765, he noted that this fading year had been "the most remarkable" of his life. After all the rallies and the rhetoric died away, he concluded that the crisis had caused "the people, even to the lowest ranks," to become "more attentive to their liberties, more inquisitive about them, and more determined to defend them, than they were ever before." Half a century later he still believed the year 1765 had given birth to the "child Independence," for the "minds and hearts of the people" had been transformed. Curiously, Adams later remembered the writs of assistance case in 1761, not the Stamp crisis, as the time when his own thinking turned. He recollected attending those court sessions daily. It was Otis who moved him with the most electrifying speech he had ever heard and who convinced him of the danger of British designs. But whatever the significance of the writs case, it was Samuel Adams's teachings about the Stamp Act and the meaning of American resistance that fleshed out for John the lessons he had learned from Otis. And it was Samuel Adams's example during the protests in 1765 that made John, for the first time, long to be active in the popular cause.[14]

John Adams was active in the cause during 1765 and 1766, but his role was relatively minor and inconspicuous. He drafted a resolution for the town of Braintree, a statement necessitated by the town's wish to instruct its delegate to the Massachusetts General Court, the province's legislature. He wrote the remonstrance in a candid and sinewy manner, mincing no words and denigrating the act both as an unconstitutional measure and as one certain to produce "a convulsive Change" within the empire. In addition, he published several works in the *Boston Gazette* in which he commented on the tax.

Beginning in August 1765, two days before Samuel Adams's first mob took to the streets of Boston, the first of four installments of John's "A Dissertation on the Canon and Feudal Law" appeared. His work appears to have originated in discussions earlier in the year at Sodalitas meetings; its inception owed nothing to the Stamp Act, about which the colonists knew almost nothing when he began writing his essays. As a result, the earliest essays were silent with regard to the protest. Only in the final paragraph of the last treatise, published on October 21, did he comment specifically on the tax. Nevertheless, he developed several ideas to which he often returned during the rebellion against British policy. He wrote of the first colonists as political and religious refugees from British tyranny. Their "love of *universal Liberty*" led them to emigrate and to establish in America "plan[s] both of ecclesiastical and civil government, in *direct opposition* to the *cannon* and the *feudal* systems" that prevailed in England. This is what he later referred to as the "American Revolution," the creation of an alternative and freer system than that existing in the parent state; in these pieces he lauded the sacrifices of his ancestors—they "bought [freedom] for us, at the expence of their ease, their estates, their pleasure, and their blood"—both by migrating to the American wilderness, then by fighting to win control of the region. And he made it clear that his generation might also have to make sacrifices to retain their hard-earned liberties. He went on to speak obliquely about British "insults and indignities," most likely a reference to what he much later denigrated as the unconscionable manner in which British officers had treated American soldiers during the French and Indian War, but he specifically identified only one great threat. In October, with the turmoil brought on by the stamp tax all about him, he wrote of a "formal design" contrived in London to "enslave all America." The "design"? A plan to impose an Anglican bishop on America. Finally, virtually appended to his last essay, were a few sentences regarding the Stamp Act. While much that John had hitherto written in the "Dissertation" was reminiscent of the language of a Samuel Adams essay, his comments on the Stamp Act differed significantly from those of his cousin. He did not see nefarious designs in the tax. Here was no plot to enslave America. There was a swipe at royal officials in America who had "trifled with, browbeaten, and trampled on" the colonists—the genesis of his later view of a plot by Hutchinson to tyrannize Massachusetts—but the Stamp Act itself was apparently only a misguided act, one that should be repealed because of the damage it would cause to American commerce and the problems it would create for lowest economic orders within the colonies.

In January 1766 Adams published three additional essays in the *Boston Gazette,* each under the name "Clarendon." His compositions were drafted in response to an essay by "William Pym," an anonymous English polemicist whose work had appeared in another Boston newspaper in November. Pym had written that the colonists were dependent upon Britain; he portrayed Britain's victory over France and Spain in the French and Indian War as due largely to British sacrifice, and he contended that the colonists must now pay for the benefits that had been won for them. Otis was first to answer Pym, refuting each of his arguments. Adams followed the next month, but his essays were turgid and discursive, and unlikely to have made a significant impact on popular thinking. He became bogged down over the peripheral issue of courts without juries and said little about British taxation. What he did have to say was not unlike his remarks in the "Dissertation" essays, although he spoke of the British tax as a dangerous threat to the colonists' "Rights and Privileges," and, as in his draft statement for Braintree, he castigated the measure as unconstitutional. Once again, however, he conveyed the impression that he looked upon the tax as merely a misguided act by an ill-informed British ministry.[15]

Adams clearly believed the Stamp Act was wrong and he lauded the colonists for their "gallant Struggle . . . founded in Principles so indisputable" against the measure, but he appears to have been uncertain about his role in the protest movement. He confessed his longing—curiously, he referred to it as his obligation—to "exert the Utmost of [his] Abilities" on behalf of the resistance, and he seems to have wrestled with his conscience over whether to commit himself more openly to the opposition. "At Home, with my family. Thinking," he wrote in his diary. "At Home. Thinking, reading, searching, concerning Taxation without Consent," he noted a few days later. Ultimately, he limited his role to that of composing the Braintree resolution and contributing the anonymous newspaper essays.[16]

It was no fault of Samuel Adams that John did not play a greater part in the Stamp Act protests. Impressed by the intellectual capabilities of his younger cousin, Samuel sought to recruit him for an active role in the popular movement "by a constant whispering at his Ear," as a Massachusetts Loyalist once suggested. John himself remembered that Samuel habitually watched for young men of promise and respectability whom he might "court" and "cultivate" for the patriot cause. In fact, Samuel probably played a considerable role in bringing the promising young attorney Josiah Quincy, Jr., and two of Boston's leading physicians, Benjamin Church and Joseph Warren, into the fold. According to John's account, Samuel also played no little part in encouraging the wealthy John Hancock to stand with the protestors. Experienced and adroit in the art of moving others, Samuel surely varied his tactics with each catch, using cajolery here, flattery there, pledges and promises elsewhere. In the case of John Adams, Samuel clearly had taken the measure of the man he courted. John's reputation would be enhanced, he would become more widely known, Samuel explained, if only he would fully commit himself to the popular protest. And if John harbored ambitions for a political career, Samuel went on, those would be furthered as well by the renown he would achieve by challenging British policy.[17]

But Samuel's skills proved deficient in this instance. John refused to be led into a more open role in the movement. Despite Samuel's claims that his legal business would improve in direct relation to his activism, John was convinced that just the opposite would result. His practice had grown appreciably by 1765. His caseload in Suffolk County had increased, and he had acquired clients whom he represented in inferior court in Taunton, Plymouth, Bristol, Barnstable, Middlesex, and Pownalborough in Maine. His prospects were promising, yet he remained only a junior attorney within Boston, and, after all the years of difficult preparation, he was loath to risk everything in a movement likely to disappear as soon as the Stamp Act crisis was resolved. Then the most visible dissenters probably would be looked upon as irresponsible, especially in Braintree, he believed.

Adams's reticence to fully commit himself to the popular protest stemmed from another factor, too. While he agreed that the Stamp Act threatened "irretrievable destruction" for the colonies, he was troubled by the direction the movement had taken in 1765. Not only did the violence of that summer concern him, but he privately wondered whether the protest was designed more to further the interests of the leaders than to secure the repeal of the objectionable tax. Whether he was thinking of Samuel Adams is not clear, but it should be remembered that John and Samuel were not close in 1765. That would come later, when John would refer to his cousin as "my Brother." At this point, however, much divided the two men. They were separated in age by thirteen years, often a vast chasm when one man is yet in his late twenties, as John was during that turbulent summer. The two hailed from quite different backgrounds. Samuel was a Boston Adams; John, his country cousin. So urbanized was Samuel, in fact, that he did not even know how to ride a horse until John taught him in 1775. Although both had been educated at Harvard, John was drawn to more intellectual pursuits, whereas Samuel was more the activist. Diligent and hard-working, John was succeeding in his chosen field, but Samuel had failed in business and as a tax collector, and, indeed, his shortcomings in the latter endeavor had very nearly resulted in his being tried for embezzlement during the previous year. John's diary during these years suggests that he saw signs of duplicity in his cousin that aroused his concern. John praised Samuel as "zealous, ardent, and keen," as "staunch and stiff and strait and rigid and inflexible" in the popular cause, but his doubts about the motives of the "designing persons" who orchestrated the protest were so sweeping that not even Samuel was excluded. Nor was the private Samuel Adams exempt. In public Samuel "affects to despize Riches, and not to dread Poverty," but, in fact, John claimed, "no Man is more ambitious" for an elegant life style.[18] It should not be inferred that John thoroughly distrusted his cousin, but he was solicitous of his future and not yet ready to make a commitment to a cause that might result in great personal harm.

On November 1, the day the duty was to take effect, there were neither stamp collectors nor stamps to be found. In some places trade continued without the stamps, but the port of Boston and several others were closed by government decree. Newspapers were not published, and the business of the courts was suspended. The port of Boston remained closed for six weeks, but on December 17 it was reopened by order of the Admiralty Court. Three days later a town meeting selected three attorneys to appear before Gov. Francis Bernard to request permission to conduct legal business once again. Gridley, Otis, and Adams were the three lawyers chosen. Without much time to prepare, Adams, garbed in the scarlet robe and powdered wig that barristers customarily wore when arguing before the superior court, stumbled a couple of times during his presentation, though he probably performed better than he imagined. At any rate, the governor was unwilling to defy the Crown. The courts remained closed.[19]

Adams was thus unemployed. Of course, he was unable to abandon his work. When at home he closeted himself for long hours in his study, reading and preparing for the day when he could resume his practice. He also seized every opportunity to speed away to Boston, one day to lunch with an important politician, another day to dine at the elegant table of a powerful merchant, and on still other occasions to spend convivial evenings with leading activists in the popular movement. He did devote some time to his chores at home, although now that he was more affluent he employed two servants and two hired hands to look after the house and the farm. Besides, he thought it Abigail's responsibility to superintend day-to-day operations at his little estate. That winter, however, both she and Nabby fell ill with the whooping cough and John not only assisted in looking after them but also oversaw the business of the farm. It was a bitter winter, and on occasion he was compelled to work in the numbing cold, even to trudge through waist-deep snow in order to drive his cattle to water.[20]

When Abigail recovered, they frequently entertained, inviting the Congregational minister or Braintree's physician and his wife, or perhaps Abigail's uncles, Cotton Tufts, a physician in Weymouth, or Isaac Smith, a prosperous Boston merchant and shipowner. Even Master Cleverly, still a teacher in the village, was a frequent guest. Mostly, however, Abigail found this to be a time of solitude and loneliness, for she now realized that John's consuming work habits and his ambitious yearnings took precedence over all other matters. Above all, it was a time of heavy responsibility, particularly for a young woman who had just celebrated her twenty-first birthday. She watched over the domestic help, did much of the cooking and sewing, worked some in the vegetable garden, and tended the endless demands made by little Nabby. In addition, she handled the shopping, for the Adamses were prosperous enough to pur-

John Adams in 1766, aged thirty-one. Portrait by Benjamin Blyth. *Courtesy: Massachusetts Historical Society.*

Abigail Adams in 1766, aged twenty-two. Portrait by Benjamin Blyth. *Courtesy: Massachusetts Historical Society.*

chase items like candles and soap and much of their clothing, and, like almost everyone else in New England, they too bought spices, fish, and some of their beef and pork. On top of everything else, Abigail was living away from home for the first time, and though John often drove her to Weymouth to visit her parents and younger sister, Betsy, she remained lonely, especially missing her other sister, Mary. Twice in 1766 John and Abigail made the long trek to Salem, the new home of Richard Cranch and Mary. These were enjoyable moments, a time to gossip about old friends and to swap stories about the children, about their ailments and their mischievous antics, about the joys they had brought to their parents. On one of these trips John and Abigail had their first portraits painted, sitting for Benjamin Blyth, a local artist.[21]

At thirty Adams was pudgy and jowly. In fact, Abigail described him as "so very fat"; he referred to himself as "short, thick, fat."[22] He looked soft and flabby, and together with his pallid countenance it was obvious that he was unaccustomed to physical labor and was confined by his occupation to indoor surroundings. He struck a serious pose for the artist. A habitual dissembler, John no doubt hoped to be captured as the sober, legal scholar. He succeeded too well. He also took on the look of a spoiled, humorless, priggish dilettante.

Abigail, only twenty-one, did not reflect a girlish air. She seemed to evoke the essence of maturity and responsibility, of intelligence and probity. There was neither coquettishness nor haughtiness in her bearing, but an unmistakable beauty and charm showed in her soft features, classical lines, and luminous, flashing sable eyes, which complemented her silky black hair. Without a hint of dissonance, Abigail somehow seemed at once soft and plucky and tenacious.

Signs that life had begun to return to normal were evident by spring 1766. In May news arrived that Parliament had repealed the Stamp Act, triggering festive celebrations throughout Massachusetts and most other colonies. Adams, back in his office now that the courts at last had reopened, drew two conclusions from the recent events. He surmised that repeal had been brought about only by "what has been done here—the Riots and Resolves." In addition, he deduced that the colonists' outlook had changed. He was correct. When the General Court assembled it clearly was a different body. Purged were vast numbers who had supported the governor during the previous year; elected in their stead were men who had resisted the new British policies. Thomas Cushing, a Boston merchant who had attacked the Stamp Act, was chosen Speaker of the House (after Governor Bernard vetoed the selection of Otis, the first choice of the body), and Samuel Adams, who for the first time had won a seat, was chosen clerk. Even John Adams, despite his meager activity, had emerged from the crisis with an enhanced reputation. His tour of the judicial circuit that spring was akin to a triumphant procession, for in each village he was feted and huzzahed by admiring crowds.[23]

But things were different in Braintree, or so he believed. The village was "insensible to the Common Joy," Adams raged. It had not even celebrated the news of the repeal, whereas many hamlets had marked the occasion with bonfires and the pealing of church bells. His ire was more deeply aroused by what he saw as a personal repudiation, however. Adams had dared to hope that his recent activities, limited as they were, might earn him a seat in the General Court next to Otis and Samuel Adams. Instead, Braintree reelected Ebenezer Thayer. To be overlooked was painful enough for Adams, but to witness Thayer's latest triumph was especially irksome.[24]

From the moment Adams returned to Braintree seven years earlier, he had laced his diary with invidious remarks about Thayer. Thayer was both a militia officer and a tavern owner, the former an achievement likely to arouse envy or guilt in Adams, the latter a calling that provoked his contempt. Yet it was Thayer's insistence upon practicing the law without formal training that principally quickened Adams's resentment. Young John regarded Thayer and his ilk as "pettifogging Dabblers," although to his mortification Captain Thayer—who was fifteen years his elder and more experienced before the bench—had on occasion outshined, and even embarrassed, him in the courtroom. Now Adams was mortified not just by Thayer's election but by the realization that "while allmost all the zealous opposers of the Stamp Act [were cheered] by their Towns . . . [he] was like to be neglected . . . in [his] own Town."[25]

Adams's cant was not entirely honest. In March, Braintree created two new selectmen posts. Adams won election to one of the seats; he garnered one vote more than was necessary to avoid a runoff election, but he won, in large measure because of the astute political machinations of his brother Peter and one or two additional operatives. The victory was a source of great pleasure, he admitted privately, though he would have been happier had he been rewarded with a seat in the legislature. But he took heart. A selectman oversaw the public schools, passed on road construction, and voted money for "Services of many Sorts." The value of such a post was not lost on Adams. "It will increase my Connections, with the People," he noted dryly.[26]

That sort of thought gave Adams more anguish than comfort, however, arousing in him disturbing doubts about his motives not only in seeking political office but also in having played a role, however modest, in the recent Stamp Act imbroglio. His rejection of Samuel Adams's counsel disturbed him, as well. Had he chosen the proper course? Samuel's electoral success in late 1765 indicated that he understood the political process far better than John. Once again he turned inward, introspectively examining his behavior as he had done when he agonized over his selection of a career. His diary again was his battleground. "To what object, are my Views directed? What is the End and Purpose of my Studies, Journeys, Labours of all Kinds of Body and Mind, of Tongue and Pen?" The choices that he permitted himself were stark. "Am I grasping at Money, or Scheming for Power? Or, Am I [a political activist for] the Welfare of my Country?" The likely answer filled him with dismay. Indeed, he eschewed an answer to his questions, claiming that he lacked the time even to think the matter through. In fact, he had not found the answer he sought, the rationale that would permit him to play the activist role he yearned to undertake. For the next half decade he would wrestle with the dilemma, seeking, as he had ten years earlier, to convince himself that his goals were not ignoble, that he was guided by ends more virtuous than the pursuit of mere "Self Love" and the "pungent, excruciating Pangs of Ambition [and] Avarice."[27]

Adams soon discovered a means by which he might retrieve some of the personal gains of which Samuel Adams had spoken, while at the same time he could work through some of his myriad thoughts. The opportunity arose during the winter of 1766–67 when his old friend Jonathan Sewall, writing as "Philanthrop," authored a series of essays that sought to defend the conduct of both Governor Bernard and Lieutenant Governor Hutchinson. Sewall employed a curious logic. He suggested that the two officials had found Britain's legislation reprehensible, yet from a sense of duty they had sought to enforce the law. Authority and subordination must exist if government and society were to survive, he argued. Otherwise, mankind would descend into the chaos of nature. To Sewall, therefore, Bernard and Hutchinson were the real patriots, while the foes of government were but petty and villainous men who had jeopardized the public welfare in quest of their own narrow ends.[28]

Writing as a suddenly urbane "Humphrey Ploughjogger," as well as under the pseudonyms "Misanthrop" and "Governor Winthrop," Adams answered Sewall's attack with eleven essays, five of which were published in the *Boston Gazette* in January and February 1767. His position was clearly enunciated in the first paragraph of his initial essay: the protestors had acted selflessly to secure the freedom of America, while Massachusetts's royal officials, a "restless grasping turbulent Crew," had sought fame, power, and fortune by perfidiously seeking to enforce the will of their masters in London. The defenders of government were "artful designing Men," mere "Pretenders to Patriotism." To Adams, therefore, the rulers had posed the greatest danger to society. The real heroes and patriots were those who had resisted the looming tyranny.[29]

Adams's logic was impeccable, yet he had failed to convince himself. Even the act of writing these tracts aroused uncertainties within him. Was it his motive to win public favor through these essays? Did he write merely to enhance his legal practice? His answers were equivocal. "There is a sense . . . in which my Professions are sincere." He believed the British actions a threat, yet he seemed to doubt the popular party's rhetoric of ministerial plots and their wild talk of designs to enslave the colonists. Perhaps it did not matter. The Stamp Act had been repealed; the crisis was over. "Since the Stamp Act is repealed," he told Cranch, "I am at perfect Ease about Politicks." It was true. In these months his writings reveal a man who, despite some misgivings over his role in the late crisis, was largely untroubled and caught up in the swirl of his business endeavors.[30]

For more than a year following the repeal of the Stamp Act, Adams ignored politics. He devoted time to his little farm, a gainless spread that often must have seemed to be more trouble than it was worth. In 1767 he owned only two horses (and one of those, according to Abigail, was "a *Mare,* a poor lame hip'd spavell'd, one eye'd mare"). He also had three cows, two calves, twenty sheep, and one rooster. The farm itself, excluding the land about the house, amounted to about thirty acres. Six or eight acres were planted each season, usually yielding fodder for the livestock, as well as small amounts of grain that could be exchanged at market for household necessities. An apple orchard splayed over another portion of the property, a grove that furnished the family with a generous supply of cider. Adams never looked on his estate as a real farmer would have viewed his property, as a George Washington, for instance, regarded Mount Vernon. He kept no ledgers of his crops, engaged in no agricultural experimentation, and, at best, he was an infrequent reader of agrarian treatises. His diary contains only an occasional farm-related entry. Before 1767 there are notations of his involvement in driving his cattle to water or of participating in the autumn slaughter of his livestock; afterwards, the entries involve orders given to his workers: construct a pond, prune trees, gather the manure.[31] Although his little estate was poor and infecund, Adams took great comfort in the place. It was ancestral property for one thing, and it was a refreshing alternative to the grimy, often sordid world of Boston. But it was more than that. It was a retreat, a haven from the pressures and tensions of the world, a place with fields to walk and hills to climb, a serene refuge for body and mind.

Adams's law practice absorbed most of his energies. By 1767 he knew that he was an accomplished lawyer. Privately he ranked himself—together with one or two others—as one of the most talented young attorneys within the province. His earnings had grown steadily, too, so that his family lived quite comfortably, if not opulently. As he took stock of his life near the end of 1766, he appeared to be relatively contented. He fretted over the long separations from his family that his profession required, and he admitted that his work was often lonely and boring. But against those drawbacks he acknowledged that his calling afforded long periods of quiescence and ample time for contemplation, luxuries available in few other undertakings.[32]

In 1767 Adams once again was made painfully aware of the anguish of separation from his family. Late in 1766 Abigail realized that she was pregnant again. She quickly visited her parents while she still could travel comfortably. In April, in the absence of John, who was on the circuit, the Cranches came to visit and to help a bit, although Mary also was pregnant. In July, with the birth imminent, Abigail returned to Weymouth, and there, with John once again abroad on his legal errands, she bore a son, John Quincy, named for his great-grandfather. John got home as quickly as he could, but soon he was on the road again, wandering from one alien village to another, all the while aching to be at home with his wife and daughter and tiny son. Somewhere along the circuit a letter from Abigail reached him, a missive with the news that forlorn little Nabby rocked her brother, singing to him: "Come pappa come home to Brother Johnny." "What a desultory Life," John afterwards grieved, a "rambling, roving, vagrant, vagabond Life," first one town then another, a week "at Sessions, then at Pleas, now in Admiralty, now at Superiour Court, then in the Gallery of the House. What a Dissipation. . . ."[33]

In fact, it had become more and more commonplace for John and Abigail to be separated, and not just because of the demands of his law practice. Adams found it increasingly difficult to escape the lure of Boston. Frequently he spent long days in the city talking shop with other attorneys, and often he passed the evening hours at the table of a friend or in a tavern with political activists, listening to their bombast and intrigue, perhaps venting his own notions, then returning the ten miles to distant Braintree in the late night hours.[34]

Adams's wanderings and his sense of isolation in remote Braintree prompted an important decision. In April 1768 he moved the family to Boston, renting a clapboard house on Brattle Street, a place known locally as the "White House." He and Abigail and the children lived there for a year, then moved to Cold Lane; still later they moved again, to a larger house in Brattle Square in the center of the city. The move to the city, he hoped, would leave him with more time for the family. At least the weary rides from Braintree to courts and clubs in Boston would be eliminated. The move placed Adams in the midst of the vibrant axis of the province. It also placed him squarely amid still another imperial crisis.[35]

News of the repeal of the Stamp Act in 1766 had restored tranquillity to the colonies, a torpor undisturbed either by the Declaratory Act that accompanied repeal—legislation in which Parliament claimed its unlimited power over the provinces—or the Revenue Act of 1766, a law that posted a tax on all exports of sugar. Increasingly, the Stamp Act crisis appeared to have been an anomaly.

But in the summer of 1767 the atmosphere changed. Word of new British measures reached America's mercantile centers. The Townshend Duties sought to raise revenue for the parent state by imposing levies on the colonists' importation of British glass, lead, paint, paper, and tea. Though obviously a tax, London justified the impost as an "external" or an "indirect" tax, ignoring the quite lucid statements of the assemblies and the Stamp Act Congress, which had drawn no distinction between internal and external taxes. Nor did the ministry stop with the new taxes. To facilitate the enforcement and collection of the duties, it created a five-member board of customs for Boston; in addition, the ministry suspended the New York Assembly as punishment for its evasion of the Quartering Act of 1765, a measure that had sought to force the province to help pay for the maintenance of the British army headquartered in New York City.[36]

Protests against these measures occurred at once. A spate of critical newspaper essays and pamphlets soon appeared. John Dickinson's *Letters from a Farmer in Pennsylvania* was the most popular of these tracts, a series of essays that cogently expressed the constitutional position that had crystallized throughout America during the Stamp Act crisis. An air of mellow confidence seemed to abound in the Whig strongholds, for most who were troubled by the legislation still seemed confident that peaceful remonstrances would be heard and acted upon favorably in London. Surprisingly, even Boston was calm in 1767. Upon receiving news of the levies, several prominent members of the popular movement urged Governor Bernard to call the General Court into special session, but when he refused, the dissenters only grumbled. The notion of defying the chief executive through an illegal session of the assembly was too radical to be countenanced. Moreover, when the assembly met as scheduled that winter, the best the Whigs could attain was the passage of a "Circular Letter," a resolution merely urging each colony to petition for repeal.

Mob action soon altered the situation. At first the demonstrations were peaceful, although the reports of the governor and the customs men make clear that they were badly shaken by the sight of throngs of men, including many who were well-oiled with spirits, marching past their doors, bawling out threats and insults. Matters finally turned violent, however, when the customs officers impounded John Hancock's vessel, the *Liberty,* on a charge of smuggling numerous pipes of Madeira wine into the province, as well as for allegedly having reloaded the vessel with oil and tar without having given bond. Within minutes a howling mob had gathered, provoking a melee in which two agents were injured. Another mob turned out that evening. It destroyed some royal property, as well as the pleasure boat of the king's collector of the port of Boston. Seizing the moment, the Sons of Liberty called a public meeting a day or two later. When nearly a thousand Bostonians turned out for the affair, the popular leaders simply declared the gathering to be an official town meeting and utilized the forum to revive talk of an economic boycott of the parent state. During autumn 1767 both the Boston town meeting and the General Court had rejected such a course, and an informal agreement among some of the city's merchants to boycott English imports collapsed when Philadelphia and New York refused to participate. However, in this stormy atmosphere, momentum for a boycott grew. Success of a sort finally was attained after weeks of agitation. On August 1, 1768, the Sons of Liberty sponsored another mass rally. Delegates to the meeting, held at Faneuil Hall, voted to institute another trade stoppage, although the boycott once again hinged on the participation of New York and Philadelphia. That the embargo ever succeeded was due less to the actions of Boston's radicals than to the ministry's ill-advised rejoinder to the Massachusetts Circular Letter and the *Liberty* riots.[37]

Adams appears to have played a minor role in the initial stages of the *Liberty* affair that produced these changes in Massachusetts. In the first days after Hancock's vessel was seized, he was selected by the Boston town meeting to draft instructions to the city's representatives in the provincial assembly on how best to thwart the customs officials. But two weeks after the *Liberty* was taken, Jonathan Sewall, the advocate general for Massachusetts took steps to secure the forfeiture of the sloop for having violated Britain's Acts of Trade. Adams may have assisted in the defense of Hancock; if so, he was unsuccessful, for in mid-August 1768, the *Liberty* was declared forfeit and subsequently used by the British as a revenue cutter. Successful in this prosecution, Sewall initiated further action against Hancock in the fall. He sought to compel the merchant to pay a fine of nine thousand pounds for having engaged in a smuggling operation. Adams was retained as Hancock's chief counsel.

Although he took the case, Adams seems not to have been happy with his role as the defender of the very symbol of resistance to the imperial trade laws. He admitted that he looked upon his duties in this matter with "disgust" and that he found the case to be "a painfull Drudgery." In all likelihood, he agreed to represent the defendant both because of the handsome fee that he could expect and from fear of the consequences of refusing the entreaties of someone as popular and powerful as Hancock. Despite Adams's reluctant involvement, all turned out well for Hancock. Four months after bringing charges, Sewall abruptly withdrew his suit, probably because of insufficient evidence.[38]

As important as these occurrences in Boston were, it was London's addled response to the events in Massachusetts that proved to be decisive in shaping America's resistance to imperial policies. Slighting the remonstrances from the other provinces, the ministry sought, through Lord Hillsborough, the Secretary of State for American Affairs, to isolate the Bay colony. Hillsborough deemed Massachusetts's protest to be dangerous and illegal, and he demanded that the General Court rescind its earlier denunciation of the Townshend Duties. But it was his next two moves that proved to be especially inflammatory. He dispatched a circular letter of his own in which he threated the dissolution of any provincial assembly that petitioned for repeal of the imperial taxes. He also ordered Gen. Thomas Gage to send three regiments of British regulars to Boston.[39] The Hillsborough Letter reached Boston about six weeks after John and Abigail and their children had moved back to the city.

The last thing that Adams had in mind when he returned to Boston was proximity to the resistance movement. Indeed, the vertiginous events that occurred just as he moved—he was packing when the *Liberty* incident flared—caught him off guard. Boston generally had remained calm for nearly two years, its radicals sputtering ineffectually. Adams certainly did not expect a repetition of the frenzied days of the Stamp Act upheaval, and like many others he still was naive enough to believe that London surely would act favorably upon the colonists' peaceful protests. His aims remained what they had been a decade before when he had taken up the study of the law. He continued to seek recognition as a lawyer, thinking that the esteem he earned might someday help him attain public office. But he remained what he had been at the time of the Stamp Act crisis: cautious, apprehensive that political activism might be detrimental to his legal practice, and ever conscious of how he was seen, unwilling to sully his image as an emerging lawyer of consequence by acting the part of an agitator or mischief-maker.

There can be no question that Adams was philosophically at one with the popular party. Indeed, had he put renown and material reward above conscience, he could have enjoyed instant gratification during the summer of 1768. Sometime during the proceedings against Hancock, Jonathan Sewall, who had accepted an appointment as Judge of Admiralty in Halifax, urged Adams to consider succeeding him as the solicitor general of Massachusetts, the royal governor's chief legal officer in the province. Adams spurned the offer to serve the Crown "in an instant," he said later. For numerous reasons he rejected Sewall's tempting offer, made at the behest of Thomas Hutchinson. He would not—could not—sever his deep emotional ties to Otis and Samuel Adams. He wanted no part of Britain's imperial policies, which he looked upon as misguided and harmful. Moreover, while he was friendly with Sewall, he loathed many officials in the Court party, none more so than Hutchinson, of whom he had once remarked: "I . . . thought, that his Death in a natural Way would have been a Smile of Providence upon this Public."[40]

There can also be little doubt that Adams secretly longed to play a major role in the popular movement, but it was a commitment he could not make at this juncture. Years of legal study and practice had left him not only deeply respectful of the parent state and its institutions but also with a reverential attitude toward the sanctity of the law. To defy lawfully constituted authority was an almost unthinkable proposition. Nor was Adams's turn of mind uncommon. Approximately one-half of the lawyers known to have been practicing law in Massachusetts at this time ultimately remained loyal to Great Britain during the Revolution, or they refused to support the American resistance movement. Nor was that all. Adams's diary reveals that he shrank in horror from the "Curses, and Imprecations" that the royal officials had heaped upon Samuel Adams, and that he was profoundly troubled to discover that Otis's public role had severely damaged his private law practice.[41]

Adams sought, therefore, to play a discreet role in this protest. He was confident that Britain would quickly back down as it had two years before and that when tranquillity once again prevailed, he and his career would remain unscathed. He wrote an anonymous newspaper essay on British "mischiefs," helped draft a Sons of Liberty communique to radicals in London, and participated in the drafting of Boston's instructions to its representatives on the General Court.[42]

Given his belief that Britain would capitulate in the face of the colonial protest, Adams must have been startled by the Hillsborough Letter. Britain had not retreated. Nor did the General Court capitulate to the secretary of state. It voted 92–17 not to rescind its Circular Letter. Another full-blown crisis was at hand.

Massachusetts's defiant mood quickly spread. Legislatures throughout America spurned Hillsborough's message. At public rallies bibulous celebrants raised their glasses in tribute to the "Glorious 92," those Massachusetts assemblymen who had defied Hillsborough. This time, moreover, New York joined Boston in its boycott, whereupon Philadelphia also agreed to participate in another embargo of British trade.

Events in 1768 furthered the ideological transformation that had been set in motion during the Stamp Act crisis. Many now were convinced that a plot, a conspiracy, existed among diabolical British ministers to subvert liberty both in Britain and the colonies. It was in this grim atmosphere of tension and paranoia that a British fleet was spotted entering Boston harbor, carrying the regiments of the "redcoat dragoons," as the Whig newspapers had taken to calling the soldiers. For weeks the city had known the troops were coming. Instead of their grievances being redressed, they were to be "red-dressed," or so one Boston preacher wisecracked.

The troops landed without incident, but the presence of the soldiers aroused considerable anxiety among a citizenry bred to look upon a standing army as the monarch's agent for tyranny. Nevertheless, after the first tense days life resumed its normal pace, interrupted only by an occasional incident. Local rowdies often tried to provoke difficulty, egging on the redcoats with jeers and curses, and sometimes short-tempered soldiers retaliated. These chronic happenings were like manna for the radicals. The Sons of Liberty began to document the bellicose conduct of the troops. In a newborn newspaper, "A Journal of the Times," the radicals published accounts of alleged depredation and hooliganism. Nor was there a dearth of lurid accounts of soldierly outrages in the traditional press. In addition, both newspaper essayists and members of the clergy—the "Black Regiment," as they later would be called—inundated the population with warnings of the threat to American liberty posed by these invaders.[43]

Adams was at court in Worcester (defending a slave owner against charges of mistreatment brought by his bondsman) when the troops arrived in Boston. Upon his return to Boston, Adams resumed the role that he had previously played in the popular movement, an activism largely concealed beneath a cloak of anonymity. He assisted the Boston Sons of Liberty with some propaganda treatises, and he was part of a team that instructed Boston's representatives on the General Court to vote against appropriations for the maintenance of the British troops within the province. In addition, he probably helped draft a petition of the Boston town meeting to King George III, a somewhat qualmish document urging the monarch to recall the troops.[44]

Adams could have played a more public role in this crisis. Shortly after the British troops landed in Boston, Otis and Dr. Joseph Warren called on him. They implored him to address a Boston town meeting—to "harrangue" the crowd, was the way Adams described it—on the dangers posed by ministerial policy. Adams steadfastly refused. "That way madness lies," he told the popular leaders, and years later in his memoirs he intimated that Boston's radical chiefs had sought to use him to "deceive the People," to "conceal from them . . . essential truth[s]." Privately he resolved not to become "subservient to their Crimes, Follies or Excentricities," though he merely told his visitors that he regarded petitions for redress to be the only legitimate means of protest.[45] The rancor of Adams's private comments—his suggestion that Otis and Warren, close friends and older men whom he admired, were engaged in nothing less than criminal activity—reveals that he was no less mortified in 1769 and 1770 by the designs of the most radical protesters than he had been in 1765. His actions suggest beyond a doubt that he abhorred British policy; nevertheless, he still believed that London was merely misguided, not despotic. The Hillsborough Letter notwithstanding, he evidently continued to believe that the ministry could be made to rescind its ill-advised policies; the great danger, therefore, lay in the path proposed by the extremists, for the course they advocated would only push Britain into more provocative acts, perhaps leading inevitably to unthinkable consequences.

Samuel Adams also called on his cousin. Historians can only wish that a transcript of their conversations existed to know what was on Samuel's mind. Subtle, careful, crafty, masterful in his political inclinations and actions, he must have hurried over to smooth ruffled feathers, following the visits by Otis and Warren. He certainly could not have desired John's alienation from the popular movement; knowing John quite well, Samuel—we know from John's diary—sought to reassure his cousin by telling him that he sought no private gain through the protest movement. Samuel surely had other intentions, too. He wanted John to play a more visible role, though not the sort envisioned by other extremists. Unlike the others, Samuel probably hoped to preserve John's public reputation as a somewhat disinterested and high-minded neutral; later, when the time was right, a man with such a reputation—and one somewhat beholden to Samuel Adams—could be most useful. First, however, John's reputation required some immediate patching. Samuel Adams had heard whispers concerning John's commitment to the cause; even John had heard the rumors. Samuel therefore beseeched John to attend a public rally of the Sons of Liberty. That would lay the tattle to rest.[46]

Adams petulantly agreed to accompany Samuel and Otis to a meeting in Dorchester, south of Boston. He went, he told his diary, because it "was my Duty to be there." Over 350 men attended, dining in an open field under an awning, then being entertained by rousing speeches and a local wit who mimicked lawyers and imitated the ritual hunting of a vixen. The meeting concluded with the obligatory toasts and a few energizing stanzas of some popular liberty songs. Adams neither particularly enjoyed the proceedings nor saw much reason for his attendance. He was, he told himself, "more sincere and steadfast" toward the popular cause than most in attendance.[47]

As the 1760s drew to a close, John Adams was aware of his accomplishments. He had begun the decade as a struggling young lawyer; he completed it a prominent, rising Boston attorney. In 1760 he had been a lonely, single young man. Now he was a happily married man with a family that he treasured. Uncertain and troubled by the career he had chosen at the beginning of the decade, he was confident and relatively contented with his course. He was equally pleased with his conduct in the two great public crises of the 1760s.

Advising a young cousin at this moment, he recalled the admonition of Shakespeare: "This above all, to thine ownself be true."[48] It was a credo that he believed he had lived by, especially throughout the recent tumultuous years. But Adams knew that in the incendiary atmosphere that enveloped Boston at decade's end, such virtuous behavior would be ever more difficult. He knew as well that it would be no less arduous—as Shakespeare also had cautioned—to have "no Guardian but your own Honour, and no Monitor, but your own Conscience."[49]

CHAPTER 4

*

The Scene of Action

"Our City is yet a Garrison filled with armed Men," the Boston Sons of Liberty informed a sympathetic politician in London as the decade of the 1770s dawned. Ominously, they predicted that "America [is] on the point of bursting into flames."[1] Uneasiness over the presence of the troops had grown, and not just because of the fear of standing armies. Redcoats had been permitted to take part-time jobs in their off-duty hours, wrenching precious work from the unskilled, especially along Boston's waterfront. Further enmity was aroused when young soldiers began dating young women in Boston. By early 1770 the frequency of troubling incidents was increasing. On several occasions in January and February, crowds of citizens voiced their displeasure, congregations often, though not always, spurred on by inflammatory meetings held the previous evening. The potential for real trouble was always present, although the protestors usually disbanded peaceably. February 22 was different.

A crowd gathered that morning to demonstrate before the offices of a merchant suspected of having transgressed the trade embargo with England. All was calm until the arrival of Ebenezer Richardson, an informer for the customs service who had previously called attention to himself by openly denouncing the popular faction. Injudiciously, Richardson, a man with a reputation as a foolish loudmouth, shouted epithets at the impassioned protestors. Predictably, they turned their fury upon him, chasing him into his nearby home. The armed mob then pelted his residence with garbage and stones, one missile even striking his terrified wife in the head. Richardson retreated to the second floor, soon to appear at an open window, brandishing a musket. That only added to the crowd's frenzy, prompting a few zealots to attempt to break down his front door. Richardson, angry and panicky, fired into the crowd. A young boy of eleven or twelve, Christopher Seider, was killed. Men raced up the stairs and overpowered Richardson. Some were for lynching him immediately, but the mob leaders prevailed. Richardson was turned over to a justice of the peace for trial.[2]

Passions in Boston now ran at a white-hot pitch. Fights between local rowdies and soldiers seemed to occur daily, and fresh mobs formed just as regularly. The town was aroused by the killing, an event the Sons of Liberty were not about to ignore. Young Seider's burial was a masterpiece of propaganda. "My Eyes never beheld such a funeral," noted John Adams, who stumbled upon the ceremony as he was returning home from a court session in Weymouth. Over two thousand people marched in the procession, a carefully orchestrated spectacle in which up to five hundred boys paraded before the bier, followed by an even larger multitude on foot and in carriages.[3]

What happened a week after the funeral, though unplanned either by the radical leaders or by the redcoats, was not entirely unanticipated. Both civilians and soldiers had been predicting trouble, and Gen. Thomas Gage, the commander of the British army in America, long since had concluded that the ministry had blundered terribly in ordering troops to Boston. On Monday, March 5, a raw, late winter night, mischievous crowds gathered at three separate locations. One throng congregated at the redcoats' barracks near the Draper's Alley–Brattle Street intersection, just down the way from John and Abigail's home. About eight o'clock they began to engage in a noisy—though nonviolent—altercation with the soldiers. Adams heard none of this. He was on the south side of town attending the monthly meeting of Sodalitas. Abigail, seven months pregnant and alone except for a female servant and two infant children, did hear the ruckus, and she was terrified. Then, abruptly, the turmoil ceased, silenced by an alarm bell pealing disconsolately in the center of the city. Knots of men and a few women raced downtown, converging on the Town House, then eddying off in the direction of the Customs House, where a club-wielding crowd already confronted eight British soldiers and their commander, Capt. Thomas Preston, a forty-year-old Irishman.

It was a tense scene. The British soldiers formed a semi-circle and wielded bayoneted muskets at a jeering, taunting crowd of perhaps four hundred. Several anxious minutes passed. While some ignoramuses in the crowd dared the soldiers to shoot, more sensible bystanders, like the young bookseller Henry Knox, talked with the British commander, urging him not to give the order to fire. Preston seemed dazed and frightened, caught in a nightmare that he hoped soon would end, and end peacefully. It did not.

A hothead in the crowd threw a club, which struck a soldier. Immediately a shot rang out, followed by a pause of about six seconds, followed in turn by a round of shots. Several men in the mob were hit, five mortally. Preston, enraged that his men had fired without orders, ran down the line screaming for the shooting to cease. Once he restored order, Preston reassembled his men and marched them away, leaving the Customs House more vulnerable than ever. The troops departed unmolested, for the shooting had stunned and immobilized the crowd. The wounded were carried off. Men milled about, recounting in unstrung voices those few terrifying seconds; no one seems to have thought of sacking the undefended building. But, after an hour or so, the situation once again grew ugly. More people had arrived, including fresh British troops. Loose talk abounded. Additional violence seemed certain but was averted largely due to the courage of Thomas Hutchinson. Already the victim of one mob, he nevertheless agreed to come to the scene. Someone showed him the frozen blood stains on the snow, and many witnesses, eager to tell someone, anyone, what had happened, spilled out their accounts. He listened patiently, then took charge. Climbing onto a second-story balcony of the Town House, he calmly told the crowd that he would guarantee that Preston and his men would be tried. Satisfied, its mottled fury at last spent, the mob dispersed.[4]

On the other side of town, John Adams and his companions heard the ringing of more alarm bells about nine o'clock. Believing the city's inhabitants were being summoned to fight a major fire, the men grabbed their hats and coats and dashed for town. They had not gone far before they learned of the shooting; they continued on to the site of the bloodletting, arriving a few minutes before Hutchinson, and they observed the new British troops that had been called up. Adams, wisely, did not linger. Besides, he was concerned about Abigail, and he hurried home, where he found her shaken by the pandemonium and the ominous news of this frenzied night.[5]

John and Abigail sat up for several hours that night of the "Boston Massacre" (what John all his life called the "slaughter in King Street") discussing the tragedy, doubtless anxious lest still more incidents occur. Violence was in the air, and in this white-hot atmosphere further bloodshed must have seemed inevitable. None occurred, however, in part because Hutchinson agreed to use his power to secure the removal of the British troops from Boston to Castle William, far out in the city's harbor. Order also was maintained because the Sons of Liberty realized that it had a remarkable propaganda victory within its grasp; its leaders did not wish to forfeit their good fortune with misguided action. Indeed, with the streets peaceful, Samuel Adams and his forces waged a furious battle for the minds of the citizenry.

Spectacular funerals for the victims of the shooting soon followed. Not far behind these carefully staged events came a radical pamphlet, *A Short Narrative of the Horrid Massacre in Boston,* which argued that the events of March 5 resulted from a conspiracy between the customs commissioners and the army, a plot the radicals alleged was hatched to intimidate them into silence. Calm prevailed, although for days the situation remained so tense that men organized nightly patrols to maintain the peace. John Adams took his turn one cold March night, walking the lonely, quiet streets of the city from dusk until dawn, ready to report the making of a dangerous mob.[6]

It was in this atmosphere that the wheels of justice began to turn. Before the end of the month, a grand jury had indicted Captain Preston and his men, as well as two customs men accused of having fired into the crowd from a window in the Customs House. The court appointed Adams's old friend Samuel Quincy as special prosecutor to try the case; he recruited Adams's one-time nemesis Robert Treat Paine, now a prosperous attorney in southern Massachusetts and Rhode Island, for his team. The defendants, meanwhile, desperately sought counsel. The customs agents apparently never succeeded in securing representation; ultimately, each stood trial without a lawyer at his side. Preston reportedly approached several attorneys before he secured counsel. After what must have seemed an eternity to the frightened soldiers, Adams agreed to head their defense. He was to be assisted principally by Josiah Quincy, the brother of both the prosecutor and of John's first love, Hannah; nine years younger than Adams and his former next door neighbor in Braintree, Quincy had come along under the benevolent tutelage of Oxenbridge Thacher. Sampson Salter Blowers, Quincy's dour partner and later a Loyalist, and Robert Auchmuty, already a suspected Tory and a judge on the Boston Vice Admiralty Court, completed the defense team.

But why did Adams and Quincy, neither of whom were sympathetic toward miniterial policies, agree to defend men charged with killing five Bostonians? Adams later remembered that he had taken on this responsibility out of his belief that all men were entitled to a fair trail. While he surely felt strongly about their need for representation, incontrovertible evidence exists that Quincy agreed to take the case after being urged to do so by the leadership of the Sons of Liberty; it is more than possible that Adams likewise was retained following similar urgings. But why would Samuel Adams, who only recently had been concerned about rumors of John's passivity, suddenly wish for his cousin to defend the perpetrators of the massacre? Why would John Adams agree to such an unpopular assignment, one that could adversely affect his practice? As historian Hiller Zobel has speculated, Samuel Adams and the radical leadership must have believed that no Boston jury would acquit the soldiers, regardless of the quality of their counsel; indeed, if convictions were handed down even in the face of a defense by the best lawyers available, it would inevitably lead the general public to embrace the Sons of Liberty's argument for overwhelming evidence of an army-customs conspiracy. Moreover, if Samuel Adams was endeavoring to further his cousin's reputation as a man who stood nobly above the fray, he could hardly have found a better cause for advancing such an image. The reasons for John's acceptance of the case are more difficult to deduce. While he believed that Preston and his men deserved equal justice, he knew this was a case fraught with danger. Not only might his income suffer, but—though the peril was remote—he also knew that he would run the risk of "incurring a Clamour," that is, of being waylaid by a hooligan or of having his house set upon by a mob. Weighed against these hazards was the possibility of gain in the long run. When tempers cooled and normalcy was restored, he might be remembered as a man who had put the law above hate. Such a benefit, conjectural and at best remote, hardly seemed worth the peril, however. Adams must have been enticed to play this role by a promise of immediate gain. In all likelihood, he was encouraged to take the case in exchange for political office, for when one of Boston's seats in the legislature opened three months later, John Adams was the town's first choice to fill the vacancy.[7]

It has been suggested that historians have exaggerated the power of Samuel Adams. Certainly, he did not singlehandedly produce the American Revolution, as both his fellow colonists and royal officials in London sometimes believed. But he wielded enormous power in Boston. He controlled the streets of Boston—and through the streets, Boston itself—during both the stamp protests in 1765 and the frenzied days of February and March 1770. Both Hutchinson and the head of the British army in Boston acknowledged in the spring that "government is at an end," that the Sons of Liberty controlled the city.[8] Samuel Adams lacked the power simply to make a seat for his cousin in the assembly, but when James Bowdoin relinquished his seat in June in order to move up to the Council, he would have had little difficulty in securing the vacated post for John. Nor can there be much doubt that John Adams, consumed as he was with ambition and a passion for achievement and renown, would have accepted such a bargain.

The trials of the British soldiers did not begin immediately. Gen. Thomas Gage, the commander of the British army in America, urged Hutchinson to procrastinate until passions cooled, and the lieutenant governor seized upon every procedural opening to delay the legal action until the autumn. Arraignment did not occur until early September. Six weeks later, before a large crowd of spectators in a second-floor courtroom of Boston's new courthouse, the soldiers' trial at last was gaveled to order.

The defense scored an immediate victory, a success that set the tone for what lay ahead. Adams sought to gain a separate trial for Captain Preston. He was not accused of killing anyone, so the defense would seek to prove that he had not ordered the shooting. Later, in the trial of the men, Adams tried to show that in shooting into the crowd on March 5, they had merely been following the orders of their captain. The magistrate ruled that Preston was to be tried separately.

Preston's hearing was over in five days. The prosecution called fifteen witnesses (one of whom was Adams's law clerk) to establish that Preston had ordered his men to fire upon the crowd, but under cross-examination their testimony often appeared feeble and contradictory. The defense produced twenty-three witnesses. They painted a picture of total chaos on the night of the incident, and each stressed that the soldiers had been baited and intimidated by a huge, frenzied mob. Neither Preston nor any of his men testified. The jury took just three hours to acquit the British officer of the charges.[9]

Within minutes a happy John Adams left Boston for the Cambridge judicial sitting. Salem came next on the circuit, then it was back to Boston in late November for the trial of the soldiers. Their defense had been complicated by their commander's acquittal, for prospective jurors might now be inclined to think that if Captain Preston had not ordered the soldiers to fire, the men must have been responsible for the mayhem. Nevertheless, the prosecution's case again was weak, and it started badly. The first witness acknowledged that he had not even been present on King Street the evening of the tragedy, and several other early witnesses damaged the state's case through their admission that people in the crowd occasionally shouted "Fire! Fire!" at the edgy soldiers. Adams also secured an admission that the redcoats had been struck repeatedly by objects hurled by the crowd. Samuel Adams, who attended each session of the trial, was so exasperated by such witnesses that he once passed an acerbic note across the courtroom to Paine, complaining that the attestation thus far had succeeded only in establishing that the "Inhabitants [were] the Aggressors." Matters did not improve much for the prosecution thereafter. The well-prepared defense team hammered away at the notion that the scene on the night of the shooting had been riotous and threatening, and that the British troops would have risked injury had they not fired. The law was clear, Adams told the jury in his summation. If the soldiers were endangered, they had the right to fire in self-defense; if they were provoked, though not endangered, at most they were guilty of manslaughter. The jury agreed with the counselor. Six of the soldiers were acquitted and two were found guilty of manslaughter (those two pled "benefit of clergy" and escaped with only the branding of a thumb).[10]

The trials had resulted in a great judicial victory for Adams. Indeed, his handling of the two cases demonstrated why he had risen in a short time to an important position within the community of lawyers in Boston. In Preston's trial, he expertly exercised his right to challenge individual jurors and contrived what amounted to a packed jury. Not only were several jurors closely tied through business arrangements to the British army, but five ultimately became Loyalist exiles. As Hiller Zobel, the scholar who has most closely studied these trials, concluded, "we can probably be fairly sure that before a single witness had been sworn, the outcome of the trial was certain." Because the court restricted the number of challenges to which Adams was entitled in the soldiers' trial, the jury "was not so good," according to Hutchinson, as that which had acquitted Captain Preston; nevertheless, not one juror was a resident of Boston. While Adams surely benefited from both the state's weak case and the prosecution's pedestrian management of the facts at hand, he still performed brilliantly. His most difficult task, perhaps, was to avoid antagonizing those jurors who sympathized with the popular protest. Consequently, he gingerly cross-examined state witnesses; against Josiah Quincy's wishes, he even resisted the temptation to introduce evidence that would have demonstrated how Boston's mobs had habitually insulted the British soldiery. Quincy played a greater role in the soldiers' defense, but Adams's summation to the jury was a masterful speech.

Adams had begun his career by closely observing the oratorical accomplishments of his legal mentors, astutely understanding that, properly refined, his
own rhetorical talents might speed his success. Over the years he honed his
skills and at the end of his career, as he looked back over his achievements, he
thought many of them due to his faculties as an orator. The challenge he faced
in arguing on behalf of the soldiers was formidable: blood had been spilled, and
someone was responsible; but a jury of patriots was not likely to believe that
the citizenry of Boston bore responsibility for the tragedy. Adams took the tack
that it was better to protect innocence than to punish guilt. He also succeeded
in shifting to London much of the blame. It had been a mistake for the British
to send an army to Boston, he maintained. An army was a notoriously poor
instrument for maintaining order; the presence of this army had, indeed,
provoked disorder. And in the face of the breakdown of law and order, these
soldiers, threatened with harm, had been compelled to protect themselves
from "a motley rabble of saucy boys, negroes and mulattoes, Irish teagues and
outlandish jack tars." It was a clever, impassioned, and compelling speech but
was also one that was carefully bridled and one that, for its ultimate effective-
ness, earned the praise of Thomas Hutchinson.

Adams surely harbored many misgivings about accepting this case, but
aside from some rumors of his Toryism—which caused him little concern—he
emerged unscathed. By the time the cases were closed near the end of 1770,
tranquillity had been restored to the city. Not only had Parliament repealed all
the Townshend Duties save for the tax on tea, but British troops were no
longer seen on the streets of Boston. The jury verdicts, undoubtedly to the
surprise of many, engendered remarkably little protest. More than anything,
the public, at least for the time being, seemed to want to forget the tragedy;
indeed, as one Bostonian told Benjamin Franklin, many might secretly have
been happy with the verdict because the acquittals demonstrated that the
inhabitants were not a "violent and blood thirsty people."[11]

By fall 1770 John Adams had every reason to be pleased with his situation.
Not only had his fears over taking the soldiers' cases proved groundless, but his
reputation as a lawyer of sagacity had been bolstered by the much publicized
trials. Moreover, he now sat in the Massachusetts House of Representatives,
having won the seat by receiving four-fifths of the votes cast.

In addition, everything, and more, that Adams had dreamt of regarding his
career had come to fruition. Within ten years of establishing his practice he had
one of the heaviest caseloads of any lawyer in Massachusetts, annually handling nearly 450 cases. Among his clients were many of the colony's elite,
including the Bowdoin family, a clan that recently had produced two Speakers
of the Massachusetts assembly. He also represented John Hancock and numerous other wealthy merchants; Harrison Gray, the treasurer of the province; and
Sir Francis Bernard, the former royal governor of Massachusetts. He even had

represented John Wentworth, the governor of New Hampshire. To handle such a heavy business Adams now employed two and often three law clerks, usually recent graduates of Harvard College who were completing their legal apprenticeship. Adams's booming practice also resulted in a handsome income by 1770. Not only did he own a house and additional real estate in Braintree, he also possessed a dwelling in Boston, an expensive pew in his church, and a large and growing library. As his reputation grew, the recognition that he had incessantly sought also emerged. Besides serving a term on the board of selectmen in Braintree, he had been chosen to be the initial secretary of Suffolk County's new bar association.[12] His elevation to the House of Representatives was but the latest—and greatest—indication of his success.

Adams's success in his public pursuits appeared to be matched by felicity at home. Abigail gave birth to a second son, Charles, near the end of May 1770. It had been a gloomy and anguishing pregnancy for her, especially in light of recent tragic events in the family. Not long after the family had moved back to Boston she gave birth to another daughter, Susanna, or "little Suky," as John called her; the child had been ill continually, and shortly after Abigail realized she was pregnant with Charles, little Susanna, only a year old, died. Charles was healthy, however, and gradually as the year wore on, Abigail's spirits rose.[13]

Adams began the year in high spirits, but a few weeks into 1771 he fell ill. It was a brief, alarming illness, and it came on without warning. One evening in mid-February, after dining at the home of John Hancock, he noted that he was troubled by both a "great anxiety and distress" and "pensive" feelings. Before the end of the week he collapsed. He fell sick with a general discomfort in his chest and what he believed to be heart pains. He described himself as exhausted and feeble, and during one long wrenching night he was convinced that death was imminent. He had never experienced greater misery, he later wrote, and he added: "God grant, I may never see such another Night."[14] His spirits sank so that for two months a melancholy Adams was incapacitated, unable even to maintain his diary.

Adams offered two explanations for his illness. Initially he feared that he had suffered a heart attack. Later, he attributed his problems to the "Lord of public and private Care what has for some time oppressed me."[15] The second explanation is more likely accurate. Adams had probably collapsed from exhaustion.

Many of the public cares of which Adams spoke are readily apparent. In addition to the demands of his legal practice, he was an officer of the local bar association and until a few weeks before, he had been immersed in the stressful Boston Massacre trials. His most recent public activity, however, was service in the provincial assembly.

Adams had entered politics with deep misgivings. He feared that holding office would lead "my family to ruin and myself to death." Abigail shared his apprehension, and she had burst into tears upon learning of his decision to

seek office. Adams soon discovered political life to be even more troubling than
he had dared imagine. The legislature met in four brief sessions in 1770–71,
convening for short periods sandwiched into the judicial calendar. With the
economic boycott occasioned by the Townshend Duties still in effect during
the earliest conclaves, most of the assembly's business revolved about attempts
of the Whigs to injure and embarrass the provincial government. The burning
issue: the governor's decision to move the General Court from Boston to
Harvard College in nearby Cambridge, a transfer designed to prevent the
legislators from falling thrall to the populace in Boston. The radicals seized
upon the transplacement issue, hoping to create the impression that some
devious, conspiratorial design between London and the royal executive lay
behind the decision. The popular party repeatedly demanded that Hutchinson
make public his orders from Lord Hillsborough, and when these importunings were rejected, the radicals launched a campaign of invective against the
governor, depicting him as the very embodiment of deceit and as a mere lackey
to his wicked masters across the sea.[16]

Adams worked with the popular party in its crusade of vilification and
character assassination. He despised Hutchinson, a man who had always
struck him as the very symbol of one of the worst features of the British system.
For an enterprising man with excellent family ties, such as Hutchinson, the
possibilities of gain were enormous. What greater proof was needed than that
Hutchinson, a man without formal legal training could become the chief
justice of the province. As early as the time of the Stamp Act protests, Adams
had seen Hutchinson as a man of "unbounded Ambition" and "Avaricious
Disposition." Once he even had insisted that Massachusetts had "more to fear
from [this] one Man . . . than from all other Men in the World." Nevertheless,
Adams was not comfortable with his role as agitator. He saw the contest for
what it was. Lacking a substantive issue and dismayed by the temperate mood
that had prevailed in the province since the repeal of most of the Townshend
Duties, the radical leadership hoped to make gains through the politics of
confrontation. Adams thought this was a "laboured controversy," and a disagreeable one at that. There can be no doubt that Adams shared most of the
precepts of the radicals. He acknowledged that Otis and Samuel Adams had
shaped his constitutional views; he believed, as they did, that once the colonists
submitted absolutely to British sovereignty, their freedoms would be imperiled. To him, no less than to Samuel Adams, the presence of the British troops
in Boston posed a danger to American liberties. He concurred with the protests against Britain's stringent enforcement of its mercantile policies; in fact,
he had written that London's "army of revenue Officers and . . . Fleet of small
cruizers and cutters" pursued their American "prey as if cruizing upon a
foreign enemy."[17]

Adams had no problem with any of this. But after 1768 many of the popular
leaders had moved to even more radical ground. Historian Pauline Maier has

demonstrated that there was nothing in the writings of Samuel Adams prior to the arrival of the British troops in Boston in 1768 to suggest his desire for American independence. Thereafter, he changed. He spoke first of independence as a possible result of imperial problems should Britain not return to its traditional policies; by 1771, however, he increasingly expressed his belief in the inevitability of independence.[18] This was a plateau which John Adams had not yet climbed. He continued to believe that Britain's actions since 1763 had merely been misguided. He saw no evidence of a British plot to destroy American liberty. Where Samuel Adams's writings now suggested the need to contemplate separation from the parent state, John Adams's writings continued to praise the British Constitution. Profoundly conservative, John Adams still spoke of the need for "perfect Submission to Government"; he remained steadfast in his belief that it was iniquitous to disturb the "internal Peace . . . and good order." On the day after Samuel Adams had delivered his first mob to the streets to protest the Stamp Act, John had privately called the demonstration "a very attrocious Violation of the Peace" and an action of "dangerous Tendency and Consequence."[19] His attitude had not changed.

To John, the campaign against Hutchinson in 1771 was a mere contrivance to perpetuate the Anglo-American imbroglio, to pour fuel onto a barely smoldering fire in the hope of igniting a general conflagration. This "Contention," he prophesied, "will never be fully terminated but by Warrs, and Confusion and Carnage." The implications of radical strategy deeply troubled him; his complicity in their secret machinations unsettled him even more. The anxiety and stress that Adams felt contributed to his physical exhaustion. Indeed, not only did he fall seriously ill, but he soon announced that he would not seek reelection. Once again, he had decided to quit politics.[20]

Adams also attributed his woes to "private" anguish. What domestic cares were so burdensome as to provoke such a crisis? During the previous year he and Abigail had lost a child, and in bearing Charles she had undergone a difficult pregnancy followed by a slow, painful recovery. In addition, passages in his diary and a coolness in his correspondence with Abigail in this period hint of strains at home.

The conclusion of scholars who have assessed the early relationship of John and his wife have varied from that of Charles Francis Adams who found their initial decade together to contain nothing "worthy of recording" to the view of Charles Akers—clearly the prevalent view—that Abigail "had adjusted successfully to life with a husband driven by profound anxiety for his future." Historian Paul Nagel concluded that a strongly companionable bond was formed and that the first ten years of the marriage were the best, at least for Abigail. Lynne Withey found that although John suffered occasional "twinges of guilt" over his frequent absences, Abigail adjusted quite well to her husband's work and rather indulgent habits. Phyllis Levin painted a different picture. To her, Abigail was initially overawed by her husband, but after two years of marriage she not only was seized by the melancholy conviction that the most enjoyable moments of her marriage already were behind her, but she seemed to have "sadly aged" as well.

Considering that the marriage of John and Abigail brought together two strong-willed individuals, it is somewhat surprising that both adjusted so well to the vicissitudes of the union. There was much happiness in the marriage. John found his wife to be bright, attractive, capable, companionable, and more than a bit accommodating. He too made concessions, with the result that Abigail attained an equality with her husband that was extraordinary for the times. But clashes were inevitable. Adams was a private man. He was not a loner, but he was the type who liked to closet himself in the sanctuary of his study for hours on end, there to work, to think, to write. He must have been frustrated by the lack of privacy at home. Instead of a retreat, his house was also home to a wife starved for adult companionship and three bawling, troublesome youngsters ever able to create a noisy, distracting environment.

Within the first years of the marriage, Abigail had begun to grown restive. She was left at home alone for weeks at a time while her husband rode the legal circuit or attended sessions of the assembly; even when John was not called out of town, he frequently disappeared at night to attend meetings of Sodalitas, to seek fellowship over ale and a pipe with friends, perhaps to dine at the home of clients or popular leaders. Many years later, one of the Adamses' daughters-in-law, a woman who spent considerable time in the company of John and Abigail, remarked that the Adams men were "peculiarly harsh and severe" toward their wives, displaying "no sympathy, no tenderness." Perhaps she overstated the matter, but, in part, she surely referred to John's self-centered nature and to his penchant for ignoring his spouse as he pursued the fulfillment of his own longings. It was probably this inattention that most annoyed Abigail, but there was more as well. Bright and well-read, she had begun to question convention. "[I wish to] stretch my pinions," she said. "[T]ho like the timorous Bird I fail in the attempt and tumble to the ground," she added, she never doubted that "the Effort [was] laudable." Pressed and anxious for his independence, Adams ultimately sought a remedy for his domestic inconvenience: he moved Abigail and the children to Braintree, but he kept his office in Boston. "I shall spend more Time in my Office than ever I did," he noted on the day of the family's move. "Now my family is away, I feel no Inclination at all, no Temptation, to be any where but at my Office. I am in it by 6 in the Morning—I am in it, at 9 at night. . . . In the Evening, I can be alone at my Office, and no where else. I never could in my family."[21]

At the beginning of June, Adams decided to leave everything behind—family, politics, business—and seek a cure for his woes at the Stafford mineral springs in Connecticut. The springs, on the highway from Worcester to Hartford, only recently had grown popular among Bostonians, but once established it quickly became the fashionable place to seek relief for a multiplicity of ills. Dr. Warren prescribed a trip to Stafford for many of his patients, and he regularly took a dip there, too, as did the president of Yale College and many of New England's wealthier merchants. In all likelihood it was Warren who advised the convalescing Adams to make the journey, perhaps hoping to get him away from the stresses of Boston as much as to get him into the waters.

Traveling by horseback, Adams proceeded at a leisurely pace, enjoying the lush roadside vegetation and the colorful spring wildflowers. On the fourth day of his trek he reached his destination. Hurriedly, he checked into his lodging a mile or so from the springs, then scurried for a look at the waters. The springs, he discovered, were at the foot of a steep hill, adjacent to Connecticut's Thames River. Not knowing quite what to expect, he was a bit surprised to discover patients both drinking and immersing themselves in the clear, placid waters.

Adams returned to the springs that same afternoon and twice the following day, but he immediately seemed uncomfortable, even embarrassed, there. This was a place for the "Halt, the Lame, the vapoury, hypochondriac, scrophulous, &c.," he concluded. It was not for him. By the third day in Stafford he did not even venture to the bath, remaining at the inn, lolling away the afternoon in political discussions with other visitors. On the fourth day he briefly visited the springs one final time, but even then he spent more time talking with a local lawyer than dipping. "I begin to grow weary of this idle, romantic Jaunt," he confessed. "I want to see my Wife, my Children, my Farm. . . . I want to hear the News, and Politicks of the Day." He was so anxious to get home that he packed his belongings and set out for home on the morning of his fifth day in Stafford. But after three days in Braintree he was gone again, off to tend his legal pursuits.[22]

En route home from the springs Adams purchased a copy of the *Boston News Letter,* one of the city's weekly newspapers. What he read must have given him great comfort. The journal reported the "melodious Harmony" that had been reestablished with Great Britain. More than a year before, Lord Frederick North had formed a ministry and, ironically, on the very day of the Boston Massacre his government had moved to repeal the Townshend Duties, save for the tax on tea. The popular movement had huffed and puffed about continuing its protest, but, in fact, the Whig resistance seemed to have spent itself. Into 1771 the colonists had responded with almost total indifference to this sole remaining imperial duty. It was at this nadir of radical fortunes that the Whigs had met at Hancock's to plot a strategy to revive their cause, the agitation that had pushed the anxious, guilt-plagued Adams to his collapse. He felt better now, and he could only have rejoiced at the *News Letter*'s conjecture that "America is not [again] to become an Object of Parliamentary Attention."[23] The imperial crisis surely must be over, Adams exalted, a turn of events that he viewed no less personally than he had the news of the Stamp Act a few years before. It was as though a heavy burden had been removed from his shoulders.

"A fine Morning," Adams bouyantly announced to his diary when he awakened following his first night back in Braintree in June 1771. Eighteen months later, on New Year's Day 1773, he recorded that he had "never been happier." He said, "I feel easy, composed and contented."[24] This was indeed a time of contentment for Adams. He was in good health, he was happily married, and after the strains brought on by the Boston Massacre trials and his one term in the House of Representatives, he must have been delighted with the general tranquillity that prevailed in public affairs throughout most of 1771 and 1772. Nevertheless, happy though he was, Adams was not altogether untroubled.

Ambitious as ever, he no doubt sorely missed the recognition that had come with political office. But he remained confident that his resignation from the assembly had been the prudent course. He had acted patriotically during the Townshend Duty crisis, he told himself in his diary. "I have served my Country . . . at an immense Expense, to me, of Time, Peace, Health, Money, and Preferment," he added. It was not a view that all activists shared. James Otis, unstable and given to half-mad palaver, once turned savagely on Adams, accusing him of having repeatedly shrunk from the cause, of having provided little or nothing to the popular movement. You have spent your time "dancing from Boston to Braintree and Braintree to Boston," Otis railed, "moaping about the Streets of this Town . . . and seeming [indifferent toward] every Thing, but to get Money enough to carry you smoothly through this World."[25] Adams was speechless. Even if Otis was disturbed, Adams found it painful to hear such a bitter accusation from a man he revered.

Otis's wild cant was made the more troubling because Adams could not be certain that his old mentor was wrong. Once again, his diary became a battleground as he poured over both his own conduct and that of the activists. Adams saw himself as being above the fray. How else could his role in the Boston Massacre trials be explained, he asked. Of course, he could not say that of the royal officials. Bitter denunciations of Governor Hutchinson became more frequent in his diary. Hutchinson, he charged, had accumulated one office after another and he had ladled out posts to relatives and friends; in the process, he had amassed not only a fortune but authority and obeisance as well. There was nothing new in his attack on Hutchinson. What was new and significant, however, was that Adams levied similar charges against some of the popular leaders, especially Otis, once his role model. Otis, like Hutchinson, he now concluded, had been seduced by the "Charms of Wealth and Power." This man who had first sounded the clarion against the threat posed by British designs had made a "turn about." During the Townshend Duty crisis he had "rant[ed] on the Side of Prerogative." Adams was somewhat willing to attribute Otis's apostacy to his mental instability, but he also saw therein a crass self-serving. Otis, he charged, had treacherously switched sides in order to secure appointive offices for his brother, two brothers-in-law, and his father. By implication, Adams's outlook had remained virtually unchanged since 1765: full of distrust of the popular leadership. Nevertheless, as Otis's stature declined in his eyes, Adams's earlier reservations about Samuel Adams appeared to wane. Increasingly, John saw him as tireless and unbending, as selflessly devoted to the patriot cause, as "cool, genteel . . . and restrained in his Passions."[26]

Nor was it his political role alone that troubled him. Adams, who turned thirty-six in fall 1771, felt unfulfilled. His life probably was half completed, he complained, and he had little to show for it. Although he acknowledged greater earnings than most of his old college chums, he grieved that he had not grown wealthy. Even the practice of law had lost much of its charm. The majority of Adams's cases stemmed from commercial transactions and often involved Boston's merchants, their clients, and their trading partners in Europe, England, and the West Indies. But his was a varied practice. Property disputes involving both realty and personality figured heavily, and he represented several clients in defamation of character cases. Criminal law also constituted a large percentage of his business; he defended clients accused of murder, rape, assault, larceny, and counterfeiting, as well as defendants charged with crimes arising from mob activity, including men indicted for rioting and tarring and feathering. He was retained in tax cases, and he appeared in the imperial Admiralty courts on several occasions. Adams even handled some cases that were exceedingly rare in eighteenth-century America. He defended at least one client in a divorce case, and he once successfully represented a husband who charged another man with having "trespassed" against his wife and caused her to become pregnant. On a few occasions he served as counsel for slaves who sought their freedom.

But for every exciting legal battle, he complained, he faced a score or more of banal and dreary cases, often to be tried in some barely familiar courtroom far from home. By the 1770s he had long since wearied of his repeated odysseys on the judicial circuit, the daylong horseback ride from Boston to Salem, the six arduous days astride a mount to reach Falmouth, Maine, and the cold or wet or brutally hot hours endlessly traveling to reach Worcester, Ipswich, Taunton, Plymouth, or Martha's Vineyard. He traveled with other lawyers and even with judges, sometimes sharing accommodations with them, but their company was not a fair substitute for the comforts of home. Too often the journeys became—as did one in the summer of 1771—"flat, insipid, spiritless, tasteless . . . melancholy" treks that were devoid of companionship and amusement. Adams longed to spend more time at home, but once home, he again decided he had to be in Boston. After having lived in the capital, he had grown disenchanted with Braintree; his hometown, he now declared, was just

another small village inhabited by farmers with "vulgar, rustic imaginations."[27]

In August 1772, therefore, Adams moved his family back to Boston. For
£533—four years' earnings for many Boston craftsmen—he purchased a large
brick house on Queen Street, not far from his office, and he and his clan
returned to the city. The move signaled not a resolution of his troubles but his
belief that Anglo-American tensions would not recur. It was his intention to
practice law and look after his family, returning occasionally to Braintree to
superintend operations on the farm. He would brook no other activities. In
particular, he would shun politics. "Above all Things," he wrote, "I must
avoid Politicks, Political Clubbs, Town Meetings, General Court, &c, &c,
&c." He believed he could succeed, for—according to this new John Adams—
his "Heart [was] at Home," where he would devote his time to Abigail and the
children, hoping that through his sacrifice they might enjoy a "happier Life"
than before. Adams ignored the fact that it was not a good time to move.
Abigail had just given birth to a third son, Thomas Boylston, and she still was
quite weak.[28]

Adams was barely settled in his new residence before his mettle was tested.
A month after his return to the city, Samuel Adams called at Queen Street
imploring him to speak at the annual ceremony commemorating the Boston
Massacre. John refused. At thirty-seven he was "too old to make declama-
tions." In 1773 he did attend the triennial memorial service of the shooting,
but his diary entry that evening indicated he was moved less by the speeches
than by the recollection that his action in defending the soldiers had been "one
of the most gallant [and] generous [of] many disinterested Actions of my
whole Life."[29]

While Adams succeeded in remaining politically inactive, he was on the
verge of a profound change in outlook, a metamorphosis that was brought to a
climax by events that unfolded in the year following his return to Boston, as
well as by important changes that occurred in the popular viewpoint of his
fellow citizens.

Curiously, the issue that first galvanized Adams to action aroused little
interest within the general population. Just before the Adamses moved from
Braintree, word arrived in Massachusetts that henceforth the Crown, not the
provincial legislature, would pay the salaries of the superior court justices in
the colony. The surfacing of some opposition could not have surprised London, for two years earlier the General Court had denounced the Crown's
decision to place the governor on the civil list, thus making him economically
independent of the assembly. London undoubtedly anticipated only a minor
ruckus, just as the opposition to a Crown salary for the executive had been a
low-key affair; the radicals, on the other hand, sought to galvanize the populace
into a full-blown protest of imperial policy. The ministry was more realistic.

Town meetings in Boston and Cambridge villified the Whitehall decision, but elsewhere the general public found the issue dismayingly arcane.

Adams's initial reaction to the new imperial policy was no less indifferent. He neither made any public pronouncements nor any diary entries concerning the matter for more than two months after news of the ministry's plan reached America. Adams acted only when the moderator of the Cambridge town meeting, Maj. Gen. William Brattle, heretofore thought to be a staunch Whig, published a defense of the Crown measure. In the first two months of 1773 he answered Brattle in seven newspaper essays that appeared in the *Boston Gazette*. By Adams's candid admission, it was a "tedious," legalistic dispute, one that the populace did not follow closely. It was Adams's contention that Britain's new policy would destroy judicial independence, making America's justices susceptible to the whims of the Crown. Brattle countered that magistrates who held office for life, upon good behavior, were well insulated from the caprice of Crown officials. Adams wrote in a learned, scholarly manner, and his essays were anything but propaganda pieces. Indeed, he scrupulously avoided even the suggestion that the ministry sought to reduce the independence of the judiciary, implying only that such an outcome might be the result of this misguided policy. Ultimately this obscure flap became a significant event both for Adams and the general public when it was accompanied by another, more riveting constitutional debate and by a sensational scandal, both involving the higly visible royal governor of Massachusetts. In tandem, these events nurtured festering suspicions about Great Britain's intentions.[30]

Five days before the appearance of Adams's first essay on the independence of judges, Governor Hutchinson addressed a special session of the Massachusetts General Court. Although he responded primarily to the declarations of Boston and Cambridge regarding judicial salaries, Hutchinson also wished to broaden the debate by raising the matter of Parliament's authority over America. Undertaken without London's authorization, this was a risky step for the governor, one that invited a full airing of rival positions on the fundamental question of sovereignty within the British empire. It was fraught as well with the potential for rekindling the fires of resistance within Massachusetts.

Governor Hutchinson delivered a learned treatise to the assemblymen but one that added little to what ministerial defenders had said for a decade. Parliament's sovereignty over America, Hutchinson argued, was unlimited, and any attempt by a colonial government to exert its alleged rights at the expense of the powers of the parent state would be illegal and unconstitutional. No middle ground existed. The colonies must either be dependent or independent.[31]

At Hutchinson's invitation, both houses of the legislature responded. The Council drafted an immediate reply. The House acted more deliberately. It first endeavored to procure the assistance of Daniel Dulany of Maryland, the author of a widely read treatise on the Stamp Act, then it sought the aid of "The Farmer," John Dickinson of Pennsylvania. When both men declined to join the fray, the House settled for a committee of its own members. That panel in turn implored John Adams to assist in preparing a response, undoubtedly turning to him not only because he had addressed constitutional issues in his recent newspaper essays, but also because he had considered the question of American rights in Braintree's statement on the Stamp Act eight years earlier.

Adams agreed to their entreaty. Over several days he, together with Samuel Adams and Joseph Hawley, an attorney and assemblyman long active in the popular cause, drafted a resolution that the House of Representatives ultimately adopted. It was a bold riposte. The colonial charters, it asserted, granted the colonists sovereign legislative powers. If pushed, the House warned, the colonists would choose independence to tyranny.[32]

Hutchinson was badly wounded by the exchange. Adams had understood intuitively that the governor could not win the fight. "He will not be thanked for this" by his masters in London, Adams had predicted, and, indeed, the Earl of Dartmouth, the minister responsible for American affairs, privately admonished Hutchinson for his "imprudence." Hutchinson's "Ruin and Destruction must spring out of it," he additionally forecast. Adams was correct on that count as well. Not only did Massachusetts fail to accept the governor's view of unconditional parliamentary supremacy, it considered Hutchinson a traitor to his native land, a man who welcomed—indeed, pleaded for—foreign rule upon New England.[33]

Hutchinson's misguided debate with the assembly proved to be a paradisaical turn of events for the popular party. For three long years they had despaired for their cause. Beset by declining political fortunes, Samuel Adams and a bare handful of activists had worked tirelessly since late 1770 to keep alive—in Massachusetts and elsewhere—both the flickering radical sentiments and the cohesiveness of the popular movement. In the aftermath of the acquittal of Captain Preston and his men, Samuel had written essay after essay warning of the dangers of standing armies, and he had orchestrated the commemorative service on each anniversary of the Boston Massacre. His master stroke, however, had been the creation of committees of correspondence, a network linking Whigs in Boston to compatriots in the hinterland and eventually to Sons of Liberty chapters elsewhere in the colonies. Through this medium, he and his sedulous assistants continued to beat the drum for the popular cause, keeping alive what Hutchinson called the radical "Contagion."[34]

But only in 1773, after three long years without a crystallizing issue, was Samuel Adams's tireless, relentless labor rewarded. First had come Hutchinson's imprudent constitutional lecture. Now, with the governor weak and vulnerable, the radicals struck again. Since early in the year Boston's popular leaders had possessed several private letters that Hutchinson and Andrew

Oliver—Hutchinson's brother-in-law and the lieutenant governor of Massachusetts—had written to Thomas Whately, an undersecretary in the imperial Treasury. The purloined communications had been provided to Samuel Adams by Benjamin Franklin, who was employed as an agent for Massachusetts in London. In June the radicals decided the time was right to act. Revealing the discovery of "letters of an extraordinary nature . . . greatly to the prejudice of the province," Samuel Adams read the missives to a closed session of the assembly. Propagandists followed with a series of newspaper articles contending that the correspondents intended to subvert the Constitution. With the public almost panting to see the communiques, the letters at last were published, though not until they had been carefully edited to maximize the desired effect.[35]

In most respects the letters were unremarkable, for they contained little that Hutchinson had not said publicly on numerous occasions. His most damning remark was that there "must be an Abridgment of what are called English Liberties." Otherwise, the thrust of his message was that the empire inevitably would crumble if America was permitted to drift ever further from the jurisdiction of the parent state. Although the letters were mostly trifling abstractions, the public treated them as sensational documents. In part this was because they were published in tandem with Oliver's less temperate correspondence, thus shrouding the communiques with a sinister aura. In addition, the fact that the governor and Oliver had expressed their views to officials in London aroused fears that a conspiracy to extirpate America's liberties existed between Hutchinson and the faraway ministry. But the letters created a tempest mostly because of the adroit management of Samuel Adams. However unscrupulous and deceitful his behavior, he had successfully manipulated popular opinion.[36]

No one was more touched than John Adams by these occurrences. Coming one atop another, London's apparent drive to deprive the provincial judiciary of its independence, the governor's intransigent position on colonial autonomy, and the revelation of a possible plot among imperial officials to destroy the liberties of the colonists, all had a transforming impact on Adams. As if by alchemy, these events changed Adams. The uncertain patriot of the 1760s was at last recast. Never again would he see British policy as merely misguided. When Great Britain next moved against the colonies, John Adams emerged as a committed revolutionary.

This has not been the view of most students of Adams, however. Traditionally, historians have looked upon Adams as an unhesitating stalwart within the popular movement from the days of the Stamp Act onward. The principal exception to this interpretation was Charles Francis Adams, his grandson and first biographer, who depicted Adams as having become fully committed to the protest movement only in the aftermath of Britain's Coercive Acts in 1774, a full year later than this study judges the transformation to have occurred. Most scholars, however, have depicted Adams as a revolutionary as early as 1765.

Thus, John Ellsworth concluded that Adams's "basic committment to resist Parliament" occurred during the Stamp Act but that his fervor subsided thereafter and was not rekindled until 1774, as Charles Francis Adams held. On the other hand, Page Smith stressed Adams's "prominent part" in the protest as early as 1765 and saw him as having philosophically "defined" the radical position even during the Townshend Duties crisis that began in 1767. Gilbert Chinard believed Adams was fully dedicated to the anti-British party by 1768, while Edmund S. Morgan was convinced of his unwavering and "outspoken hostility" to every ministerial act from the earliest days of the colonial protest. Peter Shaw accepted this interpretation, but he saw Adams as emotionally unable to cope with the "guilt" of acting as a revolutionary before 1773; thereafter, Shaw said, he "displaced" his anger upon Hutchinson and the English ministers, convincing himself that they were the revolutionaries and he was the conservator. Only through a subliminal sleight of hand, Shaw suggested, was it possible for Adams to become the fully committed patriot.[37]

Adams's version of history differed from that of all interpreters. Years after the events, he claimed to have become a committed revolutionary during the writs of assistance case in 1761. But his memory clearly tricked him, and no scholar has accepted his contention. Repeated entries in Adams's diary after 1761 make it abundantly clear that he continued to vacillate with regard to the protest movement long after the writs case had concluded. Nevertheless, if Adams's recollection in this instance was faulty, he had a much better feel for the factors that gradually shaped his thinking toward Great Britain.

To his way of thinking, no one agent was responsible for the evolution of his thought. On several occasions he hinted that he first questioned the wisdom of America's union with Great Britain as a result of the parent state's unconscionable treatment of the provinces during the wars with France in the 1740s and 1750s; his father, he said, shaped this outlook. He never failed to acknowledge the influence of Otis, Thacher, and Samuel Adams. Like other colonists, he said that he came to see similarities to his own time in the voices of Brutus and Cassius and Cicero, who in antiquity had struggled with tyranny and decadence. Of far greater importance, he noted his debt to intellectuals within the English Opposition. His views on political science, he once said, stemmed principally from "Sidney, Harrington, Locke, Milton, Nedham, Neville, Burnet, and Hoadley," a list to which he subsequently added other proponents of English reform, particularly John Trenchard and Thomas Gordon, radical polemicists who ultimately published *Cato's Letters,* a damning indictment of contemporary English politics and society. What Adams derived from these Whig pamphleteers was the notion of the existence of an insidious conspiracy against liberty throughout the English-speaking world, a plot that sprang from the corruption eating away at England's vitals. Liberty was threatened throughout the empire; the oppressive measures that the ministry had sought to implement in America during the past decade were but the most visible part of the intrigue. This was the message that Samuel Adams had long preached, but it was not an ideology John had previously embraced. In 1773, though, his varied thoughts coalesced. By 1772 he had come to see Samuel Adams in a different light; that year, for the first time, he referred to him as "restrained" and as a disinterested and patriotic leader. The churning events of 1772–73, moreover, seemed to him to have demonstrated the efficacy of Samuel's message. His writings, especially in 1773, always related the importance to him of Hutchinson's apparent duplicity and of the judicial independence crisis. He made it clear that it was at this point when he at last wholeheartedly embraced the views of the popular movement. These events, he remarked, had led him to a "grand discovery." He now saw evidence of a plot of "premeditated Malice . . . against the People in general, which in the Sight of the Law [was] an ingredient in the Composition of Murder."[38]

Yet, events by themselves are unimportant; it is the perception of events that is crucial. Adams discerned these events through the prism of the Whig outlook of the English Opposition and through the tutelage of Samuel Adams, and his views were shaped as well by a suddenly altered view of Great Britain and America that flowered in his New England. During the crisis that began in King George's War in 1745, New England clergymen succeeded in fusing traditional Puritan beliefs with certain prevailing intellectual currents of the more secular eighteenth century. The result was a perspective in which the ideals of classical republicanism were merged with the lingering remnants of Puritanism. The sense of danger posed by unrestricted individual self-interest was revitalized; in addition, the notion that the new commercial age had unleashed dangerously licentious tendencies was tirelessly expounded. Individual and civic virtue alone would serve as an antidote to the corrupting forces of modernity. New England first mobilized behind this banner in the mid-century wars with France. When the parent state committed itself after 1765 to a new imperial policy for America, the Yankee popular party interpreted ministerial actions as evidence of the triumph of profligacy within the highest ruling circles of the British empire. Once again, it was presumed that only a renewed spirit of civic virtue, reminiscent of the indomitable spirit of the Puritan forebearers who had fled to wilderness America to battle for the Lord, could thwart the enslavement of the American colonists. To adherents of this mind-set, therefore, American resistance to ministerial policy was seen as defensive in nature and as designed to preserve and maintain the colonists' threatened heritage, a struggle to salvage liberty from the threat of the suddenly corrupt rulers of the parent state.[39]

Beholding the events of 1773 from this perspective, Adams was transformed. Where once he had seen the colonies as England in miniature, or as an infant England, he now looked upon Britain as irremediably corrupt. In that faraway land "corruption is so established . . . as to be incurable," he now exclaimed. A nation of "general Depravity" and of "Luxury and Venality," the unhappy people of Great Britain groaned under rulers with "no principles of public Virtue." By contrast, Adams increasingly viewed America in idealized terms. Its very discovery by Europeans was a heaven-sent endowment, a providential act contrived to enable mankind to emancipate itself from the tyranny and slavery that haunted Europe. To America came "the slavish Part of Mankind," pilgrims animated by a "love of universal Liberty, and a hatred, a dread, a horror" of the despotism that swamped the Old World. "[O]ur fathers," men of "sturdy, manly, pertinacious spirit," secured the freedom they had set out to find and, in turn, bestowed that blessing upon Adams and his generation. It now fell to Adams and his cohorts to protect those blessings from the "cool, thinking, deliberate Villan[s], malicious, and vindictive, as well as ambitious and avaricious" sorts who occupied seats of power both in America and in London.[40]

Adams's journey to full commitment to the popular movement had been slow and tortuous, but his unwillingness to see despotic motives in London's actions was not entirely unique. George Washington, for instance, had been so unconcerned by the Stamp Act in 1765 that he had not even attended the sessions of the House of Burgesses in which the legislation was denounced. And at the height of the disturbances caused by the tax, when Adams at least was writing tracts against the measure, Washington's diary entries read: "Sowed Turneps. . . . Began to seperate the Male from the Female Hemp. . . . Seperated my Ewes & Rams. . . . Finish'd Sowing Wheat." Benjamin Franklin appeared even less troubled than Washington by Britain's new policies, trusting the parent state's wisdom and benevolence. "I am not much alarm'd about your Schemes of raising Money on us," he told an English friend at the time of the Stamp Act crisis. "You will take care for your own sakes not to lay greater Burthens on us than we can bear."[41] Such a view was never countenanced by John Adams.

The transition in his outlook complete, Adams permitted his name to be placed before the House for election to the Council, the upper house of the assembly. Rather dramatically, he pattered on about how he always could be trusted to act prudently but fearlessly. As expected, he was elected, but, as many also expected, Hutchinson promptly vetoed his selection.[42]

Adams appears to have been neither surprised nor disturbed by the governor's negation. Indeed, as if a heavy burden had been lifted from his shoulders by the transformation he had recently experienced, he and Abigail enjoyed a pleasant summer, their happiest time together in years. Both were healthy. Abigail was beginning to socialize more, sometimes even attending social functions unescorted by John. During that summer Adams's business obligations were lighter than usual, leaving him more time to spend with his wife. They made trips to the farm to oversee the crops, and they went to Weymouth to visit relatives and old friends. They entertained from time to time, and they attended parties and enjoyed the gala wedding of a good friend. For the first time since their courtship days, Abigail even accompanied John on his legal circuit.

John and Abigail walked together that summer, and occasionally they went for long, quiet rides in the family carriage, and now and then on warm, verdant afternoons they leisurely scudded about the calm azure waters just off the coast in a small boat, a purchase in which John had recently indulged himself. It was an idyllic time, a warm, facile summer that they would later cherish for its tranquillity and quiescence, for the opportunity it afforded to enjoy the very best that life could provide.[43]

Then came the news of the Tea Act, and both knew that somehow everything would have to change. "I tremble when I think what may be the direfull consequences," an anguished Abigail prophetically wrote from Boston. "[A]nd in this Town," she added, "must the Scene of action lay."[44]

PART TWO

*

An Epocha in History

CHAPTER 5

*

Tea That Bainfull Weed

NOVEMBER 27, 1773. Few Bostonians ventured out on this cold, raw Saturday night. A dreary rain had fallen off and on all day, making the autumn air feel sharper than ever. Most people preferred the snugness of home that evening, relaxing perhaps before a felicitous fire, or, if tired from a long day's labor, seeking early on the happy warmth and comfort of their bed. A few men, mostly sailors and laborers, relaxed in the grog shops near the waterfront over ale and tobacco, talking of work and women, listening to the boasts and exultant tales of the loudest, most believable roisterers.

On this Saturday night, about five miles from the city shoreline, a large merchant vessel lay at anchor, unnoticed. It was the *Dartmouth,* a three-masted constant trader, a year-old ship owned by three Quaker brothers from New Bedford. It had been shepherded to this point by the resilient beam of the Boston lighthouse, but it could go no further without the assistance of a pilot. The vessel bobbed there all night, creaking resonantly on the gentle, black waters. At four o'clock on Sunday morning a pilot came aboard. He and Capt. James Hall chatted for a few minutes, although the captain was impatient to get this behind him and go ashore. The *Dartmouth* had been on a very long voyage; normally a four-week crossing from London, this cruise had taken twice that time. At last the paperwork was completed, and the steerman returned to his guide boat. Then everyone sat again, restlessly awaiting a favorable tide and a soft, embracing breeze. At 6:00 A. M. the sails began to ripple just a bit, and the ship eddied forward, ever so slowly gliding up the narrow channel into King's Road. Within the hour the first rays of light spilled over Boston Harbor, and the early risers ashore spotted the craft. Word spread quickly about town that the *Dartmouth* was approaching. At eleven o'clock Captain Hall dropped anchor again, this time astern the admiral's flagship off Castle William, the royal fortress about two miles due east of Boston's wharves.

Several churchgoers walked or rode a few blocks out of their way that morning, stopping at the docks for a few moments to squint toward the newly landed bottom. Ordinarily, the arrival of a ship in Boston harbor would have been as commonplace as the rising of the sun and would have provoked about as much attention. But people wanted to see this craft. In the *Dartmouth's* hold were 114 chests of tea, the first shipment of the commodity to reach Boston since Parliament had passed the Tea Act.[1]

Early in 1773 the directors of the East India Company—the largest mercantile firm in the British empire, a company now nearly bankrupt through mismanagement—came to Lord North, the prime minister, for assistance. Fearful that the collapse of this giant might spawn a general economic collapse, he was not unwilling to befriend the ailing enterprise. He pushed the Tea Act through Parliament, legislation that not only maintained the threepence tax on tea established in 1767 but that also granted the company monopoly rights for the exportation and sale of the beverage in the colonies. With the middlemen eliminated, the tea could be sold quite cheaply, less expensively even than the contraband Dutch tea that the colonists had enjoyed the past few years. The company was expected to do a booming business. North also had high hopes for raising revenue. After all, the colonists had imported six hundred thousand pounds of dutied tea during the past two years; with cheaper tea in the offing, who could predict how many tons of this commodity would be sold annually in America?[2]

By late September 1773, it was widely known in America that the company soon would send over about fifteen hundred chests of dutied tea, and that New York, Philadelphia, Charleston, and Boston would be the destinations of the ships. Radicals in New York were the first to act against the new measure, flooding the streets with handbills. Their broadsides played on the two themes that would constitute the radical position in each colony witnessing resistance to the excise. If not opposed, they said, the tax on tea would be followed inevitably by other imposts, duties that would be illegal because Americans could be taxed only by their own representatives. Furthermore, the protesters insisted that if the East India Company was permitted to monopolize the tea trade, all American commerce soon would be engrossed by a few huge English companies. Not only were American liberties imperiled by the Tea Act, therefore, but colonial merchants and consumers were certain victims as well. New York's protest was carefully organized, and that colony's popular party attained its objectives with stunning swiftness. After only a few weeks the three merchants who had agreed to serve as the province's tea agents, or consignees, resigned, thoroughly terrified by the likelihood of a howling mob tearing down their businesses and residences, board by board. After blustering a bit, Gov. William Tryon likewise capitulated. He notified London that the ship bearing the dutied tea would be turned back when it reached New York.[3]

Philadelphia's radicals also succeeded in preventing the landing of the *Polly,* with its seven hundred chests of tea. The Sons of Liberty in South Carolina were less successful, although they too managed to keep the tea from being sold. The *London,* bearing 257 tea chests, docked in Charleston four days after the *Dartmouth* anchored in Boston, but as all the consignees in the South Carolina capital had resigned in fear, there was no one to vend the disputed commodity. The governor ordered the tea stored until he received further instructions from London.[4]

Of the four cities targeted to receive the tea, Boston was watched most closely by the authorities in London. Strangely, in view of its clamor against earlier British taxes, the city remained calm into the fall. As late as mid-September, Governor Hutchinson reported that the town was quiet, and well into October the provincial committee of correspondence appeared to be less alarmed at the Tea Act than at another scheme of the North ministry: a plan to add still more colonial officials to the civil list, thus paying their salaries from the revenue collected from American trade. The surface tranquillity was misleading, however. Behind the scenes the radicals were busy.[5]

Boston's radical leadership looked upon the excise on tea as manna from heaven, the issue that would enable them to revive the languishing protest movement. Quietly, men like Joseph Warren, Benjamin Church, and Thomas Young—all physicians, all radicals, all men who had won respect within the laboring classes—toiled to prepare the groundwork for renewed protest. They were joined by Ebenezer Mackintosh, the shoemaker, William Molineaux, a hardware merchant, and Paul Revere, a forty-year-old silversmith, each of whom had close ties to Boston's working class. And, of course, there was "the great Mr. Adams," as Dr. Young referred to Samuel Adams.[6]

The other Adams, John Adams, played no role in these matters. Indeed, so unaware was he of the preparations by the radicals that he believed there would never have been a protest in Boston had the Sons of Liberty not acted first in New York and Philadelphia. Indeed, his reminiscences of this period suggest that he was not yet a principal figure in the leadership circles of the popular movement. He discussed at length his role during that crucial year in representing Massachusetts's attempt to secure title to dispute western territories, and he recounted the flap over salaries for royal officials, but he did not once mention the Tea Act or any protest against that legislation.[7]

The calm that Governor Hutchinson had reported was shattered early in November. Boston's newspapers suddenly were flooded with polemics against the tea tax. Town meetings were called to explore the best course of action. Mobs of five hundred or more took to the streets, visiting the homes of the consignees. But the agents refused to be coerced. Unlike their counterparts in the three other cities, none of Boston's tea agents resigned. Nor would the governor back down. Whereas the chief executives of New York and Pennsylvania had refused to permit the tea ships to dock, Hutchinson was intransigent, as Boston's inhabitants discovered on that sunny, cold November 28, when they sighted the tall masts of the *Dartmouth* in Boston harbor.[8]

"The Tea that bainfull weed is arrived," Abigail Adams notified an out-of-town friend upon learning of the *Dartmouth's* presence. Both she and her husband now feared the worst, expecting that the radicals would seek to destroy the tea rather than permit its sale. In fact, Adams was retained briefly by the owners of the *Dartmouth,* businessmen anxious to learn whether they might be liable should the tea be seized or destroyed. John and Abigail knew, too, that the populace was behind Sam Adams and his colleagues. "The flame is kindled and like Lightening it catches from Soul to Soul," Abigail reported. Only some "Lenient Measures" by Hutchinson might avert the crisis, she told an acquaintance, although she harbored little hope for any such action. It was a forlorn, frightening situation. Rumors buzzed. The tension mounted with each passing day. "My Heart beats at every Whistle I hear," she confessed.[9]

Hutchinson had no intention of budging. Expecting trouble, he packed a few belongings and retreated to his country estate in Milton. There, in his rambling two-story clapboard, he was safe from the city mob. The decision now lay with the radicals. Either they acted, or the British Customs Service would unload and sell the tea. The radicals moved on December 16. They called a public meeting at Old South Church in downtown Boston. Over five thousand attended, despite cold, inclement weather. A succession of fiery speeches ignited the crowd's passion, until the building rocked and swayed with calls for immediate action. First, however, the leaders insisted on sending an emissary to Milton. One final attempt would be made to persuade the governor to send the *Dartmouth* back to London along with two other tea ships that had arrived during the month. The envoy set out just before noon; at 5:45 P. M. he returned and announced Hutchinson's decision to a hushed audience. The chief executive was obdurate. The law would be enforced.

Shortly after the meeting broke up, a large number of men disguised as Indians and calling themselves "Mohawks" boarded the tea vessels. They held a brief "tea party." By nine P. M. their work was done. They had demolished 342 chests of tea worth about ten thousand pounds, today's equivalent of about $1 million.[10]

The following morning, a clear day, though one made bitterly cold by a howling northeast wind, John Adams rode back into Boston, returning from a week at court in Plymouth. He had barely reached town when he heard of the previous night's events. He hurried home to see Abigail and the children and to learn as many details of the enterprise as he could. At noon Abigail's uncle Isaac Smith came for lunch, accompanied by Joseph Palmer, a glove manufacturer and Dick Cranch's brother-in-law, and Joseph Trumbull, an old chum of Adams from Harvard; they talked of nothing but the Mohawks. That evening Adams dropped in on the Monday Night Club, where he pumped the members for further news.[11]

Adams knew at once that the popular party had burned its bridges. The destruction of the tea must have "important Consequences"; this was a watershed event, an "Epocha in History," as he put it. Nothing would be the same again in public affairs nor, perhaps, in his private life as well. But, like everyone else, he could only speculate on what might be the consequences of the "tea party." He knew that London would seek to make Massachusetts pay for the tea that had been destroyed. Otherwise, he guessed, arrests would follow, and he thought it likely that the ministry might attempt to revoke the province's charter. There might be economic sanctions, too. Even at this point, however, Adams could not imagine that hostilities might occur, regardless of the retribution sought by the imperial government.[12]

Despite the inevitability of British reprisals, Adams applauded the destruction of the tea. There had been no choice, he thought, and he called the defiant boarding of the vessels and the quick obliteration of the dutied beverage the "grandest Event" in the history of the colonial protest movement.[13]

As for the future, the next move in this high-stakes game rested with the ministry.

January 19, 1774. London, bleak and sunless, lay in the grip of a damp winter chill. Early that morning the *Hayley,* an American three-master owned by John Hancock of Boston, dropped anchor in the imperial capital. Before any of the crew disembarked, the captain, pausing amid the mountain of paperwork that confronted the master of each newly arrived vessel, notified the harbor pilots and customs people of the Boston Tea Party. Like a churning wildfire, the news raced through the city, and by nightfall the prime minister and his cabinet had learned of the event. Three days later a London newspaper published the story, and the news began to course through the English and Scottish hinterland. Within another week London also knew that the incident in Boston had not been an isolated case, that protests had occurred in each city due to receive the tea.

Ten days after the *Hayley's* arrival, the ministry, with enough information to sort out a fair semblance of occurrences in America, held its first meeting to deal with the crisis. Thereafter, the cabinet met frequently to consider the matter, often even reassembling at one another's homes in the evening to continue their deliberations. Slowly, a planned response emerged: four tough, unbending retaliatory measures were to be imposed on Massachusetts.

Lord North personally shepherded the bills through Parliament between March and May. It hardly was an exacting stint. Some members questioned the wisdom of doing more than compelling Massachusetts to pay for the damaged tea, but North and his compatriots pooh-poohed the gloomy talk of those who objected to the harsher, more chastening aspects of the legislation. It was far more risky to do nothing than to act with resolve, North argued. By late spring the measures, known collectively as the Coercive Acts, were law. Despite the provocations of the other cities, only Boston and Massachusetts

were to be punished. The Port Act closed the harbor in Boston until restitution was made for the despoiled tea. Under the Massachusetts Government Act a Crown-appointed council was substituted for an elected one, the
governor's appointment powers were expanded, and the activities of town
meetings were restricted. The measures were iron-hard and intolerable,
the colonists would say. The acts raised the specter of conflict. That was
not what the ministry wanted, but it had gambled. By singling out Massachusetts for retaliation, the North government had adopted a divide-and-
conquer strategy, hoping in the process to force the other colonies into line.
If the policy failed and war resulted, the government believed it could win
that war.[14]

Early 1774 was a busy time for the Adamses. John, as usual, was on the
road frequently, tending to his legal business. Whatever changes he had experienced recently in his political outlook, his personal habits remained un-
affected. While on the circuit he longed for domestic comforts, but, inevitably,
he was barely back in Boston before he was annoyed by the distractions at his
busy home. Nabby was nearly nine now; John Quincy was seven; Charles,
four; and Thomas Boylston, two, and all were full of energy and noise and
mischief. Even Abigail, longing for companionship and anxious in her role as
the tutor of these precocious children, vexed him with demands for counsel
and solace. The commotion and disorder, the inability to think and work, the
constraining closeness, irritated him. After only one day at home following a
trip in March, he complained to his diary: "I am wanted at my Office. . . .
There is Business there, but none here. . . . I think [Abigail and the children]
must remove to Braintree."[15]

In fact, Adams had already taken steps to move his family back to Braintree.
During the winter, he purchased from his brother a tract adjacent to his
Braintree residence. This parcel included the house in which he had been born
and in which his mother had continued to reside until she remarried. John now
possessed a farm that consisted of approximately fifty-five acres and two
houses. This property had come to have a special meaning for him. Not only
was it the ancestral residence, but Adams had come to look upon the rural
environment both as a healthy alternative to the miasmic urban surroundings
and as a placid retreat from the stress and pressures of the city. Sometime in
May or June he moved the family back into the dwelling that he and Abigail
had shared since the day of their wedding ten years before.

While Adams was provoked at times by Abigail and the children, the real
source of his anxiety in spring 1774 arose from the uncertainties of public
affairs. It was his lamentable fate to live in an "Age of Tryal," he cried out, and
until London's response to the Boston Tea Party was known, his future was
uncertain. No one could predict how London's retaliation would affect the
economic health of Boston or what might become of his legal practice. But the

trial to which Adams almost certainly referred was the decision he would have
to make concerning his role in the popular movement.

When word of the Coercive Acts at last reached Boston on May 10, Adams
seemed almost exhilarated, thankful for an end to the long, uncertain wait. The
news was grim, and the atmosphere soon grew even more sullen when Gen.
Thomas Gage returned from London bearing word that Governor Hutchinson had been granted a leave of absence and that he, Gage, was the new
governor of Massachusetts. On June 1 Hutchinson sailed for England, never
to return to his homeland. On that same day Gage transferred the Massachusetts Bay seat of government to Salem, well removed from the mobs of
Boston. Yet Adams proclaimed that he felt more "Spirits and Activity" than
ever before, despite the realization that London had not acted wanly, that it
adopted tough measures and had made the commander of the British army in
America responsible for their enforcement.[17]

The popular leaders in Massachusetts instantly recognized that only con-
certed action by all the colonies might force a British retreat. The only recourse
seemed to be another trade embargo. Within two days of the receipt of the Port
Act, the Boston Committee of Correspondence, meeting with eight suburban
panels, urged such a step. The following evening, May 13, a Boston town
meeting ratified the committee's work. Boston had urged a sweeping trade
embargo, one that not only would stop all imports from Britain and the British
West Indies but also would prohibit exports from throughout America to those
places. The key to success, however, was to secure the participation of the
other northern colonies. Paul Revere and other dispatch riders immediately
scurried off to distribute copies of this Massachusetts Circular Letter.

Whatever Samuel Adams, the chairman of the committee of correspondence, had expected, the results were disappointing. Rhode Island promised
to cooperate only if other colonies joined in. Connecticut did not wish to take
any action until an intercolonial congress could meet to consider every possible
alternative, or to promulgate a national boycott. In New York, a town meeting
called to consider a boycott ended in chaos, failing to take a stand one way or
another. Not much could be expected from Philadelphia; Pennsylvania's assembly was controlled by conservative elements who feared that a trade embargo might result in war.

Samuel Adams soon faced considerable problems at home as well. Several
merchants launched a campaign to raise funds to pay for the damaged tea,
hoping such an act would result in the repeal of the Port Act; more than
seventy-five influential residents in Boston, including both merchants and
tradesmen, signed an address lauding Hutchinson's long years of service and
promising compensation for the tea. The popular party, moreover, experienced a disconcerting erosion of support. Some of its more moderate supporters defected; still others, such as John Hancock, its principal financial patron,

appeared likely to assume a noncommittal stance. There were many reasons for such hesitancy. Whereas Britain had appeased the colonists in the Stamp Act and the Townshend Duties crises, it now showed no sign of backing down; this time colonial defiance might lead to hostilities. Besides, the port of Boston might be quickly reopened and a boycott avoided altogether if restitution was made to the East India Company. Finally, there was considerable anxiety in Boston that the comprehensive boycott proposed by Samuel Adams would destroy the fishing and shipbuilding industries, as well as countless merchants. "[N]ot content with the calamities already come upon us," one former foe of Hutchinson charged, the program of Samuel Adams would add still further woes to the inhabitants of Massachusetts.

Despite these problems, Samuel Adams must have been buoyed when word of the Massachusetts Government Act reached Boston several days after the city learned of the Port Act. News of the changes in the provincial government outraged even many conservatives and took some of the starch out of the movement to submit to Britain, both in Massachusetts and elsewhere. However, as the radical leaders soon discovered, this did not mean that the boycott they cherished was yet a certainty. On June 5 the committee of correspondence adopted the Solemn League and Covenant, a pledge to suspend all trade with Great Britain and to refrain from purchasing English goods imported after August 31; this embargo, unlike its predecessors, was to be enforced by "Men stiled Mechanicks and husbandmen, the Strength of every Community." The response could not have been what Samuel Adams envisioned. While only a few towns in the backcountry endorsed the plan, nearly eight hundred tradesmen in Boston refused on June 15 to agree to the Solemn League. Little had gone well for the popular leadership in the month since news of the Port Act reached Boston. There were signs, too, that matters might soon get worse. Not only was the movement to pay restitution still gathering steam, but the radical leaders feared that the merchants might be able to control the next scheduled Boston town meeting, set for June 17. There were indications that the merchants and their allies would attempt to pack the meeting and secure passage of a resolution to "censure and dismiss" the committee of correspondence.

Faced with these threats, Samuel Adams was compelled to temporize. Early on June 17, he shepherded through the Legislature a resolution committing Massachusetts to a national congress and electing a delegation to attend such a meeting. It was a step he had hitherto resisted, fearing that it might be dominated by the most conservative elements of other, unsympathetic colonies. He made a second concession as well. The majority of the four delegates selected to attend the Continental Congress were quite moderate.[18]

Samuel Adams was the only true radical in the delegation. The others were carefully selected. Each of the other three was committed to the resistance movement and could be counted on to support a national boycott, but each was a moderate in comparison to the likes of Dr. Warren or Ebenezer Mackintosh. There were no cordwainers or silversmiths within this delegation, and with the exception of Samuel Adams, no one with the slightest connection to Boston's working class; and, his extremism notwithstanding, Samuel Adams, it should be remembered, was a cultivated, urbane man, a graduate of Harvard College. This was to be a delegation, Samuel Adams excepted, of wealthy businessmen and comfortable lawyers. Each man was chosen because of his respectability and his reputation for responsible behavior, attributes which, it was hoped, might solidify opinion within Massachusetts and at the same time allay the fears of more conservative congressmen from south of New England, delegates who might otherwise come to Philadelphia thinking that Massachusetts was inhabited by nothing but firebrands bent on war with the parent state, perhaps even on independence from Great Britain. In addition to Samuel Adams, James Bowdoin, a prosperous merchant and land speculator who once had been a political ally of Hutchinson, was also a member, as was Robert Treat Plaine. John Adams was the other member of the delegation.

John Adams, of course, agreed to serve. He had begun to play a more active role in political affairs during the previous year, although much of his activity had been behind the scenes, as in his preparation of the assembly's answer to Hutchinson or, as with the judiciary furor, had been in a contest that failed to spark much public awareness. He had stood for election in 1773, however, and in the spring of 1774 he once again was elected to the Council, although Governor Gage, like Hutchinson before him, nullified his selection. Then in the hectic weeks that followed news of the Port Act he sat on a town committee that considered a response to Britain's closing of Boston's harbor and, for the first time, served as moderator of a Boston town meeting.[19] Clearly, the John Adams of 1774 was quite different from the man who proclaimed "Farewell Politicks" in 1766 and again in 1771 and 1772.

Beginning late in 1773, Adams's diary divulges his new, unwavering commitment to the popular cause. It was as though a different person now sat at the cluttered desk in the little farmhouse in Braintree and scrawled out his defiance of imperial policies. The destruction of the dutied tea by the Mohawks had been an "absolutely and indispensably" necessary action, he wrote on the day following the Tea Party. America's governors in London were "Egyptian Taskmasters" bent on reducing the colonists to ignominy, desolation, and slavery, he went on; indeed, the ministry was in the grasp of despots whose "Innovations will be the Ruin not only of the Colonies, but of the Empire." He lauded the oration that commemorated the anniversary of the Boston Massacre in March 1774, calling it an "elegant . . . Spirited" address; two years before, he probably had not even attended the service. He continued to link Massachusetts's executive officials to Britain's "Conspiracy against the Public

Liberty," and he railed against the timorous members of the Council who would permit themselves to become the tools of the royal administration. The time had arrived, he noted in June 1774, for "bolder Councils" and "Spirited Resolves," and when Boston's calls for a national boycott appeared to meet with timidity in many colonies, he wondered whether America had "Men . . . fit for the Times."[20]

Adams said little of this in public, however, and like Bowdoin, Cushing, and Paine, he was still looked upon as a moderate in Massachusetts politics, neither an insider in radical circles nor an agitator bent on fomenting upheaval. Samuel Adams, of course, knew him well. He knew that John was feisty, impassioned, and quick-tempered. He knew too that John was firmly committed to the popular cause and that, from the vantage point of the radicals, he could be trusted. Of equal importance, Samuel Adams had to have known that John's presence on the delegation would allay the fears of the skittish at home (through his law practice, he had close ties to the merchant community and men like Hancock), while in Philadelphia, as in Boston, he was likely to be perceived—quite correctly—as a mature, stable, prudent, scholarly, judicious, and thoughtful man. John Adams would not be seen as a revolutionary. Without a doubt, however, he would be viewed as a friend of America.

No man could have faced what confronted Adams without wrestling with a multitude of doubts. He worried about his ability to fulfill his role as a congressman. Not only did he know that he lacked political experience, he also was apprehensive that he might not even adequately understand the issues in the Anglo-American quarrel. Practical concerns troubled him, too. Like most of those who packed for the journey to Philadelphia, he confronted personal fears. Would his service unduly affect his legal practice? Would a protracted embargo result in the collapse of property values in Boston and Braintree, where he owned real estate? Would war be the result of the congress? Would he be liable to a charge of treason? He was anxious lest the popular defiance of Great Britain result in unforeseen and terrible changes. What, he wondered, would "the Multitude, the Vulgar, the Herd, the Rabble, the Mob" do following his example of open resistance to constituted authority? "I feel unutterable Anxiety," he confided to his diary.[21]

In these troubled times Adams turned for comfort to Abigail and the children. During recent absences Adams had fallen into the habit of seldom writing home, but during this summer of 1774, alone on the circuit, pensive and perplexed by a thousand disquieting reflections, he suddenly dispatched more than a dozen letters to his wife. He wrote almost daily, once even sending three missives on the same day. "I want to be at Home," he admitted. "My Fancy runs about you perpetually," he confided. "Kiss my sweet ones for me," he directed Abigail, and he even expressed a longing to be home to assist in teaching the children. And, as in every previous crisis, his thoughts turned toward the pastoral life, toward his Braintree farm, where "a Frock and Trowsers, an Hoe and Spade, would do for [his] Remaining Days."[22]

But the political commitment that John Adams now had made would tie him to a centrifugal orbit for the next quarter century, a force that would steadily pull him ever further from his old life, from his family, from his Braintree haven.

CHAPTER 6

*

Until Our Rights Are Fully Restored

EARLY IN JULY 1774, John Adams was in Falmouth, Maine, for court duties. He was bored by this circuit, distracted by the prospect of the coming congress. He could not remember a more "irksome . . . and melancholy" round of business, he told Abigail, forgetting for the moment that much off his recent legal work had seemed nettlesome. Jonathan Sewall, an old friend and rival lawyer was there too, and just as lonely and anxious to get home. The two bumped into one another after breakfast one morning, and Sewall, perhaps noticing the disheartened look in Adams's eyes, asked his friend to accompany him on a stroll. Adams was delighted at the invitation. Here was an opportunity to get away from the small room he had rented and to escape briefly the arduous case he was arguing—a suit brought by a Tory whose property had been ransacked by a radical mob.[1]

The two men walked from town, climbing Munjoy's Hill above Casco Bay. There they paused momentarily to catch their breath and to behold the wondrous view. On one side, as far the eye could see, they looked down on majestic forests that marched up and down the hills, great towering trees whose foliage seemed greener than green in the mingle of rising sun and viscous shade; to the other side sprawled Falmouth, a bustling, squalid frontier village, a ramshackle assembly of clapboard and stone edifices hard against the vast, island-dotted, azure bay.

Adams and Sewall had known one another for years, John having courted Hannah Quincy in the same period that Jonathan was squiring her sister, Esther. In many ways the two had similar backgrounds. Both came from solid middle-class upbringings, and both had graduated from Harvard College; Sewall was seven years older than Adams, but a sophomoric prank had led to his expulsion for a time, so he eventually became Adams's college mate for two years. Each had taught briefly following his graduation, Sewall conducting his

Latin classes in Salem. In the late 1750s each man had struggled to establish his fledgling law practice; confronting similar problems, the two had been drawn together, each often writing the other long missives filled with the most personal observations and confessions. The two even had married about the same time. Sewall, after an even more protracted courtship than that of John and Abigail, finally married Esther Quincy. By the mid-1760s each man had begun to prosper in his profession.

There were differences, however. Whereas Adams's legal mentors were foes of Thomas Hutchinson, Sewall's benefactors had been devotees of the lieutenant governor. In addition, Sewall harbored a deep, impenetrable enmity toward James Otis, intense feelings that helped solidify his ties to the Court party. Ultimately, Sewall served under Hutchinson as the attorney-general of Massachusetts; later he served the crown as the chief justice of the Vice Admiralty Court at Halifax. By then he hobnobbed more and more with those in the ruling circle of Hutchinson, and his contact with Adams, while still cordial, was less frequent.[2]

On that cool July morning in Maine, therefore, Adams must have suspected that Sewall did not wish a mere walking companion. He was correct; Sewall wanted to talk. The Continental Congress was on his mind. There was some small talk first. Then, abruptly, Sewall warned that Great Britain would not budge from its course. If Congress attempted to resist, he went on, war would be the result, a war, he predicted, that America could not hope to win, a fight that would destroy Adams as well as his province.

Adams, his mind at last set, was just as adamant. The "die [is] now cast," he told Sewall. "[I will] swim or sink, live or die, survive or perish with my country," he added.

The men argued on, but of course neither could begin to alter the views of the other. Before starting down they experienced an awkward silence; Adams clearly realized the razor's edge upon which he was poised, and he seemed to know that war was inevitable. "I see we must part, and with a bleeding heart . . . I fear forever," he blurted out.

Afterwards the two old friends quietly walked back toward their lodgings, Adams's at one end of Falmouth, Sewall's at the other. Each man knew that his world was about to change. But neither could imagine the magnitude of the change to come. They would not see one another again for thirteen years and then in vastly different circumstances. Decisions made in drawing rooms in faraway London, as well as actions agreed upon in noisy, smoking gatherings in taverns and legislative halls throughout America, had begun to sunder old friendships as surely as they lacerated the relationship between the parent state and its colonies.[3]

Adams was home with Abigail and the children for three weeks before setting off for Philadelphia. By day he toiled in his fields, preparing the farm for the autumn harvest that would commence in his absence. At night he often escaped to his study, to read and prepare for the congress just ahead.[4]

On Wednesday, August 10, Adams said his good-byes to the children and, accompanied by Abigail, made the familiar ride from Braintree to Boston. He met Paine and Samuel Adams at the residence of Thomas Cushing—a last-minute substitute for Bowdoin, who had declined to serve because he had not yet received his smallpox inoculation. From there the congressmen proceeded to downtown Boston for a brief public ceremony, this in full view of five regiments of redcoats. Another round of farewells followed, then at last the men, accompanied by six servants, set off in Cushing's handsome carriage for distant Pennsylvania.

The ride was hot and dirty, for an oppressive August sun hung over New England, parching the farmland and transforming the compact highway into a choking, dusty thoroughfare. Villagers paused to wave as the carriage rolled past, and when the men stopped for a meal they often were joined by local luminaries, anxious for information, eager to be seen in such exalted company. The Massachusetts men spent Saturday night in Hartford and kept the Sabbath there, too, attending church in the morning and again in the evening. They also met with Silas Deane, one of Connecticut's delegates to the congress, when he arrived for a visit early on Monday morning. The delegation was in New Haven by the next afternoon, and the town rolled out the red carpet for its distinguished guests. Bells chimed and cannons roared as the carriage crept toward the village green. Jared Ingersoll, once a stamp collector, now a judge of the Vice Admiralty Court in Philadelphia and the very essence of conservatism, paid his respects; Roger Sherman, another of Connecticut's congressmen, also visited with the Massachusetts delegation. Adams had not yet met Eliphalet Dyer, Connecticut's third congressman, but he must have puzzled at the differences between Deane and Sherman. Deane, a Yale graduate was a polished, erudite lawyer; Sherman, a fifty-two-year-old former shoemaker and publisher, was less cosmopolitan, and unable to hide his dislike for his colleagues. Adams met briefly with Sherman, then he slipped away to visit the campus of Yale College. On their second night in town, while a gentle rain pierced the heat wave, the men were entertained at a lavish dinner in a private residence.

The journey continued the next day, on through village after village, pausing only in Milford to see a statue of Paine's great-grandfather, once a governor of this province. On Saturday Cushing's carriage slipped across the boundary line into New York, the first time that the thirty-eight-year-old Adams had ever been outside New England. That same afternoon, ten days out from Boston, the delegates reached New York, and like many later visitors, they paused to sightsee. The men toured the city hall and several churches, looked in on a prison and a hospital, visited the shipyards, inspected the town marketplace, strolled through residential areas (Adams found the houses to be neat and "more grand" than those in Boston), climbed to the top of the Dutch Church steeple for a panoramic view of Manhattan and Long Island, walked about King's College, and very carefully—and rather ominously—looked over the fortifications that protected the city from invasion. Between the tours and a seemingly endless round of sumptuous meals, Adams and his colleagues met each of the New York congressmen as well as one from the New Jersey delegation. The Massachusetts men had found that Connecticut's congressmen, whatever their personal differences, were eager to support a boycott of English trade. The New York delegates were a different breed, however. Not only were they uncertain about the wisdom of a trade embargo, they shared equivocal views of New England, admiring its will but anxious about its alleged democratic tendencies and its bellicose spirit.[5]

After nearly a week in town, the delegates crossed into New Jersey. They paused for two days in Princeton, looking about the college and meeting with its faculty. It was from this bucolic little college town that Adams, now three weeks into his adventure, finally wrote his first letter to Abigail. She had written to him twice already, charming notes in which she sought to appear resolute and stoically patriotic, though she succeeded in hiding neither her anxiety nor her loneliness. She also was concerned that her husband had not written; she knew that the wives of Cushing and Sam Adams had received letters.[6]

Adams and his colleagues departed Princeton early on August 29. A long day's ride followed, but, just at dark, they reached Frankford, a suburb north of Philadelphia, where they found a large party waiting to greet them. A few congressmen were present, as was Thomas Mifflin, a successful young merchant who had played a key role in the campaign to persuade the reluctant Pennyslvania Assembly to support the congress. Dr. Benjamin Rush, a leading physician in Philadelphia, also was in the welcoming party, and he invited Adams and Paine to join him for the completion of the trip into the city. They had not traveled very far before Adams concluded that Rush was a gossip, but he listened closely to the tattle, learning that Pennsylvania's delegation was not to be trusted and that even the "Farmer," John Dickinson, was far less radical than most observers believed.

Despite the fatigue of their guests, the Philadelphians ushered the Massachusetts delegation to the City Tavern on Second Street, where dusty throats could be wet down with a few mugs of ale, and where much of the real business of this congress would be transacted. Very late that night Adams finally got to bed, collapsing in his quarters at Sarah Yard's stone house across the street from the tavern, a little room at the corner of Market and Second streets that was to be his home for most of the next three years.[7]

Bounding from bed on his first morning in town, Adams set off on a long walk about the city. Philadelphia was large, the biggest city he had ever seen.

Its population of twenty-five thousand was slightly greater than that of New York, about forty percent larger than that of Boston. Despite its size, Adams soon discovered that Philadelphia was an easy town in which to get about. The thoroughfares were straight and parallel, a far cry from the helter-skelter meanderings of Boston's streets. These were busy byways, too. He saw what seemed an endless stream of activity between the town and the docks along the Delaware River and saw just as much traffic in the other direction, as dray after dray laden with commodities rolled west, destined for the huge immigrant population in the hinterland of Pennsylvania—and even of Virginia and Maryland. Adams discovered that Philadelphia's principal avenues were handsome and well kept. Tall stately trees and whale-oil lamps tended by public lamplighters lined these broad streets; brick sidewalks abutted these arteries, and more than five hundred pumps had been placed strategically for thirsty travelers and their horses.

The city was only twelve blocks wide and twenty-five blocks long, but over six thousand houses were crowded into that space. The west end, into which Adams did not venture, was squalid and home to the city's working poor. The eastern sector, the first few blocks back from the river—home to Adams, for his lodging lay just three blocks from the Delaware—was a region of shops and residences, the workplace as well as the area of residence for most of Philadelphia's skilled artisans, professionals, and wealthy merchants. Adams toured this area and was immediately impressed. He discovered that Philadelphia, like New York, was a city of greater wealth than Boston.[8]

That evening Joseph Reed and Dr. William Shippen called on Adams. Reed, a Philadelphia lawyer who had been active in the protest movement, had close ties to Massachusetts. His wife was the daughter of an English merchant who had served for several years as the Bay Colony's agent in London. He and Adams in fact had met once before, at the Dorchester Sons of Liberty conclave that John had reluctantly attended in 1769. Shippen, educated at the University of Edinburgh, was in private practice, although he occasionally lectured at the College of Philadelphia. After dinner the two took Adams for a riding tour of their city, then Shippen personally guided his guest through the Pennsylvania Hospital.

A three-story, T-shaped structure, the hospital was situated eight blocks west of the State House, set in a grove of trees behind an ambling white picket fence. Built only twenty-five years earlier, this was the oldest hospital in the colonies. Adams's tour began in the basement, a reproachful dungeon that housed the mentally ill. To his horror, Adams discovered among the caged patients a former client, a man he once had successfully defended against a horse-stealing charge. Next he followed Shippen upstairs to the wards, long rooms housing row after row of beds, upon which lay the lame and the ill. It was a "dreadful Scene," he wrote Abigail. "The Weakness and Languor, the Distress and Misery, of these Objects is truly a Woeful Sight." The tour ended in Shippen's laboratory on the third floor, where the physician, using a plaster of paris model of the human body, gave his guest an anatomy lecture. Adams was "charmed," as he put it, with his new knowledge.[9]

From the next morning, a Wednesday, until Congress assembled the following Monday, Adams seemed to spend every free moment enmeshed in politicking. Each day began with a long breakfast in the company of his congressional colleagues, meals accompanied by probing conversation. Afternoons were devoted to sipping cider or beer, porter or claret, with men from other delegations. Almost every evening he was the dinner guest of an amicable Philadelphian, and these long sumptuous meals often were followed by still more hours at the tavern, where libation and talk flowed. At these gatherings Adams learned that every colony, save faraway Georgia, would send delegates to the congress, and that one-third or more would, like himself, be lawyers. Most who were not attorneys were southern planters.

Adams was delighted to discover the existence of a broad consensus on the rights of Americans, but he also found that when the group considered the best ways of standing up to Britain, perilously close to half the congressmen were extremely cautious. Men like Joseph Galloway, Speaker of the Pennsylvania Assembly, John Jay and James Duane of New York, and William Livingston of New Jersey were formidable leaders, but each, he quickly concluded, lacked the will to resist British oppression. These men would constitute a conservative faction, delegates drawn principally from the middle colonies. Not only did these men still naively believe that London would listen to calm reason, they also dreaded a trade boycott, fearing—as had Sewall at Falmouth—that such a course might plunge America into a war with the parent state, a conflict that could only be won with assistance from Roman Catholic France and Spain. More likely, they cautioned, the war would not be won, and a victorious Britain would exact a terrible revenge. If the war resulted in a stalemate, they went on, Britain and America's erstwhile European allies would partition America, leaving some of the colonies in the possession of Catholic monarchs. Even if a boycott did not result in war, the mere thought of a trade stoppage caused handwringing among the conservatives, who apprehended that fortunes would be lost by the powerful merchants whom they represented. The recommendation of this faction, Adams guessed, would be to shun an embargo and to simply urge Britain to repeal the Coercive Acts and the Tea Act, an appeal that might be accompanied by a resolution requesting that Massachusetts pay for the tea it had destroyed.[10]

Of course, Adams found that many delegates pleased him, especially some of the planters, men whom he judged to be generally "solid, firm, judicious" types. He thought it good news to discover that the South Carolinians had lived under crown officials who seemed to have been no less irksome than Hutchinson and Oliver, but he was particularly delighted by the congressmen from Virginia, "spirited and consistent" men such as Patrick Henry. Virginia's was the most thoroughly radical and dependable of all the delegations sent from below New England. Adams soon concluded that they were willing to fight, although some among them, such as Richard Henry Lee, naively believed that the vessel bearing the tidings of an American boycott would return with the news that Britain had repealed its objectionable American legislation. Adams did not share that optimistic belief. Like many of the conservatives, he had come to believe that an embargo would lead to war, but he saw no alternative save submission to tyranny.[11]

A week of listening, talking, and observing convinced Adams and his colleagues that Massachusetts's interest would best be served if they played a passive role. Mifflin and Dr. Rush had urged such a course when they welcomed the New Englanders in Frankford, explaining that an open, defiant posture would only alienate other congressmen, convincing them that their suspicions of New England fanaticism had merit. The Massachusetts men agreed, and to achieve the more important goal of intercolonial unity, each adopted a quiescent manner. It was an act that required "great delicacy," Adams observed, but one that they performed with commendable proficiency. Pennsylvanian Joseph Reed, a savvy man who would rise to become the adjutant general of the Continental army and later chief executive of his state, was fooled into thinking that the Massachusetts delegates were mere "Milksops."[12]

On Monday, September 5, a cool, misty day, Congress at last assembled as planned at the City Tavern. Sam Adams—"cool, abstemious, polished, refined," according to John—was the first man on his feet. He proposed that the Reverend Jacob Duche, an Anglican priest, be recognized to deliver an opening prayer; it was a calculated move designed to allay the suspicion that New England was a land of religious bigotry. When Duche completed his lengthy supplication, business proceeded. Congress's first decision was to move to Carpenter's Hall, turning aside an offer from Galloway, Pennsylvania's leading conservative, to meet in the State House. Philadelphia's radical leaders had urged such a move. Meeting in the chambers of the carpenter's guild, they insisted, would symbolize the bond between the congress and America's urban mechanics, men whose assistance might well be useful before this ordeal was completed. That same day, moreover, Congress elected Charles Thomson, a Philadelphia firebrand and bitter foe of the Pennsylvania conservatives, as its secretary. There could be little doubt that the more radical delegates had pushed both issues as a test of strength; while neither decision could be interpreted as an absolute guide to the will of Congress, the Massachusetts delegates had to be buoyed by the outcome in both instances.[13]

At last ready to begin, the congressmen immediately ran into a thorny problem. How many votes should be given to each colony? Virginia pressed to give the large provinces a greater voice than that extended to the small colonies; it took two days of wrangling to agree that each colony would have one vote, a result that should have been foreseen since eight of the twelve colonies in attendance were, by everyone's definition, small colonies. That divisive matter was barely settled when a messenger was shown into the legislative chamber. He bore alarming news. The Massachusetts militia, he reported, had sought to prevent the British army from seizing the provincial arsenal in Charlestown; hostilities had occurred, and Gage, in retaliation, had ordered his fleet to shell Boston.

For almost forty-eight hours Philadelphia was animated by frenzied hysteria. Muffled bells tolled almost continuously, while militiamen assembled to drill, one-day-a-month warriors who, in their inexperience, stumbled and bumbled over one another. The reaction in Congress was of greater moment. "[E]very tongue pronouncs [sic] Revenge," Deane observed, and Adams concluded that the incident demonstrated the "Resolution, of the Continent" to resist British depredations by armed might, if necessary.

Two days after the first tidings arrived, another courier appeared with the welcome news that the story of a British attack had been erroneous. Nevertheless, this curious episode had told the radicals a great deal about the mettle of their colleagues. Valuable as this occurrence might have been for Adams and his faction, however, John had suffered through the two-day war scare terribly worried about the fate of Abigail and the children, who lived within easy striking distance of General Gage's redcoats.[14]

After its breathtaking start, congressional activity soon settled into a measured, deliberative pace. Congress created a committee—which included Adams and twenty-three others—to prepare a statement of American rights, then it adjourned to await the panel's report. While the remainder of the congressmen lolled away their time with tours of the city, Adams and his colleagues on the Grand Committee, as it was styled, met day after day. Countless hours were consumed in futile contention. Opinion within the committee mirrored the divisions within the congress. Most members shared the belief that the colonists were not subject to taxation enacted without their consent, but beyond that there was little agreement. On issue after issue, the committee split into a conservative and a radical faction. Could the colonists invalidate parliamentary legislation to which they objected? Could Parliament regulate imperial trade? What were the limits of American autonomy? Ten days of rancorous meetings—an exasperated Adams soon complained to his diary of endless sessions at which "these great Witts, these subtle Criticks, these refined Genius's, these learned Lawyers" discoursed—not only brought the committee no closer to resolving these constitutional issues, but the very existence of the congress was imperiled by needless, hairsplitting debate.[15]

It was Samuel Adams who moved to break the impasse and get Congress back on track. On September 14 he wrote the Boston Committee of Correspondence for assistance, explaining his "Impatience" with the drift of Congress. It was his opinion—and he was not often wrong in such matters—that most congressmen could be depended upon to aid Massachusetts, unless Congress first collapsed over the Grand Committee's importunate debate. What he wanted from his cohorts at home was something to divert Congress's attention from the committee's irresolvable and clamorous squabbling. What he sought was already on the way: on the sixteenth, Paul Revere galloped into town bearing the Suffolk Resolves, a statement written by Dr. Warren and adopted a week or so earlier by Suffolk County. When the full Congress assembled the following morning, its members expecting to adjourn as usual while the Grand Committee and its subcommittees toiled on in private, they were instead surprised to discover before them an inflammatory resolution. The Resolves urged nonallegiance to the royal government of Massachusetts, increased militia training in preparation for resistance to the "murderous" policies of the North government, and an end to all trade with Great Britain until colonial rights had been "fully restored."[16]

After all the fluff, after days of wrestling with abstractions, the real issues were at last confronted. Endorsement of the Resolves was tantamount to sanction of a boycott; a vote for the Resolves was equivalent to approval of military preparedness and defiance of the Coercive Acts. The debate that followed made it clear, if it had not been all along, that this congress would defy the parent state. How then should the more conservative delegates vote? Opposition to the trade embargo would shatter the radicals' cherished hope of maintaining a united front against Great Britain; moreover, if the conservatives voted negatively, then bolted the congress when the embargo was enacted, the entire popular movement outside New England might collapse. On the other hand, if they resisted a trade embargo, they risked political damage at home, not to mention—or so Galloway later claimed—the possibility of facing a hostile mob in Philadelphia. In addition, if the conservatives voted for an embargo, enough radical congressmen might reciprocate by endorsing their pet scheme: a plan to revise the imperial constitution, at once resolving the crisis and strengthening the Anglo-American union. The very notion was chimerical, for even if Congress agreed to such a scheme, the odds were long against London consenting to surrender even a mite of its sovereignty. Yet that was the course the conservatives chose. On September 18 every conservative congressman voted to endorse the Suffolk Resolves. It was, John Adams remarked that evening, "one of the happiest Days of my Life," and he wrote Richard Cranch that he now believed that "Congress will support . . . Massachusetts or Perish with them." On this day, the conservatives lost whatever chance they ever had of preventing hostilities with the Mother Country, although no one, of course, could see matters that clearly at the time. But years later, exiled in London, Galloway looked back on these events and tipped his hat to Samuel Adams. He had secured the radical victory, he wrote;

Samuel Adams, he went on, was a man almost without equal "in popular intrigue, and the management of a faction."[17]

The mechanics of the embargo remained to be decided. A broad consensus favored a boycott of British goods. Beyond that the issues got stickier. For instance, would the colonists also refuse to sell their commodities to the parent state? Should goods from the West Indies, as well as from Britain and Ireland, be denied entry in colonial ports? When should the embargo commence? And how could the boycott be enforced? These were not easy questions to resolve. The debate raged for weeks, tearing deep fissures within the radical faction.

Nonimportation was resolved most easily. Most congressmen wished to close their ports to great Britain soon, within thirty to sixty days at the latest. Nonexportation was a different matter. Massachusetts, which sold little to Britain, urged that all exports cease on October 1; Virginia and Maryland, whose tobacco crops would not be ready for exportation until December, argued that all restraints on exportation be postponed for a full year. Compromise was required. Finally, on October 20, one day short of a month after the subject first arose, Congress agreed to terms. Nonimportation of British, Irish, and selected West Indian goods was to commence on December 1; the embargo also encompassed a ban on the importation of additional slaves. Nonexportation was delayed until September 10, 1775. Furthermore, no British goods already in America could be sold after March 1. Congress also agreed to an enforcement mechanism known as the Continental Association; the qualified voters in each county or town in America were to elect a committee to compel adherence to the embargo.[18]

In the midst of these deliberations the conservatives struck with their plan for constitutional change in the imperial system. Galloway, the author of the plan, presented his views on September 28, confronting the radicals with what Samuel Adams later recalled was their "most alarming" moment during the Congress. The Pennsylvanian argued that a compromise was necessary, some solution by which American rights could be maintained within an existing central imperial government. His scheme was a deceptively simple contrivance. He urged the creation of a third house of Parliament, an American branch. This house was to consist of a Crown-appointed president-general and a congress elected by the legislatures in each colony, and its consent would be required for all legislation concerning the colonies.[19]

Galloway and his fellow conservatives longed to send this plan to London as an alternative to a congressional statement of American rights. Samuel Adams had good reason to be alarmed. The plan attracted a considerable following not only among the most conservative delegates but also among their colleagues who longed to send London a compromise, a reconciliationist appeal as an adjunct to the boycott. Furthermore, it was obvious that Galloway was willing to restrict American autonomy to a degree no longer acceptable to many radicals. If his plan would check the power of London, it likewise would place restraints on the provincial assemblies, subjecting them not only to the two existing houses of Parliament, but to a new American congress and still another Crown official as well. Debate on the proposal was long and heated, but at day's end the plan was tabled by a six-to-five vote. A month later, at the very end of the congress, the plan was formally rejected and stricken from the record.[20]

In place of Galloway's scheme, Congress slowly hammered out both a statement of the rights of the colonists and a list of American grievances. The Grand Committee issued its long-awaited report in late September, but that panel had become divided so deeply on some points that Congress deferred consideration for three weeks, until the split over the boycott largely was resolved. Days of testy debates and back-room compromises preceded the adoption of the Declaration of Rights and Grievances. The most radical congressmen did not get all they desired. For instance, their notion that Parliament had no rights over America was rejected by Congress, which also rebuffed the appeals of some—mostly southerners—that some objectionable British policies in effect before 1763 be denounced. Nevertheless, on whole the Declaration bespoke an ideology that had been the staple of the popular movement for years. Congress declared that the colonists had "never ceded to any sovereign power whatever, a right to dispose of" their rights to "life, liberty, and property . . . without their consent," and that they had "by no means forfeited, surrendered, or lost any of those rights." The statement additionally denounced more than a dozen acts of Parliament, including the Sugar Act, the Tea Act, and the various Coercive Acts. The thorniest matter was the issue of trade. Did Parliament have the right to regulate the trade of the colonies?

After weeks of debate Congress divided evenly on the question. In fact, the Massachusetts delegation split on the issue, with Adams probably defending the right of Parliament to regulate colonial trade. At the behest of John Rutledge of South Carolina—a man whom he privately disparaged as displaying "nothing of the profound, sagacious, brilliant"—John Adams prepared a compromise statement. So, apparently, did James Duane, whom Adams had met in New York, and whom he described as "a sly . . . little squint eyed" man of considerable talent. Congress accepted more of Duane's draft than Adams's, but its language was acceptable to Adams. From "necessity," the article ultimately read, and for the well-being of the whole, Congress assented to the regulation of America's external commerce, although it pointedly denied that Parliament possessed the right to regulate imperial trade for the purpose of raising revenue.[21]

During the eight hectic weeks that Congress was in session, Adams found himself harried by "Business, Ceremony, Visits and a thousand &cas." "My

Time," he told a correspondent, "is totally filled from the Moment I get out of Bed, until I return to it." There were the sessions of Congress itself, generally meeting from nine o'clock until three every day except Sunday; committee meetings were squeezed in when they could be, and on occasion special conclaves—once, for instance, Philadelphia's Quaker leaders requested an informal meeting with the congressmen—were held in the evening. Adams was invited to formal dinners about five nights each week. Often these were gargantuan banquets, the table groaning under hams, fish, lamb, turtle soup, sweetmeats, fruits, trifles, syllabub, and an assortment of fine wines. One night it was an "elegant Feast," the next a "mighty Feast," then a "most sinfull Feast." No matter what the occasion, breakfast or dinner, a relaxing walk or a leisurely ride, the politicking was incessant. Adams found himself endlessly supplicating, temporizing, conciliating, forever administering praise, and habitually resorting to legerdemain, all the customary artifice of the politician.[22]

Busy as he was, Adams found time for other activities. He was in Philadelphia for a week before he wrote Abigail, then for a month he averaged a letter every third day; strangely, he did not write home during the final three weeks that Congress was in session. His letters were filled with chitchat, yet they were devoid of sensuality and almost bereft of affection. Adams allotted considerable time to sightseeing and recreation. He played cards and bowled, visited an anatomical wax museum, toured the almshouse, and, for a second time, heard Dr. Shippen's medical lecture. In addition, he rode out to see the falls of the Schuylkill River, climbed to the top of the Christ Church steeple for a spectacular view of the city, and attended a session of the Pennsylvania Supreme Court. He took the opportunity to sample several churches, worshiping with the Baptists, Methodists, Presbyterians, Moravians, Anglicans, and even the Roman Catholics, whom he described as "poor Wretches, fingering their Beads" and "chanting Latin, not a Word of which they understood," although he added that he was "amazed that Luther and Calvin were able to break the Charm and dissolve the spell."[23]

Adams's confidence in his abilities steadily grew during these weeks. Before he left Braintree he had imagined that the body would be dominated by an American Pitt or a Demosthenes, and, indeed, in the early sessions he was nearly overwhelmed by the "Abilities, Learning, Elegance, Acuteness" of many of his colleagues. Congress, he wrote Abigail, consisted of "the greatest men upon this continent," statesmen who made him "blush for the sordid venal Herd" in Massachusetts politics. He was especially impressed with Mifflin and Caesar Rodney of Delaware, and by Dickinson, who had joined the Pennsylvania delegation in October and whom he described as "agreeable" and bright. No one impressed him more than George Washington, however. A member of Virginia's delegation, Washington struck Adams as a man of great virtue and toughness.[24] In time Adams came to see through some of the delegates, finding that behind the facades of guileful oratory and polished demeanors, many were quite superficial. He discovered, too, that he was the equal in learning and in preparation of the best of his colleagues.

Because the Massachusetts delegation sought to remain in the background, Adams found his freedom of action somewhat circumscribed. Nevertheless, he joined in the committee debates and on at least one occasion he inveighed the full Congress to adopt a more radical position than it was wont to take. Fearing that Great Britain might arrest American activists and transport them to London for trial, Adams sought to induce Congress to resolve that such an act would be looked upon as "a Declaration of War and a Commencement of Hostilities against all the Colonies." In the event that Britain did take political prisoners, Adams urged that Congress authorize the seizure of British officials in reprisal; these royal officials would be held hostage until the American captives were released. Even though this scheme was not adopted, Adams found that his stature grew as the meeting progressed. Gradually, others turned to him for counsel and for special assignments; he was asked, for instance, to write the final draft of the Declaration of Rights and Grievances. Many years later, reflecting on this experience, he recalled that he had "left Congress and Philadelphia in October 1774, with a Reputation much higher than ever I enjoyed before or since."[25]

During Congress's final weeks one unscheduled matter required attention. On October 6 Paul Revere again reined his mount before Carpenter's Hall. This time he brought news that General Gage had begun constructing fortifications around Boston. It seemed apparent that Gage suspected imminent hostilities. After much wrangling Congress sent the British commander a letter urging him to take no action before London responded to its work, also warning that any attack on Boston would be resisted by "all America." During the debate on the letter to Gage, the radicals sought to capitalize on the renewed concern that the British soon might use force by securing a congressional endorsement for the arming and equipping of the militia in each colony. While the Massachusetts delegates remained in the background, several of Virginia's congressmen led the fight. Richard Henry Lee introduced the motion, and Patrick Henry urged its adoption, claiming that "A Preparation for Warr is Necessary to obtain peace." That was further than this Congress wished to go, however, and the radicals were rebuffed.[26]

Afterwards, Congress tidied up. It dispatched a letter to the people of Great Britain, a missive couched in such soothing tones that the boycott was characterized merely as a petition for redress, and it sent a propitiating appeal to King George III—Congress pointedly ignored the Parliament—which urged his assistance and pledged loyalty to the monarchy. Adams, a member of the committee that prepared the petition to the King, saw both endeavors as exercises in propaganda and as mere "Dress and ornament" to appease the timid at home. That was not the case with still another appeal that Congress adopted. The delegates beseeched the inhabitants of Canada to join in the embargo. Finally, on October 26, with many congressmen already drifting home to tend their farms and businesses, Congress adjourned, though not before it resolved to meet again, if necessary, in early May.[27]

Adams had remained until the end, but he was no less anxious than the others to return home. He had enjoyed his stay in Philadelphia. He had been especially impressed with the elegant life-style of the gentry and the polite hospitality of his hosts, and he had savored the opportunity to experience a novel culture. Even so, his provincial ways hardly were overcome. He told friends back home that he believed Bostonians were better mannered and more urbane than the inhabitants of Philadelphia, and that New Englanders were not only a more attractive people than the Pennsylvanians but also had laws and an educational system superior to those of their neighbors to the south.[28]

As Adams packed for the trip home, he could only have been happy with Congress's achievements. Those ends that the popular party in Massachusetts had hoped to secure had been realized. Not only was a national boycott in place, but the heart of the Declaration of Rights and Grievances, Congress's most important statement, was consistent with the aims and philosophy of the popular movement in Massachusetts. Nevertheless, some matters troubled him. More than ever, he now believed that war was inevitable, but in the weeks following the radicals' heady triumph in the Suffolk Resolves matter, he grew less certain of America's resolve to fight. The delegates to this Congress, he came to believe, "Shudder[ed] at the Prospect of Blood" and longed to prevent "Hostilities and Ruptures." In all likelihood, they would come to the aid of Massachusetts only if Great Britain clearly was responsible for the outbreak of war.[29]

On October 29, while a cold autumn rain soaked the city, Adams oversaw the securing of his luggage, then clamored into Cushing's carriage for the long journey home. He had little idea what the future held for him, but of one thing he seemed certain. It is not very likely, he wrote in his diary that evening, "that I ever shall see this Part of the World again."[30]

CHAPTER 7

*

We Shall Do Something in Time

THE MASSACHUSETTS DELEGATION did not tarry in its return home. Bumping along, making thirty-five to forty-five miles each day, the congressmen reached New York after three days. They remained there only one night, then sped on. Two days later the villagers in one small Connecticut hamlet urged the travelers to pause for a thanksgiving banquet, but the weary congressmen declined the invitation.[1] After a three-month absence, these men were anxious to see their families.

None was in a greater hurry to reach home than John Adams. Whatever had prompted the aloof, reticent air in his few letters to Abigail, Adams now was eager to be with his wife. Abigail's epistles to her husband must have quickened his impatience for the home fires. Long, desirous, tender missives, her letters would have captivated the coldest of men. During the early days of his absence, when no letters arrived from her husband, she poured out her worries and anguish in several letters. At last, thirty-six days after he had departed Boston, when a letter from John reached her door, she was overcome by "such a flow of Spirits that I was not composed eno to sleep." She addressed her letters to "My Much Loved Friend," and she closed with the reminder that the "tenderest regard evermore awaits you from your Most Affectionate." The thought of your presence, she wrote, "plays about my Heart, unnerves my hand whilst I write, awakens all the tender sentiments that years have encreased." She prayed that John would have similar feelings when he read her letters. Her prayers were answered.[2]

After thirteen days on the road the congressmen rumbled into Boston, and later that day John and Abigail had the rendezvous that each had so long awaited. Everything must have looked wonderful to John. The harvest was in, the children were fit, and his wife—healthier and more contented than she had been in years—had never seemed more elegant or more fetching. In one of her letters Abigail had teasingly promised never again to share John with anyone or anything, and she had vowed to make him stay at home for two weeks when he returned from Philadelphia.[3] That she accomplished, barely.

Adams had been at home for three weeks when he was selected Braintree's representative to the Massachusetts Provincial Congress, the colony's extra-legal assembly now that the General Court had been suspended. Adams attended its sessions in Cambridge for about ten days, but he played only a minor role in its deliberations. Near adjournment time the body selected its slate of delegates to attend the Second Continental Congress in May, substituting only Hancock for Bowdoin.[4]

During that winter Adams was elected to a second office. The Braintree annual meeting chose him one of its nine selectmen, although he had not held such a post for nearly a decade and, in fact, for the past eight years had not even attended a town meeting in that village. A toilsome job in the calmest of time, it now fell to selectmen throughout the province to superintend the local enforcement of the national economic boycott. Actually, their mandate was considerable. In Braintree, for instance, the board of selectmen rode herd over schemes to prevent the wanton slaughter of livestock, a safeguard against potential future food shortages; in addition, the board improved plans to foster domestic manufacturing and took steps to control prices. The selectmen also commenced the systematic observation of the Loyalist population, pledging to publish the names of all violators of the boycott so that they might be "publicly known and universally Contemned." Adams had one additional board duty. He was named to the committee supervising the creation of the minutemen. In October the Provincial Congress had recommended that each village detach one-quarter of the troops from its normal militia units, organizing these citizen-soldiers into units that could march "at the shortest notice." Braintree created three such companies that winter, with Adams's committee sorting out the details of their pay and training, ultimately decreeing that they were to drill one afternoon each week for four hours.[5]

This activity, this management of minutia, must have been a disagreeable duty for Adams. More scholar than tactician, he heretofore had concerned himself largely with the constitutional and legalistic aspects of the imperial feud. Samuel Adams and Dr. Warren were better suited for the day-to-day organizing and scheming. Adams, therefore, must have been delighted that winter at the publication of a bevy of pamphlets critical of the work of the recent congress. Their appearance afforded him the opportunity to retreat to his study and pen a Whig retort.

Since the days of the Stamp Act crisis, the most conservative colonists generally had been silent, unwilling to defend unpopular British legislation. Now, however, they leaped into the fray, certain that a boycott meant war. Joseph Galloway, their spokesman at the congress, issued the most sensational tract, a potentially damaging piece that revealed the fissures and debates that had occurred behind closed doors in Philadelphia. Galloway and other conservative pamphleteers hammered away at a few familiar points: a sovereign head must exist in each polity, lest chaos result from competing governments; America must be subordinate to Parliament and the Crown; America derived great benefits from the Anglo-American union; the empire faced a bright future, a future of prosperity and aggrandizement as the colonists, augmented by the strength of Britain, would expand rapidly to the Pacific, then sweep across the Spanish dominions to the south. Most of all, however, the conservatives argued that Congress's boycott raised the specter of war. It was unlikely that America could win a war against the professional army and huge navy of the parent state, they wrote. A defeated America would face reprisals that would make the stamp taxes and Tea Act appear insignificant by contrast. But what if the colonists did win a war with Great Britain? America's problems would only have just begun. Weak and unprotected, they would lie vulnerable to plunder by the major European powers; in a brief time, America would be partitioned by the giants of Europe. Or, they alternately asserted, civil war would inevitably follow the disappearance of Britain's restraining hand. Powerful, democratic, land-hungry New England, they predicted, would invade the South; Americans would fight one another for control of the tramontane West, until the map of North America resembled that of Europe, a region of small nations, each distrustful of its neighbors, all groaning under despotic governments inevitably and interminably trapped in ruinous warfare.[6]

The *Massachusetts Gazette,* always friendly to the Country party—it had even defended the Coercive Acts—hurried into the fray with a series of essays authored by "Massachusettensis." Adams was certain that these pieces were the work of Jonathan Sewall, so reminiscent were they of the cautious admonitions that his old friend had expressed that summer day in Falmouth. In fact, they were produced by Daniel Leonard, a friend of Adams. Leonard was a lawyer and assemblyman from Taunton, a man who had married into considerable wealth and who, as a consequence, was the only lawyer in the province riding the circuit in an expensive carriage. Before 1774 he had been more active than Adams in the popular cause, but the sudden prospect of war caused him to reconsider his principles, whereupon he accepted appointment to the Council.[7]

It was to Massachusettensis that Adams replied. Writing as "Novanglus" ("New Englander"), Adams's riposte came in twelve letters published between January and April. He was but one of several Whigs who replied to the polemics of the conservatives, or Tories, as the radicals now called their foes. Charles Lee, an acid-tongued former officer in the British army who had emigrated to Virginia in 1773; young Alexander Hamilton, still an undergraduate at King's College—now Columbia University—in New York; and John Dickinson penned the best rebuttals, although none contained much that was new, save for Lee's vibrant defense of colonial soldiers, who, he maintained, could defeat a British army with a poor record of achievement in

America's irregular wars. Had Adams not risen later to considerable prominence, his Novanglus pieces would no longer be remembered. His efforts demonstrated that he had little facility for writing propaganda or even for communicating with a broad audience. No rejoinder was more learned than his treatises, but none was so unreadable. Penned in the same solemn, pedantic manner he might have utilized in the preparation of a legal brief, Adams droned on and on ("I have rambled after . . . ," he confessed from time to time), often flushing out some tangential legalism, grasping it, fighting it, finally subduing it after a Herculean feat of erudition. In an age when fewer than one percent of the male population attended college, how widespread could the readership have been when faced with creations such as this: "Another instance to shew, that the king by his sole authority, whenever he pleased, made regulations for the government of Ireland, notwithstanding it was annexed and subject to the crown of England, is the *ordinatio facta pro statu terrae Hiberniae,* in the 31 Ed. I. in the appendix to Ruffhead's statues, p. 37."

Novanglus drew upon and fleshed out arguments that went as far back as Adams's earliest legalistic essays of the mid-1760s. In addition he dilated upon the arguments he had propounded in the assembly's response to Governor Hutchinson two years before. Two principal arguments emerged from these dozen essays. For the first time in his public writings Adams laid out the argument that America was imperiled by a conspiracy spawned by a venal British ministry. Corrupted by the "luxury, effeminancy and venality [that] are arrived at such a shocking pitch in England," the ministry and its executive lackeys in the colonies—whom he now referred to as a "junto"—had sought to plunder the colonists as they had previously ravished Ireland. Unless the despots were stopped, he said, Americans might "subsist as well as our fellow slaves in Ireland, upon Spanish potatoes and cold water." There was no time to waste. A stand must be made. Every day that this corrupt ministry governs America, he said, their evil influence "Like a Cancer . . . eats faster and faster," destroying step by step America's "virtue, public spirit, simplicity, frugality," threatening to reduce the colonists to the same level of "luxury, foppery, selfishness, meanness, and downright venality" that was devouring the parent state.

Adams's second contention drew upon the writings of English Opposition figures, as well as European legalists and theoreticians such as Hugo Grotius and Samuel Puffendorf. He argued that sovereignty resided in the hands of the people. Adams was not the first to make such a point, but his justification for the premise was novel. America, he maintained, was not part of the British realm; therefore, it was not subject to British taxation. At the time of colonization, he contended, England, Ireland, Scotland, Wales, and the various components of the realm in 1775 had existed separately. Upon acquisition by conquest, each province owed fealty to the British monarch, but Parliament had no authority in any of these regions until the inhabitants consented to such sovereign power. At the time of the colonization of America, he went on, the settlers agreed to a compact with the monarch in the form of colony charters. However, Parliament's power over America did not extend beyond its authority to regulate the commerce of the empire, a right to which America had long acquiesced but to which it had formally consented only at the recent congress.[8]

Adams completed his last Novanglus essay—a thirteenth, which was not published—in March or early April. Off and on during that dreary winter he had been putting his office in order. There appeared to be no way to avert war, and war would mean a protracted absence while he served in a congress that met hundreds of miles from his home. His spirits soared briefly when he learned that the colonial assembly in Jamaica had urged the monarch to mediate the dispute; grasping at straws, he let himself believe that London's hand might be stayed by such importunings from its valuable sugar islands. For a time, too, Adams and others even embraced the illusion that the English people might revolt, toppling the government under which they and the colonists allegedly groaned. But word from his friend Josiah Quincy, visiting in London at the time, disabused him of that dream. "Hope nothing from the people here," Quincy advised, and his prediction soon was borne out by news that the British elections late in 1774 had resulted in a victory for the North government. The final hope for peace—the capricious notion that the king might block North's use of force—also was dashed when word of George III's autumn speech to Parliament reached America. The monarch had wholeheartedly endorsed the policies of the ministry. "The die is cast," Abigail wrote upon reading the king's remarks. It "seems to me," she added, that "the Sword is now our only, yet dreadful alternative."[9]

The North ministry had realized that the Coercive Acts might lead to war. In December 1774, when word arrived that the American congress had chosen defiance over submission, the government had to decide between hostilities or retreat. The issue was never in doubt. The ministry had made its decision a year earlier when it agreed to the Coercive Acts. To North the issue no longer concerned only the power of Parliament to raise revenue in America. The question now was whether the British government retained any authority in Massachusetts. The ministry marched toward the abyss certain that the heart of the disaffection was confined to New England, confident that every avenue toward peaceful reconciliation had been probed, assured that to appease the colonists once again would constitute a greater jeopardy to the empire than that posed by going to war, convinced that the resulting war would be a short, relatively bloodless affair.[10]

Late in January the Earl of Dartmouth, secretary of state for American affairs, dispatched the orders that would trigger the conflict. General Gage was directed to suppress the rebellion by force and to sieze the leaders of the radical movement. Reinforcements were on the way, Dartmouth advised, though, for the time, Gage would have to make do with about six thousand men, hardly a handicap since the colonists acted "without plan, without concert."[11]

Gage did not hesitate. On April 14, 1775, Dartmouth's orders reached Boston. Four days later, on a dark Monday night, Gage moved, dispatching a large force of nearly eight hundred men to Concord, a village twenty miles west of Boston. Their targets were the arsenal, the colonists' stockpile of weapons and powder, and the Provincial Congress, all of which were situated in Concord. The success of the operation hinged on the maintenance of secrecy. The luckless troops never had a chance. The citizens of Concord knew seventy-two hours in advance that its arsenal had been designated for destruction. Throughout the black evening, as the soldiers descended on the village, dispatch riders, men like Paul Revere and William Dawes, sped ahead of them, alerting the citizenry and the citizen-soldiers in countless farm villages that the British army had been unloosed.

A little after daybreak the first confrontation occurred. The militiamen of Lexington, the first village out from Cambridge on the Concord Road, had awaited the British arrival for several hours. Just at sunrise they heard the unmistakable cacophony of marching men, the thud of heavy boots, the rattle and clamor of ammunition boxes against powder horns, the discordant jangle of metallic paraphernalia against blue-gray musket barrels. It required all the resourcefulness each man could muster just to stand steady. Then, from around a bend, the trainbandsmen had their first glimpse of crimson. The British soldiers looked larger and fiercer than ever.

After that, everything happened quickly. Outnumbered nearly ten to one, the colonists withdrew from the road, opening the way for a peaceful passage by the British force. But when the British commander ordered that the militiamen be disarmed, a shot rang out, then, after the briefest hesitation, still more shots. Another pause, then came a volley of fire from a British platoon. Then order; the incident was over. But eight militiamen were dead, and nine others had been wounded. The commander of the Lexington unit had been shot, then bayoneted. One British soldier had sustained a superficial wound.

The British hurried on to Concord, where they succeeded in destroying only a portion of the arsenal. Even that limited success was accomplished at a terrible price. By the time the redcoats started for Boston, seven were dead and five wounded, victims of a confrontation with a large force of colonial militia that had gathered in Concord during the early morning. And that was just the beginning. The retreat to Boston rapidly became a bloodbath. Colonial sharpshooters repeatedly ambushed the king's men, exacting a devastating toll. Seventy-three British regulars died that day; two hundred were wounded or missing. The colonists had suffered nearly one hundred casualties.[12]

John Adams was in Braintree preparing to set off for Congress when news arrived of the bloodletting. He was seized by an impulsive need to visit the scene of the clashes, and on April 22 he rode by horseback to Lexington, then meandered down the bloody lane that led to Concord. Before he returned to Braintree to complete preparations for his journey to Philadelphia, he introduced himself to many inhabitants in the two towns and listened carefully as they rehashed their tales of the grim events of that day.

Adams quickly put his affairs in order when he returned home, but a sudden illness delayed his departure for Congress. He spoke of a "fever" and described his symptoms as "allarming," evidence too sketchy for drawing any conclusions regarding the nature of the malady.[13] But he was bedfast briefly, and he certainly felt too ill to accompany his colleagues when they sped off late in April. Not until two days after their departure was he well enough to set out, although he remained so weak that concessions had to be made in his travel plans. He eschewed another long ride on horseback and traveled instead in a sulky owned by Abigail's father; Abigail also induced the son of a neighbor to accompany him and act as his servant. The ride down to Connecticut was pleasant enough. Adams found his helpmate, young Joseph Bass, to be a mature, intelligent young man whose good sense—and whose ability to listen to the congressman's endless monologues—made him an excellent traveling companion.

At Hartford they caught up with the rest of the Massachussetts delegation. The party moved slowly on toward New York, feted along the way as they had been the previous fall. As they entered New York City the delegates discovered that a huge crowd, including several militia companies, had turned out to welcome them. Adams's exuberance at this attention quickly was dashed, however, for the day very nearly ended in tragedy. Only briefly into the parade, the horse pulling Adams's small carriage bolted, spooked by the sudden influx of people and undoubtedly annoyed and frightened by the blasts from the militia's drum-and-fife corps. The carriage overturned as the horse reared, then was dragged several feet, eventually smashing into a tree, where it was totally destroyed. Fortunately, Adams had shifted earlier to the vehicle bearing his comrades, and, luckily, young Bass suffered only some superficial cuts and bruises. That evening John wrote home about the incident, adding that he and Abigail must compensate her father for the loss. "But in times like these," he added, "such little Accidents should not affect us." In the long run, in fact, it did not affect his pocketbook; he eventually induced Massachusetts to pay for the ruined carriage.[14]

Adams's recent illness caused him no problems during the long journey. Indeed, he seemed more spirited than he had been in months, even writing five letters to Abigail during his first week away from home. What seemed most to exhilarate him was the animated spirit of resistance and the sense of union that he had discovered as the Massachusetts delegation plunged farther south. In the wake of Lexington and Concord he found that "the Jerseys are aroused" and that "North Carolina has done bravely" in defying its governor and re-electing its delegation to Congress; the "Tories . . . durst not shew their Heads" in New York, he reported. Connecticut, he informed Abigail, planned to raise an army of six thousand; Rhode Island, a force of fifteen hundred. It was with a mixture of joy and relief that he reported the onset of the war actually strengthening the fragile young union of colonies. Of course, Adams also enjoyed the adulation of the crowds and the special attention he received, including the nightly posting of two armed guards before his room during his stay in New York. In a euphoric mood, Adams, riding in a cavalcade that included almost all the northern delegates, completed the trip from New York to Philadelphia, arriving on May 10, the very date scheduled for the opening of Congress.[15]

This congress had a different look about it; there were several new faces. Not only had Massachusetts added John Hancock to its delegation, Thomas Jefferson was also in attendance from Virginia and James Wilson from Pennsylvania; New York had sent George Clinton and Philip Schuyler, and Georgia—alone among the mainland colonies in lacking representation at the initial congress—now had a delegate in place, Lyman Hall. There were some missing faces, too. Joseph Galloway, for instance, declined to sit in a congress that would wage war against the parent state. Even the setting was different. This congress shifted from Carpenter's Hall to the more spacious Pennsylvania State House next door.

The problems that now confronted Congress were strikingly different from those with which the delegates had wrestled the previous fall. The proposed boycott had been the central issue before the First Congress. Now America was at war, and a New England siege army of 16,500 pinioned the British in Boston. The war was not an issue among these congressmen, however; they were willing to fight. But the aim of the war was a different matter.

It quickly was obvious that Congress was divided into three large factions. One group, the conservatives, of whom John Dickinson was perhaps the most articulate spokesman, held fast to the Declaration of Rights adopted by the First Congress and fought to compel Great Britain to return to pre-1763 conditions, a time when imperial restraints had constituted a light yoke for the provincials. Dickinson's *Letters From a Farmer in Pennsylvania,* published in 1768, had made him one of the three or four best-known Americans; his skill and charm made him an adroit politician. Scion of an affluent farmer and slave owner, Dickinson had studied law at the Middle Temple in London, returned to marry into a wealthy Quaker family that had been part of the Pennsylvania elite for three generations, and eventually established a thriving legal practice in Philadelphia. Tall, thin, and gray, at age forty-three—three years older than Adams—Dickinson managed to look every inch the squire that he was yet give the appearance of a handsome, good-natured, benevolent gentleman. Indeed,

Adams found him an agreeable, eloquent, retiring individual, somewhat awkward physically, and entirely too "moderate, delicate, and timid" for his tastes, yet clearly a deft, tactful, ingenious leader.[16]

A second group had moved beyond the imperial conception of the First Congress. Their position was outlined by Jefferson in *A Summary View of the Rights of British America,* a pamphlet he had written the previous year. The "British parliament has no right to exercise authority over us," the Virginian had boldly stated. In short, the king was the sole—and final—link holding the empire together. Considered too radical a stance in 1774, this was the position of a congressional majority in May 1775. A third faction, surely including Samuel Adams, and perhaps John as well, already favored independence for America, although it still was impolitic to mention such an idea publicly. It was not yet clear which faction ultimately would dominate. "The Congress will support Massachusetts" in its war, Adams immediately concluded. Beyond that, nothing was certain.[17]

During its first month Congress moved cautiously, its debates punctuated by the sounds of marching soldiers, for twenty-eight infantry companies had been raised in Philadelphia, and each drilled daily, often just outside the windows of the State House. The more conservative delegates usually had their way in these early weeks. For instance, when news arrived that British troops soon would be sent to New York, Congress cautioned against resistance, unless the redcoats attempted to seize the property of the citizenry. A few days later when the Massachusetts delegation urged Congress to requisition military supplies from throughout America, it voted instead that the siege army before Boston should be provisioned only by the four New England colonies. Some matters were beyond their reach, however. When it was learned that a joint force of New England militia, led by Benedict Arnold, and Yankee ruffians, commanded by Ethan Allen, had seized Fort Ticonderoga near the Canadian border, the conservatives reacted with horror, but pragmatism dictated that Congress agree to keep the fortress; in fact, it requested that Connecticut send reinforcements to hold the installation.[18]

When Congress first assembled, Adams had complained that there was so much to be done, "We know not what to do first." In fact, he knew precisely what he wished to do. He and his comrades from Massachusetts were anxious for Congress to create a national army to supplant the New England siege army before Boston. Before that could be effected, however, the conservatives sought to once again have Congress petition the king. Dickinson had come to Congress with the idea firmly fixed in his mind. Believing that Great Britain would be horrified at the news of the colonial resistance at Lexington and Concord, he viewed the petition as the first step in opening negotiations to restore peace; he urged the adoption of a "humble and dutiful" remonstrance, one to be carried to London by selected congressmen.[19]

No one was more disturbed than Adams by such a notion, and he termed the very idea of such an appeal a "measure of Imbecility." To cavil once again before the monarch would be fruitless. In addition, not only might America appear to be weak and spineless, but Great Britain might seize upon the petition to exploit the schism among the colonists. Adams took the lead in opposition to Dickinson's scheme, and in the process he antagonized the "Farmer." At one point in the debate Dickinson intemperately charged that the New England delegates would have "Blood . . . on their own heads" if they pursued the war without making another sincere effort to peacefully redress their grievances. Later, after a vitriolic speech by Adams, Dickinson trailed him into the hall and confronted him: "What is the reason, Mr. Adams, that you New Englandmen oppose our measures of reconciliation? Look ye," he demanded, if "you don't concur with us in our pacific system, I, and a number of us, will break off from you . . . and we will carry on the opposition by ourselves in our own way." Adams was outraged, not by the threat but by the tone in Dickinson's voice. He felt that Dickinson had addressed him as a schoolmaster might speak to an unruly young student. He never again spoke to Dickinson. A few months later a private letter in which he had referred to Dickinson as a "piddling Genius" who lent a "silly Cast to our whole Doings" fell into the hands of the British; they, of course, gleefully published the missive, and it was the "Farmer's" turn to be insulted. He never again spoke to Adams.[20]

Aware that some of the more cautious congressmen had begun to suspect the radicals of secretly supporting independence, Adams and his colleagues dropped their opposition to Dickinson's enterprise, and the "Olive Branch Petition," as it was called, was approved by Congress. The king's "most dutiful subjects" urged his cooperation in finding a solution to the Anglo-American conflict; instead of congressmen carrying the remonstrance to London, however, Richard Penn, the former proprietary governor of Pennsylvania, agreed to present the document to George III. "We shall do something in Time," Adams stormed to a friend at home, but it was clear that Dickinson and his tentative comrades first would have to be appeased. For the sake of unity, he told Abigail, the "fleetest Sailors must wait for the dullest and slowest." Later he put it another way. When a coach is drawn, he said, the "swiftest Horses must be slackened and the slowest quickened, that all may keep an even Pace."[21]

Nevertheless, by early June, three weeks after Congress had convened, Adams and his fellow New Englanders grew impatient for meaningful action. Not one concrete step had yet been taken to assist the diminutive New England army before Boston. No colony outside the region had yet volunteered to commit troops to the conflict. As in Philadelphia, militia companies had been formed in several colonies and there was much marching and shooting, but only South Carolina had taken systematic steps to organize its own defense, and it had no intention of sending its men to Massachusetts. Nor were the conservatives in Congress anxious to act before the king had been given the opportunity to respond to the Olive Branch Petition.[22]

The breakthrough was triggered by an appeal from Massachusetts. Just as Suffolk County had nudged the First Congress, the Provincial Congress, now meeting in Watertown, took the step that moved this one to act. On June 2 word arrived that the resistance government in Massachusetts desired Congress's assistance. It beseeched Congress to take control of its little siege army. In short Massachusetts had appealed for the creation of a national army with which to conduct a national resistance against the parent state. Congress appointed committees to study the matter, then acted in stages. First it voted to appropriate six thousand pounds to secure provisions for the army. On June 14 it voted to commit troops from outside New England; six companies of Pennsylvania, Maryland, and Virginia riflemen—marksmen who "can kill with great Exactness at 200 yards Distance," Adams gushed—were to be raised and sent to Massachusetts. The following day Congress resolved to name a general to command the new Continental army. The first great goal that Adams sought had been realized. The strategy of not pushing the conservatives too quickly had succeeded, he told Abigail. Congress, slowly, meticulously, and prudently, had come around to the view of New England that only "Fortitude, Vigour, and Perseverance can save Us."[23]

Who would command the army? John Hancock, who had been elected president of the Congress, longed for the post, but he had never soldiered. Philip Schuyler had considerable military experience, but he had not been a delegate to the First Congress, and he was not well known outside New York. Congress also was inclined to name a native-born American to this post, thus eliminating Charles Lee and Horatio Gates, former officers in the British army who now resided in the colonies. That left only two real possibilities. Artemas Ward of Massachusetts, a veteran soldier, Harvard graduate, businessman, and assemblyman who was in command of the siege army, was the choice of many in New England and some congressmen from outside the region. George Washington of Virginia also had considerable support.

Washington was the most imposing delegate at the Continental Congress. At six four, he towered above his colleagues, and although he was forty-three years old, he remained lithe and trim, a strong and graceful man who today would be called athletic, bearing little resemblance to the paunchy figure in many Charles Willson Peale portraits of this era. But it was not just the figure he cut that impressed Adams and so many of his fellow congressmen. Washington was a man, Adams thought, of "excellent universal character" who possessed "Skill and Experience as an Officer." Adams did not speak idly. Since the first sessions of the Congress during the previous fall, he had made a point of observing and speaking with Washington, seeking to learn as much as he could of this quiet, formal, and distant man.

Adams must have discovered early on that Washington was very different from himself, perhaps from any other colonist he knew. One of the wealthiest men in Virginia, Washington owned and managed Mount Vernon, a vast empire on the Potomac River that spanned nearly eight thousand acres and was worked by a corps of approximately one hundred slaves. His economic interests were far-flung. He grew wheat and tobacco, sold cloth made by his chattel, operated a small fishing enterprise, owned an interest in a lumbering concern, was the absentee owner of a frontier farm, and speculated in western lands, having secured title to about sixty thousand acres in western Virginia and the Ohio Country.

Washington had ascended from affluent origins, and his youth bore little resemblance to that of Adams. The Washingtons were an old and respected family in Virginia by the generation of Augustine Washington, George's father, who, through planting and the successful operation of an iron industry, grew considerably wealthy. But when Augustine died suddenly while still a young man, George, the third son, was left with only a modest inheritance and a future that promised a comfortable existence but little hope for great wealth or real power, or, consequently, notoriety. Like Adams, who was three years younger and growing up five hundred miles to the north, Washington was most interested in renown.

Adams's springboard to recognition would grow from his excellent formal education. Washington, however, was deficient in this regard. Augustine's untimely death deprived him of the English education the family had planned, an advantage that his older brothers had enjoyed. Instead, George was self-taught, reading self-help manuals and a smattering of the popular literature of his age, but also turning to geography and history, especially biographies of great leaders and soldiers; to a considerable degree, however, Washington learned through observation, scrutinizing the wealthy displays by his older half-brother Lawrence, and the glib, sophisticated, assured members of the Fairfax family, Lawrence's neighbors on the Potomac and the wealthiest clan in the Northern Neck of Virginia.

Lacking a formal education, Washington turned to surveying at age sixteen. It was the course others—including Thomas Jefferson's father—had taken to accumulate land and secure a more elevated status. But soldiering afforded an even better chance for renown, and when the opportunity presented itself in 1754, Washington became an officer in the Virginia Regiment. At age twenty-two, an age when Adams was reading law under James Putnam in Worcester and longing to bear arms, Washington became the commander of his colony's little army, a post he held for nearly five years during the French and Indian War. He served with great valor. Countless times he rode down dark and lonely wilderness trails, an inviting target for ambush should his adversaries be skulking nearby in the enveloping forests, and he displayed greater courage even than some British professionals on that ghastly day in 1755 when Gen. Edward Braddock's redcoats were decimated by a French-and-Indian force on the Monongahela. Something deep within Washington's inner being made him relish danger. Once he "heard the bullets whistle," he confessed, he discovered "something charming in the sound."

Washington had thought his military career was over forever when he resigned in 1758 to return to Mount Vernon. He married and settled into a life as a grand planter, the hallmark of which was his election to the Virginia House of Burgesses. But uncertain of himself in the presence of so many well educated assemblymen, Washington for years remained an indifferent legislator, a backbencher who sponsored no important legislation and who held only insignificant committee assignments.

Before 1769 Washington appears to have been less troubled than Adams by the Anglo-American upheaval. Rich and contented, he sought merely to grow richer, modeling his life-style on the pattern of an English country gentleman. But the Townshend Duty crisis had a transforming impact upon him, although the reasons for his alienation from the parent state differed somewhat from those of Adams. While he too concluded that a corrupt British ministry sought to exploit the colonists, Washington was principally motivated by the ideal of an America capable of acting independently, unhindered by the policies of "our lordly Masters" in London, as he put it. Where Adams thought principally in terms of the preservation of the colonial traditions of liberty, Washington had grandiose dreams. Years in the West had left Washington with a vision of an American empire unfolding across the sprawling prairies beyond the mountains, an idea whose fulfillment might be checked only by ministerial limitations. But there was more. Washington was utterly exasperated at foreign constraints of any kind, an exasperation that ran deeper than his cherished western aspirations and was more fundamental than his objection to ministerial taxes. For Washington the question was stark: would Americans possess the autonomy to act as they pleased?

But it was the Townshend Duties—"They have no right to put their hands in my pockets," he announced—that served as the catalyst for his activism. In 1769, years before Adams was fully committed to the popular movement in Massachusetts, Washington played a leading role in organizing his colony's boycott of English imports. At that early point in the resistance, moreover, Washington had spoken of the possibility that America might someday have to take up arms against the parent state. As the likelihood of armed resistance grew following the enactment of the Coercive Acts, Washington's role in Virginia's protest increased. By 1774, moreover, his thoughts and those of Adams regarding policy toward Great Britain appear to have been identical. Staunch resistance was essential, even if that course led to war and independence. Once again Washington led the movement to boycott the products of the Mother Country, and he assisted in the establishment of a militia system in his neighborhood.

Adams met Washington for the first time during the sessions of the First

Congress. He found him handsome, elegant, graceful, noble, and selfless, and he was moved by the Virginian's willingness to risk his great fortune in this rebellion. Washington, he also discovered, was cordial, but there was a grave, cold formality to him. He was, said one observer, "repulsively cold." He distanced himself from others, as if he was wary lest they discover some flaw in his makeup. In the real sense of the word, Washington was friendless. He saw other men as either his loyal followers or his foes, never as intimates in whom he could confide. Only with women, who of course would not have been seen as competitors, could he relax and joke and appear to be fully human.

Adams was also impressed by Washington's singular leadership abilities. By study and observation, and by the hard experience of having had power—real life-and-death responsibilities—thrust upon him when he was still a young man in his early twenties, Washington had learned the secrets of inducing others to follow his lead. Washington probably knew more about leadership before he celebrated his twenty-fifth birthday than John Adams discovered in his lifetime. Washington said his success sprang from his example of courage under fire, combined with an "easy, polite" manner of a "commanding countenance" and the maintenance of "a demeanor at all times composed and dignified." He was formal, and that formality kept others at a distance; but when blended with his other attributes it led most observers to describe him as "stately," a man who inspired their "love and reverence." Adams, too, found "something charming . . . in the conduct of Washington." Over the years he devoted considerable attention to the matter and frequently discovered qualities in Washington that he had not noticed previously.

But of all the virtues exhibited by Washington, those impressing Adams most were his "noble and distinterested" tendencies. Adams was convinced that Washington understood fully the potential for harm that he would hold in his hands as commander of the American army. After speaking with Washington and after quizzing his fellow Virginians about his mettle, Adams and others had reached the conclusion that Washington could be trusted with the command of the army, an awesome power to entrust to any mortal.[24]

There were additional reasons for Adams's support of Washington. A non-New Englander, his appointment would broaden support for the war, pulling the Chesapeake provinces and perhaps the more southerly ones into the fray. In addition, some colonies feared New England, a populous—indeed, overpopulated—region with a long military tradition; according to Eliphalet Dyer, a Connecticut congressman, the worst nightmare of some middle and southern provinces was that a victorious New England army, commanded by "an Enterprising eastern New England Genll," might humble the redcoats, then sweep across America and claim the continent for itself. The appointment of a non-New Englander would allay that concern. Adams, therefore, knew that there would be little opposition to Washington, but he also knew there was certain to be some opposition to demoting General Ward. For this reason it was imper-

ative that a New Englander introduce the motion nominating Washington. He
and Samuel Adams discussed their strategy, then decided that John should
take the lead.[25]

On June 14, the morning air heavy and sticky as a southerly breeze blew in
a tropical front from the Chesapeake, Adams was the first congressman on his
feet. He made his motion, lauding Washington's "Skill and Experience as an
Officer," as well as his "excellent universal Character." Samuel Adams seconded the motion. Washington fled the room as the debate began, but the
question was never really in doubt, and on the following afternoon Adams's
motion was accepted. Adams could not have been more delighted. This was
proof that the "whole continent" was "bestirring itself."[26]

The much more difficult task of selecting the inferior general officers began
the next day. Congress voted to create two major generals, an adjutant general,
and five brigadier generals. Three appointments were easy. Artemas Ward was
designated as first major general, and Charles Lee and Horatio Gates, with
Washington plumping for them, also were appointed. Lee was contentious,
acerbic, perpetually unkempt, and given to the habits of what the twentieth
century would call bohemianism (he never married, worked with great reluctance, thought nothing of borrowing money from his acquaintances, and traveled with a great pack of dogs who slept and scuffled at his feet, ate off his plate,
and, of course, showed him the proper deference). He had a proclivity for
annoying people, but he had spent nearly twenty years in the British army and
was reputed to be without peer in knowledge of military tactics and history.
Gates, gray and overweight, with spectacles habitually perched on his nose
(his men later called him "Granny Gates"), hardly looked like a soldier, but he
too was a veteran of many years' service in the British army, having resigned his
commission in 1769 in despair of further advancement; he had emigrated to
Virginia three years before the war broke out.

Following the rapid appointment of these men, Congress soon found itself
bogged in a seemingly endless wrangle over the selection of the remaining
general officers. The experience was the most painful ordeal in Adams's brief
congressional career, he told a friend at home. It was not that the men nominated were thought to be incompetent but that every delegate wished to have
friends and favorite sons named to high places. Ultimately, Congress sought an
escape from an otherwise insoluble dilemma by creating additional slots. It
now agreed to have four major generals and eight brigadier generals.
Schuyler—a tall, handsome, aristocratic New York assemblyman who had
soldiered for several years during the French and Indian War—got one of the
posts, as did his fellow New Yorker Richard Montgomery, a former British
officer who, like Lee and Gates, had resigned his commission and moved to
America. But the lion's share went to New England. In addition to Ward,
Massachusetts grabbed posts for Seth Pomeroy, William Heath, and John
Thomas. Connecticut secured the appointment of Israel Putnam, Joseph

Spencer, and David Wooster. John Sullivan of New Hampshire also was approved. The last officer named was Nathanael Greene of Rhode Island; a man of limited education and military experience limited to two years of peacetime militia duty, he nevertheless was destined to be the best of the lot.[27]

John Adams had not been a key player in the First Congress, but his role in the selection of Washington symbolized his emergence as a force in this one. He was finally more certain of his abilities. Now that war had erupted, moreover, there was less reason to adopt the passive stance that had characterized the behavior of all the Massachusetts delegates in 1774. While neither the reconciliationists nor their foes had formal leaders, within a month of the opening of Congress it appeared clear that Dickinson and Adams had emerged as the most forceful and articulate spokesmen on each side. Adams had little experience working with others in a legislative setting, and his obdurate manner and natural impatience did not fully suit him for such an undertaking. Yet, his courtroom skills and his pluck or "pertness," as he referred to it, served him well. Mostly, however, Adams's star rose because of other factors. The very force of his intellect was crucial to his emergence as an important force in Congress. At each step of his ascent, Adams's acuity and his imposing intellectual grasp had impressed others. Convinced of his talents, his mentors at Harvard had steered him toward legal studies; the leading men in Worcester had sought to persuade him to practice in their town and the most influential barristers within the Boston legal establishment appear to have have been quickly taken with his abilities. Both Hutchinson and Samuel Adams had identified him as a potential asset and had sought to lure him to their side. Now, although Congress fairly teemed with lawyers, savvy politicians, and articulate men far more accustomed to leading than was John Adams, he began to stand out. He was sober, learned, reflective and meditative, and his colleagues increasingly turned to him as each congressional decision seemed to lead toward still another dark, unexplored path. Adams's other great attribute was his incredible proclivity for work. The same reservoir for labor that had seen him through earlier studies and emergence as a successful lawyer facilitated his rapid rise within Congress. In the next two years he would sit on ninety committees, chairing twenty-five. No other congressman came even remotely close to carrying such a heavy work load. Soon he was acknowledged "to be the first man in the House," as Benjamin Rush reported.[28]

The evolution of Adams's thinking during this period is impossible to discern. He was discreet, recognizing that it could be impolitic to be too candid in the congressional debates; in addition, after some of his private correspondence fell into the hands of the British, he realized that he was not free to express his views even in the letters he sent to his wife. What seems to be clear, however, is that until the war began he thought that reconciliation was both possible and desirable. He had come to the First Congress brimming with the zeal characteristic of a recent convert. He indicated that the conservatives of 1774, men like Galloway and Duane, were no different than Hutchinson and Oliver, and he denigrated such men, telling Abigail that "Spiders, Toads, Snakes, are their only proper Emblems."[29] Yet at that point his views were close to those of Dickinson. He sought repeal of objectionable ministerial policies, but he continued to see positive benefits for America within the empire.

Adams had clearly reconsidered some matters by the time the Second Congress met six months later. Meeting with other disaffected colonists in Philadelphia, especially the stalwart Virginians, had been a transcendent experience, helping him to overcome any lingering uncertainties that the New England view of a ministerial plot might have been due to regional prejudices. The outbreak of the war also had a radicalizing effect upon him; he looked upon Britain's use of force as additional confirmation of the existence of a conspiracy to thoroughly subjugate and exploit the colonies, of a web of intrigue spun with the complicity of the monarch. From his willingness to accept Parliament's regulation of American trade, a right that he accepted as late as his Novanglus essays written on the very eve of hostilities, Adams had moved in the early months of the war to the view that America's sole link to the realm were its surviving ties to the Crown. Reconciliation no longer seemed as desirable as it once had.[30]

On June 23, just as the first rays of sun began to appear in the eastern sky, General Washington was up to supervise the loading of his carriage. Soon Joseph Reed and Thomas Mifflin, selected by the general to serve as his aides, arrived to accompany him to the front, as did Generals Lee and Schuyler. In the half-light of early morning, contingents of Philadelphia militiamen, resplendent in their new uniforms, also assembled, prepared to march at the head of the general's entourage. Many congressmen were there as well, including the entire delegation from Massachusetts.

The horses pranced and minced nervously. There was an air of excitement and apprehension among the men, too, a sense that Washington's departure amounted to nothing less than a great turning point in history.

Soon the preparations were complete. The men said their good-byes, wishing one another well. Washington climbed onto his horse; Adams pulled himself into a sleek, light phaeton, so that he might ride with the generals to the edge of the city.

A band struck up, then the procession slowly began to rumble forward, bouncing and clattering over the cobblestones, past the still-dark shops and the dimly lit dwellings, on and on through the empty streets, rattlety-banging into the brightening countryside. The commander of the new American army was on his way, off to wage war against a formidable foe.[31]

"Our Hopes and our Fears are alternately very strong," Adams noted simply later that day.[32]

CHAPTER 8

*

Oh That I Was a Soldier!

ADAMS HAD ARRIVED in Philadelphia in May in high spirits and good health, evidently recovered from the brief illness that had struck just prior to his departure. Within three weeks, however, his health declined. At various times during the summer of 1775 he described his condition as "miserable," "completely miserable," "not well," "worn out," "quite infirm," "very bad," and "low in spirits and weak in health." He was, he said, afflicted by "Fidgets, Pidlings, and Irritabilities." He complained of an inability to sleep. He was afflicted by mysterious rashes. He feared that he was going blind.[1] To read Adams's diary and letters during these months is to read the lamentations of a man under extraordinary stress. It has been suggested that Adams's woes stemmed from feelings of guilt arising from fears that "personal disappointment lay at the root of his public temper."[2] There is another explanation.

The surface causes of Adams's anxieties are not difficult to discern. Every activist knew the penalty for treason. Every congressman knew that prison, perhaps death, would be his reward if the American rebellion failed. In addition, Adams bore a staggering work load. Congress's interminable meetings and its ubiquitous committee assignments brought out his penchant for overwork; his was a burdensome schedule that ran from early morning until late at night, leaving him little time for sleep or relaxation. Nor was he comfortable with the condition of his wife and children, ensconced as they were near the powder keg of Boston. It was anything but reassuring to have to tell one's wife, in "Case of real Danger . . . fly to the Woods with our Children." He also fretted that his sons' education might suffer because of his absence, and he worried endlessly over the likelihood of damage to his farm, including the possibility of the loss of his extensive law library, which had been moved from his office in Boston to his estate.[3]

Adams, like most of his colleagues, also soon discovered that serving in Congress could be a lonely experience. Faced with a protracted separation from family and compelled to dwell in an unfamiliar small apartment for months on end, many congressmen suffered bouts of homesickness and of terrible melancholy. Adams may have been more lonely than most delegates, however. Indeed, Samuel Adams appears to have been his only close confidant. His heavy work load left him with little time for socializing; moreover, his propensity for angry outbursts, his sardonic, deprecatory manner, and his habit of speaking his mind frankly and boldly surely antagonized many of his colleagues. Furthermore, when Tory newspapers in the summer of 1775 gleefully published his captured letters—the missives containing his captious comments about Dickinson—Adams briefly found himself a bit of pariah, a man shunned by some of his comrades. Dr. Rush saw him "walk[ing the] streets alone, . . . an object of nearly universal detestation."[4]

Adams's most burdensome concerns, however, stemmed from the dreadfully difficult public problems with which he had to deal. From the beginning he knew that the business of the Second Congress would be more "affecting and hazardous" than that of its predecessor. The demands placed upon its members because of the war, he wrote, would be "as great and important as [ever were] intrusted to Man." Adams did not question the validity of the war. This was a just war, he believed. It was a "people's war" against evil. Men had a "moral duty" to resist despotism and slavery. He even argued that struggle and sacrifice would strengthen his fellow colonists; this "Furnace of Affliction," he suggested, would "refine and redeem" American society.[5]

But if Adams was certain of the necessity of the war, he found it difficult to reconcile himself to the role he should play in the conflict. Could he morally order other men to risk death on America's battlefields if he did not likewise face harm? Should he bear arms? Was he less than a man if he did not soldier? Adams struggled with these matters. For a sensitive man such as John Adams, it produced a terrible quandary. Together with his other burdens, his loneliness, his fears for his family, and his exhaustion, Adams's uncertainties produced ineffable stress, accompanied by the mannerisms common to a mildly hysterical disorder.[6] During this difficult summer of 1775, he repeatedly evinced surface conflicts, including recurrent illnesses, periods of black despair, dermatological blights, insomnia, headaches, and groundless fears of blindness.

At times Adams sought to escape his dilemma by convincing himself that the "Pride and Pomp of War . . . [had] no Charms for [him]." It was not a successful gambit. He also sought to persuade himself that through his congressional activities he was able to furnish a greater service to mankind than that provided by the most valorous soldier, but he did not find his own argument to be terribly convincing.[7]

The soldier will always "Wear the Lawrells," he knew, but never had those who bore arms been treated as greater heroes than during the "Rage Militaire" that swept America in 1775. Indeed, his generation not only lionized soldiers, it also attributed to those who bore arms the very traits it esteemed as proper for manly behavior, making the warrior the embodiment of strident masculinity; by implication, the civilian represented something less than virility. Adams shared these views about soldiers. He admired men such as Washington and Gates. He thought of them as courageous men who exemplified the virtuous ethic of brave and selfless public service, and he especially revered Gen. Charles Lee, whom he thought combined the attributes of a "Schollar and a Soldier."[8] He longed to do his duty, and he yearned for the recognition that was the soldier's reward.

On the eve of the hostilities, Adams had begun to fret over his role in the likely war. In January he thought the odds were considerable that he would someday have to fight. When the war began, he wished aloud that he could have been at Lexington and Concord, and from Philadelphia he wrote Abigail that he had "bought some military Books and intend[ed] to buy more" so that he might prepare himself to lead men into battle. By late May, upon seeing how others referred to Washington, as well as upon learning that Dickinson, his nemesis, had become a colonel in the Pennsylvania militia, he bawled: "Oh that I was a Soldier! — I will be. — I am reading military Books. — Every Body must and will, and shall be a soldier." But he did not become a soldier, and as he watched first Washington, then others, ride off to the front from Philadelphia, his spirits sank to a low ebb. "I, poor Creature, worn out with scribbling, for my Bread and my Liberty," he lamented, "must leave others to wear the Lawrells which I have sown; others to eat the Bread which I have earned."[9]

On August 10 a grief-stricken Abigail Adams sat at her desk, trying without success to find an easy way to inform her husband that his brother Elihu lay near death. A captain in the Braintree trainband, Elihu, thirty-four years old in 1775, had fallen victim to dysentery, an inevitable plague in the army camps of the eighteenth century. As she labored with these sad tidings Abigail had no way of knowing that her husband was but a few miles away. Congress suddenly had adjourned in late July and the entire Massachusetts delegation rushed home, anxious after a four-month absence to see their families and to attain a firsthand assessment of the war and the new army. Adams had intended to pop in unannounced at his farm, but en route the congressmen learned that the Provincial Congress was sitting in Watertown. Without pausing to see his family he proceeded instead to that hamlet. In the course of the three weeks that he was in Massachusetts, Adams saw his wife only on weekends and during the three days she spent with him in Watertown.[10]

What had seemed an aberrant separation the previous fall had become commonplace. During the next quarter century John and Abigail would live apart more than they would live together. Except for those moments of acute anxiety when he desperately longed for his wife's comforting presence, this was not an entirely unpleasant arrangement for Adams; for a man attuned to the single-minded pursuit of a goal, a wife and children sometimes were an intolerable interference. Abigail had little choice but to accede to this turn of events, but, gradually, subtly, their relationship began to change. She slowly grew more independent. When her husband once again departed for Philadelphia, her letters came less frequently; whereas in July she had confessed that she did not "feel easy more than two days together without writing" to him, that autumn she wrote only about once every ten days. She no longer praised and lauded her husband, as if his activities were the center of all that was important in her life. She began to write mostly of her business, her woes and anxieties, her afflictions. Nor did her missives any longer overflow with the tender, amorous tidings or the volcanic, passionate urges that characterized her earlier correspondence. However, she continued to experience a sense of personal achievement through his activities and she persisted in encouraging him to play the role he wished to play. In good faith she could acknowledge:

Though certain pains attend the cares of State
A Good Man owes his Country to be great.[11]

But she could also ruefully exclaim: "O Ambition how many actions dost thou make poor mortals commit!"[12]

On at least one occasion Adams slipped away from the Provincial Congress to call on General Washington and to poke about the army camp, talking with several officers and reviewing the troops. For this man who so longed to soldier, it was an important, fulfilling day. So too were those few days when he returned to his farm. He relished those moments for the opportunity to be briefly with his "little prattling Brood of Children" and to ramble over his estate, ranging through the meadows and into the hills, there to look quietly upon the pastoral splendor of his little farm and gaze beyond to the great azure bay to the east. Not coincidentally, while he was at home he noted for the first time in months that he was "entirely free" of his chronic physical ailments.[13]

Adams's vacation, such as it was, ended quickly, and late in August he set out along the now familiar, weary route to Philadelphia, this time making the trek in fifteen days, all of it astride his favorite horse, and in the company of Sam Adams, who had just learned to ride. He had barely returned to Congress when disquieting news from home reached him. Dysentery had struck at his farm only hours after his departure. First a hired hand fell ill, then Abigail. Soon thereafter two servants were afflicted; three-year-old Thomas was next. "Our House is an hospital," Abigail reported. Only the ill remained. Nabby, John Quincy, and Charles had been sent away while well, leaving those who recovered, however slightly, to minister daily to those who remained in the grip of the malady and to wash down the walls of the house with warm vinegar, a preventive measure against the likelihood of secondary infections. At times it seemed to be a losing battle. Each day brought word of contagion, then reports

of the mounting death rate. Parents watched helplessly as their children succumbed; men saw their wives perish. Most anguishing, perhaps, was the
plight of Thankful Adams, Elihu's widow, who had hardly buried her husband before she lost her infant daughter to the same awful disease. During the
first week in September, eight died in Braintree; one hundred or more lay ill.[14]

Abigail and Tommy were among the fortunate who survived. But a family
servant, Patty, died after a five-week ordeal, and during the first week of
October, Abigail was rocked by the news of her mother's death, sixteen days
after having been felled by the disease. Wan and eviscerated from her own
illness, Abigail thought she might break under the terrible strain, especially as
she was compelled to endure alone. She wrote to her husband, "[I am] seperated from thee who *used* to be [a] comfortar towards me in affliction."[15]

Three hundred miles from Braintree, there was little that Adams could do
but pray. Of course he sought to reassure Abigail with comforting letters, and
he lauded her fortitude in the face of the crisis. For a time he thought of dashing
home; he could return to Philadelphia within six weeks, and with three other
delegates from Massachusetts in attendance, he acknowledged that his presence was not absolutely crucial. But he could not cut his ties with Congress,
even in this family emergency. Indeed, strangely, in the very midst of this
personal crisis, Adams noted that his health had improved, and he confided to a
friend: "I am very happy—how it is I know not—but I am very happy."[16] The
answer to the riddle, perhaps, is that his family's afflictions served as a balm for
his own problems, enabling him to see his service in Congress as all the more
sacrificial and virtuous, and to view his grief as the equivalent of the cares
borne by those who soldiered.

When Adams returned to Congress in September he remained impatient to
move ahead. The legislators, he believed, had a continent to fortify and to
defend, crucial commercial decisions to make, and, once independence was
proclaimed, a national government to create. How quickly Congress might act
on the last matters was conjectural, but Adams knew that the military situation
must be tended immediately.

Throughout the long summer General Washington had forwarded plain-
tive letters cataloging an abundance of problems: disputes over rank had
created a sea of contentiousness among the officers; a census of the new army
revealed the force to be about one-quarter smaller than originally believed;
only enough powder was present to provide each soldier with thirty rounds of
ammunition. More ominously, Washington now wrote that the army verged
on disintegration, for few of his soldiers had agreed to serve beyond the end of
the year. Congress must act immediately to raise a new army, he warned, or the
"Army must absolutely break up." Congress rounded up clothing, pork, and
flour for the men, and it created a committee to search out other provisions,
including powder. It also dispatched a committee to discuss each issue with the

commander. Congress could hardly have been more proud of itself. "I doubt not," a New Englander wrote to Washington, "but . . . that by the opening of the next Campaign you will have the finest Army under your Command, which ever was formed in America."[17]

Indeed, by late in the year, the military situation seemed to have improved. Not only had the colonists dispatched an army to wrest Canada from Great Britain's grasp, but in Boston the besieged British army had begun to endure great hardships, including food and fuel shortages and an epidemic of smallpox that swept through their barracks. Much of Adams's information about matters in Boston came from Abigail, who by mid-October was well enough to pay several visits to General Washington's headquarters. Lonely and depressed, she looked forward to invitations to dine with the principal officers, much as they must have anticipated an opportunity to talk with an intelligent, attractive woman. One day she dined with General Sullivan of New Hampshire, whom she discovered to be pleasant, although she found a hard side to his temperament faintly unsettling. Hirsute and eccentric Charles Lee, surrounded by his ubiquitous dogs, was captivated by Abigail, even ordering his favorite hound, Spada, to shake hands with her. General Washington, whom she first had met in July, made the greatest impression on her, however. He was dignified yet modest, she wrote her husband; "the Gentleman and Soldier look agreeably blended in him," she added.[18]

Pleased with the course of the war, Adams also was convinced that Congress was moving in the proper direction in its relationship with Great Britain. "Reconciliation if practicable," he said publicly, yet in private he agreed with Benjamin Franklin's observation—also made in private—that independence was inevitable. By the fall of 1775 no one in Congress labored more ardently than Adams to hasten the day when America would be separate from Great Britain.[19]

An inquiry by New Hampshire first offered a fresh opportunity to widen the split between the provinces and Great Britain. In October that colony asked Congress whether the time had arrived to scuttle its colonial charter and establish a new government. It was not a new question; Massachusetts had first raised the matter six months before. At that time Congress categorically instructed the provinces to live under their colonial assemblies, although they need not submit to Crown-appointed officials. Adams had not been happy with the original decision, and when he was named to a committee to scrutinize New Hampshire's query, he made the most of the occasion. To remain under the old charter governments was to risk several evils, he counseled. When links with the Crown persisted, he warned, Tory espionage, or even Loyalist insurrections, might be encouraged; moreover, no foreign nation was likely to succor governments whose magistrates continued to pledge allegiance to the British monarch. Adams urged that each colony be encouraged to call popularly elected conventions for the purpose of establishing new governments. In part because of his "haranguing," as Adams later characterized his speeches, the committee, and subsequently Congress, agreed that New Hampshire should create a new government that would derive its powers from a "full and free representation of the people," a long step toward independence.[20]

During that autumn much of Adams's time was taken up by maritime concerns. With nonimportation now a year old, Congress was under increasing pressure to open American trade with nations outside the British empire. Adams favored such a course, though the more conservative delegates were horrified by the prospect and many moderates insisted that trade with Europe should be limited to absolutely essential military supplies. Adams preached that negotiations should be opened immediately with France and Spain for the purpose of securing commercial treaties, but his views were too extreme even for a majority of his own province's delegation. After days of debate Congress voted to continue its ban on all foreign trade for the next four months, by which time the military situation might be more clear.[21]

Adams was more pleased by the action of Congress in another maritime area. The legislators created an American fleet during these weeks. Actually, two important steps had already been taken. In July Congress had advised each colony to arm small vessels for the protection of its trade, and in September General Washington independently created a small privateering fleet manned by soldiers from the port towns of New England. But two incidents in October finally moved Congress to act definitively. On October 3 a dispatch arrived from Rhode Island requesting authority to commence the construction of heavy, armed warships. Almost simultaneously Washington wrote that he had learned Britain was sending two transports laden with munitions from Nova Scotia to Boston. Congress immediately created a committee to plan for the interdiction of the British vessels, a panel that eventually would be enlarged and known as the Naval Committee. Adams was one of its original members and one of the most vocal in urging the creation of an American fleet. What he sought was a small navy, one that existed for purely defensive purposes. "God forbid," he once raged, "that American naval power should ever be such a scourge to the human race as that of Great Britain has been." Much later, Adams remembered that throughout his career he had "always cried Ships! Ships!" He viewed this aspect of his service in Congress as among the most important undertakings in which he had ever been engaged.[22]

But it was the momentum of events more than the presence of Adams that moved the committee forward. Early in November word arrived that George III had rejected the Olive Branch Petition and proclaimed the colonies to be in a state of rebellion. Three weeks later, Congress learned that the royal governor of Virginia, the Earl of Dunmore, had offered to free all slaves who rallied to the Tory army he was raising; Dunmore, with a modest navy on his side, was invulnerable, given the Virginian's lack of a naval arm. Spurred by these incidents, Congress quickly accumulated a little fleet of seven vessels, allocated funds for the construction of thirteen additional ships, and raised two battalions of marines. These steps paid an immediate dividend. During the final weeks of the year, America's diminutive fleet garnered prizes totaling £20,000, including the *Lee's* capture of an ordnance brig bearing 2,000 muskets, 100,000 flints, 20,000 rounds of shot, and 30 tons of musket balls.

As a member of the Naval Committee, Adams drafted rules for regulating the new navy, an action whose influence would be long-lasting. After some minor alterations by the committee, the articles were adopted by Congress in late November and were in the hands of the fleet officers within ten days. Adams clearly adapted the American articles from acts of Parliament and Britain's "Rules of Discipline and good Government to be observed on Board His Majesty's Ships of War"; in fact, nearly one-third of the articles were taken verbatim from the British sources. Adams did provide some significant modifications, however. Officers were admonished to see that seamen be "justly paid" their due wages, a stipulation not included in the English laws. In addition, the British punishment code was much harsher. It provided for the death penalty for twenty-four offenses, while under the American articles a sailor could suffer death only for murder; the American code was silent regarding punishments for buggery, spying, or aiding the army. The American articles also mandated a more charitable allotment of provisions for crewmen, including meat six days each week, whereas British sailors were to receive meat only four times per week.[23]

At the end of the first week in December, Adams requested a leave of absence so that he might return home. It was an unexpected and somewhat mysterious petition. "As to coming home, I have no Thought of it," he had written his wife only five days before. Affairs of state had reached such a critical juncture, he had added, that he "could not reconcile it to [his] own Mind to be absent from this place at present." Why, then, did he suddenly depart? Years later Adams attributed his decision to a desire to escape the constant fatigues of Congress. But as complaints of weariness were notably absent in his correspondence that autumn, there must be a better explanation.[24]

Two weeks earlier Adams had learned that the Massachusetts Congress had appointed him chief justice of the provinces' supreme court. He had accepted the post, but it was not an appointment that he desired. Not only had he grown weary of jurisprudence after fifteen years' practice, but he had discovered his new political career to be far more exhilarating. The issues with which he dealt in Congress were ripe with momentous consequences and offered the prospect of tempering affairs in Massachusetts and the greater world beyond. Of course, at an early moment in the Anglo-American crisis, he had instinctively understood that this upheaval afforded the opportunity for fame and recognition, in the same manner that "Your Clarendons, Southamptons, Seldens, Hampdens, Faulklands, Sidneys, Locks, Harringtons" had gained renown as "consummate statesmen" in Britain. But there was far more to Adams's outlook than a vain longing to be remembered. For the past eighteen months he had been actively engaged in the defense of America. Now he stood on the precipice of performing an even more seminal act. He longed to give birth to an independent America. This would be the paramount event of his time, perhaps the most consequential and magisterial happening in America for generations to come. The choices soon to be made, and especially the decisions with regard to the nation's fledgling government, would be crucial, for the "Form of Government," he believed, "gives the decisive Colour to the Manners of the People." Within his grasp would lie the opportunity to banish the inherently "vicious and foolish" qualities of every monarchical system and to erect instead a system that would call forth from his countrymen the greatest wisdom and virtue. Before him lay the chance to play "the Part of a great Politician" and to do nothing less than "to make the Character of his People . . . and to create in them the Virtues and Abilities which he sees wanting."

In addition, Adams's outlook had grown increasingly more national in scope, impelling him to play on the continental stage rather than at the provincial level. In time his inclination would distinguish him from many of his colleagues of 1775. Jefferson and Henry would return to Virginia in 1776; only the former would ever again be a truly national figure, and then only after a lapse of seven years at home. Likewise, Hancock would immerse himself in the politics of Massachusetts after 1776, and even Samuel Adams would largely turn his back on national concerns long before the end of the war with Great Britain.

John Adams was different. In part, this was because he had played only a limited role in the political affairs of Massachusetts. Adams had virtually entered politics at the continental level, and the experience shaped his thinking, often compelling his ideas with regard to the ultimate aims of the Revolution to flow along lines at variance with those who had come of age enmeshed in the affairs of their province. For instance, whereas Samuel Adams was captivated by the prospect of the extirpation of Massachusetts's old aristocracy—that he felt had ruined "that Sobriety of Manners, that Temperance, Frugality, Fortitude and other Manly Virtues which were once the Glory and Strength of my much lov'd Town"—John Adams looked forward to the opportunity to spread across the land the virtues that lingered in the breast of every right-thinking New Englander. For him, as for Samuel, the American Revolution offered the chance to supplant those "few opulent, monopolizing Families" whose "insolent Domination" had spread such grief. But John also saw the Revolution as the occasion when "a more equal Liberty, than has prevail'd in other Parts of the Earth, must be established in America," a liberty that might flow from the republicanism indigenous to New England until even "our Southern Brethren . . . annexed the Same Ideas to the Words Liberty, Honour and Politeness that we have."[25]

Of course, affairs in Massachusetts could not be ignored, and political concerns within the province in late 1775 might also have induced Adams to hurry home at this moment. The divisions in Massachusetts, apparent in the struggles during 1774 over the proper response to the Coercive Acts, widened and deepened as new issues arose in the aftermath of the First Congress. During the long, cold winter before the outbreak of the war in 1775, towns in the western backcountry, in particular, had begun to push for military preparedness and a rigorous enforcement of the boycott adopted by Congress. These towns now were heard from as never before, for in the political void left by the destruction of the old colonial government by the Massachusetts Government Act, county conventions had sprung up throughout the province, new and far more representative governments than any previously seen in the colony. The demands that had emanated from the western conventions before the incidents at Lexington and Concord were not especially unique. But once the war broke out, the West moved to new ground. Calls for American independence and domestic reforms began to be heard from the backcountry. Specifically, the West cried out for Massachusetts to once again take up its charter of 1629, the frame of government that the Puritans had brought with them to America; such a move not only would be tantamount to virtual independence, it also would bestow upon Massachusetts a government in which all public officials were popularly elected.

The demands of the West provoked immediate alarm in the eastern coastal towns. During the spring and summer of 1775 many eastern moderates came to see American independence and domestic reform as twin issues. Fearing the possibility that independence would result in a western-led, popularly impelled movement for sweeping internal change, resistance to separation from Great Britain had begun to build in the eastern merchant-dominated centers. The divisions at home, in fact, were apparent within Massachusetts's congressional delegation. John and Samuel Adams, although hardly proponents of social change, remained confident that republican virtue and a well-structured government could restrain the most licentious, and therefore they continued to play leading roles in the separatist movement within Congress; Cushing, Paine, and Hancock, however, generally sided with the reconciliationists.

The growing factionalism in Massachusetts aroused considerable concern within John Adams, but ultimately this threat to the independence movement had been defused, at least temporarily, during the previous summer. Through the Provincial Congress that had governed the colony since the news of the Coercive Acts, the conservative East had turned to Congress for protection. In the spring the Provincial Congress had requested instructions from the Continental Congress with regard to the establishment of a government for Massachusetts. The national Congress, as the moderate easterners had expected, had proved to be their salvation. It recommended that Massachusetts establish a government complying with the Charter of 1691, a document under which

the franchise was restricted, many offices were appointive, and eastern pre-
dominance in the assembly was assured. Both John and Samuel Adams had
shepherded this recommendation through Congress. John's motivation had
been twofold. Like his wife, who, about this time deplored the fact that her
husband had to "combat not only other provinces but [his] own" in the
campaign for independence, John had acted to ease the factionalism at home,
recognizing that separation was impossible without the consent of the rich and
powerful in eastern Massachusetts. In addition, he feared that should western
Massachusetts secure its desired reforms, potential friends of independence
outside New England might be alarmed and veer toward the reconciliationists. The independence movement, therefore, remained alive and well
within Massachusetts, but resistance to separation persisted in some powerful
circles; and when Adams learned from Elbridge Gerry early in December of
renewed "Dissention" within the province promising "the most unhappy
Consequences," he probably decided to have a firsthand look and to mend his
political fences.[26]

By late 1775 Adams may also have sensed the growing changes in Abigail's
disposition, prompting him to return home to assess the situation. While
Abigail had been a prolific letter writer during his earlier absences, only two
missives from her had arrived during the six weeks before he decided to hurry
home. Her few letters seemed to manifest a different tone, though it was less
apparent in what she said than in what she left unsaid. Her earlier missives had
been surfeited with long sections in which she expressed her passionate longing for him, but such passages no longer adorned her correspondence. "My
Evenings are lonesome and Melancholy," she wrote, but they were spent in
pining for her mother, not for her husband. One of her letters had even
contained a most cryptic remark: "You will think me melancholy. Tis true I am
much affected with the distress'd Scenes around me but I have some Anxietyes
upon my mind which I do not think it prudent to mention at present to any
one."[27]

Adams left Philadelphia on horseback at noon on December 9 to commence
the long, cold ride home, a wearying journey of thirteen days through familiar,
desolate countryside. What he found when he alighted at his doorstep on
December 21, aside from a wife who was startled at his unexpected arrival,
cannot be ascertained. It is clear that he seldom was at home during his stay in
Massachusetts. Four days after his arrival he was gone again, once more setting
out for nearby Watertown where the Provincial Council remained in session.
There he remained for all but about one week of his twenty-nine days in
Massachusetts.[28]

Adams served on eight committees while in Watertown, assignments that
must have seemed trivial in contrast to his recent activities in Philadelphia. His
work included the investigation of an alleged spy case, preparation of several
resolutions, and the formulation of a plan for outfitting the province's armada.

But the drudgery of his undertakings must have been mitigated by the realization that his goal of remaining in Congress had been realized, for upon his arrival in Massachusetts he discovered he had already been reelected. Indeed, he had received more votes than Samuel Adams, though less than Hancock, the only member of the delegation to have been elected unanimously.[29]

In January 1776 Adams set out again for Philadelphia. This time, however, he rode north from Braintree. His route took him to Cambridge, where he and Elbridge Gerry, Cushing's replacement in the Massachusetts delegation, conferred with General Washington and a dozen or so Indian chieftains who had called on the commander. The next morning, accompanied by their servants, Adams and Gerry rode out through the pickets, on past the long rows of trenches and fascines, past the men huddled about small campfires, on and on toward the south, until all reminders of this very real war seemed to vanish. Theirs would be a fifteen-day trek through bone-chilling cold, impenetrable mud, and ice-slick roads.[30] John Adams would not return to the area for nearly a year, nor see his wife and children for nine months.

"French & Spaniards do not seem inclined to furnish us with military stores," Francis Lightfoot Lee of Virginia grieved in the last half of January 1776. "Their politics," he continued, "plainly tend to drive us to extremity, that we may be forced to break off all connection with G.B. and join with [France and Spain], which they know nothing but hard necessity can ever effect."[31]

Hard necessity!

The reality of this war was beginning to sink in. While Adams was still riding southward, word had reached Congress that the American invasion of Canada had failed. General Montgomery had been killed and Colonel Arnold badly wounded in an assault on Quebec. Many of their men had fallen or were languishing in captivity in Britain's cold prisons. That news came hard on the heels of other ominous tidings. British warships had leveled Falmouth, the rude Maine village that Adams and Sewall had stood above during their anguished debate over America's future just fifteen months before; similarly, Lord Dunmore, Virginia's royal governor, razed Norfolk. In addition, on January 8, Congress first saw the text of the king's speech opening Parliament during the previous autumn. His remarks fell like a sledgehammer blow upon those who yearned for reconciliation. His speech had been tough, "full of rancor and resentment," as Washington put it; the monarch had encouraged the use of force and had denounced the colonists as traitors. Whatever America had believed previously, it was clearly in for a long, difficult war. Hard necessity, as Francis Lightfoot Lee had said, almost certainly would require foreign assistance, and no help could be expected from any European power as long as America's goal was to be reconciled with Great Britain. As never before, John Adams discovered in the course of his long, wretched ride from Massachusetts, the word "independence" had been dragged from the shadows and thrust into the mainstream of the public debate.[32]

Thomas Paine, a staymaker and former tax collector, a drifter and lethargic visionary, was, however, the individual most responsible for thrusting the notion of independence before the public. In *Common Sense,* a brilliant pamphlet published in Adams's absence, Paine denounced both monarchical and aristocratic government as productive of little save repetitious warfare and tyrannical rule. In a style both enraged and euphoric he urged separation from the corrupt parent state, insisting that independence was crucial not only for the colonists but for the sake of liberty everywhere; indeed, the American Revolution, he said, offered the last hope for the survival of freedom. Independence could be won, he went on, secured with the assistance of European nations that would help America as soon as it declared itself separate from the British empire. Independence would bring peace and prosperity, Paine assured, and the yoke of government would be lightened, for America could establish a decentralized government, entrusting most of the power to the states and vesting a unicameral national legislature with just the power required to protect the new nation's commerce. Paine's ideas circulated quickly. More that 150,000 copies of the pamphlet were sold, reaching an audience roughly 100 times bigger than that of Dickinson's *Pennsylvania Farmer* tract, previously the largest-selling American polemic.[33]

Adams was one of those who purchased *Common Sense,* acquiring two copies—one for himself and another for Abigail—when he passed through New York on his return to Congress. He rejoiced at the new mood it had helped to spawn, and he was especially delighted to learn from home that "independency . . . seems to be the ardent wish of almost all" in Braintree. He was flattered, too, to learn that many in Massachusetts presumed that he was the author of the piece. He laughed at such an idea, and he confessed to William Tudor, his former law clerk, now judge advocate in the Continental army, that he could not have accomplished "the Strength and Brevity of [Paine's] style, nor his eloquent Symplicity, nor his piercing Pathos." On the other hand, he regarded Paine's attack on the monarchy as the product of an untrained intellect, and he disagreed vehemently with his appeal for a unicameral legislature.[34]

For all the fuss over *Common Sense* and all the dire news from the war front, Adams discovered that Congress had taken no bold initiative during his two-month absence. Nevertheless, he found evidence of a changing mood in Philadelphia. News of the king's bellicose speech had led the conservatives to push for a congressional resolution disclaiming America's intention of severing its ties with Britain. Their ploy failed, an indication that by early 1776 the separatists had become the majority faction within Congress. Yet, the non-separatists remained a powerful minority, probably still in control in four colonies: New York, New Jersey, Delaware, and Pennsylvania. Ironically, too, the conservatives were bolstered by news of the American Prohibitory Act, which reached Congress two weeks after Adams's return. The legislation was aimed at stopping all American commerce, and it was accompanied by a ministerial announcement that twenty-five thousand additional troops would be sent to suppress the rebellion. But the act also provided for commissioners who were to be sent to treat with the colonies. Whereas Adams saw the act as nothing less than a declaration of war, the reconciliationists seized upon the hope that the dispatch of emissaries might indicate that Britain was yet willing to negotiate a settlement. Until those commissioners arrived, Adams realized, unanimous consent for independence was out of the question.[35]

Adams also knew that the commissioners were "a Messiah that will never come." The hope of the conservatives that Britain might compromise was illusory, he said, but while he had "laugh'd at it—scolded at it—griev'd at it— and . . . rip'd at it," there was nothing to do but wait out Lord North's emissaries. Even so, the news was not all bad from his perspective. In a sense the Prohibitory Act had ushered in de facto independence. Congress had immediately responded to Britain's act by throwing open its ports to the commerce of the rest of the world, a step it had declined to take in the fall. In addition seven colonies had granted letters of marque to privateers to prey upon British shipping. Independence was almost within sight.[36]

One additional step in the march toward independence occurred early in 1776. Word reached America that Britain had hired German mercenaries to assist in the suppression of the rebellion. This seemed to be further confirmation of ministerial treachery, that the North government's plan, as Tom Paine had remarked, was "Conquest, not reconciliation." Within a few days better news arrived in Philadelphia: on March 17 the British army had been evacuated from Boston. Washington and Gen. William Howe, the commander of the British army, had struck a deal that saved the city. In return for the unmolested removal of his troops, Howe promised not to put Boston to the torch. The siege had been a success. The British occupation—which the locals traced back to 1768—at last had come to an end.[37]

Adams rejoiced at the news. Never in the course of this struggle had he radiated more confidence. Although he knew that a long war lay ahead, he was certain that independence was inevitable, but he did not know precisely when that "mighty Revolution"—his term for independence—would occur. "Perhaps the Time is near, perhaps a great Way off," he wrote in April 1776.[38]

CHAPTER 9

*

A Total Absolute
Independence

A "PEOPLE MAY LET A KING FALL, yet still remain a
people, but if a king let his people slip from him, he is no longer a king.
And as this is most certainly our case, why not proclaim to the World in
decisive terms [our] own importance?"[1]

Abigail Adams put that question to her husband early in May 1776.

"I think you shine as a Stateswoman," he responded gleefully. The goal she
sought was nearer than she realized, he added, for recent events in Pennsylvania had brought America to the verge of "a total absolute Independence."[2]

By early 1776 New England and the South were ready to separate from
Great Britain. The middle colonies were not so inclined, however, and in no
province was the battle over independence more strident or more in doubt
than in Pennsylvania. Reconciliationists dominated the colony's politics. Men
such as Dickinson had been pushed and nudged by a radical faction within the
province into some changes since the outbreak of the war; since early 1775
Pennsylvania had instituted an ironclad boycott of British commodities, disarmed its Loyalist population, and even introduced the secret ballot in Philadelphia's spirited election campaigns. Nevertheless, the reconciliationists retained a comfortable majority in the assembly.[3]

No one had been more exasperated by Pennsylvania's obduracy than
Adams. Even so, from the beginning he had expected that the province sooner
or later would come around, and he even conceded that its slow drift toward
independence might be beneficial. To force the issue, he remarked, would be
to provoke deep divisions that would only haunt the state during the "long,
obstinate, and bloody War" that lay ahead.[4]

Late in the winter of 1776 Pennsylvania's radicals—those who favored
independence—seemed to have made the breakthrough for which they had
labored. Unable to push the assembly to accept separation from Britain, they

had succeeded in passing a bill that would enlarge the legislature. If the separationists won the elections that followed, they would control the assembly, and Pennsylvania's delegates to Congress could then be instructed to vote for independence. Adams closely followed the election campaigns that spring, keeping his fingers crossed that a new majority would repeal the assembly's present "deadly Instructions" to resist independence.[5]

The canvass came on May 1. To the surprise of everyone, the radical scheme failed. While the reconciliationists's majority was whittled—the proindependence faction captured thirteen of the seventeen contested seats—the radicals narrowly failed to gain control of the assembly. The radicals did not surrender, however. They turned to their allies in Congress, none of whom offered more help than John Adams.

Adams first sought to induce Congress to discourage all colonies from instructing their delegates. Congress would have nothing of that. On May 10 he introduced a congressional resolution that urged the colonies to create new governments if their old polities were not equal to the exigencies of the times. This, of course, was a thinly veiled ploy to enable Pennsylvania's radicals to reorganize their provincial government, discarding the recalcitrant assembly. Congress accepted the resolution with little fuss. Five days later, for good measure, Adams secured the passage of a preamble to his resolve that boldly stated the necessity of extirpating all governments whose legitimacy hinged on a grant of authority from the Crown. Dickinson might have sought to block this measure, but he was absent on business in Delaware. The preamble was accepted. Adams now regarded America as independent in all but name. Immodestly, that same evening he wrote his friend James Warren that the enactment he had sponsored was "the most important Resolution, that ever was taken in America."[6]

Adams's action did open the floodgates in Pennsylvania. On May 20 an open-air conclave in Philadelphia attended by four thousand—including Adams—voted to call a provincial convention for the purpose of preparing a new constitution. A few moderates in the assembly waged a rearguard fight, but their resistance now was futile. With barely a whimper the assembly, which Adams once had accused of being "exceedingly obnoxious to America in General," soon quietly released Pennsylvania's congressmen "to concur with the other delegates in Congress" on the question of independence. The Pennsylvanians did not have long to wait. Virginia had already instructed its delegates to vote for independence; "like a Torrent," as Adams put it, other colonies quickly sent similar directions to their congressmen.[7]

The final showdown in Congress began on June 7. That morning, bright and sunny, the last vestige of spring still in the air before another humid summer descended upon Philadelphia, Richard Henry Lee of Virginia offered three resolutions: that the colonies were in fact "free and independent States" and were absolved of all allegiance to Great Britain; that the independent states seek to form foreign alliances; and that the independent states establish a plan of confederation. John Adams seconded the resolves. Consideration of the first proposition commenced the following morning, a Saturday.

A bitter debate raged all that day and again throughout Monday's session. Nothing was accomplished. On Tuesday, Congress agreed to postpone further debate on the topic until July 1. In the interim a committee was to prepare a declaration of independence. As usual, Congress structured a committee to ensure representation from every section. Adams was named to the committee, along with Sherman of Connecticut, Franklin of Pennsylvania, Robert Livingston of New York, and Jefferson from the South. Adams was exultant. "All Ideas of Reconciliation . . . seem to be gone with the Years before the Flood," he told a correspondent.[8]

At the initial meeting of the panel, Adams was offered the assignment of drafting the declaration. He declined. No one, least of all Adams, imagined the immortality that such an act would bring; after all, who remembered the Declaration of Rights and Grievances that he had authored for the initial Congress in 1774. Besides, his work load already was stupendous. Indeed, he was named to three other committees during the same week that the independence panel was established. The committee next turned to Jefferson. A graduate of William and Mary College and a lawyer, he had come to Congress in 1775 with "a reputation for literature, science, and a happy talent for composition," Adams later remembered, and, in fact, he had previously been selected to draft congressional statements. Jefferson accepted the offer.[9]

While Jefferson prepared his draft in the solitude of his rented chambers, the remaining obstacles to independence continued to tumble. During those warm June days Delaware and New Jersey reversed themselves and, like Pennsylvania, authorized their delegates to vote to break away from the British empire. Maryland, which Adams once had feared would never consent to independence, soon followed suit.[10] But stumbling blocks remained in the path of a unanimous vote for independence.

New York, with its large Tory population and a conservative leadership that had never sought more than reconciliation, constituted one formidable roadblock to unanimity. The other barrier came from a handful of congressmen who ignored the fact that their provinces now were committed to independence. By late June it remained clear that opposition from Pennsylvania and South Carolina ensured some negative votes for separation. Moreover, it was rumored that Delaware and New York would not vote at all.

In the past, the desire for unanimity had kept Congress from acting. That no longer was the case. The Molochan disaster that had befallen the American army in Canada and the news that Britain had hired German mercenaries illustrated the pressing need for foreign assistance. Significant aid, everyone agreed, was unlikely to come so long as America's aim was to remain part of the British empire.[11]

Early on the morning of June 28, two days ahead of schedule, Jefferson submitted a Declaration of Independence prepared by his committee. The panel had completed its work in a little more than two weeks. Working alone, Jefferson had prepared a draft, but he requested that Adams peruse the document before it was released to the full committee. Reluctant to ignite a semantic battle that might further delay the vote on independence, Adams recommended only a few stylistic alterations, then passed the Declaration on to the full committee, which made a few additional changes. These modifications were inconsequential, however, and the Declaration that Congress received was clearly the work of the Virginian.

In his old age, a querulous John Adams sometimes was critical of Jefferson's masterpiece, carping that it was "a juvenile declamation," even contending that his colleague had been inspired by the language of resolutions that he, Adams, had previously authored. He was both right and wrong. The document did contain little that was new, but that was one of the triumphs of the piece; it would have been impolitic—not to mention imbecilic—to introduce a strange ideology in defense of a revolution that had been years in the making. Adams's belief that his writing had influenced Jefferson was simply inaccurate; not only was the Declaration derived from a century-old tradition of natural-rights theories and Whig ideologues, but the core of the ideas that Jefferson expressed had appeared earlier in his own writings. What was uniquely, and happily, Jeffersonian was the literary style of the document. The Declaration rang with a simple eloquence that Adams could never have mustered, with a spirit of felicity and optimism that captured not just the temper of contemporaries but also the hearts of generations yet unborn in America and around the world.[12]

On the first morning in July, certain to be a hot, lazy summer day, Adams was up early, and as light began to streak the eastern sky, he wrote a long letter to a former congressional colleague from Georgia: "This Morning is assigned the great debate of all," he reported. At last Congress was to begin its last confrontation on the issue of independence. The next two days, Adams went on, would determine the matter. "May Heaven prosper, the new born Republic," he added, acknowledging that the outcome of the debate was already decided.[13]

The mood in the Pennsylvania State House on July 1 was expectant and somber, the more so because word had recently arrived that a British invasion force had been spotted off Long Island. John Hancock gaveled the session to order promptly at ten o'clock. Charles Thomson, the secretary, read Lee's motion calling for independence. The congressmen voted to consider the issue as a committee of the whole. The moment the vote was taken, John Dickinson was on his feet, denouncing the motion. What followed, Adams told a correspondent that evening, was a waste of everyone's time, for nothing was said "but what had been repeated and hackneyed in that Room . . . an hundred

Times [before] for Six Months past." But Dickinson, so pale and gaunt that some thought him near death, plunged on in his forlorn battle. He even acknowledged his certain defeat, and with it the demise of "my once great and . . . now diminished popularity." But principle counted for all.

The "Farmer" played on a simple theme: there were no advantages to separation, whereas independence was fraught with potential trouble. Independence would cause Britain to throw off all restraint. New York City might be destroyed. The Indians might be unloosed on the frontier. Foreign assistance could be attained without independence, he continued; American military success would attract the aid of Britain's rivals in Europe. But even foreign aid, he warned, could not procure victory. The best America could hope for was a stalemated war, a war without victors. In Europe, he cautioned, such wars ended in partition treaties. That, Dickinson cried, would be America's fate. When the guns finally were silent, Britain would have some of North America, but so would France and Spain and God knew who else. Some colonists would have bled and sacrificed, and in the end would have exchanged the light yoke of Great Britain for the heavy dominion imposed by an alien European power.[14]

It was a very long speech, delivered in an emotional but polite manner. Even Adams thought it a brilliant, gracile stroke.[15]

A long silence followed Dickinson's address. Would no one answer? Finally, fubsy, garrulous John Adams rose. He spoke extemporaneously. There was no need for notes. He had made the same speech, more or less, for a year. Jefferson, perhaps used to a different style of oratory in Virginia, later said that Adams was "not graceful or elegant, nor remarkably fluent," but others would speak of "the magic of his eloquence," his "genuine eloquence," his "resistless eloquence"; it was even said that his speech was "higher than all "eloquence." Calm, assured, Adams nevertheless began by wishing aloud for the deftness of the great orators of antiquity. Proceeding in a tone that he later characterized as courteous, he reiterated the proindependence case, an argument every bit as familiar as the one that Dickinson had just presented. Separation would be beneficial to America. The new nation could chart its own course. Peace and prosperity would be the great rewards of independence. Unlike Dickinson's remarks, resonating with a fear of the unknown, Adams's muted address rang with palpable contempt for the present while exulting in the possibilities of the future.[16]

Sometime in the midst of his speech a courier arrived with significant news: the delegates from Maryland had been freed by Annapolis to vote for independence. Still later, he was interrupted by the arrival of three new delegates from New Jersey, men who had been elected after Congress recommended the creation of new state governments. All were proponents of independence. Once the delegates were introduced and greeted, Adams resumed his speech, this time going back over some of the earlier ground in order to educate the new congressmen. Altogether that day, he spoke for more than two hours. Finally, past two o'clock, drained and utterly exhausted from his effort, he slumped back into his chair.

It was the greatest speech that Adams ever delivered. He was "our Colossus on the floor," Jefferson said later, adding that Adams had spoken "with a power of thought and expression, that moved us from our seats." Richard Stockton of New Jersey, one of those who had just entered Congress, was mesmerized by Adams's speech. The "force of his reasoning" made it clear that there was no choice but independence, he wrote to his son. "The man to whom the country is most indebted for the great measure of independency is Mr. John Adams of Boston. I call him the Atlas of American Independence."[17]

Other speakers followed Adams, all urging independence. At last, however, late in the day, later than usual, for this had been an extraordinarily lengthy session, Congress took a procedural vote. It was not an official vote on independence, but it revealed where each delegation stood. Adams was too good a politician to have been greatly surprised by the result. Nine colonies favored severing their ties with Great Britain. As expected Pennsylvania voted against separation. New York's congressmen abstained and Delaware's two delegates split their votes, denying the province a voice on either side of the issue. The unexpected vote was that cast by South Carolina: it voted no, although privately its delegates agreed subsequently to vote yes if every other colony opted for independence. Before any further action could be taken, the South Carolinians asked that the official canvass be postponed until the following day. The majority hastily agreed, hoping that it might use the next few hours to somehow procure a more nearly unanimous vote.

That night there was much politicking and considerable soul searching. And during the warm night a dispatch rider galloped to nearby Wilmington to fetch Delaware's third congressman, Caesar Rodney, known to favor independence but languishing in a sick bed at home.

The session of July 2, conducted while gentle summer showers bathed the city, was anticlimactic. The momentous decision was made quickly, unceremoniously. Rodney was present and voted for independence; Delaware, thus, was catapulted into the affirmative column. Pennsylvania's Dickinson, Morris, and Wilson had voted against independence the previous day. On this morning, however, Dickinson and Morris did not attend, and Wilson reversed his vote; Pennsylvania had joined Delaware in voting to separate from the British empire. New York abstained, but South Carolina made the turnabout it had promised. The final vote was twelve in favor of independence. No state voted against independence.[18]

Back in his little chamber, made cooler at last by the quenching rain, Adams wrote home to tell Abigail of the resolution of the "greatest Question." A tide of emotions swept over him now that the long fight was at an end. Had the colonies voted to separate when he first had recommended such a course, he alleged—his invidiousness showing through—French help not only would have been available for the pending battle for New York, but Quebec and the rest of Canada also would be in the hands of the United States. On the other hand, he admitted, there was one great advantage to having delayed the vote. The vote came only after everyone knew that the North ministry would not compromise. Coming when it did, independence would not rend America as it might have in January or during the previous summer. In fact, Adams was so convinced that independence gave America a positive goal to pursue that he exclaimed: "This will cement the union."[19]

Transported with the moment, he rejoiced that July 2 would always be remembered as the most revered day in American history. It must be both a day of worshipful thanksgiving to God for having made the event possible and a day of bumptious joy, an occasion for parades, "games, sports, guns, bells, bonfires and illuminations, from one end of this continent to the other, from this time forevermore."[20]

Independence had been declared, but the Declaration of Independence was yet to be considered. Congress wasted no time in turning to Jefferson's hand-iwork. The very next day and again on July 4, the legislators explored, de-bated, and contoured the document, eventually making about thirty changes to those previously recommended by Adams and his fellow committeemen, alterations that reduced the original by nearly twenty-five percent. Congress engaged in some substantive pruning in the second section, the bill of indict-ment of Great Britain and its monarch, striking redundancies and rhetorical fluff as well as a portion that unctuously inveighed against the king for al-legedly having imposed the slavery of Africans upon the colonists. However, the best-remembered section of the Declaration of Independence, the docu-ment's second paragraph, the portion articulating the Whiggish defense of the right of revolution, escaped with barely a half-dozen semantic modifications. At the end of the day on July 4, Robert Treat Paine's diary entry succinctly summarized the events of the date: "Cool. The Independency of the States Voted & declared."[21]

No evidence exists that Adams played any role in Congress's consideration of the Declaration, and in all likelihood he remained inactive during this final battle. Not only did he misjudge the importance of the Declaration, but he had already participated in the preparation of the document.

There were many roads to independence. Opportunism, a glimpse of per-sonal gain through separation, was the driving force for some. Personal bitter-ness influenced others, including Franklin, "a man nursing a deep hurt," according to his most recent biographer, because of the humiliations he had experienced at the hands of British officials; even Washington expressed his disgust with British functionaries, perhaps thinking of the imperial re-strictions that hampered the colonists' freedom of action, or perhaps remembering, as did Franklin, the often demeaning manner with which he had been treated by haughty British officials during his youthful days with the Virginia Regiment. Rage drove others, a deep smoldering anger born, as Bernard Bailyn has written, of a conviction that the British government was "stupid and cruel and that it survived only because of the atrocities it systematically imposed on humanity." A fear that Britain's invidious adulteration would defile America impelled some toward independence, while still others, such as Jefferson, simply spoke of the "abuses of monarchy." Finally, some saw a dream in independence, the dream articulated by Thomas Paine, the notion that the fate of liberty hung in the balance, the belief that a free and independent America might be a haven to the oppressed of the world, the expectation that independence would usher in a halcyon era of peace and prosperity.

No one gave more thought to the causes of independence—or of his own personal reasons for making a commitment to separation—than John Adams. Frequently during the week that Congress acted, and on numerous occasions in the ensuing years, Adams looked back on the tumultuous events that had led to the creation of what he called this "Child Independence." He offered many explanations for the colonists' alienation from the parent state. Events surrounding the wars with France that began in the 1740s were partially responsible, he said. "A mighty impression was made upon my little head" by King George's War, he once remarked of a conflict that had erupted when he was only ten. During that struggle, as well as in the French and Indian War that followed in the 1750s, the British, according to Adams, behaved scornfully toward the provincial officers and men, treating them as cowards and incompetents and assigning them the most meaningless and distasteful tasks. The British haughtiness angered the colonists and "made the blood boil" in his veins, he recollected years later. He also charged that, following these wars, many in New England grew alarmed at the sight of British diplomats manipulating issues at the bargaining table; shocked by what seemed to be Britain's unprincipled diplomacy, some were troubled lest the day might arrive when a chastened London agreed to cede New England to some victorious European power. Finally, like many other New Englanders, Adams believed that the British armies had performed incompetently in these wars, leaving the provincials to defend themselves. To his mind, the colonists were largely responsible for having driven France from North America; they had proven that they could defend themselves. Indeed, he once characterized the expulsion of France from Canada as the first act of the American Revolution, for freed at last from their historic fear of French invasion or encirclement the colonies no longer needed to cling to Britain's protective cloak.[22]

Of course, Adams looked upon Britain's improvident treatment of the colonists, which he dated from the writs of assistance incident in 1761, as the immediate cause of the spiral toward independence. But he saw other, more complex reasons for the break as well. "The Revolution was effected before the

War commenced. The Revolution was in the Minds and Hearts of the People," he once said. The "radical change in the principles, opinions, sentiments, and affections of the People, was the real American Revolution," and that had occurred in the course of living apart from Great Britain since early in the seventeenth century. He also embraced a cyclical theory of history. History, he believed, flowed in cycles. Infant nations were virtuous and uncorrupted, but with age they grew tainted, eventually falling into decline and succumbing to their encumbering maladies and vices. The colonies still were young; Britain, old and corrupt. What had occurred, therefore, was the inevitable yield of historical circumstance. Yet he also viewed these events with a certain mysticism. History, he sometimes thought, was only the expression of providential resolve. The American revolt was part of God's master plan, a means of compelling the American people, yet in their infancy, to endure the "Furnace of Affliction" so that their impurities might be burned away; someday, he thought, the American people would understand that their present struggle was necessary for the attainment of "an Augmentation of [their] Virtues."[23]

As for his own motivation, Adams acknowledged the influence of Samuel Adams and James Otis, especially Otis, who had shaped his constitutional outlook. For the most part, however, he always suggested that he had broken with Great Britain as he came to realize that the parent state was a prideful and supercilious nation that held the provincials in great contempt, and that the conscientious virtue of the colonists could never be reconciled with the ineffable corruption that prevailed across the Atlantic. But to the end he refused to see himself as a revolutionary. When he was in his seventies, a quarter century after the successful conclusion of the War of Independence, he persisted in portraying his actions as that of a man who had "resist[ed] rebellion," who had struggled against a corrupt and tyrannical ministry bent on subverting the English Constitution. It was Great Britain, not John Adams, that had changed.[24]

Historians have not agreed entirely with Adams's assessment of his motives for independence. Peter Shaw found him to be "a radical in spite of himself." To the end, he argued, Adams's intellectual stance on the question of independence was fraught with ambiguities, but he ultimately embraced this course largely because "his whole life was caught up in the Revolution," and he had discovered that through his linkage to the creation of an American nation he could achieve the recognition he so desperately sought. Gilbert Chinard rejected personal ambition as a prime motivating factor. To him, Adams was a man of "fundamental intellectual honesty" who concluded that independence was an unavoidably essential act for the people of America. Page Smith agreed, although he thought Adams was "driven" somewhat reluctantly to independence. With reconciliation impossible because of British iniquities, independence ultimately became a necessary course, both as a vehicle for winning the war and for the simple management of order throughout thirteen diverse and turbulent colonies. Charles Francis Adams also portrayed Adams as a reluctant revolutionary. He had supported the war in 1775 because "no escape was left with honor" and, similarly, because Britain's "evil counsellors" made it clear that to remain part of the empire would be a "calamity" for America. Richard B. Morris discovered a more willing advocate of independence, but a man who, like Smith's Adams, had become irreconcilably opposed to the empire because of its propulsive corruption. Finally, Edmund S. Morgan saw in Adams some of the same drives that Shaw captured. The "achievement . . . of independence became inseparable from his own ambitions," he asserted, but he also concluded that Adams acted from a mixture of rage—he was "passionately bitter against Great Britain"—and from a conviction that the "conservation of freedom" hinged on American independence.[25]

To discover that John Adams acted from personal motives could hardly come as a surprise. Indeed, to deny that his conduct was fueled by personal indulgence would be to strip him of his very humanity. Adams would have been—was, in fact—the first to agree with such a proposition, and in his later writings he endlessly propounded the notion that chief among man's causal agents were the drives of ambition, greed, and a lust after fame. However, to see Adams as embracing independence with reluctance, or to find his radicalism rooted largely in his quest for celebrity or exaltation, either consciously or subliminally, is to misconstrue the man. Adams had been slow to fully embrace the ideology of the popular movement, but once he did so he never wavered and he probably was one of the first to accept the conviction that independence was desirable. A native-born American whose Massachusetts ancestry went back nearly a century, Adams looked upon his America as a revolutionary enterprise. Here, his Puritan ancestors had gained religious freedom. Here, government based on the consent of the governed had achieved a status unimaginable in England. Here, not only his ancestors but he too had enjoyed the opportunity to rise above his birthright. This was the American Revolution of which he spoke. Once he came to believe that this way of life was threatened by British corruption and ministerial plots, there could only be one path for America to take. Adams was a conservative, the great conservator of what had been achieved in America before the onset of the troubles with the parent state. In one respect, however, his vision was as radical as that of Thomas Paine. Adams shared Paine's vision that independence would sustain the liberties that had grown and flourished in the course of the colonial era. Separate from England, America might escape the corrupting influences that threatened the triumph of tyranny, and, as his Puritan ancestors had argued in another context a century and a half before, the new nation, by its very example, might serve to liberate humankind. With independence, he said joyfully, the "Decree is gone forth, and it cannot be recalled, that a more equal Liberty, than has prevail'd in other Parts of the Earth, must be established in America." For Adams, independence was a revolutionary act to be welcomed with ebullience, for it was only through independence that his countrymen's "more equal Liberty" could be preserved.[26]

"To form a new Government, requires infinite care," George Washington counseled on the eve of independence as state after state rushed to substitute new constitutions for the old colonial charters. John Adams could not have agreed more thoroughly with the general. The Revolution now entered into its second stage, the creation of independent America's own institutions. This phase, said Adams, would be "the most difficult and dangerous Part of the Business." What particularly concerned him was that the "People will have unbounded Power" to fashion the new government. He did not fully trust the judgment of the people. The people being "extremely addicted to Corruption and Venality . . . I am not without apprehension," he confided to Abigail.[27]

Probably no activist in America had thought more or spoken more openly about matters of governance than Adams. His earliest published views on government had appeared more than a decade before. He had frequently lectured Congress on political theory, first when Massachusetts and New Hampshire had sought Congress's consent to replace their colonial governments with polities of their own choosing, then in rebuttal to the views on government that Thomas Paine had expressed in *Common Sense*. In a brief section in his famous pamphlet, Paine had urged that America's new governments consists of unicameral legislatures and weak executive officials. Adams was horrified. He called Paine's views everything from "inadequate" to "despicable" to "ignorant." If heeded, he warned, Paine's thoughts "will do more Mischief . . . than all the Tory writings together."[28]

At least four congressmen found Adams's views to be so convincing that they urged him to commit to paper his ideas on government. He did so in separate letters to these colleagues, each missive a bit longer and more thoughtful than its predecessor. So impressed was Richard Henry Lee with his letter that, with Adams's consent, he had it printed. Published anonymously just after mid-April 1776, it was titled simply *Thoughts on Government* and styled as "a Letter from a Gentleman to his Friend." Of all the millions of words that Adams wrote and published, none came close to rivaling the impact or the enduring influence of this pamphlet.[29]

The purpose of government, Adams began, is to promote happiness, and the best polity is that which secures happiness for the largest number of its citizens. A republican government is best suited to these ends, he continued. The structure? He recommended a bicameral legislature balanced by executive and judicial branches. Bicameralism was superior to unicameralism, he went on, for two houses were less subject to avarice, less likely to act in the grip of passion. One house should be more democratic than the other, its members elected by the qualified voters; this house, in turn, should elect the second house. An executive of roughly coequal powers should be chosen by the assembly. He urged veto powers for the executive, and he was willing to make him commander in chief of the armed forces; there were dangers, he acknowledged, but he believed that annual elections would teach the executive the "great political virtues of humility, patience, and moderation." Indeed, annual elections would check the "ravenous beast of prey" that lurked in the breast of each man. However appointed—either by the legislature or jointly by the executive and the assembly—justices should serve for life.[30]

What Adams had described closely resembled the colonial governments of New England, especially that of Connecticut, devoid of the customary royal intrusiveness. The American base of these governments had been strongly republican. "The Spirit of the People, among whom I had my Birth and Education . . . was always republican," Adams told a congressman, and the governmental scheme that he recommended urged a persistence of that tradition. One reason the British empire in America had collapsed, he said, was because the colonists had been given an insufficient vote in their own affairs. The new American governments must not make the same mistake. But when Adams referred to popular government, he thought of participation as being limited to property owners. The propertyless were "too dependent upon other Men to have a Will of their own," he went on in private. Indeed, he even said that Britain had made it too easy to own land, with the result that the electorate had grown too large. Restraint in opening new frontiers should be exercised, he suggested.[31]

Paine's plan of government was more daring, more radical than that of Adams. Paine had more confidence in the people, in their ability to judge properly, and he would have imposed fewer restraints on their freedom of action. Adams trembled at the thought of the dark side of man's nature. His government included safeguards against precipitate action; he sought mechanisms to balance power, to prevent any one branch—or any one class or individual—from exercising untrammeled authority. Paine's thoughts on government had been shaped by the tradition of English radicalism; Adams drew on his New England experience, and as a conservative he sought to contain change that would result from this revolutionary upheaval. Adams sought to preserve intact much of what existed in 1776, save for the British presence. The American Revolution, he believed, had occurred before the first shots of this war were fired at Lexington and Concord. He did not wish further sweeping changes. Separation from Britain he wished for, but for little else, and the newly independent governments must be so contrived as to make truly revolutionary change unlikely.

The one change that Adams hoped for was that New England's republican tradition would take root in every section of the country. He was convinced that unless the middle and southern states embraced the republicanism of his native region, union could not endure. He was not optimistic that other states would alter their ways. For instance, he attributed Dickinson's opposition to independence to his fear of republicanism, and he believed that gentlemen from the southern states were apprehensive that their aristocratic, slave-owning ways would crumble before republican institutions. When he dispatched what would become known as his *Thoughts on Government* to colleagues from the south of New England, therefore, he acted in the hope that his views would not only serve as an antidote to Paine's radicalism but also might nudge other sections toward republicanism.[32]

To his considerable surprise, most southern and mid-Atlantic states prepared constitutions that closely resembled the formula he had prescribed. By year's end nine states had completed, or nearly finished, their work. All of them established republican governments; most of them separated powers between an executive and a bicameral assembly. Although most states reduced property qualifications for voting and established more representative legislatures than had existed in the colonial era, Adams was pleased.[33] Only the constitution of Pennsylvania and, to his great mortification, affairs in his own state, gave him concern.

"Good God!" he cried when he learned of Pennsylvania's new fundamental law. This was not a constitution prepared by conservatives and moderates. Indeed, Dickinson and his ilk were swept aside soon after July 4. Pennsylvania dropped the "Farmer" from its congressional delegation, whereupon he resigned his seat in the state assembly and left for the front to bear arms for Pennsylvania, eventually becoming a private in the state militia, serving with some distinction, even volunteering for combat duty. Triumphant at last, the radicals produced the Pennsylvania Constitution; Thomas Paine even had a hand in its preparation, and the result was a charter that was far more democratic than anything that had been suggested in *Common Sense*. Not only were all adult male taxpayers permitted to vote, but power was vested in a unicameral assembly. In what must have been a most strange sensation, Adams soon found himself hoping that Dickinson would regain a preeminent position in Pennsylvania politics.[34]

Affairs in Massachusetts were of greater concern to Adams. Since the fall of 1774, he had been bombarded with anguished reports that the province was spinning into chaos. Letters from home, many from a friend, James Warren, catalogued riots and threats to private property and even warned of the possibility of military dictatorship. These grim tidings were mostly alarmist tattle. Massachusetts was experiencing a budding reform movement. Accounts of imminent class warfare, or even of sweeping social change, sprang from the fevered imagination of those in the East who had for so long enjoyed unhampered sway over political life in the province and who, as independence neared, feared the loss of their hegemony in the event of a new state constitution.[35]

Eastern moderates had preserved their control over the province during the summer of 1775 through the establishment of a government based on the Charter of 1691. Drawing upon every skill they possessed, the East solidified its control in May 1776 by pushing through the General Court legislation that gave greater representation to the larger towns in the province; the chief beneficiaries, of course, were the older, more populous centers in the East. Having secured its hold on Massachusetts, the East thereafter resisted the West's calls for the immediate adoption of a new constitution. By temporizing, the East had the opportunity to act without western interference while it sought to put the state's shaky, war-torn economy in order; in addition, as Adams's friend John Lowell told him, the Eastern moderates resisted every call for a constitution until they had seen the constitutional handiwork of other states.[36]

Adams, who had encouraged other states to proceed quickly with the drafting of their constitutions, offered no such advice to his friends at home. Advance "Slowly and deliberately," he suggested instead. Beyond that, the suggestions he offered could only have been welcomed by Eastern moderates, for he made quite clear his loathing of "that Rage for Innovation" advanced by "disaffected Persons" from the West. He recommended the drafting of a constitution that would have changed little or nothing, for it would have retained the basic features of the Charter of 1691 and of the new law of representation adopted that spring, merely making provision for the selection of an executive. But if Adams did not endorse the views of the innovators, he made it clear that he believed a government of balances was necessary to protect the general citizenry from the great merchants. Only "order and Firmness" balanced between a bicameral legislature and a strong executive could check factionalism, he said. Three interests would compete for power in Massachusetts: merchants, farmers, and tradesmen alike were "addicted to Commerce" and would seek to advance themselves though the assistance of the government. While Adams believed that every man "must seriously set himself to root out his Passions, Prejudices and Attachments," this was not always feasible. Thus, without the proper constitutional restraints, he went on, "there is great Danger that a Republican Government"—especially a republican polity—"would be very factious and turbulent," and probably end in failure.[37] But Adams would have a wait before his state acted. Only at the end of March 1777 would the General Court begin to prepare a constitution.

But a new constitution would mean little if America did not win the war. Throughout the spring and summer of 1776 Adams remained ebullient about the course of the conflict. He knew that victory could come only through a long, difficult war, but he believed that America could wear down the British. Time was on America's side, he insisted, because the new nation's greater virtue would render it more likely than Great Britain to make the selfless sacrifices required by a protracted war.[38]

Adams's reassuring view of America's military prospects was not matched by a similarly sunny assessment of his own role in this war. The part he was to play in the bloody conflict once again became a source of torment. As news of the Continental army's debacle before Quebec reached Philadelphia, his old misgivings and uncertainties, largely laid to rest in the buoyant last months of 1775, resurfaced. Within a few weeks he again spoke of what he called his "nervous" disorders, and he remarked to a correspondent, "My Face is grown pale, my Eyes weak and inflamed, my Nerves tremulous." Once again he began to voice his yearning to soldier, but, as in the first year of the war, he searched for some exculpatory vindication for his failure to bear arms. He was too old, he said, although he knew that other congressmen who were nearly his age—Dickinson and Henry, for instance—were serving with their provincial trainband units. They could have made a better contribution as statesmen than as soldiers, he assured himself. Unconvinced, perhaps, he next suggested that he could not soldier because his years of study had ruined his health. The anguish remained. "I wish every Man upon the Continent was a Soldier, and obliged upon Occasion to fight," he once said. "We must all be soldiers," he remarked later. "I hope there is not a Gentleman . . . who thinks himself too good to take [up] his Firelock and his Spade" in defense of the country.[39]

Adams vowed that he would serve if a true emergency threatened. But with the American army in desperate retreat from Quebec during the winter of 1776 he declined Congress's invitation to undertake a somewhat risky mission to Canada to win the inhabitants of that province to the American side. He would have gone, he told Abigail, but his knowledge of French was inadequate, a curious excuse in light of his subsequent diplomatic activities in Paris. Benjamin Franklin, almost thirty years Adams's senior, agreed to head the mission.[40]

As in earlier times of considerable stress, Adams's thoughts turned increasingly toward his farm and family. I long, he said, for "my rural Pleasures, my Little Property." He coveted only his "Farm, Family, and Goose Quil," he added.[41] And to Abigail he wrote: "I want to Walk with you in the Garden—to go over to the Common—the Plain—the Meadow. I want to take Charles in one Hand and Tom in the other, and Walk with you, Nabby on your Right Hand and John upon my left."[42]

By the summer of 1776 Adams had begun to cope more successfully with his travail. His health was good, surprisingly so, he acknowledged. He had pulled himself through the crisis by utilizing a familiar strategy. He had sought to convince himself that his service was every bit as sacrificial as that of the men who bore arms. He had no personal life, no liberty, he cried. His only interest was "the great Object" of his country. His was a "solitary, gloomy" existence. His lot was to endure the noise and pollution of the city, the loneliness of separation from his family, the black intrigue of his fellow congressmen. His regimen was destructive of his health, he asserted. Indeed, he even maintained that it was more dangerous to serve in Congress than at the front lines! And all this sacrifice was made, he said, merely to secure happiness for others.[43]

By July Adams appeared to be more at ease with himself, a turn undoubtedly assisted by a new assignment undertaken a month earlier. On June 12 Congress created the Board of War and Ordnance, a panel designed to insure legislative oversight of the army and the conduct of the war. Adams was named president of the body and served in that capacity until late the following year. This added enormously to his already staggering work load, which he now commenced at four o'clock in the morning and continued at until ten at night. In addition to his usual congressional duties he met twice daily with the Board of War to superintend matters as diverse as logistical problems, promotions and appointments within the officer corps, recruitment procedures, and the treatment and exchange of prisoners of war.[44]

Already renowned as a hard worker, Adams undertook his new commitment with a verve that was astounding. In no time he became a "kind of *de facto* Secretary of War," according to one scholar. Another writer has labeled him a "war department" unto himself, while still another historian noted that in supervising the war effort he worked like a "galley slave bent on his oar." His extraordinary burdens—his work load far surpassed that of the great majority of congressmen—enabled him to see himself as facing every bit as much danger as a soldier at the front. He looked upon his life as an "affliction." His walked daily upon an "ordeal Path," he said. He had compromised his health "beyond Prudence, and safety." "What have I not hazarded," he asked. He even equated himself with Cincinnatus, the legendary Roman who abandoned his farm to bear arms in defense of the state. Like the men in the trenches, he remarked, he too was "running dayly Risques" of his life.[45]

Adams was equally distraught during these months by his continued absence from his family. The seemingly endless separation caused him to "feel like a Savage," he said that summer.[46] He soon felt even worse when he discovered that his family once again was confronted with great danger. A sudden smallpox epidemic had struck the Boston area.

Without consulting her husband, Abigail decided to undergo inoculation for the dread disease. She simply decided to act, and quickly. She hastened to Boston to stay with relatives during the immunization ordeal, taking a cow to ensure fresh milk. She underwent inoculation with sixteen other persons, including her children and two servants, as well as Richard and Mary Cranch and their children. Save for being uprooted from her home, it was a relatively uneventful experience for Abigail, but eleven-year-old Nabby fell quite ill, while little Charles, only six, was inoculated unsuccessfully three times, then contracted the ailment by contagion. Three days after Charles's first symptoms he ran a dangerously high fever; then for more than forty-eight hours he was delirious. Adams learned of his son's grave condition through a letter from Abigail, a missive that struck him like a body blow. Two days later, however, happier tidings arrived. Charles was better; he would survive. "My sweet

Babe, Charles," his exultant father sighed. "I did not know what fast Hold that little Pratler Charles had upon me before."[47]

The independence that Abigail displayed in submitting herself and her children to the smallpox immunization was no longer unusual. Before this she had journeyed by herself to Plymouth to visit with her old friend Mercy Warren. By summer 1776 she had been separated from her husband for nearly twenty of the past twenty-four months, and like countless other women throughout America she had been compelled to assume responsibilities once borne by her spouse. She had become "quite a Farmeress," she told John in May, and, indeed, her letters now abounded with reports on the crops and the livestock, the work of the hired hands and the servants, even on her handling of the family's money, including the buying and selling of horses and real estate. That spring, for instance, Thankful Adams, John's widowed sister-in-law, had offered Abigail the opportunity to purchase twenty-eight acres of land. She inspected the site, checked the land deeds office to see what the property originally cost, and—as she was legally forbidden to complete the transaction herself—recommended that John acquire the tract. He consented.[48]

The farm flourished under her care. In fact, when James Warren saw the estate he was surprised to discover that it was in better shape than ever before. It was not simply an idle remark then when Abigail, with a mixture both of pride and irascibility, informed John: "[I] have supported the Family."[49]

A bristling, restive air soon appeared in her letters. "I miss my partner," she austerely remarked a few weeks after his departure early in 1776. When John did not return in the spring as he had promised, she none too coyly asked: "Shall I Expect you, or do you determine to stay out the year?" On another occasion she told him that she had permitted ten days to lapse without writing, saying, "I have not felt in a humour to entertain you. If I had taken up my pen perhaps some unbecoming invective might have fallen from it."[50]

In response, John, desperately seeking to cope not only with his sense of guilt but also with Abigail's seeming reproof of his behavior, postured as if he was a soldier under fire. "I cannot leave" the Congress, he wrote. To desert Congress would cause "more Injury to the public" than she could possibly imagine. He pleaded with Abigail to write more frequently, and after receiving a particularly cold missive from her, his next closed with a rare salutation: "My dearest Love to you all." But his only apparent concession was to vow to bring the family to Philadelphia on his next return trip.[51]

America waited that summer for its adversary's blow to fall. Following Gen. William Howe's evacuation of Boston in March, the British army had repaired to Nova Scotia to await reinforcements. While Howe's redcoats lay idle, the war proceeded with mixed results for the colonists. What remained of the American army in Canada was routed and compelled to retreat into New York;

at the same moment, however, the British sought without success to seize Charleston, South Carolina.[52]

Washington's intelligence reports in the spring indicated that Britain's next major objective would be New York, and when Howe and his brother, Adm. Richard Howe, docked at Staten Island in mid-July, it was clear that the army's assessment had been correct. After taking New York City, the Howe brothers planned to seize the Hudson River, thus isolating New England by land from the colonies to the south; a naval blockade of the New England coast would prevent supplies from the outer world from reaching the beleaguered region. Ultimately, General Howe planned to invade New England.

Through the spring Adams had remained sanguine about America's prospects in the pending campaign. By midsummer, however, his optimism had given way to a growing concern. Martial fervor remained high and, in fact, was boosted by Britain's failure at Charleston. But Howe had a larger force at his disposal than Adams previously had believed possible, and Washington was having difficulty filling his troop quotas in several states, including even in New England. "May Heaven grant us Victory, if We deserve it," Adams prayed; "if not, Patience, Humility and Persistance under Defeat" was the best he could hope for.[53]

Defeat it was, a drubbing so egregious that with better luck and a bit more enterprise the British might have turned the engagement into a decisive conquest. Late in August, Howe struck at the American army at Brooklyn, on the western tip of Long Island. In no time Howe routed his amateur foe. More than three hundred Americans died and three times that many were taken prisoner, including two general officers. For a time Washington's army was pinioned against the East River, although when Howe paused before attacking, the American commander seized the opportunity and, under cover of a heavy fog, extricated his army.

While Britain's triumph had not been as complete as it might have been, it nevertheless was a stunning victory, and the Howes took this opportunity to open talks to end the war. Sent to America as peace commissioners as well as commanders of Britain's armed forces, the Howe brothers probably did not believe that Congress was ready to capitulate, but they wished to test the waters. Soon after the fighting ended on Long Island, they dispatched General Sullivan, one of the American generals captured at Brooklyn, to request that Congress send emissaries to a formal conference. Adams opposed discussions with the British, fearing that the Howes would use the occasion to drive a wedge between the proseparatist Americans and those who, even after independence, continued to hope for a reconciliation upon satisfactory terms. Congress debated the issue, then agreed to send three deputies to Staten Island, not to negotiate but to determine whether General Howe and his brother were empowered to conclude a peace treaty with America. Adams was chosen, together with Franklin and Edward Rutledge, to meet with the British commanders.[54]

The three set off on their journey to New York on September 9, each man and his servant occupying a separate coach. After a long, hot day of bouncing along dusty roads, they passed the first night in Brunswick, New Jersey. Because of the shortage of chambers at the only available inn, Adams and Franklin shared a room. It was not a pleasant evening for the finicky, fussy Adams. Franklin badgered his colleague into sleeping with the windows open, and, though it was a mild summer evening, Adams fretted that the nocturnal air was a purveyor of fevers. If that was not enough, Franklin also kept his exhausted younger cohort awake far into the night with an interminable disquisition on colds. After a second night in Amboy, the delegates were ferried across to Howe's headquarters, situated in a modest dwelling on Staten Island.[55]

Adams was understandably nervous as he passed through a line of grenadier guards—men who looked "as fierce as the furies," as he put it—to enter Howe's residence. But Admiral Howe, a cultivated gentleman who had studied at Westminster and Eton, quickly put his guests at ease, and the envoys soon joined several British officers for a lunch of claret with cold ham, tongue, and mutton, served in a room oddly decorated with moss sprinkled across the hardwood floors and with sprigs of green shrubbery adorning the walls and windows.[56]

The talks that followed the repast were amiable but unproductive. The Americans learned that the Howes were the peace commissioners so fervently awaited by the reconciliationists. They also discovered that the commissioners were empowered only to proclaim peace "upon Submission" of the colonies. The congressmen listened politely as Howe delivered what Adams thought was a windy, rapacious discourse, then Rutledge asked bluntly whether the admiral possessed the power to repeal the Prohibitory Act and to renounce Parliament's right to tax America. Howe confessed that he did not. Shortly afterward, the meeting ended. "They met, they talked, they parted," a member of Howe's staff noted that evening in his diary. "And now," he added ominously, "nothing remains but to fight it out against a Set of the most determined Hypocrites & Demagogues . . . that ever was permitted by Providence to be the Scourge of a Country."[57]

The fight to which he referred ensued almost immediately after Adams and his colleagues departed. In mid-September the British invaded Manhattan Island, striking at Kip's Bay on the East River. Another American disaster resulted. Washington's defenders broke ranks and scattered in panic, permitting the British and Hessians to land virtually unopposed. Washington succeeded in reuniting the various parts of his army, but he remained in desperate straits, ensconced on an island from which all avenues of escape might be blocked by the British navy. Once again, a resourceful General Howe might have delivered the decisive blow, but, as at Long Island, he inexplicably delayed, permitting a month to elapse before he at last struck. By then it was too late. Early in October, Washington's army fled its trap, escaping to the mainland above Manhattan.

Adams watched the campaign in New York closely, and he appeared to grow angrier by the day as the disaster unfolded. Soon he was furious at the performance of America's armed forces. Washington and his principal general officers had been "out generalled," he remarked, but his real anger boiled over at the news that entire companies had ignominiously fled in the face of the enemy. That most of the units abandoning their posts were New England outfits only added to his wrath. "I can bear . . . almost any thing . . . better than disgrace," he wrote. The officers were to blame for what had occurred, he raged. Granted they were inexperienced, but there was "a dearth of Genius among them" as well. He urged his friend Warren, president of the Provincial Congress in Massachusetts, to open an inquiry into the conduct of the state's officers, and he not only advocated the death penalty for any officer guilty of cowardice but also suggested that being taken by surprise during combat should be made a capital offense.[58]

The military disaster in New York served one useful purpose. For some time Adams had realized that discipline and adequate training could be instituted only in an army of lengthy enlistments. Following the debacle at Brooklyn he prepared a plan that offered substantially greater cash bounties and land grants to those men who volunteered for the duration. Congress quickly adopted the measure and revised the Articles of War as well, approving a draft prepared by Adams and Jefferson. The Articles now provided for far more Draconian punishments. The limit of lashes was raised from thirty-nine to one hundred, and the number of crimes considered as capital offenses was increased as well. During the course of this war more than twenty—perhaps as many as forty—American soldiers were to be executed; no officers suffered the death penalty.[59]

The bleak showing of American arms aroused panic in some sectors, although Adams, while redolent with fury, seems not to have been unduly alarmed. He referred to the situation as "extremely critical," but he was convinced that the United States would survive to fight another campaign. Of necessity, he wrote, Howe had so divided his army that he was unable to make a telling strike. Besides, he had sized up the Howe brothers and found "nothing of the vast" in either man. In fact, Adams worried less about the British adversary than about the possibility that the Continental army might simply vanish for lack of enlistments in 1777. But that, he knew, was not too likely given the new incentives for recruitment that he had ushered through Congress. With considerable optimism, therefore, he reported, "We shall do well enough." Indeed, if Washington got his men, the British would be "ruined."[60]

In mid-October Adams suddenly obtained a leave of absence from Congress and departed for home. His decision, as during the previous autumn, was sudden and unexpected. Throughout the summer and early fall he had indicated repeatedly that he could not leave, and, in fact, only two days before he left Philadelphia he had urged Abigail to write frequently, an indication that he had no plans for a journey to Braintree. What adds an additional air of mystery to this trip is that Adams informed his wife that the trek would require three weeks or more—instead of the customary twelve to fourteen days—for he would be "obliged to make stops by the Way."[61]

No record exists of Adams meeting with anyone while en route to Massachusetts, but the journey did require twenty-four days. The unusually lengthy journey could have resulted from traveling a strange route to Braintree. Indeed, one can safely guess that he was compelled to alter his itinerary in the course of the trip. Riding north he would have discovered that General Howe's army had landed on the mainland, at Throg's Point north of Manhattan. With his customary route through Connecticut blocked by the enemy, he must have continued on farther north, probably crossing the Hudson at Poughkeepsie, then riding through the lower Catskills, perhaps toward Hartford in central Connecticut. In his capacity as head of the Board of War, he may also have paused along the way to meet with state officials and army commanders regarding the conduct of the war.[62]

But why did Adams jettison his plans for remaining in Philadelphia? While his sudden interest in returning home cannot be determined, it probably was due largely to matters before the Massachusetts Provincial Congress, sitting in Boston that autumn. A letter from James Warren probably convinced him to start home. Although Warren wrote urging Adams to remain in Philadelphia because of the critical nature of events, he also mentioned that the Provincial Congress had declined to elect additional representatives to Congress. Adams badly wished to keep his seat in Congress, but he also desired greater financial assistance so that he could bring Abigail to Philadelphia. He would go home, he must have decided, to plead for help; if denied the necessary stipend, the Provincial Congress would have to turn to "Men of fortune, who can afford" to sit idly in Congress.[63]

In a sense, Adams's decision to return home symbolized for him the end of the most idealistic phase of the American Revolution. The remarkably virtuous, sacrificial Revolution that Adams had perceived in the colonies since the summer of 1774 had vanished in the autumn of 1776, replaced by a most customary spirit of venality. The cowardly conduct of American soldiers had shocked him, as had the reluctance of many farm boys and artisans to bear arms in the struggle for independence. He found it even more appalling that many men of affluence had abandoned public service in order to resume their careers, and that workmen on the home front, given the wartime shortage of labor, had begun to demand greater wages for their services. He feared that human nature had proven "to be the same in America as it had been in Europe."[64]

Adams was fully aware that he too must look into his own "private Affairs," for his finances and his family had changed in the two years since he first had come to Philadelphia. It would be difficult for him to plead for assistance, however; acutely sensitive, he feared his motives and fretted that he was elevating his own selfish interests above those of the public good. He required a foil to justify his action, and he discovered it in the very men whom he would have to approach. The members of the Provincial Congress had been "very willing that [he] should be Sacrificed to protect them in the Enjoyment" of their personal endeavors, he raged. While he had left his family "to Starve," they had been insensitive to his suffering.[65]

Adams was compelled to convince himself of these men's callous indifference in order to carry out his own act of uncertain propriety. "I am ashamed of the Age I live in," he confessed.[66]

The next day he made the decision to ask Congress for the leave of absence.

CHAPTER 10

*

To Leave This Station with Honour

Few of New England's gaudy autumn leaves remained on their branches when Adams rode the last weary mile through Braintree and, at last, alighted at his front door. After a long, loving reunion with his wife and children, a joyous moment of hugs and kisses, of looking in wonderment at how the kids had grown, of listening to the youngsters' rapid-fire reports of their recent activities—all babbled at once, of course—John regained a measure of silence by distributing gifts to everyone. Then, although tired and dusty from the final leg of his long journey, he and Abigail surely sought to be alone to talk and to get to know one another again after a separation of nearly ten months.

Adams had come home to stay or to find the means of fetching his family back to Philadelphia. But in the end he did neither. After nine weeks at home, a period when, for a change, he seldom was apart from his wife and his farm, he returned to Congress—alone.

His departure aroused terrible anguish, especially within Abigail. After her husband's repeated declarations that they would not again be separated, he once again was gone. This time, moreover, he left behind a pregnant wife.

Abigail evidently sought to persuade John to remain at home, but whatever his initial intentions, he missed his public role, with its accompanying sense of fulfillment. Public affairs "wore so gloomy an aspect," he argued, that he must hasten to Philadelphia. Both knew that a return was unlikely before the onset of the next winter's icy blasts.[1]

It was less surprising that Adams should have resumed his duties in Congress than that Abigail should be pregnant. She had endured five pregnancies in the first seven years of the marriage, but for the past five years she had expressed no desire to have another child, and she, or John, evidently had successfully practiced some form of birth control. Abigail's earlier pregnancies had been quite difficult; on two occasions she nearly died at childbirth or from subsequent complications. Faced with still another protracted separation—and probably not the last one, it must now have been clear—Abigail may have sought the company and the distraction afforded by an infant. Moreover, although only thirty-two and with many years remaining during which she could yet bear children, Abigail might have reasoned that she would never again enjoy such good health at the outset of a pregnancy. Then again, this pregnancy might have occurred as part of a desperate design to keep her husband at her side or at least to induce his return to Braintree no later than the summer. Or Abigail might simply have become pregnant through accident.[2]

John's departure was the most grievous of any she had experienced, Abigail reported. It was difficult for him as well, and he spoke of the "cruel Parting" and of how he had labored to appear composed as he said his final good-byes. Very soon thereafter, however, Adams remarked on his "good Spirits," for whatever the doubtless pain at his absence from his wife and children, he was happy to be enmeshed once again in his political activities, the focal point of his life.[3]

Adams remained an ambitious man, and, his repeated protestations notwithstanding, the compelling need to remain active politically was certain to triumph over every competing alternative. No one understood that better than his wife. She maintained that he would have remained in Braintree had she insisted, but she said it without much conviction. She also asserted that had he agreed "to leave the Field"—even she had begun to adopt metaphors that cast his service in military terms—his action would have been a disservice to the cause. The remark was revealing, as was her declaration: "Were I a man I must be in the Field." She had begun the emotional process of compensating for the loss of her husband by seeking to convince herself of the utter necessity of his political activities. By making his service appear to be indispensable, she elevated her own contribution and ennobled her personal sacrifice.[4]

John Adams's life was nearly half over on that cold, dreary January day when he set out from Braintree. If, during his long journey south, he contemplated the time he thus far had been allotted, he must have been quite pleased with his accomplishments. Had he taken the first position dangled before him, he might now have been an unknown lawyer in the small country town of Worcester. Instead, he had grown to be one of the most successful lawyers in Boston. Not only that, he had become an important figure in the political life of his province, and more recently he had emerged as "the first man" in a national assembly. His success was due to an extraordinary single-mindedness, a quest that had resulted in the sacrifice of much that stood in his path. He was aware that he had forfeited considerable material benefits, as well as his leisure, and he believed that his health had been put at risk by his activities. Now, too, his family once again was required to make way for the inner fires that consumed him. He did not see it that way, of course, and many historians, like Adams himself, have preferred to ignore that side of his character, stressing only his public role. But the public man also had a private side, and sometimes that dimension of a person's character can disclose as much as one's external conduct.

Adams's friends admired his intellect and dedication. Most viewed his conduct as "disinterested," and his associates marveled at his seemingly boundless capacity for work. Upon becoming a member of Congress, Benjamin Rush assayed many of his new colleagues and found most blemished by—among other things—ignorance, cowardice, and laziness. But he had only praise for Adams, a man possessed of the rare ability to view "the whole of a subject at a single glance," and a man with the courage to express his convictions. Most of Rush's fellow congressmen shared his feelings about Adams; one, Nathan Brownson of Georgia, was so impressed that he once remarked that when Adams spoke he "fancied an angel was let down from heaven to illumine the Congress." Adams's great failing seemed to be his volcanic temper, which could explode with such suddenness and with so little provocation that some of his colleagues feared that passion occasionally eclipsed reason. Adams would not have disagreed with such an assessment. In middle age he still excoriated himself for his "rash . . . boyish, raw, and awkward Expressions," his "Flights of Passion," and "Starts of Imagination." When asked later in life by a correspondent to describe his temper, Adams replied that he was by nature "tranquil, except when any instance of madness, deceit, hypocrisy, ingratitude, treachery or perfidy, has suddenly struck me. Then I have always been irascible enough." His quick temper notwithstanding, other congressmen learned to turn to him when a compelling issue demanded study or when an urgent document required an author. They did not, however, see him as their leader.[5]

Adams thought his appearance, particularly his height, was a curse that deprived him of those charismatic qualities necessary to lead men. That was unlikely, however. Although he was not tall and statuesque as was Washington, his features were not terribly different from those of many—perhaps most—other important Revolutionaries. Adams once described himself as "short"; on another occasion he said he was five seven or five nine in height, unsure which was accurate. In the John Trumbull, the Robert Edge Pine, and the Edward Savage paintings of the members of Jefferson's Declaration of Independence committee, Adams appears to be of average stature. In the former work he is the same height as two of his three colleagues who are standing; in Trumbull's painting, he is just barely shorter than Franklin, who was five ten and a head beneath Jefferson, who was six feet two inches tall. Adams, thus probably stood at least five seven, the approximate mean height of native-born American males of his generation, and he was quite accurate when he said of himself: "By my Physical Constitution I am but an ordinary Man."[6]

But if Adams was of average height, there was an air of softness about him, and he was overweight, though he would be accurately described as portly rather than terribly obese. His corpulence caused him to move awkwardly, and that clumsiness, in conjunction with the pallidness that arose from his habitual indoor regimen, gave him the look of a man in poor health. Nor did his red, watery eyes, the result in all likelihood of a chronic allergy problem, contribute to an image of robustness.

Adams pondered the success of such diverse men as George Washington, James Otis, John Dickinson, Patrick Henry, and Samuel Adams. For some, he thought, it was a posture, a contrivance, or an artful countenance that enabled them to lead men; for others, a fiery eloquence. He never believed that he possessed those qualities. Instead, he saw himself as slow to come to a decision and as languid in his actions, a man of no particular distinction. He knew, too, that had the extraordinary events of his era never occurred, he would have remained a provincial lawyer, unknown beyond Braintree and Boston. "Times alone have destined me to Fame," he once remarked, adding as an afterthought that hard work—not "Sloth, Sleep, and littleness"—had assisted in his rise.[7]

Adams struck many people as vain, irritable, irascible, supercilious, and even tactless. He maintained a stiffly formal and aloof demeanor, what one acquaintance called a habitually "ceremonious" manner. Adams acknowledged that this indeed was his mien, although he thought it characteristic of all New Englanders. There was also a "natural restraint" about him, according to one friend, which was often mistaken by casual acquaintances for an air of withering snobbery and scornfulness. Abigail once scolded him for his tendency to indulge in "intolerable forbidding expecting Silence[s]" while in the midst of a conversation; "tis impossible for a Stranger to be tranquil in your presence," she cautioned. Adams was well aware of his idiosyncratic ways. As a young man he had repeatedly excoriated himself for having acted with too much constraint and formality. "My motions are stiff and uneasy," he would scold; he often vowed never again to exhibit so "stiff a face and air and tone of voice" while with his friends. If he felt ill at ease with close acquaintances, he was terribly uncomfortable with strangers. "There are very few People in this World, with whom I can bear to converse," he once admitted. He could talk about business with colleagues, he said, "But I am never happy in their Company. This had made me a recluse." Social gatherings were maddeningly disagreeable ordeals for him. He lacked the facility for making small talk; he refused to flatter others; he was not in the habit of swearing or telling off-color tales; because he did not like to talk about horses and dogs, music and women, he once said, he could think of little to say. When he did talk, he could be quite tactless. No one was more aware than him of this shortcoming. "I am obliged to be constantly on my Guard," he admitted, lest he act inconsiderately. But his vigilance did not always succeed. To his own surprise, the "Heat [seemed to] burst forth at Times," he admitted, and before he realized what had occurred he had spoken again with brusque insensitivity.[8]

Adams's proclivity for truculence and curtness probably emerged early. Uncertain of his abilities and laboring under an exaggerated sense of inadequacy, he probably fashioned such an aggressive manner as a defense mechanism. His early diary makes it clear that he consciously modeled himself upon elements within the styles of Gridley, Otis, and Thacher, and perhaps even of young colleagues such as Sewall or Robert Treat Paine, as he searched for the persona that might facilitate his success. His stiff, ordered comportment and dignified carriage might have impressed judges and juries with his maturity and sagacity, while his cold, curmudgeonlike manner was useful in keeping others at arm's length, far enough removed that they were unlikely to discover any blemishes on close scrutiny. Once a peer acknowledged his superiority or equality, however, Adams usually abandoned these annoying habits. His wife, of course, recognized his behavior for what it was, and Dr. Rush, who initially had been put off by this "cold and reserved" man, soon discovered a humorous, satirical, even self-effacing side to Adams.

Indeed, if the first impression that Adams conveyed was that of one who was cold and contemptuous of others, he was not a man without friends. He claimed, probably correctly, to have had many close companions as a lad, and as a collegian he established close relationships that were to last a lifetime. In addition, despite the adversarial nature of his work as an attorney, he developed a friendly bond with several fellow lawyers; even as a congressman, he made the acquaintance of men who considered him an ardent friend. In fact, he once remarked that he had differed politically and philosophically with many men without experiencing "the smallest personal altercation" and without the slightest "diminution of esteem." It was not easy to get close to him, but those who did broach the barriers he erected discovered in Adams a basic decency that earned their respect. Moreover, once Adams acquired a friend, he had the felicitous habit of maintaining his ties with the individual; he was not the sort to use acquaintances, then cast them aside when they were no longer of use. By nature a rather self-contained and solitary individual, Adams enjoyed his privacy and solitude, but he sometimes relished the company of others, especially if he could surmount his ingrained sense of guilt at taking the time from his work or study in order to engage in social amenities. Thus, a club such as Sodalitas could be justified, as could the endless round of dinners while Congress was in session.[9]

Adams was most at ease in the company of men. Aside from Mercy Warren, an outgoing woman who obviously luxuriated in the male world of politics, he appears never to have been close to any female outside his immediate family. Some contemporaries once compared him with Washington, who never felt more comfortable than when he mixed with attractive women. Adams, they said, was just the opposite; indeed, it was whispered that he did not know how to talk with the ladies. When he learned of the gossip he huffily dismissed such talk, but late in life he privately conceded that those observers had been correct. He had no idea how to conduct a conversation with a female.[10]

In some respects Adams's views on women were advanced for the time. He entrusted Abigail with enormous responsibilities, more akin to those exercised by the mistress of a southern plantation than by a New England farmer's wife. He expressed his admiration for Catherine Macauley, the radical English polemicist and historian, whom he regarded as every bit as talented as any man he had ever met. It was his view, too, that women were "better than Men in General." Females were more virtuous and clearly more observant than males, he once remarked, and he added that throughout history it was rare to find a successful man who had not benefited from the assistance of a talented woman. He listened carefully to the advice that Abigail proffered, even if he did not always heed it, and during his protracted absences he valued above all others her accounts of conditions in his home province.[11]

In most ways, however, Adams was every inch a man of his times. His life-style was quite conventional for a man of his station. He remained in the church in which he was raised, faithfully attending worship services each week. His political philosophy was anything but daring or innovative. He accepted un-critically the prevailing customs regarding intercourse between the various social classes. There were limits, too, to the changes he could envision with regard to women. For instance, with independence near, Abigail had written to him to suggest that Congress should "Remember the Ladies" as it discussed the rights of Americans. Because men were "Naturally Tyrannical," she said, women must be protected from men's "unlimited power." Her husband did not take her remarks seriously. "I cannot but laugh" at such notions, he responded, as he gently chided her for being "so saucy."[12]

The one area in which Adams somewhat broke with convention concerned slavery. While slave ownership was not widespread in the northern provinces, many of Adams's prominent acquaintances, men such as James Otis, John Hancock, and Benjamin Franklin, owned slaves; in fact, even Parson William Smith, Abigail's father, was the owner of two slaves. John and Abigail could have afforded to purchase a slave or two as well, an investment that might have resulted in a financial saving when compared to the cost of free labor. But both thought the practice immoral and contradictory to Christian principles. Abigail best expressed their objections. She wished slavery would be banished in Massachusetts, she said. It was a system for the "daily robbing and plunder-ing from those who have as good a right to freedom as we have." For Adams, however, the matter was a private affair. As a lawyer he occasionally defended slaves, but as a politician he made no effort to loosen the shackles of those in bondage. Like virtually every other revolutionary leader, Adams subordinated the issue of slavery to the quest for independence. In fact, he appears to have been overly zealous in guarding against the intrusion of slavery into public councils. He urged the defeat of a bill in the Massachusetts legislature that would have abolished slavery; "We have Causes enough of Jealousy Discord and Division," he said. He brushed aside other proposals for the emancipation of slaves and he opposed the use of black soldiers in the Continental army, suggesting that such a practice would make southerners "run out of their Wits at the least Hint of such a measure." There is no evidence that he ever spoke out on the issue of slavery in any national forum or that he ever entered into a dialogue on the subject with any of his southern friends.[13]

Perhaps as with most people at most times, ambivalence characterized Adams's outlook toward some orthodoxies of his time. Perhaps he shared with Abigail a feeling of outrage at much of the discrimination practiced by society against its free black inhabitants. When officials objected to the enrollment in a local school of a black youngster who worked as a servant in the Adams household, Abigail bristled, saying the lad was as entitled to an education as any white boy. "I have not thought it any disgrace to my self to take him into my parlour and teach him both to read and write," she added. John did not object to her defiant stand. On the other hand, both John and Abigail were products of their age and both unthinkingly accepted some of the intolerant ways that prevailed. Abigail recoiled in "disgust & horrour" at witnessing a black man touch a white woman when she attended a performance of *Othello*. John laughed at and ridiculed some of the practices of Quakers and Roman Catholics, and he once remarked, "[I believe] the Hebrews have done more to civilize man than any other nation. . . [but] I cannot say that I love the Jews very much."[14]

Adams was a very private person. In fact, he characterized himself as reclusive by nature. All his life he adhered to the habits he had learned in his youth on the family farm, customarily rising about four A.M. and retiring at ten or later in the evening. As a congressman he used the still dark early morning hours for reading, tended to his public duties thereafter, and returned to his chamber in the early evening to look after his extensive correspondence. The hours he devoted to his correspondence would have exhausted many men, for he not only wrote numerous letters but wrote many twice, once in rough form, then again in a final, clean state. During the nearly eight months of 1776 that he lived in Philadelphia, Adams is known to have written at least 190 letters. Approximately 40 percent of these missives—roughly two letters a week— were written to Abigail; many others went to relatives and old friends, but most went out to public officials, especially to military figures. Curiously, during his long absence in Philadelphia he appears to have written only once to his surviving brother, Peter Boylston, and never to his mother, now, in 1777, sixty-seven years old and living not far from Abigail.[15]

When Adams found the time to read, he sought to stay abreast of the news by reading both newspapers and newly published pamphlets. He could purchase several newspapers in Philadelphia, and he had access to the Boston press through Abigail's mailings. For handy reference and to help pass the long, lonely hours away from home, he brought some of his favorite books from Braintree. His correspondence suggests that he must have had works by Alexander Pope, John Milton, Joseph Addison, Jonathan Swift, and Shakespeare at his fingertips, as well several volumes penned by the most revered political philosophers. The bulk of his library remained at home, of course, and consisted principally of his legal books, numerous histories, some theological tracts, and a few novels and works of poetry, although he once admitted that upon reaching middle age, poetry no longer held any fascination for him.[16]

The books that Adams devoured were typical fare for a well-educated man of his time. The areas in which he displayed little or no interest, however, set him apart from many of his activist colleagues in this Age of Enlightenment. Nowhere was this more true than in the realm of science. To men like Jefferson and Franklin, scientific inquiry was not merely an engaging diversion, it was a quest to know nature so that man could harmonize with it. Men of this temperament read and wrote about natural history, and experimented, observed, and sought to explain natural phenomena. Ultimately their investigations led them to establish schools and libraries and scientific societies; their curiosity also caused them to examine—and in many instances to repudiate—much of the conventional, until in the course of prying open their new vistas, they often remodeled themselves.

By contrast, Adams never participated in a scientific expedition, never tinkered with scientific exploration at home, never displayed any inclination to practice scientific agriculture on his farm, nor ever evinced much interest in scientific pursuits in his correspondence. Apparently, Adams did not possess the innate curiosity that led men such as Franklin and Jefferson, and even Washington, to probe the mysteries of the weather or to investigate land forms and soil conditions encountered in their travels. Nor did Adams display much interest in artistic expression. He played no musical instrument and unlike Washington, Franklin, and Jefferson, who purchased instruments for the youngsters in their homes, Adams seems never to have encouraged his children to develop an appreciation for the art. He did not regularly attend concerts—in fact, there is no evidence that he ever attended the theater or any musical performance before he resided in Paris—and he seems not to have been moved even by the graceful, lusty hymns of his church. Adams was never a collector of art, and, indeed, he exhibited no interest in the achievements of the great painters of his age. The only works of art that were the least useful, he said, were those that provided moral instruction; he absolutely detested landscape painting. Of architecture he said little. On his initial visit to New York he was impressed by the cost of the structures that he viewed, not their style, and it was Philadelphia's streets—not its buildings—that most struck him upon his arrival in that city in 1774. His uneasiness with his limitations might be gleaned from the comment that he made in 1780: "I must study Politicks and

War that my sons may have the liberty to study Mathematicks and Philosophy. My sons ought to study Geography, natural History, Naval Architecture, navigation, Commerce and Agriculture, in order to give their children *a right* to study Painting, Poetry, Musick, Architecutre, Statuary, Tapestry, and Porcelaine."[17]

Adams spoke of his Braintree farm with love and affection, but he was never a true farmer. "My Gardens and my Farm, are complaining of Neglect, and Disorder," he acknowledged one spring long before politics intruded upon his time, not the sort admission likely to be heard by a genuine son of the soil; he even complained of the inroads made upon his time by the necessity to tend his fields. During his painfully long absences, Adams longed to see his "Grass and Blossoms and Corn," but "above all except the Wife and Children," he admitted candidly, "I want to see my Books." The farm was merely of utilitarian value to him.[18] It was a refuge, a retreat from the pressures of the outside world, as well as a source of security for his old age and a means to a supplemental income.

Without realizing it, John Adams had grown to be a one-dimensional man. As a young man, he had spoken often of achieving recognition. He had succeeded, far beyond what he must have dreamed possible during his days as a Worcester Latin master or while he struggled as a young lawyer in Braintree. He stood as the "first man" in the Congress, and his understanding of political theory was lauded as unsurpassed among activists in the colonial resistance movement. But his achievements had come at a high cost. By his middle years he was a man with little time for his family, a man given to incessant labor who disavowed virtually all earthly pleasures and distractions, an individual unable to function in certain social settings, a restricted human being whose goal was the solitary pursuit of self-fulfillment, a fulfillment that could only be realized through a popular recognition that John Adams was indeed a great man.

When Adams rode out from Braintree that bleak January morning, his destination was not Philadelphia but Baltimore, the new and temporary home of Congress. Accompanied by his servant and James Lovell, a new Massachusetts delegate, Adams was compelled to traverse a different route than he had taken in October, for a series of military reverses late in 1776 had left eastern New Jersey in British hands. Indeed, the redcoats had pushed so deeply into New Jersey that the jittery congressmen had forsaken Philadelphia for a safer haven in Maryland.[19]

Traveling in extremely cold and inclement weather, the worst he had ever experienced, Adams said, the party rode to Hartford, thence to the Hudson and across to Hackensack, from there to the western edge of New Jersey, and ultimately into Pennsylvania at Easton. They skirted Philadelphia, passed through Wilmington, and finally, on the twenty-fourth day out of Braintree, reached Baltimore. The uneasiness he felt at this separation from his family was obvious. He had rarely written home in the course of his previous travels. This time he sent Abigail seven letters before he reached his destination.[20]

Adams found Baltimore pleasant and attractive. It was about half the size of Boston, and roughly one in ten of its residents was enslaved, but the free inhabitants were "all good Whiggs," he reported. The cost of everything was "monstrous," however, and, only a month after his arrival, Congress took advantage of an improved military situation to return to Philadelphia.[21]

By the time Congress moved, Adams once again was deeply enmeshed in his congressional duties. He sat on twenty-six committees, chairing eight of them, during this session, but as in the previous year it was the Board of War that consumed most of his energies.[22] Much had transpired in the war during the roughly one hundred days he had been absent from Congress. The United States had suffered one catastrophe, the loss of Fort Washington on Manhattan Island, a terrible defeat resulting in the loss of more than three thousand men, mostly as prisoners of war. Charles Lee, the general above all others in whom Adams expressed confidence, had been taken captive as well, he by his own haphazard and indifferent behavior.

The new year had been ushered in on a bright note, however. After a summer and fall of indecision, General Washington at last had acted with boldness. In two separate strikes, at Trenton and at Princeton, he had seized the initiative and in masterful operations had inflicted stunning blows upon the adversary. The British and their mercenary allies lost nearly fifteen hundred men in the two engagements.

For Adams, the return to Congress was tantamount to a return to the war front, and his old anxieties immediately reappeared, beginning with fresh worries over his eyesight. Soon, he once again rehearsed all the familiar arguments about soldiering. In one breath he lauded soldiers and exalted the character of men molded by martial experience, but alternately—and without much success—he sought to persuade himself that he did not wish to bear arms. "The Pride and Pomp of War . . . have no Charms for me," he exclaimed in a letter to Abigail, although in the margin of the rough draft of that missive he noted: "But is not the Heart deceitfull above all Things?"[23] Unconvinced by such disclaimers, he fell back upon a familiar tactic. He next sought to convince himself that his burdens matched, perhaps even surpassed, those borne by America's soldiery. Not only had his congressional service resulted in the destruction of his health, he claimed, but it had robbed him of life's every pleasure. His was a life of misery, he said. He was oppressed with work, compelled to live "meanly and poorly," subjected to a life that he hated. "Oh that I could wander, upon Penns Hill, and in the Meadows and Mountains . . . free from Care! But this is a Felicity too great for me."[24]

Whatever his concerns over the role he played in this conflict, Adams was pleased with the course of the war. Throughout 1777, in fact, he radiated confidence. If Great Britain had been unable to defeat America in the first two years of the war, he remarked, it now was even less likely to put down the rebellion. Moreover, while London crowed about the acquisition of additional German mercenaries, Adams correctly predicted that their numbers would be insignificant. Finally, he had concluded that Sir William Howe, the British commander, was an ineffective leader. Though brave, Howe not only was a laggard and a bumbler, but, worse, he was a profligate and a vain, avaricious scapegrace "doomed to defeat."[25]

Adams was also optimistic that Britain's principal European rivals soon would enter the contest. France or Spain, or both, would seize upon Britain's weak and overextended situation to inaugurate a conflagration in Europe. In short order, too, he reasoned, the United States might commence a lucrative trade with the French, as well as with Prussia and Holland, commerce that would include life-sustaining military supplies.[26]

Adams naturally felt some apprehension as the campaign of 1777 loomed. Recruiting lagged throughout the early months of that year; indeed, to his mortification the New England states brought up the rear in meeting their quotas. He railed at the "Lassitude and Torpor" that had seized the region and, vitriol dripping from his pen, he wondered if all "New England Men [were] Sons of Sloth and Fear."[27] The leadership in the army disturbed him as well. He did not question Washington, whom he valued as a brave and trustworthy commander and as a man who set "a fine Example" by his austere and sacrificial habits, but his patience was exhausted with some officers. Were the decision his alone, he would not have tolerated Schuyler, Putnam, Spencer, or Heath for another day. The army would be better off, he once remarked, if Congress evaluated all the general officers at the end of each year, elevating those who had distinguished themselves and sending the others home. He even suggested that it might be good policy to occasionally "shoot a General." That would get everyone's attention. "We must trifle no more," he demanded. "We have suffered too many Disgraces to pass unexpiated. Every Disgrace must be wiped off."[28]

His position as chairman of the Board of War afforded Adams a unique vantage point from which to observe the course of the war. Earlier than any other civilian, in all likelihood, he was able to accurately anticipate Britain's strategy for 1777. Early in the year he predicted that Howe would seek to take Philadelphia; he also presumed that a redcoat army would descend on the United States from Canada, hoping, as in 1776, to seize the Hudson River and isolate the New England sates from their brethren to the south. From the beginning, he advised Abigail that Boston was safe, at least for that year. "You may now sit under your own Vine, and have none to make you afraid," he reassured her. Correct about the safety of Massachusetts, Adams nonetheless erred in his estimate about when the fighting would begin. He expected the British to begin offensive operations in the early spring, but April and May came and went, and Howe remained nestled in New York. Even into July,

Howe had not stirred. Nor had Washington been active, to Adams's consider-
able annoyment. "It is high Time for Us to abandon this execrable defensive
Plan," he railed. "It will be our Ruin if We do not." As week after week passed,
Adams grew more puzzled, wondering if both armies might "lounge away the
Remainder of the Campaign."[29]

While the year slowly oozed away, Adams remained busily engaged in
Philadelphia. Upon returning from Baltimore, he had found an apartment on
Walnut Street, a short walk from the State House. The surroundings were
pleasant, and the company of his landlady's family—which included three
children—as well as the company of old friends such as Samuel Adams, who
lodged down the street, all helped mitigate his loneliness. But the novelty of
his congressional duties long since had turned to tedium, to long days of
tiresome debates and wearisome committee meetings. Nor did Philadelphia
offer much relief. Once a lively, energizing city, it now was a somber and
lusterless place. The affluent revolutionaries, those families who in earlier days
had lavishly entertained the visiting congressmen, had moved into the countryside, hoping to escape before Howe arrived. The Quakers had stayed on, of
course, but Adams found them to be "as dull as Beetles."[30]

Tiresome as his routine was, the Board of War assignment occasionally
thrust Adams into a new undertaking. He attended ship launchings, visited
foundries and ordnance facilities, and one day in June, accompanied by Generals Benedict Arnold and Philippe du Coudray, one of a growing number of
French volunteers who arrived that spring and summer, Adams inspected the
fortresses and the *chevaux de frise,* sunken booby traps, designed to prevent the
British fleet from using the Delaware River should an attack on Philadelphia ever occur. For all his talk about the need to fashion a callous, steel-
like wartime character, he scrupulously avoided the public execution of a
convicted Tory spy, and when his committee work necessitated a visit to an
army hospital and cemetery, he was shaken by the experience, admitting to
Abigail that the experience plunged him into a mood of black despair and
melancholy.[31]

But those were mere interludes in his more customary activities, a dreary,
repetitive routine to which he could see no end. Unlike the past two years, he
did not tantalize Abigail with notices that he might soon be able to return
home. Indeed, he informed her that he would not get to Braintree before the
end of the year, if then. That realization only made it more difficult for Adams,
who experienced more than usual distress during this long absence; for the
first time since the early years of his marriage, Abigail was pregnant. "My
Mind runs upon my Family," he often noted with obvious sincerity. "My Mind
is Anxious, and my Heart in Pain for my dearest Friend," he added. "I wait
with Impatience for Monday Morning, when the Post is to arrive."[32]

The early weeks of Abigail's pregnancy were uneventful, but, by late January, she had begun to experience some accompanying illness. Still, her health remained as strong as in her previous pregnancies, and her spirits often soared. On occasion she experienced "sensations of tenderness which are better felt than expressed," she wrote. Her "situation," as she called it, also served as "a constant remembrance of an absent Friend." But April, a cold gray month in Braintree, began with Abigail in a gloomy mood, and ten days later her moroseness turned into a bottomless depression when a neighbor and friend died bearing her child. For a time she considered pleading with her husband to return home, an urge that she mentioned to him, perhaps hoping that it would fetch him to her side. She also candidly told him that she was left to her fate in "Solitary confinement," a happenstance, she added, that even most animals avoided. But in the end she bore her isolation stoically, viewing her suffering as a patriotic sacrifice.[33]

"I look forward to the middle of july with more anxiety than I can describe," she wrote her husband about six weeks before the likely date of birth. Strangely, Adams's return letters displayed little sensitivity. His missives of that spring rarely inquired about her health and were virtually devoid of solace. He avoided comment altogether when he received her most disheartened letters, instead packing his responses with a catalogue of his own woes and ills, ailments that never failed to elicit consoling remarks from Abigail.[34]

The closest that Adams was able to come to an expression of endearment appeared in his letter of June 21. The missive began: "My dearest Friend." His first letter to Abigail upon leaving Braintree in January had begun: "My dear." No letter during the six months that followed contained a salutation. Abigail, anxious and despondent, was overcome by even this meager show of affection. "That one single expression dwelt upon my mind and played about my Heart," she responded, and she went on at some length about the "tender soothings" of her husband's communication.[35]

A month before the anticipated birth date, Abigail fell into a renewed depression. Sleep came with difficulty. Gripped by "melancholy reflections," she sat up through long, warm nights trying not to think about death, reading and rereading old letters from her husband, seeking to remember earlier, more joyful times.[36]

Beginning about the end of June, Abigail once again began to feel sickly, and during the evening of July 8 she experienced a "shaking fit." The next morning she wrote to her husband of her apprehension, believing the child was lost. For a time her physician disagreed, but within a week Abigail's fears were confirmed.[37]

"Never in my whole Life, was my Heart affected with such Emotions," Adams wrote upon receiving the sad tidings from Braintree. His next letter, written two days later, began: "I am sorry to find by your late Letter what indeed I expected to hear, that my Farm wants manure." He did not inquire about Abigail's health or spirits.[38]

Two days before Adams learned of the death of their unborn baby, the news reached Philadelphia that the British army was on the move. Although July was nearly spent, the campaign of 1777 was at last under way. General Howe had packed his army into the sweltering holds of an armada in New York harbor, prepared to sail for a destination that Washington could only guess. Some thought he would take his army to New England and seek to link it with a British force under Gen. John Burgoyne, who had just begun an invasion of New York from Canada; others thought he would sail for Charleston or Philadelphia. Days of uncertainty passed. Not until August 23 did Adams know for sure. Howe's fleet had been sighted in the Chesapeake. Philadelphia was to be his target.[39]

Washington brought his soldiers south to defend the capital, and, with Adams a part of the large throng that watched, the Continental army paraded through Philadelphia on August 24. As the inevitable clash neared, Adams radiated optimism. He had been impressed by the sight of the army. Howe "will make but a pitifull Figure," he predicted. So long as Washington could maintain his army, the British would remain empty-handed. If the redcoats suffered a drubbing on the battlefield, Britain would be ruined. If Howe took Philadelphia, what would he have gained? Possession of the city "would employ his whole Force by Sea and Land to keep it," Adams prophesied. Caught up in the carnival frenzy that permeated the war zone, Adams spoke of his "strong Inclination" to fight. But that was idle talk, and he knew it. "If Howe comes here I shall run away" with the other congressmen, he finally admitted. "We are too brittle ware you know to stand the Dashing of Balls and Bombs."[40]

On September 11 the two armies finally collided on the banks of the Brandywine Creek, a few miles west of Philadelphia. Howe got the best of it, although Washington's army was still intact as twilight forced an end to the encounter. A week later the British slipped unopposed across the Schuylkill. Now there was nothing to stop the redcoats' advance on Philadelphia. General Washington hurriedly sent a messenger to alert the congressmen, most of whom were aroused from their beds in the still dark hours of early morning; they were told to pack and leave. Adams traveled on horseback to Trenton with Henry Marchant of Rhode Island, where they lingered for two nights. On the twenty-seventh, the day after the British at last entered Philadelphia, Congress assembled at Lancaster, but three days later it moved again, this time to York, a German-American hamlet west of the Susquehanna, about seventy-five miles from Philadelphia.[41]

"The Prospect is chilling, on every Side. Gloomy, dark, melancholly, and dispiriting. When and where will the light spring up?," Adams wrote in his diary just after the Battle of Brandywine. The light that he longed for came a month later. In mid-October, sixteen days after Adams reached York, Burgoyne surrendered his invasion army to an American force commanded by Horatio Gates. The British lost fifty-eight hundred men at Saratoga. At once, Adams knew that a great turning point in the War of Independence had been reached.[42]

The dark clouds vanished immediately. New England now faced no danger, and though Howe had entered Philadelphia, a long bitter fight remained before he secured the Delaware River, his lifeline to Great Britain. Adams was secretly overjoyed that Washington had not scored a great victory. Not that he was hostile to Washington; indeed, he defended the Virginian when Dr. Rush wrote him disparaging Washington's abilities and hinting that Gates would be a better choice to command the Continental army. "The Idea that any one Man alone can save Us, is too silly . . . to harbour for a Moment," Adams retorted. He praised Washington's courage and skill and pointed out that Gates had been more fortunate to fight Burgoyne's army, the weaker of the two forces fielded by Britain in 1777. Nevertheless, Adams was delighted at Washington's failure to score a magisterial victory, an event that might have produced a dangerous degree of "Idolatry, and Adulation." Now, he added, General Washington can be thought "to be wise, virtuous, and good, without thinking him a Deity or a saviour."[43]

Adams had once written that he would lay down his congressional responsibilities when he could "leave this Station with Honour." That time would come, he added, when "Our Affairs are in a fine prosperous Train." By midautumn, 1777, that time, at last, had come. Although the tribulations of the war were far from over, the news from the battlefield had been good; moreover, Congress was about to complete its work on the nation's first constitution, the Articles of Confederation. A congressional committee, of which Adams was not a member, had prepared a draft proposal in the summer of 1776, and from time to time thereafter Congress debated the matter. Adams characterized the establishment of the national government as "the most intricate, the most important, the most dangerous and delicate Business of all," but, with the Board of War taking up virtually all of his time, he played little or no role in shaping the constitution, although he did postpone his departure for Braintree until Congress had very nearly completed its work on this matter. He was untroubled by the fact that the new central government would be weak— almost powerless, in fact. When Adams thought of politics, it was from the perspective of what a government might do *to* the people, not what it could do *for* the people. A system of state sovereignty was fine. Liberty could be better safeguarded at that level. On November 17 Congress completed its work on the Articles; six days earlier, almost ten months to the day since he had left home, Adams had set out on horseback for New England, accompanied on this ride by Samuel Adams.[44]

Home! Home, at last. But for how long? Before departing York, Adams knew that Congress was likely to recall Silas Deane, one of its diplomats in Paris. He knew, too, that many in Congress wished to appoint him as Deane's replacement; over the past eighteen months many of his colleagues had spoken with him about diplomatic assignments. It was the role that some observers, including his good friend Mercy Warren, had predicted he would eventually be called upon to undertake.[45]

As he made the long, weary ride home, Adams must have known that the question was not whether he would be offered the diplomatic post but whether he would accept the assignment. And on that point, there could be little mystery.

PART THREE

*

Safe and Glorious in the Harbour of Peace

CHAPTER 11

*

A Man of No Consequence

JOHN ADAMS LATER RECOLLECTED that he had come home to stay. He told Abigail that it was his intention to refuse reelection to Congress. That much was true. However, he did not mention that he might be selected as an emissary to France.[1]

Adams remained at home barely two weeks, surrounded by his "Parcell of chattering Boys and Girls." (Since he had only one daughter, he evidently included Abigail among the females who were "chattering" at him). On occasion he escaped into Boston to meet with important persons in the city, and he made a point of speaking with some of his neighbors in Braintree, learning, not surprisingly, that the subjects of taxation and the scarcity of essential commodities were the most important matters on their minds. It was a "blissful" time, he said, but the felicitous interlude ended on the fifteenth day. He set out on horseback for Portsmouth, New Hampshire, to represent a client in a maritime case. Adams's decision to take the case has been seen by some scholars as proof that he planned to return to the private sector.[2] It can as easily be interpreted as a step toward putting his financial affairs in order before he embarked on what was certain to be quite a protracted absence.

Adams had been gone from Braintree only a few hours when letters arrived from the president of Congress and from James Lovell, a delegate to Congress from Massachusetts. Fearing the communiques might contain urgent tidings, Abigail ripped them open. What she read was startling. Two weeks after his departure from York, Congress had elected her husband to replace Silas Deane. He was being asked to journey to France. Lovell's accompanying letter pleaded for Adams's acceptance. Dr. Franklin was old, and some doubted Arthur Lee's capabilities, he wrote. And, he added, "We want one man of inflexible Integrity" among the United States deputies in Paris.[3]

Abigail was stunned. All her hopes and plans were in jeopardy. This would mean still another separation. Moreover, if public service in Philadelphia had necessitated absences of nearly a year, how long would her husband be in Europe? Indeed, would he ever return? A transatlantic crossing was no trifling matter. A voyage made in wartime was even more perilous. And what of the family finances? Already they were reduced to a "very loose condition." What of the children? Would the children grow to adulthood without knowing their father?[4]

Abigail did not forward the correspondence to her husband. Instead, she wrote letters of anguish to others. She knew John would accept the appointment, she told Lovell, and she raged at him for his complicity in the congressional decision, virtually exclaiming that she could never forgive his act. "[How] could you contrive to rob me of all my happiness," she demanded. This "is the hardest conflict I ever endured," she told another. Then she turned to Mercy Warren for guidance, perhaps because it was no secret that Mercy had been unwilling to surrender her husband to the state.[5]

Advice from Plymouth arrived after John returned from New Hampshire, and it probably was not what Abigail expected to hear. Although the separation would be a difficult trial, Mercy Warren wrote, Abigail could take comfort in the knowledge that she was married to a man whose "Learning, patriotism And prudence" was so universally recognized. Ultimately, too, she went on, Abigail and the children would profit from this sacrifice, for not only would John's public and private careers be enhanced, but, she seemed to hint, in the long years ahead he would treasure a wife who had assisted in his fulfillment.[6]

Adams knew of his appointment before he returned home, having learned the news from a vacationing New Hampshire congressman. One can only guess at the anguished scene that must have occurred upon his return to Braintree. One thing only is clear. Within twenty-four hours of his arrival, Abigail had consented to his acceptance of the diplomatic mission, but she also had made clear her intention of accompanying him to Europe; Adams, however, was opposed to having her and the children face the multiple dangers of an ocean crossing.[7]

Over the next few weeks the issue was resolved. John prevailed. Abigail would remain at home. The danger of her capture on the High Seas was too great, and the likelihood that she would be subjected to merciless treatment while in British captivity was too considerable, he argued, to permit his consent. More likely, he feared the decline—perhaps the loss—of his little farm if she also was absent from its premises. John did wish for company, however, and he longed to be with his eldest son, now ten, a lad whom he had hardly known for the past three and a half years; John Quincy, bright and eager to learn, would accompany him, John decided.[8]

Forty-five days remained before the *Boston,* a twenty-four gun frigate, would sail, time for Adams to put his affairs in order and to acquire and pack the many provisions he and his son would require in a strange land. It afforded time, too, to reflect on the diplomatic exigencies that he would likely encounter in Paris and Versailles.

The American government did not begin to realistically confront the diplomatic ramifications of its struggle with Great Britain until a full year after the commencement of hostilities. Until then, Congress had done nothing more than dispatch an agent to Paris. That agent, Silas Deane, was directed to purchase goods with which to bribe the Indians into neutrality or cooperation, and to seek from the French government outlays of arms, munitions, and uniforms for the Continental army. He arrived in Paris in the summer of 1776.

Deane's mission was not entirely a shot in the dark, however. France had watched closely the vertiginous American protests since the days of the Stamp Act upheavals. When war erupted, the French Foreign Minister, Charles Gravier, Comte de Vergennes, not only hinted to American businessmen in Europe that France might be willing to help the colonists, but in the fall of 1775 he sent a special agent, M. Achard Bonvouloir, to Philadelphia to encourage the American war effort and to intimate that French assistance was possible. At the same moment, Vergennes, through intermediaries, undertook a campaign to convince Louis XVI that France could benefit from Britain's woes and that it should secretly assist Washington's army. The French monarch demurred, at least until the sentiments of his ally, Spain, could be ascertained. But when Spain approved assistance to the American army—largely in the hope that Britain and the colonists would bleed one another to death, enabling Madrid to benefit from their exhaustion—Louis consented to Vergennes's wishes.

However, because the French navy was unprepared for war, neither Louis nor Vergennes gave any thought to open assistance, a belligerent act certain to result in a British declaration of war. Instead, it was decided that the goods would be sent clandestinely, through the dodge of a private and, of course, fictitious commercial enterprise, the so-called Roderigue Hortalez and Company. France's decision was reached even before Deane arrived in Paris; shortly thereafter, the windfall was in his hands. The first shipments of French goods, mostly arms and gunpowder, were speeding across the Atlantic as Washington's little army retreated across New Jersey in the fall of 1776, nearly a year and a half before Adams sailed on the *Boston*.[9]

Deane should have stopped with this triumph. Instead, he received legions of ambitious Frenchmen, mostly career militarists who, whether from adventurism or avidity, saw the war in America as an opportunity not to be missed. He soon erred egregiously. Without congressional authorization, he commissioned four French army officers as major generals in the Continental army and casually awarded lesser rank to several other Gallic soldiers. To put it mildly, Deane's impudence aroused bitterness among America's officers. In autumn 1777 two of General Washington's favorites, Nathanael Greene and Henry Knox, threatened to resign rather than submit to the indignity of being outranked by French officers who had only recently arrived in America. The crisis in the army was costly to Deane, but suspicion about his financial undertakings while in Paris proved to be his undoing. Although allegations of his peculation remained unproven, he had become expendable, because in the fall of 1776 Congress had added Franklin and Arthur Lee to its diplomatic team in Paris. In November 1777 Deane was recalled. One week later Adams was elected as his replacement.[10]

The selection of Adams was not due to mere happenstance. He had been one of the first congressmen to give any thought to America's diplomatic needs. During the first autumn of the conflict, he had reached an important conclusion. The colonists' military success, he came to understand, was contingent upon expanding American trade; otherwise, Washington's army would never possess the resources needed to overcome Britain's powerful army. But no foreign power, he also knew, would engage in commerce with America—and thus risk war with Great Britain—unless the colonists were "determined to fight it out with G.B. to the last." That is, until America declared independence, trade with the major nations of Europe was unlikely. Over the next few months, Adams's views along these lines crystallized. By spring 1776 he was openly advocating on the floor of Congress the proposition that independence was necessary in order to establish trade and that trade was essential for the actual attainment of independence. Moreover, he urged the negotiation of a commercial treaty with France.[11]

Adams's appeals aroused a furious response among the more cautious delegates. In order to procure French aid, America would be compelled to make damaging concessions, some asserted. Others feared precisely what Spain hoped for. Madrid and Paris "will rejoice to see Britain and America, wasting each other," they warned. Once again, Adams played the leading role in attempting to quell such fears. "I wish for nothing but Commerce, a mere Marine Treaty with them," he responded. "And this they will never grant, untill We make the Declaration [of Independence], and this I think they cannot refuse, after We have made it."[12]

Others agreed with Adams. The resolutions offered by Richard Henry Lee of Virginia on June 7 urged not only independence, but treaties of foreign assistance. Congress quickly appointed committees to consider each issue. Adams, an outspoken advocate both of independence and of a commercial treaty with France, was named to each panel; Franklin, Dickinson, Benjamin Harrison of Virginia, and Robert Morris of Pennsylvania were appointed with him "to prepare a plan of treaties to be proposed to foreign powers."[13] The members immediately urged Adams to prepare the draft statement, turning to him, in part, because Harrison and Morris were relative newcomers, Franklin customarily eschewed such work, and Dickinson opposed independence, without which, of course, a treaty was impossible; principally, however, Adams was their choice because he had clearly given the matter the greatest thought.

While Jefferson labored over the Declaration of Independence, Adams worked on what would later be called the Model Treaty. In the preparation of his draft, he utilized three printed compilations of English treaties and commercial laws, one a volume lent him by Franklin containing the trade agreements concluded between France and England in 1713 following what Americans called Queen Anne's War. Primarily, Adams relied on these references to assure the proper—or, at least, the customary European—form of treaty provisions.[14]

The Model Treaty, which the committee agreed to in mid-July and which Congress adopted in September 1776, sanctioned a commercial agreement with France. It contained no provision permitting political or military ties with Paris. According to this plan, the ports of the two nations would be opened and each partner guaranteed the right of never having to pay higher import duties than that required of the natives. France would be asked to renounce all claims to Canada and Florida, but, should it enter the war against Great Britain, it would be permitted acquisitions in the West Indies. French fishing rights were to be restricted to the waters specified in the Treaty of Paris of 1763, the accord that had ended the French and Indian War. If possible, France was to protect American commerce in the Mediterranean from the Algerine pirates that preyed off the Barbary coast. It was stipulated that France was not to charge duties on molasses exported from the Caribbean. The doctrine that "free ships make free goods" was to be incorporated in every treaty. Therefore, each side was to recognize the right of the other to trade with any nation, with only contraband excluded; the Model Treaty specified sixty-eight items (mostly weapons and materials used in the making of munitions and weaponry, but also included tobacco, salted fish, cheese, butter, beer, wine, sugar, and salt) that were to be considered contraband. Finally, the United States would pledge not to assist Great Britain against France in the event that a Franco-American treaty resulted in a British declaration of war.

Once the Model Treaty was adopted, Adams, absorbed by his responsibilities on the Board of War, seldom spoke out on diplomatic issues. Congress, however, turned to him when it sent emissaries to meet with the Howe brothers in New York. When Deane, the lone New Englander among America's three envoys in France, was recalled, the choice of Adams as his successor was surprising in only one respect. The conditions of mid-1776 dictating the terms of Adams's Model Treaty had changed significantly by late 1777. Congress's earlier reluctance to join in a military alliance with France had long since vanished. The defeats inflicted on General Washington in New York and New Jersey in 1776 made it quite clear that this would be a long, difficult war; in addition, while Gates's great victory at Saratoga had nurtured hopes of an ultimate American victory, the nation faced numerous problems as 1778, the fourth year of the war, loomed. Great Britain held New York, Philadelphia, and Newport; unless the United States acquired the assistance of a foreign navy, those cities could not be retaken, and others, such as Boston or Charleston, might soon be lost. Moreover, America's finances were in tatters, and a general war weariness had begun to set in, supplanting the heady euphoria that reigned in the early months of the war. These mounting difficulties converted most congressmen, perhaps most Americans, to the belief that the Model Treaty should serve only as a guide for the postwar era. In the present life-and-death struggle, military assistance was urgently needed, and the recent capitulation of Burgoyne's army just might induce France to provide such aid.[15]

Adams's last days at home went quickly. He tidied up his affairs, made some arrangements concerning the farm, avidly studied French, and devoted every spare moment to Abigail and the children. But soon time ran out, and on the fiftieth day after he had written to Congress to accept the diplomatic post, he and John Quincy, accompanied by a servant, left their bright, warm home.

John and Abigail said their good-byes at home. It was easier that way, if, indeed, parting could ever be called easy in the face of such uncertainty. Then father and son were gone.

A brisk February wind tore though John and John Quincy as they stepped outside for a brief ride to Mount Wolleston and the home of Norton Quincy, Abigail's uncle. They had barely arrived before Capt. Samuel Tucker, commander of the *Boston,* joined them. The men dined with the Quincys, then went on their way. In the last rays of winter's daylight, the passengers, clad in warm watch coats provided by the ship's crew, were rowed out to the great frigate. It was nearly five o'clock when they struggled on board the vessel that would be their home for the next several weeks.

High winds and a squall prevented the *Boston* from sailing for thirty-six hours, but just at sunrise on a cold Sunday morning, February 15, the two travelers heard the unmistakable clang of the anchor being raised, then the rustling of fervid activity in the masts. Soon, a tug of movement, followed by a gentle, gliding motion. Father and son emerged into the brisk early light to watch, entranced by the crewmen's labors and responses to orders barked in a strange idiom.[16]

The vessel moved quickly, so quickly that the familiar shoreline of Quincy Bay and the distant hills beyond Adams's little farm soon disappeared. Sight of the coast was not lost that day, however, for the craft plowed only as far as Marblehead, just above Boston, where it anchored to take on additional crew. The stop resulted in an unscheduled delay. Before the vessel could take its leave, more foul weather pushed in, this time engulfing eastern Massachusetts in a heavy snowstorm. Forty-eight hours passed and the *Boston* was unable to move. His nerves already stretched to the breaking point, Adams raged in his diary about the stupidity of making this stop. Congress and the Navy Board would hear of these delays. But, at last, near sunset on Tuesday, more than four days after he had left Abigail, Adams's voyage really began.[17]

One can imagine his anxiety at this moment. Danger attended every ocean crossing, and never more so than at this season, when the normally restless, thrashing Atlantic was likely to fall into the grip of a winter tempest that could suddenly transform the sea into a raging, howling monster, bashing and tossing even a large ship as if it were a mere toy. To that peril was added the danger brought on by war. British warships patrolled the waters through which the *Boston* would sail, and if an enemy vessel spotted this frigate Adams might face the unsavory prospect of instant death or protracted captivity. As the *Boston* moved out to sea that cold Tuesday afternoon, Adams must have felt helpless, suddenly stripped of all control over his destiny, as if in the grasp of a claw from which he would not be released until the anchor again was claimed by blessed land.

The best one could hope for was a voyage of about twenty-five days. Adams's journey lasted just one day short of six weeks, not an uncommon length for a crossing. His passage included moments of drama and danger. Less than forty-eight hours after clearing Marblehead, the *Boston's* lookout sighted three ships on the horizon, one of which gave chase for nearly two days. It never closed to a point of attack, although on the second day when it began drawing unnervingly near, a sudden, fortuitous storm erupted, separating the vessels forever. On four occasions the *Boston* became the hunter, in pursuit of prizes. It claimed only one of its prey, a London merchant ship, the *Martha*. That acquisition nearly cost Adams dearly. As the *Boston* closed on its quarry, Captain Tucker ordered his important passengers beneath deck. Adams obeyed for a time, but when no one was looking he reappeared. He had just come topside when the *Martha* suddenly fired. The ball screamed past, just above his head, tearing through the mizzen yard behind him. Tucker, not accustomed to being disobeyed, hurried angrily toward Adams and demanded to know why he had exposed himself to danger. The captain later recollected that Adams smiled and remarked, "I ought to do my Share of fighting."[18]

The bulk of the voyage was less exciting. Day after day was uneventful, a "dull Scene," Adams complained, having discovered that a "Ship at Sea is a kind of Prison." Most days were worse than monotonous to Adams. They were useless. Although he had brought along several books, he found reading and contemplation impossible. The constant tossing and heaving of the ship was distracting, and he was plagued by occasional bouts of seasickness. To make matters worse, he soon was bored with sightseeing. "We see nothing but Sky, Clouds and Sea, and then Seas, Clouds and Sky," he complained. At least he and John Quincy found company aboard. Young Jesse Deane, the son of Silas Deane, a lad only a year older than Master Adams, was a passenger, as was William Vernon, a recent graduate of Princeton College and a scion of a member of the Navy Board. Adams especially enjoyed the company of Dr. Nicholas Noel, a French surgeon, and he got on well enough with Captain Tucker, though he privately carped that the mariner was not well educated. He conversed some with the captain of the *Martha,* now a prisoner of war. Also on board were thirty members of a French company of engineers, part of the soldiery hired by Deane, which now had to be returned to France at the expense of the United States.

Adams dined daily with Captain Tucker, and he spent considerable periods observing the crewmen. He was intrigued by their strange superstitions and games, although he found them to be a coarse breed. He lolled away numerous hours observing the marine life, searching for schools of fish, amused by the frolicking of bonito and porpoise. One of the real highlights of the voyage came when a crewman caught a Portuguese man-of-war and hoisted it on board for the passengers to inspect.

In between the sea chases, however, the days dragged by slowly and, usually, uneventfully. More often than not, even the weather was without incident, mostly remaining calm and frequently as warm as that of early summer. Only one storm seized a portion of the Atlantic on this voyage, although it was a hard blow. This was the blast that struck early in the journey while the *Boston* was fleeing the unidentified ship on the distant horizon. The storm hit in an area that the crewmen called the "Squawly Lattitude." A "Dangerous Sea Running," the captain laconically noted in his log. Dangerous it was. The foresail was badly split by the howling gusts, and three crewmen were struck by lightning, one suffering a fatal injury. For most of three days and two nights the vessel was hurled about. Eating was difficult. Sleep was impossible. Everything and everyone was wet. Only praying came easily. Then suddenly the tempest ended. "I was myself perfectly calm during the whole," Adams claimed, and he lauded the behavior of his son, who had acted in a "manly" way throughout.

On March 23 a lookout sighted the Spanish coast, and four days later France came into view. Thereafter, the maritime traffic increased. French vessels were everywhere, and the haunting fear of attack or capture at last was laid to rest. If less dangerous, this was the most frustrating part of the voyage. Unfavorable winds suddenly arose, pinioning the *Boston* only thirty miles from Bordeaux. A day passed, then a second. Finally, the wind rose and the vessel once again proceeded. As it neared Bordeaux, a French pilot came aboard. The passengers, hungry for news, gathered round him. And he did have news! Four days before, he reported—quite incorrectly, Adams later discovered—France had declared war on Great Britain.[19]

Adams spent many of his final hours on the *Boston* watching as the French countryside drifted past. He was awestruck. "Europe thou great Theatre of Arts, Sciences, Commerce, War, am I at last permitted to visit thy Territories," he wrote in his diary that night.[20]

With John Quincy and Master Deane in tow, Adams spent four busy days in Bordeaux. His escorts were two businessmen who resided in this active French city, one from Quebec, the other from the United States, men he had met before he left America. Adams saw a play and his first opera, and enjoyed both. He attended a dinner at which fifteen toasts were made, including one to Abigail and one to himself, but what he remembered most was the "surprizing and shocking" behavior of the ladies in attendance. In the course of the meal, the woman seated next to him struck up a conversation.

"Mr. Adams, by your Name I conclude you are descended from the first Man and Woman. . . . [Perhaps] you could resolve a difficulty which I could never explain. I never could understand how the first couple found the Art of lying together?"

Adams must have been mortified. He blushed but stammered cleverly, or so he remembered, that the first couple surely "flew together . . . like two Objects in electric Experiments."

"Well," the lady responded, "I know not how it was, but this I know, it is a very happy Shock."[21]

Adams's pleasant stay in Bordeaux concluded on a Sunday. Early in the afternoon he and the boys set off for Paris, ushered out of town by a huge and enthusiastic crowd, his ears ringing with the sound of thirteen booming cannon fired in his honor. Adams was amazed at the speed with which they completed their journey to Paris; their four-day trip would have required ten or more days to travel the same distance on America's primitive roads. He remained in awe of the beauty he beheld, but of all that he observed, two things struck him most. After the great unoccupied stretches of rural America, he was surprised that every field in France was under cultivation. In addition, he had never before seen so many beggars.[22]

Once he reached Paris, Adams allowed himself only a few hours to look over this magnificent city, just then exploding into its annual spring splendor. Paris was twenty-five times larger than any city in which Adams had ever lived, a metropolis of approximately 650,000 souls; haphazardly constructed about the meandering blue waters of the river Seine, Paris was a booming, bustling, sprawling municipality dotted with grandiose churches; stately public structures; lovely, manicured gardens; many elegant mansions; forlorn stretches of blighted, impoverished neighborhoods—all ringed by handsome, diminutive middle-class suburbs. Exhausted from the journey and a long afternoon of sightseeing, Adams and the boys enjoyed a good night of sleep, but morning came quickly, even for an early riser like Adams. He was startled awake by the noise in the streets beneath his hotel window, the bustling sounds of a busy city beginning a new day.

Adams dressed hurriedly, gathered the boys, ate a quick breakfast, and set out by carriage for Franklin's residence in Passy, a small suburb situated on the road to Versailles. There he found Franklin and Lee about to depart for a luncheon engagement with Jacques Turgot, France's minister of finance. Adams tagged along, and that evening, somewhat puffed up by the experience, he noted in his diary that he had dined that day with "twenty of the great People of France." When the repast with Turgot concluded, Adams returned with Franklin to Passy, where he hoped to learn what had occurred in America's foreign affairs since the previous summer, the last time period for which he had seen any official documents.[23]

One can only wonder what Adams thought of Franklin at this moment, a man he had not seen for eighteen months, a person he had never known well. He knew of course that he was in the company of a celebrity and an extraordinarily popular individual. In the France of this time, Adams subsequently wrote, "there was scarcely a peasant or a citizen, a *valet de chambre,* coachman or footman, a lady's chambermaid or a scullion in a kitchen who was not familiar with [him], and who did not consider him a friend to human kind." Whether Adams at this moment believed that Franklin deserved such accolades is unclear, but later he bitterly attributed Franklin's popularity to an alleged propensity toward courting and "piddling" with the common folk.

That Franklin might have sought to do such a thing was but one of a multitude of differences between the two men. The age difference—Franklin was almost thirty years older than Adams—would have immediately struck both men. And, although both were natives of Massachusetts, they had grown up in quite different circumstances. Born in Boston, Franklin was one of seventeen children, the youngest of the ten sons of an immigrant tradesman. Like George Washington, Franklin was virtually self-taught; his formal schooling lasted only two years, and by age ten he had been put to work, helping at his father's candle shop.

Franklin's rise from his humble origins, therefore, was more impressive than that of Adams. Some luck was involved, of course. He was fortunate to have as a father an intelligent man—indeed, a "mechanical genius," according to Franklin's later recollections—who sought to "improve the minds of his children" in the only way possible, by encouraging probing, frequent, freewheeling discussions; although he did not think so at the time, young Franklin also was blessed to be apprenticed in his brother's print shop, where he learned a craft through which an ambitious man might prosper. But his rise was not due to happenstance alone. As Esmond Wright, his most recent biographer, has demonstrated, the Puritanism of the Boston of Franklin's youth left a deep imprint upon him, stamping him with a diligence, industry, frugality, and bent for self-scrutiny that would serve him well. So driven to better himself that he left home at age seventeen with his "pocket . . . stuff'd out with shirts and stockings" but almost devoid of money, Franklin journeyed alone to Philadelphia, where he did not know a soul. A year later, still not much better off, he sailed for London.

At the same age that Adams believed he had ruined his health by carrying a military dispatch from Worcester to Newport, Franklin had traveled alone from New England to Pennsylvania, then had made a round-trip crossing of the Atlantic, returning to Philadelphia in 1726 after an eighteen-month residency in England. Back in the colonies, he entered upon the trade he had learned in Boston; soon, he lived comfortably, though hardly ostentatiously. By his thirtieth birthday, an age when Adams's law practice was beginning to flourish, Franklin and his wife, Deborah, still were unable to afford servants, and their diet remained "plain and simple," breakfast, for instance, consisting of bread and milk—"no Tea," he said pointedly—consumed from earthenware, while his wardrobe of homespun shirts and wool stockings hardly differed from that of any other artisan.

But if Franklin's ascent did not occur overnight, it was nonetheless steady. He appeared to possess an uncanny ability to prosper in every endeavor that he undertook. In addition to his newspaper, the *Pennsylvania Gazette,* he printed books, operated a stationer's store and bookstore, and, after 1731, published *Poor Richard's Almanack.* He succeeded with it all, and at age forty-two he retired from his printing press, able to live off the sales of his almanac and other writings, and the income he derived as postmaster at Philadelphia. His material success was one of the reasons for his popularity, especially among his fellow tradesmen, who saw in him a man who had bettered himself. So, too, were his achievements in science. He was best known for his electrical experiments, but he had also devised a new, more efficient candle and a wood-burning stove; had invented bifocals and a smokeless chimney; and had written on myriad topics, from air currents to eclipses, from diseases to geography. In addition, he had worked tirelessly to improve the quality of life in Philadelphia. Franklin touched Philadelphia in a profound manner, to a degree that few other individuals have ever influenced life in the city in which they lived. From libraries to fire stations, from deicing streets to illuminating the city's thoroughfares, from founding schools to establishing hospitals, Franklin's hand was everywhere. And through *Poor Richard,* he touched the popular culture of his time. One person in every hundred living in America in the quarter century after 1731 purchased his almanac and read his maxims and proverbs, and, presumably, imbibed his admonitions that self-reliance and enterprise would lead to personal freedom and material rewards.

But in the long second life that began in 1748, following his retirement as a printer, Franklin turned mostly to politics and statecraft. A quarter century after he started down this road, his path and that of Adams crossed for the first time. They met at the Second Congress in May 1775. There is no hint of problems between the two at this juncture, but this was an environment in which Franklin was out of his element (he was a poor orator and so uncomfortable with his surroundings that he asked a colleague to read the most important speech he prepared as a congressman), and Adams was clearly a predominant player. Those differences presaged other dissimilarities in temperament that separated these two men. Franklin had a well-deserved reputation as a womanizer and hedonist. He also possessed a remarkable facility for making friendships. There seemed to be a magnetism and charm about him that lured others into his company. Perhaps it was because he hated contention and went out of his way to avoid any appearance of acerbity; in fact, many described him as a relaxed, humorous sort, "all jollity and pleasantry," as one acquaintance put it. Surprisingly, Franklin was quiet and customarily spoke only when asked to do so, and he could be extraordinarily gracious and polite, with a facility for putting others quite at ease. Well-read, glib, and affable, he was a man of wide-ranging interests who could expand with equal confidence on science, religion, politics, or literature. A lifelong urbanite and a resident of London for sixteen years during three separate periods, Franklin was a man of cosmopolitan style and manner who found it easy to mix with others, seemingly indifferent to the educational, social, or economic background of his companions.

For all their differences, however, Adams and Franklin were alike in some ways. Both were driven by a passion for self-improvement, and both mapped out remarkably similar plans to facilitate their ends. Franklin, at age twenty, pledged to be sincere, rational, industrious, patient, and never "to speak ill" of any man. Although Franklin was better-rounded than Adams, he too was self-centered and consumed by a single-minded pursuit. Franklin craved material comforts and social acceptance in his early years, leisure, adulation, and the indulgences of a voluptuary in his second career. Each man was willing to abandon his family to chase his dreams. In the case of Franklin, his wife, Deborah, was left behind in Philadelphia in 1764 and died ten years later without ever again seeing her husband, despite her repeated entreaties for him to return to America.

There were similarities as well in the political lives of Franklin and Adams. Like Adams, Franklin turned to public life only in middle age. In addition, Franklin also only slowly came to see a threat to America in Britain's new colonial policies. Adams understood earlier than Franklin that there must be constitutional limitations upon Parliament's authority over America, but at about the same time both men beheld the alleged peril to the colonies from English corruption; in all likelihood both came to embrace the idea of independence sometime in 1774 or early 1775, later than radicals such as Samuel Adams but earlier than the reconciliationists who had constituted such a powerful faction in Congress even after the commencement of hostilities. Franklin favored separation from Britain for many of the same reasons that motivated Adams, although, as Wright pointed out, there was also something quite personal in his decision. Franklin was a man who "could be bitter and could nurse a grievance," and in 1776 he was "clearly a man nursing a deep hurt." An indignant British government had publicly humiliated Franklin in 1774 for his part in the Hutchinson letters incident and had stripped him of his lucrative position as deputy postmaster-general for America. Thereafter, he was finished in the politics of the empire, and he knew it. Like Adams, he was never by disposition "a revolutionary, and certainly no grand incendiary," but Franklin had come to find it both expedient and desirable to commit himself to the movement for independence.

Whatever their other similarities and differences, Adams could never hope to match Franklin's facility for diplomacy in the France of the late 1770s. Franklin, a conciliator by nature, was suited temperamentally for such an assignment. He was experienced, too. Between 1766 and 1775 he served in London as the agent for four colonies, and in the spring of 1776 he accompanied Samuel Chase and Charles Carroll of Carrollton on the mission to persuade Canada to join in the rebellion, the assignment that Adams had declined. These attributes were served as well by his fame. Franklin's name was already well known when he landed at Auray in December 1776. His writings and the knowledge of his experiments had long before preceded him to the shores of France, where he was looked upon from the moment of his arrival as "the first of Men" in the hearts of Americans. To *philosophes* and enlightened government officials alike, he often was seen stereotypically as the very embodiment of the new man who had emerged from the innovative, noble experiment that was America, the revivification, said Comte de Ségur, of "classic Simplicity" in contradistinction to "our effeminate and slavish age, the eighteenth century."[24]

Franklin had been feted in Philadelphia when he entered Congress in 1775, but his stature then, Adams discovered during his few days in France, in no way compared to the way in which he was exalted by the French in 1778. But it is conjectural whether Adams considered any of this on that chilly April evening in Passy, his second night in the environs of the French capital, as, over a light dinner of cheese and beer, he listened to Franklin's account of occurrences in American foreign affairs during the past several months. What Franklin divulged came as a jolt to Adams. France and the United States had signed treaties of alliance and commerce about ten days before Adams left Braintree. Moreover, while the commercial agreement contained everything that Franklin could have desired, the Treaty of Alliance was cause for concern. Not that Adams was especially surprised to learn of the treaty. As early as July 1777 the United States envoys in Paris had expressed an interest in something more than the commercial pact called for in the Model Treaty. France was moving in a similar direction, but it responded cautiously to America's entreaties, watching the summer military campaign before it made any commitment. It used the time to complete its naval reforms and to importune Spain to enter the war. Spain demurred, but the news of the American victory at Saratoga moved France to act. Not only had Gates's triumph seemed to demonstrate that Britain could not suppress the rebellion, but the French expected London to follow its defeat with some sort of peace terms for America. If

France was to gain from this war, it had to move rapidly. The American envoys just as quickly moved to accept the French offer.[25]

If Adams was not surprised by Franklin's revelation of the military pact, he was distressed to discover that the treaty did not stipulate a date for France's entry into the war, an omission of some importance in as much as France still had not declared war on Britain, the excited rumor-mongering of the pilot in Bordeaux notwithstanding. Adams's discomfort on that point was mollified considerably, however, by his discovery that the accord stipulated that neither party would conclude a separate peace with Britain, and that both would remain at war until Britain formally recognized the independence of the United States.[26]

During their long, private conversation that evening, Franklin also confirmed a disturbing rumor that Adams had heard in Bordeaux. Immediately upon landing, Adams had been told that the three American diplomats were badly divided. Before the end of Franklin's monologue, Adams was painfully aware that a deep personal friction separated the venerated old Doctor and Lee. The Virginian had not gotten on with Deane either, but that envoy had departed for America just before Adams's arrival. Lee was "very disagreeable," Franklin stated bluntly. He was suspicious and querulous, a dark, moody sort whose fiery temper constantly was stoked by the machinations of other Americans in Paris.[27]

That day, which had begun with Adams's buoyant ride to Passy, had ended on a deeply distressing note. When Congress learned of the alliance with France, it was certain to question the usefulness of maintaining three emissaries in Paris; Adams had to have known, too, that it was unlikely that Franklin, a man revered in France as the rustic philosopher, the very embodiment of all that enlightened Frenchmen most prized, would be recalled. Nor was Lee, whose brother was a congressmen, likely to be recalled before Adams. But, useless as his assignment suddenly had become, Adams did not wish to return home. The thought of another hazardous voyage so soon must have been daunting. To quit his post, moreover, was certain to rankle some in Congress. If France's entry into the war—surely it would occur shortly—did not have an immediate impact on the battlefield, it surely would have a substantive effect in the diplomatic corridors of Europe; a role of importance for him might soon materialize. Finally, there was John Quincy to consider. A stay in Europe would benefit him.[28]

So Adams remained. He did suggest to Congress that only one commissioner be retained in Paris, but between the lines of his early correspondence he subtly campaigned to convey the impression that his presence was necessary, or, should Congress see matters differently, to secure for himself some other post of consequence. He reported that financial affairs were in a "State of confusion and darkness," a slam not only at Deane but at Franklin and Lee, who had watched the expenditure of "Prodigious Sums" without keeping

"Books of Account." He also intimated that a vast amount had been spent on personal indulgence, then added: "Few Men in this World are capable of living at a less Expence, than I am." He suggested that Congress consider posting envoys in other European capitals, where aid might also be attained. In the meantime, he declared, he would labor to correct his predecessors' "Abuses" and "seek to bring [their] Affairs into a little better order."[29]

Adams soon checked out of his Paris accommodations and moved into quarters in the small garden apartment where Franklin lived, a modest dwelling on the grand Chaumont estate, the Hotel Valentinois, a magnificent hilltop château with a courtyard, a lake, and four lovely gardens surrounding an octagonal pond. This was a measure of economy, he later said. Deane had remained in Paris, surrounded by furniture that he had purchased and charged to the American taxpayers, attended by his own staff of servants, and conveyed in an expensive carriage that he had put on the public tab. By dwelling under the same roof as Franklin, Adams wrote, he neither paid rent nor acquired furniture, and he was served by the same retainers and traveled in the same vehicle as his colleague. Adams also quickly enrolled his son in a private academy. John Quincy would live there through the week, but the school was near enough that he could spend every weekend with his father.[30]

As soon as he was settled, Franklin and Lee escorted Adams to Versailles to meet Comte de Vergennes and the monarch, Louis XVI, who impressed the new envoy with his mild, even innocent, demeanor. The three Americans also jointly drafted a communiqué to the government of the Netherlands, the first step, they hoped, in a campaign to secure a commercial pact between that nation and the United States. After that, Franklin, Lee, and Adams seldom did anything together.[31]

Nevertheless, Adams remained extremely busy. His activity has been characterized as strange for an emissary of such high rank. One scholar has contended that he occupied himself with tasks that "other men would have relegated to their clerks." Not only did he tear into the backlog of paperwork that had accumulated over the past eighteen months, but he prepared the final drafts of much of the commissioners' correspondence in 1778, and he even acted as a bookkeeper for the delegation. In reality, however, as the editors of the Adams Papers have observed, Adams emerged as the commission's chief administrator, imposing order and method on their affairs, a service for which both Lee and Franklin were unsuited.[32]

As Franklin and Adams lived together at Passy, they saw one another frequently. Lee remained in Paris, however, and scarcely was in the company of his colleagues. Only when some urgent matter arose, as when Franklin was to meet with Vergennes—at the foreign minister's request, Franklin alone was to represent the Commissioners—did Lee journey to the Hotel Valentinois for consultation.[33] These strategy sessions often degenerated into acrimonious clashes between Lee and Franklin.

The problems between these two men went back nearly a decade, to the time when each served in London as an agent for Massachusetts. From then until Franklin left England on the eve of the war, Lee suspected that his colleague was only a lukewarm supporter of the American cause. By 1778 Lee's doubts about Franklin's loyalty evidently had been removed, but he harbored a deep resentment toward his colleague. From the beginning of his diplomatic service, Lee found his role to be little better than that of an insignificant bystander. Deane had preceded him to France by six months and had established—then monopolized—important contacts in government circles. Franklin simply monopolized the affection of the French. Not only was Lee's presence of little use, but his inconsequence was underscored when Deane and Franklin customarily sided against him on nearly every important matter. Lee, proud and cantankerous by nature (Adams thought him honest, but a man of violent temper and bitter disposition, while Franklin characterized him as a man with a "sick mind" whose proclivity for malice was unequaled) turned on his fellow diplomats. He thought both men guilty of peculation, but he pressed that charge only against Deane, and it was his charge of malfeasance as much as anything that led to Deane's recall. Toward Franklin, he was merely uncivil.[34]

Both Franklin and Lee must have welcomed the arrival of Adams and sought to make an ally of him. Arthur Lee knew that Adams had been a political consort with his brother, Richard Henry Lee, while he served in Philadelphia. Franklin, on the other hand, had gotten on well enough with Adams during the eighteen months that they were fellow delegates in Congress. Franklin appeared to have the advantage in this contest. Lee, distant, captious, and contrary, was not adroit at the delicate art of winning friends; the best he could hope for was that Adams would grow to share his hatred for Franklin. The old Pennsylvanian was more wily. The panoply of guile that he turned on Adams will never be fully known, but there is reason to suspect that, among other tactics, he sought to purchase the favor of his colleague. Adams had been in Paris for only a month when Franklin, through an intermediary, offered to give him a share in the Vandalia Company, an enterprise that speculated in western lands. Adams, of course, rejected the gift and sought to adopt a truly neutral position between his fellow commissioners. But the Franklin-Lee imbroglio placed him in a nasty situation. The two men differed on every issue, forcing Adams to cast the deciding vote on each matter that came before the commissioners. He had become "an Umpire between two bitter and inveterate Parties," he wrote; regardless of his vote, he was certain to be "censured and misrepresented" by one of the other of his colleagues.[35]

Adams grew to dislike both men. He eventually came to characterize Lee as acrimonious, obstinate, overly secret, jealous, and indiscreet. Lee was unsuited for diplomacy, he reported to friends in Congress; not only was it impossible for colleagues to work with him, but foreign statesmen easily took advantage of his imperfections. His disapproval of Lee notwithstanding, it was for Franklin that he reserved the greatest calumny. One student of Adams has suggested that "Franklin posed Adams with the deepest personal challenge of his life." That surely is an overstatement, for unlike his feelings for Hutchinson, whom he deeply hated, and for Dickinson, to whom he refused to speak, Adams actually worked rather closely with Franklin during 1778 and 1779; excluding Lee, the two cooperated in several endeavors, including intelligence-gathering matters and discussions concerning the exchange of prisoners.[36] Nevertheless, the visceral, slanderous comments that Adams continued to utter about Franklin nearly thirty years after their joint service—and almost two decades following Franklin's death—reveal the keenly acrid feelings he harbored toward his colleague.

Adams dismissed Franklin as "the Old Conjurer," someone who slid by on guile, not merit, a mere actor who sought to deceive everyone with whom he came into contact. Franklin's talents were chimerical, he thought. His command of French was poor (a fact that he candidly lamented to Adams). He was but a hoax when he postured as a philosopher, Adams also charged. Even Franklin's dress irritated Adams. He eschewed the powdered wig of the diplomat and left stored in his chest the abundance of elegant silk coats and lace shirts that he had purchased during his residence in London, preferring instead a simple, unembroidered brown coat. Franklin was a charlatan, Adams raged, a master at charming the French, especially when he adopted the simple philosopher persona. Such "fullsome and sickish" behavior, Adams remarked with disgust.

Franklin's personal habits aroused even greater ire in Adams. Franklin lived the grand life of a sybarite, attended by nine servants, feasting daily from a table generously laden with unimaginable delicacies, in command of a wine cellar stocked with more that one thousand bottles, and borne about Paris and Passy in an elegant carriage driven by a uniformed coachman. The Doctor was in the habit of rising late, often sleeping until eight. Following a leisurely breakfast, he devoted hours to those who called on him: French politicians, philosophers, scholars, and artists—even adoring Parisian women and children—each anxious merely to share his company for a brief moment. Almost every evening Franklin was invited to dinner, a whirlwind schedule that sent him to mingle with the illuminati of this proud nation, to dine, play cards or chess or backgammon, then to listen to their music, or to flirt with their women, to kiss and embrace them and to tell them his thousand and one stories, so many which could be interpreted as slightly off-color. Old Dr. Franklin would "come home at all hours," Adams went on, not dragging in until as late at nine o'clock, or even later. Franklin's busy social calendar left little time for work, Adams charged, upsetting his schedule and Lee's as well, and if Adams is to be believed, producing maddening delays in the transaction of official business.[37]

But Adams soon found more than Franklin's life-style to be a matter of grave concern. Unfairly, he quickly concluded that the tactical approach that Franklin employed toward the French court and in his dealings with Vergennes was ill-advised, perhaps even dangerous to the United States. Clearly, Franklin did not wish to push too hard on America's new ally. Franklin was confident that he could satisfy his country's needs "by endeavoring to please this court," as he put it. He sought to inspire Vergennes's confidence by avoiding confrontation, shrill blather, and supplication, and he was the very epitome of patience as he ever so gently, subtly, congenially, and soberly pursued the fruits of French benevolence. Adams recoiled from such an approach. There is "too much Timidity . . . too much Diffidence . . . too much Complaisance for the Court," he charged; he feared that what he saw as Franklin's fainthearted, pliable praxis would unavoidably give France "too much Influence" over American foreign policy, with the result that "too much will be demanded of Us." Should that occur, he went on, another danger loomed. As a client state of France, Americans could but helplessly watch the slow erosion of "the Simplicity of our Manners and . . . the Principles of our Constitution" as the new nation was frenchified. Adams thus counseled that wisdom dictated that the envoys bring to bear every possible pressure on its ally.

The tactical differences espoused by the two envoys grew from conflicting views of France's relationship with the United States. Franklin not only appears to have looked upon France's commitment to America as somewhat mercurial, but given his assumption that Anglo-American difficulties would outlast the Revolutionary era, he thought it essential that nothing be done to antagonize France. "We know not," he warned, "how soon we may have a fresh Occasion for Friends, for Credit, and for Reputation." Contrarily, Adams believed that "common sense" would compel Versailles to remain closely tied to the United States. Adams was correct. As historian Jonathan Dull has pointed out, by the early 1770s France found itself isolated and without an ally among the great powers in Europe. Vergennes saw the salvation of his country in the weakening of Great Britain, and the most promising way to achieve that end was through close ties with the United States; indeed, the French foreign minister knew that to incur the wrath of the United States was to run the risk of driving the new nation back into the arms of London. Adams was no greater nationalist than was Franklin, but he probably saw France's dilemma in this era in more realistic terms than did his colleague. One thing is certain, however; whereas it has been almost commonplace among historians to attribute Adams's opposition to Franklin's style of diplomacy to simple jealousy, in fact Adams also was critical of his fellow envoy because of a genuine concern that America might be ruined by anything less than a wary, coequal, unbending relationship with its new ally.[38]

Adams, of course, was envious and jealous of Franklin. He quickly realized that he was overshadowed by Franklin, and he soon understood that neither the French government nor French society ascribed any importance to him.

When he arrived in France some mistook him for "*le fameux* Adams," Samuel Adams, while others thought him the author of the celebrated pamphlet *Common Sense*. When those errors were rectified (Adams was convinced that Franklin had no little hand in clarifying matters), he was looked upon as "a Man of no Consequence—a Cypher." Adams would have been less than human had he not been somewhat envious of the adulation in which Franklin basked. Yet he also was magnanimous enough to realize that Franklin's popularity stemmed from his "long and great Rep[utation]," whereas he had only recently begun his public career. Thus, despite his ire, Adams had been at Passy barely a month before he wrote home to ask that Congress name Franklin its sole ambassador to France and to request that it recall or reassign both Lee and himself.[39]

Adams was not big enough, however, to see that some of the whispers about him were true. He could never succeed in France, it was said, because he was "deficient in the *je ne scai quoi* so necessary in highly polished society." His one-time friend, Jonathan Sewall, put it a bit differently. Upon accepting a diplomatic assignment, he said, Adams had risen to a point where he was "quite out of his element. He cannot dance, drink, game, flatter, promise, dress, swear with the gentlemen, and talk small talk or flirt with the ladies," he suggested. The tragedy of it, Sewall added, was that the average diplomat had neither one-tenth the intellectual capability of Adams nor "a spark of his honesty."[40]

Adams had always endeavored to surmount imposing obstacles through hard work and, once again, he chose that path toward success. He now sought to become Franklin's coequal and perhaps America's most useful emissary by reintroducing the tactics that had resulted in his earlier achievements. Always before, his star had risen through a regimen of hard work and study, even if such a life-style had entailed considerable self-denial. Now, in Passy, he remained within his apartment and went to work. He purchased the best French texts to facilitate his study of the language. He quizzed the literati about the best French histories, and he acquired and read those works. He labored to compile the commission's papers. Nothing was allowed to stand as an obstacle to his labors. He declined social invitations so that he might work, although he attended the theater with even greater frequency, an excess that he justified with the rationale that it might assist in his struggle with the language. Soon, he hoped, his command of French would outpace that of Franklin so that he might be able to converse in fluent, flawless French with the learned men of Paris. It could not be long, he imagined, before the French government discovered "that the Business of the Commission would never be done, unless [he] did it." Already—because Franklin and Lee canceled one another— Adams's vote was the most important, regardless of the issue. It was only a matter of time before everyone recognized his importance and realized that, in his own way, he made a greater contribution than Dr. Franklin ever could.[41]

This time Adams's endeavors were unsuccessful. He could not supplant Franklin, even though his command of the language surpassed the haphazard usage of the "Old Conjurer," and despite the fact that his work habits were more businesslike than the bohemian traits of his colleague. Franklin not only better understood the French temper, he realized that for the moment the most important role the American envoy could play was that of actor, not diplomat. The delegation's immediate task, Franklin knew, was to convince the French of the accuracy of their Enlightenment image of America as the land of civilized simplicity, a land whose emissaries were but simple and unsophisticated products of that faraway and primitive continent.[42]

A heavy, fatiguing work load bore down on Adams throughout his ten-month stay in France. In addition to the clerical, accounting, and administrative chores that he took on, Adams was faced with numerous official problems. There were endless reports to Congress. Adams had barely moved into the Hotel Valentinois before he began to communicate intelligence to Philadelphia on the Carlisle Commission, envoys dispatched by Lord North's government to offer America terms of reconciliation. Adams accurately reported that Great Britain did not desire peace. In reality, he said, North's objective was to "introduce disorder," to provoke a split between those in Congress who might prefer an accommodation with the parent state and those who preferred the continuation of the war alongside France. Overall, the tone of his early reports was unfailingly optimistic. Adams concluded that peace was within sight and that the end of the contest would be glorious. He based his feelings on the victory at Saratoga, the alliance with France and her certain entry into the war, the expectation that Spain also would join the war against Britain and that Holland might, too, and even that a general European war might soon erupt and compel North to withdraw from America. Indeed, Adams not only believed that America would win the war, he forecast that Great Britain would be considerably weakened by its trial, leaving the United States with nothing but splendid prospects for the postwar era. Adams expressed gloom with regard to only one principal matter. "Loans in Europe will be very difficult to obtain," he predicted in August 1778; "Taxation, deep and broad Taxation, is the only sure and lasting Remedy."[43]

Some problems faced by the commissioners were interminable. Prize cases and incidents between American merchants and Barbary pirates, for instance, cropped up repeatedly.[44] But no problem required as much attention as that of American prisoners. Shortly after Adams's arrival, a thorny case arose. John Paul Jones had captured two hundred British prisoners on the high seas. He could not take them to America, and France was reluctant to confine these captives because it was still technically at peace with Britain. The commissioners sought to prevail upon its ally to retain these luckless British sailors so that they might someday be exchanged for American captives, but while the matter dragged on the United States paid for their incarceration in Brest. The issue was resolved when France entered the war; Paris, moreover, eventually was persuaded to compensate the United States for the costs it had incurred in the affair.[45]

The gravest problem in this regard, however, stemmed from Britain's alleged treatment of its American captives. Adams had become thoroughly aware of the matter while in Congress. Stories of inhumane treatment surfaced during the first year of the war; men were starved and compelled to live in indecent accommodations, it was said, and some were even "constrained by cruel usage and whippings to enlist with the British Troops." Many Americans wished to retaliate in kind; others were restrained, either from humanitarian motives or from pragmatism, as far more Americans than British languished in captivity. Adams took a tough stand, however. He advocated that the United States threaten retaliation upon British prisoners when evidence existed of deliberate cruelty inflicted upon Americans. "The end of Retaliation . . . is to prevent an Injury, and it seldom fails of its design," he counseled. If the United States pursued such a course, he went on, any "disagreable Consequences . . . will be wholly chargeable on the Enemy."[46]

The course that Adams recommended ultimately became American policy, and while captives on both sides continued to endure inadequate rations and unfit shelter, neither belligerent pursued a policy of deliberate horror with regard to its prisoners. Still, much suffering existed, and one of the first acts of the commissioners following Adams's arrival was to protest to Lord North the treatment of American prisoners "in a manner unexampled, in the practice of civilized Nations." "Retaliation will be the inevitable Consequence," they warned.[47]

The commissioners took three concrete steps with regard to American captives. They secretly routed some public money to the captives, which then was used to bribe guards into permitting their escape and to procure passage from England to the continent, and thence to France. Once in France, the fugitives received some assistance on which to subsist while awaiting their return to America. The commissioners' greatest efforts, however, were made to arrange prisoner exchanges. The first successful exchange was achieved in September 1778, but in January the commission succeeded in placing an agent in England to negotiate further exchanges. During that winter and spring Adams himself engaged in exchange negotiations in Brest, Nantes, and L'Orient.[48]

For all their multifaceted work, the primary focus of the commissioners' efforts was directed toward relations with France. Ten days after Adams moved to Passy, he and his colleagues urged France to convoy American commercial shipping across the Atlantic. Such a step, they said, would reduce insurance costs and drastically curtail losses; France, they added, would be the great beneficiary, for a "considerable Commerce" soon would result. They even sought to persuade the Ministry of the Marine to provide frigates to the largest private French firms engaged in the American trade. The American envoys had little success in either instance. The French could not spare its naval vessels for such matters, the government responded, although Adams—not entirely incorrectly—believed the navy had scotched the idea because it regarded such duty as "disgracefull Service."[49]

On occasion, the Commissioners sought to press a military action upon France. In the fall of 1778, for instance, Franklin and Adams communicated intelligence on the location of the British whaling fleet and sought to convince the French government of the wisdom of seizing these vessels. The ships and cargoes would be of inestimable value, they argued, and the men—up to 450 sailors—could be exchanged or incorporated into the American merchant marine. Not much came of the recommendations, although late that year France captured three British whalers en route to waters off the coast of Brazil.[50]

At the end of 1778 the commissioners embarked on a new course. They sought to persuade France to make an ever greater naval commitment. No one was more responsible for this departure than Adams, and in this instance no one's views had changed more significantly than those of Adams. During 1775 and 1776 he had urged only a commercial agreement with Paris, asserting boldly and openly that French military assistance was unnecessary for an American victory. He welcomed French aid by the time of his arrival in France, however, and within a few months of reaching Passy he wrote that the "longer I live in Europe . . . the more important our Alliance with France appears to me." When France finally entered the war, he rejoiced because it meant that Great Britain "is no longer Mistress of the Ocean." But his initial optimism gradually turned sour during the course of 1778. Contrary to his initial reports, Great Britain showed no signs of leaving the war; Adams, in fact, came to realize that Lord North feared that the loss of the United States would hasten Britain's collapse in Canada, Nova Scotia, Florida, and islands in the West Indies. Britain would not "quit the united States," he now said, "untill they are either driven out or starved out of them." Nor was the war going according to plan. Spain had not entered the war, and by fall Adams knew that Holland also was unlikely to become a belligerent. Moreover, while he continued to believe that France would "support [the United States] to the last," he had grown to believe that it could do more. For instance, its commitment to privateering against British shipping was lackadaisical, he charged. In place of the heady optimism of the spring and summer, Adams, by September, spoke of the "great Difficulties and Dangers" that lay ahead, adding that America was "a great Way" from victory. However, he now concluded, should France augment its navy in American waters, the war could still be brought to a speedy end.[51]

Adams still had to convince his colleagues of the wisdom of making such an entreaty to Vergennes. It was not easy. From the start, Franklin feared it unwise to push too hard at Versailles. Nor was this an auspicious time even to hint that France could do more. During the summer a Franco-American campaign to take Rhode Island had ended in disaster. The commissioners knew, too, that Charles Théodat, Comte d'Estaing, the commander of the French fleet in America, had been subjected to considerable abuse in the American press after that failure; Franklin may have feared that an appeal at this moment for additional assistance would be interpreted as a criticism of the French commander and might arouse French enmity. On the other hand, Adams could easily have demonstrated that the military situation had not improved. To bolster his case, moreover, he spoke unofficially about the matter with Edmé Jacques Genêt, the chief of the translator's bureau within the foreign ministry and editor of *Affaires de l'Angleterre et de l'Amérique*. Adams told him that a significant augmentation of the French fleet "would probably destroy the British Power in America;" Genêt agreed, and urged Adams to press upon his colleagues the necessity for communicating such a request to Vergennes. Finally, Adams had Lee's support. Thus, Adams prevailed in what likely was his first real clash with Franklin over a substantive issue of policy, although he did acquiesce to Franklin's wish to moderate the tone of the draft. In December or early January 1779, the commissioners urged the French government to send to America "a powerful Fleet sufficient to secure a naval superiority." The moment that Britain lost its naval dominance, the envoys argued, it would be compelled to end the war.[52] The appeal did not persuade Vergennes. He dreamed instead of a joint Franco-Spanish invasion of England.

Quite aside from his official duties and his problems with Franklin, much of Adams's time was consumed with worries about Silas Deane, the commissioner whom he had replaced. Deane had reached America in the summer of 1778 and had immediately appeared before Congress to defend himself, but his was a weak defense, for he had left all his financial records in Paris. Nevertheless, Congress was in a bind. To find against Deane would be to denigrate his associate, Franklin; to find for him would be to impugn Lee and his allies. Congress backed and filled, unwilling to act. Deane was willing, however. Intemperately, he took to the newspapers and published a bitter account of events, sparing neither his foes in Congress nor their friend Arthur Lee. His most alarming allegation was that Lee's financial ties in London had resulted in his disloyalty to the very nation that he represented.[53]

Adams had known from the outset that he opened himself to attack by doing nothing more than replacing Deane. "I never in my Life knew a Man displaced from a Trust, but he and his Friends were angry with his successor," he said shortly after reaching Passy.[54] Indeed, he soon was aware of whispers that as a congressman he had conspired to bring down Deane and have his post, and in August 1778 a London newspaper had published a captured letter written to Deane by his brother, Simeon, which said, "[the] two Adamses are both strongly against . . . yourself. God knows what lengths they intend." Adams wondered as well to what lengths the "Weathersfield Family"—the Deanes hailed from Weathersfield, Connecticut—would go to "dishonour" him. He sought to distance himself from the bitter furor that ensued following the publication of Deane's charges. He sent no materials to Congress with regard to the matter for more than a year, and his comments—he now characterized Deane as "wicked" and as a man who conducted himself as might a "wild boar"—were confined to his diary and to letters to very close, trustworthy friends.[55]

In addition to the personal threat posed by the Deane-Lee Affair, Adams feared that the imbroglio could cause irreparable damage to the United States. An irremediable chasm between the North and South might result from this clash, he predicted. Moreover, Spain might be persuaded not to enter the war. His greatest fear, however, was that French suspicions of the United States might be increased as a result of Deane's incredible assertions.[56]

Adams's fears were not the product of a fevered imagination. But for all the danger, there was opportunity, as well. Lee clearly was discredited at Versailles. Franklin, because of his close ties with Deane, might be badly harmed, too. Only Adams had never been part of this mess. Quietly, without informing Franklin, he requested a private meeting with Vergennes. Officially, he acted in the hope of dispelling the damage wrought by Deane. Unofficially, Adams must have seen this as the opportunity to supplant Franklin in the eyes of Vergennes. But his plans went awry even before Vergennes received his communique. The day after Adams wrote the foreign minister, word from Philadelphia arrived in Paris that Franklin had been named the sole minister to France.[57] Adams's proposed meeting with Vergennes never took place.

The news of Franklin's appointment was not a surprise. Unofficial word of Congress's action, transmitted by Deane, had reached Passy weeks before. Thereafter, rumors buzzed that Adams would be sent to Austria or Holland, perhaps even to Tuscany; word had it, too, that he would be called home. He was in terrible suspense. "We wait and wait and wait forever, without any News," he lamented. But when word of Franklin's appointment arrived in mid-February, Adams still knew nothing of his fate. Congress had said nothing. Not even a mention of Adams. "The Congress I presume expect that I should come home," he said. As the days passed, his rage grew. "The Scaffold is cutt away, and i am left kicking and sprawling in the Mire," he fumed. His purple fury was warranted. His treatment had been contemptuous, not least after the dangers of a wartime ocean crossing and the pain he had suffered during twelve months' separation from his family.[58]

Adams was going home. Congress's failure to give him an assignment was tantamount to a recall. He broke the news to Abigail in a letter, telling her—as he often had in the past—that his political career was over. The family would move to Boston, and there he would return to his legal practice. "I will draw Writs and Deeds, and harrangue Jurys and be happy," he mused.[59]

Adams wrote that letter one year and seven days after he last had seen his wife. He knew, too, that several additional weeks must pass before he finally reached home and was reunited with a wife that he feared had grown apart from him during the long separation.

While on this mission, Adams's behavior toward Abigail was perplexing. He wrote to her with less frequency than during any previous absence. He did not even bother to send tidings of his safe arrival until two weeks after he reached France and, thereafter, wrote home only once every two or three weeks, whereas he had written two or three times each week while in Philadelphia. Of necessity, his letters were brief and sterile. The danger of interception by the British was too great for him to divulge secrets or to express unfriendly thoughts toward France. He even told Abigail that he could not be candid in expressing his feelings about her, fearing that if captured and published it would make him appear to be "very ridiculous." Besides, he said, such expressions of tenderness "will do for young Gentlemen," but "Old Men . . . can no more amuse themselves with such Things than with Toys, Marbles and Whirligigs."[60]

But as the months wore on, Adams began to worry about his relationship with his wife. He grew "uneasy" about the lack of letters from home. He received only eleven letters from Abigail in the first twelve months they were apart. Some of her correspondence had miscarried, he knew, but he also realized that she no longer wrote as frequently as during the years of his congressional service. The letters he did receive, he fretted, contained "a Strain of Unhappiness and Complaint" that he had never previously discerned. One missive cut so deeply that he destroyed it. For the first time in all their years apart, he began to suspect that someone had "whispered in [her] Ear Insinuations." And for the first time since the early months of their relationship, he found himself writing that his love for her would never die.[61]

Indeed, more than Adams could know, someone had whispered to Abigail. More than he could realize amid the swirl and excitement that surrounded him in his exotic post, Abigail was overcome with a protracted despondency, the likes of which she had never experienced. Just four days after the *Boston* had stood out in the cold Atlantic breeze, James Lovell, Adams's colleague in the Massachusetts delegation to Congress, had written Abigail offering to assist her in every possible way during her husband's absence. In many ways, Lovell was much like Adams. One year younger than John, he was a graduate of Harvard College and a former teacher. Bright, abrasive, reputedly a very hard and diligent worker, he had served in Congress since shortly after being released from a British prison in Halifax, where he had been incarcerated following his arrest on a charge of spying during the first year of the war. In making contact with Abigail, Lovell advised her to "command me freely." "Be assured," he added, "I shall be gratified in executing your Commands." Abigail did not respond immediately, but sometime in the spring of 1778, still unaware that the *Boston* had reached France safely, she wrote to Lovell to inquire if Congress had received any word on the fate of the vessel and to express her fear that John was dead or in captivity.[62]

Her missive seemed to stoke an inner fire in Lovell, prompting an immediate answer to "lovely suffering . . . Portia," as he called her, appropriating the very pet name by which John had so long privately—very privately—addressed his wife. He made little attempt to hide his feelings for her, even admitting his "*secret* Admiration" for this anxious woman and, curiously, acknowledging that her distress caused him "*Delight.*" He was, he already had told Abigail, a man of "the most tender Sensibilities."[63]

"[Y]ou are a very dangerous man," she responded. He was also a married man. But she signed the letter "Portia," and she continued to write, dispatching about one letter each month before her husband's return to Braintree in the summer of 1779. Dangerous though Lovell may have been, within two months Abigail lauded his "Native Sensibility, tenderness and Benevolence," qualities she noted that would "ever attach the fair Sex" to him. For the most part, however, her letters were discreet, even businesslike missives in which she sought information and Lovell's "kind attention" from afar during her long, lonely, anxious months alone.[64]

Lovell sent fewer letters to Abigail than he received in return. His favors, too, exuded more an air of friendliness than enchantment, particularly after both he and Abigail learned of John's safe arrival in France. Nevertheless, his flirtatious manner occasionally was evident. If "'ye were mine . . . how dearly I would love thee,'" he wrote, quoting the Scottish poet Allan Ramsey, and he confessed his "blasted Hopes" at her prudent response to his overtures.[65]

Abigail also carried on a lengthy correspondence in this period with John Thaxter, Jr., her cousin, a young Harvard College graduate who had studied law in Adams's office and who, thanks to Adams's assistance, now served as a clerk in the Continental Congress. He wrote about twice each month, long letters in which he kept Abigail abreast of affairs of state and sought to answer her inquiries about congressional activities. Thaxter was a very different sort than Lovell. Not only were his letters almost barren of personal comment, but when Abigail inquired about his success with the ladies of Philadelphia, he responded tersely that "a cold phlegmatic frame has . . . render[ed] me invulnerable" to feminine charms. Nevertheless, she enjoyed his communiques, for this up-and-coming young man was a surrogate for her uncommunicative husband, a sober, industrious, and grim sort, not unlike John, and an activist who flattered her by his willingness to accept her as an intellectual equal.[66]

Adams and his son hurried from Passy to Nantes in March 1779, to secure passage to America on the *Alliance*. They need not have been in any haste, for the vessel had been detained elsewhere. Aside from a brief trip to Brest, father and son spent weeks in a hotel, passing their evenings at the opera, at the theater, over long dinners with French officials and American businessmen, or in their separate studies. One of the merchants with whom the Adamses passed the time was Joshua Johnson and his four-year-old daughter, Louisa Catherine. Their paths would cross again; sixteen years later, she and John Quincy would meet again and marry.[67]

Not until April 22, almost fifty days after their departure from Passy, did the Adamses board the *Alliance,* but even that proved a false start. Before weighing anchor the captain of the vessel received new orders. The *Alliance* would not sail for America! Adams was outraged, and he convinced himself that Franklin had used his influence to prevent the vessel from sailing. He was certain that Franklin feared his return to Congress to "tell some dangerous Truths." But Adams was wrong. The *Alliance* had been added to a squadron under John Paul Jones and Lafayette, which was to attack the west coast of England.[68]

Adams and his son quickly departed Nantes for L'Orient. From there they would take *La Sensible* home, though not any time soon. Nearly two full months passed in that old harbor town before their voyage commenced, a tedious time of waiting and waiting, and still more waiting, the monotony broken only by several convivial evenings spent in the presence of John Paul Jones, and a day or two in the company of Jones's officers aboard the *Bonhomme Richard.*[69]

The delay in sailing was occasioned by the tardy arrival of the Chevalier de la Luzerne, France's new minister to the United States, who also had reserved a berth on *La Sensible*. At last the envoy arrived, accompanied by his secretary, Barbé Marbois, and two clerks. All was in readiness. On June 17 the anchor was hoisted; the vessel creaked and swayed and finally began its run toward America. Ironically, at almost the same moment the *La Sensible* sailed, Abigail, three thousand miles away in Braintree, was taking a summer ride in her carriage, a leisurely trip cut short when she learned through a messenger that a packet of letters had arrived during her brief absence. "My spirits danced," she later recalled, but to her disappointment the packet was from Lovell. In her anguish she wrote a long, soulful letter to her friend in Philadelphia. "Six Months and not one line" from John, she raged, after which she encouraged Lovell to write again soon, promising that she would never again be angry with anything he said.[70]

After Adams's danger-fraught crossing eighteen months earlier, this voyage was tranquil. One scholar has suggested that Adams concluded that Franklin contrived to put him aboard this ship, which was weaker than the *Alliance,* in the hope that he would be killed or captured during the crossing. That is a misreading of Adams's letters. He suspected no such thing. *La Sensible,* in fact, was a large, powerful craft. Numerous privateers were spotted in the course of the voyage, but none dared challenge this vessel. Situated in a commodious—and private—cabin, Adams experienced a pleasant voyage. He passed the long daylight hours in conversation with his traveling companions, occasionally venturing onto the deck to observe the crew and to bathe in the warm summer breeze. Long meals with the officers punctuated the evening, followed by a retreat to his quarters for his customary late night stint of reading. *La Sensible* made normal time, favored throughout by felicitous weather and favorable winds. Only as the vessel approached St. George's Bank, about one hundred miles east of Cape Cod, did the weather suddenly turn nasty and foggy, but even that normally unwelcome occurrence proved fortuitous, for this region was regarded as the most dangerous stretch of the journey, and the inclement elements shrouded and safeguarded the ship from enemy vessels. On August 3, nearly eight weeks after departing L'Orient, *La Sensible* entered Boston harbor, and as quickly as possible thereafter, perhaps the same day even, Adams and his homesick young son were greeted at home.[71]

Abigail was not taken entirely by surprise at the sudden appearance of John and her son. Only a week before she had learned from Lovell—whom else?—that John Quincy and his father were rumored to have been in a French port in March awaiting embarkation. It was the first word she had received that he might be coming home, his letter of February 20 evidently having miscarried. The word from Lovell, she confessed, caused feelings within her that had "almost subsided" to well up again.[72]

Probably three days before Adams reached Braintree, Abigail received reliable word that her husband had been awaiting passage on the *Alliance* during the first week in March. That news was a mixed blessing. He was definitely coming home, but a voyage that commenced in March should have culminated weeks before—if it ended safely.[73]

Then, suddenly, the long, lonely wait was over. John and John Quincy were home. This time, surely, her husband was home to stay.

It was the loveliest time of the year. The days were mellow and warm, the nights pleasantly cool. It was good to be at home, to eat the vegetables from Abigail's garden, to once again taste his favorite food and sleep in his own bed. After such a lengthy absence, it was a joy for Adams to go into his fields, even to work for a spell under an energizing sun. It was grand, too, to find that his estate had flourished under Abigail's care. Indeed, it looked better than it had when he departed, better even than when he had managed the farm before politics pulled him in other directions.[74] It was a good time for visiting friends and relatives, for becoming reacquainted with the children, and for spending as much time as possible with his wife. Weeks passed. John wrote few letters. He made no entries in his diary. He simply remained close to home, close to his family.

Politics soon intruded, however. A Braintree town meeting asked him to serve as a delegate to the Massachusetts constitutional convention, scheduled to meet in Cambridge in September. This was to be the second attempt to secure a constitution for the state. In the spring of 1777, while Adams still sat in Congress, elections had been held in Massachusetts that empowered the House of Representatives to sit in a convention for the purpose of writing a state constitution. Adams had been delighted that his state at last was to act on this urgent matter, but the House, sidetracked frequently by the crucial day-to-day business of the war, had proceeded so slowly that its work was completed only after Adams's departure for France. Friends at home had sent him a copy of the proposed constitution and kept him abreast of the fight to ratify the document, but Adams wisely refused to enter the fray. His only comment on the matter concerned his disapproval that the Constitution of 1778 was submitted to a popular vote; nor did he respond when James Warren, who had approved of the proposed constitution, reported its defeat in the summer of 1778.[75]

Massachusetts thus remained under the Provincial Congress that had emerged in 1774 in protest against the Coercive Acts, but in February 1779, about the same moment that Adams departed Passy, the state assembly requested that the people, through town meetings, vote on the desirability of a constitutional convention. By a two-to-one majority the towns urged such a gathering. By happenstance, Adams arrived back in Braintree just as the village was preparing to select its representative to the convention.

Adams, as usual, pleaded his inability to cope with such an assignment, but he quickly accepted the appointment. He hurriedly prepared by rereading the Virginia constitution of 1776—one of eight state constitutions written and adopted since independence—and his own *Thoughts on Government,* as well as *Oceana,* a tract on empire and property written a century before by James Harrington, the English republican. On September 1, he was one of 313 delegates who assembled in Cambridge.[76]

Adams looked upon the adoption of a proper organic law as an especially urgent matter. Although he had been home only a brief time, it had been long enough for him to become deeply troubled at what he had seen. He feared that the western push for reform—more elective offices, an expansion of the suffrage, and majority rule—would dangerously divide the state. But he was no less alarmed at trends in the East. The interests of the mercantile East, including the commercial elite of Boston—whose calls for moderation in the aftermath of the Coercive Acts had ultimately gone unheeded before the crush of the popular party—had, of course, regained their hegemony during the spring of 1776. Eastern delegates now sought a charter that would guarantee its continued domination. John Hancock had emerged as the leading light of this faction, and during Adams's time in France he and others had worked assiduously to weaken the hold of the old popular movement. Their tactics included *ad hominem* attacks on Samuel and John Adams, popular leaders who had consistently remained independent of the merchants and who, in addition, had unwaveringly argued that harmony was essential and that interest politics were to be avoided at all costs. The Hancockians thus had floated the scurrilous tales that Samuel was part of a cabal to depose General Washington and that John had conspired to dismiss Silas Deane so that he might have his post in France.[77]

Adams understood the nature of the interest politics that had emerged within his province. He realized that at bottom the divisions often were based on class and economic interests, so that in his letters during this period he sometimes spoke of differences over issues such as "Paper Money" and taxation, as well as over the desires of the "stockjobbers" and the "mercantile Speculators" to use government in the pursuit of their narrow ends. Unless checked, these divisions, which he saw as only a recent development with Massachusetts, threatened the existence of republican government. What Adams sought, therefore, was not something new, but the preservation of what he regarded as the best of the old way. His was an ideal rooted in the past. He looked back to a time when government had supposedly been "in Miniature, an exact Portrait of the people at large," to a time when social deference, stability of leadership, and consensual politics had prevailed. His principal object in 1780, as it always had been, was to secure a constitution of balances, the sole hope of restraining "those who corrupt our symplicity," the last remaining prospect, he thought, for checking the divisions that had emerged in revolutionary America and for maintaining—recapturing, actually—a way of life he believed had once been held intact through bygone virtues.[78]

Adams soon had his chance to act, for the Hancockian campaign to deflate his and Samuel's influence clearly failed. At the end of the first week of its deliberations, the convention created a thirty-member committee to prepare a draft document; it names James Bowdoin, the convention's president, and the Adamses to actually do the work. Bowdoin and Samuel Adams immediately prevailed upon John to undertake the assignment. By week's end he was at work in his study in Braintree.

Adams's draft became the core of the Massachusetts Constitution of 1780. What he wrote in the seclusion of his home during those bright, summery days indicated that his views had not changed substantively since the appearance of his *Thoughts on Government* five years earlier. He continued to believe in the basic decency of humankind, and after a brief preamble his draft included a Declaration of Rights, which he modeled on the bill of rights included in several other state constitutions. These rights stated that all power resided in the people; his Declaration guaranteed free elections; offered protection against unreasonable searches and seizures; promised trial by jury; stated the right of free speech, press, and assembly; protected the right to keep and bear arms; and listed among mankind's "natural, essential, and unalienable rights . . . the right of enjoying and defending their lives and liberties; that of acquiring, possessing, and protecting their property."

Adams believed, however, that some structure was required to keep the darker passions of humankind in check. He provided for two elected legislative houses, the one to check the other in the course of making, changing, and repealing legislation, the most important function, he thought, in government. His two houses represented different social "orders," for the Senate was based on counties, the House of Representatives on towns. To qualify for sitting in the House, a man must own property valued at one hundred pounds; senators were required to possess a freehold worth three hundred pounds. The executive was crucial, too, for Adams saw this official as the engine that was to surmount the assemblymen's more petty, localistic concerns. Thus, the governor was to be both powerful and independent of the legislature, for only then could he play his assigned roles, an equipoise to the assembly and the primary spokesman for and defender of the public weal. Only those who possessed property valued at one thousand pounds could qualify to serve as governor. The governor was to be elected at large, and he was to be assisted by a council of nine elected by the Senate from within its own membership. In Adams's *Thoughts on Government* in 1776 he had proposed that only the lower house be directly elected; it was to elect the members of the upper house and the two legislative branches were to elect the executive. In 1780, however, he proposed the direct election of both legislative houses and the governor. Adams defined qualified voters as adult males who owned property with a minimum valuation of sixty pounds. But if assemblymen and governors were elected, Adams provided that judges were to be appointed by the executive and to serve "during good behavior."

In October, Adams submitted his handiwork to his two fellow subcommittee members. With slight alterations, they passed the document on to the committee of thirty, which in turn recommended the draft with only minimal changes to the full convention. Ultimately, the convention made some substantive alterations to Adams's draft. It provided for a legislative override of the governor's veto, somewhat weakening the strong executive that Adams had envisioned, and it permitted the election rather than the appointment of militia officers, broadened the property qualifications for holding office, and deleted his reference to free speech in the Declaration of Rights. Nevertheless, the Constitution of 1780 bore the clear imprimatur of John Adams. The document, moreover, occupies a crucial place in American political history, for it ended the period of legislative-centered government that had prevailed since news of the Coercive Acts reached America, the pattern that had characterized most of the earlier state constitutions; it inaugurated the era of the system of checks and balances represented by the presence of popularly elected executives and independent judges, which were to exist coequally with bicameral assemblies. In addition, the Constitution of 1780 was the beginning of the end of the problems that had divided Hancock and his faction from John Adams. Hancock, who easily won five successive gubernatorial elections beginning with that of 1780, discovered that the mercantile elite would have no difficulty living under an organic charter embraced by Adams, and as new issues and eventually new political parties arose over the next few years, the Hancockians and John Adams learned that they agreed with one another more than they disagreed.[79]

Adams soon found his time consumed with other matters. While he was drafting the constitution, Congress voted unanimously to appoint him minister plenipotentiary to negotiate an end to the War of Independence, should Great Britain agree to approach the bargaining table. Word of the appointment reached Braintree in mid-October, and its meaning was unmistakable. As the end of the war did not appear to be in sight, this mission was virtually certain to entail an absence of several years.

Henry Laurens of South Carolina, once president of Congress, wrote to urge Adams's acceptance of the post. His first mission had ended "without censure or applause," Laurens wrote apologetically, but he promised that Adams should not again suffer such a fate. Adams's acceptance would "make the true friends of American Independence happy, and [would] abate their apprehensions from incompetency or negligence in other quarters," a reference, undoubtedly, to Franklin and Lee.[80]

Adams decided immediately, perhaps even on the day that word of his appointment reached Braintree, to accept the tender. There never was a serious doubt that he would refuse. Bruised by his recent treatment, he yearned for vindication; driven by an insatiable ambition, the opportunity could not be ignored. He sought to soften the blow for Abigail by telling her that someday "We shall yet be happy." That was not much comfort to her, however, for she soon discovered that his pending absence reawakened old feelings of bottomless despair. In fact, she even began to refer to herself as a widow. She could not understand her fate. Why, she asked, was it her lot to be "so often . . . call'd to struggle" with the loss of a husband? What she did understand was how very differently she and her husband looked upon matters. "Honour and Fame" moved him. "Domestic happiness" was paramount for her.[81] Whereas he could never again find fulfillment in the ordinary pursuits of a Boston lawyer, even a successful one, she was unlikely to be contented in any capacity save that which was traditional for a woman in late eighteenth-century America: wife, mother, and manager of the home, each role undertaken with her husband at her side.

This time Abigail did not try to dissuade her husband from leaving. She simply sought to cope with her pain in private, searching for some way to "Give sorrow vent," as she put it. Her search led her back to James Lovell, to whom she soon wrote and to whom she candidly admitted that the trial she now faced might "distroy a tabernacle already impaired."[82]

CHAPTER 12

*

My Business Is Peace

JOHN ADAMS HAD BEEN HOME FOR seventy-one days when he again said his good-byes. This time he was to be accompanied by little Charles, not quite ten years old, as well as John Quincy, now twelve and already something of a well-traveled young sophisticate. Left behind were Nabby, fourteen now and likely to be a grown woman when she next saw her father, and Thomas, only seven, not far enough along in his schooling to be taken. Abigail, too, would remain in Braintree.

John Quincy left a day earlier than his sojourners, escorted to Boston by John Thaxter, Abigail's timorous, ramrod-straight cousin who had agreed to serve as John's private secretary. At midmorning the next day, November 13, Charles and his father set off, the former after picking and nibbling anxiously at his breakfast, the elder only after a long, painful, disquieting farewell. Once in Boston, Adams stopped at the residence of Isaac Smith, Abigail's uncle, to collect John Quincy and Thaxter, and just before sunset the party boarded *La Sensible,* the same vessel that had borne John home only a few weeks earlier.[1]

Although now something of a veteran sailor, Adams seemed especially ill at ease prior to this voyage. However, once he settled into the ship's routine, he grew more relaxed. He took his old quarters, sharing the tiny cabin with Charles, while John Quincy boarded with Thaxter. The last of several passengers arrived in the course of the next day, the most important being Francis Dana, eight years younger than Adams, also a Harvard College graduate and a congressman since 1777, now the newly appointed secretary to the legation. During the day, James Warren came aboard to bid the travelers a safe journey; he remained until well past dark, engaged in conversation, finally leaving an expectant but cheerful Adams. About ten the following morning, November 15, 1779, a sunny, chilly, breezy autumn day, the voyage at last began.[2]

La Sensible made a fast run, reaching the continent in twenty-three days but landing in Spain rather than Brest, the original destination. The first ten days of the crossing were thought to pose the greatest danger from enemy craft, but though two British frigates were known to be about, the *Sensible* safely cleared the Grand Banks on November 25. The sea and the Atlantic winter offered far greater peril. One day beyond the Banks a savage, mauling storm struck the ship, tossing about passengers like ragdolls, leaving many terribly ill and all thoroughly frightened. After three days the storms abated, but the vessel was battered and water seeped into its entrails through two large fissures. Pumps were established and each adult passenger was compelled to manually operate the equipment during four assigned shifts each day. *Sensible* was saved, but it was limping so badly that it lacked the mobility to defend itself. About the end of November its captain altered course for Ferrol, the nearest friendly port. An additional week of anxious sailing lay ahead until, just before noon on December 7, land—gorgeous land—was sighted.[3]

Adams languished in Ferrol for a week, awaiting word on the seaworthiness of *La Sensible*. When it was learned that the vessel could not soon be repaired, he organized what promised to be an arduous journey by land to Paris. The trek proved more difficult than Adams could have imagined, an adventure that he later called the most severe trial of his life. The party of Americans—the three Adamses, Thaxter, Dana, two servants, and two additional residents of Massachusetts who had booked passage on the *Sensible*—set out by mule, making what Thaxter called a *"Quixotik Appearance."* Led by two Spanish guides, the van wound from village to village, making only a few miles each day, sometimes traversing poor, dangerous, mountainous roads and often forced at night into beds infested with fleas and lice. Dreary, cold, foggy, inhospitable weather was their constant companion, and within a few days each person in the band was sneezing and coughing. More than a month was required merely to reach the French frontier. Late in January the party reached Bilbao, where after a few days' rest the travelers left their mules behind and boarded a chaise for the last leg of the trip. On the afternoon of February 9, more than two months after landing at Ferrol, the party, all in "tolerable Health," according to Adams, arrived in Paris. The journey by land had consumed twice the time required for the ocean crossing.[4]

Characteristically, Adams wasted little time before getting to work. On his first full day in Paris, he crossed to Passy, first to enroll his sons in an academy, then to call on Franklin. Despite his hearty dislike for his fellow envoy, Adams was cordial, though he was careful not to divulge the purpose of his mission, for fear that an envious Franklin would utilize all his artful skills to "strike Mr. Adams out of existence as a public minister and get himself into his place." He also was careful to situate his headquarters as far removed from Franklin as possible. After lodging briefly at the Hotel de Valois, he soon established his legation in a house adjacent to the hotel.[5]

The next day, accompanied by Franklin and garbed in a powdered wig with a sword strapped to his side, Adams called at Versailles. As he made the cold ride under scudding wintry clouds, past the barren forests and the brown, vacant fields, Adams might have reflected on how the war had changed in the two years since he first had ridden at Franklin's side along this very road.

Twenty-four months before, at the time he had landed at Bordeaux on his initial mission to France, it had been difficult for an American not to exude a heady optimism. Flushed with its recent triumph at Saratoga, the United States had just signed treaties of alliance with France. Surely, many had believed, the war would soon end victoriously.

But 1778 had been a year of few achievements for the allies. In June a French fleet under Comte d'Estaing had reached America, but by year's end he had failed to capture a single British ship of the line, and he and his American allies had been unsuccessful in their attempt to retake Newport. In the final days of the year, in fact, the British captured another American seaport, Savannah. D'Estaing enjoyed some success in the West Indies that winter, but his attempt to liberate Savannah in October 1779, failed. Nor did France succeed in its aims in Europe in 1779. Louis XVI's war ministers sought to reduce Portsmouth, a conquest that they hoped would leave France in control of the English Channel; that triumph was to be followed by raids against Bristol and Liverpool. But as 1780 dawned, the English flag still flew over those cities. In America, moreover, British armies were on the offensive. At the very moment Adams rode toward Versailles, a British armada bore down on Charleston, set to put in motion Whitehall's new strategy of reducing the South. Aside from having kept Britain from winning the war, the allies could point to only one real achievement. Spain had entered the conflict in 1779, although it had refused to ally with the United States.[6]

By the spring of 1780 the war was five years old. It also had become a world war. And it was a stalemate. Unless one side scored a dramatic victory, attrition would settle the matter. The war would continue until one side was too debilitated to continue, then the diplomats would decide the issue. In Europe's posh drawing rooms, three thousand miles from the grime and stench of any American battlefield, the ministers would bargain and haggle, and the war would end in a negotiated settlement.

Each side sought leverage for that eventuality. Great Britain hoped to reclaim the Carolinas and Virginia; it also looked about for an ally in Europe, and, at the same time, it began to pressure the Netherlands into ceasing commerce with the Franco-Spanish allies. France, which originally had believed that its navy alone could secure the independence of the United States, recently had decided to dispatch an army to America to assist General Washington.

Adams was aware of all this. He also knew that his mission had little chance of immediate success. Indeed, he even feared that his presence as a peace negotiator might be viewed by London as a sign of American weakness.[7]

The roots of Adams's appointment went back to early 1779 when Congress, at the behest of Vergennes, the French foreign minister, had begun to consider the ends it hoped to secure in this war. Independence was the only goal that all congressmen could agree on. Eight months of bitter wrangling passed before

Congress reached a decision on its other aims. Ultimately, it stipulated that Britain must relinquish to the United States all territory westward to the Mississippi River and southward to the thirty-first parallel, as well as southern Canada; Britain must also concede America's right of access to the Newfoundland fisheries. Furthermore, Congress stipulated that it wished to negotiate a postwar treaty of commerce with the former parent state. Having at length agreed upon these objectives, Congress selected Adams to be the United States's sole minister to negotiate both the peace accord and the commercial pact.[8]

If Adams was aware of what he must seek from Great Britain, he also knew that he could not negotiate a separate peace treaty. Article eight of the Treaty of Alliance with France mandated as much. The war would continue until the allies agreed mutually to end hostilities with Britain. Hence, Adams was anxious to call upon Vergennes, not just as a matter of courtesy, but to coordinate matters with his ally.

There was much on Adams's mind. As early as fall 1778, he had reached the conclusion that the war could be won if only France would agree to send a greater naval force to American waters. Within another six months, he had even begun to recommend that France dispatch an army to America; should France send five thousand troops across the Atlantic, he said in February 1779, the allies "must infallibly succeed." Instead, France had sought without success to invade England, and during 1779 Adams watched in dismay as the British were both more active and more successful than the Allies. In addition, the conditions that he must have discovered during his brief sojourn in America could only have convinced him further of the imperative need for a greater French military commitment. After years of hostilities, danger signs were visible throughout New England. In Massachusetts, inflation was rampant; labor was scarce; farm animals were few; men were away at war and unable to tend their farms; and people sometimes went hungry. Everywhere, it seemed, lives were disrupted by a war that seemed endless. Adams seems to have been surprised that the "Spirits of the People [remained] high and their Temper extreamly firm," and he certainly did not doubt that victory could be achieved, but he appears to have returned to France with the understanding that something must be done quickly to break the military deadlock. The steady collapse of Continental currency, the remorseless inflation, the habitual logistical problems that plagued the Continental army, and the deadly factional strife in Congress that had been spawned both by the Silas Deane Affair and the legislators' attempt to determine the conditions of peace had made a severe impact on public morale. If the war did not turn around soon, the future might be gloomy. But what Adams found upon his arrival clearly cheered him. The French were pursuing the war with a renewed vigor. A greater fleet than had ever previously been sent to America was being outfitted; the French "are determined to maintain a clear Superiority," he reported. Along with this,

Vergennes was sending an army to America. Donatien de Vimeur, Comte de Rochambeau, was gathering four thousand men at Brest and soon would depart. Adams's dreams appeared to be coming true. British confidence would be shattered, he predicted. London would fight on for awhile, but soon enough it would realize the folly of continuing the war.[9] Buoyant with optimism, Adams was convinced that the time had come to open talks with America's ally in preparation for eventual negotiations with Great Britain.

The Versailles that Franklin and Adams entered that cold February morning was not yet the stately museum that we know today. Elegant and magnificent, yet neglected, it was, as Franklin said, a palace of "shabby half Brick Walls and broken Windows."[10] The American envoys were shown through the corridors, past office after office, down hallways busy with officials and clerks, until they reached the chamber of the foreign minister. There was a brief wait outside Vergennes's office, then they were ushered into his presence. The minister received Adams with the same reserved, cool, even patronizing manner with which he had bade him farewell almost exactly one year before. Then Vergennes sat back to listen as Adams explained the purpose of his mission. What he heard must have come as a surprise. Adams merely requested permission to write him concerning the cause of his undertaking. Obviously, he did not wish to have Franklin intruding in any way in the execution of his assignment. Although not happy with this strange request, Vergennes nevertheless consented.

The next day brought Adams's letter. He sought Vergennes's consent to inform the British ministry of his powers to engage in peace negotiations.[11]

Vergennes moved immediately to quiet Adams. He cautioned the American to be circumspect, lest Whitehall and the European neutrals drew the conclusion that the allies were desperate for peace; he warned, too, that any entreaty by Adams would only stabilize the North government, for it could point to his eagerness to talk as evidence that its war policies were succeeding. In reality, however, Vergennes was troubled by something else. Haunted by the prospect of a separate Anglo-American peace, he hoped to forestall all contact between the United States and London, fearing that the result might be a reconciliation between the former colonists and their parent before France had achieved its objectives in this war. Adams, he instructed, was to publish a statement merely indicating that he had been sent to conduct "the future pacification"; moreover, the draft of that announcement must be cleared by the French foreign ministry prior to its publication.[12]

Adams had no choice but to consent. He could hardly antagonize his nation's sole ally.

Chastened, Adams divided his time that spring between looking after his sons and tending his public responsibilities. The boys were enrolled in L'École de Mathématiques, the same school that John Quincy had attended in 1778, an academy esteemed by the American residents in Paris. Although they lodged at the school, Charles and his brother spent the weekends with their father, a time the three used for sightseeing, an undertaking that was now easier for Adams, as he no longer was quite so perplexed by the strange language and cultural differences within Paris and the surrounding countryside. Now and then, the Adamses visited some nearby provinces, but primarily they took in the sights in Paris, seeing places that John had never found the time to visit on his first mission. One weekend, they attended the museum, another the mint, and on still other occasions they toured gardens and public squares, or viewed statues, then it was on to Bicetre, an institution for criminals, the insane, the ill, and infirm. It was a fine education for the boys, a good complement to their formal instruction, and the rapid progress of the two left Adams a happy father. Charles, especially, was a delight. Father and son had been separated so much that Adams barely knew the boy, but now that was changing. He was a strong, tough, bright youngster, said the doting father, a boy that everyone liked. "He is a delightful, little fellow. I love him too much."[13]

Adams closely followed the boys' education, once advising John Quincy not to spend much time on such subjects as geography, geometry, and arithmetic, later instructing the headmaster not to waste the youngsters' time with lessons in fencing and dancing. A little art and penmanship was fine, he agreed, but most of his sons' attention was to be focused on the study of Latin, Greek, and French. Adams put John Quincy in charge of little Charles during the week, and he clearly expected much from his older son. Once when he received a note from the boy, Adams admonished him for having hurried off the missive in a slapdash manner. Write more legibly, he ordered. "Cant you keep a steadier Hand?" On another occasion, Adams refused to send along a letter that the youngster had written to a friend in Massachusetts. The communique was sloppily written, Adams remarked testily, adding that the "Letters [were] badly made, the Lines as crooked as possible." Rewrite the letter, he ordered, and this time take greater care to write more legibly.[14]

When John Quincy's redrafted missive was ready, it went into a packet of letters that Adams had written to friends and his wife back home. Surprisingly, however, he wrote to Abigail only infrequently during this period, sending her a letter about every ten days. Often his letters were accompanied by packages laden with fabric, tea, glassware, silverware, and china. "We married men who run away from our Wives and Children must send them something, to alleviate the pains of Solitude," he explained to the captain of a vessel transporting one of his bundles of commodities. In fact, the goods were not intended for Abigail or the children. He expected his wife to sell the items so that the family might keep up with expenses and she might be able to purchase a "genteel Chaise," the sort of vehicle an affluent French family surely would possess.[15]

During the week, Adams devoted his days to his official duties. Following Vergennes's directive, there was no official business to transact. Nevertheless,

Adams remained busy. He filed report after report with the Congress, averaging about five communications each week he was in Paris, mostly lengthy résumés of intelligence gathered from the British press and from his contacts in Paris. He met often with private citizens and French officials, sometimes in their offices, usually in their homes; of course, he entertained frequently at the simple American legation, careful to serve his guests, which included, among others, the Comte d'Estaing—recovering from the wounds he had suffered at Savannah—only the "very best Quality Bordeaux." Adams additionally expended considerable energies as a propagandist. With the sanction of the French government, he wrote occasional anonymous essays for a weekly Paris newspaper, *Mercure de France,* pieces that sought to counter British stories of discontent within the Franco-American alliance or of "drooping Spirit[s]" in the United States. Quite without French authorization, he published in British newspapers as well. He wrote under a pseudonym, although it probably was not difficult for French intelligence officials to learn the identity of the author, as he not only revealed the purpose of his mission but also divulged details of his arduous journey through the Spanish mountains. Many of these essays sprang from his desire to refute the pamphlets of Joseph Galloway, his former colleague in Congress, now a Loyalist refugee in London. Galloway ground out one tract after another in an effort to sustain public interest in the war and to persuade the British of the necessity of holding onto the colonies. Adams responded by showing that an independent America and imperial Great Britain could coexist and prosper from a flourishing trade. He placed his articles through Edmund Jenings, a native of Maryland who had remained in England following the completion of his studies at Cambridge and the Middle Temple. Adams, who probably met Jenings through Arthur Lee, a relative, was convinced of his contact's commitment to the American cause. He may not have been correct, and the candor with which he communicated frequently with Jenings may have been unwise.[16]

During the spring of 1780, Adams's views began to change, as they often had during the past five years. The ebullience that he had radiated in February following his arrival in Paris faded. While Rochambeau and his army (he actually had fifty-five hundred men, a force about one-quarter larger than Adams realized) sped off for America in the late spring, French naval reinforcements, to Adams's dismay, went to the West Indies, not to the United States. As it was likely that the French army and navy would hope to act in concert, he concluded—quite correctly—that the armies of Washington and Rochambeau would remain idle for still another campaign. Two years after the Franco-American alliance had begun, he ranted, "nothing has yet been done . . . that seems decisive." Spain, he noted, had been in the war for only a few months, yet it had already scored a victory at Mobile and now was likely to garner East Florida and West Florida in the postwar settlement, a region that many Americans coveted; why, he wondered, could France not act with such vigor.[17]

For the first time, the tiniest hints that he doubted the inevitability of victory began to show through in his private writings. He spoke of "artful and sensible men" in America who wished to reunite with Great Britain. Victory would go to the side that could "hold it out longest," he said, and he believed that America, France, and Spain could outlast Britain, if, of course, the French ally and co-belligerent Spain remained in the war. His previous expectations that Britain would soon be brought to the peace table had vanished by late spring, the result both of allied inactivity and the news that British forces had invaded South Carolina early in the year. No end to this interminable war was in sight, he wrote to friends at home, also seeking to prepare them for the reality that America might ultimately have to win the contest on its own. For the first time in years, he castigated as "unmanly" those who might not wish to fight on. "Americans must be soldiers, they must war by sea and land, they have no other security," he had begun to counsel by the spring of 1780.[18]

As these views began to take shape in Adams's mind, it is apparent, too, that he grew increasingly suspicious with regard to the nature of America's partnership with France. Despite the cavernous differences in strength between the allies, Adams from the beginning had looked upon France and the United States as equal partners in this alliance. It was "a natural alliance," as he put it in May 1780, an instance of two nations drawn together through "mutual wants and interests." Similar fears and hatreds of Great Britain had helped weld the union, but commercial and agricultural opportunities for both had also played a role. In the light of events since February, however, Adams saw that France treated the United States not as an equal but as a dependency. France "ought not to have so undue an influence upon an Independent Nation," he remarked. Indeed, in such an unequal partnership, two fears began to root in his breast. Lest a victorious America conclude a separate peace and leave France alone to fight on against Great Britain, was France dragging its feet in America until it secured its aims elsewhere? Or, if France achieved its ends elsewhere, would it abandon America before independence was recognized? In either case, subservience to Versailles meant that the interests of France would be served, but those of the United States might be imperiled.[19]

There seemed to be little that could be done to alter this situation, however. Not only did Adams have no contact with Vergennes, but he also had long since concluded that Franklin could not be counted on to take a strong stance in his communications with the foreign minister. In their clash over the wisdom of urging a more active role upon France eighteen months earlier, Adams had concluded that Franklin was fearful of pushing too hard. Adams had often spoken of Franklin's servile, obsequious manner toward French officials and once he even told Congress that "Dr Franklin is as good an index of [Vergennes] as I know." Later, he charged that Franklin thought American "affairs in Europe ought to be under one direction, and that the French court ought to be the centre." These were mendacious charges. Franklin simply believed that a respectful, almost deferential, manner (what he called a style of "Decency and Delicacy") was more likely to secure greater assistance for America; dogged assertiveness, he thought, might result in French calumny.[20]

Much to Adams's surprise, an opportunity to express his views to Vergennes suddenly presented itself in early summer 1780. But, as historian James Hutson has demonstrated, what Adams did not understand was that he was being manipulated by the foreign minister. Through his intelligence sources, Vergennes had learned of Adams's activities, including, in all likelihood, his essays in British newspapers and his indiscreet correspondence with residents of England. Too, through his first minister to the United States, Conrad Alexandre Gerard, he discovered that Adams had even contemplated a trip to London to present his credentials. Vergennes, as distrustful of America as Adams was of France, concluded that Adams constituted a menace to French plans and must be removed.

An opportunity to act against Adams occurred in June. In the spring, Congress had devalued the dollar, an action certain to cause harm to French merchants. When businessmen in Paris beseeched Adams's assistance, he turned a deaf ear to their entreaties. Vergennes saw his chance. If Adams remained unwilling to aid the French, perhaps Congress would recall him as an obstacle to Franco-American relations.[21]

Vergennes, thus, opened a correspondence with Adams, requesting his assistance with Congress in securing special financial considerations for French businessmen. It was his first contact with the American envoy in four months. To what must have been the utter surprise and amazement of the minister, Adams not only wrote extensively about American monetary policy, but he once again urged upon France a greater naval commitment in American waters and he reopened the issue of approaching London with regard to opening peace negotiations.[22]

There can be little doubt that Adams ultimately injured himself by resurrecting these issues. What led him upon such a course? Some scholars have attributed his action to naïveté and diplomatic inexperience; by implication, it has also been suggested that his towering vanity and deep hatred for Franklin compelled him to seek an ever greater role for himself, even if his actions antagonized America's French ally. But to portray Adams as an awkward, callow bungler is to overlook the fact that his years in Congress and in Paris had provided him with considerable seasoning in the arts of politics and statecraft. Moreover, to attribute his motives during his embassy to his dislike of Franklin is to ignore the consistency in his foreign policy outlook. He was America's first great nationalist. "I was John Yankee and such I shall live and die," he remarked in 1778, and, indeed, from the first he had looked with distrust upon all foreign powers and had sought to structure an American foreign policy that would result in the true independence of the nation he represented.[23]

Adams had to have known the risk he ran in his renewed entreaties to Vergennes, but he feared that remaining silent would place the United States at greater peril. He believed that the worst crisis in this interminable war had arrived. The military stalemate must be broken; if the war continued to drag on without a greater promise of victory, American independence would be jeopardized. Once suspicion set in that victory was a mirage, numerous dangers might emerge. British energies would be redoubled. France's staying power could wane. The accommodationists in America might be revived. Not least, the noncombatants throughout Europe likely would pressure Britain and France to conclude the contest. Adams thus seized upon what he saw as the golden opportunity afforded him by Vergennes to push for an immediate commitment of greater French naval forces, the one thing that would enable Washington and Rochambeau to take the offensive, perhaps besieging the British in New York, or perhaps invading Canada as a means of luring Gen. Henry Clinton and his army from New York. Adams knew, however, that entreaties alone were unlikely to move Vergennes. He sought, instead, to use the one small bit of leverage he possessed. Adams attempted to play on Vergennes's fears that America might seek a separate peace, that France might be left alone to wage its war with Great Britain. Only that prospect, Adams appears to have concluded during the spring of 1780, could move France to a more vigorous prosecution of the war, the one thing that could save the Revolution. It was a desperate gamble, and, for Adams, one that resulted in bitter failure.

Seven letters from Adams were all that Vergennes required to accomplish his ends. Adams's final communications were the most damaging. His first letters dealt only with America's currency regulations, but his fourth communique was given over entirely to a lengthy rumination on the course of the war, in which he made it quite clear that he did not believe that France was doing all it could to bring the war to a conclusion. Before Vergennes could respond, he wrote again, proposing, as he had in February, that Britain be apprised of his mission to negotiate a settlement. The foreign minister's response to Adams's lecture about the war was gentle. The "King is far from abandoning the cause of America," he replied. But his reply to Adams's entreaty with regard to approaching London was savage and mocking, rendered in a tone that resembled the scolding an insensitive schoolmaster might give to an ignorant pupil. Such a course could "serve no good purpose." It would convince Britain that America harbored "an irresistible predilection for her." London would not negotiate; Adams would be made to appear "the laughing-stock of all nations." Adams had to have the last word. In a tone that was nearly as sarcastic as that employed by the minister, a manner that he might have used before a Boston jury but one certainly inappropriate in these circumstances, he sought to counter point by point Vergennes's refutation. His principal argument hinged on the notion that North would reject negotiations but that his rejection would divide public opinion and strengthen the peace movement within Great Britain. With that, Vergennes terminated the correspondence and passed on Adams's communiques to Franklin, adding that he hoped the materials would be sent to Congress, which could judge whether Adams was suitable for such a crucial diplomatic assignment. Meanwhile, he wrote Luzerne, his new minister to the United States and Adams's traveling companion on the *Alliance* during the previous summer, to gently broach the idea of Adams's recall or, failing that, to request that Congress provide him with a "colleague capable of containing him."[24]

The United Provinces, the Netherlands, had been on Adams's mind for some time. A confederation of seven semiautonomous states, the Netherlands was a faded world power, although it yet possessed a string of colonies that stretched from present-day Indonesia to Ceylon, and from southern Africa to the West Indies. Officially, the Dutch had refused to be drawn into this war. In theory, an ally of Britain, the States General, the national parliament, had steadfastly remained neutral, although neutrality had not been without its difficulties, especially once France and Spain joined the war. Britain had an obvious interest in preventing Dutch transports laden with naval supplies from reaching the ports of its adversaries. On the other hand, the Netherlands realized that it might profit from a diminution in Britain's colonial power in America. As the number of incidents on the High Seas increased, American officials—including Adams while on his initial mission to France—sought to cultivate the Dutch, a ploy that was not entirely unavailing, as powerful dissenting forces within the country indicated a willingness to open trade with the United States. Consequently, when Congress selected Adams to negotiate the peace, it also named Henry Laurens as its envoy to the Netherlands. His mission was to negotiate a treaty of amity and commerce and to seek a loan of $10 million.[25]

By July 1780, however, Laurens had not yet arrived in the Netherlands. Indeed, although Adams was unaware of it, Laurens was only just leaving South Carolina on an ill-fated journey. Three weeks into his voyage, the little brigantine upon which he was a passenger was seized by a British frigate; he was taken to London, where he would languish for fifteen months in the Tower.[26] What Adams did know by July was that he could do nothing in Paris. As early as March, in fact, he had sought a French passport to travel to Holland, where he might begin to do some spadework for Laurens. Vergennes, fearing that Adams would only cause mischief, blocked his trip. Nor was Franklin supportive of such an undertaking. "I have long been humiliated with the idea of our running from court to court begging for money and friendship," he told Adams; arms and money, he went on, were more likely to be withheld "the more eagerly they [were] solicited." Adams likely saw in this still further confirmation of Franklin's unwillingness to defy Vergennes. But he was convinced—even more so now that France had rebuffed his appeal for a greater military commitment—of the need to secure a Dutch loan. He brushed aside Franklin's reservations and once again raised the matter directly with Vergennes. Probably unwilling to risk arousing American enmity over this matter, Vergennes relented. Before the end of the month, Adams and his sons moved to the Netherlands.[27]

When Adams took up residence in Amsterdam, he knew that he had no power to talk with the Dutch. Nevertheless, through his intelligence sources he knew that the Dutch government might permit a loan to the United States, a loan that would accomplish two objectives. First, the funds might permit the United States to be more independent of France. In addition, a Dutch willingness to become involved with the United States might force London into peace talks. With his own mission thwarted, he believed that he might plant the seeds that Laurens, or whoever, could someday cultivate.[28]

Adams settled in Amsterdam in mid-August, after brief stops for sightseeing in Brussels, Antwerp, Rotterdam, and The Hague. He immediately took a fancy to the place. He found the inhabitants frugal and serious, much like the natives of New England; he also discovered that a small, convivial band of Americans resided in the city, mostly businessmen who had come to this city in search of commerce, a tiny community within which he could relax, converse, and entertain. With its coursing canals and Old World architecture, Amsterdam was a beautiful city, although its frequently damp, gloomy weather caused him some discomfort. Still, he liked the city, and after a few months he admitted that he found it preferable to Paris, or even to Philadelphia.[29]

A month after his arrival Adams learned that Congress had placed Dutch affairs temporarily in his care, but his official status did little to further his ends. Actually, Adams initially thought the likelihood of his success was quite good. During his first days in Amsterdam he spoke with several influential figures who led him to believe that Dutch financiers and businessmen not only would provide a loan but shipments of stores and clothing as well. His exuberance soon faded, however. One delay after another arose. At first he attributed every hindrance to the language barrier; he did not speak Dutch, his Dutch contacts spoke no English, and neither spoke French very well. In time he better understood the complexities of the situation. Dutch assistance almost certainly would provoke British retaliation, not a prospect that many in Amsterdam welcomed. Nor did the news from America help his efforts. First had come word of the fall of Charleston. A few weeks later, tidings arrived that General Gates had suffered a stunning defeat at Camden, South Carolina, leaving America's southern army in tatters. Worst of all was the discovery that the British had found evidence within Laurens's papers suggesting that the Dutch had conspired for two years or more to aid America. November brought still more bad news. Benedict Arnold, one of America's most prominent general officers, had conspired to commit treason against his country.[30]

Great Britain did not go to war with the Netherlands, at least not formally. It did issue an order-in-council authorizing reprisals against Dutch shipping, with the effect, said Adams, that the Dutch were so apprehensive that every thought of aid was banished. By early 1781, five months after his arrival in Amsterdam, Adams still had not met with a single government official. He now knew full well that there was no immediate hope of such a meeting. Characteristically, he recanted the nice things he had previously said about Amsterdam. He wished he were in Paris, or even Passy, he said. This city was the "capital of the reign of Mammon."[31]

Bleak as matters seemed to be, Adams still saw a ray of hope. During the previous year the Russian empress, Catherine the Great, had announced the formation of a League of Armed Neutrality. Sweden and Denmark joined immediately, followed by Portugal, Prussia, and Austria. All were neutral nations who chose to associate with one another to protect their commerce, particularly in the Baltic, from marauding British warships bent on crippling French trade. Adams knew that the League was neither an anti-British nor a pro-American alliance, but he was confident that in time British depredations would pull these powers into the conflict. Sooner or later "England will be ruined" by the neutral states, he proclaimed. Indeed, he embraced the hope that someday the neutral states would recognize American independence; the moment that occurred, he predicted, Britain would lay down its arms.[32]

Late in the winter Adams was flattered to learn that in view of Laurens's misfortune Congress had named him commissioner of the United States to the United Provinces. Within a few weeks he decided to approach the Dutch government, announcing his appointment and seeking to negotiate a treaty of commerce. He could not be dissuaded from acting, although the French especially sought to restrain him, thinking the time was inappropriate for such an act. France had just learned of a Russian offer to mediate the undeclared Anglo-Dutch war. With the Russian offer on the table, the French insisted, nothing good could come of Adams's initiative. St. Petersburg, likely to believe that Versailles was pulling Adams's strings, would of necessity conclude that France had sent the American envoy into action to foil the Russian mediation. Catherine would be mistaken, yet alienated. Nor did the Dutch wish to deal with Adams, for by the time he got around to acting, Britain had rejected the Russian offer to mediate; if Adams stumbled into the picture at this juncture, the Dutch government feared, Catherine might seize upon his offer as a convenient pretext for jettisoning the Netherlands and avoiding war with Britain.[33]

But Adams could not be deterred, despite the Herculean efforts of the French. The Duke de la Vauguyon, who was aware of Adams's intention, urged his counterpart to come first to the French legation in The Hague for an urgent conference. Adams obliged, and the two spoke for two hours on April 19 and four more hours the following morning, but no amount of pleading or

cajoling could dissuade the American diplomat. "Determined, and unaltera-
bly determined I am," he pronounced.[34]

While he did not expect immediate success, he was certain that the Dutch
could be persuaded eventually to aid the United States. He would convince
them that Britain could not crush the American rebellion. He would make
them see that the Dutch people and the inhabitants of the United States shared
many common bonds, including an abiding faith in republican government,
similarity in religious persuasion, and a desire to escape British commercial
restraints. He could make them understand the benefits of a free trade with the
United States.[35]

As Adams prepared to approach the Dutch government, he relied heavily
on Charles W. F. Dumas, a Swiss national who had resided for several years in
the Netherlands and who, since 1777, had been a secret agent for the United
States. Dumas advised the envoy, established contacts in official circles, and
spoke in advance with Dutch luminaries. But Adams made ready as well. He
acquired a large house on the Kiezersgragt, an abode with good kitchen
facilities and suitable rooms for entertaining. He purchased decorous furnishings and tasteful table linens and napkins, and he hired an excellent chef and
three efficient servants. He now had a place that was "decent enough for an
character in Europe to dine with a Republican citizen," he remarked. In
addition, he obtained a handsome, sleek chaise, a team of horses, and the
services of a coachman. Then he set to work to cultivate influential Dutchmen
from among the states least committed to the Stadtholder, the pro-British chief
executive. He wined and dined them in his comfortable residence and he called
on them in his sparkling new carriage, hoping in that manner to vanquish the
notion that the United States was merely a weak, bankrupt client state of
France. Adams relished his new life-style, and he appears to have been happier
than at any time since his initial posting in France two years before. He had
come to Europe with a grant of power and a more exalted position, he believed,
than had been given even Washington.[36] Indeed, living and acting amid the
flourishing swirl of a dazzling European capital, far removed from the mun-
dane work of a Boston lawyer and the isolation of a rural farm, living a life so
different from that of the tedious, corporate lot of a congressman, Adams seems
to have known a contentment that he had not experienced in years.

By the spring of 1781, as Adams prepared to present his memorial to the
Dutch government, a year and a half had elapsed since that cold autumn day
when he had left behind a wife and two of his children in Braintree. Separation
from Abigail now had become a commonplace of his life. In fact, he had been
apart from her so often—about ninety percent of the time during the past
seven years—that he rarely complained any longer of his lonely existence. He
no longer even wrote home very often. While some letters have been lost, it is

known for certain that he sent only six letters to her during the initial nine months of 1781. Abigail did not receive a single letter from him between the last week in December 1780 and the final week of September 1781. Strangely, he never wrote to Nabby or Thomas during this period.[37]

Abigail never grew accustomed to living without a mate. She continued to speak of her "many solitary hours," and she fervently believed that she suffered from the separation to a far greater degree than her husband. Generally, however, she was able to keep her disappointment and depression in check, although at times—as on Christmas Day 1780—her pain showed through. "I feel the pangs of absence sometimes too sensibly," she admitted, only to quickly reproach herself for such a "repineing thought." She made no attempt, however, to hide her anguish at the absence of her sons. She fretted especially over "My delicate Charles," aware that John Quincy was older and used to living apart from his parents, and she confessed that her "two dear Boys cannot imagine how ardently I long to fold them to my Bosom."[38]

With two children at home—one an eight-year-old—and myriad other responsibilities, Abigail had her hands full. She had leased the farm to tenants, removing that daily care from her schedule, but she managed the family's finances, vended the goods that John succeeded in getting to her, and speculated in public securities and real estate, purchasing tracts of land both in Braintree and faraway Vermont. The latter acquisition perhaps grew from a forlorn hope that she might someday induce her husband to a frontier farm, far from the distractions of public life in Boston. If so, Adams never remotely shared her sentiments. In no uncertain terms he told her to forget Vermont. "I must be within the Scent of the sea," he said.[39]

Abigail wrote to her husband about once each month during this absence, sending along news of the war, the weather, and, of course, family matters. She conveyed the sad tidings of the death of John's sister-in-law, Mary, Peter's wife, who died of complications at childbirth, and of the demise of John's stepfather, John Hall. Abigail also wrote often of the declining health of John's mother, now seventy-two, reporting that "the Good Lady . . . bids me tell you not to expect to see her again." Letter after letter contained information concerning her fiscal management, but she merely reported her endeavors. She no longer required her husband's advice.[40]

Abigail's numerous responsibilities—and especially the care demanded by the children—would have overburdened a lesser person. Not only did Nabby and Thomas require considerable attention, but for a time one of Peter Adams's youngsters moved in following his family's tragedy. She bore the strain well, however. Of course, she was assisted by servants, but she was also in good health. Save for what must have been an allergy-induced illness each October and one minor bout with arthritis, she experienced no physical ills during these years. Time was her greatest enemy—long, lonely, empty hours of solitude. Getting away from the farm from time to time helped. She did not leave Braintree during the first six months of her husband's absence, but thereafter she escaped on occasion. More than once she rode to Cambridge to visit Francis Dana's wife, Elizabeth, and once she even journeyed to Plymouth for a stay with the Warrens; early in 1781 these old friends purchased Hutchinson's former country home on Milton Hill overlooking Quincy Bay and Boston, and thereafter they frequently played host to Abigail, who made the short ride from Braintree in the "genteel Chaise" that she at last purchased for $300. Many old friends cheered her with frequent visits to her residence. Elizabeth Dana and the Warrens called on her, as did the Warren's sons. Richard and Mary Cranch came often, too, and on occasion dignitaries such as Gen. Benjamin Lincoln and Col. John Laurens paid their respects.[41] Otherwise, she worked and read, and she maintained a voluminous correspondence with John and the boys, and once again with James Lovell.

Once before when her husband was gone, Abigail had remarked laconically: "I shall find some excuse or other to write him [Lovell] soon, I suppose." On this occasion she waited only five days after John's departure to renew her correspondence with the Massachusetts congressman. During the next two years, until Lovell departed Congress and returned to Massachusetts, the two wrote frequently, each averaging about one letter a month. Abigail hid behind the fiction that she had approached Lovell, who chaired the committee on foreign relations, merely to secure information concerning congressional policies and politics. In fact, he rarely contributed much to her knowledge of such matters, and from the beginning she found Elbridge Gerry much more useful in this role. Lovell did assist Abigail in the procurement of items she sought to vend, but clearly her real tie to the congressman was more an emotional bond than a business arrangement.[42]

"In truth Friend thou art a Queer Being," Abigail once told Lovell, a reference to the fact that although married—for the third time—he had not seen his wife for four years, preferring to remain in Philadelphia while she resided alone in Massachusetts. Lovell, as Abigail knew quite well, had a reputation as a paramour, and dark rumors circulated of his filiations and escapades. Once he even told her, "the Nights they are ten times more ruinous to my health" than daily political responsibilities, and he confessed that he hurried to his lodging to "hide myself . . . within the Bed Curtains the moment that *public* duty is discharged." Nevertheless, she was drawn to him, flattered that such a worldly man—in this respect so unlike her husband—evidently was just as taken by her.[43]

His reputation to the contrary, it was Lovell who seems to have acted with the greater discretion. Abigail initiated the renewal of the relationship, knowing full well the dangers involved in corresponding with any man while her husband was absent. Lovell, too, was aware of the dangers, and he often wrote Abigail in a cypher, a safeguard in case his letters fell into the wrong hands; she refused to use such a precaution, however, and when one of her missives was intercepted and delivered to a Loyalist publisher in New York, she faced weeks of anguish, although, curiously, the newspaperman never printed the letter. Lovell's earliest letters, moreover, could not have been more businesslike, but as the correspondence continued he began to warm up, and soon he was referring to Abigail as "lovely Woman," "Lovely Portia," "most lovely," and even as a "Saucy-box." Abigail quickly admonished him for his advances. "[W]icked Man," she scolded.[44]

Lovell responded by not writing for weeks, until Abigail once again urged him to resume the correspondence. When his letters that followed were unusually formal, she criticized his "Laconick" manner. She told him that she loved his "Letters when they are not too sausy, or do not border upon what I never will pardon or forgive." She watched the mail daily in the hope of hearing from him, she confided, and she often complained of the lapses between his letters. She admitted that she read and reread his messages. She probed to learn more of Lovell's relationship with his wife. She even coyly sought to learn from Lovell the truth of his allegedly scurrilous behavior with the Philadelphia ladies, adding that she did not believe the tales of his activities, and confessing her inability to "withdraw my esteem" from the congressman.[45]

"I shall find you out by and by," she told Lovell, and, in part, that was what the correspondence was about. Intrigued by this rakish man, she sought to know more of him. Mostly, however, she was desperately lonely. "Domestick happiness" was all she ever desired, she admitted to Lovell, but her husband's vain lust for notoriety had left her cloistered alone, ignored, isolated, useless. Only thirty-five years old when her husband departed on his second mission to Europe, Abigail was young, attractive, and, as she put it, "widowed." She was flattered that a dandy such as Lovell was obviously attracted to her. He provided an escape of sorts, offering attention, enchantment, an air of mystery, and the safe allurement of forbidden excitation. But despite their mutual attraction and affection, their relationship almost certainly remained an emotional bond rather than a physical liaison. Indeed, before Lovell returned to Massachusetts in 1782, and perhaps even afterward, the two were in the presence of one another only twice, including once in the company of several other persons at the Cranch's residence.[46]

It is unlikely that John Adams had an emotional need for a similar relationship to see him through the protracted separation from Abigail, although month after month of living alone would have tested the mettle of even the most disciplined man. At times Abigail appeared to believe that the fame and attention showered upon her husband was likely to be fulfillment enough, but in other moments she wondered whether her husband might be tempted by the dark lures of Paris and Amsterdam, and she and Elizabeth Dana conferred about the likelihood that their mates might stray. It was a thought helped along by Lovell, who once hinted darkly that he had heard rumors of indiscretions by

John. Abigail rejected such a notion. "[M]y confidence in my Friend abroad is as unbounded as my affection for him which knows no limits. He will not injure me even by a thought," she shot back to her friend in Philadelphia. But during the long stretches without a word from her husband, Abigail was left to wonder in private at his feelings. Had she said something that caused him pain or anger? If so, it was from the "ardour of affection." "You well know I never doubted your Honour," she told him.[47] And, she added: "Be to my faults a little Blind / Be to my virtues ever kind."[48]

The new spring foliage in 1781 gave a bright, cheerful look to Amsterdam, but it did little for John Adams's spirits. The fears that had haunted him during the previous year with regard to the course of the war continued without abatement. He had watched as the languid military efforts of the allies in 1780 produced little of significance, just as he had cautioned Vergennes during their heated exchanges during the past July. In fact, while Washington remained inactive outside New York City and Rochambeau sat idly in Rhode Island, ominous tidings had arrived from America. On the heels of the news of Arnold's treason came word of mutinies early in 1781 within the Continental army. Adams now had fresh reasons to worry about his "countrymen . . . deluding . . . themselves with dreams of peace," and he spoke of a rising tide of accommodationism in America, an "enemy more pernicious to us than all [the British] army." Nor was it just the spirit of America that concerned him. He remained troubled by France's staying power. If "we can carry on the war forever, our allies cannot," he warned, "and without their assistance we should find it very difficult" to continue the conflict. In his despair, he spoke for the first time of returning to America. Perhaps he could do more good there, he remarked; perhaps he could "wake up [his] countrymen out of their reverie about peace."[49]

If matters were not already sufficiently grim, a message from Vergennes that arrived one month after the presentation of his memorial to the Dutch government only further sank his spirits. The foreign minister wished to consult with Adams about a proposal to mediate the war. In the past thirty months, three unsuccessful offers to mediate the conflict had been proposed; in April 1781 a fourth proposal, this by Russia and Austria, was communicated to the European belligerents. The United States was not approached. In this latest proposal, the American "colonies" and Britain were to first agree to a one-year armistice, then the two would seek to negotiate their differences. Afterwards, the European combatants would gather at Vienna for the purpose of mediation. Adams did not have to see this offer to know that it posed great danger for the United States.

He hurried to Paris early in July, then journeyed to Versailles twice during the next five days to meet with the Foreign Minister. It was then that Adams first learned the details of the Russo-Austrian plan, what he would subsequently call their "wild propositions." Initially, however, he confessed that he did not know how to respond, and when he did reply to Vergennes, he appeared to be confused, taking one position, disavowing it three days later, then returning to his original stance later in the week. Writing from his temporary lodging at the Hotel de Valois in Paris, Adams began by telling Vergennes he would agree to talk with the British only if London first recognized the independence of the United States and removed its troops from American soil. But on July 16 Vergennes received another communique from Adams. In this note Adams indicated that he would not insist upon British recognition of American independence as a precondition to peace talks; he went on to say that he would not agree to an armistice before the commencement of talks, nor would the United States ever accept a peace based on *uti possidetis*—the concept that the belligerents would retain the territory held by their armed forces at the instant of peace. Before Vergennes could digest this response from Adams, still another reached his desk, this one composed on July 16. Adams now returned to his original position. Britain, he stated, must recognize the independence of the United States before talks could begin.[50]

Adams's two weeks in Paris caused him "many anxious hours," he said later, an unnecessary period of stress. He also later claimed credit for having thwarted mediation. Only his resolute stance during this crisis, he recollected, had prevented a turn of events that would have resulted in "chicaning the United States out of their independence." In fact, the peace conference was never held because Great Britain rejected the co-mediators' proposal.[51]

A weary John Adams returned to his post in Amsterdam at the end of the month. About three weeks later, in August 1781, he fell desperately ill. In recent years two scholars have attributed his woes to "a major nervous breakdown," the "most severe breakdown of his life."[52] A persuasive case can be made for such a conclusion. Adams had been subjected to considerable stress since his return to Europe eighteen months before. He had been rebuffed and treated with insolence by Vergennes; he was suspicious both of Franklin and the French, and he was apprehensive with regard to the course of the war. Never had the strain upon him been greater than during the summer of 1781.

First came the crisis over mediation. It was a prospect he had long feared. "I should dread a truce ten times more" than a continuance of the war, he had remarked in the fall of 1780, for he understood that mediation would pose two profound dangers for America. An armistice would precede the international mediation conference, and Adams knew that once the fighting stopped, it could be resumed only with great difficulty, even if the mediation had not been in America's favor. Furthermore, Adams knew full well that France would hold America's fate in its hands during a mediation conference. It was not a path he wished to follow. Adams suspected the worst from France. Only "total silence and impenetrable mystery" emanated from the foreign ministry, he said, and by mid-1781 it had caused him to conclude that France now sought a graceful exit from this stalemated war. Although he did not know it—nor would he ever learn the truth—his judgment was correct. Vergennes was prepared to consent to a long term truce *uti possidetis;* a diminutive United States would have existed, but Great Britain almost certainly would have retained Maine, northern Vermont, the Carolinas, Georgia, the tramontane West, and portions of New York, including New York City, and New England doubtless would be denied access to the Newfoundland fisheries.[53]

Adams's cares were not alleviated by his return to Amsterdam. In fact, not long after he returned, letters arrived from Passy that brought bitter disappointment. The first communication led Adams to believe—incorrectly, it would turn out—that Franklin, through whom the French paid the upkeep of America's diplomats and their legations, had cut off his funding. Franklin, he once said, had sought to "Sweep Europe clear of every Minister but himself, that he might have a clear unrivaled Stage." Adams jumped to the conclusion that Franklin and Vergennes had at last found a way to be rid of him.[54]

Soon after Franklin's first letter arrived, a second missive from Passy was delivered. This packet contained dispatches from Philadelphia indicating that Congress not only had stripped Adams of his authorization to negotiate a commercial treaty with Britain, it had expanded the peace commission to five members. Adams was to be a member, but he was to be joined by Jefferson, Jay, Laurens, and Franklin.[55] For a man of Adams's vanity, for a man who had sacrificed so much to return to Europe in the belief that he was to play a huge role in securing American independence—a role second only to that of General Washington—this news had to be cataclysmic, to be nothing less than a staggering refutation of all that he had done and sought to do.

Solid evidence exists that Adams had begun to exhibit the unmistakable signs of accumulated stress even before the events of July and August. An American physician who resided with him briefly in the late spring found that he alternated between long periods of shunning human contact and moments of emerging from his self-imposed isolation to rant and rage in the most frightening manner against his enemies. The doctor spoke of Adams's "inexpressible" anxiety, and he noted that even his features seemed to have become distorted; he commented on Adams's "protuberant eyes," as if the strain bore down upon his appearance every bit as much as it did on his personality. Nor was the doctor alone in detecting indications of Adams's stress. Adams, himself, spoke of his "nervous" state. His writings during this period, moreover, reveal a man who had not only grown suspicious of almost everyone about him but who had even begun to believe that he was the likely target of assassins.[56]

That Adams fell ill in the midst of such a personal trauma, that the illness struck immediately after he learned the news of the change in his diplomatic status, and that he had collapsed once before, in 1771, makes the "nervous breakdown" theory an alluring conjecture. However, Adams was treated during this illness by Dutch physicians, who concluded that he had fallen victim to malaria, not an uncommon malady in the Netherlands. Adams later said that he was insensible for a week and that his recovery was so slow that he could not write his wife of his misfortunes for two months. While the precise symptoms of Adams's illness are unknown, it is known that malaria can cause high fever, headache, loss of appetite, nausea, general aches and pains, abdominal pain, occasional respiratory difficulties, weakness, vertigo, nosebleeds, diarrhea, jaundice, pallor, and skin eruptions. In some instances, the body can fight off the parasites that have invaded it; the body's fight can also be assisted by drugs, which in the eighteenth century consisted principally of Peruvian bark—quinine—and which could result in remission and recovery.[57]

Adams often spoke of his ailment as a "fever," a term that in his lifetime could mean almost anything. But, others within his household also soon fell ill with what he called "fevers," what the doctors called malaria. Several things suggest that Adams's physicians may have been correct in their diagnosis: he was insensible for several days, which might indicate the presence of a severe fever; he remained, according to his subsequent letters, "feeble" for months; he suffered from memory loss and experienced skin disorders during the next few months; and years later he continued to mention afflictions that he traced back to 1781.[58]

By October, when his recuperation had reached a point that he could resume his correspondence, Adams's spirits appeared to have improved. Occasionally, his disappointment in having been removed as America's sole peace negotiator was clear, as when he compared himself to a sheep that had been fleeced or when he spoke of how he would like to return to Congress and settle old scores, but for the most part he resigned himself to the change in his status. Indeed, he almost seemed happy that the enormous burden of acting alone had been removed. The collective wisdom of the envoys would probably result in a better treaty for the United States, he said, and now that that each section of the nation was represented on the peace commission, everyone should be happier with the finished product. He even suggested that he perhaps lacked the "faculties" necessary to be an extraordinary diplomat. "My talent, if I have one, lies in making war," he added, a reference to his far more distinguished service as a congressman.[59]

While Adams returned to his duties in the fall, he remained an ill man. It was only in early 1782, nearly twenty months after the onset of his ailment, he said, that his condition improved significantly, and even then he continued to speak of his eviscerated condition, especially of weakness in his legs and feet.[60] During much of this time, Adams had to care for himself. Thaxter and his servant were felled with fevers that autumn—Adams now blamed the rampant sickness within the legation on the "tainted Atmosphere" of Amsterdam—and neither of his sons was present to attend to him. Adams had brought both boys with him when he moved to Amsterdam in mid-1780, but when John

Quincy quickly clashed with his new teacher, still another schoolmaster was found in nearby Leyden. John Quincy soon flourished and early in 1781, just before his fourteenth birthday, he was admitted to the University of Leyden, one of Europe's finest centers of higher education. His stay was short-lived, however. Early in the summer, just before his father had been summoned to France to meet with Vergennes, Dana learned that Congress had commissioned him to journey to St. Petersburg to seek the recognition of the empress Catherine II's government, and Adams had permitted young John Quincy to go along as both the secretary and the companion of the envoy.[61]

Charles's stay in Leyden was even more brief. In April he too fell seriously ill, perhaps with some sort of viral infection, although his father was told that the lad was suffering from seizures. The attending physicians suspected a rare form of malaria; curiously, John once even referred to the boy's malady as a "Wound." Whatever the problem, within a month the youngster, only eleven, was better, but desperately homesick for his mother and little friends in Braintree. Indeed, he had never wished to leave home in the first place, and now with his brother gone to Russia, he was even more miserable. Realizing that it was pointless to keep the boy in Europe, Adams placed him in the care of a young physician who was returning to America, and just a few days before his August illness, the sad, apprehensive father watched as the boy commenced his perilous journey. Charles's voyage began aboard the *South Carolina* and concluded on the *Cicero,* which he boarded in Spain. It was a safe crossing but terribly long. He did not reach home until January 1782, nearly five months after his embarkation in France.[62]

The news arrived in Amsterdam on or about November 26. Other than word of Charles's safe arrival in Braintree, these were the tidings that Adams had most longed to hear. In Virginia, in the low country on the York peninsula below Williamsburg, only a short distance from where Britain's colonial experience in America had begun almost two hundred years before, Franco-American forces had caught and captured the army of the earl of Cornwallis at a place called Yorktown. In mid-August, Washington and Rochambeau had learned that a French fleet under the Comte de Grasse was sailing from the Caribbean to the Chesapeake. They quickly moved their armies to Virginia, and soon Cornwallis found himself trapped. De Grasse blocked his rescue by sea, the allied armies prevented his exit by land. A siege operation had been instituted late in September; twenty-one days later, on October 19 Cornwallis capitulated. While a British band allegedly played a march tune, "The World Turned Upside Down," 7241 British soldiers surrendered their arms.

The great allied victory, and the manner of the conquest, in a sense vindicated Adams, for he had never wavered in his belief that the key to victory lay in French naval power. More than three years had passed between the time he first pressed this course on Vergennes and the triumph at Yorktown. The combination of a French fleet and a Franco-American army "must infallibly succeed," he had long ago sought to convince the French, but the French naval presence was the most important of the two. Once French superiority "in the American seas" was established, he had predicted, the war could be won. A great victory could be achieved, perhaps in New York, maybe in Canada. It made no difference. The "British Possessions in America depend upon each other for reciprocal support," he had said, and once the British fell in one sector, their other dominions would inevitably begin to fall like a row of collapsing dominoes.[63] With justification, Adams's diplomacy has been severely criticized by historians, but his understanding of what was required to bring this war to a successful conclusion could not have been more correct. While he watched in dismay, France had sought in 1778 and 1779 to win this war through an invasion of England. When that proved a chimera, France augmented its forces in America, but even then, in 1780, Versailles still believed that victory would be had through a Franco-Spanish war of attrition against the British in the Caribbean. Adams had seen matters more clearly. Had his way been attempted, this long, bloody war might have been shortened and countless lives saved.

News of the British debacle coursed like a whirlwind through the capitals of Europe, touching off a string of momentous events. For one thing, the success that had previously eluded John Adams in the Netherlands soon was achieved. Adams had not expected immediate results when he presented his memorial in spring 1781. They "will deliberate, and deliberate and deliberate," he had correctly predicted. After Yorktown, the Dutch at last were prepared to assist the United States. Britain's problems partly accounted for the change in Dutch thinking, but pressure from France was even more important. Versailles was in a position virtually to dictate to the Netherlands. Not only was France assisting in the protection of several remote Dutch colonies, but it had recaptured from Britain, St. Eustatia, Demarara, and Essequibo, all former possessions of the Netherlands. If The Hague played its cards properly, the Dutch empire might be preserved, even restored. Before the country's famous tulips emerged to brighten the dreary late winter landscape, the Dutch government had made its decision. It would formally recognize the United States. The ceremony was held on April 19, the seventh anniversary of this war's initial engagements, the confrontations at Lexington and Concord in faraway Massachusetts, and the first anniversary of the presentation of John Adams's memorial. A commercial treaty followed, and, that, in turn, after months of difficult negotiation, was followed by a loan for the United States, extended by a consortium of Dutch bankers. That accord was signed in the autumn of 1782.[64]

Subsequently, Adams took credit for solidifying the ties between the Netherlands and the United States. He spoke of his "signal Tryumph," of having "done great Things," of his "success," and he called this accomplishment "the happiest Event" of his life. The reason for his elation is not difficult to fathom. It was a mission that he had embarked upon in the face of opposition from both Franklin and Vergennes. Now his name was celebrated throughout the land. In all the Netherlands, he reported to Abigail, no one was as feted as "Mynheer Adams." Adams had worked tirelessly for this moment, yet it stretches credulity to imagine that a nation could be nudged into such substantive changes by the savvy of a foreign envoy. In fact, he remained so ill during the months when the decisive diplomatic maneuvering was taking place that he had little idea of exactly what was occurring. But even had he remained healthy, his actions, however adroit, would have been unavailing had Cornwallis's army not been captured on Virginia's sandy York peninsula. It was that brilliant Franco-American military success, in conjunction with French leverage, that ultimately moved the government of the Netherlands to change its course.[65]

In the winter Adams learned that Congress had named him minister plenipotentiary to the Netherlands, supplanting Laurens, who continued to languish in the Tower. He hurried to The Hague and acquired a residence that would serve as the new United States embassy, a dwelling he shared with Charles Dumas and his wife, who served as hostess at diplomatic receptions. He was happy to escape the climate in Amsterdam, although The Hague also lacked the "pure Atmosphere of America," as Thaxter put it. By June, Adams felt better than he had since he began his first mission to France, better, in fact, than since before the outbreak of the war in 1775. He suddenly was well enough to resume his morning horseback rides, a ritual he had always enjoyed for both exercise and relaxation. He undertook a ceaseless round of entertainment, as well. Almost every day there were "Sups and Visits at Court among Princesses and Princes, Lords and Ladies of various Nations." He had become a courtier, he remarked, and he loved every minute of it. His stature in Holland was equal to that of Franklin in France. He lived in a regal manner to which he was unaccustomed. He entertained in a salon that featured a huge turquoise rug, marble tables, and a gilded mirror, all set beneath a large canopy of red damask; dinner was served at a dining-room table that could accommodate sixteen guests; he slept in a green-and-gray bedroom furnished with mahogany tables, bureaus, and a secretary. No longer was he the "Grumbletonian Patriot, always whining and snarling," he confessed. Now he was "complaisant, good humoured, [and] contented."[66]

When Adams moved into the "United States House," or the "New World House," as he variously referred to the embassy, he predicted that it would be his residence for only a brief time. He believed that peace talks would soon commence, although he thought the discussions would be long and difficult. Negotiations would not begin in earnest, he said, until all British troops had been removed from America, and even then he expected months to pass while Great Britain maneuvered to divide the allies. He suspected that Britain would seek a separate peace with the United States so that it could pursue its war with

France unhindered by the engagement in America. That ploy would not work, he declared shortly after learning of Cornwallis's misfortune. The United States would not desert its ally.[67]

Sometime in May, Adams learned that a British envoy had arrived in Paris and was talking with Franklin. About the middle of the month he received a call from the Doctor requesting that he come to France and participate in the discussions. But Adams refused to leave The Hague. He first wished to conclude the commercial treaty and to secure the Dutch loan. Besides, he would come to Paris only if Britain first recognized the existence of the United States.[68]

In early autumn, at last, the word that he had awaited arrived. It came from John Jay. Come to Paris "soon—very soon," Jay urged. Britain had agreed to negotiate with the "Commissioners of the United States of America."[69]

Adams soon was on his way, traveling in a rented coach. He was about to engage in the peace talks for which he had been sent to Europe. It was almost three years to the day since he had left Braintree in quest of this moment.

CHAPTER 13

*

Thus Drops the Curtain

THE NEWS OF BRITAIN'S HUMILIATING defeat at
Saratoga in 1777 had provoked fears within the ministry, lest those in
charge of the government might, as one witness noted, "lose their heads as well
as their places." While those apprehensions were exaggerated, Cornwallis's
surrender at Yorktown in 1781 did prove to be fatal, although only to the life of
the ministry. Lord North took the news "as he would have taken a ball in the
breast," according to Lord Germain, the American secretary. His ministry
lingered in its death throes for a few weeks, then on March 20, 1782, it
tumbled down, and on the day that North departed, after a reign of more than a
dozen years, the Commons adopted a resolution that declared anyone who
should in any way attempt to wage war in America for the purpose of securing
the submission of the colonies to be an enemy of the King.[1] At last, diplomacy,
not further war, would resolve the Anglo-American difficulties.

The marquis of Rockingham, whose first ministry had been in office just
long enough to repeal the Stamp Act in 1766, formed the new government,
and discussions with Franklin in Passy commenced soon thereafter. Lord
Shelburne, Germain's successor, was responsible for the negotiations. A native
of Ireland and a former army officer who had served with distinction in the
Seven Years' War, Shelburne was secretive and distant, a man with few friends,
yet an official with nearly twenty years' experience in dealing with the American colonies. From the outset, Shelburne's objectives were clear. He wished to
divide America from France, thwart France and Spain's territorial ambitions in
North America, retain Gibraltar, and reestablish Britain's commercial dominion over America. From the outset, too, Shelburne knew that the recognition
of the independence of the United States could not be avoided.[2]

Shelburne selected Richard Oswald to conduct the preliminary talks in
Passy. At age seventy-five, Oswald was but one year younger than Franklin. A
merchant much of his life, this Scotsman often had engaged in commercial
dealings with America, mostly selling military supplies and slaves to the
colonists. He owned real estate in the colonies and some of his family still
resided in America. In April, accompanied by Henry Laurens, recently re-

leased on bail from London's Tower, Oswald crossed the Channel to begin the negotiations that might finally end the seven-year-old war.[3]

In Ostend the envoys separated, Oswald continuing on to France while Laurens looked in on affairs in the Netherlands, his destination two years earlier when he had been captured. His successor, John Adams, had mixed feelings upon seeing Laurens at the door of the American legation. He was delighted, of course, that his countryman's long captivity had ended; on the other hand, he looked upon Laurens as a rival, an interloper who might intercede to gather the harvest that he, Adams, had so patiently, so frustratingly, cultivated over the past twenty months. Upon learning of Laurens's release, Adams had told a friend that he would step aside immediately if the South Carolinian wished to claim his commission as the United States representative to Holland. He never seriously entertained his threat to resign, however. In fact, despite Adams's surface cordiality, Laurens was made to understand that his presence in The Hague was not desired. Adams told him forthwith that his "attention [not only was] not requisite," but that he would only add an unnecessary expense to the maintenance of the mission. After the sacrifices that he had made for his country, Laurens was enraged by what he regarded as Adams's "imperious treatment," but probably questioning the wisdom of his ever having departed South Carolina, he soon left for France. He did not forgive Adams for his coarse behavior, however. He continued to seethe with a black rage and early in 1784 he even considered—albeit only briefly— challenging Adams to a duel.[4]

Alone at The Hague, Adams had labored through the spring and summer of 1782 to bring his enterprise with the Dutch to a successful conclusion. Meanwhile, he had listened for word from Passy. He was not optimistic that peace would occur soon, and, in fact, until the very eve of his summons to Paris, he predicted that there would be no peace treaty before 1784. Initially, he seemed to believe that Whitehall had opened the discussions merely to prevent the collapse of the English stock market, and as late as midsummer he believed the Rockingham ministry lacked the stability to recognize the independence of the United States. But when he learned in July that the prime minister had died suddenly and that Shelburne had become the titular head of the government, Adams grew more hopeful of success. Shelburne was a thoughtful man with "well digested" notions, he remarked. If his government survived, Adams predicted, "he will be the Man to make Peace." Indeed, as the summer wore on, Adams fretted less over whether the war would end than over whether the diplomats could obtain a satisfactory accord. He worried especially that Franklin might sabotage America's interests.[5]

Adams can be forgiven his pessimism. For months the preliminary talks in Passy had moved nowhere. Oswald first met with Franklin in April; he learned quickly that the allies would treat for peace only in concert with one another.

Not until mid-July did the discussion pass from a very preliminary stage to a semblance of negotiation. Oswald broke the ice by requesting that Franklin— "as a friend"—lay out America's objectives, and the Doctor responded with a document that catalogued his country's demands. Recognition of the independence of the United States, the removal of British troops from American soil, a favorable settlement of the Canadian boundary, and freedom to fish on the Newfoundland Banks were "necessary." In addition, it was "advisable" that Britain not only indemnify those residents of America who had lost property during the war, but reestablish full Anglo-American trade, surrender Canada to the United States, and offer some acknowledgment of its error in having waged the war. Although Oswald was unaware of it, Franklin made these proposals without first having consulted Vergennes.[6]

Franklin was optimistic that his "hints," as he referred to these proposed terms, might immediately lead to open, substantive negotiations. He was disappointed. Oswald did send Franklin's suggestions to London, and, in turn, Shelburne empowered him to conduct discussions on the hints. But there was a snag. Oswald could negotiate only with the commissioners of the "colonies or plantations." While Vergennes and Franklin were willing to accept that, deferring the British recognition of United States independence until the peace treaty itself, Jay—who had arrived in Paris in June and who knew that John Adams was in his corner—was unyielding. These two saw what Franklin could not understand. Shelburne hoped to use the enticement of independence to seduce America to accept otherwise "bad conditions." Independence must be granted before serious talks commenced. Jay thus would not budge, even if Congress had instructed the envoys to be guided by the French government.[7]

In fact, as the summer wore on Jay grew ever more contumacious regarding Congress's directive, for he, like Adams, had become steadily more suspicious of France. He was certain that France and Spain desired to prevent the United States from acquiring the tramontane West; he also concluded that they preferred that Britain retain the area north of the Ohio and between the mountains and the Mississippi River, while Spain should gain the region south of the Ohio. Jay's deductions were quite accurate. Spain's incentive was obvious. France, on the other hand, believed that if Britain was left with Canada and much of the West, the United States would be forced to continue its ties with Versailles. When Jay learned in early September that Vergennes's private secretary had departed for talks in London, his worst suspicions were further aroused. Nevertheless, he saw in these French machinations an opening that he could play. Bereft on its rightful territory, he warned Oswald, the United States would of necessity remain linked to Britain. The implication was clear. The United States was ready to move ahead in the talks, even at the expense of risking a rupture with its ally. Shelburne had it within his power to sever the Franco-American bond. Desiring that end, and anxious for peace, the ministry moved quickly. By the end of the month Oswald was authorized to treat with the commissioners of the United States, whereupon Jay dispatched his "come soon—very soon" appeal to John Adams.[8]

Adams remained at The Hague for two weeks following the receipt of Jay's summons, after which his journey to Paris—which with luck might have taken seventy-two hours—required nine days. It has been argued that Adams had an "unconscious" motive for the painstakingly, deliberately slow pace with which he moved toward France. Supposedly, he feared that Vergennes and the ever-servile Franklin would conclude a bad peace for the United States; by absenting himself from such chicanery, he could not be branded as responsible for the treaty.[9] Yet, while it is true that he continued to distrust Franklin, Adams would have known that by staying away he would have had no part in a good treaty, and he believed that the United States was in an excellent position to attain most of what it desired in a peace accord.

Adams, in fact, was slow in reaching Paris for the simplest of reasons. He did not wish to leave The Hague before the commercial accord was signed. He knew that the negotiations in Paris, as was the way with all diplomacy, would be a protracted affair and that nothing would be conclusive until he put his signature on the document. That allowed him time to wrap up his business in Holland, which he correctly regarded as a matter of urgency, for there was no assurance that the Paris talks would actually result in peace. When he at last departed The Hague, his still-fragile health dictated a slow pace; heavy rains, poor roads, and a broken carriage axle that required extensive repair during the course of the journey added to the length of the trip. Adams, together with his traveling companions, Thaxter and Charles Storer, a distant relative of Abigail, who had come to Europe following his graduation from Harvard in 1781, traveled a few miles each day, then rested by visiting cathedrals, castles, art collections, historical sites, gardens, and even a race track.[10]

It was after dark on October 26 when Adams's party reached Paris, where Adams checked into his usual accommodations at the Hotel de Valois. The next morning he took care of pressing business. He bathed in a public bath house of the Seine and called on a tailor, wig maker, and cordwainer in preparation for the coming negotiations. Then, before he met with Franklin and Jay, he set out to gather some information. He knew that Laurens had declined to participate and that Jefferson had never left the United States, but evidently wishing to learn as much as possible about his colleagues in Paris, he called on Matthew Ridley, a man with whom he recently had corresponded. An agent sent to France by Maryland, Ridley, he thought, was a knowledgeable and trustworthy outsider.[11]

From Ridley he learned that Franklin had been ill. Afflicted both with kidney stones and the gout, Franklin had been forced to bed in August. For the past month or more, everything had been in the hands of Jay, who, Ridley remarked, could not have been more firm in his dealings with Vergennes. The news was good, yet Adams continued to fret. Franklin, he wrote in his diary that night, "will intrigue, he will maneuvre" to "divide Us."[12]

Adams called on Jay the following afternoon. It was an engaging session, and he departed in sweet ecstacy, having discovered that his comrade shared his suspicions about the policies of Vergennes. For some time Adams had suspected that the French not only would seek to prevent the United States from utilizing the fisheries off the North American coast but would endeavor to confine the new nation to the territory east of the mountain barrier. Jay agreed. In fact, his tales of collusion by Madrid and Versailles to perpetuate America's impotence and maintain the new nation's dependence on France must have raised Adams's temper to a fever pitch. Adams was as intuitive now as he had been in 1779 when he had first expressed his skepticism about the French. He sometimes exaggerated and saw French duplicity where Vergennes was blameless, but in its bare essentials Adams's habitual distrust was not misplaced. France indeed wished to keep its weak ally enfeebled so that the United States would be compelled to remain the client state of its powerful European partner.

Jay evidently said nothing untoward about Franklin, but visiting the Doctor was not something that Adams looked forward to. In fact, although he had not seen Franklin in more than two years, Adams was so steeped in bitterness that he initially refused to ride to Passy to make even a social call. He relented only when Ridley convinced him of the damage that could result should Britain learn of divisions within the American negotiation team. At the end of his third day in Paris, therefore, Adams rode to Passy to pay his respects to the man he so bitterly hated. He managed to be cordial, and Franklin, feeling a little better, likewise succeeded in being "merry and pleasant."[13]

The following day the three American envoys met together and Adams learned what had occurred in the five months or more since Franklin's initial meetings with Oswald. What he heard must have relieved some of his anxieties. He discovered that Jay and Oswald had signed a preliminary draft accord ten days before his departure from The Hague, a pact that secured vast stretches of the tramontane West for the United States. For the first time, too, he learned of the congressional directive to the negotiators to adhere to the "advice and opinion" of the French government. Adams expressed his outrage at this curious abnegation of sovereignty and vowed to resign if congress held the diplomats to such a course, but he also was relieved to discover that neither Jay nor Franklin intended to abide by the instruction. Indeed, his colleagues had ignored the order since the inception of the talks with Oswald in the spring.[14]

There was much to worry about, however. While he had grown to believe that France badly needed the American alliance, his worst suspicions of Vergennes's duplicity had been confirmed. He and Jay could not both be wrong.

Adams also discovered that Jay had made concessions detrimental to the interests of Massachusetts. He had tentatively agreed to set the boundary between Maine and Nova Scotia considerably below the Saint John River, the site that Adams regarded as the true northern limit of his province. In addition, Jay had agreed to surrender the privilege of America's fishermen to dry their catch on the shores of Newfoundland, although they retained a capability of fishing off the Banks. And there was more. He had known for some time that the French navy had suffered a drubbing at the hands of a British fleet in the West Indies in April; now there was news that a Franco-Spanish armada had failed in an assault on Gibraltar. He could only speculate on how those setbacks might influence negotiations. Finally, he realized that because of the poor health of both his colleagues—Franklin was still in great pain with his stones, and Jay had fallen ill with influenza weeks before and scarcely yet possessed the strength to write—much of the labor in the remaining negotiations might fall upon his shoulders.[15]

Adams was prepared for such a responsibility. As early as 1775, Congressman James Duane of New York, once a follower of Joseph Galloway and long a reconciliationist, had paid Adams a supreme compliment. "We all agree," he had remarked, "that you have more fully considered and better digested the subject of foreign connections than any man we have ever heard speak on the subject."[16] Four long years at the courts of Europe had caused Adams to reflect further on the role of an independent United States. He came to the Paris peace talks with clear views on the interests of the United States.

Adams's principal concern, once independence was recognized, was the maintenance of the true independence of the United States. Despite his travail with Vergennes and his ally, France, it was Great Britain that gave Adams the greatest concern in the postwar world. Three days before independence was declared, Adams had counseled a friend not to expect to see peace with Great Britain followed by a restoration of the "Happiness and Halcyon days" that once had existed. Instead, he foresaw an "incurable Animosity" between the two nations that would endure for generations. Nothing that occurred after 1776 altered his thinking. In 1780 he still spoke of the "perpetual rivalry" between Britain and the United States, and reflected on the former parent state's enduring "hatred" for America. Problems with Great Britain would endure, he said, because the nation was "blind and vindictive," and would seek revenge for its mortifying losses in America. He believed too that immigration from Britain to America would be a continuing source of friction; vast numbers of residents of Britain would seek to flee to America in search of land and freedom of religion, and, he predicted, Britain would ever seek to stanch the flow of its peoples. Boundary disputes between the United States and Canada would aggravate matters as well. But commercial rivalries would be the principal cause of discord. Adams expected an ever-powerful and expansive United

States to compete for the same markets that Britain desired. As a result, Adams saw Great Britain as the "natural enemy" of the United States.[17]

But Britain was also the natural enemy of France, and that meant the United States could look forward to the continued assistance of France in the postwar world. The linkage between American agriculture and French manufacturing would help sustain friendly ties between the two countries, yet British actions would be the crucial element in the preservation of sound relations with France. In fact, France would need America more than the United States would require France. France could not tolerate a resurgence of British power in America, and the "natural and continual jealousies of England" toward France would compel Versailles to "stand in need of America."[18]

Once the War of Independence was brought to a successful conclusion, Adams believed, the United States could look toward a glorious future, one crowned by peace and prosperity. The greatest danger to the true independence of the United States would stem from its citizens who would seek once again to be close to Britain, from those who might be so unwary as to desire—whether from a cultural, religious, or economic impetus—to return to the protective umbrella of the former parent state. But if Americans could "wean [themselves] from the little remainder of affection and respect for that nation," and if, as he had counseled repeatedly during this long war, his fellow countrymen would understand that France pursued its own agenda for its own selfish ends, the security of the new nation should be assured.[19]

Peace and true independence, therefore, should reign following the conclusion of this war. Adams discovered several reasons that led him to conclude that it was in the interest of Europe collectively to maintain the independence of America. All the major powers would hope to benefit from American trade; should any one nation secure dominion over America, the result would be "an absolute tyranny upon the ocean," an event that Europe would find intolerable. An independent America, moreover, would be fertile ground for foreign investment, because the new nation would inevitably and quickly "arise out of the distresses of the war to affluence." An independent America would pose no threat to Europe. Primarily an agrarian nation, the United States would merely seek to sell its farm produce, asking only that it be permitted to trade with all on the basis of "equality, freedom and reciprocity." In addition, the European states would realize that the United States had no designs on their territory. So long as "we have land enough to conquer from the trees and rocks and wild beasts," he reflected, there would be no incentive to expand beyond North America. Finally, the European nations, which so often were at war, would see a neutral United States—and it would not involve itself in Europe's wars, he said—as a godsend, a nonbelligerent with whom to trade; but the European powers would realize that the United States could remain neutral only so long as it was independent.[20]

To reach that point, however, the War of Independence had to be brought to a successful conclusion. For Adams, this meant that, independence aside, the United States must secure three items in the peace accord. Without possession of the tramontane West, the United States would be trapped. Poor and over-crowded, its liberties and republican traditions would be jeopardized; in addition, it would, of necessity, remain a dependent upon France, which alone could offer protection against the towering British empire encircling the enfeebled new nation. The United States must additionally possess the right of navigation on the Mississippi River. Denied that avenue to eastern and foreign markets, what farmer would desire to live in the West? Worse, the nation that controlled the Mississippi—certain to be Spain because of its victories in America in 1779—could use its power as a lever with which to pry western farmers away from the United States. Finally, Americans must have access to the fisheries. The fisheries were crucial to the New England economy and he knew full well that "the New England People" had from the outset of the war "eagerly embraced" the hope of someday regaining their Atlantic fishing rights. But the fisheries, he added, were "a Nursery of Seamen and a source of naval Power" that could not be replaced. Not just for the benefit of his own region, but for the well-being of all America, the new nation must have access to the fisheries.[21]

Adams entered the talks convinced that these concessions could be won from Great Britain. It was America's ally, France, that concerned him. "Our Allies dont play us fair," Jay had told him, when they first had conferred, and Adams could not have been in greater agreement. On the eve of negotiations Adams's great fear was that Vergennes would use his powers, especially his alleged sway over Franklin, to deny America what it needed to become truly independent. It was his resolve, he told the president of Congress at this juncture, to use every fiber in his being to prevent the United States from being "duped out of the fishery, the Mississippi, [and] much of the western lands."[22]

On October 29, the Tuesday following his Saturday night arrival, Adams met his counterparts for the first time. The British delegation made a social call at his lodging. Over tea the men chatted amiably, though neither Adams nor his visitors made any attempt at hard bargaining. The next morning, the real business resumed. Adams and Franklin, who had made the uncomfortable ride from Passy, arrived at Jay's residence at the Hotel d'Orleans just before eleven. Shortly thereafter, three British envoys arrived. In addition to Oswald, there was Henry Strachey, whom the ministry had recently dispatched to take charge of its delegation; he was a dignified undersecretary of state in the Home Office. Also present was Benjamin Vaughn, a young gadfly friendly with both Shelburne and Franklin, a Jamaican whose mother was a Boston Hallowell. Alleyne Fitzherbert was not present this day, though he would later join in; he was a twenty-nine-year-old career diplomat who had been transferred from Brussels in July to conduct peace talks with Vergennes. Aside from Strachey, an experienced politician and bureaucrat, though a man with little diplomatic experience, and Fitzherbert, who ultimately played only a minor role in the talks with the Americans, the British delegation was undistinguished. There was little reason for Vaughn's presence, while Oswald, according to a recent student of the proceedings, already was in the clutches of senility. Against these men were the wily and experienced Franklin, as well as Jay and Adams, both adept lawyers, skilled politicians, and, by now, veteran diplomats.[23]

Intensive negotiations consumed the next six days and resulted in several tentative agreements, although the British envoys were forbidden to consent to anything without London's formal approval. During the second week in November, therefore, Strachey raced home for instructions, not to return until November 25. The brief interlude was a pleasant time for Adams. Not only did he have a rare cordial meeting with Vergennes, but the French minister invited him to a sumptuous lunch, so anxious was he to discover what the American diplomats were up to in their negotiations. In a last-ditch effort to make Adams more malleable, every effort was made to flatter and coddle him. Even Vergennes's wife was enlisted in the project. She first insisted that Adams sit next to her, then she proved "remarkably attentive" to him throughout the festive evening, listening rapturously to his discourses and laughing promptly on cue at his every witticism. At times the French laid it on a bit thick, lauding Adams's accomplishments in the Netherlands and repeatedly toasting him as "the Washington of diplomacy." Adams credulously accepted every bit of it. If only Franklin could have been present to hear what the French thought of him, he noted that evening in his diary. But if he permitted himself to believe the blandishments, he kept his head and revealed nothing new about the course of negotiations.[24]

Adams relaxed as he awaited Strachey's return, walking, riding, reading, sightseeing, occasionally attending a formal dinner, and from time to time even meeting informally with Oswald and Vaughn. He also met with Franklin, who made the painful ride into Paris to call on the younger envoy, hoping to make peace with his colleague before the next round of talks commenced. In the short run Franklin's visit paid dividends. He convinced Adams that the two men were not far apart on what they hoped to see included in the final accord, prompting Adams for a time to speak of the Doctor's harmonious inclinations and of his "able and usefull" talents. As always, Adams gave over some time to worry during these weeks. He knew that peace was near, but only if the Shelburne government survived, and he held his breath lest that ministry, shaky since its inception, should collapse before an accord could be signed.[25]

Strachey at last returned to Paris at the end of November and the final round of negotiations opened. Beginning with a session in Oswald's lodgings, the talks continued during five of the last six days of the month, beginning daily about ten and continuing until well past dark. While gray, cold, scudding clouds hovered above wintry Paris, the diplomats—including Laurens, who showed up on the next to last day of the bargaining just in time to gain the insertion of an article that compelled the British to return all slave properties to their lawful owners—made their final arguments, their last concessions.[26]

By this time only two major problems remained to be resolved: the thorny question of fishing rights and the issue of the compensation of the Tories, the most divisive and perplexing issue that plagued the envoys. Most of the other matters had been settled in earlier talks. Adams had played a substantive role in the resolution of the northern boundary issue, getting back some, though not all, of Maine's northern reaches that Jay had earlier conceded; he agreed to the Saint Croix River as its uppermost limit. The resolution of the prewar indebtedness problem removed another difficult obstacle. Adams was flexible on this point. He believed it necessary for America to meet its debt obligations, and he ultimately broke down both Franklin's and Jay's reservations on this matter.[27]

Adams was unyielding on the fishing question, however. Indeed, he was so determined to protect New England on this issue that he hinted to the British that if America got its wishes in this regard the new nation might detach itself from the French alliance. The British envoys were not deceived by such a blatant ploy, but in the end Adams obtained some of the concessions that he sought. The United States received the "liberty" to fish not only on the Newfoundland Banks but in the Gulf of Saint Lawrence, and it secured the right to dry its catches only on the uninhabited coasts of Nova Scotia, the Magdalen Islands, and Labrador.

The Tory question produced more acrimony than any other matter. The British sought restitution for the property taken from the Loyalists. Adams would have agreed to compensation had he been the sole negotiator, but Jay and Franklin were intransigent and the best the British could secure was a meaningless provision in which Congress was to request that each state legislature provide compensation for the Loyalist losses.[28]

The talks concluded on November 29. In the waning moments of that resplendent late autumn day, as the last warm, ocherous rays of sunlight spilled across the table at which the envoys sat, the final obstacle was surmounted. "Tom Cod," as Adams referred to the fishing question, was the last item resolved. That evening, relaxed and in joyous spirits, Adams, dining with Ridley, laughingly rejected an entree of fish, quipping that he "had a pretty good Meal of them today."[29]

While Adams enjoyed his dinner, Franklin, the minister to France, carried out a distasteful chore. He rode to Versailles to inform Vergennes that the United States envoys would sign a preliminary accord the next day. Vergennes, understandably, was bitter at the news of the separate peace, a palpable violation of the Franco-American treaty of alliance and of the instructions of the

American Commissioners at the Preliminary Peace Negotiations with Great Britain.
By Benjamin West, about 1783. *Courtesy: Henry du Pont Winterthur Museum.*

United States Congress. But all he could do was reprove Franklin, who, nonplussed and brazen as ever, concluded the meeting by requesting a French loan of twenty million livres.[30]

The following afternoon, a Saturday, the Americans met at Jay's suite, then proceeded to Oswald's apartment in the Grand Hotel Muscovite, on the rue des Petits Augustins, to sign the preliminary treaty, an accord that would go into effect when ratified in London and Philadelphia, and when Britain and France concluded peace. The signing ceremony was brief and simple, after which the diplomats from both sides adjourned to Passy for an evening repast at Franklin's residence. "Thus drops the Curtain upon this mighty Trajedy," Adams noted with a sigh of relief.[31] More than seventeen years had passed since the Stamp Act had been promulgated, setting afoot, as thirty-year-old John Adams had predicted, "[his] Ruin as well as that of America"; seven and one-half years had elapsed since the war's beginning in the sleepy little crossroads villages of Lexington and Concord, and three years, almost to the day, had passed since Adams had left his wife and children in Braintree to pursue this very moment.

The treaty was a triumph for the United States, the fruit of the "sure genius" of the American negotiators, in the words of the dean of United States diplomatic historians, Samuel Flagg Bemis. Franklin, Jay, and Adams understood the distresses of Europe's great powers and turned those woes to America's advantage. Great Britain, they knew, sought peace to escape the unremitting financial burdens caused by this war. Moreover, as Adams once said, Whitehall knew that United States independence now was in its interest, for an independent America possessed of the trans-Appalachian West would possess the strength to stand alone, without need of French assistance. France, on the other hand, troubled by nightmares of the eventual reunion of English-speaking America and Great Britain, could only acquiesce in the separate peace that the American diplomats negotiated. Indeed, it even granted the loan that Franklin had had the temerity to request.[32]

Adams believed that Jay had been the most important of the three American envoys, but he acknowledged that Franklin too had been "very able" at the bargaining table. Each of the three, in fact, had played a substantive role. Adams was most responsible for securing American fishing rights, something Massachusetts had considered lost forever five years before. In addition, he had played the principle role in breaking the deadlock on the debt issue. Franklin was most intransigent on the Loyalist problem, and he and Jay were most responsible for the various boundary settlements and for the procurement of the trans-Appalachian lands. As successful as they were, however, the American team might have gotten even more. There is evidence that Britain was prepared to cede a portion of present-day Ontario; in addition, the envoys undoubtedly erred in permitting the use of the word "liberty" instead of "right" in regard to certain fishing interests. Nevertheless, the American diplomats had secured the aims that Congress had set forth in 1779, save for some territory about the fringes of the suddenly distended new nation.

Adams knew that it was a magnificent treaty, a pact, as he put it, that had secured "the Cod and Ducks and Beavers" for the United States. More importantly, of course, the accord brought independence—real independence, Adams remarked—to the United States. For too long, he often had said, America "had been a Football between contending Nations." While still colonies, the provincials had repeatedly been dragged into Britain's plundering wars. After 1778 it had been a mere client of France. At last, however, he now dared to believe that the United States could stand alone, escaping the conflicts of Great Britain and France, and having "nothing to do but in Commerce with either of them." America also had some breathing space, for the great powers of Europe were too exhausted at the moment to embark on new adventures. By the time the British had gotten "a little refreshed from the fatigues of the War" and again was ready to make trouble for the United States, he added, America would be strong enough to stand alone.[33]

The first payoff for America came five days after the signing ceremony. On December 5, 1782, George III alighted from the royal carriage before the fog-shrouded doors of Parliament and hurried inside the chambers of the House of Lords to address the legislators. Seated before his audience, adorned in flowing burgundy-and-blue robes, the king read from a prepared speech. He had ordered an end to the prosecution of offensive war in America. Moreover, to fully secure a "candid reconciliation" with his former subjects, King George III now "did not hesitate to . . . offer to declare them free and independent States." He closed with a prayer that the United States should not suffer unduly from its want of a monarchy.[34]

With the signing of the preliminary treaty, Adams began to speak more frequently of his desire to return to his family. "My farm and my family glitter before my eyes every day and night," he often remarked. But his expressions were hollow. There can be no doubt that Adams missed his wife and children, but still only forty-seven years of age and hardly a wealthy man, he could not yet contemplate retirement. Yet, his interest in the law, either as a practicing lawyer or as a magistrate, had slacked, and the thought of serving again in Congress, especially in a generally powerless, peacetime Congress, held little allure. But the diplomatic life had gotten into his blood; a good diplomatic assignment brought recognition and respect. He found the work to be "singular and interesting," employment that offered excitement and the reward of providing an essential service to the public, yet which left the official with time for thought and reading.[35]

Adams coveted the appointment as America's first minister to Great Britain. The assignment would be tantamount to an affirmation of his prior service. He longed, too, to play a role in the restoration of harmonious relations between the two nations. A good relationship with Britain was crucial for the well-being of the new United States. The resulting trade would strengthen the new nation economically, while the normalization of relations would permit the United States to become truly independent of France. Adams believed that he deserved the appointment, but he feared that the pro-French faction in Congress would send "some booby" who would only antagonize the British government.[36]

In January 1783 Adams resigned his commission, but he told Congress he would remain in Europe until he learned that his resignation had been accepted. At the same time, he began to lobby openly for the post in London. The assignment, he wrote to Congress, should go to a mature, experienced diplomat with a background in the law, a man with a classical education who was knowledgeable in English and French history, a person of "independent spirit." So transparent was Adams that James Madison, a congressman from Virginia, remarked with some disgust that the envoy had delineated a "character in which his own likeness is ridiculously and palpably studied."[37]

In the meantime, Adams could only await Congress's decision and the completion of the final peace settlement. One of the hurdles that blocked the conclusion of the definitive treaty fell quickly in 1783. In mid-January, six weeks after the conclusion of the Anglo-American accord, Britain reached armistice terms with France and Spain. General discussions commenced soon thereafter. As pleased as Adams was by these events, these months were not without their moments of anxiety. Indeed, he spoke of being even more apprehensive now that peace was so near, yet so far, from being realized. His greatest concern was aroused by the collapse of the peace-minded Shelburne government and the emergence of a new ministry headed by a revivified Lord North and Charles James Fox, a turn of events initiated largely by Parliament's displeasure with the terms of the preliminary peace, especially the prime minister's abandonment of the Loyalists. Oswald, who was responsible for the preliminary accord, was recalled, and David Hartley, a member of Parliament, was dispatched to conduct the final negotiations with the American envoys. But the new government was no less committed to peace. Indeed, disgust with the war was so pervasive throughout England that the ministry had no choice but to pursue a final peace.[38]

Nevertheless, Adams's fears were not entirely misplaced. The collapse of the Shelburne government did end all hope that the United States might secure better terms in the final treaty. Hartley, a foe of the British war effort since the outbreak of hostilities, arrived in Paris late in April and got down to business immediately, meeting with the Americans every evening at six o'clock in Adams's residence. Hartley, it turned out, wished to tinker with the preliminary peace only in a modest way. He sought the inclusion of an article to protect British fur traders who had been conducting business in what suddenly had become the United States; he and his masters in London knew that the Loyalist cause was hopeless. What was really on Hartley's mind was the establishment of a federal alliance with the United States, an arrangement characterized by a mutual defense pact—which, of course, would shatter the Franco-American alliance—and a return to the commercial ties of the colonial era. It was a forlorn hope. Not only would Congress never have agreed to the commercial concessions that such a neocolonial arrangement would have entailed, but the American people, having just fought a war to escape British hegemony, would not have stood for the slightest diminution of American independence. Once Adams and his colleagues understood Hartley's intentions, they made it clear that they would agree to nothing but the provisional treaty.[39]

The sporadic talks with Hartley were a treat for Adams, for, during most of the ten months that followed the preliminary peace, he found himself crushed under what he called a "total Idleness." It was the "most insipid . . . Time . . . imaginable," he exclaimed. But it was also a time when his personal demons restored their hold on his emotions. He stewed and simmered as he witnessed almost daily reminders of Franklin's popularity with the French, an approbation that only grew with the successful conclusion of the war. Adams convinced himself that America would give Franklin sole credit for the peace treaty. His own achievements would be forgotten; his patient, virtuous sacrifices would have been for nothing. Falling into a mood of black despair, he reflected upon what might have been, had his commission as sole negotiator not been stripped from him. His loss of power was the work of Franklin and his allies and lackeys in Congress, men whom he characterized as motivated by "envy and green eyed jealousy," but he also saw the hand of the deceitful Vergennes in his political fall, though, of course, the foreign minister had succeeded only through the cooperation of his "Satellite," the Doctor.[40]

To all who would listen, he told of Franklin's alleged perfidy, and he set about to convince his acquaintances that he and Jay, not Franklin, had been responsible for the successful negotiation of the preliminary peace. So bitterly disappointed was Adams with his neglect, that he acted irresponsibly, sharing information with the British envoys concerning his commission to secure a treaty of commerce, and even divulging information with regard to differences within the American delegation and divisions between the allies. Soon, in a torrent of invective, he denigrated Franklin's very character. His earlier charges against the Doctor reappeared in his correspondence. Franklin's reputation as a genius was spurious. The Doctor was a man of "cunning without Wisdom." Franklin was an impostor, as well as a rake, a liar, a cheat, a troublemaker, even a traitor. So consumed with hatred was Adams, and so indiscriminate was he in his remarks, that Franklin inevitably learned of the calumny of his colleague. He dismissed these "Ravings" and "Fancies" as the product of Adams's "troubled Imagination," and at about this same time he remarked that Adams meant well, was always honest and often wise, "but sometimes, and in some things, [he was] absolutely out of his senses."[41]

Adams's woes in 1783 included a mild recurrence of the illness that had afflicted him two years before, a relapse that had probably occurred naturally, although it might have been aided by the stress under which he appears to have labored that spring and summer. Suddenly, he spoke of "weakness and pains," as well as of debilitating fatigue, an inability to sleep, the onset of nervous tremors, and the appearance of "Sharp fiery humours," eruptions that broke out on his neck and body.[42]

Adams might have been saved from even more severe physical problems when public business drew him away from Paris in July. News had arrived a few days earlier that Whitehall would not permit United States ships to conduct trade in the British West Indies. With all hope of Anglo-American commerce extirpated, he returned to The Hague in the hope of stirring up Dutch trade for America's merchants and to investigate the possibility of commercial intercourse in the Dutch West Indies. It was not only a pleasant break from the pressures of Paris but also something of a rejuvenating experience. He received a warm, effusive greeting from the Dutch, and he was reunited with John Quincy, who had only recently returned from Russia to Holland.[43]

Adams remained in the Netherlands for only two weeks, then, accompanied by his travel-weary son (John Quincy's recent trek from Russia to Holland had required nearly six months), he returned to Paris. The word that he had awaited so long followed soon thereafter. Late in August word came that Whitehall was willing to accept the terms of the provisional treaty. Peace—the final peace—was at hand. The diplomats wasted no time. On September 3, 1783, in David Hartley's hotel room, in a ceremony evidently so simple that Adams failed even to make note of it in his diary, the treaty ending the war between Great Britain and the United States was signed. Later that day, with much greater pomp, Britain signed definitive treaties with France and Spain at Versailles.[44]

Four days later, word arrived from Philadelphia that Franklin, Jay, and Adams had been appointed to negotiate a treaty of commerce with Britain. Disappointed that he had not been named the sole envoy, Adams nevertheless was overjoyed to learn that he had been made head of the troika of commissioners. He flippantly attributed his appointment to Congress's fear that he would "do them more harm in America than in England," but in private his pride showed through. He knew that Congress was extending its recognition of his earlier successes.[45]

If Adams celebrated, however, it was from a sick bed. A few days after the peace treaty with Britain was signed, Adams, transported with jubilation, saw John Thaxter—a copy of the accord in his pocket—off to America. But shortly thereafter he fell seriously ill, the victim of a scourge of influenza that had invaded Paris, pitilessly afflicting about one-fifth of the population before it reached Adams's hearth. Adams was seriously ill for only three or four days, a period when he was treated without charge by a friend, Sir James Jay, the physician-brother of the envoy. While he recuperated, caring friends moved him to quiet Auteuil, above the Seine on the outskirts of Paris, thinking the serenity of the place would be an antidote to frenetic Paris. (Adams once had complained that the traffic beneath his window sounded like the roar of Niagara Falls.) By month's end he felt better, well enough, in fact, to undertake twice-daily horseback rides and walks of up to five miles, both part of the therapy recommended by his physicians.[46]

Adams could hardly have found a more attractive setting in which to recover his strength. From his new lodging he could look upon rivers, forests, and hills; the towers of two castles and the spires of a nearby church also could be seen, as could the little village of Issy. But it was the bucolic countryside that most enchanted him, and on his long, solitary, recuperative rides he delighted in spotting an occasional deer or rabbit or game bird. The pastoral environment reminded him of rustic Braintree, and, during the long moments that he was alone in the forests and on the rural trails, his thoughts increasingly turned to his wife and children, whom he had not seen in four years.[47]

This separation from her husband, especially the summer of 1781, was a terribly difficult time for Abigail. The ineradicable pain was almost unbearable, for in addition to John's absence she also discovered that Congress had stripped him of his diplomatic commissions. "[W]hen he is wounded I bleed," she exclaimed, although it was the apparent meaninglessness of his mission— and of their separation—that now was most grievous. The betrayal of her husband by Congress meant that her "domestick pleasure" had been forfeited unnecessarily. Worse still, she learned of John's fate at a time when she had not received a single letter from him for nearly a full year.[48]

Initially, her rage and frustration was subsumed somewhat by her long, anxious wait for the safe arrival of little Charles. When he did not arrive in the late summer as expected, she grew more fearful, even expressing frequent "slight indispositions," which she immediately attributed to the appalling stress under which she lived. At long last, however, her son landed safely. Yet Charles's arrival sparked fresh anxieties, for through him she learned of her husband's first serious illness, the breakdown that he suffered in Amsterdam in August 1781. Actually, Charles had sailed three weeks before his father had collapsed, and he could provide only the sketchiest of details, which he had garnered during a long stopover in La Corununa. More months would pass before she knew that John was largely recovered, though still enfeebled.[49]

But the realization that she had nearly lost her husband in the course of his interminable mission seemed to stoke the fires of rancor within her breast. In earlier letters she had merely inquired about the likelihood of his return. In spring 1782 her wrath poured out. For eight years, save for a week here or a month there, she had been compelled to live apart from her husband. Evidently, she wrote, he found their separation less disagreeable than she. Had his service not been adequate? Could he not serve as well at home as abroad?

Would his reputation be tarnished by retirement from public office? Cincinnatus, the ancient Roman warrior who, after long service, had resigned his public office to return to his plow without forfeiting his honor. With peace, could he not also return to his home? Indeed, if peace were attained and he did not return immediately, she wrote, "I could not forgive you." Unless, of course, she could come to him.[50]

Since 1779 Abigail had often dreamed of traveling to Europe, but an Atlantic crossing unescorted by her husband was not something she had thought possible. A woman was too delicate to undertake such a journey without a male escort, she had remarked; besides, she added, the "many Dangers we are Subject too from" males made such an an undertaking unthinkable. In August 1782, however, Benjamin Waterhouse, the physician who had resided briefly with Adams in Amsterdam fifteen months before, called on her and suggested just such a venture. Her presence was essential to John's health, he advised. Peace might still be years away; if she did not join her husband in Europe, she would not see him for years, if ever again. For the first time, Abigail proposed that she and the children, or at least she and Nabby, be permitted sail for Holland, adding: "I fear neither the Enemy or old Neptune." If you accept my proposal, she wrote, "one Letter will be sufficient. If it is rejected, one Letter will be too many."[51]

Three months before Abigail expressed her yearning to make the voyage to Europe, John had written, "[I] must go to you or you must come to me." The loneliness had become unbearable, he had said. But when he learned of her willingness to come, he sought to dissuade her. Since early in 1783, in fact, he had vacillated on the matter of his wife's coming to him, at times even writing as many as three contradictory letters within the space of a week. Mostly, however, he urged her not to come. He would be home soon, he often wrote. If she sailed for Europe, he cautioned, she might land only to discover that he had departed for America. He also warned that if he stayed on in Europe she would find Holland to be terribly unhealthy, while in London both he and she might face incessant harassment. She would be terribly unhappy abroad, he told Abigail, faced with living a life of "hideous Solitude" in an alien culture.[52]

Abigail's response was ingenious. She seized upon those letters that urged her to come and largely ignored the others. During 1783, therefore, she told John that she wished he would come home to Braintree, but for the first time she made it clear that she was prepared to cross the Atlantic. Dr. Waterhouse's counsel was a crucial factor in her decision, but of greater importance was John's admission that he desired a ministerial post in London. By midyear Abigail knew that if her husband was sent to the Court of St. James, years would pass before he returned to America.[53]

Most historians have been loath to acknowledge that John Adams did not want his wife at his side. Yet, he had not permitted Abigail to join him in Philadelphia, and he was no less tenacious in his refusal to permit her to come to him in Europe. But why would Adams have chosen such a course? He may have settled into the comfortable habits of bachelorhood, undistracted by an incessant domestic bustle. This had been his way of life for years, since his departure for the first Congress in 1774. Indeed, since their marriage in 1764, the couple had lived separately almost one-half of the time. His concern for the survival of the farm must have been a factor in the course that he chose, too, as was his concern for the safety of his wife and the well-being of his children.

Yet, there must have been another factor that moved Adams, for abruptly in the autumn of 1783 he called out to Abigail to join him. With the war at an end, it was safer for her to travel, and the boys, even the youngest, were old enough to be left with relatives in America. But it was Adams who was most liberated by the end of the war. His compulsive need for personal sacrifice in lieu of soldiering had vanished. During the long conflict with Great Britain he had twice faced peril in the Atlantic, forsworn handsome earnings, and endured a long and painful separation from his wife and children. But now he need no longer pay such a price. He had proven his manhood to himself.

Immediately upon signing the definitive treaty, Adams wrote Abigail to urge her to join him that very winter in Europe. Bring Nabby and one or two servants, he advised, but leave the boys with relatives. "I will fly" to you wherever you disembark, he added, meaning it literally, for he told her that he would come to her in one of the new-fangled aerial balloons. At last, he told a friend, he once again was about to be a married man.[54]

So anxious was Adams to be reunited with Abigail that he immediately wrote her a second time exhorting her to hurry across the Atlantic. A few weeks later he fired off a third letter in which he implored his wife to come to his side, dashing off this missive, curiously, just after having completed a tour of the bedchamber of the queen of England. Dr. Jay, who had practiced in England before the war, had recommended that Adams journey to Bath, the famous health resort, as the final step in his recuperation from the influenza. Adams required no coaxing. Together with John Quincy, he departed Auteuil in mid-October, and for three days the two travelers bounced and clattered noisily over France's flint-stone highways before reaching Calais, from whence they crossed on the Channel packet to Dover. Two days later, October 26, he arrived in London. Adams was excited and moved to be in this city of which he had often dreamed, yet surprised and comforted by the discovery that so many things—the language, of course, but the people's manners and even the furnishings in his hotel on the Strand—were so similar to the America that he remembered.[55]

Adams was so taken by this vast city with its 750,000 inhabitants that he appears to have temporarily forgotten the ills that had occasioned his journey. He lingered in London for two months, occupying much of the daytime with sightseeing forays. He busily darted from historic churches to natural history museums, from public buildings—including Windsor Palace—to noted schools. He visited the Wedgwood pottery, delighting in the opportunity to watch exquisite china being produced before his eyes, and he attended the opening of Parliament, where, bunched together with other curious onlookers, he watched and listened as George III addressed the legislators. Part of his time was consumed in sitting for Benjamin West and John Singleton Copley, two famous expatriate American painters, but that was relaxing compared to the badgering to which he was subjected by American petitioners, down-and-out fellow countrymen who somehow had succeeded in getting marooned in London during the war and who now beseeched his assistance in arranging their return to their homeland.[56]

On Christmas Eve 1783, still "feeble, low and drooping," Adams at last arrived at Bath in the West country. But he tarried in the resort village only briefly, testing the constant 116-degree waters just three or four times before urgent public business called him away. Word came that a full-blown crisis had developed in Amsterdam. The American loan had gone unpaid; the credit of the United States was in jeopardy.

Although fearing that his health could not tolerate another journey, Adams immediately hastened to the Netherlands. He crossed England to the coast, where he again took the packet to the Continent. The voyage was a nightmare, three days of terror in a January storm. Finally on the eighth, the little vessel, battered and beaten almost beyond endurance by the vicious winds, put ashore on the desolate coast of a small island off Zeeland. Though weakened from a seventy-two-hour bout of seasickness, Adams was compelled to walk four miles through snow and ice to reach Goeree, the nearest village. There, he and John Quincy found warm lodgings and a decent meal, his first in days; he also rented a wagon and a team of horses for the trip to east coast of the island. From there the weary travelers sped to the mainland aboard an iceboat, but even in this more populous region the only conveyance that Adams and his son could locate was a Dutch peasant's cart, in which they continued their journey until they found a handsome carriage that finally conveyed them to Amsterdam.[57]

After such a harrowing and fatiguing journey, the diplomatic labors that followed must have seemed a mere trifle. Within a few days he secured an urgent new loan for the struggling United States, although he was compelled to accept an unusually high interest rate of 6 per cent. As usual, Adams was comfortable in Holland and he opted to remain there rather than to return to the stress of Paris, leaving it to Jay and Franklin to conduct the preliminary— and certain to be futile—talks with the British. Adams relaxed, recuperated, read, got to know his rapidly maturing son a bit better, and awaited the arrival of Abigail and his daughter.[58]

By the spring of 1784 Adams knew that his wife was coming to Europe, although he did not know when or where she would arrive. In fact, Abigail would not depart until June, preferring to wait until that time of the year when the treacherous Atlantic storms normally were most rare. She had decided instantly to go to her husband. Indeed, not only was she terribly anxious to be reunited with John, but she also had another reason for making the journey. She was anxious just now to remove her daughter from Massachusetts. During the last half of 1782, Nabby, a young woman just turned seventeen, had begun to see Royall Tyler, a twenty-five-year-old Braintree attorney. Within weeks he was calling almost daily, and it was obvious to all that the young couple were quite serious about one another.[59]

After some initial reservations, Abigail had grown fond of her daughter's suitor. The valedictorian of his 1776 Harvard College graduating class, Tyler possessed the mind and charisma to effect a handsome legal business someday; despite persistent rumors of earlier irresponsible and rakish behavior (he once had been expelled from Harvard and admitted to having squandered a modest inheritance), he appeared to have grown into a mature and trustworthy adult, even if he did not study as diligently as Abigail thought prudent.

But Abigail's fondness for Tyler did not mean that she approved of her daughter's marriage to this charming young gentleman. She feared that his law practice was not yet sufficiently established to permit him to support a wife, and she believed that her daughter was too young to marry. In addition, she continued to worry about the rumors concerning Tyler, which buzzed about Braintree, including a tale that he had fathered a child by a housemaid at Harvard. More than anything, perhaps, Abigail was influenced by the reaction of her husband. John categorically refused to consent to the relationship. He had scant respect for the Tyler family, and he too doubted that his daughter— whom he continued to regard as the thirteen-year-old child he had left behind in 1779—was old enough for matrimony. In fact, he was so outraged at the very idea of Tyler's courtship of his daughter that his initial reaction was to scold Abigail for not keeping the two apart from the outset. Abigail responded to the crisis by sending Nabby to Boston for a protracted visit with relatives. But when her husband summoned her to Europe, Abigail envisioned a better solution. Nabby, still unmarried, would accompany her. They were likely to be gone for a year, perhaps even two; by the time they returned, Tyler would be better situated and Nabby would be about twenty, the age at which Abigail had married. Nabby acquiesced in the decisions made for her, although by the time she and her mother departed she was just a few days shy of her nineteenth birthday, an age when many young women were already married and some had borne their first child.[60]

Leaving fourteen-year-old Charles and twelve-year-old Thomas in the care of her sister's husband, John Shaw, a Haverhill parson who agreed to oversee the boys' final year of preparatory schooling before they enrolled at Harvard, Abigail and her daughter, accompanied by two servants and a cow, boarded the *Active* on the first day of summer, 1784. She could have sailed in the company of Thomas Jefferson, recently appointed to succeed Jay on the commission to negotiate with Great Britain, had she been willing to postpone her departure for two weeks. But she eschewed the pleasure of his company rather than put off her reunion with John even for a few additional days.

On a breezy, delightfully warm Boston morning, the *Active* began its trek. Ironically, soon after Nabby and her mother commenced their adventure, Royall Tyler heard from John Adams. He had reconsidered, he said, and he gave his blessing to the marriage of his daughter and this promising young attorney.[61]

This voyage of the *Active* was routine and relatively rapid. Abigail immediately found the customary aroma of the ship to be "excessive disagreeable," a bane that soon worsened when its stench was compounded by the pungent odor of whale oil leaking from the cargo hold. In addition, she and Nabby fell prey to seasickness before the run was two hours old, a malady that plagued them for more than ten days; throughout the voyage the persistent dampness of the vessel caused Abigail to endure rheumatic aches, while the nagging anxiety occasioned by such a voyage resulted in frequent nervous headaches. When she was well enough to eat, she found the ship's food to be worse than awful, inedible concoctions prepared by "a lazy dirty Negro, with no more knowledge of his Business than a Savage." Her miseries were compounded by an inability to bathe, which left her feeling dirty and unkempt. Abigail and Nabby were distressed too by their lack of privacy, for the door separating their bunks from the men's quarters had to be left ajar at night to cool and ventilate the compartment. But the male passengers were polite, and when Abigail was not reading she spent much of her time in affable conversation with several of the men. Ultimately, she concluded that a ship was like a prison, and an experience that "a Lady" ought to avoid, for it was impossible to maintain the "Decency and Cleanliness which ought to be an inherint principal in every female."[62]

On the twenty-eighth day out of Boston, land was sighted. At last, she noted in her diary at that very moment, "am I Gracious Heaven . . . then to meet, the Dear long absent partner of my Heart?" It was at once a joyous and a frightening prospect. "How many[,] how various[,] how complicated my Sensations," she confessed.[63]

The reunion was not quite as imminent as Abigail expected when she glimpsed her first view of the English landscape, the white Dover cliffs, on July 18. Three more weeks would pass before she was again with her husband. After landing on the Kent country coast, about sixty miles from London, three days were consumed in a carriage ride to the capital. To their great disappointment, Abigail and Nabby discovered that John was not in London. He had remained in Holland since early in the year. Abigail took rooms in the Adelphi Hotel, where she had expected to find her husband, and sent word immediately to The Hague announcing their safe arrival.

Meanwhile she waited anxiously, as first ten days, then twenty passed with no word from John. All the while, she was apprehensive at what she would find after such a long separation. "Heaven give us a happy meeting," she prayed, not knowing what to expect.[64]

John Quincy came first, sent by his father to fetch the ladies to The Hague. Before they could depart, however, John came, too. He had learned of Jefferson's arrival in Paris; as his presence in the French capital was not urgent, Adams decided to come to London and personally escort his family to France.

At noon on a cool, late summer Saturday, August 7, 1784, nearly five years after his departure from Braintree, Adams reached the Adelphi Hotel in busy downtown London. At last, he was reunited with his wife and daughter. "I had the satisfaction of meeting my friends," he curtly said of the occasion.[65]

Good "poets and painters wisely draw a veil over those Scenes which surpass the pen of the one and the pencil of the other," was Abigail's more fitting and tasteful comment regarding the reunion.[66]

CHAPTER 14

*

High against America

THE REUNION OF John and Abigail Adams ended one age and commenced another in their lives. The terrible strain and travail imposed upon this couple by the Revolution and the war, and by John's decision to live for years apart from his wife and family, had slowly wound down in the months and years following the British debacle at Yorktown, until, abruptly, it came to an end at the Adelphi Hotel on that happy, tender August forenoon in 1785. The long, harrowing era—the epoch in history, as John had immediately called it—that had commenced a dozen years before with the Boston Tea Party had at last come to an end.

But John and Abigail faced an uncertain future. Directly ahead were talks with Great Britain, an assignment likely to be the work of a year, perhaps eighteen months. Thereafter, they would certainly return to Massachusetts, but to what fate? Perhaps Adams would resume his legal practice. He might reenter provincial politics. Or, he might sit in the national Congress for another term. He might consider a judicial appointment. But the future had seldom seemed so murky.

The Adamses were hardly reunited before they set out for France, traveling in a somewhat shabby, thoroughly uncomfortable carriage. It was a lightning journey, as they raced over as much as eighty-five miles per day. The travelers reached Paris on August 13, where they paused for four days, dividing their time between shopping and sightseeing. John served as tour guide, escorting the ladies through famous public buildings and gardens, to the cathedral of Notre Dame, the Palais de Justice, and the Tuileries, still green and verdant in this summer season. Then it was on to Auteuil and the residence that John had inhabited for the better part of the past year, the lovely mansion that would be home to the Adams family until the following spring.[1]

While John plunged ahead with his work, the women began the process of settling into their new environment, a transition in life-styles that proceeded far more smoothly than John had anticipated. Nabby complained that many rooms in the mansion were too small, ignoring the fact that there were fifty rooms in the house, about forty-four more than in the homestead in Braintree. Abigail found the lodging "gay and really beautiful," with its red tile floors and its huge salon and a dining room that opened onto a magnificent courtyard and lovely gardens. But her frugal Yankee upbringing left her unprepared to cope with the seven servants that waited on the family, or to purchase from her husband's meager salary—only two hundred guineas a year—the accoutrements essential for entertaining dignitaries; nor did it comfort her to know that the china and silver and linen that she acquired could have been purchased in Boston at about one-third their cost in Parisian stores. Because of their inability to speak French, the two women seldom strayed from their home, although on occasion John or John Quincy accompanied them on forays into the city. There they shopped, attended the theater and opera (which "made a great deal of noise" and was "ridiculous" in Nabby's eyes), trekked to the royal palace to watch the "Dauphin," the heir to the throne, at play on the lawn, were among the ten thousand spectators who turned out to observe a manned balloon being launched at the Tuileries, and visited the art galleries in the Palais Royal.[2]

Abigail and Nabby adjusted to French culture more rapidly than had John upon his arrival in 1778. The more liberated manner of French women—the facile manner with which they greeted male friends and their open, frank conversational habits at social gatherings—came as a shock initially, but soon even a conventionalist such as Nabby lauded the "French ease" as a welcome break from the "stiffness and reserve" she beheld among Americans. Open prostitution in Paris was something to which they could not become habituated, however, nor could they accept the lively holiday atmosphere that accompanied the Sabbath in Catholic France. Still, both women soon accepted most of the ways of the French, and Abigail, who had come to Europe with a low opinion of the Gallic demeanor, even came to appreciate much that was customary in this strange land. In fact, more than anyone in the family, according to Nabby, Abigail's mind had been "Metamorphosed" during her first weeks in France.[3]

The Adamses had a busy social schedule. Diplomats had to be feted. American sojourners often paid their respects, too, including men such as John Paul Jones and Col. David Humphreys, once an aide to General Washington. Acquaintances made during Adams's lengthy stay in France were entertained as well; none were more welcome than the Marquis de Lafayette and his young, congenial wife. Dr. Franklin rarely rode out from nearby Passy, so great now was the discomfort he experienced from "the stone," as he referred to his malady. Yet he came to Auteuil on four occasions (Adams claimed these were the only times the Doctor left his residence for more than a year), and the Adamses dined with him at Passy an equal number of times. Franklin appears to have made a genuine effort to overcome Adams's enmity, and he sought, too, to make the Adams women comfortable in this strange land. Not only did he

The mansion of the Count de Roualt, the Adams residence in Auteuil, near Paris, in 1784. *Courtesy: Massachusetts Historical Society.*

see them about once a month, but he endeavored to be a good companion, putting them at ease with his endless array of stories and even giving Abigail a book of sermons, so that she might have something to read on Sunday mornings in lieu of attending a strange Roman Catholic worship service.

Although Adams was never able to forget the sleights that he believed he had suffered at the hands of Franklin, he grew to feel a deep compassion for his afflicted rival, a man often subject to great discomforts and who, he reported, would pass blood after even the shortest carriage ride. Abigail shared her husband's aversion, if not his enmity, toward Franklin, but Nabby rather liked him, finding that he inspired respect by his venerable appearance, and noting that he was "always sociable, and . . . very satirical, always silent, unless he has some diverting story to tell, of which he has a great collection."[4]

The Adamses grew closer to Jefferson than to any other person during this period. In fact, Thomas Jefferson and John Adams would seem to prove the validity of the old adage that opposites attract; except for an interest in the literature of classical political theory and a facility for charming Abigail Adams, these two dissimilar men somehow forged a bond of close friendship. The two could not have come from more strikingly different backgrounds. The Virginian was the son of a wealthy planter, Peter Jefferson, a self-made man who as a surveyor and land speculator had risen from the overseer class to the upper class, a position he solidified and enhanced through marriage into the elite Randolph family. In 1743, when young John was already eight and struggling with the demands of his father to master his early Latin lessons, Thomas was born at Shadwell, within sight of the Blue Ridge Mountains on Virginia's frontier. He was the eldest son in a family of eight living children. Beginning at about age five, Thomas was taught at home by a tutor, at age nine was placed in a Latin school operated by a Scottish clergyman in Goochland County, and at age fourteen was removed to the care of an Anglican mentor who ran a log schoolhouse a dozen miles from Shadwell.

That same year, 1757, when Adams was completing his first year as Putnam's apprentice in Worcester, Peter Jefferson died. At "14 years of age," Jefferson later remembered, "the whole care and direction of my self was thrown on my self entirely." While not entirely true, Jefferson had nevertheless lost a strong-willed father who had given direction to his life; in addition, he was compelled to begin making at least some decisions in the management of Shadwell and its army of slave laborers. Unlike George Washington's experience following the death of his father, Peter Jefferson's demise did not end the formal education of his son. Thomas continued his preparatory education until he was nearly seventeen, when, a bit late by eighteenth-century standards, he enrolled at the College of William and Mary in Williamsburg. Like Adams, who remembered that he had begun to flower intellectually only during his college years, Jefferson responded to his new environment in dramatic fashion; largely because of the influence of Dr. William Small of Scotland, under whom he studied mathematics, ethics, rhetoric, and literature, Jefferson was trans-formed at William and Mary into a man of passionate intellectual curiousity, a man with an abiding interest in natural science.

Jefferson completed his college studies in just two years. At age nineteen, he might have returned home to manage his estate and live the life of a gentleman planter. But he wanted something more than the sameness of life on a plantation, a life-style in which, he said, "All things . . . appear to me to trudge on in one and the same round." Like Adams, he chose to study law. His professors, like John's, urged such a calling upon him; as with John, moreover, Jefferson saw the law as the most direct route to public office. Off and on for a period of five years, he read law under George Wythe in Williamsburg. By the time he had completed his studies and was licensed to practice, he had reached his majority and inherited Shadwell. In 1767, at a time when Adams was emerging as one of the leading attorneys in Boston, Jefferson commenced his career. Already, he was the owner of a plantation of five thousand acres and twenty-two slaves.

Within three years, Jefferson established a successful law practice. But his style was quite different from that of Adams. Jefferson was uncomfortable as an orator and he found it difficult to address juries; his strength lay in his careful preparation and in his intellectual grasp of the law. By his third year of practice, Jefferson, like his father before him, had been elected to the House of Bur-gesses. He entered public life, therefore, in the midst of the Anglo-American crisis. His experiences in this regard were quite unlike those of Adams, how-ever. Jefferson was still a student in Williamsburg during the Stamp Act crisis and he merely observed the great orations of Patrick Henry at the session of the Burgesses that passed the Virginia Resolves. The first session that he attended as an elected assemblyman came in 1769, the session at which Washington helped organize a boycott against his "lordly Masters" in London who had imposed the Townshend Duties upon the colonies; a newcomer, Jefferson could play only a small role.

During these years Jefferson began to construct his home, Monticello, the mansion that would become his obsession and masterpiece and would occupy his attention for the remainder of his life. In 1770, in addition, he began to court Martha Skelton, the daughter of a planter in Charles City County, near Williamsburg. Until then, Jefferson, like young Adams, had been an unsuc-cessful suitor. Despite years of dancing lessons and tutoring in the other social amenities that were supposed to make him a well-rounded young man, Jeffer-son appeared strangely confused and ungraceful when in the company of young ladies. But with Martha, widowed for three years when he met her, all went well, and on New Year's Day 1772, when Jefferson was twenty-eight, a bit old by the standards of the Virginia planter class, but a year younger than John had been when he wed Abigail, Jefferson was married. With his wife's estate coupled to his own, Jefferson now owned over 11,000 acres and more than 150 slaves.

The material differences between Jefferson and Adams were matched by other dissimilarities. According to most descriptions, Jefferson was tall and slender, probably standing over six feet. He was indifferent to his appearance, often affecting a rumpled, slapdash look in habitually ill-fitting, old, thread-bare, even stained, clothing, and striking observers as somewhat disheveled because his sandy red hair seemed never combed. His was a perpetual "state of negligence," said an acquaintance. With a ruddy complexion, a rather long nose, and a somewhat jutting chin, Jefferson was rarely described as hand-some; he was more often characterized as earnest and thoughtful. He was shy by nature, but people seemed to be comfortable in his presence, perhaps because of his "mild and pleasing countenance," as one observer put it, or perhaps because he conveyed the air of a gentle man who usually greeted others with a pleasant smile and a mild manner. Not handsome, not dynamic, not witty, not intimidating, not obstreperous, not acerbic, Jefferson—as much for what he was as for what he was not—had found the means of putting people at ease. Nevertheless, to be comfortable with Jefferson was not to know him. He was an extremely private man, so much so that the inner Jefferson re-mained impenetrable to outsiders. The one thing that every observer dis-cerned, however, was his intellect. Virtually every description by a contempo-rary acknowledges two aspects of his intellectual capabilities. He almost always was described as "a truly scientific and learned Man," and the breadth of his intellectual accomplishments also deeply impressed many acquain-tances. Here was a "Musician, Draftsman, Surveyor, Astronomer, Natural Philospher, Jurist, and Statesman . . . finally a Philospher," it was said.

But if Jefferson was comfortable in the companionship of men, his relations with women took on a mixed quality. Following the death of Martha after only ten years of marriage, he never remarried, a decision in all likelihood that stemmed from the storehouse of more unpleasant than pleasant memories of matrimony; in fact, he once described marriage as "moments of ex-tasy . . . ransomed by years of torment and hatred." Jefferson seemed almost to fear city girls and he expressed his dislike for well-educated females, yet he was even less fond of women who acted from emotion rather than reason, an attribute that he thought was endemic to the sex. While Jefferson had little or nothing to do with single women, over a period of years prior to his own marriage he had endeavored to foist his amorous affections upon the wife of a close friend, and, as a widower, he did have a brief, passionate affair with Maria Cosway, the blonde, coquettish wife of a foppish English artist. Rumors circu-lated in his later years, moreover, that he had a lengthy affair with one of his female slaves, by whom he had allegedly sired several children, but the alle-gation remains unproven.

Much of Peter Jefferson's success had been due to his facility for hard work, and son Thomas exhibited the same penchant. He found idleness intolerable. He rose each morning before the sun and pursued his work according to an ordered, systematic plan. By the time he first met John Adams in June 1775 at the Second Congress, he had, through constant labor and diligent study, developed a deserved reputation as a brilliant thinker and accomplished writer. Adams, in fact, read Jefferson's *A Summary View of the Rights of British America,* published the previous year, and remarked on his "peculiar felicity of expression." Others perceived the same talent and the Congress in 1775 and 1776 often turned to him to draft its pronouncements, as it had turned the previous year to Adams, by then terribly busy with committee assignments. The crystallization of his views on independence were not unlike those of Adams; although he appears to have been more advanced in his notions on the degree of American autonomy in 1774, both men probably decided upon the wisdom of separation from the empire at about the same time. But the decision came for different reasons. Jefferson was more the revolutionary. He wished for independence because, for him, it meant the liberation of the individual, the opportunity, as Edmund Morgan suggested, for the "individual to manage his own life with the minimum of interference from governments."

Jefferson became linked with a philosophy quite distinct from that of Adams. He came to be seen as engaged in the emancipation of humankind, preaching that change should be easy to effect and that great change should occur with each generation. For Jefferson, the American Revolution was waged to remove aristocratic privilege and to limit governmental power. In the course of the Revolution, he proposed that land be given to the free population in Virginia so that each adult white male might possess fifty acres. He advocated what was tantamount to universal manhood suffrage for Virginia's white males. He urged the abolition of entails and primogeniture lest his state's republican experiment collapse before the crushing power of its planter aristocracy. He pressed for a system of public education that would provide free schooling for three years for the children of all citizens. He called for reform in the criminal code, urging the reduction of capital crimes to just two offenses, treason and murder. Perhaps the most important change for which he was largely responsible during the Revolution was the enactment of Virginia's Statute for Religious Liberty, an act providing for both freedom of religion and freedom from religion.

Despite his magnificent record of reform, Jefferson arrived in France with a reputation as something of a failure. He had been elected governor of Virginia in 1779, succeeding Patrick Henry. He came to power at perhaps the darkest hour of the war. Probably no one could have coped successfully with the desperate situation that confronted his state in this period, but Jefferson, who demonstrated serious deficiencies as an administrator, certainly was unable to press the war to Virginia's advantage. In the last hours of his governorship he was forced to flee from British troops who had reached his very doorstep at Monticello; had it not been for Cornwallis's fortuitous surrender four months later, Jefferson would have been subjected to a legislative inquiry into the failures of his administration and, possibly, a public censure that could have ended his political career. As it was, he left public life after this episode and might not have returned, had it not been for the death of Martha in late summer 1782. Soon thereafter he agreed to serve once again in Congress, and a year later, in May 1784, he was appointed minister plenipotentiary in Europe with Adams and Franklin.[5]

Jefferson and his daughter, Martha, arrived in Paris about two weeks after Abigail and Nabby reached London. They took up residence in the city, initially on the Left Bank, later in a house that he refurbished on the Cul-de-sac Traitbout, near the Opera. Jefferson maintained a cordial, though never close, relationship with Franklin that winter, coming instead to depend on the Adamses to provide the hospitality and conviviality for which he longed, and he reciprocated not only with dinner parties of his own—the meals were prepared by a slave whom he apprenticed to a French chef—but also by escorting seventeen-year-old John Quincy and nineteen-year-old Nabby about the city. Jefferson and Abigail, who first had met only on the eve of her voyage, immediately liked one another. It was the most rare of relationships for Jefferson, who normally disapproved of intelligent, opinionated women. Perhaps this instance was different because only a year separated them in age, and because she was kind, gentle, and garrulous, but not overbearing. Clearly, Abigail took a fancy to the Virginian. She pronounced him to be "one of the choice ones of the earth," someone with whom she could converse, look after, pamper a bit (he was ill during much of his first year in Paris), and even console, for during that terrible winter Jefferson learned that he had lost to whooping cough a two-year-old daughter left behind in Virginia. Jefferson and John got on well together, too. Adams once remarked that Jefferson was "but a boy to me," although, in fact, only eight years separated them, and Jefferson was a mature man of forty-one. But Jefferson almost habitually deferred to older, successful men, and in this instance he often sat quietly, nibbling at Abigail's New England meals of "plain beef and pudding," and listening respectfully to Adams's long monologues. The working relationship that developed between the two was a far cry from the tempestuous affiliation that had existed between Adams and Franklin. In fact, Jefferson was so successful in smoothing over some of the smoldering animosity that lingered between those two that Adams marveled at the sudden "wonderful Harmony, good Humour" that now existed in his dealings with Franklin. Adams also remarked that he had never had such a congenial relationship with any colleague as that which developed with Jefferson, a man whom he praised for his industry, talent, and integrity.[6]

John and Abigail found their nine months in Auteuil a happy time. Their anxieties at what they might discover in one another upon being reunited apparently had been exaggerated. In addition, they were comfortably situated with an endless array of intriguing diversions available at their fingertips. The one disappointment for Adams in these months was his lack of success in his public responsibilities. He and his colleagues were to arrange commercial treaties with as many European nations as could be induced to open trade with the United States, but after several months only Prussia had agreed to admit American goods to its ports. Great Britain, the biggest prize, refused to budge. An attempt by young William Pitt to repeal all laws prohibiting trade with America was overwhelmingly rejected in the spring of 1783. Instead, the Fox-North government repealed the Prohibitory Acts so that British merchants could sell their wares in American ports, but an order-in-council issued in July 1783 prevented American ships from bringing American goods into British ports, including the West Indies, where New England merchants had vended enormous quantities of grain, fish, and lumber before 1775; the only commodities excepted by this decree were American oil, naval stores, and tobacco.[7]

At the outset Adams was not terribly ruffled by the British trade embargo. He expected most of Europe to open ports to ships flying the Stars and Stripes, and he predicted that Whitehall's policy ultimately would be fatal to Great Britain without causing much harm to the United States. In the meantime, he proposed two strategies that might compel London to repeal its restrictions. Show her "that you can do without her," he advised. In other words, sever all trade with Britain until its government reestablished full economic intercourse with the United States. Second, he urged that his government send an ambassador to each European capital, including the Court of St. James. Dispatch them with sufficient funds so they could court the powerful and seek to influence public opinion, he added, saying success would come.[8]

This was hardly a disinterested proposition, of course, but Congress soon agreed, though less because of Adams's suggestion than because the British government ultimately urged that an American minister be sent to London. Late in the winter Congress selected Adams to be that minister. The New England delegates shepherded his selection through a barrage of flak in Congress. Even Adams acknowledged that some of the opposition was merited. His acerbic manner had made enemies over the years; many also detested his vain countenance, a quality that showed through in his letters to Congress (he had not tried to hide the silly "Washington of diplomacy" title that the cunning Vergennes had laid on him, for instance). Moreover, his ill-concealed hatred of Franklin had provoked many of the Doctor's friends. But some of the opposition was unwarranted. Some southern congressmen, for instance, suspected that Adams would not work to secure compensation for their lost slave property. Nevertheless, despite the resistance to naming Adams, there were pragmatic reasons for his appointment. To have selected another—the names of John

Rutledge and Robert Livingston, formerly the secretary of foreign affairs, had been placed in nomination—not only would have antagonized New England but would have invited retaliation on some future issue. Besides, most congressmen had to admit that Adams's work in Holland and in the peace negotiations had been admirable. Thus, Adams secured the assignment that he had coveted for the past thirty months, receiving the news late in April when Col. William Stephens Smith, named secretary to the legation in London, arrived on his doorstep in Auteuil bearing a packet bulging with congressional documents.[9]

The Adamses completed their business in France during the next three weeks. John had a final, cordial meeting with Vergennes, who was relaxed and expansive, and who advised his guest that it was "a great Thing to be the first Ambassador from your Country to the Country you sprung from. It is a Mark." Characteristically, Adams responded that such matters did "not weigh much with me." John and Abigail also said good-bye to Jefferson. He would remain in Paris as Franklin's successor, having been appointed ambassador to France at the same time Adams was chosen for the position in London. With far fewer regrets, Adams bade farewell to Franklin, too, who had asked to return to Philadelphia after spending the past ten years—and nearly twenty-five of the last twenty-eight years—abroad. John and Abigail's most burdensome task was deciding what to do with John Quincy. For Abigail the decision was especially difficult, as she had been reunited with her son for only nine months. John, however, argued that it was essential to educate the lad in the country in which he would live and work, and he prevailed. Passage on a vessel bound for America was arranged on short notice, and the young man, just a few weeks short of his eighteenth birthday, sailed alone for Massachusetts and Harvard College, where he would complete his formal education. Shortly thereafter, on May 20, 1785, the three remaining Adamses, together with their two servants and plentiful trunks and bundles, and the pet songbird Abigail had purchased in Paris, departed Auteuil for London, and for a new chapter in their lives.[10]

John Adams was forty-nine years old that spring. From two paintings for which he sat during this period—one rendered by John Singleton Copley during his first brief visit to England in 1783, the other completed in 1788 by a young American artist, Mather Brown—we have an idea of Adams's appearance at this juncture. Adams was critical of Copley's effort, probably because the artist captured his tenacious pride. Abigail, on the other hand, thought it "a most beautiful painting" and a good likeness.[11]

Copley represented Adams as the statesman. Sword at his side, Adams stands before a globe and a table laden with maps. He is clutching a document. Behind him is an open window, through which can be seen a statue of a Roman statesman holding a cudgel in one hand, an olive branch in the other. Adams is

John Adams in 1785, aged fifty. By Mather Brown. *Courtesy: The Boston Athenaeum.*

unsmiling, though a hint of a smirk seems to steal across his face. He seems cocksure, perhaps a bit arrogant, and he exudes an air of smug self-satisfaction. Not long before, he had claimed that he, together with Samuel Adams and John Hancock, had "set the World in a blaze." The Adams on Copley's canvas appears complacent and vainglorious, powerful and forceful, a man who at once saw himself as the instigator of a mighty revolution and as the envoy responsible for American independence.[12]

Brown's work, of which Adams was fond, depicts the subject as a sedate, reflective sort. He sits at a desk clutching his correspondence, a quill conveniently at his fingertips. He slumps a bit in his chair, a man bowed slightly from his years of wretched cares and tribulations. His face bears a meditative cast, but it is dominated by large eyes that appear tired yet convey the impression that this is a gentle, compassionate, and quite sober man.

In both paintings Adams appears to be in good health, although Copley's was painted while he was in England for recuperative purposes. In the Copley oil he is overweight, perhaps by as much as twenty-five pounds. Adams does not appear to have aged prematurely, nor, despite his slightly sagging posture in Brown's portraiture, does he evince any signs of debility or the residual effects of undue physical or emotional stress. What does seem clear is why he preferred the one painting to the other. That he wished to be seen as Brown captured him is manifest, yet no one who reads his letters and diaries is likely to conclude that Copley failed to render the very essence of his subject.

Abigail, at forty-one, also sat for Brown during their stay in London. Her appearance was matronly, but quite attractive. Middle-aged, she is slightly plump and gray-haired, but her face retains the thin, sharp appearance that was evident in her first portrait made more than twenty years before. Her features are dominated by her eyes—dark, clear, lustrous eyes that seemed to betray tenacity as well as compassion and tenderness. It was a "good likeness" according to both John and Nabby.[13]

Brown, who was kept busy by the Adamses, also painted Nabby in 1785. His canvas was exquisite, according to her proud father, for it captured both her meek and her droll qualities. Barely twenty when she sat for the artist, Nabby at first glance appears even more matronly than her mother, but upon greater scrutiny she clearly seems bright and attractive, and lurking behind an evident shyness is a whimsical disposition struggling to become manifest.

The Adamses reached London late in May and soon found accommodations in a large townhouse on one corner of Grosvenor Square, a handsome area developed about sixty years before. Only a short walk east of Hyde Park, it was home to numerous titled noblemen, including Lord North and Lord Carmarthen, the foreign secretary. The Adams house was roomy. There were three floors for the family and their guests, a kitchen in the basement, and servants quarters on the fourth floor. Immediately upon moving in, Abigail set

Portrait traditionally said to be that of Abigail Adams, completed in 1785 when she
was forty-one years of age. Oil on canvas. Artist unidentified, but thought to have
been Mather Brown. *Courtesy: New York State Historical Association, Cooperstown,
New York.*

Abigail Adams Smith ("Nabby") in 1785, aged twenty. By Mather Brown.
Courtesy: U.S. Department of the Interior, National Park Service, Adams Historic Site, Quincy, Massachusetts.

about hiring a large staff of servants, while John presented himself to the English government, calling on Carmarthen at his office in Cleveland Row, then, a few days later, visiting the king's closet.[14]

His formal appearance before the monarch was a moving experience for Adams. Once a rebellious subject, Adams, his voice quaking nervously, now spoke of the desire of the United States for friendship with Great Britain. The king responded that he had failed to prevent America's separation, but now that it had been accomplished he too yearned for amity. The meeting ended quickly, George III signaling by a stiff royal bow that Adams was dismissed. The envoy bowed three times, as protocol demanded, and backed uncertainly from the chamber. The next issue of the *London Chronicle* reported that "his Excellency John Adams was . . . most graciously received." The *Public Advertiser* was less charitable, assailing the receipt of an ambassador from the United States, especially one who had been a rebel bent on "cutting her [England's] throat."[15]

Adams's audience with the king formally inaugurated his embassy to England, a mission that would last just thirty days short of three years. After the stress of the past few years, this was a happy period for Adams, a time of liberation from the psychic adversity occasioned by the presence of a rival such as Franklin; in addition, Adams was delighted to escape the invidiousness with which he believed he had been treated at Versailles. Furthermore, he basked in his selection to the ambassadorial post, an event he interpreted as a congressional endorsement of his earlier labors. Moreover, while separated from his three sons during this period, he had Abigail at his side. Finally, as the urgency of the war years vanished, his burdens, physical and emotional, lightened. The pace of his life seemed more measured, marked by occasional meetings with British officials, frequent social contacts with envoys from other nations, considerable time for reading, reflecting, and writing, and ample opportunity to vacation and take in the sights in the company of his wife. The result was that Adams enjoyed better health than he had in years, apparently suffering nothing more serious than an infrequent head cold and some minor discomfort in his extremities, the latter a lingering effect of the catastrophic illness that had befallen him in 1781.[16]

On many days Adams was able to revert to the daily schedule he had enjoyed as a young man struggling to establish a legal practice. He rose early, breakfasted with Abigail, adjourned to his study for several hours' work, rejoined his wife in the early afternoon for a light lunch, walked briskly for nearly an hour, and finally returned to his library to complete the day's labor. At times, however, Adams must have wondered if a diplomat could ever experience an evening alone with his family. Lord Carmarthen and other British dignitaries supped at his table, and, as was the custom, he was expected to entertain each nation's ambassador to the Court of St. James. He sought out influential writers and scientists, as well as prosperous merchants and high-ranking church officials, for dinner engagements in the hope that they might sway public opinion or influence government leaders. Adams also welcomed Englishmen with whom he had established a warm personal relationship, particularly Edmund Jenings, his British contact and correspondent during the years he spent in France and Holland.[17] The most common guests, however, were other Americans. The legation became headquarters for the American community in London, and a steady stream of sea captains, businessmen, students, and weary travelers anxious to converse with fellow countrymen paraded through the Adams dining room and parlor.[18] While Abigail clearly would have preferred to have resided with her entire family on her Braintree farm, there is no evidence to suggest that either she or her husband chafed at the social responsibilities inevitably accompanying diplomatic service. Indeed, both John and Abigail were self-assured individuals who long since had become habituated to the company of strangers, including prominent and imposing sorts.

Other Americans—the less influential citizens—called on Adams during the daytime, to seek assistance in the resolution of myriad problems. His most painful duty occurred when an American exile appeared pleading for assistance. Approximately seven thousand Tories of a total of perhaps eighty thousand who fled their homeland resided in England, principally in London, and at times it must have seemed that each of these displaced persons called at the legation. Abigail took a cold view of their plight. They were "very desperate bitter and venomous" people who "would devour us yet if they could," she remarked. Whatever her husband felt, there was little he could do, for the United States was not obligated to compensate or assist the Loyalists for suffering incurred in the Revolution.[19]

One Loyalist received a call from Adams. Jonathan Sewall, Adams's old friend from Massachusetts, agreed to receive the envoy. The two had not seen one another since the eve of the First Congress a dozen years before, when on that cool summer morning in Falmouth, Sewall had taken Adams atop the bluff overlooking Casco Bay and exhorted him to renounce the resistance movement. When Adams was ushered into Sewall's library, he took him by the hand and exclaimed: "How do you do my dear old friend." For the next three hours, according to Sewall's recollection, the two conversed easily. Thereafter, Adams sought to rekindle the friendship with frequent meetings, but Sewall, bitter and melancholy at his fate, declined to see Adams or any other Americans, even fellow exiles.[20]

Both John and Abigail made every effort to overcome the English Channel's barrier to their friendship with Jefferson. The envoys exchanged numerous letters, mostly of a business nature; Abigail, meanwhile, dispatched twenty missives to her friend within two years, and he responded with almost one letter a month. Abigail initiated the correspondence within a week of her arrival in London, and she and the Virginian kept the postman busy with affectionate epistles full of gossip, news of America, and treatises on the culture, habits, and politics of their host countries. They exchanged gifts and even shopped for one another, Abigail sending, among other things, table-cloths and nutcrackers, Jefferson reciprocating with china figurines and fine fabric.[21]

Despite a reserved tone in Adams's correspondence with Jefferson, it is clear that he, as well as his wife, remained close to their new friend. The diplomats agreed to share the expense of commissioning the renowned French artist Jean Antoine Houdon to complete a bust of General Washington, whom Jefferson revered and Adams admired. In March 1786, moreover, Jefferson journeyed to London, called by Adams in anticipation of the formal signing of a commercial treaty with Portugal. The Virginian stayed on for six weeks, and while he did not lodge with the Adamses, he visited their home frequently. In addition, he and John undertook a seven-day excursion to observe England's most famous gardens, even squeezing in a guided tour of William Shakespeare's house at Stratford-upon-Avon.[22]

A year later Jefferson wrote Abigail to ask that she look after his daughter, eight-year-old Mary, or Polly, as everyone called her, who was due to arrive in England in the company of an older, trusted servant. As soon thereafter as possible, Jefferson explained, he would fetch her to Paris. In June 1787, the little girl arrived, confused, suspicious, and frightened, and accompanied only by Sally Hemings, a fourteen-year-old mulatto whom Jefferson owned. Abigail immediately swept little Polly under her wing, loving her and furnishing her with new clothes, books, and toys. Ten days later, when Jefferson's Parisian servant arrived to gather Polly to her father, Abigail could barely consent to part with her new friend, and John, too, soon acknowledged that he missed her, for she was the most "charming Child" he had ever encountered.[23]

Adams's sojourn with Jefferson into the English countryside was not his only trek during these years. Twice he and Abigail undertook extended trips throughout England. In the summer of 1786 they simply took a sightseeing vacation; the following year, soon after Polly left them, they escaped London on the advice of their physician, seeking a more salubrious summer climate. In between these journeys the couple spent two weeks at Bath, and Abigail accompanied her husband on a business jaunt to Holland, one of three such trips that he undertook while on duty in London. The Adamses also visited the sights within London, touring gardens and public buildings, and often attending the theater, where they enjoyed serious drama, vaudeville, opera, and ballet, although Abigail was put off by the latter, finding the skimpy costumes worn by the dancers too shocking for her Yankee tastes. Finally, because of her husband's position, Abigail at times attended state functions, and on one occasion she was presented to the King and Queen.[24]

Although she was able to travel on occasion, Abigail's mobility was somewhat limited during these years by recurrent health problems. For a child supposedly afflicted with numerous and chronic frailties, Abigail had been a remarkably healthy adult, withstanding several pregnancies and a long, arduous ocean crossing. Indeed, until just before her fortieth birthday she had suffered nothing more than an occasional "slight indisposition." Thereafter, however, she began to experience the discomforts of rheumatism, a disorder ill suited to London's damp climate. By 1786 she also alluded vaguely to frequent bouts with debilitating fevers.[25]

Her physical woes might have been alleviated somewhat had she been happy in England, but almost from the beginning she was homesick and put off by what she saw as the callous arrogance and haughtiness of the English. Everyone with whom she came into contact, she insisted, manifested a demeanor of "studied civility and disguised coldness." She additionally was affronted by the manner in which the English elite treated their own people, and she expressed particular shock at the squalid living conditions endured by a large percentage of the population. She thought England a hopelessly, corrupt country. Of course, she acknowledged her affinity for the pleasures London offered, and she admitted she preferred the climate in England to that of Massachusetts, where for nine months of the year "we must freeze or melt." Nevertheless, she had hardly unpacked her luggage before she announced that she had little desire to play the role of a diplomat's wife, and within six months she had begun to speak frequently of her longing to return to America. The thought of going home to a life of "feeding my poultry and improveing my garden has more charms for my fancy, than residing at the court of Saint James's where I seldom meet with characters so inoffensive as my Hens and chickings, or minds so well improved as my garden."[26]

The one really happy occasion for Abigail during these years was the resolution of Nabby's matrimonial concerns. When she sailed with her mother in June 1784, Nabby had expected to return to America sometime the following year, whereupon she would marry Royall Tyler. However, several occurrences in the year following the voyage of the *Active* led to an alteration in her plans. Tyler's strange behavior contributed to Nabby's change of heart. While she and her parents wrote frequently to the young man, he failed to answer any of their letters; moreover, Tyler abused Nabby's confidence by publicly displaying some of her missives. In addition, Aunt Mary Cranch, with whom Tyler occasionally boarded, often dispatched word—much of it based on gossip—of Tyler's alleged immaturity, instability, and spendthrift habits. But perhaps the most crucial incident occurred when Col. William Smith entered her life.

Selected by Congress to serve as Adams's secretary, Smith—a thirty-year-old bachelor who was veritably tall, dark, and handsome—had a distinguished background. He had graduated from the College of New Jersey (now Princeton) and had served briefly as an aide-de-camp to General Washington. His first meeting with Nabby occurred less than a year after she last had seen Tyler.

Abigail immediately recognized the powerful emotional changes occurring within her daughter; John, immersed in his work and evidently kept in the dark about Mary Cranch's detective work, was unaware of these happenings.

By the end of her first autumn in London, Nabby had made her break with Tyler. Her mother could not have been more approving. Colonel Smith, she said, was "a man of strict honour"; she looked upon him as a "Dutiful Son." By early 1786 Nabby was engaged to Smith and in the spring became his bride. Eleven months later, in April 1787, John and Abigail became grandparents for the first time when Nabby bore a boy, William Steuben Smith.[27]

Abigail's disenchantment with England soon was matched by that of her husband. Adams's first duty in his capacity as America's minister was to negotiate a commercial treaty with Britain. In addition, he hoped that several other lingering trouble spots from the revolutionary war years might be repaired, thus paving the way for normalization of relations between the two countries. His wishes were dashed, however, leaving him embittered and apprehensive for the future of the United States.

A long period of peace was America's most pressing need, Adams believed, a breathing space during which time the young nation could collect itself and repair the wounds of the long, destructive war. The resolution of the vexatious issues dividing the United States from Britain would minimize the danger of renewed conflict, and a lucrative trade with America would diminish London's inclination toward adventurism in Europe, thereby lessening the likelihood of still another Anglo-French war into whose vortex America might be sucked. Both nations would profit if Adams had his way. America would enjoy peace. Britain would avoid a ruinous war and resume a close relationship with the nation "destined beyond a doubt to be the greatest power on earth, and that within the life of man."[28]

Within four months of his arrival in England, Adams realized that his chances of success were minimal. Everyone he encountered, from ministerial officials to influential private citizens, treated him with the "same uniform tenor of dry decency and cold civility," but no one embraced the opportunity to reestablish cordial ties with the United States. Indeed, he soon came to understand that the official air of solicitude masked deep-seated anti-American feelings. The "popular pulse seems to beat high against America," he told John Jay, now the secretary of state, and he even reported that many Englishmen desired another war with America if only some means could be found by which France might be neutralized during such a conflict.[29]

Adams's first objective was to open British ports to American ships. America must fight fire with fire, he counseled. Should Congress pass a navigation act excluding British imports, the ministry would be compelled to open its ports to American commodities. But Congress refused to take that step, for the foes of centralization in the United States thwarted every move in the mid-1780s to grant the national government the power to regulate foreign commerce. Unofficially, Adams also suggested private boycotts and, most interestingly, federal subsidization of American manufacturing so that his country's businessmen might undersell their English competitors in the United States market. But no such steps were taken, and with his leverage diminished, the failure of his embassy was assured.[30]

From his first meeting with Lord Carmarthen, the foreign secretary, Adams also sought to compel British adherence to the Treaty of Paris. Once again, Adams was placed in a weak position. At that initial meeting, Carmarthen, a "modest, amiable man," according to Adams, greeted the American minister by reminding him that the United States had not honored the commitments it made in that same treaty. America had neither begun to liquidate its prewar debt nor permit Tory exiles in some states to return to their homeland. Having thrown his counterpart on the defensive, Carmarthen sat back to listen as Adams dilated upon the sins of the British. He assailed the ministry's failure to withdraw its army from United States territory and criticized its inattentiveness to the treaty provision stipulating that slave owners must be compensated for the loss of their property. But Adams knew that British compliance was out of the question unless the United States also honored the accord, and he understood too that America lacked the power to compel British observance.[31]

Carmarthen merely listened to the effusive minister. The first conversation and most that followed were "all on one side," an exasperated Adams informed Jay. Consumed with bitterness for America, yet uncertain of what steps to take, Britain, he concluded, had decided to do nothing for the time being. He feared, however, that Britain ultimately would forge an alliance with Prussia and Holland, then assail France. While American neutrality was most desirable in such an eventuality, he felt, the United States could not afford to see France destroyed, lest the weak, new nation be left to stand alone against a victorious Britain. The best antidote for such a disastrous turn of events, Adams advised, was for the United States to maintain close ties with France, Holland, and Spain, for if confronted by a phalanx of these four former co-belligerents, Whitehall was likely to be deterred from another round of war. Yet, Adams despaired, any spark might plunge Europe into war. The most likely catalyst for another round of warfare, he predicted, was revolution in Spain's South and Central American colonies, but whatever might be the next source of trouble, he saw his era as a time of maximum danger for the United States. Not until about 1800, he maintained, would the United States overcome its post-Revolutionary enfeeblement and be truly able to stand alone.[32]

Other diplomatic matters also fell to Adams during his stay in London. He participated in the negotiations of commercial treaties with Portugal and Prussia, and on three occasions he traveled to Holland to secure American loans. He dispatched a steady stream of information and opinion to secretary Jay concerning America's problems in the Mediterranean, where the rulers of Algiers, Morocco, Tripoli, and Tunis sought to extort money from the United States in return for protecting American sailors from attacks by the Barbary pirates. He thought it sensible to simply pay the bribes; as distasteful as such a course might be, it was less costly than sending a large navy halfway round the world, a conclusion that many European powers had already reached. Accordingly, early in 1787 he and Jefferson signed a pact with Morocco, committing the United States to pay for such protection. Adams additionally worked on behalf of New England whalers, searching for new markets for the industry and, perhaps misusing his office, providing business tips to a cousin based on information he gleaned from contacts in London.[33]

As the inevitable failure of his mission became apparent, Adams began to contemplate a return to the United States, and early in 1787 he requested that the Congress name his successor be named in his place. In the seven years that had elapsed since his arrival in Paris, Adams had rarely commented on the domestic concerns of the United States, although through the letters of well-placed friends at home he had managed to keep abreast of the events and trends in America. Charles Storer, who had accompanied him to Paris in 1782, and John Thaxter, who had carried the peace treaty home the following year, wrote frequently, as did Cotton Tufts, a Weymouth physician and Abigail's uncle by marriage, and Elbridge Gerry of Marblehead, who had first entered Congress in 1776. Innumerable visitors to the legations in Amsterdam, Paris, and London also transmitted information, as did American newspapers, which friends regularly dispatched. Moreover, from his own experience—his victimization, he might have said—he had intimate knowledge of affairs in Congress,[34] knowledge that often troubled him.

The steady erosion of the republican virtues that had accompanied the opening of the revolutionary struggle caused him great dismay. The spirit of selfless service for the public weal had been supplanted, in his estimation, by an acquisitive factionalism that had emasculated Congress and jeopardized the conduct of foreign policy. Nowhere was that more evident than in Congress's decision in 1781 to surrender to Versailles the management of the nation's diplomacy. The news from Massachusetts late in 1786 only heightened his concern, for that fall, word arrived in London of serious disorders within the state.

Led by Daniel Shays, once a captain in the Continental army, Massachusetts farmers, burdened by an indebtedness that threatened their very existence as yeomen, had taken up arms in the autumn of 1786, seeking to prevent both foreclosures against their possessions and the collection of debts. The uprising had been suppressed by a Massachusetts army, but not before the most politically conservative elements had fancied the onset of anarchy and class warfare. Adams was troubled by the turbulence, calling the farmers' action "extremely pernicious," but he did not exaggerate the importance of the event. "Dont be allarmed" by the news, he advised Jefferson; "all will be well," he went on, even predicting that the government would be strengthened by the experience. His reaction was far less hysterical than that of Abigail. "Ignorant, wrestless desperadoes, without conscience or principals," she told Jefferson, had "led a deluded multitude to follow their standard, under pretense of grievances which have no existence but in their imaginations." She breathed a sigh of relief at the news that "the mad cry of the mob" had been stilled. But some good would come of Shays's actions, she added, if only someone would conduct a learned inquiry into the ills plaguing America, the bane "which have produced these commotions." Although she did not mention it to her friend in Paris, Abigail of course knew that her husband had launched just such an investigation.[35]

Indeed, by the time Abigail wrote Jefferson, Adams had completed a manuscript and dispatched it to the printer, who would issue it early in 1787 as the first volume of *A Defence of the Constitutions of Government of the United States of America*. More manuscripts followed, as did two additional volumes, the last appearing early in 1788.

Several factors induced Adams to undertake such an endeavor. It is often assumed that he wrote the *Defence* in response to Shays's Rebellion.[36] But Adams had already begun work on the treatise when he learned of this disturbance; other factors led him to this task. One, at least, was personal. Now that he knew he soon would be going home, Adams reverted to the course of action that had previously served him well. Just as his earliest writings had facilitated his rise as a Boston lawyer and as his published essays and outspoken comments had enhanced his standing within the Congress, Adams sought through the *Defence*—a thoughtful, reflective commentary by an elder statesman who had served his country continuously for fifteen years—to reintroduce himself to his countrymen, from whom he had so long been separated.

There is evidence as well that Adams saw the *Defence* as a response to what he believed were dangerous tendencies in French thought, ideas that without doubt would be welcomed in some circles within the United States. Since first coming to Paris in 1778, he had carefully followed the debate among the *philosophes* over the reformation and democratization of French institutions. He shrank in horror from the demands of the radical reformers, and, at least in part, he intended the *Defence* as a response to the writings of the French minister and reformer Baron Anne Robert Turgot, who urged democracy and virtually unbridled authority for the legislative branch in the French polity. But if the radical French theorists disturbed Adams, the other side in the debate—that taken by the conservative reformers—exerted a powerful influence on him. He was swayed by their argument that in an age of absolutism throughout Europe, the people of England had largely succeeded in remaining free of oppression; and, like the French conservative reformers, he was convinced that it was the English constitution that had spared Englishmen from the iron hand of despotism. No writer influenced Adams more than Jean Louis De Lolme, a Swiss national who, following his immigration to London, had authored *The Constitution of England.* For De Lolme, the secret of England's success was power balanced among three branches of government— monarchy, aristocracy, and commons—each of which represented a different order within society.[37]

The French debate rekindled concerns within Adams that he had permitted to lie dormant during his diplomatic missions. Since at least 1777 he had perceived a decline in America of what he had always referred to as "virtue," a selflessness in those who served the public. "I am not . . . of [the] opinion that the Independence of our Country, entirely depends, on a Harmony and Unity of sentiment," he said but had nevertheless been shocked when, with the question of independence behind them, many of his colleagues in the Congress had begun displaying a "Stream of Some Impurities," a "Depravity" that threatened the very existence of republicanism. Jockeying for personal enhancement or acting blatantly in the interest of a narrow segment of the population, these selfish men had ceased to "promote the Happiness of the People [and] to increase the Wealth, the Grandeur, and Prosperity of the Community." As he waited in Braintree to depart for Europe on his first diplomatic mission, Adams, perhaps able to see things more clearly in the solace of his little farm, had raged at the depredations of "the richer sort" against the great bulk of Americans. "Every Mans Liberty and Life, is equally dear to him," he had said, but he saw increasing evidence that those in positions of authority, like their counterparts in England against whom the Revolution had been waged, were bent on "robbing and plundering all whom they think in their Power." These awful tendencies had, for the first time, caused him to think that the constitutional prescriptions he had offered in his *Thoughts on Government* might not be entirely adequate. Substantive modifications beyond those undertaken in the first bloom of the Revolution might be required, for a system that tolerated such injustice mocked the concept of republicanism, the notion that sovereignty truly resided in the people.[38]

In 1777 Adams had restricted his concerns to the privacy of his correspondence with close acquaintances. In the *Defence,* completed eleven years later, he publicly aired his views. Readers discovered a considerable continuity in Adams's thought, going back to his pre-Revolution publications. He remained committed to a balanced government and to a government with strong executive authority; he also continued to oppose hereditary monarchy and hereditary nobility. But striking departures in Adams's views had occurred since *Thoughts on Government.* An optimist at the beginning of the struggle with Great Britain, Adams had presumed his countrymen possessed the virtue to safeguard their liberties. The venality displayed by opportunists almost from the first days of the Revolution disabused him of that notion. Initially, too, Adams believed that the great danger of despotism came from craven individuals, men such as Hutchinson and Oliver. What he saw as a congressman, together with his firsthand scrutiny of European societies, had led him to a different conclusion. He now was cognizant of the danger arising from the competing interests of various, antagonistic social orders.

In the *Defence,* Adams set out to find the means by which society could be protected from the self-serving social orders. The principal problem of government throughout history, he argued, was that fundamental inequities existed in every society. Unalterable human nature produced these disparities. Nature drove men to seek wealth. Some men were successful, others were not. The result was that every society included the very wealthy and the abjectly poor. Moreover, even those who succeeded—the best and most talented among men, he believed—would never be satisfied but would lust after still more possessions, while those without property would seek the belongings of the affluent. In other words, class warfare was an ever-present danger.[39]

To this point, what Adams argued was very much within the mainstream of eighteenth-century Whig thought. What did set him apart, however, was his belief that the wealthy few posed even greater dangers to the public weal than was likely to be wrought by the multitudinous poor. History demonstrated that the wealthiest in every society inevitably secured power, Adams argued; history also taught that the wealthy, if unchecked, would utilize that power to suppress their chief rivals, the mass of society. Adams did not ignore the dangers that he presumed to exist in popular rule. The common people were "of the same clay" as the few, and, if they held untrammeled power, despoilation would reign. More dangerous, however, was the class war that would ensue, for the aristocracy would fight to save itself; always, he warned, the few would prevail over the many, and, if given a free hand, they would impose monarchical government—and a tyrannical monarchy, at that—upon society.[40]

The inevitability of such a catastrophe grew from the gloomy perception of human nature that dominated in Adams's time. While some writers harbored a charitable view of man's nature and his rationalism, and others believed that tainted mankind could be perfected through the reformation of his iniquitous environment, most theorists, like Adams, were less optimistic. Man's prevailing features, they thought, were dark and sinister. Most saw the side experienced by Voltaire's Candide and Pangloss, the nature of man that perpetrated pillage, butchery, tyranny, and war.

But how could this monstrous side of man be controlled? Adams had confronted this problem in *Thoughts on Government* and had urged a three-tiered, balanced constitution as man's salvation from himself. The constitution he had authored for Massachusetts in 1779, moreover, fashioned that very superstructure as its barricade against despotism. This multilayered separation of powers remained in the *Defence,* but it was altered significantly. Influenced by De Lolme, Adams now argued that one house of the bicameral legislature must be the preserve of the many, the commoners. The few, those he variously termed "the natural aristocracy," the "rich and the proud," and the "rich, the well-born, and the able," men of wealth, education, and talent, must possess the other chamber, a house that would be their preserve because entry would be regulated through the maintenance of rigid property qualifications. But the key—Adams called it the "essence"—to his system was the third branch, the executive branch. It alone could maintain the equilibrium and prevent a descent into the nightmare of despotic class rule. Adams proposed that this chief magistrate by given an absolute negative over the legislature, a power virtually tantamount to coequal lawmaker with the other branches. The executive, in brief, was the people's last best hope for protection from autocratic governance by the elite.[41]

As Adams was drafting the *Defence,* he told Jefferson that he was undertaking a "hazardous Enterprize" that would cause him to be unpopular. But had he known the full extent of the damage to come, especially when seen in the light of some of his subsequent writings and statements, he might have resisted the urge to continue.[42] Had he stopped, too, to remember just how long he had been gone from America and that he might be out of touch with the intellectual currents abroad in his homeland, he might have at least waited until he returned to Massachusetts before completing his tract. His hand was not stayed, however, and the work he produced was not only dated but filled with concepts alien to an America about to enter the final decade of the eighteenth century. Not only had Adams's treatise appeared to be a clarion call for a fearfully strong executive, one who might have in his hands all the resources for evil necessary to subjugate the freedoms of his subjects, but he had clearly raised the specter of aristocratic domination, never an inherent feature of political life in America. Worse still, however, was the fact that Adams appeared to understand republicanism in a manner foreign to that of his countrymen. Where most Americans—and certainly the Federalist authors of the new Constitution—saw the people as the source of political power and sought representation in each of the three branches of government, Adams saw the people as sovereign; but he sought to divide power between the two orders he believed constituted society—the rich and the poor—then to create a magistrate, supposedly above the fray, who would inevitably have the greatest power within his construct.[43]

Adams had struggled and sacrificed in quest of an independent, republican America. Now he believed that everything secured by the Revolution was being jeopardized by an elite potentially more threatening than the North ministry and its lackeys had ever been. While there were many in America who shared his fears, they possessed what they regarded as a better and safer blueprint against the dangers of chaos and despotism: the new Constitution produced by the Philadelphia Convention in 1787 and ratified the following year, the year that Adams completed work on the *Defence.*

Early in 1787, when Adams had requested an end to his embassy, he had explained to Secretary Jay that he and Abigail hoped to embark for America by the following spring, at the latest. There were many reasons why John and Abigail longed to put England behind them. The frustrations occasioned by his mission, as well as Abigail's health problems and homesickness, were not the least consequential factors. In addition, both longed to see their sons. By 1788 three years had elapsed since they had seen John Quincy; Thomas and Charles, who had been left with their aunt in Haverhill, had not seen their mother in nearly four years, and both looked upon their father as an utter stranger. Charles had been eleven when he last saw John; he turned eighteen in 1788. Thomas, two years younger, had not been at his father's side in nine years, since he was a little boy of seven, and now, confused and disconsolate at his abandonment, he refused to write to either parent.[44]

One item of official business remained in 1788 before the Adamses could depart. In March, Adams rushed to Amsterdam for the last time, there to meet Jefferson and negotiate still another loan, this to enable the United States to meet its existing debt payments of Dutch bankers. It was a whirlwind trip, as much as a journey through the heavy Channel seas and across the primitive English and continental highways could be. Only the ceremonial farewells awaited him upon his return to London, for, in his absence, Jay's letter sanctioning the termination of his three-year mission had arrived.[45]

Late in April, beneath a mottled sky, and filled with the feverish apprehension that flooded the breast of every Atlantic mariner, John and Abigail, and their servants, John and Esther Briesler, boarded the *Lucretia,* the vessel that would transport them home to sons they barely knew and to a future that had never appeared more uncertain.

PART FOUR

*

One Man of Inflexible Integrity

CHAPTER 15

*

Much to Be Grateful For

NEVER IN HIS WILDEST DREAMS had John Adams anticipated the fuss that was made over him when the *Lucretia* docked in Boston harbor. Almost no one had noticed when the creaky *Sensible* bore him away nine years before, but on June 17, 1788, a delightfully cool, breezy, summer day, Adams returned to find an emissary of Gov. John Hancock waiting to greet him at the gangplank. He and Abigail were escorted to the governor's mansion, where they were invited to lodge temporarily. Along the route from the harbor, thundering cannon and the decorous peal of church bells greeted the returning native son. It was only the beginning. During the next few weeks, he was approached about holding virtually every important office in the land, each of which —save for the presidency of the United States, which was reserved for George Washington—appeared to be his for the asking.[1]

Adams made no immediate commitments. A virtual stranger to America, he first wished to assess the situation. He was even uncertain which would be most prestigious, a state office, or a federal post under the new constitution written at Philadelphia during the preceding summer but finally ratified only days before the *Lucretia* landed. Of course, he also wanted to relax and tend to personal business, which included moving into a new residence.

Six months before their departure from London, the Adamses had purchased a new home. Apprised by Dr. Tufts that a spacious house once owned by Royall Tyler was on the market, the couple had eagerly completed the transaction. Situated on eighty-three acres and lying about a mile north of the cramped little saltbox John had first occupied at the time of his marriage in 1764, it was described by a local newspaper as a "very Genteel Dwelling House, and Coach House, with a Garden, planted with a great variety of Fruit Trees [and] an Orchard." That was apparently how John and Abigail remembered the estate, too, and they quickly deemed it an ideal choice for them, spacious enough for the numerous pieces of furniture they had collected in Holland, France, and England, and quite satisfactory for entertaining guests, including relatives and grandchildren. They paid six hundred pounds—the

Peacefield, or The Old House. The Adams residence in Quincy, Massachusetts, after 1788. Sketch by E. Malcolm, 1789. *Courtesy: U.S. Department of the Interior, National Park Service, Adams National Historic Site, Quincy, Massachusetts.*

equivalent of a decade's wages for a skilled artisan—and Abigail quickly sent instructions to Tufts regarding the painting and carpentry work that she wanted done before her return.[2]

As always seems the lot of new home owners, the workmen had not yet finished when the Adamses arrived. In fact, not only were sawhorses and uncut lumber strewn about, but the place was not quite as Abigail remembered it. She had recollected it as elegant and capacious, and indeed it was, in comparison to the Braintree dwelling she and John had previously shared. But after the mansion at Auteuil and their lovely townhouse in London, this new house seemed dark and confining, with quite low ceilings that put her in mind of soldiers' barracks or a "wren's house." She was dismayed as well at the sight of the neglected lawn and garden, although she knew that with care the grounds could be made to look bright and charming. And, in fact, she and her husband adjusted quickly. Indeed, John, who seems not to have been disconcerted by what he found, soon fell in love with his new home. He named it Peacefield, for after the frenetic bustle that had characterized life in the legations abroad, the day-to-day pace in this dwelling seemed the very essence of tranquillity. Other members of the family frequently referred to the estate as "The Old House," while many in Quincy continued to call it the "Vassall-Borland House," after the family who had constructed and maintained this country villa for half a century.[3]

While still enjoying Governor Hancock's hospitality, the Adamses were reunited with their sons. Charles, outgoing as always (he "wins the heart, as usual," Abigail remarked) and brooding Thomas Boylston, both students across the Charles River at Harvard, hurried over for the reunion. Arriving a few days later was John Quincy, who had finished second in his graduating class the previous summer and now clerked in the law office of Theophilus Parsons in Newburyport, about thirty miles north of Boston. It was the first time in nine years that all three boys had been together with their parents. Only Nabby was missing. The Smiths had sailed from England a few weeks after the departure of the *Lucretia* and had settled in Jamaica, Long Island; Colonel Smith was busily searching for a government job.[4]

By July, Adams and his wife were in their new home, although disconcerted by painters, plasterers, and carpenters who continued to work around and amid them on into the autumn. Even so, the master of Peacefield was happy. He enjoyed the deference and respect that he encountered everywhere. He made plans for the rejuvenation of his neglected farm lands. On pleasant days he walked briskly about his estate, acquainting himself with its every nook and cranny, and on several occasions he climbed the familiar hills overlooking Braintree, seeking out old haunts and gazing down upon his little village and the great azure bay that lay just east of town. Before the winter set in, he spent some time with Richard Cranch and other old friends; he was reunited with his brother Peter Boylston and with his mother, now nearly eighty; he saw Abigail's sisters; he welcomed the boys home from time to time and accepted visits from old partisans and chums from the days of the rebellion—men like Hancock, Knox, and Lincoln—but after a decade he had returned to find one-third of his old friends dead, one-third senile, and one-third "grown unpopular."

Adams did not wish to sit idle forever. Pleasantly surprised by his reception in America, Adams quickly decided to remain in public life rather than resume his law practice. The question was not whether he might accept an office but which position he thought suitable for a person of his stature. Within a month of reaching America, he made his decision: he would accept nothing but the vice-presidency of the United States. Any other office was deemed "beneath himself," as Abigail put it.[5]

Adams's election was not assured. Governor Hancock had some supporters, as did Knox and Lincoln, although once Adams made clear his interest in the post, their candidacies vanished overnight. John Jay's name also was mentioned. Like Adams, he had served abroad for several years; upon his return he had become secretary of foreign affairs in the last years of the confederation and had played a major role in the ratification of the new federal constitution. George Clinton, the governor of New York, also was considered an aspirant for the position. But Jay and Clinton were bitter rivals in New York, and the governor's strength was such that he could easily thwart the ambitions of the former diplomat. Clinton, on the other hand, was an unlikely choice because he recently had opposed New York's ratification of the Constitution.

Adams, meanwhile, possessed some important advantages. New England would cast a huge bloc of electoral votes, and there was little doubt whom the region would support. Adams was universally regarded as a man of integrity; he was known to respect Washington and was thought able to work well with the first president. His *Defence,* moreover, had won him allies among the ascendant conservative forces that had spearheaded the movement for the new constitution. Among such men, Adams was viewed as safe, a kindred spirit in that he too wished to arrest the changes unleashed by the American Revolution. He had one additional advantage. As James Madison suggested, Adams, the only candidate who did not presently hold a public office, was the person most likely to relish the "unprofitable dignity" of the vice-presidency.[6]

As Adams's opposition collapsed during the autumn of 1788, some of Washington's supporters expressed the fear that he and Adams might receive an equal number of electoral votes, forcing the issue to the House of Representatives, an occurrence that most hoped to spare the general. This likelihood arose from the voting procedure mandated by the original constitution. Under that document, each elector cast two ballots without designating which was for the presidency and which for the vice-presidency. The individual receiving the largest vote total, if it amounted to a majority of the ballots cast, became president; the runner-up, vice-president. To remove any possibility of the canvass being left to the House, some political leaders, principally Alexander Hamilton in New York, labored throughout the winter to strip Adams of a vote here and there in order to ensure Washington's unanimous selection.

Hamilton's machinations were quite successful. When the returns of the Electoral College—which met in March 1789—were opened, it was discovered that Washington had received sixty-nine votes from sixty-nine electors. Adams, with thirty-four votes, finished second, well ahead of the ten other men who garnered second-place votes, and, hence, became vice-president.

His election notwithstanding, Adams, apparently unaware of the backroom maneuvers of Hamilton and others, was deeply wounded to learn that less than half the electors thought him entitled to the nation's second post. He could not understand why the public refused to elevate him to the same status it accorded Washington and Franklin. In a bilious mood, he spoke of the election as a "stain" upon his character, and he even entertained the thought of refusing the office. Soon, however, he abandoned such a notion.[7]

Whereas some of Adams's earlier decisions to accept overseas appointments had occasioned rancorous disputes within the family, Abigail fully supported her husband's decision to stand for the vice-presidency. Even Nabby encouraged her father to take the post. While both understood the man and realized how badly he coveted the office, each had an ulterior motive. With the national capital established in New York City, Vice-President Adams and his wife could live near Colonel and Mrs. Smith. Abigail and Nabby, never really separated before the *Lucretia* sailed in April 1788, missed one another terribly. Indeed, barely four months after her arrival in Boston, Abigail set out for Long Island to be with her daughter, who again was pregnant. Little John was already born by the time she arrived, but Abigail stayed on for some time, a mother who sought to help her daughter through the period of recovery, and a worried, intrusive parent apprehensive for her child's well-being, more so now than ever before, for Colonel Smith still had no clear career prospects.[8]

Adams departed for New York in mid-April 1789, beginning what was to become both a long, frustrating epoch in his career and a period of relative happiness. He was given a hero's send-off in Boston, and as he passed through the little New England villages en route to the capital he was feted and cheered in a manner he had seldom experienced. Adams reached New York a few days before General Washington, but he was immediately sworn in as vice-president. The ceremony, performed in Federal Hall—New York's former City Hall, recently refurbished and enlarged to serve as the nation's new Capitol— was simple. Only the members of the Senate were present, and they alone heard Adams deliver what Pennsylvania's Sen. William Maclay described as a dull and uninspiring inaugural address.

At month's end Washington at last arrived from Virginia, and on April 30 the first president was inaugurated in another simple ceremony. Festivities commenced with morning prayer services at nine, followed at noon by a

parade from Washington's residence to the Capitol. Adams waited in the
Senate chamber for the president-elect, and upon his arrival opened the ritual
with a few remarks; witnesses described the vice-president as nervous and
trembling so badly that he spoke only with difficulty. Washington then stepped
onto a balcony overlooking Broad and Wall streets, where he took the oath of
office. When the cheering stopped, he returned to face the joint Congress and
slowly, almost inaudibly, read an address of only seven paragraphs. At the
conclusion of the ceremony, which had lasted barely twenty minutes, the entire
government walked a half mile to St. Paul's Chapel, an Anglican church, for a
brief service.[10]

This inauguration, unlike all that have followed, not only installed a president but also symbolically launched a new government under a new constitution, a new federal government that was to be far more powerful than its
predecessor. Adams had first read the Constitution a few weeks before he
sailed from England and for the most part had warmly applauded the handiwork of the framers. He had objected that the president would be too weak
and the Senate too strong, yet the essential framework of the United States
government was so similar to the plan he had outlined in his *Thoughts on
Government* that he could only be happy, perhaps even flattered. From the
beginning, moreover, he had championed the new government because in the
tradition of revolutionary America, it recognized that power was derived from
the governed. Finally his belief that another round of European warfare was
imminent led him to conclude that the American states must remain confeder-
ated in the face of the foreign danger; the new constitution, he felt, offered the
best hope of preserving the Union.[11]

In the weeks that followed, the new president pieced together his administration. Alexander Hamilton, who had been an obscure twenty-two-year-old
aide to Washington when Adams had sailed on his first diplomatic mission, got
the key post of treasurer. Bright, loquacious, and genial, Hamilton was loyal to
Washington and had worked tirelessly to strengthen and centralize the national government. Washington had a habit of turning to Hamilton when he
required assistance, and he sought out the young New Yorker—a man
thought to have a keen grasp of fiscal matters—to map the fledgling nation's
economic course. The president named Jefferson his secretary of state. He
trusted and admired his fellow Virginian, America's ranking envoy among
those in Europe's capitals. Adams was happy with that choice, and he was
delighted to learn of the selection of two other acquaintances, Knox and Jay;
Knox was to be secretary of war, a post he had held in the last years of the
Articles of Confederation period, and Jay was named to the Supreme Court.
Only Hamilton was a stranger to Adams. All he knew was that the young New
Yorker was supposed to be bright and energetic, and close to Washington.

While the president pondered his appointments, Adams was besieged by
people in search of a position in the new federal government. Relatives such as

Richard Cranch, his brother-in-law, called on Adams, seeking a good job for his son. Numerous strangers and many old acquaintances sought favors, too. Robert Treat Paine and James Lovell beseeched his assistance. Ebenezer Storer, the second husband of Hannah Quincy, with whom the young Adams had been madly in love, petitioned for employment. Down on his luck, Storer confessed his family's desperate plight, but evidently there was little Adams could do except devote "many melancholy hours" to fretting over Hannah's misfortune. He seems to have devoted greater energy toward securing a position for General Lincoln, a friend and an important political ally who had labored in Massachusetts for his selection to the vice-presidency. Nonetheless, Adams's efforts in Lincoln's behalf bore little fruit and only succeeded in arousing considerable bitterness among the general's foes in Boston.[12]

Actually, Adams possessed little patronage power, and he simply referred most of the applicants to President Washington, sometimes with a positive recommendation but usually without comment.[13] Adams found the entire process distasteful, a squalid, time-consuming exercise, an undertaking likely to win him few friends and many enemies. In fact, the disappointed ones often "Spit fire at Adams," as he put it, whether or not he was to blame. Among the supplicants who grew terribly embittered with him were the Warrens, his old friends from Plymouth. Not long after Adams reached New York, a letter arrived from Mercy Warren in which she obliquely petitioned for posts for both her husband and son. It was hardly an unreasonable request. James Warren had been active in the colonial protest movement and in the war that followed, and she had risked the family's welfare by publishing anti-British tracts. In addition, the Warrens had often welcomed the Adamses into their home, and they and their sons had frequently visited Braintree, including out-of-the-way sojourns to look after Abigail's welfare during John's long absence. Although Mercy was too proud to have addressed the point, a government sinecure would have been most helpful, for her husband, now past his sixtieth birthday, suddenly found himself shunned as a relic and an embarrassment to the Hancock political machine in Massachusetts.

Adams might simply have responded to Mercy's entreaty by divulging his powerlessness in such matters. Instead, he used the letter to criticize General Warren for allegedly having sided with the Shaysites three years before. It was as though he had said that he would not—rather than could not—assist these dear old acquaintances in a time of tribulation. Adams's letter was uncharacteristic. Acerbic as he was, he normally eschewed such a manner when writing to friends and equals. That his response was couched in such visceral terms suggests the depth of his enmity toward the rebel farmers and those who defended them. The contumacious tone of his missive drove a wedge between the two families that eventually grew into a gaping chasm, causing much grief on all sides.[14]

At the same moment that he succeeded in antagonizing the Warrens,

Adams managed to harvest even greater political hurt through the stance he took in the Senate's debate on the proper title for the president of the United States. The matter seems trivial today, but contemporaries saw in this issue nothing less than a statement of the republicanism of the new government. Washington, conscious that his every act likely would establish an ironclad precedent for his successors, was uncertain about his conduct, especially on the simplest of matters. For instance, should he accept dinner invitations to the homes of friends? Would it be proper for him to invite acquaintances to dine with him and the First Lady? In short, should he make the presidency into a formal, aloof, virtually monarchical office, or should he strive to bring forth an open, accessible chief executive? He elicited the advice of his closest advisors, as well as that of Vice-President Adams on these matters, and in the end—largely because of his own personality and preconceived notions—he sought to make the presidency not just an office of dignity and authority but one with an aura of the regal, the potentate, the distant and lordly suzerain. It was a conception with which Adams found no fault.[15]

Sen. Richard Henry Lee, a friend of the president, brought up the matter of the chief executive's title—probably at the behest of Washington—a few days after the inaugural ceremony. In the debates that ensued, Adams, who under the new constitution was the presiding officer in the Senate, clearly sought to lead, not merely to officiate. Seated before a score or so of senators, looking out onto a small rectangular room ensconced beneath a ceiling mural of a sun and thirteen stars, Adams urged that the chief executive be called "His Highness, the President of the United States of America, and Protector of the Rights of the Same," and he differed sharply with those who took issue with such a monarchical title. In private he plumped for "His Highness" as the very minimum title due the presidency, and once he even urged the foolish-sounding honorific, "His Most Benign Highness."[16]

Such titles seemed silly, dangerous even, to many, but to Adams, who had spent the past decade amid the formal trappings of Europe's royal courts, they were normal and necessary. Without realizing the change that had come over him, Adams—who in his days in the popular movement against Hutchinson, had declared his repugnance toward magisterial trumpery ("Formalities and Ceremonies are an abomination in my sight. I hate them.")—now took the elitist position that they were essential for sustaining deference, respect, and hierarchy throughout society. A royal title, he said, could elevate the dignity of the presidency, investing the chief executive with a regnant aura that could assist in making the new national government truly sovereign over the state governments.[17]

Coming from another source, Adams's suggestions might have been shrugged off as ill-advised, or, at worst, as "superlatively ridiculous," as Jefferson said of them. Indeed, most Americans appeared not to notice that President Washington resonated a cold, formal, dignified, almost royal air, the very

John Adams in 1793, aged fifty-eight. Oil on canvas by John Trumbull. *Courtesy: Harvard University Portrait Collection. Gift of Andrew Craigie, 1794.*

sort of manner that Adams had urged. But when Adams proposed the adoption of pompous titles and an imperious demeanor for America's officials, the suggestion aroused scorn and ridicule, and cost him dearly. The author of the *Defence* was, after all, a man who had the rather silly habit of presiding over the Senate adorned with a powdered wig, who routinely appeared on ceremonial occasions with a sword strapped to his waist, and who rode to work each morning in a large, expensive carriage attended by a driver in livery. Adams became an object of derision, lampooned as "the Duke of Braintree" and "His Rotundity." He waged a losing fight, too, for the Senate ultimately rejected his unrepublican-sounding designations in favor of an imminently simple title: "The President of the United States."[18]

Adams claimed that both the *Defence* and his proposed titles had been misunderstood, and he assured his friends that he remained the same staunch republican that he had been in 1776. He told Franklin that the scheme of balances he had championed in the *Defence* was a plan of republicanism in "the only sense in which I am or ever was a Republican." Logically, therefore, he referred to Britain's government as a "monarchical republic." He also predicted that the United States would eventually fully embrace the British system. The elected chief executive, he believed, already was a limited monarch, and he forecast that the presidency and the Senate would remain elective bodies only until "intrigue and corruption" reached such a state that hereditary institutions would be erected as a "remedy against greater evil." He was untroubled by such a prospect. Not only was hereditary rule unavoidable, it eventually would be welcomed as a corrective for the certain ills that accompanied democracy.[19]

Adams's statements on republican government were contradictory. "I was always for a free republic, not a democracy," he once remarked, but he also told a correspondent that he never knew the meaning of the word "republicanism," and, he added, "I believe no other man ever did or ever will." Such a remarkable comment laid bare his inability to grasp the ideological consensus that had propelled the American Revolution. No one can fail to see ambiguities in the revolutionary ideal, yet behind the differences were shared assumptions: this revolution amounted to an assault upon slavish reliance on hereditary government and on the courtiers whom the privileged—with no pretense of popular sanction—placed in power; it was a blow against royalism and a strike for the principle of popular government for the popular good; and it represented a ringing endorsement of the notion of equality based on merit.[20]

Adams continued to share the popular enthusiasm for most of these precepts, but the anti-royalist fires that once raged within him had died. The emergence of what he regarded as an iniquitous, extravagant, avaricious spirit as the driving force in revolutionary America had led him in the *Defence* to search for a means of controlling this vice. Events in Europe after 1789 produced still more changes in his outlook. It soon was apparent that the

John Adams by Charles Willson Peale. The date of this painting is unknown, but it is thought to have been completed in the early years of Adams's vice-presidency, probably within a year or two of the painting of John Trumbull. Adams was between fifty-five and sixty years of age at this time. *Courtesy: Independence National Park Historical Collection.*

French Revolution, which had begun to crystallize during the very week Washington was inaugurated, would witness sweeping change, much of it instigated from the bottom up in what Adams would call a "democratical hurricane." The events that rocked the France he had known a decade before, and which grew from the republican society in place after 1789, had a profound impact on Adams's thinking. As a result, the difference that now existed between Adams and a traditionalist such as Washington was considerable. Where the vice-president had come to see royal governance as a blessing, Washington spoke of "painful, sensations" caused in him by the talk of monarchy, and he exclaimed: "I am told that even respectable characters speak of a monarchical form of Government without horror. . . . [H]ow irrevocable and tremendous! What a triumph for our enemies [the Tories] to verify their predictions! What a triumph for the advocates of despotism to find that we are incapable of governing ourselves, and that systems founded on the basis of equal liberty are merely ideal and fallacious!" In private, Washington ridiculed Adams for his "ostentatious imitation [and] mimicry of Royalty."[21]

The views of many revolutionaries had changed between 1776 and 1789. Jefferson once remarked that upon his return to the United States in 1790 he had discovered that "a preference of kingly over republican government was evidently the favorite sentiment" among most members of President Washington's administration and with the elite in New York.[22] Adams, therefore, had many intellectual soulmates. Most, however, closely guarded their thoughts, and pragmatism suggested that it would have been prudent for him to sequester his views as well, especially in light of the damage he had suffered in the bruising fight over the presidential title. Instead, like a moth to a flame, he improvidently aired his ideas in a string of lengthy newspaper essays titled "Discourses on Davila," the first of which appeared late in 1790. In part, he published his thoughts under the misapprehension that he could explain himself to the American people and that popular opinion would swing back around to his side. In addition, the surging radicalism of the events in France had caused him to rethink a portion of his premise in the *Defence;* "the wild idea of annihilating the nobility" and monarchy had created a situation of such gravity, he thought, that he must convey his reassessment to the American people.

In the *Defence,* Adams had stressed the inevitable dangers posed by wealth. In the wake of the street-inspired terrorism in France, "Davila" placed much greater emphasis on the dangers posed by unbridled democracy. This led Adams once again to explore human nature. Humankind could be affectionate and benevolent, as well as bruitish and selfish, he said. But the one yearning in every persons' breast, he went on, was the "passion for distinction," the need to be noticed by others. Such a passion often led to the most meritorious and laudatory behavior. But ambition could also be dangerous, for anarchy was certain to be the result if individuals were unrestrained in their pursuit of notoriety. Government, Adams wrote, should take care not to hinder the beneficent qualities in human beings, but at the same time it must provide safeguards against their iniquitous propensities. A government of balance, he added, was best designed to regulate every human urge. There was little that was new in these reflections. He had said much the same thing in the third volume of the *Defence,* as had countless other writers in his time. But the direction in which these thoughts now led Adams made the difference, although he took some pains to camouflage his ultimate destination. "Davila" was conceived as his ruminations upon historian Henrico Caterino Davila's discourses on the French civil wars in the sixteenth century, but it was clear that Adams saw parallels between the events in the France of his day and those of which Davila had written; it would have required considerable myopia, moreover, not to have recognized that Adams was forecasting that human nature would inevitably pose the same problems in America as in France. To forestall the occurrence of disorders similar to those raging in France, changes should be made, he appeared to be saying. The elite, society's bane in the *Defence,* should be recognized as the source of stability within society, he now stated. As in the *Defence,* though obviously for quite different reasons, he appeared to urge the establishment of an aristocratic branch of government within the American republic. His American aristocracy was to be nonhereditary, to be sure; it was to consist of the wealthy and most talented within the society. Nevertheless, this segment of the public was to have a branch of government to itself, obviating the notion of the popular will, the hallmark of the rebellion of 1776.

Similarly, to delegate the executive authority to someone with "an illustrious descent," a royal lineage, he appeared to suggest, was essential. Invest that office with a royal title, surround the ruler with pomp and circumstance so it will "glitter with the brightest lustre in the eyes of the world," he suggested, and the mass of people will happily and affectionately accept the official and will also live vicariously through such a majestical figure. Such an office, he went on, would have the additional benefit of eliminating elections, occasions that "produce slanders and libels first, mobs and seditions next, and civil war, with all her hissing snakes . . . at last." Hereditary monarchy was attended by "fewer evils" than a republican chief executive. "This is the true answer, and the only one," he concluded in his last Davila essay.[23]

How had Adams arrived at such views? The self-indulgent behavior of so many of his countrymen in the course of the long Revolutionary War had convinced him that human nature was universal, that the American people were no more virtuous than others. The civil disobedience of the Shaysites offered further proof of the rapid erosion of the "discipline, and subordination" needed to prevent anarchy. Moreover, he had grown disillusioned with the elective process, having observed not only the bribery and scandal in English polls, but the jaded contortions to which an old colleague such as Warren had been reduced in his desperate attempt to remain in office. Even his own behavior, he may have thought, was a compelling reason for a system of hierarchy and balances. Virtuous as he must have seen his own conduct, he never denied being driven by the engine of ambition from his days in Worcester to this very moment. He appeared to feel that only a blend of monarchy—with its almost magical capability to induce subservience—an aristocratical house—better because it eschewed elections and brought forth men of merit—and a popular house could hope to avoid the "Pyrrhorism, anarchy, and insecurity of property" certain to consume mankind in any other system of governance.

Despite the reactionary edge to Adams's views, there was an element of continuity in his thought that stretched back to the moment of his halting involvement in the colonial protest movement. From the beginning of what we now call the American Revolution, he had sought little but American independence, and even much later he would insist that the "real American Revolution" had consisted almost solely of a mere change in the "sentiments, and affections of the people" toward the parent state. Activism even in the early resistance movement had been difficult for Adams. He was uncomfortable with the mob activity and the propandizing that had accompanied protest, and it was not until nine years after the passage of the Stamp Act that he was fully committed to the popular movement, but even then his politics left him plagued by such deep-seated guilt that he was nearly overwhelmed by periods of terrible, punishing anxiety. Adams was never committed to the egalitarianism spawned by the upheaval, urging the leaders of the popular movement to "guard against this Spirit and these Principles." In 1776 he had worked simultaneously for independence and the establishment of stable American governments, so that the citizenry could "glide insensibly"—his very choice of words conveys his sense that little should change—"from under the old Government, into a . . . contented submission to new ones." These governments were to resemble the colonial regimes, with the role of the people expanded somewhat and all hereditary and monarchical features eliminated. With that accomplished, the revolution in America would stop. That it did not cease was the reason for his *Defence* and "Davila" essays, and indeed, a partial reason for the new government and the Washington administration.[24]

Adams was hardly alone in his views. He represented a strain of conservatism that had existed since the beginning of the protest movement against Great Britain and that had grown in strength in the course of the 1780s. Adams and others of this persuasion looked forward to the emergence of the United States as a modern nation-state with a centralized government capable of raising sufficient revenue, regulating trade, conducting foreign policy, and, for some, organizing a standing army. While Adams was abroad, the movement that culminated in the Constitutional Convention of 1787 originated among these conservatives, deriving support from among northern merchants disenchanted with a government too weak to compel Great Britain to open its ports to American vessels, and from among southern planters distraught with a government powerless to open the newly acquired tramontane West. The centralists, or Federalists as they would style themselves, also included financiers, slave owners, and many of the most affluent property holders, North and South, who were alarmed at the nature of the some of the measures under consideration by several state legislatures, "calamities" (James Madison's phrase) that included inflation of the currency, abolition of debts, and a more equitable division of property. It was Shays's Rebellion that galvanized the diverse elements among the conservatives into the unified force that wrote and ratified the new national constitution. "Good God!" Washington exclaimed when he learned of the disorders, for like many among the nation's elite and privileged, he looked upon the protestors as farmers who believed the lands of America "to be the *common property* of all."[25]

While Adams shared most of these fears and hopes, his views included distinct qualities. This stemmed in part from his lengthy absence from America and his isolation from the vertiginous strains coursing through conservative thought during the late stages of the war and the postwar 1780s. His long residence abroad and his observation of European courts and society were important as well. Finally, his views reflected the deeply ingrained, gloomily sullen view of the human character that had always lurked in a corner of his mind, a legacy of the Puritan thought that had continued to surfeit the Massachusetts in which he had come of age. The result was an apprehension so exaggerated that he was moved to urge even more safeguards against popular change than had been built into the new constitution. His views were too extreme for most of his countrymen, and some were prompted to accuse him of favoring a hereditary, monarchical system for America modeled on the English constitution. James Madison, for instance, reported to Jefferson that Adams was "getting faster and faster into difficulties" for his "unpardonable" ideas and "obnoxious principles," beliefs, he said, which had "produced . . . a settled dislike among republicans every where." To Madison, Adams's views, despite the vice-president's disclaimers, were "monarchical principles." Adams treated such recriminations as if they were ludicrous. But, despite his belief that the new constitution should have a "fair play" before any alterations were attempted, Adams privately expressed his belief that hereditary rule was inevitable. "Our ship must ultimately land on that shore," he predicted.[26]

While this storm raged about him, Adams took comfort in the conviction that the country was in capable hands during the Washington presidency, and he loyally and cheerfully supported the administration's principal domestic and foreign policies. Some contemporary political leaders—Jefferson, for instance—revered Washington, and others, such as Aaron Burr, and perhaps even Hamilton, disliked him or thought him unimaginative and lacking in talent. Adams, however, respected and admired the president, and, toward the end of his vice-presidency, he remarked that his constant support of Washington and his policies had been the "Pride and Boast" of his life. In private he sometimes carped at the excessive adulation of Washington, once even enviously charging that the "History of our Revolution will be one continued lie. . . . The essence of the whole will be *that Dr. Franklin's electrical Rod smote the Earth and out sprung General Washington. That Franklin electrized him with his Rod—and henceforth these two conducted all the Policy, Negotiations, Legislatures and War.*" But Adams's envy of Washington's popularity did not diminish his appreciation of the Virginian's talents. He never questioned Washington's courage or his generalship during the recent war. Adams found Washington's decision-making processes somewhat slow, although he believed the president usually made the proper choice. He praised Washington's facility for self-control and his ability for self-knowledge. Adams was certain that the president was unequaled when it came to intuitively understanding others. Washington possessed "Talents of a very Superior kind," the vice-president concluded. "I wish I had as good."[27]

Washington and Adams jointly executed many more of the executive branch's ceremonial undertakings than would be likely for a contemporary president and vice-president. For instance, Adams frequently attended Washington's levees and dinner parties, accompanied the president on a portion of his tour of New England in the fall of 1789, and even appeared with him at a commencement exercise at King's College, now Columbia University. The contrast between these two men must have startled their audiences. Washington was graceful, tall, and well proportioned (six four and only 210 pounds, even in his last years), while Adams was considerably shorter and portly. The two were quite different in other respects as well. Adams was contemplative and something of a loner, whereas Washington was an aggressive, energetic businessman-farmer who read relatively little and was happiest when he was physically active. Because of their differences, the two were never close friends, but they enjoyed one another's company. Adams sometimes dined alone with Washington and the First Lady, and when Abigail or one of the boys was in the capital, the entire family occasionally was invited to dinner at the presidential mansion. From time to time Washington requested the vice-president's presence for a late afternoon cup of tea, and on several occasions Adams was the president's companion on long horseback rides and on evenings spent at the theater.[28] Yet in spite of their cordial relationship and Adams's long years of public service, the vice-president played virtually no role in the administration's decision-making processes.

Adams's few powers, therefore, were almost entirely confined to his constitutional role as presiding officer of the Senate. During the first session of the First Congress, he sought to expand his authority by participating in an occasional debate, but the practice irritated many senators, who believed that his conduct was an abuse of his prescribed duties. During that initial session, Adams also fell into the habit of lecturing his audience, often attempting to explain the customs of the British parliament, no doubt hoping the Senate would adopt the time-honored practices of that distant legislature. His listeners resented these homilies even more than his involvement in their deliberations, and soon Adams forswore all activity except that of actually presiding over this body and voting when the Senate was "equally divided," as the Constitution put it.

Adams cast the tie-breaking vote at least thirty-one times during his eight years as vice-president, often on matters that strengthened the powers of the new national government. On five separate occasions he was compelled to decide the fate of the Residence Bill, legislation seeking a permanent capital for the United States. And it was Adams's vote that defeated a navigation bill James Madison had shepherded through Congress, a decision that indicated he had changed his views on an important question of the day. Washington and Hamilton opposed such a bill, as did Northern mercantile interests. Trade was flourishing in the early 1790s in comparison to the previous decade, some of it growing out of the reexport of British goods; besides, many not only feared British retaliation in the event that America chose such a course, but some also were anxious lest a navigation policy prematurely trigger American manufacturing. Perhaps his most important tie-breaking vote authorized presidential removal of joint executive-Senate appointees, a grant of power bitterly resisted by many senators who believed that an individual placed in office through the "advice and consent" of the Senate could be dismissed only if the Senate confirmed such a step.[29]

President Washington and his cabinet rarely sought Adams's opinion. Washington looked upon Hamilton, his treasury secretary, as the linchpin of his administration. The president's goal was to create a sovereign central government capable of "vigorous execution," the sort of entity he had yearned for since those bleak days during the war when he was compelled to look upon his cold, hungry, unpaid, and potentially unwilling soldiers. Hamilton set out to fulfill Washington's desires and, in the process, to recapitulate the British system. The new constitution already had done much of the work; Hamilton sought one additional change to complete the new system. By creating a new debt with which to eliminate the old, Hamilton endeavored to attach firmly the new propertied elite to the new government, its unswerving allegiance a guarantee of stability and an assurance that the refractory among the privileged would be kept in their proper place.

Adams played no role in the preparation of the funding, assumption, and banking measures introduced in the first years of the Washington government, nor was he involved in the congressional battles that these measures stirred. He was troubled by some aspects of Hamilton's economic schemes, however, and he recoiled from what he called the "mercenary spirit of commerce" that pervaded the secretary's program. Later, he spoke of Hamiltonianism as a "swindle" of the poor and middle classes and he raged at the "gangrene of avarice" unleashed by the Federalist party's economic policies. He understood that Federalism would, among other things, enrich the few, leading to a growing concentration of wealth in the United States. From the outset of his public life, he had suspected that businessmen must be subjected to careful public scutiny and control. In the course of the war he had advocated the enactment of sumptuary laws in order to prevent the excessive accumulation of wealth; there was no reason to believe that his attitude had changed since 1776 when he had maintained that "Frugality" would banish "vanities, levities, and fopperies, which are real antidotes to all great, manly, and warlike virtues." Nevertheless, he chose to watch passively as each of Hamilton's plans was enacted. The one aspect of the administration's economic program that Adams did support was its principal revenue-raising measure, an excise tax on whiskey, and when in 1794 the government raised an army to suppress the farmers in western Pennsylvania who refused to pay the duty, Adams defended the president's decision to use force against this "wicked rebellion" staged by "miserable" pro-French democrats.[30]

By the time Hamilton's economic program had been enacted, the president was preoccupied by foreign policy concerns. During the week of Washington's inauguration, the French parliament, the Estates General, met for the first time in 175 years, called into session in the hope that it could find the means to extricate France from staggering indebtedness. Soon, however, the reforms initiated by the Estates General touched off the second great western revolution of the eighteenth century. Within three years France was at war with its neighbors, including Great Britain. France had launched this great conflict both to export its revolutionary ideals and to prevent the reactionary monarchies of Europe from destroying the French Revolution. The conflict between France and Britain, two great powers with possessions and ambitions in North America and the Caribbean, inevitably affected the interests of the United States.

Adams's views appear to have been sought on only two foreign policy matters during the entirety of his vice-presidency. During a war scare between Great Britain and Spain in 1790, Washington twice conferred with him; Adams urged United States neutrality should hostilities commence between those European powers. Three years later, difficulties stemming from the mission of the French minister, Edmond Genêt, once again prompted the president to seek Adams's counsel. Genêt arrived in Philadelphia in mid-1793 and immediately took action designed to rally the supposedly nonaligned American people behind beleaguered France. By year's end, moreover, he was actively seeking to raise an army of southern frontiersmen to attack Spanish Florida. Washington might have turned to Adams in this instance because of his experience with the French; the president might even have believed Adams was likely to be more objective than Secretary of State Jefferson, who was suspect in some circles because of his affinity for the French and their revolution. Perhaps Adams's views were elicited because he had been friendly with Genêt's father during his embassy to Paris in 1780–81. Whatever the reason, Adams and Washington met twice and conferred for several hours in an "affectionate" manner, as the vice-president described the sessions. It is not clear what Adams recommended, but his advice was of no consequence, for within hours of the second meeting word arrived from Paris that Genet had been recalled.[31]

Adams's presence was not even acknowledged when the administration grappled with the great foreign policy issues of the day. The vice-president played no role in the decision to proclaim the neutrality of the United States during the war in Europe. Although Adams had served as his country's first minister to Great Britain, Washington did not ask his advice about sending John Jay to London on a peace mission in 1794. Nor did the president consult Adams before he submitted the Jay Treaty to the Senate for ratification, even though the vice-president presided over that body.

Similarly, while the president and his advisors were compelled to make many difficult decisions concerning Indian policy, Adams was never brought into the discussions. Washington succeeded in peacefully securing lands from the Creek Indians, which opened vast stretches in Georgia and the southeast, but the president resorted to force to secure the lush, flat tramontane lands north of the Ohio River. Two armies dispatched into this bloody region suffered devastating losses; ultimately, a force commanded by Gen. Anthony Wayne defeated the tribesmen in 1794 at Fallen Timbers near Lake Erie. Although not consulted, Adams defended Washington's policies.[32]

Given Adams's experience, his positive feelings for Washington, and his unswerving endorsement of the president's policies, it is surprising that he was not permitted to play a greater role in the formulation of administration policy. Of course, any leader must find advisors with whom he can work comfortably, and Washington relied more on Hamilton and Knox, whom he had known and trusted in the continental army, and on Jefferson, a fellow Virginian with whom he had become familiar before his presidency. By contrast, Adams and Washington had served together briefly in the Congress in 1774 and 1775, but they had not shared committee assignments or grown close, nor were they ever in one another's presence during the dozen years preceding Washington's inauguration. Adams's manner, moreover, was frank and candid, frequently even piquant, and Washington preferred more deferential habits in those close to him. There is even a possibility that Washington was unaware that he and his vice-president shared many views. In the spring of 1796, the seventh year of the Washington presidency, Adams dined with the chief executive one evening and to his amazement he discovered, as he put it, that Washington's "opinions and sentiments are more exactly like mine than I ever knew before."[33]

It is possible too that Hamilton, who looked upon Adams as a rival to lead the Federalist Party in the post-Washington era, might have subtly used his influence to block the vice-president's access to the president. Adams seems not to have suspected such behavior by the Treasury secretary, however, and their relationship—what there was of it—appears to have been cordial but formal. Adams lauded Hamilton as a man who was "able and has done so well," and he supported his economic programs.[34]

That Jefferson largely ignored Adams is perhaps more surprising than Washington's disregard of his vice-president. Within a month of assuming office, Jefferson solicited Adams's opinion concerning a Canadian-United States boundary problem and more than a year later he sought out the vice-president's view on a relatively minor matter pertaining to France. No evidence exists that he ever again requested Adams's advice on any foreign policy matters. In fact, relations between the two men cooled after the spring of 1791, when Jefferson not only publicly lauded Thomas Paine's newly published *Rights of Man* but also endorsed it as especially refreshing in light of the "political heresies" lately published in America. The remark could only have been a jab at Adams's recently published Davila essays, and, indeed, Jefferson had complained to Washington of the vice-president's "apostacy to hereditary monarchy and nobility." Additional damage soon resulted when John Quincy Adams—writing as "Publicola"—published a series of essays that struck at Paine and, by implication, at Jefferson. The Publicola series not only angered the secretary of state but was counterproductive in further convincing the public that Vice-President Adams was a monarchist.[35]

The rift grew even wider after 1792 when Jefferson and Madison established a newspaper, the *National Gazette*—edited by Philip Freneau—in which to air their views against Hamilton's economic policies and to inveigh for their vision of America as an agrarian, republican society. This was an early step in the eventual emergence of formal political parties. Once crystallized, Adams found himself in the Federalist party, while Jefferson assumed the lead in the Democratic-Republican party. The two factions represented a fundamental division in the ideology of activist Americans, including Adams and Jefferson.

The rival parties reflected deeply encrusted ways of thought. Many who were drawn to the Federalist party not only thought in terms of established authority but would also have been uncomfortable with anything but the orthodox and the conventional. Many who came naturally to the Republican party looked irreverently upon the past while gazing toward a future in which they expected to see progress. Contrasting views of the nature of humankind lay at the base of the differences. Most Federalists believed that humans could never escape the influence of their innately base passions, especially the uncontrollable urge for wealth and power. This faction sought to use government to check evil propensities. Most Republicans, on the other hand, believed that humans possessed the capacity for great good if the proper environment could be structured to facilitate their virtuous side. The solution of the Republican party was to rid society of evil, including the worst of all evils, a large, powerful government.

But there were other significant differences between the parties. The Federalists yearned for an American society and a national government established on the model that had evolved in England since the Glorious Revolution late in the previous century. The key to realizing this goal, as Hamilton saw it, was a system in which all classes were collectively fettered to the new federal government. The reduction of the Revolutionary War debt was the vehicle he selected to obtain his ends, for the revenue to be used for the eradication of America's indebtedness, aside from that derived through the whiskey tax, was to be procured largely through duties on imports from England. Such a scheme demarcated and proscribed national policy. Deviation from the institutionalized system that Hamilton had fashioned would threaten the superstructure upon which all else rested. National bankruptcy might result from either sweeping changes at home or a worsening of relations with Great Britain, a catastrophe that might jeopardize the very existence of the fragile American Union.

Republican resistance to the Washington-Hamilton policies drew on the model of the English Opposition's fight to forestall the establishment of such a system. From John Locke and James Harrington, among others, the Jeffersonians borrowed the notion that the happiest state could be realized in an agrarian atmosphere characterized by widespread ownership of property. Agriculture would predominate; commerce would exist to serve a nation of farmers. The Hamiltonian system that fostered corruption by encouraging man's appetite for ambition and avarice would be banished. Gone, too, would be the need for a strong central government and its attendant danger of invidious monarchism, a Federalist creation that some Jeffersonians viewed as nothing less than a betrayal of the American Revolution, at least if the powers of the new government were strictly construed. The Jeffersonians looked upon their alternative as the means to real independence, for their farming society would have no need to be bound to any foreign power.

But the Jeffersonians were not merely tied to the past. They perceived the dawning of a new age characterized by increased democratization, the means by which the citizenry might escape the authority that government had traditionally wielded over their lives. Sturdy yeomen with a stake in society—the bulk of the free populace—would exercise power as never before. Moreover, like the Federalists, the Republicans were modernists who welcomed capitalism and who were willing to use the new national government to further their ends. They would spend federal dollars, too, but their expenditures would be designed to open quickly the recently procured western lands for settlement, to link by federaliy funded transportation arteries the nation's farmers and the commercial hubs of the East, and to open new foreign markets to grains and cereals grown on American farms from the Chesapeake to the tramontane West.

John Adams was not comfortable with the entirety of Federalism. He blanched at the close ties with Great Britain that Hamilton and others favored. He disliked the standing armies that the Federalists envisioned. Not only had he never liked banks, but as a Puritan descendant who had never betrayed his concern for a virtuous citizenry, Adams feared that Hamilton's economic schemes would inevitably invite both corruption and an increased danger of aristocratic usurpation, the great evil for which he had sought a cure in the *Defence.* Nor should it be forgotten that while—like most Federalists—he wished to protect the rich from the poor, Adams—unlike most members of his party—feared the wealthy few as much as he was disturbed by the humble. Finally, he felt a decided measure of discomfort at finding himself in the same party with numerous former Loyalists (who seemed to flock to Federalism with the same regularity that immigrants were drawn to Republicanism), as well as with those who had come to support the Revolution only at the last moment and usually, he thought, with considerable reservations and little enthusiasm.

On the other hand, Adams was a representative of New England, a region whose traditional leadership had recently been badly frightened by Shays's Rebellion, a land with poor prospects for commercial agriculture and states that contained not only commercial towns and thriving shipbuilding and fishing industries but also a powerful mercantile elite with strong ties to English capital. More importantly, however, he shared with most Federalists a fear of democracy and anarchy, and he doubted whether his countrymen any longer were sufficiently virtuous to sustain the kind of republic envisioned by the Jeffersonians. Like many Federalists, Adams was a student of the classical theorists of balanced government, but he and most New England Federalists also believed that the traditional deference of the many to the few offered the only hope of reconciling virtue with liberty, and of preventing liberty from degenerating into licentiousness.[36]

As the Republican party crystallized, Jefferson resigned from Washington's cabinet to return to Monticello, his hilltop mansion in Virginia. During the next three years, he and Adams seldom saw one another. Their correspondence subsided as well. Once close friends, these two proud, stubborn men exchanged only fourteen letters between 1794 and 1812.

There was one additional reason why administrative officials perhaps ignored Adams. He was absent from the capital for long stretches during the Washington presidency. Washington got away to Mount Vernon when he thought he could, but he usually was in the capital during ten months of the year, and on one occasion more than a year and a half passed between his visits to Virginia. Adams, however, spent almost three-fourths of each year on his farm in Quincy, as Braintree was now called. That Washington might have turned to Adams more often is evidenced by his remarks during a foreign policy crisis in 1791. In that instance, Washington notified his cabinet: "Presuming that the Vice-President will have left the seat of government for Boston, I have not requested his opinion to be taken. . . . Should it be otherwise I wish him to be consulted." Adams, it turned out, had already departed, and he played no role in the administration's deliberations.[37]

Adams had not commenced his duties in such a manner. He remained in the capital during the initial two years of his term, save for a few weeks in 1789 when he accompanied Washington on a portion of his tour of New England. Abigail had cheerfully been at her husband's side during this period, having moved to New York a few weeks after Washington's inauguration. The couple had rented Richmond Hill, an elegant, two story, columned mansion that overlooked the Hudson River about a mile north of the city. It was a happy time. Both were fond of the house and its thirty acres, which Abigail described as the "most delicious spot I ever saw." Both were also delighted to be within commuting distance of Nabby, whom they saw frequently. If the vice-presidency was an office without power, it nevertheless was a high office, and both John and Abigail relished the deference that it brought and the opportunity it afforded for mingling with the most-acclaimed citizens of the new nation. But, fifteen months into Washington's presidency, Philadelphia was named the temporary national capital, after which the government was to move to a site on the Potomac.[38]

Abigail was disconsolate at the prospect of the move. She once again would be separated from her daughter. She fretted too over the expense of the undertaking, a burden she was not sure the family budget could sustain. Nevertheless, in November 1790, accompanied by mountains of crates and chests, she sailed to Philadelphia and took up residence at Bush Hill, a handsome dwelling on the outskirts of the city. But she remained only six months before departing for Quincy. Abigail returned to the capital in the fall, but after only a few months she once again departed for home, this time vowing never to return to Philadelphia. It was a pledge that she kept during her husband's vice-presidency.[39]

Economic considerations influenced her decision to remain in Massachusetts. The burden of maintaining two residences, even on the vice-president's annual salary of five thousand dollars, was considerable. She also feared for the well-being of Peacefield during her absence, especially since it was still undergoing restoration from its previous neglect. In addition, she not only had wearied of the entertaining incumbent upon the wife of a high official, she also longed for her privacy and for the opportunity to pursue her own interests. Her declining health was still another factor in her decision not to return to Philadelphia. For some time she had been afflicted with rheumatism, a malady that had grown steadily worse, beginning with her stay in damp London; by the beginning of her husband's vice-presidency, when Abigail was forty-five years old, she at times endured excruciating torments. She lost weight, and there were days when the agony was too great to arise from bed. The thought of a jostling ride over the primitive roads from Quincy to Philadelphia was too much to bear.[40]

For the final five years of his vice-presidency, therefore, Adams lodged alone in Philadelphia. He usually left Peacefield late in November, sometimes traveling in his own carriage, sometimes in a public conveyance, or often sailing to New York, where he caught the stage for the capital. In Philadelphia he rented rooms at a boardinghouse occupied by several congressmen, remaining in the capital only until Congress adjourned, usually early in March, whereupon he returned home for the next nine months.[41]

It is customary to depict the powerless and ignored Adams as a feckless and bitterly unhappy man during his vice-presidential years. Certainly, he required only a few weeks in office to discover the impotency of his post. "[M]y Burthens are not very heavy," he remarked soon after being sworn in. Later, he complained that the office "renders me so completely insignificant." Other petulant outbursts followed. "I am weary of this Scene of Dullness," this life of "dull Solitude," this existence of "tedious days and lonesome nights," he added in numerous letters. He occasionally spoke of resigning the office, but that was the sort of bluster he had uttered during good moments and bad in earlier days. He had never carried through on such a threat, nor did he in this instance, even though he might have done so and returned to Massachusetts to be considered for the governorship or the United States Senate. Indeed, he might have stepped down at the end of his first term. Instead, he sought reelection and easily outpointed the Republican party candidate, George Clinton. There can be little doubt that Adams saw the vice-presidency as his best means by which to succeed President Washington. To further that end, he soon eschewed his powdered wig, ceremonial sword, and handsome coach.[42]

Despite his frequent complaints, Adams often exhibited a bright side, a more contented and optimistic visage than he had displayed in years. He seemed grateful for all he had achieved, telling John Quincy that his life story had been an instance of "Success almost without Example." His had been a full life, too, he thought. He told a correspondent, "[I view] the Adventures of myself" as "a kind of Romance." He thought himself akin to a medieval knight who had been compelled to struggle against great odds but who ultimately had flourished. Never had Adams seemed so complacent with his lot as in these years. He marveled at the respect and deference shown him. He also acknowledged that Washington indeed should have been the first president, and he took great pride in his elevation to the second spot under the Constitution.[43]

Of course, Adams hoped to succeed Washington, a prospect he thought would be his likely reward for having spent eight years in the vice-presidency.

Compared with the travail and isolation he had experienced in much of his earlier public service, Adams did not find the vice-presidency an unpleasant position. As a member of the Continental Congress, he had often spent ten or more months in Philadelphia while his family remained in Massachusetts. His first diplomatic mission to Europe had occasioned an absence of nearly sixteen months from his wife; his second embassy forced a separation from Abigail that lasted nearly five years. After 1792, however, John normally was separated from Abigail for only a few brief weeks each year. In addition, his life-style in Philadelphia was more subdued than in the bustling legations in Amsterdam and London, affording him ample time to read and write.

On a typical day Adams rose early and read the morning papers, took a brisk horseback ride for exercise, attended the Senate session, read public documents in the later afternoon, and spent his evening alone tending to his correspondence and his books. On occasion he socialized over dinner and cigars with a European envoy or with acquaintances in the government and the city. He was close to several members in the Massachusetts and Connecticut delegations to Congress and he enjoyed a long, intimate friendship with Benjamin Rush, Philadelphia's most famous physician. During nearly half of Adams's vice-presidential years, his son Thomas Boylston lived in the capital, where he was completing his legal apprenticeship; the two got together frequently, sometimes for dinner, sometimes so that John could assist with son's legal studies. Adams enjoyed Philadelphia, too. He described it as "a great City" of beauty, charm, and edifying opportunities, a cultural hub with twice the population of Boston, ten newspapers, a college, a public library, a hospital, two theaters, a museum, and a philosophical society.[44]

Adams's health was always a good barometer of his state of mind, and his health was seldom better than during these years. Although he was sixty-one in 1796, his last full year in the office, he said that he did not feel a day over forty. "I feel bold and strong," he added, attributing it to his daily exercise. Only in his first year in office did he allude to any lingering problems from his serious illness in 1781, although he did acknowledge that he was unable to control a chronic tremor in his hands, a quivering that the observer at Washington's inauguration mistakenly attributed to nervousness. After 1792 he fell victim to pyorrhea, which resulted in the loss of several teeth; the latter affliction not only altered his facial appearance but caused him to speak with a pronounced lisp.[45]

Adams's greatest unhappiness in these years appears to have been occasioned by the brief annual separations from his wife. Indeed, a profound change occurred in the relationship between John and Abigail in this period of their lives. He now seemed to need her at his side as never before. When she did not come with him to New York at the outset of his term, he pleaded for her presence in almost hysterical terms. She must come to be "my Physician and my Nurse," he wrote. Living without her had done "great dammadge" to his health, he added unconvincingly; "I cannot consent to your delaying any longer." Borrow money if need be in order to make the journey, and borrow it at any rate of interest, he added, but come immediately. She did come, and she remained with him for three years.[46]

When she could not, or would not, return to the capital during the last years of his vice-presidency, Adams responded as never before. He remained at home with her most of the year, turning his back on whatever opportunity existed to play a greater role within Washington's administration. When Congress was in session and he dwelled alone, he seemed to pine for his wife as he had when they were newlyweds. He also beseeched her to join him. They could live in inexpensive rooms rather than renting a large, expensive house, he advised. Unable to persuade her to leave Peacefield, he poured out his feelings in letter after letter. "I want my Wife to hover over and about me," he wrote. "I want my Horse[,] my farm[,] my long Walks and more than all the Bosom of my friend," he told her in another missive. When she turned a deaf ear to his entreaties, he added: "I know not what to write you, unless I tell you I love you. But that will be no News." Once, upon learning that she had been ill, he confided that he had known telepathically of her distress. On another occasion, upon arriving alone in the capital, he cried out: "Three months before I can see you again. Oh! What to do with myself I know not." What he did much of the time was write home, dispatching an unprecedented number of letters to her. In previous absences he rarely had written home more than once a week, sometimes only once every two or three weeks. From the outset of this separation, however, he wrote twice each week, and by early 1794 he was mailing three letters a week to Abigail. During the congressional session of 1794–95 he sent her twenty-seven letters in December and January. But she would not budge from Quincy, and during the twelve to fourteen weeks each year that they were apart Adams had to be content to wait for her letters, which usually arrived each Monday and Thursday via the New York stage.[47]

The change in Adams's feelings surely stemmed in part from the comfort he derived from Abigail's presence during a time when he was ignored by those in power and left without a significant public role to play. Yet the transformation also reflected something deeper. Uncertain of himself when he had first entered public life, Adams appeared to have withdrawn into himself, seeking insulation from those nearest to him, punishing himself. But upon his return to America he had discovered public applause for his revolutionary accomplishments. First had come the hero's welcome when he reached Boston harbor. Then, the second office in the land—second only to that reserved for the exalted, revered Washington—had been bestowed upon him. At last he had achieved the recognition he had so long sought. His identity was established; he had more energy for dealing with his internal world, and in turn he sought more opportunity and stimulation from that internal sphere. More sure of himself, more happy with himself, more genuinely loving of himself, he was able to overcome the distantness that characterized his relationship with Abigail during his struggle to establish his career and succeed as a political leader. At last he was capable of realizing with Abigail the real intimacy that had for so long eluded him.

In addition, Adams was experiencing a transformation that is not uncommon among men in their later adult years. An older man by the time of his vice-presidency (he was fifty-three when he took office), he was gripped with a sense of urgency about the time that was left to him. He was more aware of life. He grew to see himself and others differently. He appeared to realize the hurtful things that he had done to Abigail, and he sought to build a new life structure, one that would include a more intense and sensual relationship with his wife. This was a John Adams who was more passive and dependent, a John Adams who required the nurturance that only his wife could provide.[48]

But Abigail had changed as well. The habits of independence that had grown during her long separation from John were ingrained. She sought to maintain the enhanced autonomy over her life that she had achieved during her "widowhood." For the first time in their relationship Abigail wrote less often than her husband. Twice each week John eagerly awaited the New York stage, hoping it would bring another letter. Often he was disappointed. During his absences in 1793 and 1794, for instance, she wrote approximately one letter to her husband for every two that she received. In addition, her communications lacked the spark of his effusive missives, or of those she had written when she was younger. Typically, during his first winter alone in Philadelphia, she responded matter of factly to his expressions of desire: "Years subdue the ardour of passion but in lieu thereof a Friendship and affection Deep rooted subsists . . . and will survive whilst the vital Flame exists." Although she added that she believed their "attachment" would continue to increase, it was Adams's fate to have finally broken the restraints inhibiting his achievement of full intimacy at the very moment his wife had come to a very different understanding of their relationship.[49]

Back in the United States and with his sons nearby, Adams was anxious to help, even to guide their development. John Quincy seemed to command the lion's share of his attention. Adams not only knew him better than the younger boys, but he saw vast potential in the young man, more than he could expect, he thought, from his other sons. John Quincy completed his legal training and in 1790, at age twenty-three, opened a law office in Boston. His father helped him in every way he could, making available his large law library, offering advice, even subsidizing him with a handsome annual stipend of one hundred pounds, the equivalent of a year's income for many skilled artisans. Nevertheless, this was a difficult period for John Quincy. He was not happy practicing law. Moreover, like any young man, he was anxious to establish his own life independent from parental intrusion. Submissive by nature, John Quincy found it difficult to effect a separate identity. When he fell in love with a young lady from Newburyport, for instance, he mutely permitted his parents to quash the relationship; marriage might interfere with the advancement of his fledgling law practice. With little will of his own, and locked into a career that he pursued because he believed his parents expected it of him, he was a most unhappy young man, corpulent from overeating to allay frustration, often depressed, besieged by insomnia, and occasionally dependent on tranquilizing opiates. But in 1794 his life changed drastically. He learned that President Washington had named him minister president to The Hague. Although besieged with mixed feelings about such an abrupt career change, he accepted the appointment; his parents could only burst with pride.[50]

Thomas Boylston, whose bitterness had led him to refuse to write his parents in London, graduated from Harvard at the same time that John Quincy was establishing his law practice. He had no desire to practice law, and even John Quincy thought him ill suited for such a calling. Ultimately, however, he relented to parental pressure and moved to Philadelphia where arrangements were made for him to begin his studies. He appears to have been no less unhappy than his older brother, but fortune smiled on him, too. He was still engaged in his legal studies when the opportunity arose to serve as John Quincy's secretary in The Hague. Thomas seized the moment, apparently with the blessing of his mother, who had also begun to doubt his capacity for the law and who hoped he might learn something of the banking business while he lived abroad. He sailed for Europe in July 1794.[51]

Charles caused his parents even greater concern. From the time he reached his mid-teens, John and Abigail looked upon him as a troubled youngster. At first glance, he seemed to be filled with winning qualities. Bright and affable, so charming that he immediately won over everyone with whom he came into contact, his prospects for success appeared to be unlimited. But there was a dark side to his makeup. Early on, Abigail concluded that he was terribly unhappy, a lad who was "not at peace with himself." She and her husband were heartbroken to discover that as an undergraduate at Harvard, Charles had exhibited the unmistakable signs of a drinking problem, an affliction that had caused the early death of Abigail's brother. Nevertheless, Charles completed his studies and in 1789 moved with his parents to New York where, like his brothers, he commenced legal studies under a tutor. He progressed more rapidly than Thomas; in 1792 he was admitted to the bar.

John and Abigail continued to worry over their son's alcoholism, and they were outraged when he squandered some of John Quincy's money that had been entrusted to his care. But something else concerned them as well, although their correspondence and that of Charles's siblings contains only dark hints and allusions with regard to this other, unspecified behavior. There are references to his alleged proclivity for consorting with men whom his parents regarded as unsavory. John Quincy, who remained a close, tolerant older brother through thick and thin, urged Charles to "be more cautious" and prayed that his conduct would remain within "the limits of regularity." By the early 1790s, such references may have been occasioned by the fact that Charles was living in New York with an old revolutionary war general, Baron Friedrich von Steuben, who is now thought by some to have been homosexual. Charles clearly adored Steuben—"My dear Mamma there is something in this man that is more than mortal," he told Abigail—and he was grief stricken when the old man retired to a farm in upstate New York. Following Steuben's departure, Charles announced his intention of marrying Sally Smith, the sister of his brother-in-law, Colonel Smith. Whereas his parents often interceded in John Quincy's and Thomas's matrimonial concerns, the vice-president and Abigail seemed almost relieved at their son's decision. Even Nabby breathed a sigh of relief. After "all the Hair breadth scapes and iminent dangers he has run, he is at last Safe Landed," she exalted.

It was during this period that John and Charles's relationship first exhibited signs of great strain. At first, the vice-president lectured and scolded his son, evidently with regard to his personal behavior, although most of the letters he wrote to Charles have disappeared, virtually the sole portion of Adams's vast correspondence that apparently was not carefully preserved for posterity. Through Charles's rejoinders, some of which are extant, the reader can discern a distraught son anxious for his father's approval. Why do you believe the calumny that you hear about me, he asks his father. Many "things have been told respecting me which are false," he writes. But John, intrusive, demanding, and anxious for his son to succeed, persisted until Charles retorted: "Your letter if it was intended to give pain had the desired effect." For a time thereafter the vice-president did not write at all, which led Charles to confide to his mother that he desperately wished to hear from his father. Plaintively, Charles also exclaimed to Abigail that there "is something more endearing in a mothers love than in a fathers."[52]

The three boys were not the only the parental cares that faced John and Abigail. By the early 1790s it was quite apparent that Col. William Smith, Nabby's husband, was not the prize that he at first had appeared to be. Indeed, within a few years Smith had become the embodiment of the very worst that the Adamses had perceived and feared in Royall Tyler. The "poor Girl," Abigail wrote of her daughter. "Poor Nabby!" the vice-president added, as Smith sank deeply into debt. The Smiths were compelled to abandon construction of a mansion modeled on Washington's Mount Vernon, and Nabby was left alone for long periods while her husband chased desperately after speculative ventures in England and the American West. Nabby and the children settled into an isolated existence in quite modest surroundings, living in an area so remote that neither churches nor schools were available. "I have

had so many trialls and struggles," Nabby confessed, "that I only wonder that I
have retained my senses." One thing that helped her state of mind was that
President Washington, at the vice-president's request, felt obliged to appoint
Colonel Smith federal marshal for New York in 1789; two years later the
president appointed Smith supervisor of revenue for New York.[53]

When Adams returned from Peacefield for the annual session of Congress in
December 1795, he learned that President Washington planned to leave office
at the expiration of his second term, a little more than a year away. Martha
Washington first dropped a hint of her husband's intention, then early in
January a cabinet official confirmed the news in a private conversation with the
vice-president. "You know the Consequences of this, to me and to yourself,"
Adams hurriedly wrote to Abigail. "We must enter upon Ardours more trying
than any ever yet experienced."[54]

From the first, Adams expected that Jefferson would be the choice of the
Republican party to succeed Washington. By the third week in January 1796,
he also believed that his party, the Federalists, regarded him as the heir apparent to the president. For once, being the vice-president was important. In
addition, he had the support of New England and some strength in the South,
where neither Hamilton nor Jay had a following. But the South, he knew, was
basically anti-Federalist and longed to see Jefferson in the presidency. Thus
there was a real possibility that he might finish second to Jefferson and face
four more years as vice-president.

Adams decided quickly that he would not serve under Jefferson. In fact,
from the outset of his term in 1789 he had indicated that he would occupy the
vice-presidency only under Washington. No other man could equal his record,
he believed. No one had served longer. No one had faced greater personal
dangers. No one had made such a huge personal sacrifice. Besides, the friction
that had developed between himself and Jefferson made it unthinkable for him
to serve under the Virginian. Rather than be vice-president under Jefferson, he
said, he would seek a seat in the House of Representatives.[55]

The immediate question that confronted Adams, however, was whether to
stand for the presidency. There can be no question about his inclination,
although he once again rehearsed the familiar pattern of doubt and equivoca-
tion. He spoke of retirement. It would be the "happiest Portion of my whole
Life," he said. He and Abigail could be "Farmers for Life," living out their days
in Quincy in "a very humble Style." On the other hand, the new nation needed
his service, he remarked. By early February he cautioned Abigail to keep their
sons' letters confidential lest they contain something that might injure him
politically. A week later he acknowledged his weariness with politics, but he
confided that he did not know how he could "live out of it." After another week
he was fretting over whether to serve four or eight years in the presidency.[56]

The possibility that her husband might be elevated to the presidency could hardly have come as a surprise to Abigail. For the past eight years she had lived with the realization that he would become president immediately should Washington suddenly die, an event that seemed likely during two serious illnesses that he suffered in the course of his tenure in office. But seeking the presidency was another matter, and Abigail was not happy with the prospect of several additional years of public service. It meant protracted separations from her husband; it also meant that she would be compelled to return to Philadelphia. She knew too that her husband would be exposed to barbs and calumny to a degree that would be difficult for him to withstand. She also feared for the health of her husband, who would be sixty-two years old when he entered office.

But she did not resist his aspirations. "My Ambition leads me not be first in Rome," she remarked cooly, yet she knew that her husband's ambition was less easily satiated. She told him that the presidency would be a "flattering and Glorious Reward" for his years of toil and unselfish service, the capstone on his career. He was ecstatic upon receiving her "delicious Letter." "Hi! Ho! Oh Dear. I am most tenderly . . . ," he very blithely closed his next missive.[57]

Adams was convinced that he was prepared for the presidency. He was healthy, he said. He knew that he was honest. He did not think of himself as a malevolent person. There were weaknesses in his makeup, he acknowledged, but timidity was not part of his character. Nor, in his view, was he an intemperate man. More than anything, he believed that he possessed the inner strength to withstand the ordeal.[58]

John Adams had only to be elected to the presidency, a far from certain prospect. In fact, as the election year of 1796 began, Adams was convinced of only one thing. This election, he said, would be decided by the House of Representatives.[59]

CHAPTER 16

*

An Office of Hard Labor and Severe Duty

JUST BEFORE HE RETURNED to Quincy in May 1796, Adams expressed his indifference to the outcome of the election. He "really, truly, and sincerely" did not care whether he won the contest, he claimed.[1] His disclaimer was unconvincing.

Adams spent the summer and most of the following autumn at Peacefield, torpidly looking after his farm and enjoying the pleasure of his wife's company. Aside from occasionally welcoming important New England politicians who were certain to work for his election, he was not active in the canvass. "I am determined to be a Silent Spectator of the Silly and Wicked game" he remarked at the outset, and he was good to his word.[2]

Thomas Pinckney, a South Carolinian, was chosen by Hamilton and the Federalist moguls—apparently without consultation with Adams—for the second slot on the ticket. His selection was dictated by "his southern position," Jefferson noted sagely, but he did have a distinguished record, having fought with valor in the War of Independence (he suffered both a wound and capture at Camden in 1780), and later having served the Washington administration as minister to the Court of St. James and as a very successful envoy extraordinary to Madrid.[3]

To oppose the "British party," or "Anglomen," as their adversaries had taken to referring to the Federalists, the Republicans selected Jefferson, the only administration foe possessed of the prestige to defeat Adams. Aaron Burr, who had followed his service in the late war with a distinguished legal career in New York and a term in the United States Senate, was the party's choice to run with Jefferson.

Other than lining up the candidates, the parties gave little evidence before late September that an election was imminent. On the nineteenth of that month, however, Washington published his Farewell Address in a Philadelphia newspaper, making public what insiders had known for months. The two parties were left with about ten weeks for campaigning before the Electoral College met.

Among the four candidates, only Burr was active. It was customary in Adams's time, and would remain so throughout most of the nineteenth century, for political aspirants to look upon electioneering as an unseemly endeavor. But friends of the candidates openly campaigned, and the party presses, well versed in the black art of invective, also sought to sway the voters in the sixteen states. The Federalists painted Jefferson as a Francophile, charged that he was indecisive, and even obliquely questioned his courage by making repeated reference to his flight from Monticello in the face of an invading British army in 1781. The Republicans portrayed Adams not only as an Anglophile, but as a monarchist, and one handbill even alleged that John Quincy would seek to succeed his father and establish an Adams dynasty.[4]

Everyone agreed that the returns from the Middle Atlantic states would determine the election, for Adams was certain to carry New England, while Jefferson would win the South. Everyone also agreed that covert machinations in the middle states might affect the outcome of the election. Should improbity occur, the opinion seemed nearly universal that Alexander Hamilton would have had a hand in the artifice.

If young John Adams lacked the advantages of such planters' sons as George Washington or Thomas Jefferson, the conditions of his youth would have struck young Alexander Hamilton as heaven-sent bounties. Of all those of the revolutionary generation who rose to an exalted position, none began their climb from a lower depth than Hamilton. The son of a woman with a penchant for taking up with ne'er-do-well men, Alexander was the offspring of an adulterous tryst between Rachael Lavien and James Hamilton, a Scottish merchant who had temporarily dropped his anchor on Nevis, a British-held island in the West Indies. When Alexander was ten, in 1765, his father moved the family to Saint Croix, a Dutch possession; the following year, James abandoned his wife and two sons.

Hamilton's youth has often been depicted as a struggle against grinding poverty. That was only partly true. While James was around, he evidently provided for his family, even paying for young Alexander's preparatory education in a small Jewish school on Nevis. Once James left, the family's fortunes deteriorated and Rachael was compelled to run a general store in Christiansted, a small business at which eleven-year-old Alexander was put to work keeping the books. The job did not last long. In 1768, when Alexander was thirteen, Rachael died. Stained by his illegitimate birth and now orphaned, the youngster faced a bleak and uncertain future. But gloomy as matters must have seemed, he was fortunate. Whereas his older brother was apprenticed to a carpenter, Alexander, probably because of the two years he had worked in his mother's store, secured work as a clerk in a mercantile firm operated by immigrants from New York.

Alexander worked for this enterprise from age fourteen, the age at which young Adams had entered Harvard College, until he was almost eighteen. He hated the life he led, especially the "grov'ling condition"—the lower-class status—to which he was subjected. Hamilton appears to have spent a considerable portion of his time dreaming of an escape from the chains that bound him, but he probably never imagined that it would come as it did. Impressed by Alexander's capabilities, one of his employers, Nicholas Cruger, agreed to finance the completion of his education. Alexander sailed for the mainland in 1772, arriving in Boston on almost the very day that James Otis elsewhere in the city was excoriating Adams for his lack of involvement in the popular protest movement. Hamilton quickly made his way south, and after a brief period in a preparatory school in Elizabethtown, New Jersey, enrolled at King's College in New York City. During his sophomore year in 1774–75, the precocious Hamilton joined in the spate of pamphleteering touched off by the First Continental Congress. He published two essays in response to the Tory attacks on America's boycott of Great Britain, works that lacked the intellectual resonance of Adams's "Novanglus"; nevertheless, Hamilton, not quite twenty years old, exhibited a talent that Adams would never match, the unerring touch of the master propagandist.

Throughout his life, Hamilton had a facility for enlisting the aid of older, powerful benefactors. Whereas Cruger paid for his education, John Jay, who had learned of Hamilton through his essays, agreed to use his influence in 1776 to secure the young man's appointment as captain of an artillery company. Recent research has demonstrated that Captain Hamilton saw no military action in the Battle of New York or subsequent engagements that autumn, but he was with the Continental army as it reeled in retreat across New Jersey, and in December and January he was part of the fighting at Trenton and Princeton. On March 1, 1777, he received the opportunity of a lifetime. He was appointed as an aide-de-camp to General Washington.

Only five years before, Hamilton, in Saint Croix, had complained, "My Fortune . . . condemns me" to an unhappy future. His rise had been rapid, and over the next dozen years he would as steadily and spectacularly continue his ascent. Hamilton remained at Washington's side as long as it was useful to do so, for the most part serving in an armchair capacity as the general's secretary and confidant, although during the siege at Yorktown he commanded under fire. But Washington was not the only person Hamilton courted. After telling a friend that he was looking for a wife with money and influence, he married into the Schuyler family, a wealthy and powerful clan in New York, and he used his post at headquarters to ingratiate himself with preeminent men in business, the army, and Congress. Although nothing came of it, his powers of persuasiveness were such that some of his new friends even mentioned his name with regard to the post of minister of finance in the new government under the Articles of Confederation; Hamilton was twenty-six years old at the time.

After Cornwallis's capitulation late in 1781, Hamilton could discern no more worlds to conquer in the army. He returned to civilian pursuits. In the almost unprecedented time of three months, he completed his legal studies and was admitted to the New York bar; in an equally record time his law firm was flourishing with a heavy caseload of business brought by wealthy merchants and large landowners. Nor did he ignore public affairs. He served briefly in Congress and, of course, he played a crucial role in the adoption of the new federal constitution. When John Adams alighted in Boston in June 1788, Hamilton, whose name he had never heard before making his initial mission to France ten years earlier, had emerged as a major political figure. Indeed, playing the role of virtual premier in the administration of President Washington, Hamilton, younger still than Adams had been when he at last committed himself to public life, would hold far greater power in the new national government than the vice-president.

Hamilton, like Adams, was driven by a lust after fame, but he also craved wealth and power, especially the latter. Probably because of the penury and the perceived ignominy of his Caribbean youth, Hamilton sought to assure that he would never again confront the destitution and despair that once had enveloped him. Power was his obsession, for it not only gave him a hold over other men, it was the level that could procure the adulation, notability, and grandeur after which he yearned.

Hamilton had attained considerable authority before his thirty-fifth birthday. It came as a result of his erudition, his boundless, restless energy—focused endlessly, interminably upon power—together with a nearly unerring intuition for the proper political course. But it was his utter ruthlessness that was most responsible for his extraordinarily rapid rise. Behind a facade of cordiality and eloquence, beneath an exterior of garrulous charm and amicability, skulked the reality of low, cunning dishonesty. Jefferson thought him "a man whose history . . . is a tissue of machinations." To John Quincy Adams, who as a young adult saw Hamilton in action, he was "little scrupulous of the manner which he used against those who stood in the way of his ambition." Yet he is better remembered for the chicanery with which he manipulated those who could be of assistance, especially George Washington. Although he privately acknowledged his dislike of Washington (he thought the general was indelicate and ill-tempered), he buried his contempt in order to serve this man whom the nation lionized, persevering to assist in building Washington's reputation and just as sedulously turning his talents toward the destruction of those who might prove a threat. Washington, he once remarked coldly, "was an Aegis very essential to me."

There were many philosophical similarities between Hamilton and Adams, and each man longed to achieve fame, but in temperament and personality there were worlds of differences. However, the great chasm that separated these two was an ethical one. It is as inconceivable that Hamilton might ever have kept a diary in which he expressed his guilt over his desires for acclaim as it was that Adams might have sought by cunning to exploit for his own selfish ends a major figure such as Samuel Adams. For the one, the possession of power was everything. For the other, holding power was justifiable only if the means by which it was gained were honorable and if the uses for which it was employed were virtuous. Jefferson told a story that revealed much of Hamilton. Once, when Hamilton visited Jefferson at the State Department, he asked the identity of the men in three portraits he saw in the secretary's office. Jefferson responded that these were paintings of the "three greatest men the world has ever produced, Bacon, Newton, and Locke." Hamilton immediately replied: "The greatest man in history was Julius Caesar."[5]

This was the Hamilton whom many suspected of chicanery as the election campaign of 1796 commenced. Rumors buzzed that autumn that he was conspiring to assure that Pinckney would finish ahead of Adams. There were numerous reasons for such suspicion. Many believed that Hamilton had acted duplicitously with regard to Adams's candidacy in 1788. Moreover, with Washington's retirement, Hamilton must have felt power slipping from his grasp. He was not close to Adams; indeed, he barely knew the vice-president and could hardly expect to be his confidant. More than all the other factors, however, Hamilton knew quite well that Adams was a fiercely independent man who could never be manipulated. Pinckney, it was believed, was more "discreet and conciliatory," more easily exploited.

There is evidence of treachery in this canvass, but Hamilton does not appear to have been guilty of seeking to assure Adams's defeat. He feared a Jefferson administration more than he dreaded an Adams presidency, and he appears to have labored "to support Mr. Pinckney equally with Mr. Adams." This was the very conclusion that Adams reached. A week after acceding to the presidency, Adams remarked that he believed that Hamilton "wished me to be P. and Mr. Pinckney V. P."[6]

In fact, some Federalists were troubled by the prospect of an Adams presidency. The most reactionary Federalists thought him too anti-British. Some acquaintances saw him as unsteady and given to capriciousness, as likely to swing suddenly toward some imprudent course. Others feared that his "great vanity"—Hamilton called it his "disgusting egotism" and "distempered jealousy"—would lead him to act unwisely. There was talk of his "eccentric tendencies," and Oliver Wolcott, Hamilton's successor as Treasury secretary under Washington, thought Adams possessed "far less real abilities than he believes he possesses." Counterbalancing these fears—which were expressed by only a handful of influential party figures—was Adams's long, distinguished record of service. In addition, many Federalists, including Hamilton, feared that the party would be split disastrously if Adams was betrayed and was denied the presidency.[7]

Adams had heard enough rumors of backroom maneuvers to be thoroughly uncertain about his prospects of victory. He had heard speculation about Hamilton's legerdemain and he had even been told that John Jay was intriguing against him, an unlikely tale to which he gave little credence. He was aware of some disaffection for him within his own party and he knew that he had made enemies among both the pro-British and pro-French elements.[8]

After nearly six months at home, Adams left Peacefield for the capital in early December. Depressed at the prospect of another separation from his wife, a wet and cold Philadelphia hardly cheered him, especially when all the gossip that reached his ears revolved about Jefferson's certain victory. As usual, Adams postured that he could care less, claiming that he was "perfectly willing to be released" from the cares of public service. But his correspondence from this period bears the imprint of an unmistakable gloominess, even of anger. He dreaded the humiliation of defeat. Nor did the prospect of retirement or of living the life of a farmer hold much allurement; the resumption of his legal practice, something he had left behind more than twenty years earlier, was equally unattractive. As the campaign progressed, moreover, he grew bitter at the defection of old friends. That James and Mercy Warren had not supported him was to be expected, but he was deeply pained to learn that Samuel Adams, once again the governor of Massachusetts, and Benjamin Rush had favored Jefferson. As the day of decision neared, he spoke of the indignity of losing to Jefferson, whom he regarded as his inferior; it would be mortifying to lose to Pinckney, however, for he thought of him as a nobody. Adams continued to insist that he would resign if he was reelected to the vice-presidency, and once, while in a particularly black mood, he even said he would not serve if the issue had to be settled by the House of Representative.[9]

The presidential electors met in their respective capitals about one week after Adams returned to Philadelphia. While their ballots remained sealed until February 8, it was impossible to prevent reasonably accurate word of their transactions from leaking out. By the third week in December it was agreed that Jefferson could not win. It was not clear, however, whether Adams or Pinckney would triumph, or whether the issue would be left to the House of Representatives. Over the next few days, more definitive word arrived. It seemed clear that Adams had been elected. At Washington's final levee of the year, the First Lady warmly congratulated Adams, and told him of the president's delight at his victory. Soon foreign diplomats began to call on the vice-president, a sure sign that they believed he would be Washington's successor. But Adams did not admit what everyone else had been saying until the next to the last day of the year. He broke the news to Abigail in a radiant letter that contrasted sharply with those he had penned during the past month. "John Adams," he wrote of himself in that missive, "never felt more serene in his life."[10]

When the official tabulation was announced in February—ironically it was Adams, in his capacity as president of the Senate, who opened and read the

results of the Electoral College voting—it was learned that Adams had garnered seventy-one votes to Jefferson's sixty-eight. Pinckney finished in third
place. As almost everyone had expected, Adams received every vote from New
England, while Jefferson controlled the South, capturing fifty-four of that
region's votes to Adams's nine. Nevertheless, Adams won the election in the
southern and middle states. Jefferson lost Maryland to Adams, and the vice-
president secured one crucial vote in both Virginia and North Carolina; moreover, Jefferson did not receive a single electoral vote from New York, New
Jersey, and Delaware. Pinckney won two more votes than Adams in the
middle and southern states, but he received eighteen fewer votes than the vice-
president from the New England states. Clearly, some New England electors
had conspired to reduce Pinckney's strength, in the process depriving him of
the vice-presidency. Had he received only a majority of the second ballots cast
by New England's electors, he would have been elected vice-president; had he
received three-fourths of New England's second-choice votes, he would have
been the second president of the United States—and John Adams again would
have been elected to the vice-presidency.[11]

Several factors contributed to Adams's victory. The country relished the
peace and prosperity that had accompanied Washington's presidency. In addition, after eight years of southern rule, many in the North must have felt that it
was their turn to control the executive branch. Furthermore, Adams believed
that he had secured two or three southern votes that Pinckney might have won
simply because "Hamilton and Jay are said to be for" the South Carolinian. A
strong Federalist organization, especially in the burgeoning urban, mercantile
centers, also aided Adams. Nor can the role of the French envoy be discounted.
Adams spoke of the existence of three parties in the race, an English party, a
French party, and an American party. It was to the Francophiles that Pierre
Adet, minister to the United States since early in 1795, appealed when he
unwisely campaigned openly for Jefferson. Both Hamilton and Madison believed that his actions hurt the Virginian's candidacy. Still, Jefferson could
have carried the election had he won the two pivotal electoral votes that Adams
secured in Virginia and North Carolina. The Republicans carried both states
by overwhelming margins, but Adams won the Loudoun-Fauquier district in
Virginia, western counties that long had exhibited hostility to the hegemony of
the planter aristocracy. Adams's one source of strength in North Carolina was
in the commercial region along the coast, an area with historic mercantile ties
to England. Had Jefferson won those two southern electoral districts, he
would have defeated Adams seventy to sixty-nine.[12]

During the long, damp, winter weeks while he awaited his plunge into the
"treacherous" waters of the presidency, Adams learned through intermediaries
that Jefferson was delighted to serve under him, thus easing his mind about the
prospect of a president and vice-president from different parties. Utilizing

Elbridge Gerry as a conduit, Adams let it be known that he bore no hard feelings toward Jefferson, whom he referred to as a man of "good Sense, and general good dispositions." Adams acted in order to reduce party strife, but his feelings were unfeigned. "His talents . . . I know very well," Adams remarked to a friend, "and have ever believed in his honour, Integrity, his Love of Country and his friends." Adams's victory made his magnanimity much easier, as did his belief that the excesses of the French Revolution had proven him right and Jefferson wrong in the episode that had produced their estrangement—the Virginian's critical remarks about Adams's political theory.[13]

Adams once remarked that he was a poor politician, for he was "unpractised in intrigues for power." His ineptness was never more apparent than in his first presidential decision. He asked Washington's department heads—men whose loyalties lay elsewhere—to remain in his cabinet. It was a decision he eventually described as his greatest mistake, a blunder that, in his estimation, resulted in the ultimate destruction of his presidency. Later, he claimed that he had complied with Washington's request that he retain these men, fearing that to do otherwise would "turn the World upside down." At the time, however, he seems to have been unaware of the dangers of such an act. But others understood. The "Hamiltonians who surround him," Jefferson soon remarked, "are only a little less hostile to him than to me."[14]

Timothy Pickering of Massachusetts, who was to be his secretary of state, was certain to hold the key post in his cabinet. Although from the same state, Adams and Pickering had never been close. Ten years younger than Adams, Pickering had soldiered and served as quartermaster general while his counterpart was in Congress, then in Europe. After the war, Pickering, lacking a fortune or an alternative income, dabbled in business and real estate, then turned to the federal bureaucracy for a livelihood. In 1791 Washington named him postmaster general of the United States; subsequently, he became the nation's principal diplomat in negotiations with the Indians. In 1794, he was selected—after three others had declined the offer—to succeed Henry Knox as secretary of war, and a few months later, when a vacancy arose, he was made acting secretary of state, a post he continued to occupy during the final year and a half of Washington's administration. Tall, slender, shy and reserved, severe in appearance, and, like Adams, dour, acerbic, and querulous, he was at least his own man and not a tool of Hamilton as his foes later alleged.[15]

Nor was the attorney-general, Charles Lee, under Hamilton's thumb. The brother of Henry Lee, Washington's dashing cavalry commander, he had been elevated from the Virginia House of Burgesses to the cabinet in 1795. Washington had seen him as talented, loyal, and trustworthy, which he was; he also thought him deserving, for he had faithfully managed Federalist affairs in Republican Virginia.[16]

War and Treasury were in the hands of men who took their marching orders from Hamilton. James McHenry, who had been a surgeon before he became a wartime aide to General Washington, succeeded Pinckney as secretary of war in 1795, although the president, who knew him well, unsuccessfully offered the post to four others before he approached this Maryland Federalist. Steadfastly loyal to Washington, McHenry had served as a delegate to the Constitutional Convention, and he had worked diligently for the document's ratification; after 1791 he was among the Senate's strongest supporters of the Washington-Hamilton program. Under Washington, McHenry faced nothing more demanding than the administration of a peacetime Department of War, yet the president soon concluded that his secretary lacked the competence even for that undertaking.[17]

Oliver Wolcott, Jr., the treasury secretary was the most compliant of the four, having fallen under Hamilton's sway in 1789 when he joined the new national government as auditor of the treasury. Hamilton thereafter diligently assisted in the elevation of his protégé. He eased Wolcott into the office of United States controller in 1791, then he persuaded Washington to bring him into the cabinet in 1795. Affable and gentle in appearance, cultivated and courteous in manner, Wolcott's darker side included a penchant for scheming, a compelling urge to do whatever had to be done to get ahead—and to see that in course of things the Federalist's and Hamilton's interests were served.[18]

With the cabinet selected, Adams had only to await the inaugural ceremony. At times it seemed the day would never arrive. February, which always seems to dawdle along as an interminable barrier to the advent of spring, passed even more slowly in 1797, its gray monotony broken only be a series of parties and balls for the outgoing president, its cheerless demeanor punctured only by the euphoria that Adams experienced as a result of the deference that everyone now paid him.

Sleep was difficult for Adams on the night before his inauguration, and the next morning he found himself gripped by terrible anxiety as he waited for the last hours to pass before the ceremony. He longed for Abigail's presence, but she was in Quincy. Jefferson had called on him the previous afternoon, and friends in the Massachusetts congressional delegation probably paid their respects that morning, but he was visibly nervous as he boarded his new carriage—his first purchase with his $25,000 annual salary as President, a conveyance that cost $1,500—for the short ride to the Capitol. Dressed elegantly in a pearl suit, his hair well powdered and a sword strapped to his side, he was attended by servants outfitted in livery, which he had also purchased. He arrived at the Capitol just before noon and was escorted into the House chamber. Jefferson, who had taken his oath before the Senate two hours earlier, was seated before the Congress and galleries. Adams took a seat beside him. A minute or two later Washington was announced. He entered the hall in the rear, dressed in his usual black suit and accompanied by a retinue of servants, staff, and officials. Adams later told his wife that he felt faint and feared that he might not make it through the rites, but as the ceremony progressed his confidence grew, even though Washington's manner appeared to him to say: "Ay! I am fairly out and you fairly in! See which of us will be happiest."[19]

It was an emotional ceremony, not because of Adams's victory, but because of the pending departure of Washington, homeward bound after years of public service. It was, as everyone knew, the end of an era, a realization that made each person in the House chamber feel older and terribly mortal. There was something else that struck each spectator. The inauguration of Adams represented a peaceful transfer of power, a triumph of republicanism. It was "a novelty" in human affairs, Adams observed later, this "sight of the sun setting full-orbit, and another rising (though less splendid)." Many in the audience were moved to tears before these proceedings closed.[20]

The ceremony moved quickly to a conclusion. After Washington was seated, Adams was introduced and delivered a brief address in which he obviously sought to counter the popular suspicion about his sentiments. He traced the history of the American Revolution to the establishment of the "present happy constitution," a government well adapted to the American character, especially insofar as it rested on the consent of the governed and provided for only short terms of office. The greatest danger to the Union, he warned, stemmed from foreign powers. Their menace was not a military threat, but rather the danger that they might so influence the populace that the new nation would lose its independence. He would work to expand education and religion, and to ameliorate the condition of the native Americans, but his principal object, he said, would be to preserve the neutrality of the United States. If he succeeded, the people would remain united and "the spirit of party, the spirit of intrigue, the profligacy of corruption, and the pestilence of foreign influence" might be eradicated. Curiously, Adams did not take the oath of office until he completed the speech.[21]

After a round of bows and congratulations, President Adams led a procession of dignitaries from the House chamber. He returned to his lodgings at the Francis Hotel, where he would continue to live for the remainder of the week while the Washingtons slowly vacated the President's House. A steady stream of visitors called on him that first afternoon, most to wish him well, a few to laud his speech; one or two men with whom he was close hurried by with word that some Federalists were carping that the address had been too conciliatory toward the Republicans. Washington visited Adams later that afternoon and again toward the end of the week, and one evening in mid-week he and his wife were hosts at a dinner in honor of the new president and vice-president. Washington's visits to the Francis Hotel were principally social calls, although some business was transacted. Washington had purchased all the furnishings for the President's House from his salary as chief executive. Not wishing to bear the expense of transporting unwanted household goods back to Mount Vernon, he sought to interest Adams in the furniture. Adams did acquire some of the wares, but he declined to buy two horses that Washington also hoped to sell. Adams later intimated that the former president had sought to gouge him, and he may have been correct; Washington confided to a friend that the horses were older than he had represented them as being.[22]

Just at sunrise on March 9, a bitterly cold and windy day, Washington and his family stole out of the capital without ceremony. Shortly thereafter Adams moved into the President's House, a dwelling that he had to rent for $225 a month. The house had once belonged to Robert Morris, a Philadelphia businessman and head of the national Treasury during the last, dark years of the war; before that the mansion had been the residence of Gen. William Howe during the British occupation of Philadelphia in 1777–78. It was a wide, three-story brick structure, though two dormers facing the street announced the presence of a large fourth-floor attic. Inside, the dwelling boasted the finest mantels and moldings to be found in Philadelphia, an entrance hall outfitted with columns, arches, and pilasters, and rooms and staircases finished in rich West Indian mahogany. The house sat only a few feet from its neighbor on the east, while to the west a generous, lovely garden lay ensconced behind a five-foot-high brick wall. A kitchen, wash house, smoke house, and stables were in the rear, as was a small abode that Washington had built to house the slaves he fetched from Mount Vernon. Despite its elegance, however, Adams was shocked to find that the mansion had not been properly cleaned following the Washingtons' departure and that the former president's servants, in a drunken stupor, perhaps at the prospect of returning to a life of hard labor at their master's Potomac estate, had damaged some of his new furnishings. In addition, Adams found that several rooms had been illogically carved into small, useless chambers. While he settled into a portion of the capacious house, therefore, he ordered that minor renovation be undertaken in other wings.[23]

Settled at last, Adams turned his full attention to his duties. Matters of foreign policy immediately required almost every minute he could spare from the press of job seekers. In fact, throughout his administration grave diplomatic concerns would constitute the most difficult and chronic problem he faced. This came as no surprise to Adams. Weeks before he took office he told Abigail he would be compelled to deal with "the open assaults of France and the secret plots of England," challenges that he viewed as nothing less than threats to the very independence of the United States.[24]

Some of the nation's problems were old. Great Britain, for instance, still refused to open its ports to American shipping, the concession that Adams had sought in the course of his embassy to London more than a decade earlier. On the other hand, some old problems appeared to have been resolved, although not as satisfactorily as many people believed at the time of Adams's inauguration. For instance, the resolution of two matters that had divided Spain and the United States since the end of the War of Independence appeared to have been secured through the Treaty of San Lorenzo, negotiated late in Washington's administration by Thomas Pinckney, Adams's eventual running mate in 1796. In the treaty, Spain acceded to the administration's demands concerning the boundary between the United States and Spanish Florida; in addition, the government in Madrid granted the United States both the right of navigation on the Mississippi River and the right of deposit, or storage, at New Orleans. But while these difficult issues appeared to have been solved, Adams did not lack for troubles. His adversities stemmed largely from the vicissitudes of the French Revolution and the wars it spawned.

The European conflict that began in April 1792 had widened early the following year when France declared war on Great Britain. President Washington had immediately proclaimed the neutrality of the United States, but his policy did not stanch the popular passions unleashed by the war and the sweeping republicanization of French society. Lingering anti-British sentiment and the residual feelings of gratitude for the American Revolutionary services of French soldiers contributed to a churning pro-French attitude that swept much of the country. But that was not all. The issues raised by the sansculottes in France, as well as the deeply rooted social bitterness within America—first evidenced in Shays's Rebellion, then rekindled by the taxation policies of the Washington-Hamilton administration—led to the crystallization of a movement for domestic change. Eleven democratic-republican societies sprang up in 1793 and twenty-four more had been founded the next year. Modeled on the Jacobin Clubs of Revolutionary France and the Sons of Liberty of Revolutionary America, these societies were openly pro-French and anti-British. They scorned American neutrality, for in the victory of France's revolutionary armies they saw the triumph of what they sought: the beginning of the era in which rulers would be responsible to the needs of the ruled. Thus, French victories were hailed and celebrated, and for a time many American nationals had taken to calling one another "citizen" and "citess." Some even had worn the tricolored cockade made popular in revolutionary France. When Republican France's first minister to the United States, Edmond Genêt, the son of Adams's friend in Paris, arrived in Philadelphia during the summer of 1794, he was feted at banquets and serenaded with stirring renditions of the "Marseillaise."[25]

While Washington had endeavored to remain neutral, France remembered that it still was an ally of the United States under the terms of the Treaty of Alliance of 1778. It had sent Genêt to secure money, provisions, and military stores from the United States, the very sort of assistance called for by the military pact, although, for the most part, Paris had merely wished that the United States would abide by the Treaty of Commerce of 1778. According to that agreement, French warships and the prizes they captured were to be admitted to American ports. Washington was not amenable. He had advanced a considerable sum to Paris in 1793 as an advance on the debt owed to France, but he discontinued the payments with Britain's entrance into the war, and he declared that American neutrality would be compromised if he permitted French prizes to enter United States seaports. Intemperately, Genêt had sought to appeal over Washington's head to the people of America. Chanting crowds poured into the streets of the capital in 1794. At the time, Adams thought these protestors were terrorists, and later, as an octogenarian, he harbored the fanciful recollection of mobs that "threatened to drag Washington out of his house."[26]

Genêt's work was made easier by British policy. In June 1793, Britain announced a blockade of the French coast; that autumn the government of William Pitt the Younger promulgated an order-in-council that authorized the capture of all neutral vessels carrying goods to and from French possessions in the West Indies. Applying the "Rule of 1756," Pitt asserted that trade that had not occurred in peacetime would not be tolerated in wartime. By the next spring some of the smaller French islands were in British hands. So were approximately 250 American vessels, seized by the British navy on the translucent blue-green waters of the Caribbean.[27]

War fever gripped the land. Congress huffed and puffed from the time it met in December 1793 until the following spring, but few in authority wanted another war with Britain. Washington least of all had spoiled for a fight, and in the spring he announced that he was dispatching John Jay to London. As an envoy extraordinary, Jay was to seek to open British ports to American ships and to resolve the differences aroused by the French war. Seizing the white-hot passion of the moment, the Republicans struck to push for the passage of an American navigation act. Their bill passed the House of Representatives, but it failed in the Senate when Vice-President Adams—once a supporter of such legislation—broke a tie with a negative vote. Adams now believed that a retaliatory measure would further strain relations with Britain and drive America into the arms of the French.[28]

While the populace awaited word of the success—or failure—of Jay's mission, the national hysteria abated. A year elapsed before the long-awaited packets from the faraway envoy finally arrived. Their contents refired emotions to a fever pitch. The Jay Treaty had secured few concessions from Whitehall. Britain agreed to remove its troops from American soil by June 1796. In return, the United States had pledged not to impose discriminatory duties on Great Britain; Jay additionally conceded the right of Britain and its Indian allies to trap and trade on the rivers of the Northwest Territory, and he promised to settle the prewar claims of British creditors in America. The pact said nothing about the British practice of impressment, the habit of seizing crewmen from American ships and pressing them into the Royal Navy, nor did it address the matter of the slaves carried away by the British army during the War of Independence. Moreover, London declined to acquiesce in America's long-standing demand that English ports be opened to its commerce, save for the opening of West Indian commerce to American vessels of under seventy tons. By implication, too, Jay appeared to have assented to the "Rule of 1756." The treaty had secured little, except the prospect of peace with Great Britain. Washington clutched at that possibility rather than take the fragile new nation into still another war. He sent Jay's Treaty to the Senate for ratification, and he threw his awesome prestige behind the accord.[29]

In June 1795, Washington had called the Senate into special session to consider the treaty, causing Adams, who had been home for only a few weeks, to return to the capital. What followed was one of the most rancorous sessions in Senate history, although after thirteen days of angry debate, the Federalists mustered the necessary two-thirds vote to ratify the treaty. Only Article 12, the section that would have limited America's trade in the British West Indies to its smallest vessels, was omitted. Adams had played no role in the deliberations— it would "be less distressing or rather less insipid, if my presence here was more necessary," he had remarked at the time—but he, like Washington, had supported a flawed treaty in preference to the possibility of a disastrous war. He also had met privately with Jay during the session and emerged convinced that the envoy had secured as much as possible from the British government.[30]

Relations with France had deteriorated since the failure of the Genêt mission, but they plummeted to new depths when the United States accepted the Jay Treaty. By Washington's final year in office, Paris had come to see his administration as a puppet whose strings were pulled in London and in America's pro-British mercantile centers. In response, the Directory, France's latest government in its raging, relentless Revolution, issued a decree on July 4, 1796—it was hardly coincidental that the day marked the twentieth anniversary of American independence—that announced its intention of dealing with neutral vessels in the same manner as London treated such vessels. The move amounted to a repudiation of the Franco-American commercial and military alliance. French vessels soon began to seize American ships whose cargo holds bulged with contraband.[31]

Concerned by the action of France, Washington had not, however, been alarmed. At about the same moment that the Directory had acted, Washington had dispatched a new minister to France. Charles Cotesworth Pinckney was his choice to replace James Monroe, whose open Republican sympathies had offended many Federalists. President Washington was confident that he could work the same magic in France that his brother, Thomas Pinckey, had performed in Madrid, a view bolstered by his belief that Monroe's failure to forestall French animosity was due to personal shortcomings.[32]

If Washington had not initially reacted with apprehension at the Directory's new policy, he soon grew more concerned as mounting reports reached his desk of repeated French depredations on the high seas. About thirty days before Adams took office, Secretary of State Pickering catalogued these incidents, a long list of marauding that included the plunder of American property and the wounding—even the alleged torture—of the United States seamen. The mission of Ambassador Pinckney suddenly took on greater importance. Indeed, in the last few days before his inauguration, the president-elect was besieged with entreaties by spokesmen from both parties to send a special envoy or an extraordinary commission to Paris to seek a negotiated settlement with the Directory, just as Washington had sent Jay to London in 1794. Hamilton was one of those who favored such a mission, and he communicated his advocacy of the notion both to friends of Adams and to Washington, hoping that someone would urge the step upon the incoming chief executive.[33]

In fact, Adams had already begun to consider the idea of dispatching an emissary to Paris. The new president's foreign policy outlook was virtually identical to that of his predecessor. In Adams's opinion the expansion of United States commerce was the linchpin upon which the well-being of the United States rested. A thriving trade, he believed, would introduce sufficient capital to augment the country's manufacturing capability. In addition, the wealth derived from a flourishing trade would advance American vigor and strength. Ultimately, therefore, commerce would be the engine that could procure not only true United States independence but also the establishment of an American empire so vast and powerful that both Great Britain and France would be beholden to it. Adams did not expect to see this in his lifetime, but, like Washington, he understood that a misstep at the beginning of the national adventure could delay—even thwart—the realization of an American empire. A war at this point could be fatal, for it might result in the loss of American territory or, more likely, it could so divide the American people that the fledgling union would disintegrate. He also feared the "many bellied Monster of an Army" necessary for war, a force that might ultimately "tyrannize" the country more effectually than any foreign power. During his vice-presidency, Adams had supported Washington's neutrality, and he had castigated as "Knavish" every attempt to push the president into war. Thus, where Washington had been willing to appease British commercial interests in order to maintain peace, Adams was willing to placate France in order to avoid war.[34]

Adams's views were not new. Since the Treaty of Paris he had consistently sought a pacific resolution of America's problems, whether the antagonist was England, France, or the Algerine pirates, and during the Washington administration he had supported the president's policy of neutrality with regard to Europe's deadly conflagration. He could no more understand his countrymen's urging the United States to take sides in Europe's wars than he had been able to fathom Franklin's flippant remark that America should join France in still more wars with England.

To a remarkable degree for a person who had come of age in the anti-French environment of preRevolutionary New England, Adams had overcome much of his anti-Gallic prejudice. He disapproved of Roman Catholicism and abhorred the radicalism of the French Revolution, but he viewed France as indistinguishable from other nations. France was neither inherently more friendly nor more hostile to the United States than was Great Britain, he long ago had concluded. As with any nation state, France simply reached policy decisions based on what it determined to be in its own best interest. The United States must act similarly, and in Adams's estimation that meant an adherence to a policy of neutrality. He stated repeatedly that he did not desire war with France; he could not have been more truthful. "I am not Scared" of war, he protested shortly before his presidency began, but he promised that under his stewardship the United States would go to war only if hostilities were forced upon it. He prayed, therefore, that the French would not push America "beyond [its] bearing."[35]

By the time he took office, Adams had decided to nominate a plenipotentiary who might resolve the differences with France. Two days before the inaugural ceremony, Jefferson called on the president-elect, the first time the two men had met in more than three years. The following afternoon they met again, this time in the vice-president's apartment. At one of the meetings, probably the first, Adams proposed that Jefferson journey to Paris as an envoy extraordinary.[36]

Adams may have simply hoped to put his vice-president to better use than Washington had seen fit. More likely, he sincerely believed that Jefferson, who was admired, even widely loved, in revolutionary France, was more apt to succeed than any other individual. In fact, any accord that Jefferson brought home—even a poor one—would certainly garner sufficient support to give Adams the justification he required to avoid war. Conversely, if Jefferson failed to restore amity with the French, Adams's hand would be strengthened should the day arrive when he would have to ask Congress to declare war on France.

However, Jefferson refused Adams's offer, evidently arguing that it would be improper for the vice-president to submit to a protracted absence from the United States, and adding that he was too "sick of residing in Europe" to contemplate such an enterprise. Adams acquiesced in good humor, then sounded out his vice-president's views regarding the candidacy of Madison for such a mission, adding that he would like to name the Virginian and Elbridge Gerry, both Republicans, to accompany Ambassador Pinckney, a Federalist, to Paris. Jefferson was noncommittal, but three days later, as the two men strolled down a dark Philadelphia street following dinner with the Washingtons at the President's House, he reported that Madison would refuse such an assignment. By then Adams already knew that the Virginian's embassy was out of the question. When he broached the idea with his treasury secretary on the day of his inauguration, Wolcott had vehemently protested that only Federalists be sent on the mission to Paris. Wolcott even threatened to lead a mass resignation of the cabinet if Adams went through with his plan. Adams submitted to Wolcott's wishes.[37]

Dire tidings from abroad soon raised the question of the propriety of sending any commissioner to Paris. Sometime during his initial ten days in office
Adams learned that the Directory not only had refused to accept Pinckney as
Monroe's replacement, it had ordered the envoy from the country. The same
courier who brought that ominous news also bore word of the further seizure
of American vessels in the Caribbean. Furthermore, a few weeks later Adams
learned that the Directory had issued a decree on March 2 abrogating the
Franco-American treaties of 1778 and ordering the seizure of neutral vessels
transporting British goods.

The Directory obviously viewed the Jay Treaty not only as a violation of its
accords with the United States but also as a virtual declaration of war against
France. Some quick-tempered officials favored an open war with America in
retaliation for the pact with London. Others—a majority, perhaps—thought
differently. Attacks on American vessels laden with British goods, they reasoned, probably could be undertaken short of an actual declaration of war, and
such a policy could lead to favorable results. The commodities seized on
American ships could be sold in France, yielding tax revenues for a desperate,
nearly bankrupt nation; in addition, the struggle waged on the high seas
would deny Great Britain the benefit of the American merchant marine. One
other benefit to France might result from a belligerent policy. Federalist rule in
the United States might be ended. French officials were convinced that the
United States government did not represent the views of the American people.
French agents and envoys in America often nourished such a notion, although
Jefferson's troublesome "Mazzei Letter"—the missive whose publication in
1796 had strained Adams's feeling for his old friend—might have been even
more influential in shaping the Directory's understanding of American politics. In this private letter to an old friend, the Florentine Philip Mazzei—
whose first wife was buried at Monticello—Jefferson had insisted that while
"the main body of our citizens" remained committed to republicanism, "an
Anglican monarchical, & aristocratical party" had somehow gained control of
the American government. Some in Paris believed that the right pressure—
the threat of war with the old French ally, perhaps—would cause the overthrow of Federalism when Americans next went to the polls.[38]

The French action required an immediate response by President Adams.
Several options were available to him. He could still send an emissary as he had
planned. He might sever all trade with France. He might arm American
merchantmen. He could license privateers to prey on French shipping. He
could commence preparations for war. He might even opt for war. Or, some
combination of these alternatives might be pursued. Adams pondered the
matter for a few days, then he decided on still another course. He sought to buy
time. The president called a cabinet meeting for March 14, then he summoned
Congress to a special session sixty days later, on May 15. He would have two
months in which to reflect and decide on his most appropriate course.

His first step was the cabinet meeting, a session that Adams viewed as a means of debating options rather than making a final decision. In the course of the meeting, he informed his advisors that he still favored dispatching a commission of emissaries to Paris, but he asked whether such a step would be "too great an humiliation" to undertake. Once again he stressed that he was not afraid to go to war and he reiterated his preference for hostilities to "Iniquity or . . . disgrace." Few presidents have had to make such momentous decisions so soon after taking office. Holding this post, he soon realized, was "not a Sinecure." "It is an office of hard labor and Severe duty," he remarked after only a few days on the job.[39]

Whatever counsel the cabinet officials immediately provided, each member, save for Attorney-General Lee, contacted Hamilton in New York to partake of his wisdom before Congress assembled. The advice offered by the former Treasury secretary was extraordinary. He spoke of the "President's Administration" and the "*actual* administration," indicating that in this crisis it was crucial that Pickering, McHenry, and Wolcott convince the public that they, like Adams, sincerely sought to avoid war. He did not believe a special commission could be avoided, and, indeed, such a mission would be useful, for if France rejected it—and he seems to have guessed that the French would rebuff every American emissary—no one could question a decision to resort to war. He must have startled Wolcott by acknowledging his preference for Jefferson or Madison, or some other members of the opposition party, to be among the envoys, for if the diplomats were doomed to failure, he preferred that a Republican team bear responsibility.[40]

Adams had no idea that his advisors had, like automatons, immediately confided in Hamilton. In fact, he was delighted at the outcome of this early cabinet session, concluding that each man had shared his interest in peace. Most Federalists, he concluded in the first weeks of his administration, genuinely hoped to avoid a struggle with France. Only a small faction of reactionary New England Federalists, a circle that would later be called the Essex Junto, seemed bent on war, but Adams dismissed them as Tories unlikely to generate a large following. Confident that all was proceeding well, he instructed Pickering to draft instructions for the diplomats who would be sent to France.[41]

Meanwhile, Adams sought to convince the French of his pacific intentions. "I am more their Friend than they are aware of," he told Abigail, and in a long meeting with Citizen Adet, the outgoing French ambassador, Adams sought to persuade him of his desire for peace. He succeeded with that envoy, but other French diplomats in America disagreed with Adet's assessment. Joseph Philippe Letombe, the French consul in Philadelphia, informed the foreign ministry that Adams was the same suspicious, obstinate, Francophobe that Vergennes had dealt with nearly twenty years before. According to Joel Barlow, a Connecticut poet who had resided in Paris since the 1780s and who had solid contacts within the revolutionary government, many officials in Paris looked upon Adams not just as a royalist but as a man who long had borne nothing but enmity for France. Barlow's assessment may have been accurate, but within the foreign ministry a different view was emerging. Shortly after Adams's inauguration, the new French Foreign Minister, Charles M. de Talleyrand-Périgord, directed six envoys to submit appraisals of the new American chief executive. Five of the six reports concluded that Adams sincerely wished a rapprochement with France. The envoys believed that the American people were more sympathetic toward France than was the Federalist government, a view that Talleyrand, who had lived in the United States from 1794 to 1796, already harbored.[42]

As the date grew near for the special session of Congress, Adams continued to receive advice from his cabinet, much of it from Hamilton, though it was camouflaged in letters penned by the former official's puppets, Pickering and McHenry. Adams was advised to abandon his plan to placate France. Instead, he was urged to press the Directory for compensation for the property losses its merchants had suffered at French hands in the Caribbean. Hamilton's satraps also urged Adams to commence defensive preparations, including the augmentation of the navy and, at the very least, the creation of corps of artillery and cavalry. Much of what Pickering and McHenry passed on to Adams was copied verbatim from Hamilton's instructions.[43]

By the second week in May, congressmen from every corner of the nation had descended on Philadelphia, as if drawn by some gigantic magnet. With winter having departed and the miasmic summer months still ahead, with the flowers and shrubs and trees yet aglow with spring's temperate beauty, the city radiated a lush, balmy charm. But many congressmen were in a bilious mood, some upset at having been wrenched from home, while others, including every Republican, feared that the special session could only signify that President Adams planned to ask for a declaration of war against France.[44]

Adams did not go that far. At noon on the second day of the special session, he appeared before Congress to read his address. The congressmen greeted him politely, then listened in solemn silence as he delivered a brief, strident message. He expressed outrage at France's treatment of Ambassador Pinckney, characterizing the action as an attempt to produce "fatal divisions" among the American people. He also denounced French depredations in the Caribbean. Showing his pugnacious side, he insisted that the United States must defend its neutrality, and in this vein he urged Congress not only to expand the American navy and assist in arming merchant vessels but also to modernize the militia. Having made the point that he would not permit the further humiliation of the United States, he reached the key element in the address. Adams insisted on "a fresh attempt at negotiation," this to be undertaken through the dispatch of a team of emissaries.[45]

Federalists generally applauded the address, while Republicans blasted the president's course as certain to lead to war. Madison, for instance, soon referred to Adams as "our hot-headed Executive," and, indeed, the president's remarks were far more bellicose than were the assurances he had given in private to Ambassador Adet. But when Adams first divulged the names of the three commissioners whom he proposed to send to France, it was his own party that howled the loudest. A few days after his speech, Adams convened his cabinet to announce his decision to name Charles Pinckney, who was still in Europe, together with John Marshall, a Federalist judge from Virginia, and his old friend Elbridge Gerry. The cabinet exploded at the inclusion of Gerry. He was not a Federalist—though he had come out of retirement to become an elector in 1796 and cast a crucial ballot for John Adams—and he had been an opponent of the ratification of the Constitution.

The cabinet's visceral response could not have come as much of a surprise to the president. He might even have suggested Gerry just to see whom they would propose as an alternative. Wolcott suggested Rufus King, a former senator from New York and a close friend of Hamilton, as an alternative; he even proposed that John Quincy Adams be considered in lieu of Gerry. Once again, Adams took a placatory stance, backing off from his original plan. But instead of King or his son (whom he shortly named as minister to Prussia, transferring him from a less important post in Lisbon), he appointed Francis Dana of Massachusetts, a veteran diplomat—it was Dana whom the fourteen-year-old John Quincy had accompanied to Russia in 1781—and, like Marshall, a Federalist judge. Adams submitted the names to the Senate at the end of May, only to learn a few days later that Dana's poor health had made it impossible for him to serve. Without again consulting the cabinet, the president sent Gerry's name to the Senate. He was desperate to place on the commission a man in whom he had the utmost confidence. Gerry, he said, was one of the "two most impartial men" in America; Adams regarded himself as the other unbiased individual. Adams's obstinacy also showed through in this matter. He latter recalled that he had nominated Gerry because he refused to be a "slave" to his cabinet.[46]

More quietly, the cabinet approved guidelines for the envoys. The key to a rapprochement, Adams believed, was the negotiation of a new treaty giving France the same commercial rights as had been extended to Great Britain in the Jay Treaty. Otherwise, the United States insisted upon the right as a neutral to trade with whomever it pleased, and the diplomats were told categorically that America would extend neither aid nor loans to France so long as it was at war, for such steps almost certainly would drag the United States into the conflict.[47]

The divisions created by Adams's policy—no president, no policy could have unified opinion—soon were apparent. In fact, the first mention of the word "secession" occurred in the tempestuous congressional debate that followed the president's speech. In this instance a western spokesman advised New England to leave the Union and construct its own fleet, if it must have one, but not to ask the nation's farmers to pay for the navy. Nevertheless, Congress agreed to a bill strengthening the navy, although the fleet would not be as strong as Adams and the Federalists had hoped. The Republicans also defeated Federalist legislation that would have created an army of fifteen thousand, a far larger force than Adams had ever urged. Congress did sanction the three envoys whom the president had nominated, however. By the second week in July, two months after having been gaveled into session to listen to Adams, Congress adjourned. The president remained in the capital only long enough to meet with Marshall, who paid his respects and dined one evening with Adams just before sailing for France. Soon thereafter Adams departed. "I never could bear a city in the summer in the best seasons," he once remarked most sensibly, although in this instance he hurried to escape the capital before yellow fever, an almost annual summertime visitor, once again plagued the city. He was just as anxious to get back to Peacefield, which he had not seen for nearly eight months.[48]

Abigail accompanied her husband to Quincy, having abandoned past habits and come to the capital to serve as First Lady. He had continued pleading with her to come, eventually convincing her not to wait until the fall, as she initially had planned. However, she had remained at home until she found tenants for the farm and until the last of winter's icy gales had been stilled. Arriving in Philadelphia five days before Adams addressed the special session of Congress, Abigail quickly discovered that her presence did not mean seeing her husband frequently. He remained in his office throughout the day, though it made little difference, for she faced a frenetic schedule, supervising a large staff, procuring a long list of New England delicacies (cider, white potatoes, cranberries, hams, casks of tongue) that John wished to have in the pantry, receiving a steady stream of visitors for two or three hours each afternoon, hosting small dinners and well as state banquets, and two or three times each week holding levees for the public and invited guests. On a typical day she and John breakfasted together at eight and sometimes shared dinner at three. Only in the evenings, and then only for two or three hours at most, were they alone.

Abigail had been deeply depressed when she arrived in the city. En route she had spent two weeks with Nabby. Isolated in remote East Chester, Nabby had been all but abandoned by her husband, who was off on a business venture or was simply hiding from creditors—she was not quite sure which. She was terribly unhappy. Her marriage appeared to be in tatters, all her aspirations foiled by her husband's irresponsible behavior. She spoke forlornly of her seclusion and helplessness. Divorce, exceedingly rare in the eighteenth century, was a subject mother and daughter explored during that visit.

In a mood of black despair, Abigail quickly grew to detest the "splendid misery" of the presidency, imprisoned by her relentless duties and confined to "Bake House" Philadelphia, as she described the city during the first weeks of summer. More anxious than ever to return to the rural tranquillity of Quincy and to walk among her canicular flowers and delight in the balmy fragrances of a New England summer, she wheedled her husband to forsake the capital for several weeks at Peacefield, often counseling that a holiday was imperative for his health. Adams needed little persuasion.[49]

Traveling over the flat, dusty littoral that linked the capital to New York, the family sped by carriage to Nabby's residence, where the grandchildren were gathered. Then it was on to Quincy for a summer vacation. President Washington had usually returned each year to Mount Vernon for a few weeks of rest. Although some of Adams's cabinet thought it unwise of him to go in the midst of the French crisis, this was another of Washington's precedents that he was happy to observe.[50]

CHAPTER 17

*

War Is Inexpedient

PRESIDENT ADAMS REMAINED AT HOME for four months, twice as long as Washington had ever stayed away from the capital. But there was not much work to be done in Philadelphia. Since the terrible yellow fever epidemic of 1793, most government officials fled the city during the summer months; this year, as for the past five years, work would proceed at a snail's pace until Congress reconvened in December.

Adams and his wife found Quincy a delightfully restful escape from the turmoil and stress of the President's House. Not only was New England's customarily mild summer a welcome alternative to the heat and humidity of the Delaware Valley, but both had the opportunity to see several friends, John remaining at home to receive his acquaintances, while Abigail rode to Braintree, Hingham, and Weymouth to visit old companions. The president left Peacefield only once during this stay. In mid-August he was the guest of honor at a dinner organized by the elite of Boston. Best of all, perhaps, the Adamses enjoyed the rare opportunity to spend weeks with Nabby, as she and her children accompanied them to Quincy, her first extended visit with her parents since their departure from London nearly ten years before. Yet if John and Abigail regained their daughter that summer, they "lost" a son. Word arrived that John Quincy—still only a boy in their eyes—had married Louisa Catherine Johnson, the daughter of Joshua Johnson, an affluent Maryland merchant who had resided in London since the end of the war.[1]

Although he may not have recollected the occasion, John Quincy had met Louisa Catherine eighteen years before in Nantes, while he and his father awaited a vessel to bear them back to the United States. She was four and he was twelve. They met again in the spring of 1796, and this time John Quincy was immediately bewitched. Raised in Nantes and London, Louisa was an attractive, bright, refined young woman, fluent in French, talented musically, and socially comfortable in the company of the rich and powerful. The child of a father who had imprudently lavished every extravagance upon his wife and daughters, she naturally expected that her husband would do no less for her. John Quincy was neither wealthy nor given to displays of affection, but obeisance was a trait in his character. The courtship proceeded smoothly, and within four months the couple were engaged.[2]

Undoubtedly fearing his parents' objections, as they had six years earlier, John Quincy kept his intentions a carefully guarded secret. His strategy was unavailing, however. John and Abigail soon learned of his plans from acquaintances in London. The president appears to have quickly resigned himself to this development, but Abigail feared that Louisa Catherine's English background—she had lived in England since before her tenth birthday, and her mother was English—might jeopardize her son's advancement in republican America. Abigail thus dispatched several cautionary notes. John Quincy, meanwhile, was developing reservations of his own. He too was politically ambitious; moreover, he had begun to doubt whether he could support Louisa Catherine in the manner to which she was accustomed. The period of engagement, which had begun so smoothly, dragged on for more than a year, as he repeatedly refused to set a date for the nuptials. Only when pressure was applied by his fiancée's father and when Abigail at last gave her consent to the match, did he agree to marry.[3]

Early in October 1797, the Adamses' idyllic holiday ended, and the presidential party set out for Philadelphia. Leaving home was difficult, and Abigail found herself in a "dark and Gloomy" humor at the prospect of resuming her duties in the capital. But despite her melancholy mood, the journey was pleasant. Indian summer prevailed, providing the sojourners with cool, crisp mornings followed by warm, dry afternoons. Down these memorably familiar roads, John and his companions drank in the beauty of New England's radiant fall splendor, a feast of rich reds and vibrant golds mingled with maroons and ochers. The travelers paused in Hartford to visit Oliver Wolcott's wife, then it was on to East Chester, Nabby's home. There the trek abruptly stopped. About a month before his departure from Quincy, Adams learned that yellow fever had once again attacked the capital. Half the city's population fled for safe, rural environments; more than fifteen hundred houses stood empty, their windows boarded over to forestall burglars. The Treasury Department moved its operations to Gray's Gardens on the Schuylkill. The State Department transferred its operations to Trenton. McHenry, the secretary of war, fled to Downingtown, about forty miles west of Philadelphia. The customs houses set up business downriver in Chester. The danger would not end, physicians advised, until after the season's first freeze. Despite evidence that the crisis had passed by mid-October, Adams and the First Lady refused to budge. They took a room in Nabby's home, and there they remained for a month.[4]

When the Adamses resumed their journey, Abigail sought to persuade Nabby to come along, too, as company for herself and as therapy for her sad and lonely child. But her entreaties were to no avail. Nabby feared the humiliation she would face if it became public knowledge that she was living sepa-

John Quincy Adams in 1796, aged twenty-nine. Oil by John Singleton Copley. *Courtesy: Museum of Fine Arts, Boston.*

rately from her husband. Her refusal to accompany her parents to Philadelphia set the tone for the journey that followed. Dreary winter weather had replaced the lush days of autumn. Bundled against the cold, the First Family traveled mile after monotonous mile, bounced and jostled from the coastal flatlands through the rolling Jersey hinterlands, past Princeton and Trenton until, at last, they reached Philadelphia in mid-November. The trip ended just in time, for Adams had begun feeling bad as his carriage neared the capital. It was only a cold, but as a precaution his physicians put him to bed for a week.[5]

Adams must have hoped that word on the success of his envoys to France waited him in Philadelphia. Instead, he learned only that Gerry and Marshall had landed safely in Holland and that they, together with Pinckney, had set out for Paris about the same time that he had departed Quincy. There was substantive news from Europe, nonetheless. Napoleon Bonaparte, a brigadier general since age twenty-four, had become the Directory's principal soldier, and throughout 1796 and 1797 he had waged a sensational campaign in Italy, resulting in the establishment of French hegemony and security on its eastern periphery. Adams instantly recognized the potential danger that Napoleon's victories posed for America, and he fretted that all Europe, including Great Britain, soon might effect peace with the Directory, leaving Paris free to turn its unfettered gaze upon the United States. Such an eventuality, he remarked, would confront America with an "uncommonly Critical" situation. About the time he reached the capital, moreover, he learned from John Quincy of the coup d'état of 18 *Fructidor* (September 4, 1797), a complex French crisis during which the Directory had succeeded in thwarting a royalist plot, and which had altered the composition of the multiheaded French executive branch. It appeared, he now believed, that Paris was even less likely to be friendly toward the United States.[6]

News of still more Napoleonic victories reached the president early in 1798, and so did rumors that the French government had refused to receive America's envoys. Adams discounted the unconfirmed reports, but his pessimism had grown steadily since his return to Philadelphia. John Quincy had written that Gerry and his fellow diplomats surely would fail. They would have to deal with a French government composed of "the most inveterate Enemies of America," he predicted. Adams's worst fears seemed to be coming true when he learned that Austria had dropped out of the war. More disturbing were intelligence reports that suggested a French invasion of England was imminent. If Bonaparte succeeded in this endeavor, France would become a colossus, lord of western Europe, sovereign on the high seas.[7]

While Adams eagerly waited and watched, he sought to persuade Congress to prepare the United States for the worst. Congress met two weeks later than scheduled that autumn, as many of its members, like Adams, cautiously postponed their arrival in Philadelphia until they were certain that yellow fever was indeed gone. Finally, during the third week in November a quorum was attained, and on the twenty-third the president appeared before the legislators to read a pessimistic speech. He held out little hope for success for his diplomatic initiative. He did not forecast hostilities with France, but he suggested that a long period of Franco-American enmity was likely; to be ready for such an occurrence, he urged the improvement of America's naval and military defense. Congress listened politely, then did nothing, evidently unwilling to spend a cent until French policy was crystal clear. Several weeks later Albert Gallatin, a member of the Pennsylvania delegation, captured the mood when he told his wife, "[Our] greatest leisure time is while Congress sits, for we have nothing of any real importance before us."[8]

Adams had to be ready to act quickly if his envoys failed. He solicited the opinion of his cabinet, at least one of whom, McHenry, immediately sought Hamilton's fresh views on the crisis. The former secretary did not disappoint the sycophantic head of the War Department. Composing his reply on the day that McHenry's letter arrived, Hamilton counseled against war should the envoys fail to resolve the differences between the two nations. "By a formal war with France there is nothing to be gained" territorially or commercially. It would be wise to leave one envoy in Europe, he went on, for that would demonstrate the United States's continued willingness to pursue talks. Otherwise, he urged that the navy be strengthened, both by the construction of sloops in this country and by purchase of ships of the line—the behemoths of eighteenth-century fleets—from Great Britain, and that the 1778 treaties with France be suspended. Hamilton also proposed that an army of twenty thousand men be raised immediately. All this was to be presented to Congress by Adams "with *manly* but *calm* and sedate firmness & without strut," Hamilton concluded, unable to forgo giving this chief executive stage directions in the same fashion that he had often advised President Washington.[9]

McHenry obligingly passed along as his own recommendation Hamilton's suggestions for military preparations. The counsel of Wolcott and Pickering was so similar that it is difficult to believe they were not also privy to Hamilton's thoughts, though the secretary of state did take a more bellicose stance, proposing that in the event Paris rebuffed the envoys the United States should retaliate by seizing Louisiana. Adams barely had time to digest this advice. On March 4, the first anniversary of his inauguration, word from Pinckney, Marshall, and Gerry at last reached the President's House.[10]

Their dispatch actually arrived first at Pickering's desk. He did not have to decode much of the message to grasp the thrust of the envoy's report. Although a cold, still darkness had already descended upon the capital, the secretary, boiling with anger and ready for war ("*real Americans*" should seize their arms, he bristled to a friend), hurried down the street to present a summary of the tidings to the President. It was not a pretty story that Adams strained to read under the light of his flickering candle. Foreign Minister Talleyrand had refused to receive the diplomats. But his rebuff was not the worst of it. Secret agents subsequently approached the diplomats and demanded not just the payment of a bribe as a precondition to the commencement of negotiations but also the extension of an American loan to France and an apology from Adams for allegedly anti-French comments he had inserted in his May 1797 address to Congress. Adams's reaction was not unlike that of Pickering. He had no more than completed his perusal of the cryptic account from Pinckney and his companions when he sent word to Congress of the failure of his diplomatic initiative. As there was "no hope" for a rapprochement with the French government, he urged reconsideration of the defensive measures he had recommended three months earlier.[11] Significantly, however, he did not reveal the indignities to which the envoys had been subjected. He wished to manage this crisis in his own way.

While work on deciphering the message went forward, Adams polled the members of his cabinet regarding his next step. Their recommendations were contradictory. Attorney-General Lee and Pickering urged the president to ask Congress for a declaration of war. The alternative, Lee remarked, was "national ruin." Pickering additionally proposed the negotiation of a formal alliance with Great Britain. Wolcott and McHenry were less truculent. While they wished to prepare for war and advocated that the United States fleet be permitted to respond to French depredations in the Caribbean, they counseled against a presidential request for a declaration of war. Once again, their views were consistent with those of Hamilton, who, perhaps dismayed at the secretary of state's independent course, wrote Pickering to remind him of his belief that Adams should be "*grave solemn* and *firm,*" but that war should be avoided. An "attitude of *calm defiance* suits us" better than open hostilities, he instructed.[12]

The decision was for President Adams to make. The last student to study Adams's life concluded that his course in this crisis with France was filled with "inconsistency," that his was a "pattern . . . of self-righteous response to events . . . followed by ill-timed compromise," during the whole of which Adams neglected to assert his authority. In fact, from the beginning, Adams knew the direction that he wished to take—if France would permit it. Adams sought peace, believing that a war now would be dangerous for the United States. He spoke in bellicose terms and augmented the nation's defenses, but he would have been remiss in his responsibilities had he not displayed America's resolve to the leaders in Paris. He also played for time. Rather than act precipitately, he hoped that more moderate elements would eventually replace the most truculent officials within the French government. There can be no doubt that he waffled from time to time as he considered the best tactics for defusing the crisis, but he was unwavering in the pursuit of peace with honor for the United States. In this instance, therefore, he first prepared a militant and raging message to Congress. But before he submitted that address, he reconsidered and drafted a new message with a quite different tone.[13]

In the address that he delivered to Congress on March 19, Adams sought to guard against an overreaction. He stressed that Europe was caught up in a European war, not a conflict with America. He told Congress that he was recalling the three envoys and he repeated his plea that America's coastal and maritime defenses be improved, although once again he withstood the appeals of those who sought the creation of an American army. More important than anything he said, perhaps, was what he did not say. Adams did not divulge details of the deciphered reports of his three diplomats, fearing that the lurid details of their treatment in Paris would enhance the mood of war fever in some circles and push him into the war he did not want.[14]

Adams misjudged the response of Congress. Not only was its reaction less bellicose than he had expected, Congress took no immediate steps to commence the defensive preparations he had proposed. The conduct of the Republican leadership was even more surprising. Acting in the belief that the president desired war and that he had exaggerated French malevolence— Jefferson had privately referred to Adams's "insane message" to Congress— the party chiefs demanded the release of the envoys' dispatches. They were joined by a few hawkish Federalists, some of whom had been secretly apprised by members of the cabinet of the "monstrous" demands of France for "Money! Money!"—"unlimited demands of more money." In a rare display of togetherness, and with very different ends in mind, this coalition of Federalists and Republicans in the House passed a resolution demanding disclosure without deletions. The next day Adams complied, concealing only the names of the four French agents who had met Pinckney, Marshall, and Gerry. He simply listed them as commissioners "W, X, Y, and Z."[15]

The release of the envoys' dispatches—the commencement in America of what has come to be known as the XYZ affair—triggered the spasm of militancy that Adams had dreaded. The Republicans, at last aware of the magnitude of their error, desperately began to search for some means by which to extinguish the fire storm they had unleashed. Jefferson, who had previously carped at Adams's pugnacity, now claimed that the president's long record of anti-French remarks left the Directory no choice but to refuse negotiations, although in private he fixed the blame for all this on Talleyrand, a man of "most noted ill fame." The Republican press acknowledged that the affair proved the unfriendliness of the Directory, but it denied that the French government's scandalous behavior warranted a war; some editors even claimed that X, Y, and Z were not French agents at all, but sharpers and confidence men who had sought to fleece the unwary, innocent diplomats of a portion of the American treasury. The country was in great danger, one Republican suggested, but the peril arose less from France than from among those Federalists bent upon catapulting the United States into the European war.

It was to no avail. The "lower class of people," as Abigail Adams had taken to referring to most Americans, were "now roused" and, she added, had begun to abandon their "Jacobean" leanings. The Federalists, of course, welcomed the new, acrimonious mood. Some hoped the chauvinistic, cold war atmosphere would aid the party in the approaching congressional elections; some sought to ride the whirlwind to enhanced power for themselves. Many Federalists believed it made war with France inevitable, a prospect they welcomed, whether to avenge wounded national honor, to assist in destroying revolutionary France, to aid in preserving Great Britain, or to advance the national interest of the United States through open warfare with Paris.[16]

As usual, no one was more instrumental than Hamilton in shaping opinion and policy. Barely a week after the President's address, he published the first of a series of essays that he titled "The Stand," trenchant pieces in which he sought to whip up fervor against the "FIVE TYRANTS of France [who] after binding in chains their own countrymen . . . have . . . decreed war against all nations not in league with themselves." America faced a stark choice between resistance or submission to France's plundering of its commerce. He urged resistance and called for the creation of an American army of fifty thousand— previously the hawkish Federalists had spoken of a force of about twenty thousand—led by General Washington.[17]

During his initial year in office Adams had not sought a large army. In his first weeks as president he had spoken of resurrecting the cavalry and artillery, both of which had been abandoned in the diminutive peacetime army developed after 1783, but he had always stressed that a strong navy and an active militia could provide quite adequate security for the United States, especially as he believed a French invasion unlikely. The only direct threat to American soil, he believed, might be sudden incursions against the nation's coastal cities, but that danger was remote and could be met by coastal artillery and a combination of militia and regular cavalry forces. But it was not just that Adams thought an army unnecessary. He was too much a Whig not to fear the prospect of a large standing army—what he had alluded to as a "many bellied Monster"—that might become a vehicle for tyranny and corruption and might result in the sudden imposition of monarchy in the United States.[18]

But during the spring of 1798 Adams appeared to change. The pressure upon him from within his own party was enormous. In addition, he may now have concluded that war was inevitable, or at least likely; he did, in fact, tell the British ambassador he expected war with France, a view that grew in part from the advice of John Quincy, who, from his vantage point in Lisbon, had surmised that Paris planned to invade the United States in an effort to detach from the Union the sprawling region south of Pennsylvania and west of the mountains. Adams, like many Federalists, may have come to the view that a regular army was essential for the preservation of the "internal security" of the United States, something that could hardly be guaranteed once the reality of a long war with France became apparent to a people that harbored the warmest affection for that faraway nation. Or, Adams might simply have relished his new stature. Since the XYZ events had become public knowledge, people had paraded in his behalf; addresses in support of his pugnacity had poured into his office from all over the country. "The President's March," "Hail Columbia," and "Yankee Doodle Dandy," were played at concerts and even prior to stage presentations. When Adams now traveled, he, like Washington before him, was accorded "every mark of distinguished attention." When he came to New York in the summer of 1798 he received the "most splendid" reception ever given a political leader, or so one local Federalist believed. Some believed that John Adams's stature now equaled that of Washington, and one Federalist leader even predicted that "no man . . . will go down to posterity with greater lustre than John Adams — I will not even except *George Washington.*"[19]

The blandishments and the cheers were a heady experience, perhaps too much to resist for one who had so often and so fervently longed to win attention as a soldier. Adams, the commander in chief, began to appear in public wearing a full military uniform with a sword strapped to his side. His public pronouncements frequently were filled with the most bellicose rhetoric, often harkening back to the martial sacrifices of earlier generations. His ancestors would feel "disgust and Resentment" if America did not act, he wrote revealingly; not to bear arms, he seemed to say, would indicate that debasement and corruption had blanketed the land.[20]

By late May, Congress was ready to create an army. By then the rumor that a French invasion armada was gathering at Brest had swept the nation. Tales even were circulated—Pickering had a hand in the dissemination of this one— that French operatives were stirring a slave rebellion in South Carolina; newspapers reported the tattle that secret agents of the French government had been sent to torch Philadelphia and assassinate America's leaders. Abigail Adams's prediction of a swing in public opinion soon was borne out. French songs and toasts to French republicanism vanished from public display, as did the tricolored cockade, the very symbol of the French Revolution; Instead, crowds sporting black cockades—thereafter the Federalist insignia—surged into the streets bawling for war. In this milieu of nationalist hysteria and feverish anxiety, the Federalist majority in Congress enacted one defensive measure after another.

Twelve new frigates were authorized and steps were taken to augment the stockpiles in the national armories. On April 27 Congress added a regiment of engineers and artillerists to the existing army, specialists who were to prepare the seacoast defenses. During the next two months an army of ten thousand men was created, with provision for its enhancement to fifty thousand should the president regard such a step as necessary; Adams was also empowered to call up eighty thousand militiamen. Finally, Congress voted to sever all commercial ties with France. It all must have seemed anticlimatic to Adams, as he had been saying for some time now—as Abigail put it— "we already have war; the French have been at war with us for many months." Indeed, all that was left was to make war official, and that required only a presidential request to Congress. Everyone in both parties during the summer of 1798, including even the First Lady, appeared to believe that Adams was on the verge of asking Congress to declare war on France.[21]

The president gave every indication that he had decided on such a course. Between April and August, in seventy-one written responses to the patriotic messages of support that reached his office, many of which were printed in newspapers or issued as handbills, Adams struck a consistently truculent pose. Republicanism, he said, would be extinguished if the United States did not fight. It would be cowardly not to take up arms. "[N]either Justice nor Moderation, can secure Us from a Participation in the War," he told one group. War is "a less Evil than national Dishonour," he remarked to another. He exhorted his readers to adopt a "warlike Character," and he disclosed that the American people would forfeit their "Character, moral, political and martial" if they did not resist. And to the younger generation living in strongholds of pro-French opinion, he counseled that "Your Fathers and you may differ in opinion" on the issues of war with France, but "we ought to love our Country better than any other."[22]

Adams also set about administering the navy and army that Congress had created. The former was easy. Not only was the navy already in existence, but Congress had recently created the post of secretary of Navy to tend to the fleet. After being turned down by his friend, George Cabot of Massachusetts, Adams inveighed upon Benjamin Stoddert, a Maryland Federalist, to accept the secretarial position.[23] The army, however, presented numerous problems, many of which the president never imagined.

The selection of the army's officers was Adams's initial dilemma. Washington seemed the logical choice to command the new force. Indeed, given his stature, it was impossible not to approach him before any other. Besides, Adams knew the former president well enough to understand that he yearned for attention and adulation, and he must have feared that Washington would make trouble if his services were not solicited. It is not unlikely, either, that he learned through one of Hamilton's cabinet insiders that Washington once again was ready to don his Continental army uniform that had been packed away for the past fifteen years. After not having written Washington for nearly a year, Hamilton, during the mounting hysteria in May 1798, contacted his former chief to ask him to tour the South and beat the drums for military preparedness; he also urged him to accept the position of commander should Congress create a provisional army. Washington declined to take an active role in stirring up anti-French sentiment, explaining that he thought war unlikely and unnecessary, especially as he believed France incapable of invading the United States. On the other hand, he told Hamilton that he would not resist a call from Congress to assume command of the army. The knowledge that Washington was willing to serve must have been made known to the president.

It could not have been entirely unpleasant news for Adams, for if war occurred he would want to line up the old general's support for the cause. Besides, as his wife acknowledged, the president feared that if Washington was not the commander, he would be pressured into accepting Hamilton as the leader of the army.[24]

On the day that Congress authorized him to appoint the principal officers in the new army, Adams wrote to Washington, imploring him to come out of retirement and take command of the provisional force. It was a curiously maudlin letter, one in which Adams suggested that were it not for the constitutional obstacles he would ask Washington to resume the presidency while he dropped back to the vice-presidency. Almost simultaneously, McHenry wrote to Washington, pleading with the old general to play an active role during this "crisis so awful and important."[25]

Washington's response was a masterpiece of ambiguity, a facility in which he had few equals. He would accept the post of commander of the new army if an "*actual* Invasion" was threatened, although he thought the French incapable of such an undertaking, but, then again, he had to admit that this was an "Age of Wonders!" and that the "folly of the Directory" was unsurpassed. He also seemed to say—without explicitly stating it—that the commander, "be him whom he will," must have the freedom to select his subordinates; moreover, were he empowered to select the general officers, Washington went on, he would bypass the highest-ranking men of the revolutionary generation in favor of younger men of "sufficient activity, energy and health." To Secretary McHenry, whom he wrote the same day, Washington advised that younger generals were essential, for the army must wage this war differently than the War of Independence, moving and striking, thrusting and feinting, often on the move against an adversary likely to be less conventional and far more daring and energetic than had been the hidebound armies of Howe and Clinton. Washington also told McHenry that the second in command would hold the crucial post; therefore, he must be a man of enormous energy, strength, and respectability.[26]

Washington's remarkable missives raised as many questions as they answered. No one could have been more surprised than Adams at Washington's statements. Evidently expecting the old general's unequivocal assent to serve, Adams had not even waited for Washington's reply before he nominated him to be "Commander in Chief of all the Armies raised" by the United States. The Senate confirmed the appointment on July 3, the day before Washington answered Adams's appeal. Now, confounded and uncertain of Washington's intentions, the president dispatched McHenry to Virginia for a face-to-face consultation with the master of Mount Vernon.[27]

The secretary of war alighted at Washington's door late one afternoon in hot, muggy July. His pockets were bulging with communiques. Washington's commission was there, as well as another letter from Adams. McHenry also bore a note from Hamilton, written in Philadelphia, to which the former secretary had hurried, now that the crisis was simmering nicely. Hamilton importuned Washington to accept the call of Adams to take command. His refusal would "throw a great damp upon the ardor of the Country," perhaps with fatal results to the well being of the new nation; moreover, if Washington declined to serve, Adams, the commander in chief under the constitution, might meddle in martial matters, something to be avoided as his "prepossessions on military subjects . . . are of the wrong sort." Presumably, Hamilton was alluding to Adams's fancy for the navy over the army, for the militia over a large, standing army.[28]

In the secretary's satchel was still another letter, this from Adams to McHenry, in which the president listed several candidates whom he wished Washington to consider as his principal subordinates. The list included such obvious possibilities as Knox, Lincoln, Charles Cotesworth Pinckney, Henry Lee, Hamilton, and Horatio Gates, a ludicrous choice, for everyone knew that Washington hated the man. Col. William Smith, Nabby's feckless husband, was on the list, too, as were two Republicans, Aaron Burr and Frederick Muhlenberg. Adams subsequently acknowledged that the Republicans were included for political reasons. He believed appointing Burr might mollify some New York republicans, while naming Muhlenberg might win adherents to Federalism from among Pennsylvania's large German population.[29]

McHenry was a guest at Mount Vernon for three days, and, during much of that time, he and the former president spoke of nothing but the problems of command. Washington revealed that he had ruled out all but Pinckney and Hamilton for the crucial second spot, that of inspector general. Of the others, only Lee and Knox had much appeal to him; the former was another Virginian who had not risen above the rank of colonel during the war, while the latter now was so old and fat as to be almost immobile. Pinckney seemed the ideal choice. He had outranked Hamilton at the end of the war and was trusted in the South, the section where Washington believed the war would be fought should the unlikely French invasion actually occur. Moreover, to select Hamilton would probably cost the country Pinckney's services, as he likely would refuse to accept a rank beneath his former subordinate. But Washington was under pressure to choose Hamilton.

McHenry must have campaigned for Hamilton. Pickering surely did. A letter from the secretary of state arrived at Mount Vernon only hours before McHenry's carriage rolled up Washington's oyster-shell driveway. Hamilton, he wrote, "will gladly be *Your Second*," but he will accept no other position. You are aware of his "distinguished ability, energy and fidelity," he continued, and in a remark that must have stretched even Washington's credulity, he added: "even Colo. Hamilton's political enemies, I believe would repose more confidence in him than in any other military character."

At the conclusion of their deliberations, McHenry climbed back into his coach for the hot, wearying trip back to the capital. As much as he must have dreaded the journey before him, McHenry must have been delighted as he set out for Philadelphia. Washington had responded precisely as Hamilton, Pickering, and he had hoped. In James Thomas Flexner's magisterial biography of Washington, the old general is depicted as having benignly and not unreasonably demanded the choice of his own subordinates; supposedly, he had sought Hamilton's appointment because he believed that his former aide had possessed a better "opportunity to survey the whole military scene" than any other man, and because he was frightened by the thought that Hamilton might stay home" throughout this crisis. In fact, Washington's behavior in this instance was unconscionable. Whereas he had never demanded the right to select his subordinates during the War of Independence, he suddenly arrogated to himself that power, seeking now to compel the president of the United States to accept what he, a private citizen, desired. Moreover, he was motivated not by high principle but by the narrowest partisan reasons, for not even Washington had the temerity to suggest that Hamilton possessed the military command experience to deserve the post immediately beneath the highest-ranking commander in the army. Yet, within the satchel that McHenry fetched back to President Adams were two critical letters that would place the revered former general on a collision course with the chief executive. One was a communique from Washington in which he consented to accept the appointment on the grounds that he should "not be called into the field" until a French invasion actually threatened. Another letter was from McHenry to Adams. In that missive, the secretary had inserted—at Washington's insistence—the statement that the master of Mount Vernon would serve only if he could select his general officers from among a list that he, Washington, had prepared. Without specifically ranking the officers, Washington had listed as major generals the following men in the following order: Hamilton, Knox, and Pinckney. The list also included eight additional names, and each man was a Federalist. Neither the two Republicans whom Adams had suggested, nor the president's son-in-law, William Smith, Washington's former aide, were on the old general's list.[30]

When McHenry arrived at the president's House, Adams was shocked to read the letters. Not only had Washington sent a virtual ultimatum rather than the "advice" that Adams had solicited, but the effort that Alexander Hamilton had been expending to shape and control the policy of his administration now was becoming clear to him. In fact, he immediately concluded that even Washington, the most revered man in America, was but a puppet of Hamilton, a conjecture that Adams had heard whispered about but had previously refused to believe. He also now came to see Hamilton as a most dangerous man, both to the nation and to himself. Abigail said at about this moment that she suspected that the New Yorker had the makings of "a second Buonaparty." The president thought him more like Franklin. "Hamilton I know to be a proud Spirited, conceited, aspiring Mortal always pretending to Morality," he wrote, but "with as debauched Morals as old Franklin who is more his Model than anyone I know." In Adams's eyes, Hamilton had succeeded Franklin as "the most restless, impatient, artful, indefatigable and unprincipled Intriguer in the United States," a man, he began to suspect, who would have been as willing for the United States to become a dependency of Great Britain as the supposedly servile Franklin would have been for it to become a dependency of France.

There no longer were any doubts about Hamilton in Adams's mind. But, at this moment, he neither moved to deny Hamilton the military post he sought nor to root out his lackeys within the cabinet. The most recent student of Adams to investigate his failure to respond to the threat posed by Hamilton has seen the president's restraint in psychological terms. Adams, according to Peter Shaw, feared "giving vent to his true feelings" lest he be seen as excessively vain; supposedly, he habitually submitted to and forgave those who betrayed him so that he would not be harmed even more through the guilt that accompanied the act of fighting back. In reality Adams capitulated from political necessity. Defiance of Washington would have been attendant with great political risk, perhaps even the destruction of his presidency. Adams thus had little choice but to submit the names that Washington had proposed, adding only Smith's name (as adjutant general) to the roster.

The Senate immediately confirmed the nominations, save for that of Smith. His rejection has usually been laid at the feet of Secretary Pickering, who did indeed oppose his selection, feeling that Smith was an incompetent dilettante and a Republican turncoat. But Pickering lacked the power to block Smith's appointment. There were "many Secret Springs at Work," said a bitter Abigail Adams, who closely watched the debate over the nominations. Many in Congress shared Pickering's views; some dismissed Smith as a failure, a bankrupt failure by now; and some undoubtedly even crassly voted against Smith in order to strike a personal blow at the president. In addition, as Abigail also noted, some who voted to deny Smith the appointment may even have acted as "the tools of they knew not who."[31]

To this point, therefore, Adams had been willing to acquiesce to Washington's wishes. His view soon changed, however, not because of the rejection of Smith but because of the entreaties of Henry Knox. The former artillerist was mortified at his treatment, and he poured out his feelings in long, rancorous, pathetic communiques to both the president and Washington. Feeling that he had been treated most treacherously, he refused to serve under Hamilton. Shortly, the Federalist leaders in New England rallied to his support, and they made the implications of Washington's and Adams's sleight of Knox quite apparent. As Knox himself put it to Washington, only "Time will discover" whether the people of New England, "which must furnish the Majority of the Army," will serve in a force devoid of a principal general officer from any of the five states in the region.[32]

Adams was in a quandary. He neither liked nor disliked Knox. They had never been intimate friends, and while Adams thought the artillery commander had performed capably during the war, he did not stand in awe of him. On the other hand, he did not think that Knox should be "disgraced or degraded" by being offered a post beneath men whom he previously had commanded.[33]

It was not just Knox, of course. To turn one way was to risk an affront to the obdurate Washington, the one man whose symbolic presence was essential for the unification of the nation and the recruitment of the army. To turn the other way was to alienate powerful men in his own New England, extirpating his political base. Moreover, Adams feared that General Hamilton, a New Yorker, might reawaken the same sectioned passions that had confronted Schuyler, a New Yorker, when he had sought without success to lead an army of New Englanders in the War of Independence.

Initially, Adams sought to assuage New England. In mid-August he announced that each general officer's rank would be determined by the date of his commission in the Continental army. Hence, the ranking after Washington would be: Knox, Pinckney, Lee, Edward Hand of Pennsylvania, and Hamilton. Adams had the power to enforce such a decision, one that he apparently made in the belief that his cabinet would loyally assent to his will and that Washington would not risk his reputation in a clash with the president of the United States in the midst of a national emergency. He was wrong on both counts.[34]

Washington wrote once again to campaign on Hamilton's behalf, but it was a letter from a cabinet officer that determined the issue. For a time Pickering, Wolcott, and Stoddert considered a joint letter to the president urging that Hamilton be made second in command. In the end, however, it was decided that an epistle signed only by Wolcott—a New Englander, the advisor with whom the president had the closest relationship—would carry more weight. Consequently, the Treasury secretary penned an exhaustive letter to Adams, in the course of which he proposed that the matter be left to Washington, an experienced military man who was best suited to judge the merits of the candidates.[35]

Wolcott's logic gave Adams the out he needed to extricate himself from this thorny mess. He immediately signed each general officer's commission on the same day, thus capitulating to Washington and his friends. "I was no more at liberty than a man in prison," he subsequently remarked, for to have acted otherwise would have given affront to the most beloved—and most powerful—man in the United States. The president announced that he expected that "an amicable Adjustment or Acquiescence might take place among the Gentlemen themselves." There was every reason to think so. Pinckney was unlikely to run the political risk of a clash with Washington or Hamilton, while Knox's twenty-year relationship with Washington had been one of total servility. In short, Washington, not Adams, was to make the decision, and if any officer "should be so obstinate as to appeal to me," Adams privately told the Virginian, he would confirm whatever judgment Washington had made. The only surprise that followed was that Knox declined to serve.[36]

While Adams spent these torrid summer days wrestling with the appointment of the officers, the Federalist Congress seized the moment to curtail civil liberties within the United States. The XYZ affair had sent war fever and nationalist hysteria to their highest levels since the weeks immediately after Lexington-Concord in 1775. Neither the anti-British frenzy accompanying the outbreak of the war in Europe five years earlier, nor the passions aroused by Citizen Genêt and the Jay Treaty, could equal this perturbation, perhaps because in those earlier crises President Washington had used his office to counsel for peace, whereas Adams had utilized his position on behalf of pugnacity. In this moment of extreme fervor and alacrity, a Federalist caucus had even considered the possibility of declaring war—whether or not the president of the United States agreed—only to discover that the party lacked the necessary votes to undertake such a perilous course. If the caucus lacked the numbers to commit the nation to war, the group understood that the moment had arrived when it might weaken its political adversaries and at the same time mount a full-scale offensive against the ideas of the French Revolution.[37]

As the crisis mounted from May onward, Adams expressed the hope that "the prospect of a just and necessary war" might silence the foes of his foreign policy. Of course, that had not occurred. From the outset of the breach with France in 1797, most Republicans had resisted what Jefferson steadfastly referred to as the Federalist "war measures." While Vice-President Jefferson presided over the Senate, Albert Gallatin led the Republican resistance to what many saw as a headlong rush toward a Federalist-contrived war. A native of Switzerland, Gallatin had emigrated to the United States in 1780 at the age of nineteen. After spending two years as a French tutor at Harvard College, he had moved to Richmond and ultimately—about the time Adams took up residence in London—settled in western Pennsylvania atop a high bluff overlooking the Monongahela River, about forty miles south of Pittsburgh. Well-educated and articulate (though some had difficulty with his thick accent), he soon emerged as a leader on the Pennsylvania frontier. He was elected to the House of Representatives in 1795, and by 1798 this compulsive worker, a tall, thin, bald, hook-nosed man, had succeeded Jefferson, who had been immobilized by his vice-presidential post, and Madison, who had returned to Virginia, as the party's legislative leader. Indeed, Gallatin quickly gained a reputation for economic expertise, the only Republican with sufficient understanding of such matters to cope with Hamilton. The Federalists hated his brilliance, his foreignness, his politics, his religion. Abigail Adams was one of his most fervent detractors. Full of sulky malevolence toward this foe of her husband, she referred to him simply as "the Jesuit Gallatin."[38]

During the spring and summer of 1798, Gallatin led the Republican fight for peace. The defense buildup was unnecessary, he charged, except for the economic well-being of a few Eastern seaboard centers. The burden of paying for bringing this prosperity to the Federalist cities, he added, would fall upon the nation's farmers, a practice his foes had pursued since the whiskey tax days of the Washington-Hamilton administration. Consequently, he had fought both the augmentation of the navy and the creation of the provincial army. The Republican press also joined this campaign. The *Philadelphia Aurora,* edited by Benjamin Franklin Bache, the grandson of Adams's late nemesis, sought to convince its readers that the Federalists were warmongers, and as proof it published a statement by Talleyrand insisting that France did not wish a conflict with the United States. The Federalist leadership was savaged in the press as well, none more so than the president, who was castigated as the "old, querilous, Bald, blind, cripled, Toothless Adams."[39]

With a majority in Congress and the public on its side to a degree that had not occurred since the early days of the Washington presidency, the Federalists saw the opportunity to seriously weaken their adversary. For some, this was merely politics, the moment to gain an edge and to retaliate against a nettlesome foe. For others, the acts were simply war measures. Some genuinely feared public safety would suffer if the scurrilous Republican press was not silenced, or at least tempered. However, many High Federalists, as the most extreme conservatives within the party were called, had convinced themselves that the Republicans threatened the very fabric of American society. To these zealots, the Republicans were more loyal to France than to the United States; they concluded that Jefferson and his "Jacobin" followers sought nothing less than to subvert the Constitution, a document the Republicans supposedly had hated since the ratification struggle ten years before. In its place, the "Gallic faction" allegedly sought to erect a democratic, thoroughly egalitarian society modeled on the most radical of revolutionary France's governments. The most frenzied Federalists even fancied the likelihood that wild-eyed Republicans would order the execution by guillotine of Adams and his cabinet shortly after the Jeffersonians ascended to power, if, in fact, a Republican-inspired mob did not first seize and murder Adams and his family in the President's House. The hysteria reached such proportions that it intruded into the president's residence. With difficulty, Adams persuaded his servants that they were safe, although, not fully comfortable himself, he ordered a large cache of arms delivered to the presidential mansion for his protection.[40]

While Adams did not generally embrace these High Federalist notions of Republican conspiracies, he did share with most members of his party a hatred of the French Revolution. This great revolt against superstition, aristocratic privilege, and tyranny was incomprehensible to him. The most he could fathom from the events in France was a movement by the "rabble" to effect social leveling and democratic government—twin evils, to his way of thinking. He feared, too, the influence that the French experience might have on American opinion, and like most of his Federalist brethren, he fretted that the "French, Jacobinical faction" within the United States—the Republican Party—might be the vehicle for spreading the heresies of the French Revolution. In the spring of 1798, about the time Congress created the provisional army, he even expressed alarm at the possibility that Republican "Traitors . . . will unite with the invading [French] enemy and fly within the lines," moving Jefferson to remark in private that Adams inveighed more against "his own fellow citizens" than against the French threat. Jefferson grew so alarmed, in fact, that he suspected the Federalists might dispatch their new army into Virginia to suppress their foes, and he even cautioned Madison to say nothing that might provoke an invasion.[41]

In this white-hot atmosphere of "unguarded passion," as Jefferson put it, the Federalist Congress passed four separate acts within a two-week period beginning on June 18. Realizing that most foreign-born voters signed on with the Republican party, the Federalists had for some time sought to curtail immigration. Their earlier efforts had failed, but they now succeeded in passing the Naturalization Act, a measure that increased to fourteen years the period that newcomers must wait before obtaining citizenship and the right to vote. Two acts concerned aliens. The Alien Friends Act vested in the president the authority to deport any alien whom he considered dangerous; the Alien Enemies Act permitted the chief executive to deport aliens who hailed from a nation with which the United States was at war. The capstone of the Federalist bulwark against dissent was the Sedition Act, legislation that won Senate approval one day after the twenty-second anniversary of the Declaration of Independence.[42]

As a Federalist congressman observed, the Sedition Act was designed to assure that only "pure sentiments and good principles" emanated from the nation's press. Federalist magistrates and Federalist judges presumably would decide what constituted the laudable principles worthy to be read by the "sons of riot, and intemperance, and idleness, who cluster in the villages and dramshops" of America's cities. The act set punishments of a maximum five-thousand-dollar fine and five years incarceration for those who conspired to thwart federal law, and fines of up to two thousand dollars and jail terms not to exceed two years for those convicted of making "false, scandalous and malicious" statements about federal officials. As if to underscore its political intent, the Federalist Congress stipulated that the law would expire on March 3, 1801, the last full day of John Adams's term as president. Adams signed the bill into law on July 14, the ninth anniversary of the storming of the Bastille in revolutionary Paris.[43]

This legislation cannot be attributed to the long shadow of Hamilton, as Adams subsequently suggested. Hamilton, in fact, was critical of these measures. "Let us not be cruel or violent," he counseled while the Alien Enemies

Act was under consideration. Observing the Sedition Act, he cautioned: "Let us not establish a tyranny." His disapproval of these harsh measures arose less from a fervent commitment to individual liberties than to the fear that the suppression of human rights likely would "give [the opposition] faction *body* & solidarity"; nevertheless, this was one legacy of Federalist rule that can not be laid at his feet.[44] Nor were the acts entirely the responsibility of the High Federalists, for they were but a small part of a large party. Rather, this was the work of an entire political movement whose membership enthusiastically and overwhelmingly approved this effort to quash free speech and open dissent.

Adams's preeminent biographer not only sought to minimize the president's role in this matter, but he defended the Alien and Sedition acts as necessary to control and remove the many French, Irish, and English "troublemakers and revolutionaries . . . loose in the country." The "government took steps to protect itself," Page Smith added, by passing acts that were, at worst, "simply impolitic." The truth is less pretty. The acts were undertaken largely toward the goal of maintaining Federalist hegemony. The measures sought to stifle domestic opposition to a war movement that many Federalists perceived as essential for the Party's salvation. Moreover, Adams acquiesced in the statutes. He did not introduce the ordinances or play a direct role in their passage, for, as he saw a clear delineation between the executive and legislative branches in the making of laws, throughout his administration he played only the smallest role in the lawmaking process. Indeed, in this instance, his active participation was unnecessary, given the consensus within the party. But he must share complicity in the creation of the measures. By questioning the conduct of alien residents and by repeatedly warning of Republican treachery and foreign-inspired cabals, he had helped fabricate the mephitic climate of opinion in which such laws could be made. He did not oppose the legislation. Neither did he veto the enactments, and, much later, when he sought to put the blame for these acts on Hamilton, he confessed that he had agreed to the legislation because there was "need enough" to restrain those who were resisting the national defense measures then being taken. That seemed to be the prevailing mood within the President's House. William Shaw, Abigail's nephew and the president's secretary, was among the staunchest defenders of the Sedition Act. Clearly no civil libertarian, Shaw looked upon the act as a godsend, for he believed "the liberty of the press . . . is a powerful engine for the subversion of all government—a mighty lever, sufficient . . . to overthrow the social order of the world." The president's wife had urged just such a law a few weeks before the bill was introduced in the Senate. "[U]ntill congress pass a Sedition Bill," she had reflected in April, there was nothing to stop the "wicked and base, violent & calumniating abuse" of the Republican press.[45]

The Sedition Act had an immediate impact. Several frightened Republican editors either moderated their attacks or announced their intention of forswearing the publication of anything that could be construed as seditious. Many journalists were not so easily intimidated, however, and the government soon swung into action against these intrepid souls. Secretary Pickering, whose job included responsibility for all those domestic matters that did not naturally fall to the other departments, became the chief hunter of seditious prey. Grim and efficient, and relentlessly willing to prosecute editors who dared to publish even the most trifling criticism of the administration, he soon won the popular title of "the Scourge of Jacobinism."

The government did not even wait for the bill to clear Congress before it moved against the Republican press. The *Aurora's* Ben Bache was arrested in June on a charge of libeling the president; he died three months later while awaiting trial. John Daly Burk, an Irish alien who edited the New York *Time Price,* was seized in July, as was Matthew Lyon, a Republican congressman from Vermont. Burk met his bail (Aaron Burr paid it) and immediately fled to Virginia, where he vanished from sight. Lyon, an acerbic sort who had earned the enmity of every Federalist for having spat in the face of Congressman Roger Griswold of Connecticut during a heated legislative debate (thereafter referred to in the Federalist press as "the Spitting Lyon"), was charged with seditious libel after publishing a typically scathing article in the *Vermont Journal.* In the fall he was convicted, fined one thousand dollars, and sentenced to a four-month imprisonment, which he served in an unheated cell previously reserved for runaway slaves.[46]

Ultimately, the administration secured at least fourteen indictments under the Sedition Act, including suits against five of the six most important Republican newspapers. The majority of the actions occurred in 1798 and 1799, although most of the trials were held on the eve of the 1800 presidential election, timing that hardly seems coincidental. Adams neither initiated nor resisted any of the prosecutions, but he is known to have authorized at least two of the government's suits prior to the commencement of formal legal action.[47]

The enforcement of the legislation pertaining to aliens was a different matter. While chief executive Adams boasted that he was "always ready and willing to execute the Alien Law," in his retirement years he protested that he had never enforced the legislation. His recollection was correct, for he repeatedly rejected Pickering's insistent pleading to begin massive deportations. Actually, it soon was apparent that the Federalists had accomplished their goal without having to undertake the forced expulsion of aliens.

Many French aliens simply left the country after mid-1798, some out of anguish at the suddenly inhospitable environment, some to return to France, which recently had relaxed its restrictions upon the return of its émigrés, and some to return to Santo Domingo, from whence they had fled in the course of a bloody slave insurrection in 1793.[48]

The passage of the Alien and Sedition acts was the final item on the agenda of this busy congress. As soon as it adjourned, the Adamses, accompanied by four servants, set out for Quincy. John and Abigail were not only anxious to flee the torrid capital but to escape in case yellow fever struck again, as it had the previous summer. Abigail was especially anxious to return home. Without informing her husband, she had made arrangements to begin work on several minor renovations at Peacefield as well as on a major addition to the house. The kitchen floor, stairs, and servants' quarters had been painted a bright yellow. Her room had also been repainted, and a low stone wall had been erected about the periphery of the garden. She had planned to have the exterior of the house painted, as well, but shortly before leaving Philadelphia she learned that the workers had not yet gotten to that task. Furthermore, still distraught at being "so confined" in the dwelling, she had commissioned the construction of an east wing consisting of two new rooms, a parlor downstairs and a library— Abigail called it the "Book Room"—above it, an enlargement that virtually doubled the capacity of the house. While the work was expected to take some time to complete, she envisioned the fresh new look at Peacefield as a surprise for her husband, something to brighten his mood and lessen his cares. Besides, she confessed, he neither had a decorator's eye nor could he bear "to trouble himself about any thing of the kind."[49]

The trip home was a difficult undertaking. For days on end the party bounced and jostled across dust-choked roads. Their carriage shielded them somewhat from the blazing July sun, but there was no escape from the sultriness of high summer. As during the previous year's journey, the Adamses swooped down on East Chester to fetch Nabby home for a few weeks. Otherwise, they pressed on day after weary day, traveling about forty to forty-five miles before impending darkness brought a halt.[50]

Either shortly before reaching Quincy, or soon thereafter, Abigail fell desperately ill. For the past fifteen years she had experienced chronic difficulties with rheumatism, and all her adult life she faced episodic bouts with migraine headaches. Like everyone, she too was felled by an occasional virus, although for the past few seasons these illnesses had occurred annually, someti.nes attacking her twice a year. It is not clear what struck her down in August 1798. The president said she was "sick of a complication of disorders, a chronic Diarrhea, an intermittent fever & almost a diabetes." This might have been due to a virus and the complications that it produced. She might even have consumed tainted water en route to Massachusetts, falling victim thereafter to a parasite such as cryptosporidium, which can produce similar symptoms for a protracted period. The First Lady's most recent biographer hints that she may have collapsed due to physical or emotional strain, but there is scant evidence to support such a conclusion.[51]

For weeks Abigail believed she was near death, a view shared by her husband. Three weeks after reaching Peacefield, Abigail remained "in great danger," her husband thought. More than a month later, she continued in an "extremely low" state, and, fully three months after the onset of the affliction, she still was too weak to write. At the height of the crisis, Adams apprised Washington that his wife's life hung in the balance, and "mine in consequence of it," he added darkly. Near the end of what was to have been a joyous, relaxing, working holiday, Adams sat torpidly in the anxious silence of Peacefield. This was the "most gloomy summer" of his life, he remarked to a correspondent, confessing his inability to concentrate on his public responsibilities. Fortunately, only one pressing issue required immediate attention: the ranking of the general officers, a matter that Adams finally left to Washington's judgment.[52]

By mid-October, Abigail at last succeeded in fighting off whatever had felled her, although she remained too feeble to come downstairs for some time thereafter. Both Nabby and the president continued to tend her needs, yet with the hazard apparently overcome, Adams began to devote more attention to his work. He postponed his return to the capital for nearly thirty days in order to be certain that Abigail was recovering, but by early October he was devoting more time to his correspondence with the members of his cabinet and he even had begun receiving Federalist leaders at his residence.[53]

When he resumed his duties, Adams discovered that the great urgent matter with which he had to contend remained unchanged—the relationship of his country with France. As he once again resumed his duties, the president saw three choices before him. Upon his return to Philadelphia, he might ask Congress to declare war. Second, he might do nothing, continuing in the course he had pursued since March, watching and waiting, but leaving it to Paris to decide whether to move from the cold-war status of the past eighteen months to a state of formal hostilities. Or, despite the failure of two diplomatic embassies to France—one initiated by Washington, the other dispatched in the early days of his own administration—he might once again send envoys across the Atlantic in a desperate search for peace. As the burnished leaves tumbled down all about Peacefield, heralding the third winter of his term, Adams was certain only that he would not request a declaration of war. In fact, he now believed, as Washington did, that a French invasion of the United States was out of the question. "[T]here is no more prospect of seeing a french Army here, than there is in Heaven," he told McHenry.[54]

By the second week in November, still in a choleric mood, Adams was packed and ready to return to Philadelphia. Abigail now was well enough to take short rides in the family carriage, but the long journey to the capital was beyond her endurance. Adams thus rode off, accompanied only by young Billy Shaw, his secretary. For the first time since his first weeks in office, Adams would be compelled to endure the stresses of his job without Abigail's comforting presence. So lonely was he that he wrote home almost every day of the trip, sometimes penning more than one letter a day, even seizing upon a moment or two during mid-day rest stops to dash off a line or two. It was not a pleasant journey. The weather was blustery and wintry cold, and the pyorrhea, which had caused him incalculable pain and the loss of several teeth over the past few years, chose this moment to flare up again. As if these discomforts were not sufficient, he soon was afflicted with a cold that brought on a raw throat and a daily, pounding headache.[55]

By traveling unannounced, the presidential party avoided the usual plague of ceremonies in each hamlet through which it passed. That shortened the trip a bit, so that Adams's carriage arrived at the President's House on the thirteenth day out of Quincy; he would have reached the capital even more quickly had he not paused briefly in New York to visit with Charles, and had he not had to travel through early snowfalls in New Jersey and Pennsylvania.[56]

With only a week remaining before Congress was scheduled to convene, Adams summoned his cabinet on his first full day in Philadelphia. Just before leaving Quincy, he had written to his advisors requesting that they contemplate his options with regard to France. They had an answer for him when the cabinet assembled. His five advisors unanimously recommended that nothing be done. Although he continued to fret over French intrigue within the United States, especially on the frontier, and though they knew that hostilities might procure an alliance with Great Britain, they responded that an "open rupture"—a declaration of war—was "inexpedient." McHenry privately confessed that many Federalists feared the occurrence of war, and Stoddert later remarked that even a congress composed of a majority of Federalists would not declare war. What they told Adams is not known, other than that Pickering informed him simply that Congress was not ready for war.

But, if not war, what course should the president pursue? The cabinet advised against sending still another embassy to Paris. Such a step would be an "act of humiliation," they counseled. Another diplomatic mission should be considered only if "extreme necessity" so dictated, and no one in the cabinet believed that such a necessity existed late in 1798. The president, isolated from his advisors for the past five months, listened and accepted the counsel. He jettisoned the draft of an address to Congress, prepared in Quincy, turning now to Wolcott to write the speech he would deliver. He changed only one sentence in the message his secretary wrote.[57]

On December 8, five days late, Congress finally achieved a quorum and invited the president to present the long-awaited address. Drawn and thinner than he had been in years, Adams walked the short distance to the Congress, which met in the courthouse at the corner of Chestnut and Sixth streets. The president was ushered into the house chamber on the first floor, bowed to Generals Washington, Hamilton, and Pinckney, who had been in town for nearly a month to prepare the organization of the provisional army, and in the customarily nervous manner that overcame him when he was compelled to deliver a formal address, began to read his remarks.

The thrust of what he said was that there would be no change in United States policy. He did not wish for war, but he urged the continued development of America's defenses. Nor would he send another envoy to Paris; such a step would disgrace the nation. If there was a bombshell in the speech, it was in the one sentence he had added to Wolcott's draft. He divulged that he had detected signs of moderation in France, principally through intelligence suggesting the Directory was ready to receive an American ambassador. But he placed the burden of proof on France. "It must . . . be left with France (if she indeed is desirous of accommodation) to take the requisite steps" and to communicate the "determinate assurances" that would result in peace. Give us the sign, he was saying quite clearly, and peace will be at hand.[58]

Afterwards, Adams returned to the President's House, a large mansion that never before had seemed as empty as in this gray, gloomy December. Alone, save for Shaw and his familiar staff of servants, Adams's mood turned as dark and mottled as the terrible wintry weather that gripped Philadelphia. There were no pleasures in his life, he lamented. "No company—No society—idle unmeaning Ceremony . . . Extravagance, Shiftlessness and Health sinking . . . under my Troubles and fatigues." Public service produced only suffering. He could think of no satisfaction that he had ever derived from holding public office. "All my enjoyments have been on my farm," he wailed.[59]

It was a well-rehearsed litany, although one that John Adams had not broached in nearly fifteen years, since his days of travail in Paris and the Netherlands. Alone, surrounded by untrustworthy aides, aware that he had nearly lost his wife to a mysterious illness, confronted with life-and-death decisions, and desperately concerned lest he have the fortitude and the leeway to make the choices he wished to make for the new nation, the mood of contentment that Adams had often conveyed during his vice-presidential years and the jaunty air he had evinced during his early presidency vanished in those last, dark days of 1798. As in the uneasy days of earlier instances of personal crisis, Adams appeared to be slipping back into that state that could only leave him submerged in a black pool of anxiety.

CHAPTER 18

*

Thunderstruck

JOHN ADAMS HAD REACHED A CROSSROADS in his presidency. A terribly difficult decision had to be made. The walls of the president's inner being had begun to close in upon him once again. "I am old—very Old and never shall be very well—certainly while in this office," he lamented. And certainly not in the year 1799, the year of decision.[1]

Adams had told Congress that he would make no changes in American policy. In fact, something would have to be done. If nothing else, the existence of a costly army required some movement. One solution to the quandary was to give peace a chance only until the summer, watching in the meantime to see if Paris seized the proffer of a peaceful resolution held out in his recent speech. That was the recommendation of Hamilton and his men. Jefferson feared they would have their way. War could be averted, he predicted gloomily, only if the new army was unable to "raise anything but officers" to fill its ranks.[2]

Jefferson did not know that President Adams leaned in another direction. Since the inception of the crisis two years before, he had believed that war might be avoided. But only in the autumn of 1798 had he begun to see signs confirming his belief that a pacific resolution might be within his reach. For Adams, the choice had become one of moving quickly in an effort to nudge the Directory away from the brink of war or of waiting for France to display categorical evidence that it had eschewed its bellicose stance. To take the former path was to risk outpacing public opinion and acting contrary to the wishes of his own party. To pursue the latter course was to chance losing a precious opportunity for peace and, ultimately, to hazard the likelihood of being pressured into war by the sheer momentum of events. During January and February 1799, President Adams sought to control events rather than to be controlled.

Several factors induced Adams to rekindle an initiative for peace. By late 1798 he not only believed that the national ardor for war was evaporating, he understood that the war measures pursued by his administration were sowing the seeds of disunion. Part of the problem stemmed from the high cost of putting the country on a war footing. By Adams's third year in office, the federal government was spending twice the amount that the Washington administration had spent in its final year in office. Taxes increased as the national budget grew; open protest soon flared. Bucks and Northampton counties in Pennsylvania, just up the road from the President's House, witnessed the most sensational disturbances. Many home owners in those counties refused to pay the new assessments. Arrests followed. Some citizens, undoubtedly including many who had come of age protesting English taxes a quarter century before, took the law into their own hands. A mob of nearly 150 men led by John Fries, a middle-aged cooper and father of ten who had fought in the Revolution as a captain of a militia company, pushed their way into the Bethlehem jail and liberated the tax resisters.

Adams was outraged. He spoke of the "treason" of Fries, and he ordered a portion of his new army to assist the state militia in suppressing the resistance.[3]

The Alien and Sedition acts had also eroded the zeal for war. In fact, two Republican-dominated legislatures adopted resolutions (partially drafted by Jefferson) depicting the statutes as evidence of a Federalist plot to establish despotic rule. The Virginia and Kentucky Resolves did not specifically address the Franco-American dispute, but they warned that the Union could not long exist if the rights of the citizenry were abused.

However, the flagging war spirit did not trouble Adams. What grieved him was the emergence by the late 1790s of a new phenomena, the very danger, in fact, of which he had warned in the *Defence* and "Davila." He believed that a powerful oligarchic force sought to lay hold of the United States, a force created during the Federalist years. He knew that powerful families had made "monstrous fortunes" through the institutions that Washington and Hamilton had erected; in some states, power and wealth were becoming increasingly concentrated in fewer and fewer hands. He knew too that what Jefferson called a "war gentry" had sprung up in the course of his own administration, Federalists who sought to remain in power through the perpetuation of the crisis with France. This element had used the army to crush Fries and his supporters in Pennsylvania, the vice-president believed; he feared the army would next be used to throttle dissent in the South. Some worried that Inspector General Hamilton might use the army to stage a coup against the Adams administration; it was a fear expressed both by Jefferson and Abigail Adams. Adams shared some of the apprehensions of his wife and his Republican foes, and he knew full well that the imperious forces unleashed under Federalist rule would only be strengthened in the event of war with France.[4]

One solution to these domestic ills was to end the war crisis. Adams had always hoped to avoid war. Now he believed that a conflict with France might be averted. In part, his views were shaped by the reports of several individuals. In October, just before he departed Quincy, Adams was visited by Gerry, recently returned from France. The meeting caused a tempest in some circles within the Federalist party, for Gerry had won the enmity of many by refusing to return home with Marshall and Pinckney following their reception by agents "W, X, Y, and Z." He had remained in Paris as a private citizen, but he had engaged in talks with Talleyrand's low-level functionaries. Some in the President's party viewed Gerry as a traitor; more saw him as a political opportunist. Adams, however, continued to view him as a trusted friend, albeit a misguided one, and he welcomed the chance to confer with someone who possessed firsthand information of recent events in France. The message Gerry bore was that France did not desire war.[5]

Adams also was influenced by Dr. George Logan, an idealistic Quaker from Philadelphia who had undertaken a private peace mission to Paris in 1798. Arriving in midsummer, Logan had presented letters of introduction from Jefferson and other Republican officials to Talleyrand's ubiquitous secret agents; soon he was meeting with the foreign minister himself, as well as with various members of the Directory. Logan remained for only two weeks, but his venture yielded two significant results. Before the Philadelphian departed Paris, the French government released several American sailors who had been held captive for months. In addition, Logan's mission helped persuade Adams that the Directory genuinely sought to avoid war. On his first full day back in the capital following his summer hiatus in Quincy, Adams met with Logan. Over tea the president listened carefully as his guest insisted that France now was ready to receive an American minister. Adams appeared skeptical. Perhaps the French would accept you, he told Logan, or maybe Madison or some other Republican. Logan held his ground. "[W]hoever you do please to send will be received," he insisted.[6]

Other evidence that reached Adams's hands that fall mitigated his skepticism and convinced him that both Gerry and Logan had correctly apprised French intentions. Messages from America's official diplomats were the most decisive in shaping his thinking. In October the first of several important communiques arrived from William Vans Murray. This was a man whom Adams trusted. He had met Murray in London in the 1780s, when the young man was studying law. Murray clearly admired Minister Adams, and Adams clearly respected a man who was so fond of him. The friendship warmed while Murray spent Adams's vice-presidential years as a staunchly Federalist member of the House of Representatives from Maryland; in 1797 President Adams selected him John Quincy's successor at The Hague. Once in Europe, Murray and John Quincy grew close, prompting the president's son to express his appreciation of Murray's talents. The president thus was disposed to listen sympathetically to whatever this soft, effeminate—he was pretty rather than handsome—young man reported.[7]

Murray had hardly stepped on Dutch soil before he was approached by Louis André Pichon, twenty-eight years old and a member of the French legation at The Hague. Murray might have guessed that Pichon's presence and friendliness were not accidental. Soon the two young men were meeting frequently and covertly, although Pichon kept Talleyrand up to date on the progress of the talks, while Murray not only wrote directly to President Adams but to John Quincy in Berlin, who in turn passed on the envoy's private correspondence to his father. From the outset of the conversations, Murray gathered that France feared war with the United States. Not only would hostilities be unpopular in France, they would drive the United States back into the arms of Britain. Almost surely, too, war would doom France's remaining colonial toehold in North America.[8]

The reports of Gerry, Logan, and Murray were instrumental in refashioning Adams's thinking and in causing him to suspect that some of his "friends" had seized upon the crisis as a means of speeding him into a "Quixotical adventure" to advance their own ends. But still another breakthrough for the president came in January, about a month after he spoke to Congress. The news that Adams awaited was brought to him by his youngest son, Thomas Boylston, who returned to America at the beginning of 1799.[9]

In an effort to chart his own course, Thomas had traveled to Europe with John Quincy five years before, and he had served at his brother's side as a secretary in the Netherlands and Berlin. Gradually, however, he wearied of life abroad; besides, as he passed his twenty-fifth birthday, Thomas Boylston longed to return to the states and get on with his life. Late in 1798, he caught a vessel—ironically, the *Alexander Hamilton*—for America. The *Hamilton* docked in New York, and four days later, after brief visits with Nabby and Charles, Thomas was reunited with his father at the President's House in Philadelphia. One reason that he had hurried to the capital was to deliver a satchel laden with crucial diplomatic correspondence.[10]

Among the papers borne by Thomas was a letter from Talleyrand to Pichon, who had passed on his superior's communique to Murray. After some indecisiveness (he was uncertain whether the foreign minister was the actual author) Murray had forwarded it to the president. Talleyrand's epistle stated that "every plenipotentiary whom the Government of the United States will send to France . . . will undoubtedly be received with the respect due to the representative of a free, independent, and powerful country." Adams saw in this document the "determinate assurance" of France's peaceful intentions that he had requested of Paris.[11]

Early in February further confirmation arrived of France's desire to end the Quasi-War crisis. Once again, Murray was the source of the intelligence. He sent over a packet from The Hague containing still another pacific overture from Talleyrand. Adams saw this material just hours after the *Aurora*, edited now by William Duane, printed a story, based on insurance data, demonstrating that American merchants actually had suffered greater shipping losses at the hands of the British Royal Navy than to the Directory's prowling frigates.

Thomas Boylston Adams, c. 1795, aged twenty-three. Artist Unknown. *Courtesy: Massachusetts Historical Society.*

Even Pickering confirmed the reliability of the story. In fact, the High Federalists could only watch helplessly as Duane's scoop further defused the war spirit that had gripped the land.

Jefferson noted early in the year that he believed public opinion was beginning to swing. Adams, too, was aware of the change. In fact, he nurtured it. On February 2, he released for publication Gerry's notes and report on his conversations with French officials during the preceding year. The Republicans had known for months that Gerry had turned over his papers to the State Department, and they suspected that the documents had been sequestered because, as Madison remarked, the envoy's conclusions did "not favor the position which our Government wishes to take." Now everyone could read Gerry's account of the environment of conciliation that he had encountered in Paris.[12]

Late that same week, the determinative word reached the president's desk, tidings that enabled him to escape his straitjacket and act as he had long wished to act. The post brought a letter from Washington at Mount Vernon. The general had heard from Joel Barlow, well known for his Francophile views. This was not the first time Barlow had written to a powerful figure asserting his belief that France wished for peace with the United States. Indeed, the previous autumn a missive he had sent to a Georgia congressman found its way into the hands of Matthew Lyon, who had made it the basis for a pamphlet—the publication that led to his prosecution for libel, in fact—that urged Adams to pursue negotiation with the Directory. Adams had discounted the advice. While he admired Barlow's talents as a poet, Adams otherwise had no use for the man, a one-time Connecticut Federalist whose long stay in Paris had resulted—in Adams's view—in his conversion into a libertine and a democrat. He was a "worthless fellow," Adams believed, a worse miscreant even than Tom Paine, he said.[13]

It was not Barlow's entreaties that impressed Adams, therefore, but the accompanying message from Washington. The retired president insisted that Barlow correctly understood that the Directory sought peace on "terms honorable" to the United States. Not only did he believe that the American people desired peace, Washington went on, but he felt peace was essential for the best interests of "this rising empire."[14]

Adams was bolstered by Washington's communiqué. The old general's support would become an aegis for him in the rough days that lay ahead, buffering the fire storm certain to be generated within his own party when he launched a new peace offensive. But, for Adams, the meaning of Washington's commitment to a pacific policy was more profound than its mere political ramifications.

Washington's devotion to peace released Adams from the emotional shackles that had gripped him from the onset of the French crisis, restraints that had appeared to be growing ever tighter since his return to Philadelphia the previous November. During the two great wars of his life, Adams had been irresolute and deeply troubled over his failure to play the soldier, often exhibiting unmistakable signs of distress and anguish. During his presidency, that same deep, afflicting, infixed turmoil appeared once again to churn away within him as he confronted the prospect of unleashing war by his own hand.

At the outset of the Quasi-War crisis he had sought to convince himself that France bore sole responsibility for the apparently inevitable hostilities. By late 1798 he was no longer certain of his initial judgment. Signs of France's hopes for peace, nourished by the calm assessments of men like Gerry and Murray, as well as John Quincy, and heightened by the devious machinations of treacherous men during the drive to create and command the provisional army, sowed doubts in the president's mind. By early 1799, the third year of the crisis, he was haunted by a steadily growing awareness that many within his own party yearned for war or a war climate solely "for electioneering purposes." For a time, Adams had pretended to be the nation's first soldier, appearing in a uniform with a sword strapped to his waist, issuing the most bellicose statements. In part, he adopted the posture in order to prepare the nation for the possibility of war and in part to convince France that the United States would resist its depredations. But he had also struggled to convince himself that he was not afraid of war and that he possessed the "manly determination" to lead the country into conflict if no other choice existed.

In the end, another choice did exist, although choosing not to go to war was extraordinarily difficult, both politically and emotionally. There was Hamilton to be reckoned with. Adams looked upon him almost as he would a feral animal, a reckless, intriguing, megalomaniac, who, he now believed, somehow had frightened even Washington into complying with his every wish. Not even the resources of the presidency, Adams feared, would be sufficient to enable him to win a fight with the inspector general. Hamilton exerted greater control over the Federalist Party than did the president; that fact was evident not only in a negative response to Adams's December speech by the Federalist-dominated Senate but in the bitter attacks by the Federalist press on its own president for the few conciliatory remarks he had uttered in that address.

The pressures on Adams were so great that many, including the French consul, continued to believe that ultimately he would capitulate and ask Congress for a declaration of war. So heavy were his burdens, in fact, that he sometimes wondered if he could survive the ordeal. The fortuitous intervention of Washington in February was crucial, therefore, for it helped to remove the heavy emotional perturbation with which he had wrestled and instilled in him the courage to take the step he knew would doom the slide toward war. Even so, having made the decision that could result in peace, he responded to Washington the following day by decrying those who "snivel" for peace and who engaged in "babyish and womanly blubbering" for an accord with France. His sense of manhood compelled him to posture in such a manner, especially when dealing with General Washington. However, his sense of right, his understanding of the national interest, his compassion, and his horror of war and the role he would play in it, led him in quest of the very accord that he accused others of stalking in a timorous, tearful manner.[16]

Having resolved to act for peace, Adams considered at least three alternative courses. He could have quietly conducted low-level talks through Murray at The Hague, a plan proposed by John Quincy. The beauty of this choice was that a plenipotentiary would be sent to Paris only after an agreement had been secured. Curiously, the president rejected this option. He might also have insisted that Paris send a special envoy to Philadelphia as a sign of its serious desire to reach an accommodation. That notion, too, was scotched, probably because those negotiations inevitably would have fallen to Pickering, whose trustworthiness Adams had begun to question. Instead, Adams opted to dispatch still another diplomat to Paris.[17]

Murray, once proposed by John Quincy for this very sort of enterprise, was Adams's choice as envoy. The president did not consult the cabinet or any member of Congress. He simply dropped his bombshell. On February 18 he dispatched a courier to Congress bearing his message. The messenger sought out Jefferson, who interrupted the business of the Senate to read the terse remarks. It was an "event of events," the vice-president remarked privately the following day. His joy upon reading the communication must have equaled the mortification of the Federalists, who sat in stony silence listening to the remarks of their president. Murray had been appointed, Jefferson happily read on, subject to the Senate's consent and with the stipulation that he was not to step foot on French soil until he received concrete assurances from the French government that he would be formally received as the representative of a sovereign nation.[18]

Moments later, the news reached the House of Representatives, arriving, ironically, while its members debated an increase in the size of the new army. Adams's friend, Harrison Gray Otis, the nephew of James Otis and Mercy Warren, was puffily excoriating the French when a colleague, just informed of Adams's intent by a Senator, rose to say that there no longer was a need to consider the bill. Otis, visibly shaken, took his seat; the House adjourned, some to celebrate, some too angry or too sick to continue. The rancor of the High Federalists, Jefferson noted, only proved "that war had been their object" all along.[19]

The decision has "Stirred the Passions of some," Adams soon laconically informed his wife. That was not the half of it. The "federal party were thunderstruck," the British minister reported, using the same adjective that Pickering had used to express his shock at Adams's decision. Perhaps never in United States history has a party turned on its own president as virulently as the High Federalists struck against Adams. Their newspapers boiled with vituperative editorials. Anonymous threats of assassination circulated. Federalist senators and congressmen scurried to the President's House to plead with Adams to reconsider his decision. One, Theodore Sedgwick, a prosperous lawyer and landowner from Berkshire County, Massachusetts, now the Speaker of the House, became engaged in a shouting match with the president, a man whom he regarded as "vain, jealous, and half frantic." Otis questioned Adams's sanity, while the secretary of state, angry and humiliated at being ignored by his chief, wrote Washington to request that the old general use his influence to forestall the dishonor that Adams threatened to bring upon his country.[20]

Unable to dissuade Adams, the High Federalists set about to convince him to appoint additional commissioners to assist Murray. Such a move reflected the counsel of Hamilton, who felt the young Maryland Federalist was "certainly not strong enough for so immensely important a mission." Typically, Adams was unyielding at first, but, after less than a week, he relented, although he did rebuff suggestions that Hamilton and George Cabot be included among the envoys. Adams had little choice but to surrender to the clamor for a broader peace team. So much opposition had erupted that Murray's confirmation by the Senate was uncertain. On February 25, therefore, Adams announced the appointments of Oliver Ellsworth, the chief justice who had sworn him into office, and Patrick Henry. Later, when the Virginian declined the appointment, Adams selected another southerner, William Davie, the Federalist governor of North Carolina, to join Murray and Ellsworth in approaching the French government. Adams also announced that the two new emissaries would remain in the United States until France formally agreed to receive Murray with dignity. At a late Saturday afternoon cabinet meeting, the instructions for the diplomats—prepared by Pickering at the president's direction—were completed. America's demands were tough, so much so that Pickering boasted in private that France would never consent to commence negotiations. The United States would demand that France indemnify it for all the property it had lost during the Quasi-War. The High Federalists, still not very happy, had to be content with the knowledge that they had at least secured some changes. With these alterations in place, the Senate quickly confirmed the appointment of the three envoys. It was Congress's final major act before adjournment, and as the congressmen scattered to their homes, President Adams likewise hurried back to Quincy.[21]

The harbingers of spring that Adams had seen in the capital were not to be found in the cold and wet Massachusetts to which he returned in the final days of March 1799. Yet, he was delighted to be reunited with Abigail, whom he found still weak and troubled with insomnia. She was better than when he last had seen her more than four months before, but the thought of her facing a torrid summer in her delicate condition caused him considerable concern. Indeed, when a brief spell of hot days besieged Quincy in May, she seemed about to relapse, but that scare lasted no longer than the blistering weather.

Thomas Boylston was also present when his father arrived, having come home earlier in the month to visit his mother; he remained at Peacefield for only a few days after John's arrival, however, departing for Maryland to visit the Johnsons, John Quincy's in-laws, then to settle in Philadelphia where he planned to complete his legal studies.[22]

Adams's hiatus at Peacefield should have been therapeutic. Not only had he escaped a hot, fetid Philadelphia but he was able to superintend work at the farm he loved, overseeing the construction of a cider house and the completion of a new barn. Nabby was there most of the time as well, for what had become an annual visit with her parents. Adams squeezed in several public appearances that spring and summer, always a delightful experience for this man who enjoyed adulation. Dressed in full military uniform, he attended a meeting of the Artillery Company of Boston and participated in a ship-launching ceremony in Boston harbor. Later, he was an honored guest at the commencement exercises at Harvard, and still later he appeared at a July Fourth celebration.[23]

Abigail once characterized each year of her husband's life in the presidency as six months of tranquillity followed by six months of "severe duty." But that was not true of this respite at Peacefield. Even here, she discovered, he could not escape the cares of his office. At times the burden seemed too heavy to bear. His appetite disappeared; he lost weight. He feared that his life was ebbing away under the strain; in two years, he fretted, he would not be alive. A black irritability came over him. In his sour, atrabilious mood he launched prosecutions against two authors who had published attacks on his administration. At times he was so irascible that Abigail thought it unwise even to permit him to see state documents. He acted the perfect curmudgeon, snapping at his wife and the hired help and treating old acquaintances and well-wishers in a contemptible and uncivil manner. When General Knox and two others called on him, he refused to engage in conversation, reading the newspaper instead while they stared uncomfortably at one another. One morning a group of naval officers and Harvard students rode out from Boston hoping for an appearance, and, if they were lucky, a few brief remarks by the president. He did appear at his front door, but only to tongue-lash them for their insolence at coming to his estate without an invitation. The men were mortified at the president's conduct, Abigail wrote, and she was embarrassed for him.[24]

The testiness and melancholy with which Adams wrestled during his stay in Quincy grew from the realization that his presidency probably had been destroyed and, with it, the opportunity to serve a second term. It was the price he had paid, he said, for having defied the "combinations of Senators, generals, and head of departments" that had hungered for war. The fact was inescapable, and not even his bucolic farm, always a haven in times of crisis, could buffer cold reality.[25]

But Adams was not alone in witnessing the collapse of his ambitions that summer. Hamilton's schemes also appeared wrecked by the recent decision of the president, threatening his political future and that of his satraps as well. Many of his followers concluded that Adams must have lost his mind. One High Federalist, Fisher Ames of Boston, spoke of the "freakish humors" that supposedly had always been characteristic of Adams's behavior; others prayed that the chief executive's "horses might run away with him or some other accident happen to break his neck," apparently without stopping to think that such a tragedy would only elevate the hated Jefferson to the President's House.[26]

Hamilton's future, as well as that of the Federalist Party, was built largely on opposition to France. Adams's peace mission thus threatened the very super- structure upon which their prosperity stood. But peace with France imperiled far more for Hamilton. Abigail Adams once had asked: "What benifit can war be to [the president]? He has no ambition for military Glory." No one would have said that of Hamilton. The gleam reflected by Spain's New World empire had caught the eye of the New Yorker. Indeed, he had long been entranced by that luminous, precariously held entity. Nine years before, he had sought to educate President Washington on the necessity of establishing United States hegemony over the Mississippi River; long before that, in his very first political tract, published a few weeks before Lexington-Concord, he had enviously dreamed of the day when New Spain would be swept out of North America. When he became inspector general in 1798, he told one of his subordinates of the "Tempting objects" that will "be within our Grasp" should war be de- clared. Florida, lush and inviting to the south, and sprawling Louisiana to the west, were the prizes that he coveted, and war with France—tied by alliance to Spain—was the means to that end.

To capture these jewels not only would make the United States a power in the Gulf of Mexico, it would leave the nation poised on the threshold of the Caribbean. Possession of Louisiana would open a sluice into the continental heartland west of the Mississippi; it would also forestall the likelihood of the region's falling into the clutches of France. North and South would be benefici- aries, as would the Federalist party. General Hamilton, conqueror, surely would benefit as well. His grandiose vision has often led historians to compare him to Napoleon. George Washington might be a more suitable comparison, however, for his career had been launched as the soldier of a Virginia govern- ment that sought to usurp the trans-Appalachian West from the clutches of France. If all went well, Hamilton might be to his generation what Washington had been to his. Only John Adams seemed to stand in his way. By early autumn 1799, Hamilton had grown terribly anxious, for after a delay of almost six months, the president appeared on the verge of dispatching commissioners Davie and Ellsworth to join Murray in the commencement of peace talks with the French.[27]

Hamilton had not initially betrayed great alarm at Adams's sudden message of February 18. After all, the president had given his assurance that the mission would not proceed until clear evidence existed of an altered attitude in Paris; moreover, General Hamilton was confident that France would not accept the terms that America demanded for the establishment of normal relations. Sooner or later, he remained confident, one side or the other would declare war. Hamilton was further cheered when word arrived in mid-summer of the coup d'état of 30 *Prairial,* a brief uprising that toppled all but one member of the Directory. It appeared that the Directory's days were numbered and that a Bourbon restoration was imminent. Whatever else that meant, Hamilton presumed that the political chaos within France would compel Adams to direct Ellsworth and Davie to remain at home until conditions in Paris were clarified.

Adams had other ideas, however. At about the same time that word of the French coup reached Philadelphia, several dispatches from Murray also arrived. That envoy not only continued to radiate confidence in the pacific intentions of France, but his mail pouch contained still another letter from Talleyrand. The foreign minister was responding directly to Adams's February speech, and his latest statement gave fresh assurance that America's envoys would be received cordially. The president directed Pickering to ready the instructions for the envoys. He announced, too, that Davie and Ellsworth soon would sail.[28]

The secretary of state temporized, taking more than a month to complete a task that should have required only a day or two. Then he wrote the president urging that the mission be postponed. Adams should wait for word of the disposition of the post-*Prairial* government, he argued. The cabinet favored the suspension of the mission, he added, an innacurate statement since two members, Stoddert and Lee, urged the immediate dispatch of the envoys. Finally, Pickering warned that the allies were near victory, and, in their triumph, they might turn upon the United States if Adams's actions begat the impression that his government was too closely tied to France. Privately, Pickering told a friend that he thought Adams was playing to the masses. Vanity was the most dangerous attribute in a public figure, he went on, adding that he could see no other reason for the course that Adams was pursuing.[29]

In his isolation at Quincy, three hundred miles from the capital, without a single advisor present, Adams had to make each decision alone. He weighed Pickering's counsel. He accepted it. The emissaries were not to sail. Evidently, Adams decided to postpone his final decision until late November when he would return to the capital. By then, perhaps, the intentions of the new French government could be seen with great clarity. By that time, too, the improvements to the navy that he had set in motion during the previous year would be nearing completion.[30]

During Adams's long stay in Quincy, he had been well aware that his extended absence (he had been at home for six months by the time of his exchange with Pickering) had raised many eyebrows. Washington had never been away for that long, never for more than three months, in fact. Absence for such an extraordinary period in normal times would have provoked criticism; his absence from the seat of government in the midst of a crisis was, to some, tantamount to an abrogation of his responsibilities. Adams remained unmoved, however, always pleading that his wife's precarious health required that he remain at her side. Actually, while Abigail remained frail, she was able, by her own admission, to tend to the needs of her family, even to travel short distances visiting friends and relatives. Adams's stay at Peacefield, thus, appears to have been escapist. He required this asylum and he needed Abigail's comfort and reassurance to see him through the travail.[31]

Adams probably would have remained until November had it not been for the urgent appeals of Benjamin Stoddert. Late in August, the Navy secretary wrote urging the president to come to Philadelphia immediately. When Adams refused, Stoddert wrote again, this time warning that "artful designing men" sought to take over his foreign policy and destroy his peace initiative. If successful, he warned, the implications for Adams in the election of 1800 could be substantial. Adams at once agreed to come.[32]

His destination was Trenton, to which the government had moved temporarily while the capital once again was besieged by yellow fever. Although autumn had arrived, pushing the searing summer weather out of the Delaware Valley, ten to fifteen people were dying daily in Philadelphia. Adams set out about October 1. Traveling with him were Shaw and two servants. Abigail felt well enough to come too but planned to travel at a more leisurely pace, so she waited in Quincy for several more days, before beginning her journey. It was a miserable trip for Adams. Not only was he wrenched away from home before he was ready to leave, but he was made to go without his wife and to travel in intolerable conditions, for, day after day, cold, rainy weather lashed his carriage as it struggled languidly to the south. He reached Trenton on the tenth, weary and suffering from his first cold of the season. According to one eyewitness, he looked quite ill.[33]

Trenton was a little village through which Adams had often passed. Made famous by Washington's great victory at Christmas 1776, it had been the temporary capital once before, when Congress had been run out of Philadelphia in 1783 by mutinous Continental soldiers. Adams found lodging in the private dwelling of two maiden sisters. He had a small bedroom and a tiny adjoining parlor to himself. He also found that his landladies took great pride in waiting on their famous guest. One found a down comforter for him; the other located some rhubarb and calomel and urged him to use it as a cold remedy.[34]

By the time Adams left Quincy, he had decided to dispatch the envoys, and he instructed Pickering to have Davie and Ellsworth ready to sail before the end of October. His resolve was only strengthened when he discovered upon arriving in Trenton that his attorney-general, Charles Lee, strongly endorsed the mission. Lee, in fact, warned that postponing or canceling the enterprise not only would adversely affect public opinion, it might communicate such an air of hostility to Paris that the opportunity for rapprochement could be lost.[35]

Adams quickly summoned his cabinet, meeting with them several times during his first five days in town. At each session, Adams listened as McHenry, Pickering, and Wolcott inveighed against the mission, but, in the end, the president had his way. At the conclusion of a marathon session that stretched nearly until midnight on the fifteenth, it was official. The instructions for the three envoys were prepared. The draft over which Pickering had dallied so long was accepted almost in its entirety, though Adams strengthened it here and there with a subtle change of words ("seeking redress" became "demanding redress," for instance). Ellsworth and Davie were ordered to sail within the next two weeks.[36]

Undoubtedly apprised by one of his disciples of the virtual certainty of the mission, Hamilton, in desperate straits, took a mad step. Leaving his army behind in Newark, two days away at a hard gallop, he hurried to Trenton to protest the mission. He met with the president two or three times on matters pertaining to the army, then he requested one last interview, a session at which he at last got down to cases. His action presented an extraordinary spectacle: a general officer, without policy-making portfolio, arrogating to himself the responsibility of counseling the president of the United States. For such an act, another president well might have summarily ordered the soldier back to his troops. Adams, however, listened to him for several hours.

Hamilton opened with a lengthy monologue on the state of Europe, speaking in a condescending manner, as if lecturing a first-year student. Having begun in a calm, pedantic vein, Hamilton gradually underwent a transformation, working himself into a state of frenzied excitement, speaking in loud, agitated tones. Years before, Knox and General Lee had told Adams of Hamilton's tendency to grow impassioned as he argued, so, the president, well prepared, rather enjoyed this exhibition of "paroxysm," as he later called it, listening, saying nothing, probably puffing all the while on a cigar. The thrust of Hamilton's argument was that the Bourbons once again would be in command of France by Christmas and that Louis XVIII would be unlikely to receive the American envoys.

When the general completed his speech, Adams rejected his assertions. Secretly believing that this "[over]wrought . . . little man" had betrayed a "total ignorance . . . of every thing in Europe, in France, England and elsewhere," Adams told Hamilton that he did not foresee an imminent Bourbon restoration, but if it did occur he expected its foreign policy to be similar to that of the Directory.

Seeing the futility of continuing to pursue his initial course, Hamilton switched tactics. The peace mission would result in war with England, he now maintained, just as John Jay's accord with London had inaugurated America's difficulties with France. Once again, Adams rebuffed Hamilton's case. Hostilities with Great Britain would only drive America into the arms of France, as they had after 1775. Such an eventuality was the last thing that a beleaguered England could desire, he informed Hamilton.[37]

Hamilton was beaten, though he still refused to surrender. Before he returned to his army, he sought to persuade Ellsworth to refuse to sail for Europe. If he resigned, Hamilton argued, the credibility of the undertaking might be destroyed. At the very least, he went on, the mission would have to be delayed until his successor was approved by the Senate, thus postponing the envoy's arrival in Paris until the next spring or summer. Ellsworth, like Adams, listened politely, but he too declined Hamilton's entreaties.[38]

At last, Hamilton was defeated. The envoys departed from Newport, Rhode Island, on November 3. By month's end they had alighted in Lisbon, no farther from Paris than Quincy was from Philadelphia.

By the last week in October, fall's leaves almost gone, the morning nippy with autumn frost, several officials returned to Philadelphia, convinced that the danger of plague was past. Adams waited several days before leaving Trenton, delaying his departure until Abigail arrived from New York. The First Lady had left Quincy about a week after her husband, paused briefly at Nabby's residence in East Chester, then hastened into New York, hoping to see Charles. She had not heard from him for months, a likely augury of bad news; what she found when she reached his home was worse than she had ever feared. He was in utterly disastrous straits, a discovery that the president had made a few days earlier in the course of his trip to Trenton.

Stopping briefly in New York, Adams had found Charles deeply, inextricably in the thrall of alcoholism. Adams had raged at his troubled, suffering young son, accusing him of being a "Rake," a "Beast," a "Madman possessed of the Devil." Not only had he lost six thousand dollars belonging to John Quincy but had squandered the golden opportunity for a successful life, which his parents had prepared for him. John renounced his son, vowing never again to see him or to have the least contact with him, a monstrously cruel promise that he kept.[39]

Gentler and more compassionate, Abigail refused to cut her ties with her son while the faintest hope existed for his recovery. Deep down, however, she knew that her son was doomed as surely as had been her own brother, William, likewise a victim of alcoholism in his youth. Abigail found Sally, Charles's wife, and their two small daughters, at Nabby's home. They had sought refuge there from Charles and his besotted, insensate manner. Sally provided her mother-in-law with the unadorned details of Charles's deterioration. His health was sinking, his legal practice already destroyed. His wife had no idea even of his whereabouts. Months before, he had resolved to eschew drink; clearly, he had not, could not keep his pledge. He was a "graceless child," his mother re-

Charles Adams, c. 1797, aged twenty-seven. Artist Unknown. *Courtesy: Massachusetts Historical Society.*

marked, but she was moved to anguish and pensiveness, not to the unbridled rage and enmity of her husband.[40]

In his despondency over Charles and the cares Adams bore continually for Nabby, he first excoriated himself for having been separated from his children while they were growing up. Then he envied Washington. "Happy Washington! happy to be Childless," he wrote Abigail. "My children give me more Pain than all my Ennemies," he added. But Abigail would not go that far. "I do not consider GW at all a happier man because he has not children," she responded. "[I]f he has none to give him pain, he has none to give him pleasure." She could not excuse Charles's "viscious conduct," she went on, but she sought to convince herself and her husband of their blamelessness in the unfolding tragedy. Each son had received a "good & virtuous" education, and two had developed "virtuous and distinguished Characters." As for Charles, "what I cannot remedy I must endure."[41]

Charles's desperate plight was the most grievous problem raised by the children, but Nabby's unfortunate marriage provoked almost as much anxiety for her parents. The wife of "a gay, deluded boy" (Louisa Catherine's characterization) who seldom was at home and who had fallen deeply into debt in the fanciful pursuit of one get-rich-quick scheme after another, Nabby must have cursed the day that the handsome young colonel had walked into her life. Actually, though, there was a ray of hope for this couple. Smith had used the war scare and his father-in-law's influence to secure a colonelcy in the new army. Rebuffed by the Senate in his quest for a general officership, he had accepted a lower rank out of desperation, even agreeing to serve under men whom he had commanded in the last war. Adams thought him a fool for accepting such a humiliating post; it was embarrassing to him to sign such a commission, but, as an indulgent father, he did so for the sake of Nabby.[42]

Though Thomas Boylston, meanwhile, would have preferred a career in business had he possessed the capital to get started, he resumed his legal studies. Once he was ready to open a law office, both parents encouraged him to settle in Quincy. John and Abigail admitted that Philadelphia offered more fertile ground for a young lawyer with a recognizable name, but both evidently doubted their son's ability to succeed in the fast world of the capital. He was a "good amicable and virtuous" young man, Abigail said, "a comfort to his parents," save for his habitual diffidence and nonchalance. Eventually, John and Abigail relented, and Thomas opened an office in Philadelphia, although he did agree to their entreaties to move into the President's House in order to save money. But Thomas remained a concern of his father. With his practice languishing, John admonished him about his friends, uncomfortable that Thomas ran with Quakers rather than with other attorneys. He offered well-meant advice, too. He urged his son to follow the path he had blazed. Every legal establishment is dominated by three or four men, he counseled; gain the "heart, the Confidence and real friendship of one of them or you will not succeed," Adams told his son, thinking of his relationships with Otis and Gridley. The president was also troubled by his son's lighthearted manner. Once, when a "strain of levity" appeared in a letter that Thomas had written home, his father exploded. All of Thomas's energies must be directed at achieving success in his career, he advised, and that would come only with "a total Sacrifice of Pleasures and Amusements" and "with an ardent devotion to Study and indefatigable devotion to labour." Thomas, now twenty-seven years old, immediately pledged to exhibit a more august persona.[43]

John Quincy was exactly what his father wanted. "I am a man of reserved, cold, austere and forbidding manners," he once said of himself. Some observers thought his deportment keenly resembled that of his father, and many believed that he was destined, like his father, to rise in the world of statecraft. Nevertheless, he was not a happy young man. At age thirty-two he was attending to diplomatic duties in Berlin when he would have preferred to have been in London or The Hague or, better yet, Boston. But he knew that coming home would disappoint his parents. Independent conduct ran counter to his grain. For John Quincy to have simply begun to pursue the sort of life that he desired was as alien to his constitution as for a trusted old dog to eschew his master's comfortable hearth and set out on his own. Thus he remained abroad in "honorable exile," as his mother put it, enduring a sacrifice that would serve as a "future usefulness."[44]

John Quincy's public service was above reproach and his meticulous, incisive, and flawless reports were a crucial factor in shaping his father's policy during the Quasi-War crisis, but this was a cheerless time for him. Louisa did not enjoy her role as a diplomat's wife, and her woes were compounded by frequent illnesses. Although she had been married less than eighteen months by the fall of 1799, she had already suffered three miscarriages. John Quincy, uncommonly moody all his life, was so overtaken with melancholy at his wife's inability to bear him a child that he found himself unable to read or think. Abigail offered advice aplenty to Louisa's mother, bromides that might strengthen her frail, young daughter-in-law. But to her son and Louisa, Abigail merely wrote: "My love to Louisa. No little Johnny. No little Louisa. All the best, be assured."[45]

At last, after a week with Nabby's and Charles's children—during which time Abigail never saw her ill, suffering son—she set out for Trenton. Adams met her in Brunswick, and the two rode together to Philadelphia, returning to the capital during a cold, heavy rain.[46] Fortunately, the dreary weather proved not be a herald of the months just ahead. After the stormy sessions earlier in his presidency, Adams found the Congress that assembled in December the essence of tranquillity, coming and going with the usual partisan strife—after all, the election of 1800 would be held before the legislators next assembled—but with no significant new legislation. The Federalists had long since enacted their program, and with a comfortable majority they beat back the Republicans principal initiative, an attempt to repeal the Alien and Sedition acts.

Congress had hardly commenced before sad tidings reached Philadelphia. General Washington was dead, the victim it now is thought of a streptococcus infection. The general already was buried in a sealed vault at Mount Vernon when word of his demise reached the capital, but the government immediately closed for a day of mourning. Thousands gathered for a funeral procession in which the president participated, then hundreds, including John and Abigail, crowded into a warm Anglican church for the ceremony and the eulogies. That evening the Adamses held a somber dinner for selected dignitaries, including some who had come to the city for the service. The men wore black, Abigail wrote to a friend, the women white dresses with black ribbons, gloves, and flowers. For the Federalist ladies, it was a heady evening, she remarked, for many knew they would not be back for another season of public festivities after the elections in 1800.[47]

Despite the strains that had developed during the selection of the army's officers, Adams was genuinely moved by the death of Washington, a man whom he had respected and admired. So, too, was Abigail, who, since her first meeting with the general during that dark, wartime summer of 1775, had never wavered in her respect and affection for the man. No better man ever lived, she told a friend a day or two after the funeral. He had never misused his awesome power, had never acted for private gain, and had suffered the barbs of his foes in dignified silence. The Adamses dispatched Billy Shaw to Virginia to assist in whatever way he could. Thomas Boylston temporarily took on Shaw's duties as the president's secretary.[48]

When Adams had returned to Philadelphia in November, he already had considered removing Pickering from his cabinet. He had been warned by Gerry even before he took office that Pickering was deceitful and untrustworthy, but Adams had not listened. Nor did he appear to suspect the magnitude of his secretary of state's disloyalty until the fall of 1798, eighteen months into his term. Adams once described himself as "the most . . . unsuspicious man alive." While hardly true of his relationship with Franklin, he sometimes was naively trusting, as he had been with Hamilton, refusing at first to believe the stories he heard of that individual's backhand dealings, and as he had been even earlier with the spies who infiltrated America's diplomatic team in Paris.

Adams never displayed greater naivete than in matters relating to his cabinet, first in accepting Washington's men, then in believing that service in the cabinet categorically bound the official either to obedience or to the relinquishment of the post. Differences had existed between himself and Pickering from the beginning, but Adams had not wanted to surround himself with sycophants. It was only in the course of the controversy over the appointment of the army's officers that he began to think that his secretary's conduct transcended philosophical differences. He began to suspect a dark treachery within his cabinet, a cabal that sought nothing less than the annihilation of his constitutional powers. The manner in which Pickering, McHenry, and Wolcott fought his peace initiative early in 1799 confirmed his suspicions.

Thereafter, according to administration insiders, he frequently denounced Hamilton and openly questioned the loyalty of his secretaries of State, War, and Treasury. Confidants soon plied him with reports that confirmed his misgivings. By chance, some of these accounts were intercepted by Abigail, who kept them from her husband, fearing they would damage his health. But some reached his desk. So too did the urgent letters from Stoddert pressing him to come and take charge, lest the villainy of others demolish his foreign policy. Once in Trenton, Attorney-General Lee confirmed Stoddert's alarming report of perfidy within the cabinet. After he returned to the capital, an anonymous correspondent provided details of an alleged Hamiltonian plot to destroy his diplomatic initiative, then to replace Adams with a more pliable Federalist candidate in the upcoming election.

Before the end of 1799 he had come to see Pickering and McHenry as the worst of the bunch, but it was the secretary of state for whom he reserved most of his pent-up fury. He raged about his "subterranean intrigues," called him "malignant, ignorant and jesuitical," charged that he was not fit to be more than a customs collector, and characterized him as "a man in a mask, sometimes of silk, sometimes of iron, and sometimes of brass." He even alleged that Pickering hated him because, thirty years or more before, Adams had humbled and embarrassed Pickering's father in a Salem courtroom.[49]

Although as early as August 1799, the capital buzzed with rumors of an imminent purge of the cabinet, Adams moved slowly and with considerable reluctance, not acting until more than six months after his clash with Hamilton at Trenton. Abigail attributed his temporizing to his reluctance to have a cabinet filled with yea-sayers. McHenry later suggested that Adams was "actually insane" and that there was no rhyme or reason to his actions. Neither observer was correct. Between November and May the evidence before Adams of duplicity on the part of some cabinet members grew, until he came to believe that Pickering had withheld vital information from him. However, he did not act until he had absolute proof of the treachery of his secretaries of State and War. There was still another reason for his decision to finally purge those who had been so disloyal to him, one that many contemporaries noted. They discerned political overtones in his move to cleanse his cabinet.[50]

Adams wished to be reelected to the presidency, but from the outset he knew that he faced formidable odds in realizing his objective. Even at the height of his popularity during the season of "black cockade fever," he would have faced a difficult battle, but the decline thereafter of Federalist strength made his reelection in 1800 even more problematical. During the off-year elections in 1799, it became apparent that a national backlash had set in

The Executive Mansion in Philadelphia. By William Strickland (1790s). *Courtesy: The Historical Society of Pennsylvania.*

against the Federalist program of militarism, high taxes, and the denigration of civil liberties. The Republicans scored several crushing victories that year, including a triumph in New Jersey, the first time that the Federalists had lost control of that state's legislature. Federalism appeared to be on the wane in Virginia, and the party's majority had deteriorated significantly in Connecticut; in Vermont, Republicanism was so strong that the "spitting Lyon," now out of jail, easily was reelected to Congress. The news early in 1800 was even worse for the Federalists. In April their candidate for governor in Massachusetts, hitherto a Federalist stronghold, defeated Elbridge Gerry by a mere two hundred votes. More stunning news reached the President's House on May 3. The Republicans had won control of the New York legislature, the body that would choose that state's presidential electors. Everyone now knew that the Federalist party could not carry that key state in the election of 1800. By late spring, therefore, Adams realized that he could win reelection only if he broadened his political base. Perhaps the only means of accomplishing that feat at this late juncture was by purging his cabinet of the very symbols of the High Federalist faction within his party. When Adams did move against Pickering and McHenry, most High Federalists, such as Theodore Sedgwick, the Speaker of the House, believed that the secretaries had been "sacraficed [*sic*] as peace offerings."[51]

While the potency of the Federalist Party had declined, Adams's strength within the party had grown during 1799. Some reluctantly fell in behind their president. As the presidential race neared, even Hamilton observed that only Adams could "possibly save us from the fangs of *Jefferson*." Most of Adams's support, however, came as a result of his quest for peace. His announcement that he was sending envoys to Paris had "electrified" the country, as Abigail correctly put it. Fathoming the new political winds, many activists within the Federalist Party moved toward the political center; by the end of 1799 the average Federalist appeared to be closer to Adams than to Hamilton, as Jefferson observed. His observation was borne out in December when a Federalist caucus in Philadelphia agreed to support the president's reelection bid. Even embittered Speaker Sedgwick ruefully acknowledged that Adams's peace probe had "endeared him to the great body of federalists."[52]

When the news of the Federalist debacle in New York reached the President's House early in May, Adams must have realized that he had to act quickly if he was to have any chance of victory in the fall. Nevertheless, the end came suddenly and spontaneously in a moment of black, fervent passion that surprised and dismayed Adams. Darkness was closing in on Philadelphia on May 5—two days after he had learned the results of New York's election—when the president summoned McHenry from dinner. Adams wished to discuss a rather trivial matter, the appointment of a purveyor of public supplies. He may have had no intention of broaching any other subject, but something that McHenry said aroused the quick-tempered president. Almost before Adams realized what had occurred, his pent-up passion and frustration spilled out. He turned savagely on the secretary, revealing that he knew of McHenry's subservience to Hamilton, accusing him of manipulating Washington so that his real boss would become the real power within the new army. Adams rambled on wrathfully, madly charging that McHenry had acted with arrogance toward him; he had connived with Hamilton to unseat him in the coming presidential race. Hamilton, he continued, was the world's greatest schemer and plotter, "a man devoid of any moral principle—a Bastard, and . . . a foreigner. . . . Mr. Jefferson is an infinitely better man; a wiser one, I am sure." McHenry's diplomatic advice was ignorant and foolish, but that was not all. He accused McHenry of having sought to wreak his peace initiative, of having alerted Hamilton to what was afoot so that the inspector general could hurry to Trenton to campaign against sending Ellsworth and Davies to Paris. Redolent with fury, Adams denounced McHenry's alleged prejudice in the selection of the army's officers, then went on to outrightly impeach him for administrative incompetence. "You cannot, Sir, remain longer in the Office," the President closed, finally spilling out what he had longed to say for months.

Stunned by the vitriol of the man sitting across from him, McHenry was momentarily speechless. Then he sought to defend himself. But it was useless, and ultimately, as the president dismissed him, he offered to resign, rather angrily mentioning that had he known of Adams's displeasure he would never have invested in an expensive house in the new Federal City to which the government shortly would move. Adams immediately felt guilty. He apologized and, thrown on the defensive, sought to soften some of the invective that he had just heaped upon the man before him, mentioning that he had always regarded McHenry as an honest and intelligent advisor.[53]

The next morning McHenry formally resigned. Adams did not hesitate to accept, and four days later, on the tenth, he requested Pickering's resignation. Incredibly, the secretary of state refused. Displaying an arrogance that knew no bounds, he responded that he expected Jefferson to be elected in the fall and wished to remain in charge of the last gasp of Federalist foreign policy. Pickering's remarkable answer appeared to confirm Abigail's judgment of the man. Six months before, she had told her sister, the secretary is a man "whose temper is sour and whose resentments are implacable." If the president ultimately displayed some remorse at the removal of his secretary of War, he never showed any regret at discharging Pickering. One hour after he received the secretary's extraordinary communique, Adams fired him. Surprisingly, Wolcott survived. Adams still looked upon him as "a very good Secretary," but one who thereafter would be consulted only on economic matters.[54]

The President moved quickly to fill the vacancies. Samuel Dexter (his Massachusetts friends called him "Ambi"), a Boston lawyer who had served in the House and Senate, replaced McHenry, while John Marshall of Virginia, a member of the first diplomatic team that Adams had sent to Paris, became secretary of state. Hamilton at last had lost to Adams. Not only was his influence within the cabinet destroyed, but he now commanded an army that he would never utilize. On the same day that Pickering was dismissed, Adams moved to raze the provisional force. He met with little opposition; Federalists everywhere were running for political cover. Demobilization began on May 15. Hamilton's response to these events was to remark that Adams was "as wicked as he [was] mad."[55]

Having finally acted, Adams had only two matters on his schedule before he departed for another lengthy summer sojourn in Quincy. John Fries, leader of the Pennsylvania tax rebellion in 1799, had been sentenced to death in May 1799, on a charge of treason. He and two confederates appealed to the president for a pardon. Adams once again procrastinated, waiting almost exactly a year to act. Some of Adams's original advisors urged him not to grant the pardon. In late May 1800, his new cabinet unanimously voted that he permit the executions. Stronger, more independent, Adams rejected their counsel; believing that Fries had led a riot but had not sought to overthrow the government, Adams pardoned the three protestors, recommending clemency. It was the humane thing to do, and a gesture unlikely to harm him in the coming election.[56]

Soon thereafter Adams journeyed to Federal City, now almost universally being called Washington, to inspect the burgeoning capital to which the government would move in the fall. The president traveled with Billy Shaw and his servants; Abigail, not wishing to undergo an arduous journey into a southern summer, had returned alone to Quincy. It was his first trip to the South, and, aside from the fatiguing travel, he appeared to enjoy himself. Large, friendly crowds greeted him everywhere. He visited Martha Washington at Mount Vernon, was feted by Attorney-General Lee who lived near Alexandria, enjoyed a long dinner and a brief tea party at the home of Joshua Johnson, John Quincy's in-laws, and rode and walked about the gnarled, muddy landscape from which the capital city was rising.[57]

Adams liked what he saw of the capital, and, he told Abigail, he looked forward to moving to Washington. Once there, in the president's new house, the White House, perhaps for three months, perhaps for the next four years, he would "Sleep, or lie awake."[58]

CHAPTER 19

*

The Seeds of Discontent
and Division

PEACEFIELD WAS A WELCOME SIGHT for the weary, dusty president, a refuge, he must have thought, from his political worries. It was that, in fact, but it offered no escape from family tribulations. Abigail awaited him with sad tidings. During her recent stop in New York, she revealed, she had discovered that Colonel Smith was at home and once again unemployed now that his regiment had been demobilized. Once again, she was left to fret over the fate of Nabby and the grandchildren. But her news of Charles was far worse. His condition had deteriorated. She now admitted what she had previously refused to concede. "[A]ll is lost," she confirmed; she knew that "ruin and destruction have swallowed him up." It was only a matter of time. One can only guess at her husband's reaction. He had made no attempt to contact Charles during his odyssey from the Potomac. As the summer wore on, he persisted in his refusal to communicate with, or provide succor to, the tormented young man.[1]

Both Adams and the First Lady remained active through those warm, tranquil summer months. Abigail ran the house and oversaw the continuing renovation work begun the year before. John managed the farm and heeded the responsibilities of his office. Actually, there were few obligations concerning the presidency to which he had to tend. There was little news from Paris, save that the envoys had been received early in the spring and that talks were under way. Adams spent some time with reports and appeals from job seekers, but he left as much as he dared to his secretaries in the capital. One matter of public business was on his mind, however—the presidential election of 1800.[2]

The campaign was to be almost a rerun of the 1796 canvass. Adams now shared the Federalist ticket with Charles Cotesworth Pinckney, whose brother had been the other Federalist candidate four years earlier. Pinckney was a talented man who had studied in England and France, soldiered with distinction, and successfully practiced law; he was also a hero of the XYZ incident. The Republicans once again put up Jefferson and Burr. Aside from some myopic New Englanders, few thought Adams could be reelected. The best that most Federalists hoped for was that Pinckney could win, a view shared by Abigail Adams; some, like Speaker Sedgwick, believed until the end that the South Carolinian would be elected and that Adams would be returned to the vice-presidency.[3]

That was the goal sought by Hamilton, a man who at times seemed capable of moving mountains. Initially, he had counseled that Adams was the Federalist most capable of being elected to the presidency and he had urged party members to support the incumbent president. However, the firing of his friends in the cabinet, together with the pardoning of Fries and the disbanding of the army, all of which he seemed to interpret as retributive strikes by the president, caused him to reconsider. By June he had decided to seek the election of Pinckney. If his efforts divided the party and opened the door to Jefferson's election, so be it. At least Jefferson was not marred by the flaws that fouled Adams's character, the "*Vanity* and *Jealousy*," the tendency to decide great issues on "*impulse* and *caprice*."[4]

One key to Pinckney's victory seemed to lie in New England. If the South Carolinian ran well in that section, he might upset Jefferson. To effect that end, Hamilton hurried through each New England state during June. Officially, his excursion was for the purpose of disbanding the brigade stationed in Oxford, Massachusetts, but his activities fooled no one, least of all John and Abigail. The "intriguer" sought "to create divisions and Heart burnings against the president," Abigail immediately concluded, and both she and her husband believed Hamilton would succeed, especially in Connecticut, where Adams had been deserted by even his Treasury secretary, Wolcott. Both were also aware that a powerful faction of Federalist dissidents, popularly called the Essex Junto, sought the president's ouster; the junto—whose members included old friends such as Francis Dana and George Cabot, as well as John Lowell, who had taken over Adams's law practice after 1775—was thought, with Hamilton's assistance, to possess the clout to cause trouble in every New England state, save Massachusetts.[5]

Late in the campaign, Hamilton, driven by his hatred of Adams to the point that his customary highly sensitive political skills were subsumed by his irrational passion, decided to publish an open philippic against the president. Not only would he recapitulate the errors of Adams's statecraft, he would reveal to the public what he judged to be the president's emotional disorders. It was not a wise course for Hamilton to pursue, as some of his friends sought to make him aware. Wolcott, for instance, advised him to circulate his ideas privately, and only then in the Middle Atlantic and southern states. It not only was inexpedient to publish a broadside against Adams, he added, it was unnecessary. The "poor old Man is sufficiently successful in undermining his own Credit and influence." Besides, he went on, "the people [already] believe that their President is Crazy."[6]

But the frenzied New Yorker could not be dissuaded, and in October his *Letter . . . Concerning the Public Conduct and Behavior of John Adams* appeared, more than fifty pages of vitriol through which Hamilton sought to settle old scores against the president. The crux of his attack on Adams's statesmanship revolved about the current peace mission to France. Adams had acted imprudently, without consulting with his advisors, hardly the method of administration that the framers of the Constitution had anticipated in their chief executives, he charged. Hamilton went on to admit that Adams was a good theoretician, but he judged him a poor politician. He also depicted Adams as a jealous, prejudiced man whose vanity knew no bounds, a man who was indecisive, eccentric, egotistical, and abrupt and discourteous to those who worked with him. Adams, he added, was a man with an "ungovernable temper" given to "paroxisms of anger, which deprive him of self command."[7]

Adams understood immediately that the pamphlet would be as harmful to Hamilton as to himself. He also sensed that it would be injudicious for him to respond to the diatribe. He controlled his inclination to lash back at his nemesis, and, indeed, nearly a decade passed before he publicly answered Hamilton. Most Federalist leaders, even those who urged Pinckney over Adams, deplored Hamilton's act, and some even published rebuttals of the tract. The consensus among Federalists was that Hamilton's destructive, divisive maneuver inevitably would result in the forfeiture of his position as a party leader. But many also believed that Hamilton had harmed the president. That was the conclusion of Jefferson, as well. He read some of Hamilton's contumely in a Richmond newspaper, then told Madison that Adams had been mortally wounded by the treatise.[8]

Jefferson was correct, but this was not the only document to appear in the campaign that injured Adams. A private communique that had gathered dust for nearly a decade also came back to haunt him. When Washington appointed Thomas Pinckney ambassador to the Court of St. James in 1792, Adams had privately criticized the move in a letter to Tench Coxe, an acquaintance in the Treasury Department. Then vice-president, Adams made it appear that Great Britain's leaders had pulled strings to secure Pinckney's selection; in addition, he suggested that the Pinckney family had sought to have him removed as minister in London in the 1780s in order to open the post for one of their own.

During the presidential election campaign in 1800, Coxe, now a defector to the Republican Party, turned over Adams's letter to William Duane, the editor of the *Aurora,* who soon printed the document. In the interests of party harmony, General Pinckney initially dismissed the letter as a forgery, but when that line of defense foundered, he urged Adams to disavow the missive. The president responded with a public letter in which he confirmed having corresponded with Coxe, although he claimed to have no recollection of having penned the epistle that Duane had published. If he had actually written the letter, he remarked lamely, he would never have implied that Great Britain had exerted any influence with the Washington administration; if he had ever made comments critical of the Pinckney family, the remarks would have been based on rumor and would have been incorrect.[9]

Adams's letter to Pinckney, issued in the final days of the campaign, was as close as he came to openly electioneering. As in 1796, only Burr actively took to the hustings. Nevertheless, both Jefferson and Adams were more active than in their previous contest. The Virginian provided financial aid to several Republican newspapers, helped distribute political pamphlets, appealed to friends for assistance with his efforts, and wrote several letters that he undoubtedly knew would be made public and would constitute a kind of party platform. On the other hand, when Adams made his trip to Washington in May, he traversed a roundabout route via Lancaster and York in Pennsylvania; on his return to Quincy he paused in Baltimore. Contemporaries saw political overtones in the trip, as well as in his pardon of Fries and in his cabinet purge. They were not entirely incorrect.

Adams believed that open campaigning was beneath both his dignity and that of the presidency. He also thought it unnecessary. He was the incumbent president, and he knew that he would be judged on his record. Besides, his supporters within the Federalist Party were active. They sought to link Washington and Adams as Federalists and to point to the peace and prosperity that had reigned during their stewardship. More scurrilous Federalist writers depicted Jefferson as a weak, even cowardly, individual in the thrall of French Jacobinism, although the issue that received the most attention was the allegation made by some that the Republican candidate was an atheist. There were whispers, as well, about Jefferson's alleged sexual misconduct with his female slaves, rumor and speculation that the Adamses refused to believe.[10]

The Republicans fought back by denouncing the provisional army and the recent naval expansion, decried Federalist taxes, promised the speedy repeal of the Alien and Sedition acts, and alleged that the Federalist Party was pro-British in orientation. They said little about Adams, evidently believing that their adversaries were doing quite enough to vilify their own president.[11]

By remaining in Quincy through the summer and into the fall, Adams managed to escape much of the unpleasantness of the campaign that would have been his lot in the capital. But in mid-October, with Congress's opening session only a few weeks away, he was unable to delay his departure for Washington any longer. Once again, he traveled alone. Abigail had decided to remain in Quincy, then agreed to come, then decided to postpone the start of her journey until several days after her husband had left. She wished to put the house in order after he left. In addition, she recently had suffered a recurrence of her chronic rheumatic afflictions, and she wished to travel more slowly than

John Adams by Gilbert Stuart. The painting was begun in 1801 when Adams was sixty-five years of age. *Courtesy: National Gallery of Art, Washington. Gift of Mrs. Robert Homans.*

Abigail Adams in 1800, aged fifty-six. By Gilbert Stuart. *Courtesy: Massachusetts Historical Society.*

did her husband, pausing frequently and stopping early each evening. She also planned to spend a few days in New York with Nabby and, if possible, with Charles. It was not a journey that she looked forward to. The opportunity to visit her children in New York was one reason she decided to come. She also wished to see the new capital and to decorate the new White House, something she had given some thought to during the past few months. Mostly, however, she did not wish her husband to endure the agony of the election—and his likely defeat—alone.[12]

She left Quincy on the last day of October. Five days later she was in New York, where, unlike her husband, who had passed through the city a few days before, she visited Charles. She found him at the home of a friend, attended by his wife, Sally, who had returned to be with him during the last days of his illness. Before she was admitted to his room, Abigail learned from the attending physician that the end was near, probably only a few days or weeks away. Once she saw her son, she knew the doctor was correct. Charles's alcoholism had destroyed his liver. Bedfast and at times incoherent, he was jaundiced and bloated. With mingled feelings of guilt and remorse, Abigail sat at his side, and, while trying without success not to weep, spoke words that he could not hear.

After two or three days she was compelled to leave, resuming a trip that now was more melancholy than any she had ever before undertaken. She rode mile after mile haunted by the knowledge that she never again would see her son. In Philadelphia she paused briefly to see Thomas Boylston, but even that brief moment of happiness was tempered by calls from many old friends, folks she knew that she would never see again if her husband was turned out of office in March, as she expected. Soon she was on her way again, plunging into the South for the first time in her life. The experience began inauspiciously. Her driver became lost between Baltimore and Washington, and the First Lady of the United States had to bide her time as he drove about aimlessly in search of the right highway.[13]

The city of Washington to which the Adamses moved that November was not a city at all, but a collection of a few public buildings and an occasional private dwelling, most of which still were awash with carpenters and masons hurriedly attempting to complete their labors. In every corner of the burgeoning capital city, each newcomer endlessly heard the resonant thumps and rasps of the workers' tools and lived with the musty scents of brick and mortar and the sweet redolence of freshly cut wood.[14]

At the behest of Congress, President Washington had been asked in 1790 to select a suitable site on the Potomac River for a new federal city. The Residency Act had required that the new capital be ready for occupancy within ten years, and the terms of the act had more or less been met when Adams ordered the federal departments to commence operations in Washington on June 15. The move had begun shortly after Adams's spring visit to the new city; fortunately the new government was small, so tiny, in fact, that the entire archives of all the departments within the executive branch were stored in seven packing cases for the transfer from Philadelphia. The government was in place, therefore, when Adams and the congressmen arrived during the autumn.

Most of the legislators and the vice-president found accommodations in the cluster of boardinghouses erected near the Capitol or along the wide, muddy, poplar-lined thoroughfare linking the Capitol and the White House. Of course, Adams and his wife were ensconced in the new presidential mansion. It was well situated, commanding a majestic view of the Potomac, but Abigail thought the palatial structure—she called it a "great castle"—was too large. Based on a plan offered by James Hoban, an Irish native who had been trained in Dublin, the house in fact was patterned after that of an English gentryman's large country estate. It was twice the size of Abigail's church back in Quincy, she complained, and while it was a "grand and superb" building, it was poorly lighted, inadequately furnished, impossible to heat, and not even completed, as the plastering was yet to be applied in most rooms.[15]

A congressional quorum finally was attained on November 22, and President Adams rode up to the unfinished Capitol to deliver his annual message. He gave a languid performance. The sense of crisis and drama attending earlier occasions was gone, and, besides, he had nothing to report on the progress of the negotiations in Paris. He read a brief speech and departed, much to the joy of the legislators, who were happy to escape their uncomfortably cold House chamber on this nippy fall afternoon.[16]

The paramount issue on the mind of most Washingtonians that fall was the presidential election. "Election day" was December 4, the date set for the electoral colleges to assemble in the various state capitals. Only five of the sixteen states popularly selected their electors; elsewhere, the state legislatures made the choice. By December, therefore, much was already known, gleaned from counting heads in state assemblies. New England would be Federalist. New York and most of the South would be won by the Republicans. Still, there were many unresolved questions. New Jersey, Maryland, Pennsylvania, and South Carolina were too close to call. Moreover, even where the victorious party could already be identified, no one knew how many Federalist electors would vote for both Adams and Pinckney or how many Republicans would submit ballots for both Jefferson and Burr. Adams must have continued to hope against hope for a victory until the very end. Some, in fact, like Harrison Gray Otis, once the close friend of the president, believed until the night before the election that Adams would be reelected.[17]

But, by the end of election week, it was clear that Adams had been defeated. By the middle of the month everyone knew that Adams and Pinckney each had forty-seven votes to forty-six for Jefferson and Burr. However, five southern states with thirty-one votes had not been heard from. Jefferson would do well there, and so might Pinckney, but Adams could hope for little from the electors south of the Potomac. He could not win, and everyone knew it. Some, like Speaker Sedgwick, who had battled the president so often during the past two years, rejoiced. Adams could finish no higher than third place, he exalted. He had been given "sufficient notice to quit" public life, he ecstatically told friends in Massachusetts.[18]

Confirmation of Adams's defeat trickled in over the next few days. Jefferson and Burr had tied with seventy-three votes each. Adams finished in third place with sixty-five electoral votes, one more than Pinckney received. As expected, Adams had run well in New England, edging Pinckney in the region by thirty-nine to thirty-eight. But aside from four votes in North Carolina, he did not garner a single vote in the southern states.

South Carolina and New York had been the pivotal states. Pinckney was shut out in his own state, largely the result of the competent work of his second cousin, Charles Pinckney, who delivered South Carolina to the Republicans, for which he was rewarded with a diplomatic post in Madrid. Had Pinckney made even a modest showing at home, he would have succeeded Adams in the presidency. New York was the most devastating blow to Adams, however. He had carried the state unanimously in 1796, but Jefferson and Burr won every New York electoral vote in this canvass. Abigail alternately attributed the outcome to Burr's competence and to Hamilton's hostility toward her husband's reelection. Since May she had forecast that New York would determine the issue in the election of 1800. The state will "be the balance in the ~~seaile scale skaill~~, scaill (is it right now? it does not look so)" against her husband, she had predicted. Perhaps she did not know how to spell "scale," but she knew a political debacle when it occurred.[19]

Why was Adams defeated? Students of John Adams have tended to exonerate him of responsibility for the trimming he suffered in 1800, as did biographer Page Smith, who wrote that the "basic cause of Adams's defeat" was "the rancorous division among the Federalists." As we have seen, that was the view put forward by Abigail in the immediate aftermath of the contest, and it was the interpretation that Adams himself insisted upon during the remainder of his life. Adams, in fact, believed that the embittered Hamilton not only had sought his defeat but also that the disappointed inspector general had wrecked the Federalist Party with his mad designs. To make matters worse, Adams contended, Hamilton had then sought to make him, Adams, the scapegoat for the carnage. Hamilton and his cronies "killed themselves and . . . indicted me for the murder," he later charged. Until he drew his last breath, Adams never wavered from this belief, and he never doubted that he would have been reelected had Hamilton not provoked the Federalist defeat in New York.[20]

Such an interpretation is only partially accurate, however. There can be no doubt that Hamilton's open attack and back-room maneuvers harmed the president. Nor can it be supposed that the Federalist cataclysm in New York was unimportant. With the exception of New York, in fact, Adams generally was successful where he had succeeded four years earlier, while he fared badly in the same states in which he had shown poorly in 1796. Thus, with a victory in New York, Adams would have been reelected.

However, attribution of Adams's defeat in that state to the split with Hamilton cannot be substantiated. New York was lost at a time when Hamilton was still fighting diligently to maintain party unity and to elect a Federalist legislature. Adams failed in New York not because of Hamilton, but because the Federalist Party, bolstered initially by its identification with Washington and the Constitution of 1787, had steadily grown less popular. Jefferson understood this better than the president. In the waning days of the campaign, he had called on Adams and sought to convince him that this was a contest that would turn on ideology, not personalities. But consumed with bitterness and unwilling to admit his own complicity in the compilation of the Federalists' record, Adams could not see that the Republican Party in New York had been in the ascendancy for some time, especially within the working class in New York City, where voters had either increasingly embraced Jeffersonianism or simply rejected the high taxes and the threat to civil liberties that, of late, accompanied Federalist rule. Abigail once had explained the loss of New York by pointing to the "seeds of discontent" that Hamilton had sowed. But if the defeat occurred because of any seeds that Hamilton had sown, to use the First Lady's metaphor, it was the jungle-growth of repressive war measures, as well as the inspector general's Francophobia and Anglophilia, that came home to haunt the Federalist Party in 1800. Nor was Hamilton alone to blame for the loss. Adams also had to share responsibility for his own defeat, for he had acquiesced in and, for too long, abetted the very policies that ultimately devoured his presidency.[21]

Ten weeks of the presidency remained to Adams after he learned of his defeat. They were not happy weeks for him. In addition to the anguish caused by his political loss, word of Charles's death reached the White House only hours before the electors met. The end had come on November 30, about four weeks after Abigail had sat at his bedside for the final time. "Let silence reign forever over his tomb," Thomas Boylston remarked when he learned of his brother's demise, finding no words of exculpation for him. Nor did the parents publicly utter any words of forgiveness or love for their lost son. There is "nothing more to be said," John remarked. Abigail cruelly stated only that death meant that Charles could never again "add an other pang to those which have pierced my Heart for several years past."[22]

Privately, however, both Abigail and John were devastated by the tragedy, and both quietly sought to cope with and understand the calamity. Abigail was deeply distressed by the recollection of the terrible agony that Charles had suffered during his final weeks, and the "tender remembrance of what he once was" seemed to haunt her every waking moment. In a sentence in one letter, she appeared to attribute Charles's misfortune to John's injunction that the young man pursue a legal career, a path the poor boy did not wish to trod. The president—especially the president, considering his uneasy relationship with Charles—also grieved. In troubled silence he remembered their happy days together in France and Holland, a time when the young boy had been "the delight of my Eyes and a darling of my heart." A month later he remarked that Charles's death had caused the "greatest Grief of my heart and the deepest affliction of my Life." But he would not accept responsibility for what had happened to the young man, although he did write to Thomas promising to spend more time with him and confessing that his children had never had "an equal chance" to secure his attention. Not until fifteen years had passed did he frankly admit that his actions might have been partially responsible for Charles's dissolute behavior.[23]

Thomas Boylston, soft and compassionate, understood the grief that his father felt, however. While he could not find words of consolation regarding the family tragedy, he did seek to cheer his father by forwarding epistles that brimmed with tributes to the Adams presidency. Ultimately, the president would be venerated by his countrymen, he predicted, for he had eschewed caprice and intrigue in the performance of his public obligations. Were that "the only inheritance left [by you] to your family," he added soothingly, "they might esteem themselves rich in possessing this."[24]

While Thomas expressed no bitterness at his father's defeat, Abigail railed at the "calumny and falsehood" published about her husband, and she made no attempt to hide her enmity for Hamilton. Secretly, however, she was not too upset at the outcome of the election. "I shall be happier at Quincy," she confided to her sister. The president, of course, was disconsolate at the realization that he had been rejected by the American people. The defeat, moreover, confronted him with a painful decision about his future. Now sixty-five years of age, he had to decide whether to remain in public office or to retire to Peacefield.[25]

Some of his friends concocted a bizarre scheme by which he might have been able to become the chief justice of the Supreme Court, and others encouraged him to accept another embassy abroad. He ruled out both possibilities. He had not practiced law in twenty-five years, he said, and his eyesight was too poor to endure the study necessary to reacquaint himself with judicial matters. In fact, he soon offered the chief justiceship to John Jay, and, when he declined, he appointed John Marshall, his secretary of state, still young and vigorous at forty-five years of age. Adams was equally unenthusiastic about accepting another foreign assignment. He not only was too old to travel abroad again, he said, but he did not wish to undergo still another long separation from any member of his family. Other possibilities remained. He did not exclude running for governor of Massachusetts, an alternative pressed upon him by some of his Federalist acquaintances, nor did he eliminate the option of running for election to Congress, a course he had considered four years earlier when he had first run for the presidency.[26]

Within a month of his defeat, Adams began to speak of retirement from politics, a threat he had made off and again since 1765. For once, however, he seemed to mean what he said. He would finish his days alternately caring for his farm and reading what his weak eyes could tolerate, he remarked. At last, he would gladly leave the labors as well as the "great and little passions" of office to someone else. "I must be a farmer," he exclaimed, and he took to calling himself "John of stony field," the name he now occasionally used for Peacefield.[27]

His stewardship in the White House did not end with the election, however. He would be president until noon on March 4. Several matters required his attention, although on one prickly issue he wisely managed to remain aloof. He and Pinckney had lost the election, but it was not clear who had won. The House of Representatives had to choose between Jefferson and Burr, who had received the same number of electoral votes. While Abigail could not decide whom she favored (she remembered her friendship with Jefferson and thought him the "purer" of the two men, but she feared him as a visionary and distrusted his anti-Christian biases), the president immediately hoped the Virginian would win. For a time he even contemplated an immediate resignation so that Jefferson might be aided by his elevation to the presidency. Ultimately, Adams discarded that notion, if only because there was yet much unfinished business to tend.[28]

The French business, for instance, at last called for a decision. Ellsworth and Davie had reached Europe in November 1799, hoping to open talks quickly with their French counterparts. However, at almost the same moment that they landed in Lisbon, Napoleon Bonaparte had seized power in the coup d'état of 18 *Brumaire*. The Americans opted, therefore, to proceed cautiously, waiting until affairs in troubled Paris were more settled before they sought out the French foreign office. It was not until March 1800, therefore, that Ellsworth and Davie at last joined Murray in the French capital.

Both Talleyrand, who seemed always to be foreign minister regardless of who held executive power, and Napoleon, the first consul, cordially greeted the three American envoys. Talks began at once and progressed smoothly until Joseph Bonaparte, Napoleon's brother and the head of the French negotiating team, suffered a serious illness. In May discussions resumed, but suddenly the transactions stalled; Napoleon, preoccupied with his summer campaign in Italy and probably content to wait for Jefferson to take office, no longer seemed inclined to reach a settlement. But in late summer the military situation changed. The mercurial Napoleon once again grew interested in the talks. The pace of the negotiations increased. The final hurdles were cleared during the last days of September. A week later, on October 3, an accord was signed at

Château Môrtefontaine at a state dinner attended by 180 dignitaries and friends of Napoleon.

The Convention of Peace, Commerce and Navigation, variously called the Convention of 1800 and the Treaty of Môrtefontaine, was less inclusive than Adams had hoped for. While the agreement established peace between the two nations, recognized the right of the United States to trade in noncontraband with belligerents, and defined the items each regarded as contraband, it said nothing about indemnification for the American property seized by the French. That issue, as well as the question of a formal Franco-American alliance, was deferred for future discussion.[29]

President Adams knew virtually nothing of what was occurring in Paris until he read a story about the treaty in a local newspaper early in November. Thereafter, he prayed that he might receive the treaty itself before the presidential electors gathered in December. But only three terse communiques arrived that fall from Paris, and the accord played no role in the presidential election.[30]

When he finally did receive a copy of the treaty, Adams knew immediately that the consent of the Senate would not be easy to obtain. Although most Senators clearly favored ratification, the High Federalists, who looked upon a pact devoid of French compensation as "another chapter in the book of humiliation" written by John Adams, possessed the votes to deny the two-thirds majority necessary for approval. The president played a minor role in the deliberations that began in mid-December. He urged ratification when he submitted the treaty, and on the eve of the vote he publicly maintained that the nation's "honor and good faith" demanded that the accord be approved. But even had he been more active, the results probably would have been no different. On January 23 the Senate voted sixteen to fourteen for ratification. Adams and the convention's proponents had fallen four votes short.[31]

From the outset, however, even the High Federalists were prepared to vote for the treaty with reservations. If amended to terminate the Franco-American alliance of 1778 and to provide for French indemnification for United States property lost during the Quasi-War, it would be "no very bad Bargain," as Gouverneur Morris, the New York Federalist, put it. To block the accord altogether might be disastrous politically. In fact, Hamilton, callously opportunistic as always, made an amazing about-face and urged his party to ratify the treaty and then take credit for having preserved the peace with France. In future elections, he counseled, Federalists should argue that the "Foederal[ist] Administration steered the vessel through the storms raised by the contentions of Europe into a peaceable and safe port." Ten days after its initial vote, the Senate reconsidered the treaty with reservations. It passed by a vote of twenty-two to nine.[32]

Adams was not happy with the reservations, but to scuttle all that he had worked for by vetoing the amended treaty would have been an act of folly. He soon nominated James Bayard, a Federalist senator from Delaware, as minister plenipotentiary to France to pursue the additional negotiations now necessary. Yet he knew that the French crisis was over. He had, in fact, "steered the vessel . . . into a peaceable and safe port," and with justification he took enormous pride in his accomplishment. By preventing war with France, he maintained, he had kept Great Britain "in awe" of the United States, a disposition that could not have continued had America, isolated and vulnerable, slipped into hostilities with Paris.[33]

Once the Senate acted, only one month remained in his presidency. It was a busy time for both John and Abigail. The First Lady decided to start home in mid-February, three weeks before her husband. She wished to have the house ready when he returned, and she hoped to travel before the onset of the spring thaw, which usually rendered roads impassable and streams unfordable. During her last few days in Washington, she said good-bye to old acquaintances whom she knew she would never see again. One of these was Martha Washington, a sweet and kindly woman whom she had grown to love over the years. On a cold, sunny day in February, Abigail rode out to Mount Vernon, her first visit to the famous estate. She was shocked at what she saw. Only a bit more than a year after the general's death, the estate already had a tumbledown look. Abigail, nine years younger than her husband, must have wondered if she would someday endure a similar fate at Peacefield.

She returned to Washington to serve as host for her final levee, and she saw Jefferson for the last time as well, when he graciously called on her at the White House. They chatted over tea and cake for a part of one afternoon, and Jefferson once again succeeded in charming her as he had years before in Auteuil and Paris. Then, in the cold early hours of February 12, just as the first rays of lambent sunshine streaked across the capital, she departed the White House in her coach-and-four. Unattended by a male escort, she knew that she was taking her final journey to Quincy, a plunge into a frighteningly indefinite, uncertain period of retirement. But she was confident. "[O]ur desires are moderate, our oeconomy strict, our income, though moderate, will furnish us with all the necessaries, and many of the comforts of Life," she thought. She was fifty-six years old. At last, she was about to have a year-round husband, something she had known only four years out of the past twenty-six.[34]

Following Abigail's departure, the president remained at work, although there was little to do except fill numerous vacancies in the bureaucracy, the army, and the judiciary. These were posts that he filled from December onward, so that contrary to the Republicans later prattle about Adams remaining at his desk far into his last night in office in order to appoint "midnight judges," there was no last-minute scramble to get the job done. Naturally, he named members of his own party to most positions; for instance, he appointed only Federalists to serve as judges in the twenty-six new judicial circuits created by the Judiciary Act of 1801, legislation that his party passed after it lost the election of 1800. Adams also found jobs for two relatives during these last days in office. Colonel Smith was awarded a plum near his home; the president named him surveyor of the Port of New York, a sinecure that rivaled any post that Thomas Hutchinson had ever bestowed upon his kin. Adams also appointed William Cranch, son of Richard and Mary and nephew of John and Abigail, as justice of the Circuit Court of the District of Columbia. It was a godsend for young Cranch, who had lost his fortune in real estate speculation in Washington; it also was restitution of sorts to his parents, who had kept all three of John and Abigail's sons when they were in France and England in the 1780s.[35]

During his final days as president, Adams did not venture out of the White House. Grieving over the loss of Charles and bitter over his defeat, he remained isolated inside the cold, austere mansion. He refused to call on any old friends. Unlike the last days of Washington's presidency, when old acquaintances had thrown numerous parties and balls, no one sponsored any tribute to John Adams. Nor did Adams publish a valedictory address as had Washington. He simply put in the time required by the Constitution, the stress of dreadfully critical decisions long since behind him and, in truth, with little work to be done to fill each long, lonely day.[36]

One thing that Adams did during those final days in office, as he would in fact do for the remainder of his life, was ponder his presidency, seeking to sort out what he had accomplished and where he had erred. He had been defeated in the canvass of 1800, but he apprehended that he had lost something even more profound. He knew that popular opinion had turned away from the ideology of Federalism and he feared that, as a result, history would look upon his tenure as an infamous interlude; worse, he was afraid that he would be forgotten by history. He sought to be philosophical about this turn of events. When he had first entered politics, he reminded himself, he had predicted that his decision would result in his personal ruin and, perhaps, the destruction of members of his family. Sadly, he confessed, his presentiments had been borne out.[37]

Adams ultimately blamed the destruction of his administration on three factors. He attributed some of the responsibility to his own limitations. He was the first to admit that he was a poor politician, that he was naive and lacked the feel and toughness—perhaps the treacherousness and rascality—necessary for success in such a rough-and-tumble calling. His greatest error in this regard, he said repeatedly, was in not selecting a cabinet of his own men prior to his inauguration. Adams, of course, also savagely attacked Pickering and Hamilton, especially the latter, as a cause of his woes. He spoke of "subterranean intrigues" that had eroded his support. The "lies and libels" told against him by members of his own party had done greater harm than all the propaganda issued by all the Republican organs, he said. Hamilton was the chief "intriguer." For a dozen years, he raged, the New Yorker had labored "underground and in darkness" to replace him with someone less independent, more easily controlled, until, ultimately, he had brought down not only Adams but the Federalist party as well.[38]

The growth of democracy was the third factor that ruined him, Adams charged. Since before his presidency, he had written of his belief in the inherent inability of the people for restraint in government and had counseled that the executive power be taken from their hands. The "giddy, thoughtless multitude" must have representation in one house of the legislature, but the other branches must be insulated from the emotional voice of the crowd; indeed, the executive must be an "impregnable barrier" against their insensate demands, thus becoming the "patron and guardian of [the] liberty" that the ignorant masses would destroy if left unchecked. That was the role that Adams saw himself as having played as president. The nation had seethed with elements seeking their own selfish ends, he wrote. Once he listed five factions as active during his presidency: Tories, democrats, the pro-French, the anti-English-Irish, and the Hamiltonian Federalists; on another occasion, he described the country as divided between "Anti-Federalists, Democrats, Jacobins, Virginia debtors to English merchants, and French hirelings." He had sought to make the hard choices to prevent chaos and to further the national interest, he said, but his actions had alienated too many, and, as presidential elections grew more democratic—or at least more politicized—he was inevitably made the victim of the wrathfully disappointed.[39]

Nevertheless, Adams was proud of what he had done. He would leave office with a conscience as "clear as a crystal glass," he proclaimed, because rather than acting to appease the demands of a narrow faction, he had been "borne along by an irresistible sense of duty." His great act was the preservation of peace, he said, an accomplishment that he believed had resulted in nothing less than the salvation of the American Revolution. Had war occurred, the danger was too great that the Union—and, with it, true independence—would be shattered and lost forever. But war had been avoided and the nation preserved, though he had known that the course he had chosen to pursue in the face of a rancorous multitude would result in his political demise.[40]

Adams certainly would be surprised to find what historians have said of his presidency. The so-called Schlesinger Polls, two surveys of historians and political scientists made years apart, revealed that Adams was regarded by the distinguished pollees as a "near great" chief executive. Even those most critical of Federalist rule, such as Charles Beard early in this century, found little that was ill to say of Adams, save to criticize his political instincts and to point to an "austere and unbending" nature that rendered him unable to "perform an official act or make a public pronouncement that did anything to conciliate permanently the opposition party." More recently, he has been lauded by Stephen Kurtz as a "fitting successor" to Washington because he fought for

American independence in the 1790s as assiduously as he had in the 1770s; by Marshall Smelser as a "responsible statesman" who resisted the "infectious fever" of war; by Manning Dauer as a trustee of the people whose "contribution had been great"; by Ralph Adams Brown as a president who worked for the national interest "with personal integrity and the greatest possible skill"; and by Page Smith as "a popular figure with a stormy but successful administration."[41]

These assessments err only in the faintness of their praise. This is not to suggest that Adams did not blunder. A better politician and a more sagacious judge of character might have defused the strength of the dissidents within his own party. In addition, through his own strident, "grotesque" rhetoric, to use Madison's descriptive term, he actually succeeded in inflicting even greater pressures upon himself. But, against these failures, it would be wise to remember the seminal achievement of the Adams presidency.

Adams had been drawn to the Federalist vision of governance, for he saw in it the quest for stability, a goal to be achieved by balanced government as well as national prosperity, the latter built upon commerce and a sound national currency. In time, however, he came to believe that whatever such concepts as independence and prosperity had meant to the revolutionary generation, they meant something else to the new generation of merchants, financiers, and speculators. Two weeks into his presidency, he acknowledged this, saying, "From the situation where I now am, I see a scene of ambition beyond all my former suspicions and imaginations." So great was the greed he beheld, he told Abigail, he had come to fear that it threatened "to turn our government topsy-turvy." From the outset of his term, therefore, Adams saw himself confronted with the very battle that he had envisioned in the *Defence.* He must be president of both the "gentlemen" and the "simplemen"—"President of all the people," as a later generation would put it—lest the rich and powerful, or perhaps in retaliation, the pro-French Republicans, aggrandize the new nation. "Jefferson had a party, Hamilton had a party, but the commonwealth had none," he said.[42] It was his duty to stand as a bulwark of protection for the commonwealth.

Throughout his public career, Adams's thoughts frequently turned to the question of greatness in leadership. In the still-dark days of the War of Independence, with his own future clouded and uncertain, he turned again to the issue. "What is to become of an independent statesman," he had asked. His answer: "[H]e will be regarded more by posterity . . . and although he will not make his own fortune, he will make the fortune of his country." Written years before his presidency, those lines were prescient with regard to his experience as chief executive. Defeated in 1800 and forced from office, Adams now faced a life in retirement at Peacefield, a most modest estate when compared with that inhabited by every other major leader of this early national era. But he would live comfortably and in the knowledge that his indomitable independence had been a blessing for a fragile union and a new nation. Perhaps the best tribute to his presidency was offered by a contemporary essayist. "It is universally admitted that Mr. Adams is a man of incorruptible integrity, and that the resources of his mind are equal to the duties of his station," the *Philadelphia Aurora* had said upon the occasion of his inauguration. Adams, the writer went on, was a friend of peace, an admirer of republicanism, and a foe of faction. "How characteristic of a patriot," he added. By that criteria, John Adams's presidency can only be judged to have been a noble and patriotic sacrifice.[43]

In midmorning on Wednesday, March 4, Inauguration Day, militia companies from Washington and Alexandria paraded in the streets near the boardinghouse of the president-elect. At noon, Thomas Jefferson, escorted into the Senate chamber by the members of Adams's cabinet, took the oath of office.

John Adams witnessed none of this. At 4:00 A.M., while the city still slept through a black, winter's night, he had departed the White House. Like his wife, he had begun the final journey back to Quincy, the public life he had once so assiduously sought now a thing of the past.[44]

PART FIVE

*

I Still Live and Enjoy Life

CHAPTER 20

*

A Retired Hermetical Life

SHORTLY BEFORE HE LEFT WASHINGTON, Adams predicted that his retirement years would be the happiest period of his life. It is difficult to believe that he meant what he said. Bitter at his recent defeat, his very identity shattered by his public rejection, Adams for the first time in more than a quarter century seemed to be without a sense of purpose in his life. Nor could he have believed that much time remained. He was sixty-five years old when he returned to Quincy, just about the full allotment of years that a man could expect. There were exceptions, of course, including his mother, who had lived a very long life, dying at eighty-eight in the first year of his presidency. Samuel Adams was still alive at seventy-nine, but John did not look upon him with envy. Time had not been kind to the revolutionary patriarch, prompting John to pray that he would never become a similar "grief and distress to his family, a weeping, helpless object of compassion." Most people, however, did not live much beyond their mid-sixties. His father, the Deacon, had died at sixty-nine, Washington at sixty-seven, and some, like his old political allies John Hancock, James Otis, and Thomas Cushing, had passed on before reaching his present age.[1]

Abigail, happy to be home to stay and confident that the end of her husband's public service would add years to both their lives, was waiting for John when his carriage rolled to a stop at Peacefield. She was surprised at his good spirits, and over the next few days she found his frame of mind to be "beyond what you could imagine," as she told John Quincy.[2]

Actually, John's outlook was far less rosy than Abigail's depiction indicated. He faced a long and difficult period of adjustment. Weeks passed before he stirred from the house. He was languid and bored. Mostly he sat in his study staring at the drab wintry scenes beyond his window, listening to the echo of his neighbor's ax. His first stirrings came when he penned a rejoinder to Hamilton's *Letter,* but he hesitated to publish his essay, probably fearing it would only cause problems for John Quincy should he someday seek office as a member of the Federalist party. Next, he wrote to those members of his cabinet who had remained loyal to him, telling them—and himself—that he had made "a good exchange," a swap of official cares for a life of ease. A month passed before he felt like writing to family members, and nearly ninety days elapsed before he began corresponding with old friends. By then he was confessing, "Ennui, when it rains on a man in large drops is worse than one of our own North East storms." He also had begun toying with the idea of resuming his law practice.[3]

Adams was sustained through this troubled period by the conviction that while his public service had included failures, he had been guided by the purest of intentions. Always he had sought to act in the national interest, he said, not for narrow partisan ends; however others judged his presidency, he appeared to say, he could life with himself.

Living in Quincy, far from the tattle and perfidy of the capital, also helped him cope with the transition to a less-active life-style. Gradually, public matters lost their all-consuming sense of urgency and other concerns grew in importance. He waited anxiously for visits from his children and grandchildren. The relentless agricultural cycle necessitated planning. Gradually, he grew to appreciate fully the luxury of his quiet, comfortable house, the care and attention bestowed upon him by his loving wife, and the joy of his grandchildren's presence, for Charles's widow, Sally, and her two young daughters, had come to Quincy to live with their benevolent in-laws. In short, time eventually became an ally. Even so, it is obvious that for years a battle raged within him. To one friend he confided that if he had his life to live over, he "would be a Shoemaker rather than an American Statesman"; to another he confessed that he did know how long he could resist the urge to reenter public life.[4]

Adams had been home for only a few days when the members of the Massachusetts legislature journeyed to Quincy to express their appreciation for his long years of public service. He wept openly during the brief ceremony, the first occasion upon which a public body had actually honored him. But few visitors came thereafter. Unlike Mount Vernon, so inundated with guests that Washington complained that his home was more like a public inn than a private residence, Adams seldom saw anyone from the outside world. Now and then an old acquaintance who lived close by called at Peacefield, but few others came to see him. During his first four years at home, he noted visits only by Raphael Peale, son of Painter Charles Willson Peale and an esteemed artist in his own right, and David Humphreys, who briefly had been part of his "family" at Auteuil many years before. Whereas young men traveled long distances to be in Washington's company, as if the experience was the last stage of their education, Adams was ignored. He felt abandoned. "I am buried and forgotten," he lamented, and, to a friend, he cried out that he never again expected "to see any thing but [his] plough between [him] and the grave."[5]

During all his years in retirement, Adams seldom left his home, save for a walk or ride in the nearby countryside, or to visit with Parson Wibard or

Richard Cranch. There is no evidence that he ever left Peacefield during his first years at home, not even to travel the short distance to Boston. Nor was he terribly active in other ways. He made no attempt to publish essays on any topic, and his correspondence remained light. He worked a bit on the farm and often retired to his study to read and to be alone.[6] Melancholy, dispirited, rejected, neglected, unappreciated, John Adams waited to die.

The safe return of John Quincy and his family during Adams's first autumn in Quincy offered a rare joyous moment. In one of his last acts as president, Adams had recalled his son, a move that Abigail had encouraged for a year or more, an act of personal urgency for John in the aftermath of Charles's death. The summons to come back arrived in Berlin in May, and the Adamses sailed in July. When they docked in Philadelphia in September, husband and wife parted company. Louisa Catherine was anxious to see her parents, from whom she had never been separated. John Quincy hurried to be with his own family in Massachusetts, rather than accompany his wife to Washington.[7]

In the fall Louisa Catherine came north to meet John and Abigail for the first time. Four years with John Quincy and a slight correspondence with her mother-in-law had filled her with trepidation at what to expect. Her husband and Thomas were no less concerned, and both had sought to put their mother in the proper frame of mind. To the end John Quincy remained confident that Louisa's presence would bring happiness to the grim, cheerless environment at Peacefield. He was wrong. The long-awaited meeting proved taxing.

John Quincy, Louisa Catherine, and their six-month-old son, George Washington—who had been delivered by a drunken German midwife a few weeks before his parents left Berlin—arrived at Peacefield on a gray autumn afternoon. Louisa Catherine was apprehensive as she alighted from the carriage. She feared that Abigail would look upon her as too shallow, too frail, too English, and too poor to assist in the furtherance of John Quincy's career. She also arrived harboring biases of her own. While visiting with her parents, she had heard whispers that Abigail had sought to persuade John not to appoint her father to a federal post; the tattle was false, and, in fact, in the last weeks of his administration, Adams had appointed Joshua Johnson to the stamp office, but prejudices nevertheless had been sown.[8]

Louisa Catherine's apprehensions became a self-fulfilling prophecy. She soon saw in Abigail's every act studied coldness, condescension, superciliousness, and jealousy. She additionally suffered culture shock at the strange environment she encountered. She discovered that every aspect of life in Quincy was alien to all that she had ever known. The natives' accent, their diet and dining times, their sense of humor and dress, even their church service, were foreign to her. Indeed, she later compared the strange atmosphere that she had suddenly entered to the very new world that Noah must have found when he descended from his ark. The one real surprise that Louisa Catherine encountered was John Adams. Given his well-known penchant for acerbity, she had expected to fear and dislike the old man. Instead, Adams instantly took to the distraught young woman. He saw her as John Quincy must have seen her. Perhaps, too, Louisa's travail with Abigail may have caused him to see her as a kindred spirit, for he was coping with his own recent repudiation. Among all the people that she met in Quincy, John alone seemed not just friendly but caring. It was a sentiment toward her that he never abandoned and one that she reciprocated for the remainder of her life.[9]

Mercifully, John Quincy moved his wife to Boston after a difficult month at Peacefield. Without enthusiasm he returned to his legal practice. He would have preferred a life as a writer, but he knew that he lacked the financial independence for such a pursuit. Briefly, he and Thomas considered jettisoning their legal careers and moving together to the frontier in western New York, the one to write and speculate in western land, the other to launch some sort of business enterprise. Ultimately, neither could take the step. John Quincy's political fortunes appeared too good to eschew. He stayed with the law, therefore, and played an active role with the Federalist party. Soon, he was elected to the state legislature and in 1803, barely seventeen months after his return from Berlin, that body elected him to a vacancy in the United States Senate.[10]

Once he learned that John Quincy would not accompany him, Thomas abandoned his dream of moving to the frontier. He remained in Philadelphia, thirty years old in 1802, still a bachelor with a struggling law practice. Whereas the Adamses looked upon John Quincy as an exemplary individual— Abigail believed he possessed greater capabilities than "any other native American"—they saw Thomas as a frail, indifferent, ineffectual young man, one who would never succeed in the streamlined world of the capital. Although they admitted that he would be unhappy in Quincy, John and Abigail sought to convince him to come home. Back in Quincy, they thought, his law office might capitalize on the family name; in addition, he might benefit from an occasional well-meant parental nudge, and, if necessary, he might even give up the law and simply manage the farm at Peacefield. Thomas withstood his parents' entreaties for years, but eventually he submitted; near the end of 1803 he moved in with his parents and opened a law office in his hometown.[11]

Predictably, Thomas was terribly unhappy. Never particularly happy with the law, he hated this pursuit even more now that he had to scratch out a new practice after several years of laboring to become established in Philadelphia. He succumbed to bouts of melancholy, the "Blue Devils," he called these brutal low periods. The one bright ray of joy in his life was his relationship with Nancy Harrod of Haverhill, with whom he had fallen in love some time before; they married in 1805, when he was thirty-three and Nancy was thirty-one. Nevertheless, what should have been the happiest time of his life was just the reverse. Faced with real or imagined parental pressure, he, like John

Quincy, entered politics and, with his father's assistance, was elected to the Massachusetts legislature. Within a year, however, he resigned under mysterious circumstances, although his departure may in some way have been related to his alcoholism, a disease that had now begun to afflict his life, as it had unhappily struck others in this family.[12]

Time and family distractions, and almost certainly John Quincy's elevation to the Senate—the more satisfying because he defeated Timothy Pickering for the post—helped to lift John from his protracted depression. After more than two years of self-imposed isolation at Peacefield, he began to stir about. He began to appear at July Fourth celebrations in Boston. He attended each year's commencement at Harvard as well as the annual gathering in June of the Honorable Artillery Company of Boston. He was made honorary president of both the American Academy of Arts and Sciences and the Massachusetts Society for Promoting Agriculture, attending their board meetings and other functions. Ultimately, too, he became a member of Harvard's Board of Visitors. He even met with friends in the Boston business community in hope of finding a satisfactory position for either Colonel Smith—who in 1805 was sentenced to prison for indebtedness—or for his grandson, William Steuben Smith, who by the age of twenty was beginning to display unmistakable signs of having been cut from the same cloth as his tragic father.[13]

Another sign that his old fires had begun to reblaze appeared in 1802. He decided to write his autobiography. It was an undertaking, he said at the time, designed only for his children's elucidation, not for public consumption. As with so much that Adams said where his vanity was concerned, his disclaimer is not believable. He knew his acquiescent sons well enough to know that someday one of them would publish the manuscript, just as he would have disseminated his father's memoirs, had the Deacon ever composed such a document.

From time to time Adams toyed with the idea of writing a personal narrative of some of the more important occurrences in which he had been active. He once had promised to leave to posterity an insider's account of the peace negotiations of 1782 and 1783, and he may have contemplated relating his impression of the revolutionary years in Massachusetts or of the early period of the Continental Congress. That he decided to proceed with an autobiographical account in 1802 stemmed from the hurt he had suffered in his presidential years, and from his desire to rescue his reputation, sullied as it was by party invective and the treachery of his supposed friends.[14]

Working quietly in his study, Adams sputtered through only twelve paragraphs before he aborted the project. Two years passed. In 1804 John Quincy, unaware that his father had already begun such an endeavor, urged him to write his memoirs, thinking that such an undertaking would be therapeutic. Adams promptly rejected the advice. The "Mortifications, Disappointments or Resentments" would be too painful, he pleaded. But, just as promptly, he resumed work on the autobiography he had abandoned. During the next half year he carried his story through the autumn of 1776, a lengthy relation that ultimately would consume nearly two hundred printed pages.[15]

Distracted by other matters, he once again abandoned his memoirs in mid-1805, taking up the project only at the end of the following year, recalled to his labors perhaps by letters of encouragement from Benjamin Rush and F. A. Vanderkemp, a friend from the time of his mission to Holland. He worked feverishly during the next seven months or so, drafting a long account of his diplomatic activities to March 1780. Diverted by a dispute with Mercy Warren at one point, he once again put aside his treatise, never to return to the endeavor. He had planned to chronicle his activity through his presidential years, but when he again had time for the undertaking, the raging fire that had driven him to the enterprise in the first place had been largely extinguished.[16]

Adams was a marvelous letter writer and a few of his published essays were praiseworthy, although none were timeless literary masterpieces. Much of what he wrote for publication was narrowly legalistic or, as in the case of the *Defence,* clouded by a style that could only be called disordered. He was never a match for the better writers of his age. Franklin appeared to write effortlessly, and his pen was graced by a habitual wit; Tom Paine, a master of the catchy phrase, wrote in a manner easily understood by every reader; Jefferson's sentences flowed clear and untroubled as a placid summer stream; Hamilton's systematized thought enabled him to marshal argument after argument and to march his ideas across the landscape, deftly and briskly devouring everything in their path. To read Adams, by contrast, is to submit to a painstaking struggle with disarray, to face the effort of an author who too often seemed more concerned with getting something on paper than with the quality of the composition.

The *Autobiography* is no different. The work is chaotic and jumbled, much of it punctuated by unfortunate gaps as well as by long sections merely extracted from printed documents. He says little of his law practice and next to nothing of the protest movement in Massachusetts before 1773; he ignores completely the entire year of 1777, one of three full years that he sat in Congress. The work is also flawed by his unwillingness to provide detailed and revealing inside glimpses of the many famous people with whom he associated. Only Franklin is really delineated. Of Jefferson, he wrote only that he was a poor public speaker and debater and that he once had heard him deliver a speech that was "a gross insult on Religion." He carefully omitted the harsh characterizations of Washington that had begun to creep into his private correspondence. As for others, from generals to political activists, from teachers to merchants and diplomats, Adams usually—maddeningly—gave them only the most cursory treatment.

When Adams wrote his memoirs, he had virtually no others to serve as a literary guide, not even Franklin's now-famous *Autobiography*. He did not see the Doctor's memoirs until more than a decade after he abandoned work on his own recollections, and he immediately acknowledged that his work was the inferior product. Nevertheless, with all its flaws, segments of the *Autobiography* are extraordinary, especially the sections dealing with his youthful rebelliousness and his early congressional service.[17]

That his work on the *Autobiography* proceeded as far as it did was indicative that by 1807, after half a dozen years at home, Adams at last was coping better with the problems that had drawn him to this project in the first place. Not only had he chased away some of his own demons through writing an account of self-vindication, but, to his way of thinking, events since he left the White House appeared to have cleansed his reputation. Despite their rhetoric, his Republican successors had not ushered in revolutionary change. In fact, Adams had once quipped that Jefferson's most significant reform had been his abandonment of the weekly levees that his Federalist predecessors had inaugurated. Jefferson, of course, had made some important changes. Federalist taxes had been repealed; military appropriations had been slashed; the Alien and Sedition acts had been permitted to lapse; the Naturalization Act had been liberalized; new, more liberal western land laws had been enacted; and the Judiciary Act of 1800 had been repealed. But there was continuity as well. President Jefferson had followed through on ratification of the Convention of Môrtefontaine in mid-1801, the final negotiations completed for him by William Vans Murray, Adams's appointee. In the end, the accord abrogated the French alliance of 1778, a goal long sought by many Federalists, and France was excused from paying any indemnities to the United States. In the cordial relations that followed between the two nations, Jefferson, in 1803, was able to purchase the Louisiana Territory from Napoleon, an acquisition that Adams supported.[18]

Nevertheless, when Jefferson departed the White House after his second term, Adams remarked that the Virginian "leaves the government infinitely worse than he found it." He did not mean that Jefferson's presidency had been disastrous for the nation, however. He criticized his successor as "a party man full of party spirit," and he was especially upset when the Republicans repealed the Judiciary Act. But what most troubled Adams were the signs of a national malaise, a haunting, malignant devastation that he believed Jefferson had been incapable of thwarting.[19]

Adams eventually came to believe that his had been an "age of Folly, Vice, Frenzy, Fury, Brutality, Daemons." It most certainly was not an "Age of Reason," he charged, as Thomas Paine had labeled it in the great treatise of the same name he had published in 1792. Adams thought the eighteenth century preferable to what he had seen of the 19th; indeed, he believed that no previous century could match the gains achieved by mankind in the realms of science,

education, and the general advancement of liberty. Nevertheless, the perfec-
tion of human nature, the cherished hope of the Enlightenment *philosophes,*
had not occurred. Neither humankind's condition of woe nor its propensity for
unleashing misery had been ameliorated during his long lifetime, Adams
asserted. In fact, he feared that the excesses of the French Revolution, a cataclysmic event, in his estimation, had set back human progress for hundreds of
years. "[I]t was all madness," he said of the Parisian revolutionaries' attempts
to install a more egalitarian social order. The French Revolution had ushered in
only what he saw as "chaos." He understood only "order."[20]

Adams had come to fear, too, that the gains made by the American Revolution were jeopardized. He fretted not only for the survival of republicanism but
for the very existence of the Union. He was certain that southerners hated
northerners, and he was no less sure that the South—by now virtually a one-
party region—would not again submit to a northern-dominated Federalist
administration. Yet, even if the Union survived, Adams doubted that republicanism could endure in the face of the "aristocracy of wealth" that held
sway. A "monied and landed" plutocracy in the North and a "*slaved* aristocracy" in the South were unchecked, save for the opposition of what he thought
were licentious democrats. The very danger that he had sought unsuccessfully
to remedy in the *Defence* and "Davila" essays now seemed close to realization.[21]

Aristocratic hegemony was a greater immediate danger than democracy, he
thought, and his party, the Federalists, posed the most serious threat to mixed,
republican government. Largely a coalition of financiers, speculators, and
merchants, as well as an old guard whom he called "Tories" (because they had
been lukewarm at best about separating from Great Britain), the Party, he
increasingly felt, had shifted from its original goal of consolidating the Revolution to serving the narrow ends of a small elite in the northern states. The more
he thought about it, the more he believed this was what Hamilton, the Party's
real organizer and leader, had sought all along. When he had returned from
Europe in 1788, he reflected, he had found an aristocracy of commercial and
agrarian wealth deployed under Hamilton and poised to take control of the
new nation. George Washington was the means they had used to achieve their
goal.

Adams now saw Washington in a very different light than he had during his
vice-presidential years. In his present mood, he charged that Washington had
been "puffed like an air balloon to raise Hamilton" into power; Washington
was merely a "viceroy under Hamilton." Washington, he went on, had submitted because he craved the adulation of an adoring public; not very bright, he
claimed, Washington had been a sufficient actor not only to make the populace
believe that he had really possessed power but that he was actually disinterested in public affairs. Adams had come to see himself as the sole foil to the
realization of Hamilton's grandiose dreams, including war with France, al-

liance with, even vassalage to, Great Britain, northern dominion over the South, a nation in the thrall of a commercial aristocracy.

Adams would say none of this in public. He did not even make such charges in his memoirs. Nor did he ever openly suggest, as he did confidentially, that there were greater men than Washington, including some of leaders of the popular protest movement in Massachusetts, men who had performed more significant services on behalf of the Revolution than had the Virginian. But, as his views took shape, he moved away from the Federalist party. After 1804 he never again endorsed another Federalist candidate for office or appeared at their party functions. Philosophically—and quite privately—he had drifted to the Republican party, the party of Jefferson, but also the faction of Sam Adams and Elbridge Gerry and, eventually, of his son, John Quincy.[22]

By 1810 Adams feared that the great test for the survival of the Union was imminent. He saw an emerging cycle in party politics. One side would hold power for about a dozen years, as had the Federalists, then the other party would be ascendant. The change was likely to occur shortly after the party in power had scored a sweeping victory, for it then was most likely to grow "presumptuous and extravagent, and break . . . to pieces." The Federalists were the initial victim of this political law that he beheld; the Republicans, easy victors behind Jefferson in 1804 and James Madison in 1808, soon would experience the same fate. But the Federalists would be back. They knew better "how to dupe" the electorate than did their adversaries, he remarked. And when the northern commercial interests regained power, the Union well might be sundered.[23]

The best hope for the Union was a war, Adams concluded. Moreover, he came to the troubled conclusion that each generation should have to fight for its survival. The notion represented a return to his revolutionary idea that the "furnance of affliction purifies," extirpating softness and banishing the inevitable luxurious living that stole up in peacetime. In this spirit, he not only declined an invitation to join a newly formed peace society, but he welcomed the War of 1812 as a conflict that might resolidify the Union by driving the sections and classes into one another's arms.[24]

Adams had seen the war coming for several years. Great Britain's refusal to abandon its policy of impressment, which had made his blood boil while he was president, and its Orders in Council, which sought to restrict American trade with France, had made a collision between the two nations inevitable. Whereas he had struggled against great odds to avoid war during his presidency, fearful that a terribly divided Union might be shattered in the course of the conflict, he now believed that only positive benefits would accrue from hostilities with Britain. Progress could be made only through tribulation, he counseled. Once war was declared, he cheered the news of each American naval victory. He also was delighted to discover in the course of the conflict what he thought was the appearance of a "national character," a growing American nationalism that appeared to be supplanting the deadly sectionalism about which he had warned.[25]

Adams spelled out these ideas, and far more, in a voluminous correspondence that began to mushroom after he had been home for about three years. He wrote frequently to Judge Cranch, his appointee in Washington, and to Benjamin Waterhouse, an old friend and the physician who had seen him just before his illness in Holland in 1781. Letters flowed out in these first years at home to old friends and compatriots, to John Trumbull, his former law student, now a renowned poet and Federalist judge in Connecticut, to Samuel Malcolm, his first secretary during his presidency, and to David Sewall, a classmate at Harvard half a century before. He and Vanderkemp, acquaintances for a quarter century or more, wrote almost monthly, though Adams shied away from his correspondent's repeated entreaties to discuss scientific matters, preferring to discourse almost solely on politics and history.

In 1805 Adams reopened communications with Dr. Benjamin Rush. The two had known one another since that warm summer evening when Rush had escorted the Massachusetts delegation to the First Congress into Philadelphia. They had been especially close during Adams's vice-presidency but had seen little of one another since 1797, when Adams ascended to the presidency. Adams wrote first to reestablish contact with his old friend. "It seemeth to me that you and I ought not to die without saying goodbye," he began his first letter. Rush answered immediately, thus beginning a marvelous correspondence that spanned eight years, until the physician's death in 1813.[26]

Adams devoted hour upon hour to his correspondence. He wrote two or three letters each week, and many ran several pages, lengthy epistles that pondered philosophical principles and theological tenets, reflected on current affairs, or recalled the great public events and leaders of his lifetime. His was still a "retired hermetical Life," he said, but it had become an existence filled with "serenity and Tranquility."[27]

Although Adams's mood improved as the year passed, life remained filled with travail. The wayward Colonel Smith was one source of enduring worry. In 1806 he and his eldest son, William Stueben, became involved in a quixotic enterprise to liberate Venezuela from Spanish colonialism; Smith ultimately was arrested and jailed—his second imprisonment—for his complicity in this plot against a nation with which the United States was at peace, while his son, taken captive by the Spanish, was fortunate to escape execution. A few years later, despite Smith's notorious record, Abigail sought a post in the army for her fifty-seven-year-old son-in-law when the United States entered the War of 1812. Secretary of State James Monroe, whose aid she had beseeched, did not answer her appeal. Thereafter, John reconciled himself to the notion that the once-promising Smith would never again have the opportunity to play on "the Field of Glory"; he will be but a simple farmer, Adams declared. In fact, to the surprise of both John and Abigail, Colonel Smith was elected to the United States Congress in 1813.

There were other worries, great and small. In 1813 word arrived of the death of John Quincy's one-year-old daughter, Louisa. Their son's health was a source of concern, too, for Louisa Catherine hinted—mistakenly—that he suffered a serious illness, perhaps tuberculosis. Like all home owners, John and Abigail worried about Peacefield, which over the years suffered damage from two hurricanes and one major winter storm, and like farmers everywhere they agonized through episodes of drought followed by seasons of flooding.[28]

When news arrived of the death of others from among the revolutionary generation, an all-too-frequent occurrence anymore, Adams always appeared to be deeply shaken. The soldiers seemed to go first. General Schuyler died in 1804. Knox and Gates perished in 1806; Benjamin Lincoln, four years later. They joined a swelling list of political leaders who had passed on. Tom Paine, John Dickinson, William Vans Murray, and Samuel Adams all were gone by 1810, the year John turned seventy-five.

But, save for a worsening of the palsy that had troubled him since his vice-presidential years, and a gradual deterioration of his near vision, John remained in remarkably good health during his first fifteen years of retirement. Well into his seventies, he not only continued to enjoy frequent long horseback rides but also walked four miles each day that the weather permitted, and he intermittently attended the supervision of the labor in his fields. Nevertheless, some concessions to age were necessary. While he continued to smoke, he eschewed alcohol and slept more than previously; in addition, he took frequent doses of mercury and bark, and his diet now consisted of "Indian Porridge, Water gruel and mutton broth, [and] lemonade."

Abigail did not fare as well, however. She suffered through several serious illness, each of which excited alarm and dread within her husband. What may have been a bout with influenza in 1807 was followed two years later by a severe case of dysentery; in 1812 a pulmonary disorder left her so breathless that she was briefly unable to speak. She withstood each crisis, but her general health was not good. Sixty years old in 1804, Abigail was so plagued by rheumatism that the simplest activity often was wrenchingly painful. By 1808 she confessed that she was able to write only in the morning hours; thereafter, the pain was too great for her to hold a quill. The "dismalls," as she referred to her affliction, frequently confined her to bed, sometimes for days at a stretch. That she was able to get about at all, she attributed to the gruel-and-water diet and the purgatives that her physician prescribed; in fact, the opium pills that she also took may have done more to keep her on her feet.[29]

Midway through his first decade at home, Adams casually remarked that he expected his presidency to be "condemned to everlasting . . . infamy" and his services to the new nation to be forgotten. He did not really mean what he said.

Indeed, he appears to have believed that time would vindicate his conduct and that his achievements would be fully recognized and applauded. Adams was never more shocked or hurt, therefore, than when he read Mercy Warren's history of the Revolution, a tract that appeared in 1806. For years Adams had known that his old friend was at work on the project. At first he had eagerly anticipated its publication, expecting to be delighted by what she wrote, even joking with her about her penchant for criticism. Eventually, however, she and her husband had moved into the orbit of the Jeffersonians; Adams, knowing full well her caustic, barbed manner, grew more apprehensive. But never had he expected what he finally read.[30]

In her *History of the Rise, Progress and Termination of the American Revolution,* Warren told a story of betrayal. The ideology of simple, virtuous republicanism that had launched the Revolution had been thwarted by the ignoble and ambitious men who had come to direct the uprising. The great ideals of 1776 had been defaced by "a rage for the accumulation of wealth." Adams could abide much of this; it bore a considerable resemblance to much that he had said of the Hamiltonian Federalists. But ultimately the net she cast ensnared Adams. Not only did she allege that his ambition had provoked him to seek office after office, whatever the cost in the abandonment of principles, but she also charged that he had been corrupted by his long residence in Europe. His republicanism had been a casualty of those years; he had returned a monarchist. Once a great leader, she wrote, Adams in the end became another who had "forgotten the principles of the American Revolution" and who "daily sigh[ed] for *Patrician rank,* hereditary titles, stars, garters, and nobility, with all the insignia of arbitrary sway."[31]

Nothing in his retirement years had so provoked Adams. He reacted with trenchant, visceral bitterness, firing off ten long, caviling, wrathful letters within thirty days of reading her history. "What have I done, Mrs. Warren," he demanded, "to merit so much malevolence from a lady concerning whom I never in my life uttered an unkind word or a disrespectful insinuation?" She wrote in a feminine manner, he charged, and attributed her allegedly insolent and derisive tone to her gender. He blasted her work as error-prone, and he virtually accused her of having been motivated to pen this assault out of revenge for his refusal in 1789 to assist her husband in finding a federal post. He dusted off old denials of his supposed monarchist bent, denying that he had ever advocated such a government for the United States. As for her imputation of his unsettling ambition, he responded by acknowledging that he was driven to improve himself. "Ambition . . . is the most lively in the most intelligent and most generous minds," he wrote, at once a defense of himself and a slam against James Warren, who had refused to accept any office that took him away from Massachusetts and his family. "I never solicited a vote in my life for any public office," Adams added. "I never swerved from any principle . . . to obtain a vote. I never sacrificed a friend or betrayed a trust. . . . I never wrote a line of slander against my bitterest enemy, nor encouraged it in any other."[32]

Warren was not easily chastened. She fired back six rejoinders. But after his tenth letter, each voluminous and quaking with ire, she terminated the correspondence. Let the *History* speak for itself, she finally suggested. Besides, she had tired of his "rancor, indecency, and vulgarism." "[As] an old friend, I pity you," she told him, and "as a Christian, I forgive you."[33]

Warren's *History,* together with the appearance soon thereafter of an anonymous newspaper essay reviving many of Hamilton's accusations about his character, convinced Adams that if his reputation was to be saved, he would have to tell his side of the story. He began by publishing the essay he had written shortly after returning to Peacefield, the rejoinder to the vitriolic attacks made upon him by Hamilton during the election of 1800. The piece had gathered dust for eight years, but the circumstances that had influenced him not to seek its publication in 1801 had been altered substantially. Hamilton was dead, long since the victim of Aaron Burr's gunshot in their famous duel at Weehawken. In addition, that very year, 1809, John Quincy had broken with the Federalist party; he could no longer be hurt by his father's attack on Hamilton and the High Federalists.[34]

Typically, Adams did not stop with one or two rebuttals. Almost weekly for three years he sent off essays and documents to the *Boston Patriot,* pieces that were originally intended merely as a defense of his presidency, but which, in time, grew to include a general, sweeping account of his diplomatic activities in Paris and the Netherlands. This was a significant undertaking, for it was Adams's first, and only, published attempt to rehabilitate his name; for the first time, too, he aired his side of the story with regard to his differences with Franklin and Hamilton.

By 1812, however, he had wearied of writing these polemics. He had grown more fatalistic. Future generations could do with his reputation as they wished, he told Rush, hinting that he believed some historians would criticize and others defend his actions.[35] But other factors were involved as well. Having exculpated himself, there no longer seemed to be anything left to prove, and at last he appeared to achieve peace with himself. The change in his attitude, moreover, occurred during a difficult time for John and Abigail, a period of travail that left him more aware than ever of the transitory nature of this life. The year 1811 was one of tragedy for the Adamses. In October his old friend and brother-in-law, Richard Cranch, a daily companion this past decade on long walks and at the whist table, died after a lengthy illness. Two days later, his widow, Mary, quietly passed away as well, as if, upon losing her soulmate of half a century, she no longer wished to continue this life.

Their demise occurred in the midst of an unfolding catastrophe for John and Abigail. Early in the year, Nabby wrote that her physician had discovered a cancerous tumor in her breast. Following the repeated entreaties of her mother, she made the wearying ride to Quincy in July and yielded to examinations by several of Boston's leading physicians. Only one recommended surgery; most maintained that surgical treatment would be more dangerous than the malady. Although she looked "very miserable" and found it almost impossible to eat, Nabby, upon the advice of the doctors, discontinued all medication, including the hemlock that she had been taking since the spring. Late in September, however, the Adamses heard from Dr. Rush in Philadelphia, whose opinion they had solicited; even though he had never examined the patient, Rush argued for surgery. Within a few days of the arrival of his recommendation, Nabby submitted to a mastectomy, a ghastly operation performed while she was conscious. The agonies that she endured during the surgery and for weeks thereafter were unimaginable, and shook both her parents to their very core. In the first letter that John wrote following the operation, he spoke of the likely impendence of his own demise, a subject he rarely broached.[36]

Nabby's physicians—four had been present during the surgery—confidently predicted a full recovery. Enervated by her ordeal, she remained at Peacefield until the summer of 1812, when, feeling well and strong again, she returned home. But shortly after she reached New York, the deep, afflicting pains reappeared. Initially, the distress was attributed to rheumatism. Then, early in 1813, her doctor changed his diagnosis. Her suffering was from cancer. The disease was spreading throughout her body. Death was imminent.

Forlornly announcing that her final wish was to die "in her father's house," Nabby summoned her son John, the lad born about the time his grandparents had returned to America from London, and had him transport her to Quincy. She arrived late in July and lived for only two weeks. In the last days, Abigail was too distraught even to be with her stricken child, but John remained at her bedside, providing every little comfort that a grieving father could grant his dying daughter.[37]

This tragedy, and the recurrent news of the demise of old colleagues and adversaries from the days of the Revolution, changed Adams. Not only did he abandon his defense in the *Boston Patriot,* but his outlook on the contemporary party battles mellowed. What once had been important seemed less urgent. Why had he even once wished to be president, he suddenly wondered. It had signified nothing. "Vanity of vanities, all was vanity," he now admitted. He was depressed. He wept frequently. Death could not be far away, he presumed. At times he wished that a fatal accident might suddenly snuff out his life. It would be preferable to enduring a lingering, painful illness, as Nabby had suffered, or to becoming a decrepit, helpless dotard who burdened all about him.[38]

It was in this mood that he was able to reestablish contact with Jefferson, once a close friend. The two men had not been in touch since shortly after Adams had fled the capital on that cold March morning when Jefferson ascended to the presidency. Adams had written his successor shortly after his return to Quincy; Jefferson had not responded. Three years later, Abigail made contact following the death of Jefferson's twenty-five-year-old daughter, Mary, the same little "Polly" who had briefly resided with the Adamses in London in 1787. Abigail sent condolences, adding that "the powerful feelings of my heart have burst through the restraint" she felt at writing an incumbent president; she knew too well the "agonizing . . . pangs of seperation" that resulted from the loss of a child, she went on. Jefferson answered, and the two exchanged a few letters over the next several months. But the tone of their missives was stiff and formal, at times even a bit rancorous, as the president carped at the partisan appointments made by his predecessor during his last days in office and Abigail recalled the "blackest calumny" practiced by the Republican party during the election of 1800. When she evinced her intention of turning the dialogue into a political discourse, Jefferson simply terminated the exchange by not replying to her fourth letter.[39]

John had not been a party to his wife's correspondence, nor did he or Jefferson respond in 1809 when Dr. Rush, a mutual friend, moved circumspectly in the aftermath of the Virginian's presidency to reunite the two men. By 1811 the situation had changed; that was the year of the onset of Nabby's terrible ordeal. By then, too, Adams's political views had mellowed considerably, as Jefferson noted when he read reprints in a Richmond newspaper of his old foe's letters to the *Boston Patriot;* he even discovered that Adams defended him against the long-standing Federalist charge that he was a mere puppet of France. The first substantive step toward a breakthrough, however, came when John and Edward Coles, secretaries to President Madison and natives of Albemarle County, Virginia, Jefferson's home, visited with John and Abigail for two days in the summer of 1811. They evidently made it clear that Jefferson bore no ill will toward Adams, who, in turn, responded: "I always loved Jefferson, and still love him." Jefferson was moved when he learned of Adams's comment. "This is enough for me," he told Rush, who quickly dispatched word to Peacefield that "the olive branch . . . has been offered to you by the hand of a man who still loves you." Adams wrote his first letter to Jefferson in eleven years, almost immediately after he received Rush's encouraging missive, and Jefferson responded almost on the very day that Adams's first communique arrived at Monticello, thus inaugurating a correspondence terminated only by death. Typically, Adams was the more verbose of the two, but he also was in greater need of the friendship. He dispatched 109 letters in fourteen years; Jefferson, who appears to have more carefully crafted his replies and who was decidedly less contentious in his remarks, sent forty-nine responses on a weeklong journey to Quincy.[40]

Jefferson, more private, always reticent to reveal his private side in public, characteristically confined his responses largely to political and philosophical matters. Adams fell into step. At the outset, Adams's habitual testiness shone through. He sought to defend the most controversial actions of his presidency, chided Jefferson for his early support of the French Revolution and for his authorship of the Kentucky Resolutions, questioned the Virginian's handling of the neutral rights crisis during his administration, and even stridently accused Jefferson of having been indifferent to the threat of internal revolution that Adams believed had existed in the 1790s.[41]

In time, Adams changed. The connection with Jefferson took on great meaning for him, too much to endanger by dredging up ancient differences. Adams had remembered his earlier relationship with Jefferson as that of teacher and pupil. "I was his preceptor in politics and taught him everything," he once remarked in all seriousness. Now, however, Jefferson became the means whereby Adams's self-dignity could be restored. By deigning to treat with Adams, his old rival, Jefferson appeared not just to forgive but to approve of the conduct of his predecessor in the White House. Through this liaison, therefore, Adams's guilt was banished, the wisdom of his behavior was confirmed. Moreover, his association with the more popular Jefferson appeared to elevate Adams to an exalted station, one that could be inhabited only by two former leaders of the Revolution, two former presidents. It permitted Adams to tower above—and to strike back against—those who once had connived and furtively intrigued against him, those who had attacked him in their histories. In his own mind, Adams became so intertwined with Jefferson that he began to refer to Peacefield by another name. "Mr. Jefferson lives at Monticello, the lofty Mountain," he observed; "I live at *Montezillo* a little hill."[42]

After a year or so, Adams began to write three or four letters to each missive that Jefferson sent, and he suddenly avoided controversial matters, mostly thereafter focusing on philosophical or theological matters, reminiscing about the Revolution or simply responding to Jefferson's observations and questions. His terse, initial salutation of "sincere esteem" gave way to more affectionate tidings. "With half a centurys affection for yourself," he closed one letter, and he commenced another, admitting, "Every line from you exhilarates my spirits and gives me a glow of pleasure."[43]

Jefferson was Adams's most important correspondent in these years but hardly the only person to whom he wrote on a regular basis. In 1814 he began corresponding with John Taylor of Virginia, author of the recently published *An Inquiry into the Principles and Policy of the Government of the United States,* a treatise written in large part as a critique of Adams's *Defence.* Adams dispatched more than thirty letters to Taylor in about one year, each slaked with his usual verbose reasoning, none containing any substantively new thoughts. He also exchanged several letters with Thomas McKean, whom he first had met on that same August evening in 1774 when he had been introduced to Dr. Rush; for the next four years they sat together in Congress, until Adams went abroad and McKean turned to a bountiful career at the state level, serving for twenty-two years as Pennsylvania's chief justice and for three terms as its governor, first as a Federalist, then as a Republican. Adams first wrote McKean in 1812 to learn details of the Stamp Act Congress of 1765, which the Pennsylvanian had attended. The correspondence continued for the next five years.

Beginning late in 1816, Adams added Hezekiah Niles, the publisher of a popular early magazine, *Niles' Weekly Register,* to his list of correspondents. Actually, Niles first approached Adams. He urged Adams to contribute for publication in the *Weekly Register* any revolutionary era documents that he might possess. Fearing the loss of precious materials, Adams initially surrendered only some out of print essays that he had authored nearly fifty years before; later he sent along some letters he had exchanged with Washington in 1790 and much of his correspondence with McKean, as well as his own reminiscences of revolutionary events.[44]

With each of these men, and numerous others as well, including John Quincy, whom he sometimes wrote weekly, Adams poured out letter after letter, his words flowing out at a stupendous, pistonlike rate, a production all the more remarkable when one considers that he was seventy-seven years old when he inaugurated the correspondence with Jefferson.

After a decade at home, Adams was no longer the bitter, vindictive man he had been when he departed Washington. The suffering and death about him were the primary agents of the change in his outlook. Nabby's demise in 1813 was the most difficult blow with which he had to cope, although soon thereafter Thomas Boylston and Nancy lost a young son to whooping cough—the second of the Adams grandchildren to die recently. John again was plunged into grief: "Why was I preserved 3/4 of a century," he wondered, "and that rose cropped in the bud?"[45]

In addition to these family tragedies, word all too often reached Peacefield of the passing of old friends. The sudden, jolting news of Dr. Rush's death in 1813 hurt most. In his final letter, Rush had predicted that "the night of imbecility of mind or death is fast approaching," yet Adams was taken by surprise when a letter arrived from Rush's son bearing news of the physician's demise. That same year Robert Livingston died in New York, leaving only Adams and Jefferson alive from among the five who had prepared the Declaration of Independence. The next year Adams learned of the death of James Lovell, once the close friend of Abigail. During 1814 Mercy Warren, Elbridge Gerry, and Robert Treat Paine, once young John's rival and tormentor but later a cordial acquaintance and occasional colleague, passed on.[46]

From this point on, Adams dwelt more than ever on the mysteries of life and death. During his early adult years, Adams had turned away from the strict Calvinism of his youth. He thereafter referred to himself as a "church-going animal" and as "a fellow disciple" to all Christians. In his final years, however, he moved toward a Unitarian position. He continued to believe in the existence of a Supreme Creator and in an afterlife, but he rejected the notion of Jesus' divinity and denounced institutional Christianity as a purveyor of fraud and superstition. The Christian church, he declared, was the cause of much pain and suffering on earth. Nevertheless, he continued to believe that Christ's teachings and his "universal Toleration" offered the best guide to human conduct. "My religion," he remarked in 1815, "is found on the love of God and my neighbor; on the hope of pardon for my offenses. . . . I believe, too, in a future state of rewards and punishments, but not eternal." The one notion to which Adams remained committed was his belief that religion was necessary for the general populace; without some such belief system to constrain the masses, he said, "their World would be something not fit to be mentioned in polite Company, I mean Hell."[47]

While Adams's emotional commitment to current political matters waned after about 1813, he never forswore an interest in public concerns. But it was the events of the American Revolution that now absorbed his attention. He was furious that some histories of the Revolution were giving Virginia too much credit for having led the opposition to Great Britain. He tried to set the record straight in his correspondence with Hezekiah Niles. The revolution was the focal point of long letters he exchanged with William Tudor, once his law clerk, now a prominent Boston attorney, and Jedidiah Morse, a Congregational clergymen and staunch Federalist. What was strikingly different about his recollections in this era, however, was that he seldom touched upon his own role in the important events of the revolutionary period. Instead, he portrayed Otis, Samuel Adams, and, surprisingly, John Hancock as the great triumvirate that had shepherded the rebellion in Massachusetts.[48]

Adams, who once had sought and achieved virtually complete independence from his family, now found solace in a full house of kin. Peacefield was indeed a busy household. On occasion, more than twenty people were crowded under its hospitable roof. Phoebe, a black servant who had been with the family for years, always was present, as was Juno, Abigail's pet Newfoundland, who relentlessly tagged about at her heels. Louisa Smith, an unmarried daughter of Abigail's deceased brother, continued to live with her aunt and uncle, as she had since 1788; Sally Adams, Charles's widow, and her two daughters also resided at Peacefield. John, the second son of John Quincy and Louisa Catherine, lived for years with his grandparents while his parents were away in the public service, although his brother, George Washington, a hyperactive and often unmanageable child, was kept by other relatives. Thomas Boylston and Nancy lived nearby in the house in which John had been born, busily producing seven children in the space of a dozen years, each of whom spent considerable time at the mansion down the road. Of Nabby's four children, only Caroline, the youngest and probably Abigail's favorite among the grandchildren, appears to have lived in Quincy for any length of time, but all came for visits, as did a bewildering array of nieces and nephews. Even Billy

Shaw, John and Abigail's nephew and once the secretary to President Adams, dwelled off and on at Peacefield.[49]

The maintenance of such a life-style was costly, but the family managed, thanks in large measure to John Quincy. Adams had neither debts nor an income when he returned to Quincy in 1801, but his frugal habits while a public servant had enabled him to accumulate handsome savings. When he entered retirement, most of his reserves—approximately $13,000—were drawing interest in a London bank. In 1803, however, the bank collapsed, and for a time a very anxious John and Abigail feared financial ruin and the certain loss of Peacefield. John Quincy saved them. He began purchasing property that his father had accumulated, ultimately paying his parents about $12,800 for parcels of land in Weymouth and Quincy, including Peacefield.[50]

John Quincy was the great delight of his parents and not just for his benevolent intervention in this family crisis. They were extremely proud of his advancement as a public official. For a time it appeared that his political career would founder almost at its inception. In 1809, at the conclusion of his first term in the Senate, the Massachusetts Federalist party disowned him for his Jeffersonian leanings. Turned out of office, he returned to Boston, planning to resume his law practice and teach at Harvard, where for the past three years he had been a part-time professor of rhetoric. But shortly after he had purchased a house in downtown Boston, president-elect Madison offered him the post as first United States minister plenipotentiary to Russia. He quickly accepted the offer.

His father was both delighted and saddened by the development, happy at the rejuvenation of John Quincy's political career, but fearful that he would never again see his favorite son. Accompanied by Nabby's son, William Steuben Smith—his secretary—John Quincy, Louisa Catherine, and their youngest son, Charles Francis, sailed for Europe in the summer of 1809. They did not return to America for eight years. John Quincy was a witness to and a participant in much history in these years: he watched as Napoleon invaded Russia in 1812; together with James Bayard, Albert Gallatin, and Henry Clay, he served on the United States diplomatic team that negotiated an end to the War of 1812; he was in Paris in 1815 when Napoleon regained power, then lost it at Waterloo; that same year he was appointed minister to the Court of St. James, a post his father had held more than a quarter century before.[51]

Late in 1816 John and Abigail learned from newspapers that their son had been recalled to the United States to serve as President James Monroe's secretary of state. John Quincy and his family reached Quincy in mid-August of the following summer. No longer a young man himself—he had just turned fifty—John Quincy must have been surprised at the years' impact on his parents. Abigail, nearly seventy-three, had grown completely gray and fearfully thin; her vision had deteriorated, and she was somewhat forgetful as well, but it was the crippling disability produced by rheumatism that must have struck John Quincy as the most cruel change suffered by his mother. When she spoke now of being "feeble," it was no longer was merely an expression, and when, a few months before her son's return, she remarked that "a small blast would blow me away," she was simply stating a terrible truth. Although nine years older than Abigail and beset with afflictions of his own, John appeared to be in better health. Five years before, he had described himself as a "withered, faded, wrinkled, tottering, trembling, stumbling, sighing, groaning" old man. His remark was not entirely hyperbole. His palsy—he spoke of his "quivering fingers"—had worsened so that he could no longer write, and his sight had declined even more appallingly than that of his wife; for the past eight years, at least, he had been able to read for only short stretches, forcing him to conscript Abigail or one of the other obliging women in the household into reading to him. He was an "old Dotard," he remarked on the eve of his son's return, and he equated his condition with that of the Benjamin Franklin he remembered during the days of the peace talks in 1782–83, a man beset with numerous infirmities. Nevertheless, Adams was about to celebrate his eighty-second birthday when John Quincy returned from Europe, and, for a man of that age, Adams not only remained in remarkably good physical condition but showed absolutely no evidence of senility.[52]

John and Abigail had a delightful visit with their son and young Charles Francis, who had been only two when he and his parents departed for St. Petersburg. The Adamses remained at Peacefield for a month before John Quincy had to leave for Washington and his new assignment. The boys stayed behind, George Washington to commence his studies at Harvard, John and ten-year-old Charles to continue their preparatory schooling in Boston.[53]

Despite their physical infirmities, this was a happy time for John and Abigail. John Quincy was safely back in the United States and his political career was flourishing; his duties as secretary of state did not permit the indulgence of lengthy absences from the capital, although he did manage to return to Quincy during the summer of 1818 for a brief visit. Thomas Boylston was nearby and called on his parents often. George Washington rode down from Cambridge on occasion, but John and Charles came every weekend, so often, in fact, that Abigail had to ask them to come less frequently; their visits were too taxing for the elderly couple.

The best-known visitors to Peacefield, however, were President Monroe and his wife, who called on John and Abigail during their tour of New England in the summer of 1817. John was flattered at the obvious reminder that he, indeed, was still remembered. But the president's courtesy call was not as meaningful as it might have been a few years before. Adams was now more than ever detached from "the gambols of Ambition Avarice . . . and Caprice" that constituted public life. In fact, a visit a few months earlier from his granddaughter Caroline, who had married John Peter De Windt and moved to

New York in 1814, was more gratifying to him than the social call by the Monroes.[54]

The retirement years had become the happiest years of his life, just as Adams had predicted they would be. His only regret seemed to be that time was going by so quickly. Suddenly the years were "Gone like the dew," he said. "I must soon reach the Bottom," he told a friend, but, meanwhile, he had found tranquillity. He neither hated life nor feared death, he remarked.[55]

When death next struck at Peacefield, Adams expected to be the victim. He was wrong. Abigail was struck down first.

"Old Age is dark & unlovely," Abigail had remarked at the beginning of 1818. Her disabilities had increased with each year, although two years had elapsed since her last serious illness, a winter's malady that had clung remorselessly to her for weeks. Through the first nine months of 1818 she remained in normal health, escaping the harsh winter season and the sultry summer weeks that she always feared. But autumn had normally been the most dangerous time for her, and this year, less than a week before her fifty-fourth wedding anniversary, she was attacked by typhoid fever, called "bilious fever" at the time.

Dr. Waterhouse was called in. Initially, optimism prevailed. Abigail had always been susceptible to fevers, but she had always withstood their onslaught. This time, too, after four dreadful days, she appeared to rally. On October 23, 24, and 25—the last date was her wedding anniversary—she was awake and alert, though terribly weak. Still, John was sufficiently encouraged to leave her side from time to time so that he might go to his study and be read to. But on October 26 she worsened. The next morning Dr. Waterhouse indicated that there was no hope. The end came the following day, just after noon on Wednesday, October 28, 1818. She was seventy-four years old.[56]

"We shall meet again and know each other in a future State," John wrote in the grief-stricken days that followed. "I cannot conceive that [God] could make such a Species as the human merely to live and die on this Earth."[57]

On the final day of the month, an unprecedentedly warm afternoon for so late in the fall, Adams walked the half mile to his church for the funeral service. The governor of Massachusetts and the president of Harvard College were among the pallbearers. The next day, Sunday, Abigail was laid to rest beside Nabby.

Peter Whitney, the Adamses' pastor, lauded Abigail as "meek and humble," a characterization that hardly seemed apt. But he also noted that she was "one who shone with no common splendor."[58] That was an assessment with which few could disagree.

CHAPTER 21

*

A Heavy Burden to Carry

J OHN ADAMS HAD ALWAYS PRESUMED that Abigail
would live at least to his present age, outlasting him and surviving on
into the late 1820s. He was stunned and devastated by his loss, but he was able
to go on. Friends and family poured in to help him through the days and weeks
that followed. Even Hannah Quincy, his first great love, called on him. Thomas
Boylston and Nancy, together with their six children, moved into Peacefield,
or the Old House, driven there as much by their financial situation as by a
desire to help the family patriarch. Nancy and Louisa Smith superintended
domestic matters, and in due time the household—at minimum, fourteen now
shared the dwelling—again was running smoothly.[1]

John Quincy returned each summer for a visit and continued to look after
his father's financial affairs. Thomas had done a satisfactory job of managing
John Quincy's concerns during his long absence in Europe, but he was no
longer to be trusted. His intemperance had become alarming. Although his
condition never matched that of Charles, it was a matter with which John
refused to deal, perhaps because of his recollection of how sorrowfully he had
coped with Charles and his desperate struggle.[2]

Although emotionally distraught and confronted by the inescapable fragili-
ty of old age, Adams remained mentally alert and unwilling to die. "I still live
and enjoy Life," he exclaimed six months after Abigail's death. His correspondence with Jefferson helped give comfort and meaning to the time that remained. The Virginian sent his condolences when he read in the newspapers
of Abigail's death. Having lost a wife himself—Martha Jefferson had died in
1782 and he had never remarried—he told John he could feel what he had lost;
it was cold comfort to remember, he added, that following their approaching
deaths, he and John would "ascend in essence to an ecstatic meeting" with the
mates they had loved and lost.[3]

Despite the enormous vacuum in his home and life, Adams remained busy.
He began to arrange his papers—his diaries, memoirs, ledgers, and prodigious
correspondence—for the likely day when John Quincy might write his biography. He spoke of the "few intervals of light" that his eyes allowed him, yet he

worked steadily at this endeavor, and he continued to read as much as he could. Reading "has kept me alive," he remarked in 1818, but each year thereafter he found it a more difficult undertaking. His eyes were "too dim" to accomplish much, he complained, yet until he was past his eighty-fifth birthday he continued to refer to having taxed his eyes with reading or to having "whirled away the time in reading." Eventually, however, reading was beyond his capability. When he reached that point, he sought to enlist someone, anyone, at Peacefield to read to him. He would listen to anything, even sermons, although he preferred contemporary writers such as Sir Walter Scott, James Fenimore Cooper, or Lord Byron, or histories and reminiscences. Writing, too, was something that Adams could no longer accomplish, both because of his failing sight and his palsy, or "quiveration," as he referred to the condition. He dictated to whomever he could induce to take the time for the chore, unaware that the spelling that was sent out over his name was often atrocious. Thomas Cushing became "Cushion" in his final letters, John Marshall was reduced to "Martial," Franklin to "Frankline," Negroes to "Negrows."[4]

In 1819 he hired additional labor for his farm, a sign that he now recognized his inability to do the physical work, or even much of the superintendency, that he once had performed. But he could still travel. A month after Abigail's death he rode to Boston to see John Trumbull's painting depicting his and Jefferson's committee presenting the Congress with the Declaration of Independence. The following year he journeyed to Brookline to once again see the farm on which his mother had been raised. That same year, Massachusetts held a constitutional convention to revise the charter that he had played such a considerable role in writing back in 1779, and Quincy elected him as its delegate to the conclave. Adams attended only a few sessions of the two-month convention and contributed nothing to the proceedings; later he said that he felt badly at having occupied a chair that might have been better filled. He had been "the Shadow of a Man" at the convention, he said; it was an act of "imbecility" to have accepted the position, he excoriated himself.[5]

Afterwards, Adams seldom left Peacefield. He declined invitations to attend the Artillery Company's annual gathering in Boston and to participate in the city's July Fourth observances. "[V]arious infirmities" precluded such endeavors, he explained. He also refused an offer to ride on a steamboat, a fairly new invention. Given his condition, he explained, a bout of seasickness likely would be fatal. The last time Adams appeared in public was in August 1821, when the West Point corps of cadets marched from Boston to Quincy, then paraded past his residence. He emerged and spoke briefly to the assembled companies, somewhat surprisingly, given his rancor of late, encouraging the young men to model themselves on the character of George Washington.[6]

His physical woes continued to mount, although most of the new distresses were relatively minor annoyances. He spoke of enduring "Jobs afflictions." He was beset by boils, then aching joints, next a general weariness, and afterwards still another cold. He was like a watch whose various components were wearing out, he said. Not long before his eighty-seventh birthday in 1822 he told Jefferson that his "sight [was] very dim; hearing pritty good; memory poor enough." By then he was badly stooped and unable to cross the room without assistance, but everyone who saw him remarked on his "spirit" and keen mental faculties. Charles Francis, who was at Peacefield often after 1818, remembered his grandfather as a paradoxical sort. He was grave "but not unbending," happiest when engaged in conversation, and often displayed a delightful sense of humor. But he could be vindictive, "unbearing and unjust," as well, and he forever seemed on the verge of a fiery outburst. When something provoked the old man, he said, his "anger . . . was, for a time, extremely violent, but when it subsided, it left no trace of malevolence behind."[7]

On three occasions during the last years of Adams's long retirement, artists came to Peacefield to capture its famous resident. A few weeks before Abigail's death, the Massachusetts legislature subscribed a marble bust of Adams. J. B. Binon, a French artist, was retained and spent a few hours in Quincy. Adams was pleased at the attention, and he told Jefferson that he would "let them do what they please with [his] old head." The Adams that emerged from Binon's hand bore little resemblance to the infirm old man who sat for the artist; the subject appears to be garrulous, robust, strong, and, like a venerated Roman, tough and wise.[8]

Two artists came to Peacefield during Adams's last years. The contrariety within John Adams of which Charles Francis was to speak was evident in their works. John sat first for Gilbert Stuart in 1823. Seated in the parlor on his red couch, Adams appeared relaxed, comfortable, vindicated. Charles Francis had described his grandfather's eyes as "mild and benignant, perhaps even humorous," and Stuart captured that as well, for his Adams appears to be smugly laughing at a world that at last wished to acclaim his achievements. Two years later, John Henri Browere visited the ninety-year-old former president in order to make a life mask. Adams agreed to the enterprise, as Jefferson had earlier in the year. The Virginian discovered it an unpleasant undertaking. "Successive coats of thin groaut plastered on the naked head and kept there an hour, would have been a severe trial [for] a young and hale man," he reported. Adams, surprisingly, found it to be a painless, rather interesting experience.[9] The Jefferson mask that resulted depicted a gaunt, tight-lipped, contemplative subject, whereas Adams resembled an elderly, wrinkled, haughty, bitter man. Stuart and Browere worked less than two years apart, yet each seemed to have portrayed a different John Adams. In fact, their works captured the two sides of this complex man. In the one work, the bitterly resentful, acrimonious Adams is visible, the man who remains consumed by vanity and who still was vexed at those who betrayed him and at those whom the public continued to exalt above him. The other work depicts the Adams vindicated by time, the man who is certain that his public actions were proper and who

John Adams in 1823, aged eighty-eight. Oil by Gilbert Stuart. *Courtesy: Charles F. Adams.*

believes that the public now understands the wisdom of his behavior. That these two Adamses existed side by side should not be surprising. Franklin and Hamilton had seen as much in the 1780s and 1790s.

It is difficult to read Adams's correspondence from his last years without concluding that feelings of vindication outweighed the bitterness in his soul. The final acquittal, in a sense, came in the canvass of 1824. John Quincy was elected president of the United States. Although he was eighty-nine when the issue finally was decided by the House of Representatives, John followed the election carefully. Once the matter was settled, Jefferson sent his congratulations. He knew, he wrote, that the victory "must excite ineffable feelings in the breast of a father." He was correct, of course. Those who saw the old man remarked that he was nearly overcome by John Quincy's accomplishment, all the more so, one suspects, in light of what he regarded as his apparent failures with Charles and Thomas Boylston.[10]

For several years after Abigail's death in 1818, John's health remained good enough to afford a generally happy existence, although he was terribly lonely and somewhat adrift without his wife at his side. "My House is a Region of sorrow," he once said, a dwelling in which both he and Sally Adams sought to cope with their loneliness and painful memories. But after early 1823, as his infirmities multiplied rapidly, the quality of his life deteriorated. Soon his sight was nearly gone and he could barely hear. He grew so weak that he could move about only with great difficulty; he trembled so badly that he had to be fed by his niece. Largely confined to his bedroom and the parlor, he likened himself to a horse in a gristmill, going round and round over the same path as it pulled the thick pulverizing stone. At the outset of 1823 he remarked that life had become "a heavy burden to carry." That was the year his brother Peter Boylston died at eighty-five. John was eighty-eight that year, the age to which his mother had lived. Death, he knew, could not be forestalled much longer.[11]

In 1822 Adams remarked that one ought not to wish for death "till life becomes insupportable." In his senectitude he had encountered various frailties and disabilities, yet until about 1824 his mental faculties remained keen. Then, for the first time, he observed that he felt "imbecility" creeping up on him. Even so, a visitor that year testified that his mental faculties remained "wonderfully vigorous," and his letters continued to be quite lucid, although the volume of his correspondence declined suddenly and dramatically.[12]

Still, John Adams was unwilling to die. All his life he had achieved great things through extraordinary feats of will, driving himself until he became Boston's leading attorney, laboring obsessively until he was recognized as the most noteworthy among the members of Congress, almost destructively lashing himself to endure privation and danger and loneliness in order to succeed in his diplomatic missions. One goal remained. He wished to live to the fiftieth

John Adams by John Henri Isaac Browere. Plaster bust taken November 22, 1825, when Adams was ninety years of age. *Courtesy: New York State Historical Association, Cooperstown, New York.*

anniversary of the signing of the Declaration of Independence, July 4, 1826. He hoped that Jefferson, too, would live to that day.

It seemed unlikely that Adams would survive until the jubilee of independence. His condition deteriorated rapidly throughout 1825. John Pierce, a Congregational minister who had visited him annually since 1815, called on Adams shortly before Christmas in 1825 and found him to be infirm and, for the first time, disinterested in conversation. He grew weaker in the spring of 1826. By May he was so feeble that his physician doubted he could survive to the end of the month. Survive he did, but by early summer he had grown too weak to swallow normally; Dr. Waterhouse feared that Adams would suffocate in his sleep.[13]

He remained alive until July 4, however. Jefferson, now eighty-three, eight years younger than Adams, was also still alive, but his spirits and health had declined steadily since the spring of 1825. By early 1826 his daily consumption of laudanum, a painkiller he took for a chronic urinary tract disorder, had reached massive proportions. Nevertheless, he was alert and active until late June. He fell ill suddenly on June 24; his condition swiftly worsened, although he remained lucid until July 2.

Late that day, Jefferson began to drift in and out of consciousness. When awake, he inquired whether the fourth had arrived. Despite his physician's doubt that he could last, Jefferson did live until July Fourth. At 12:50 P.M. on that warm, magical day, he breathed his last.[14]

Five hundred miles to the north, John Adams lay dying.

Four days before, he had received his last visitor from outside the family, a representative from Quincy's July Fourth celebration committee. Pressed to provide remarks for the coming ceremony, Adams responded with simplicity: "Independence Forever!"[15]

Bedfast and breathing with great difficulty, he had fought to stay alive. He made it to July 4. He knew it was July 4. Early that morning, his struggle at an end, he lapsed into unconsciousness. Near noon, close to the time of Jefferson's death, he awakened and with great effort proclaimed: "Thomas Jefferson survives."

These were his last words. Immediately thereafter he sank into a coma, from which he briefly stirred only one other time.

About six o'clock, as the long, cool shadows of day's end began to envelop Peacefield, John Adams died.[16]

AFTERWORD

*

I Am Not
. . . a Great Man

ON A WARM JULY MORNING shortly after his death, services were conducted for John Adams at the Congregational Church he had long attended. Many of the citizens of Quincy moved in procession from the Adams residence to the nearby church, then stood in two lines outside the great doors to the meetinghouse, permitting visitors to pass and occupy the few seats available. Pastor Whitney preached for the better part of half an hour and prayed for what must have seemed an eternity. When he was done, Adams's body was laid to rest next to that of his wife.[1]

Adams would have been surprised at the grief and ceremony occasioned by his passing. He probably would have been even more astonished at the praise lavished upon him. "Not half an age has roll'd its winter o'er / Since hate of Adams spread to every shore," one poet remarked soon after the events of that memorable July 4, 1826; yet now, the same poet added, the people voice "an adoration [for Adams] they never felt" when he was alive and active.[2]

In his latter years, Adams had known that his reputation had begun to rise from the depths to which it had sunk during this presidency. As his era's party battles—and even his Federalist Party—faded into history, it was natural that Adams should be looked upon in less emotional terms. The War of 1812 changed the way people felt, too, provoking a national self-consciousness that resulted in the exaltation of the Founding Fathers. The jubilee of 1776 seemed to complete the transformation; after the protracted celebration of the events leading to independence, it must have seemed that every leader who was active at the nation's birth had been canonized.[3]

But if Adams had become more palatable to the public before 1826, his enshrinement as one of the early greats can be traced to the remarkable coincidence of his and Jefferson's nearly simultaneous deaths on the fiftieth anniversary of the Declaration of Independence. Cities throughout the country immediately conducted solemn services to remember the two fallen patriots;

thousands—more than twenty thousand in Baltimore alone—paraded in funeral processions in their honor. Everywhere people sensed the hand of Providence in the extraordinary circumstances surrounding the deaths of the two statesmen. In truth, it was a "strange and very exciting coincidence," as John Quincy remarked when he learned of the occurrence.[4]

Notwithstanding his sudden elevation in status, John Adams still failed to achieve the lofty status of some of his famous contemporaries. George Washington stood above all others in the popular mind. He was the "father," the "First of Men," as a eulogist had said upon the occasion of his death at the turn of the century. Franklin, the sage, the artisan who had risen from humble origins to wealth and universal acclaim, continued to be esteemed; in fact, to a nineteenth century enveloped with the industrial process, Franklin the scientist, inventor, and exponent of thrift and hard work, the very embodiment of the native religion of upward mobility, may have been even more acclaimed than in his own time. More admired in life than Adams, Jefferson remained the greater popular favorite after death. After all, he was the actual author of the Declaration of Independence. To many he was the champion of republicanism, the "Apostle of Liberty," the defender—even the savior—of the Revolution. To others, the Virginian was the promulgator of democracy and egalitarianism.[5]

John Adams was remembered fondly as an ardent exponent of independence, indeed as the very "Atlas of Independence." But alongside that image, he was quite correctly perceived as a conservator, a preceptor against change, a leader identified with the restriction of liberty, a theorist who sought to erect defenses against the expression of the popular will, and as the guardian of an English political heritage that prevailed in a dark, remote American past.

The image of each of the Founding Fathers has undergone permutations with the passage of time. Always, however, Adams has remained within the galaxy of the greatest men of his time, yet, in contrast with Washington, Franklin, and Jefferson, he has remained a cultural hero of secondary proportions. Adams had seen it coming. Shortly after the conclusion of the War of Independence he had predicted Washington and Franklin's everlasting fame; because he believed himself to be "obnoxious, suspected and unpopular," he ruefully forecast that he would be forgotten. "Mausauleiums, Statues, Monuments will never be erected to me," he had remarked. Later, in retirement, he reflected on his long public life and concluded: "I am not, never was, & never shall be a great man." On another occasion he told a correspondent: "I never could bring myself seriously to consider that I was a great man." Subsequent generations have mostly agreed. A few years ago the distinguished historian, Edmund S. Morgan, thoughtfully considered Adams and reached the conclusion that he was "very nearly a great man."[6]

But what constitutes greatness? For a statesman, the definition inevitably comes down to the ability to lead, to become what Thomas Carlyle referred to simply as a "Commander over Men." What qualities does the "great man" possess that enable him to arouse and inspire others to follow? Carlyle, again, thought it was an extraordinarily "intuitive insight and great sincerity," an ability to convince others that he is both the "strongest soul" of his people and "a son of Order, not of Disorder. . . . His mission is . . . to make what was disorderly, chaotic, into a thing ruled, regular." John Stuart Mill thought great men exhibited such exceptional "powers of persuasion" that they could foster a commitment within others to follow their "feelings," even when such a course might appear to fly in the face of reason. Sidney Hook agreed. Great men, he wrote, "can get themselves believed in." A leader, he added, achieves greatness if he can shape "an issue or event whose consequence would have been profoundly different if he had not acted as he did"; a truly great man, he went on, possesses the "capacities of intelligence, will, and character" to alter history even when the forces of his age would seem to militate against change.[7]

More recently, historian Arthur Schlesinger, Jr., has written that a great man has the facility to arouse admiration, love, and, fear in his people, then to guide his followers to the achievement of their "highest potentialities." Political scientist-historian James MacGregor Burns has argued that the great leader succeeds in uniting his followers behind a "collective purpose" designed to fulfill the "needs, aspirations, and values" of his society. To accomplish such a feat, according to Eleanor Roosevelt, a close witness to the exercise of power, the great leader requires extraordinary patience and a feel for acting at precisely the right moment. Thomas Bailey, a student of presidential leadership, stressed that the greatest men in that office knew when to act boldly, when to move cautiously; they were actors, not dreamers; and they exhibited traits of decisiveness, dedication, and humanity.[8]

To John Adams, what constituted greatness? Growing up amid the lingering Puritan strains in New England and at a time of wide acceptance of the Anglo-American Whig political science, young Adams embraced the notion that the public good was the great aim of government. The exemplary ruler was to "dare boldly" to govern in the interest of the entire society, it was said. The best ruler, declared the *Essex Gazette* in the year of the Boston Massacre, would "guard and secure the lives, liberty and property of the industrious husbandmen, the careful merchants, the diligent mechanics and laborious poor, who compose the body of the people, and are the basis of society."[9]

While still a young man and merely an aspirant to power, Adams concluded that the "greatest men have been the most envious, malicious, and revengeful." They were, he added, universally driven by the sole purpose of securing fame to themselves. As he matured and gained office himself, and as he consorted with others in a similar situation, his views moderated, and ultimately he came to see many with whom he had served—and often clashed—in a more judicious light.[10]

Adams was unyielding only when it came to Hutchinson, Hamilton, and

Thomas Paine. To the end he remained convinced that Governor Hutchinson had been "base and corrupt," a man of "deep hypocrisy" who was unfit to govern. Nor did he waver from his view that Hamilton was a scapegrace in whom he could find no redeeming qualities. Paine, he continued to believe, was a "wild man" who had caused "infinitely more harm than good in every Country in which he ever showed his hand." Otherwise, his rancor dimmed in his last years. Eventually, he even admitted that Franklin "deserved a high rank," although he did not think him a great man; in fact, Adams believed his old friend, Dr. Rush, had "done infinitely more good to America than Franklin."[11]

Adams appreciated the talents of many men with whom he had served. In his letters he lauded Oxenbridge Thacher, from whom, he said, he had learned much about politics, Roger Sherman ("the most sensible man in the World"), John Jay, Patrick Henry, Artemas Ward, Washington's predecessor as the first American commander in 1775, Dickinson, the Lee brothers of Virginia, Robert Livingston of New York, with whom he had served on the committee that prepared the Declaration of Independence and to whom he had reported during a portion of his embassy abroad, and John Rutledge of South Carolina, whom he had initially judged to be "not very promising." While oddly silent regarding Jefferson, there can be little doubt that he viewed the Virginian as deservedly one of the great men of his era. His most bewildering reversal concerned John Hancock, a man for whom he once had displayed little respect, even looking upon him before 1776 as important chiefly for providing financial assistance to the protest movement. Later, Adams had second thoughts. In 1817 he wrote: "I profoundly admired him, and more profoundly loved him."[12]

Among his contemporaries, Adams believed that only three Americans could be considered great men. Despite his vacillation, he ultimately concluded that George Washington had been a great man, though decidedly a mortal; he had earned the praise of his fellow men, not their worship, he said. Adams often puzzled over the reasons for Washington's success. He was tall, handsome, elegant, graceful, and wealthy, he said; more importantly, he understood the "gift of silence," was aware of his weaknesses, which he kept carefully hidden from others, and manifested extraordinary "self-command." James Otis was greater even than Washington. Until madness overtook him, Adams thought, Otis's intellect was such that he taught the revolutionary generation why it was imperative to resist British encroachment. Adams even went so far as to argue that Dickinson, the "Farmer," largely pilfered Otis's writings for his more popular pamphlet. He saw in Otis the very embodiment of the virtues he most prized. James Otis, he said, was "the most learned, the most manly, the most honest" person that he ever knew.

Nevertheless, Adams thought Samuel Adams was the greatest man of his era. With a steely resolution, an excellent grasp of the constitutional issues at stake, a fervent commitment to republicanism, and extraordinary courage, he had molded and led the protest movement from its earliest, most dangerous days in 1765 until independence was at last possible in 1776. He likened Otis to Martin Luther, and Samuel Adams to John Calvin. Otis, he said, was more responsible than any man for launching the American protest movement. But it was Samuel Adams who shaped and guided the resistance; Samuel Adams had done more than any other activist to secure American independence.[13]

While Adams grew to believe that his talents were superior to those of most men with whom he had served, he never argued that he was a great man. It would have been unthinkable for him to make such a boast. But with considerable justification he did claim primary responsibility for five important occurrences in his public life. The acts he described as being of the most "eventful importance" were: his fight to preserve the independence of the provincial judiciary; his authorship of the Massachusetts legislature's response to Governor Hutchinson's interpretation of the imperial constitution in 1773; his leadership in the movement to select Washington as commander of the Continental army; and his long, successful campaign to win assistance from Holland during the darkest days of the War of Independence. However, the "most splendid diamond in my crown," he said, was his preservation of the peace during his presidency.[14]

Today, some of what Adams regarded as his greatest achievements appear to have been of less consequence than he believed. For instance, while Adams undoubtedly labored tirelessly behind the scenes to prepare New England's congressmen for the elevation of a southerner, Washington, to command the new colonial army in 1775, the movement to broaden the war into a continental struggle was so widespread and popular that Washington's appointment seems likely whether or not Adams had worked on his behalf. As a result of the fight over judicial independence and Adams's artfully constructed response to Hutchinson in 1773, many articulate colonists must have become convinced of British venality; it is unlikely, however, that either issue had much impact on the thinking of the great majority of Americans, for whom legalisms and constitutional issues remained terribly arcane matters. Finally, Adams did ultimately secure assistance from Holland, but his success occurred long after the Battle of Yorktown, the one truly pivotal event of the final years of the war.

Adams was correct to label his refusal to be coerced into an unwise war with France after 1798 as an act of seminal importance. It was a courageous deed, an act of statesmanship that saved countless lives; in addition, his pursuit of peace spared the new nation unimaginable dangers—dangers to the survival of its republican experiment as well as to the very existence of the Union. Among the Federalists of the time, only Washington, the most venerated man in

America, and Adams, grittily independent, could have withstood the enormous pressures from within their own party and peacefully shepherded the new United States through this dark, dangerous crisis.

In the *Boston Patriot* essays written during his retirement years, Adams sought with justification to explain his contributions to American foreign policy. So far as foreign policy is concerned, Adams deserves to be remembered as his country's first great nationalist, as a statesman who was more consistent in his views of America's relationship with the major powers in Europe than any other Founding Father. It is a trick of history that President Washington's Farewell Address is today the best-remembered statement of early American diplomacy, for those famous remarks made in 1796 were tantamount to a compendium of the ideas that Adams had expressed since 1776.

Adams might have claimed responsibility for other accomplishments. It is curious, in fact, that he took no credit for squiring the movement for independence through Congress in 1775 and 1776, an achievement recognized by his contemporaries. Not only had he fought to separate from Great Britain when it was not popular to take such a stance, but by his example and his logic he must have altered the thinking of some of his colleagues.

Stangely, too, Adams neglected to mention his impact on the shaping of the post-independence state governments. Yet, the prescription for government that he outlined in his *Thoughts on Government* in 1776 exerted a profound influence on the constitutional writers in several states. Indeed, his teachings on checks and balances remain at the core of the American system of governance even today.

These were the accomplishments of the public man. What of the private person behind the public activities? Adams was so consumed by a vain pursuit of recognition that, for a protracted period during his adult years, his relationship with his family can only be described as indifferent, even heartless. First emotionally, then physically, he separated himself from his spouse for years on end, pursuing what he fancied, apparently insensitive to her grief and sorrow as she was left alone to cope with the children, to manage the family's business affairs, to keep matters intact until he was at last ready to return his attention to such pursuits. His self-absorption proved to be an even greater misfortune for his sons. Adams doubtless loved his children, but his compelling drives left him with no time to tend to their needs during crucial periods in their lives. If Abigail could complain of her "widowhood" during the 1770s and 1780s, it could be said that little Charles and Thomas Boylston had no father as they passed through puberty and into adolescence. This deplorable state only worsened upon his return to America in 1788, when Adams was in a better position to impose his strong will upon his sons. The result was nothing short of disastrous for Charles. Thomas and John Quincy, likewise, appear to have struggled incessantly with the terrifying burden of complying with the family's precepts of achievement, ascendancy, and preeminence; fettered with the necessity of carrying out the fantasies and aspirations of another, each young man ultimately suffered the emasculation of his autonomous will. Ironically, however, their ultimate fates were quite different. The one was destined to live an unhappy life as an underachiever in a small Massachusetts village; the other, following the model erected by his famous father, emerged as a giant of American statecraft.

There was a brighter side to the private Adams, however. He provided quite adequately for the material necessities of his family. He often was compassionate and indulgent. At considerable personal expense, he opened his home to a vast array of relatives who found themselves confronted by mountainous economic or emotional woes. He was not given to duplicity or cunning. His code of honor was such that the deceit, disloyalty, and myriad petty treacheries endemic in the world of business and politics were largely foreign to his makeup. Adams, moreover, refused to be part of a system that reduced human beings to the status of chattel. He might have owned slaves, as did other affluent northern provincials, including Benjamin Franklin, John Hancock, and James Otis, saving himself a considerable sum otherwise expended upon free labor; instead, this man who was so often ridiculed for his pomposity, eschewed the elevated station that accompanied the ownership of slaves because he found the practice abhorrent.[15] Finally, while there can be no doubt that his customary demeanor was one of irascibility, Adams was able to form deep, long-standing, close relationships with other men, indicating that those who knew him best discovered what the historian who reads his private correspondence will find: behind his bilious, churlish facade, Adams could be a kind, loyal, warm individual.

But it is on the public field that greatness in a historical figure is normally tested. How, then, to evaluate the greatness of John Adams? Was he an indispensable actor in the historical drama of his age? No, but there surely was no such man in the America of his time, not even Washington; as Adams had lectured Dr. Rush during the troubled Valley Forge winter of 1778, the American Revolution was too great an event to hang on the actions of any one man. If not an indispensable figure, Adams was not an unimportant figure in the great events of his era. He played significant roles in his province's protest against Great Britain, in the movement for independence, in the early conduct of the war, in the diplomacy of the Revolution, and in shaping United States policy during the great crisis of the late 1790s. He was an especially important congressman between 1774 and 1777. Reflective by nature, a tireless worker, and a persuasive debater and speaker, Adams functioned well in such a corporate setting; alas, his skills were so readily apparent that many of his colleagues came to look upon him as the most important member of Congress.

Were there shortcomings? Of course. He was vain, irritable, impatient, jealous, and, at times, thoroughly unreasonable, even nearly irrational. Some of those qualities may have assisted him during the negotiation of the Treaty of

Paris and in the course of his embassy in London, but they rendered him ill-suited for the delicate task of treating with the proud and powerful French ally during the war years. Furthermore, despite a lifetime in politics, he was never an adroit politician. His irascible, impulsive, indiscreet manner often proved damaging; his inability to adequately judge his confederates was a fatal weakness. His naivete was so encrusted that not even a quarter century in the public arena equipped him for the rough-and-tumble, for the backstairs machinations that went with the presidency during the turbulent 1790s. In addition, one recalls the quip of his friend Jonathan Sewall, who recognized that Adams's distaste for blandishment and wheedling, his inability to act the dandy with the ladies or prattle foolishly with men of all backgrounds and persuasions, undermined his other attributes that might have permitted him to be an extraordinary "Commander over Men," as Carlyle had put it.[16]

Adams's greatest failure, however, lay in his inability to use his talents for a greater good. He so distrusted humankind that he could countenance little within the panoply of reformism advanced by the most daring men of his time. He dreamt of liberating Americans from a distant and corrupt parent state, substituting for the governance of a faraway, arbitrary parent a system in which the "People will have unbounded Power." But those very people, he warned his wife on the day after independence was declared, are "extreamely addicted to Corruption and Venality." Because that was the focus of his thought, he could only recoil in the face of Thomas Paine's exultant cry in 1776: "We have it in our power to begin the world over again." Paine offered the hope of a sweeping reconstruction of American politics and society, but Adams could see in that breathtaking vision only a "crapulous mass" of rhetoric, ideas that he could neither understand nor abide. Later, he appeared to see only the tyranny that accompanied the French Revolution, remaining oblivious to the qualities marking that upheaval as a great event in the liberation of man. He seemed incapable of understanding the misery of the desperate who rallied behind Daniel Shays or the Whiskey rebels or John Fries; he did not lift a finger to inhibit the passage of the Alien and Sedition acts. While others looked toward an American vista that included democracy, the unencumbered supremacy of legislatures, and manhood suffrage, Adams sought the preservation of much of the old order, minus any British influence.[17]

But he never contemplated the conservation of the old order in its entirety. If his *Defence* comes uncomfortably close to a plea for monarchism, what he championed, it should be remembered, was a strong executive, but one whose authority would be counterbalanced by other branches. Nor could he countenance aristocratic dominance. "You are afraid of the one—I, of the few," he once told Jefferson. "You are Apprehensive of Monarchy; I, of Aristocracy."[18] Indeed, it was humanity's oppression at the hands of the wealthy few that Adams thought most likely, and it was that which he most dreaded. His remedy for the evils of the old order was not unbridled democracy, which, in fact, had never existed in pre-Revolutionary America; he knew that human-kind's propensity toward avarice and power could result in a tyranny as brutal as that laid down by the most despotic king or oligarchy.

Like Jefferson, Adams also sought a popular, republican government of small, property-owning farmers. Had he possessed the power to will it, Adams's republic would have been peopled by a citizenry embodying the virtues that he embraced—the noblest qualities of the Puritan strain, especially a selfless public spirit. He quickly realized, however, that his ethic asked too much. Therefore, drawing upon the teachings of history and his Puritan sense of man's sinfulness, he propounded the notion of a republican polity that might be safeguarded through a system of balances, a system that might spare his countrymen the worst evils of the past while it insulated them from the dangers of newer ways, including the new world of which the worst terrors of the French Revolution were but a harbinger. His was a great and good dream. It would have been a grander dream had he sought not merely the preservation of liberty but also its expansion.

As a young man of twenty, John Adams had fretted that he would live and die in obscurity. Half a century later, in retirement at the end of his long public career, Adams knew that he would be remembered, but he had come to fear that he would not be remembered as a great man. In fact, he was not the greatest man of his era. George Washington exerted a more profound impact on the events of the time. With prudence and courage, with industry and sagacity and selfless sacrifice, Washington presided over both the American victory in the War of Independence and the establishment of the national government in the new American Union. He was the greatest man of his age, the man who became the very symbol of his time. But Adams deserves to rank with Franklin and Jefferson, just beneath Washington. Franklin—the innovator, apostle of the self-made man, scientist, humanitarian, popular philosopher, exponent of political, economic, and scientific freedom, skillful diplomat who understood the Gallic temper and succeeded with the French foreign ministry without doing damage to his own nation's vital interests, and the civic-minded reformer—touched numerous lives, although unlike Adams, the Atlas of independence and conservator of peace, he seldom was truly a leader of humanity. Jefferson "believed, as we believe, in Man," a later president, Franklin D. Roosevelt, said, and, he added, Jefferson believed "as we believe, that men are capable of their own government, and that no king, no tyrant, no dictator, can govern for them as well as they can govern for themselves."[19] His was a dream of greater liberty for greater numbers, a vision that would serve as a beacon of liberation for generations yet unborn on July 4, 1826. But Adams's judicious counsel would also serve as a buoy to future generations, a prescript for continuity with the past as well as a guide for the preservation of the liberty that had been secured by the revolutionary generation.

Adams achieved a greatness surpassing that of the two men whom he most admired, James Otis and Samuel Adams. Otis, of course, was cheated by the early onset of ruinous mental instability. Samuel Adams was a one-dimensional figure, a masterful politician in rebellious Boston as well as in the preindependence Congress, but a man who seemed tragically lost and adrift after 1776. Contrarily, the two men that Adams most despised in his latter years, Alexander Hamilton and Thomas Paine, were greater figures than he cared to acknowledge. Hamilton played a seminal role in the establishment of the new national government after 1787, and in the economic realm his vision was as profoundly important for the nineteenth century as were Jefferson's political views. Paine's clarion call to renounce reconciliation with Great Britain, his wartime propaganda pieces, and his advocacy of personal and political freedom, all espoused in artful, popular tones, undoubtedly reached multitudes of readers who remained unfamiliar with the writings of Adams.

What was the source of John Adams's greatness? It lay in his long, tireless service, undertaken at enormous personal sacrifice, and in his steadfast commitment to liberty. It was his genius to understand that if American independence could be won, then preserved, a nation in which the "People will have unbounded Power" could realize whatever it sought. On the day after independence was declared, he wrote to Abigail that he was "well aware of the Toil and Blood and Treasure, that it will cost Us to maintain this Declaration. . . . Yet through all the Gloom I can see the Rays of ravishing Light and Glory. I can see that the End is more than worth all the Means. And that Posterity will tryumph in that Days Transaction."[20]

He had "dared boldly," as the Puritan and Whig theorists of his youth had taught. For the duration of his public career, he remained committed to the quest for that "ravishing Light and Glory."

*

Abbreviations

The following abbreviations are used throughout the notes to designate frequently cited publications, libraries, and individuals.

AA	Abigail Adams
AAS	Abigail Adams Smith
ADA	L. H. Butterfield et al., eds., *The Diary and Autobiography of John Adams*. 4 vols. Cambridge, Mass. 1961.
"Adams-Warren Letters"	Charles F. Adams, ed., "Correspondence between John Adams and Mercy Warren Relating to Her History of the American Revolution," Massachusetts Historical Society, *Collections,* 5th ser., vol. 4. Boston, 1878.
AFC	L. H. Butterfield et al., eds., *Adams Family Correspondence*. 4 vols. Cambridge, Mass., 1963–.
AHR	*American Historical Review*
Am. Antiq. Soc.	American Antiquarian Society
AQ	*American Quarterly*
ASP	Walter Lowrie and Matthew St. Clair Clark, eds., *American State Papers. Class I. Foreign Relations*. 6 vols. Washington, 1832–59.
A-J Letters	Lester J. Cappon, ed., *The Adams-Jefferson Letters: The Complete Correspondence Between Thomas Jefferson and Abigail and John Adams*. Chapel Hill, 1959.
FLJA	Charles F. Adams, ed., *Familiar Letters of John Adams and his Wife Abigail Adams during the Revolution*. Boston, 1876.
HLQ	*Huntington Library Quarterly*
HSP	Autograph Letters of John Adams, Historical Society of Pennsylvania
JA	John Adams
JAH	*Journal of American History*
JAPM	The Adams Papers, Massachusetts Historical Society. Boston, 1954–59. Microfilm.
JCC	Worthington C. Ford et al., eds., *The Journals of the Continental Congress, 1774–1789*. 34 vols. Washington, 1904–37.
JQA	John Quincy Adams

JW	James Warren
LC	Library of Congress
LDC	*Paul H. Smith et al., eds., Letters of Delegates to Congress, 1774–1789.* Washington, 1976–.
MHS	Massachusetts Historical Society
MOW	Mercy Otis Warren
NEQ	*New England Quarterly*
NYHS	New York Historical Society
NYPL	New York Public Library
PAH	Harold C. Syrett and Jacob E. Cooke, eds., *Papers of Alexander Hamilton.* 26 vols. New York, 1961–79.
PJA	Robert J. Taylor et al., eds., *Papers of John Adams.* Cambridge, Mass. 1977–.
RDC	Francis Wharton, ed., *The Revolutionary Diplomatic Correspondence of the United States.* 6 vols. Washington, 1899.
TBA	Thomas Boylston Adams
WMQ	*William and Mary Quarterly*
W-A Letters	*Warren-Adams Letters: Being Chiefly a Correspondence among John Adams, Samuel Adams, and James Warren.* Massachusetts Historical Society, *Collections.* 2 vols. Boston, 1917, 1925.
Works	Charles F. Adams, ed., *The Works of John Adams, Second President of the United States: With a Life of the Author.* 10 vols. Boston, 1850–56.

Notes

INTRODUCTION

1. On daily life in JA's time, see: David Freeman Hawke, *Everyday Life in Early America* (New York, 1988) and Jack Larkin, *The Reshaping of Everyday Life, 1790–1840* (New York, 1988).
2. C. P. Reynolds, "Benjamin Franklin: Poor Richard in Paris," *Gourmet* 50 (April 1990), 137; "Noted with Pleasure," *New York Times Book Review* 95 (Apr. 29, 1990): 47.
3. Gilbert Chinard, *Honest John Adams* (Boston, 1933).
4. Page Smith, *John Adams.* 2 vols. (New York, 1962).
5. Peter Shaw, *The Character of John Adams* (Chapel Hill, 1976).
6. JA to President of Congress, Dec. 23, 1777, *PJA* 5:367.
7. JA to MOW, Dec. 18, 1778, ibid. 7:282.

CHAPTER I

1. *ADA,* 3:256; 4:66; "Genealogical Note," *PJA* 1:351–52; Smith, *JA,* 1:7–8; Jack Shepherd, *The Adams Chronicles: Four Generations of Greatness* (Boston, 1975), 4.
2. Charles Francis Adams, *History of Braintree, Massachusetts* (Cambridge, Mass., 1981), 89.
3. *ADA* 3:261, 276.
4. Ibid., 257.
5. *ADA* 1:65–66.
6. Ibid. 3:257–58; Lawrence A. Cremin, *American Education: The Colonial Experience, 1607–1783* (New York, 1970).
7. Robert Middlekauf, *Ancients and Axioms: Secondary Education in Eighteenth-Century New England* (New Haven, 1963), 63–102.
8. *ADA* 3:257–58.
9. Ibid., 257–58, 259n.
10. Ibid., 262.
11. Ibid., 259–60.

12. James Axtell, *The School upon a Hill: Education and Society in Colonial New England* (New Haven, 1974), 201–45; Cremin, *American Education,* 330–31, 466–68, 509–15, 553–54.
13. *ADA* 3:259–62; JA to Nathan Webb, Sept. 1, 1755, *PJA* 1:1; JA to Rev. Jacob Bailey, [1756], ibid., 11.
14. Cremin, *American Education,* 554.
15. *ADA* 3:262.
16. On Deacon Adams's views on lawyers, see the words attributed to him by JA in "Clarendon to Pym, 1766," *PJA* 1:161–62; *ADA* 3:263. On the changing image of lawyers, see: John M. Murrin, "The Legal Transformation: The Bench and Bar of Eighteenth-Century Massachusetts," in Stanley N. Katz and John M. Murrin, eds., *Colonial America: Essays in Politics and Social Development* (New York, 1983), 541–42, 548–53. For JA's ambitions and his view of the law, see *ADA* 1:7, 8, 23; JA To Jonathan Sewall, Feb. 1760, *PJA* 1:41–42; Charles Warren, *A History of the American Bar* (Boston, 1911), 79–80.
17. *ADA* 1:8, 23,31, 193, 217–19, 224n; 3:263, 276; JA to Charles Cushing, Apr. 1, 1756, *PJA* 1:12.
18. JA to Richard Cranch, Sept. 2, 1755,*PJA* 1:3; JA to Bailey, Jan. [?], 1756, ibid., 11; *ADA* 1:13–14.
19. *ADA* 1:2–32, 2n.
20. Ibid., 21, 35, 39, 41.
21. JA to Cushing, Apr. 1, 1756, *PJA* 1:12–13; *ADA* 1:20, 23, 24, 31, 33–34.
22. *ADA* 1:10, 21–22, 26.
23. Ibid., 41, 42–44; 3:264.
24. Ibid., 43.
25. Ibid.

CHAPTER 2

1. *ADA* 1:2n, 3n, 9n; 3:265–66.
2. See Richard B. Morris, *Studies in the History of the American Law* (New York, 1930), 42–44, 65–67.
3. *ADA* 1:63.
4. JA to AA, Feb. 13, 1776, *AFC* 1:347; Adrienne Koch, *Power, Morals, and the Founding Fathers: Essays in the Interpretation of the American Enlightenment* (Ithaca, 1961), 97. On service in the Massachusetts armies during the French and Indian War, see Fred Anderson, *A People's Army: Massachusetts Soldiers and Society in the Seven Years' War* (Chapel Hill, 1984), 27–62, 225–42.
5. JA to John Trumbull, March 9, 1790, JAPM, reel 115. Emphasis added.
6. *ADA* 1:26, 87; *PJA,* 1:88; JA, *Thoughts on Government,* in Adams, *Works* 4:199. On society and war in eighteenth-century Massachusetts, see John E. Ferling, "The New England Soldier: A Study in Changing Perceptions," *AQ* 33 (1981): 26–45. On male-female socialization in the colonial era, see Philip Greven, *The Protestant Temperament: Patterns of Child-Rearing, Religious Experience, and the Self in Early America* (New York, 1971), 246–47, 284–85, 322.

7. [JA], "On Political Faction, Man's Nature, and the Law," *PJA* 1:88, 90n; *ADA* 3:269–70.

8. *ADA* 3:269–70; Peter Shaw, *The Character of John Adams* (Chapel Hill, 1976), 27.

9. On JA's interviews with the four distinguished Boston attorneys, see *ADA* 3:272–73; 1:58–59, 83–84. On James Otis, see John J. Waters, *The Otis Family: In Provincial and Revolutionary Massachusetts* (Chapel Hill, 1968), 62, 64, 71, 75–102, 114, 132–39, 148.

10. *ADA* 1:60, 63.

11. Ibid., 16, 44–45, 51, 59–60, 64, 71, 74, 93, 131.

12. Ibid., 45, 51, 57, 63–64, 65–68, 73, 77.

13. JA to John Wentworth, Oct. [?], 1758, *PJA* 1:26; *ADA* 1:45, 66–73, 87–88, 103–4, 108–9, 115, 119, 176–77.

14. *ADA* 1:80.

15. Ibid., 52, 63, 68, 73, 78, 84, 95–96, 98, 100, 106, 118, 133.

16. Ibid., 168, 128–30, 135–38.

17. Ibid., 193, 217–19, 224n; 3:276.

18. Smith, *JA* 1:59–60.

19. *ADA* 1:73.

20. Ibid., 45–48.

21. Ibid., 84, 96, 113.

22. Ibid. 3:273, 275; JA to Hezekiah Niles, Jan. 14, 1818, Adams, *Works* 10:276; JA to William Tudor, March 29, 1817, ibid., 247. Also see Peter Shaw, *American Patriots and the Rituals of Revolution* (Cambridge, Mass., 1981), 109–30, and James M. Farrell, "John Adams's Autobiography: The Ciceronian Paradigm and the Quest for Fame," *NEQ* 62 (1989): 505–28.

23. Trevor Colbourn, ed., *Fame and the Founding Fathers: Essays by Douglass Adair* (Chapel Hill, 1974), 3–26. The Hamilton quotation is from Hamilton to Edward Stevens, Nov. 11, 1769, in Harold C. Syrett and Jacob E. Cooke, eds., *The Papers of Alexander Hamilton.* 26 vols. (New York, 1961–79), 1:512.

24. *ADA* 3:256; 1:8; JA to AA, May 22, 1777, *AFC* 2:243.

25. Ibid. 1:108–9.

26. Charles W. Akers, *Abigail Adams: An American Woman* (Boston, 1980), 1–16.

27. JA to AS, Oct. 4, 1762, Apr. 20, 1763, May 7, 1764, *AFC* 1:2, 5, 8, 44–46; AS to JA, Aug. 11, Sept. 12, 1763, and May 9, 1764, ibid., 6, 8, 47; Hannah Storer Green to JA, Feb. 20, 1764, ibid., 11; JA to Zabdiel Adams, July 23, 1763, *PJA* 1:95; Akers, *AA,* 14–15; Smith, *JA,* 1:63.

28. Akers *AA,* 4; *ADA* 3:276.

29. JA to AA, Apr. 7, 13, and 26, 1764, *AFC* 1:16–18, 24, 38; AS to JA, Apr. 7, 12, 15, 16, 18, and May 9, 1764, ibid., 15, 25–27, 31–36, 46–47; Cotton Tufts to AS, Apr. [19?], 1764, ibid., 38–39; *ADA,* 3:280.

30. Smith, *JA* 1:68–70; JA to AS, May 4, 1764, *AFC* 1:43; AS to JA, Oct. 4, 1764, ibid., 50.

31. Smith, *JA* 1:69–70; JA to AS, Sept. 30, 1764, *AFC* 1:48.

32. AS to JA, Apr. 30, 1764, *AFC* 1:42; Lynne Withey, *Dearest Friend: A Life of Abigail Adams* (New York, 1981), 23–24; Phyllis Lee Levin, *Abigail Adams: A Biography* (New York, 1987), 8.

33. *ADA* 1:251; "A Dissertation on the Canon and Feudal Law," *PJA* 1:103–28.
34. "On Political Faction," *PJA* 1:58–94; Helen Saltzberg Saltman, "John Adams' Earliest Essays: The Humphrey Ploughjogger Letters," *WMQ*, 3d ser., 37 (1980): 125–35.
35. Akers, *AA* 18–19; Catherine M. Scholter, "'On the Importance of the Obstetrick Art': Changing Customs of Childbirth in America," *WMQ*, 3d ser., 24 (1977): 426–45.
36. Withey, *Dearest Friend,* 29–30.
37. *ADA* 1:264–65. Emphasis added.

CHAPTER 3

1. *Boston Gazette,* Oct. 14, 1765, reprinted in *PJA* 1:146–47; Clarendon to Pym, Jan. 20, 1766, ibid., 161–64.
2. Allen S. Johnson, "The Passage of the Sugar Act," *WMQ*, 3d ser., 16 (1959): 507; Lawrence Henry Gipson, "The American Revolution as an Aftermath of the Great War for Empire," *Political Science Quarterly* 55 (1950): 86–104; Jack P. Greene, "The American Revolution: An Explanation," in George C. Suggs, ed., *Perspectives on the American Revolution* (Carbondale, Ill., 1977), 56–59.
3. Jack P. Greene, "An Uneasy Connection: An Analysis of the Preconditions of the American Revolution," in Stephen G. Kurtz and James H. Hutson, eds., *Essays on the American Revolution* (Chapel Hill, 1973), 32–80.
4. Johnson, "Passage of the Sugar Act," *WMQ* 16:507–14; David S. Lovejoy, "Rights Imply Equality: The Case Against Admiralty Jurisdiction in America," *WMQ*, 3d ser., 16 (1959): 459–66; Thomas C. Barrow, *Trade and Empire: The British Customs Service in Colonial America, 1600–1775* (Cambridge, Mass., 1967), 134–37, 189–90; Merrill Jensen, *The Founding of a Nation: A History of the American Revolution, 1763–1776* (New York, 1968), 36–69; Carl Ubbelohde, *The Vice-Admiralty Courts and the American Revolution* (Chapel Hill, 1960), 44–51.
5. Jensen, *Founding of a Nation,* 70–97; JA to Dr. Moore, March 9, 1809, JAPM, reel 118; Adams, *Works* 10:248; JA to AS, Apr. 7, 1764, *AFC* 1:16. James Otis's pamphlet, *The Rights of the British Colonies Asserted and Proved* (Boston, 1764), has been reprinted in Bernard Bailyn, ed. *Pamphlets of the American Revolution, 1750–1776* (Cambridge, Mass., 1965–), 1:419–82.
6. Edmund S. Morgan and Helen M. Morgan, *The Stamp Act Crisis: Prologue to Revolution* (Chapel Hill, 1953), 53–70.
7. Stephen E. Patterson, *Political Parties in Revolutionary Massachusetts* (Madison, Wis., 1973), 33–57; *ADA* 1:226; Gary B. Nash, *The Urban Crucible: The Northern Seaports and the Origins of the American Revolution* (Cambridge, Mass., 1979), 245–46, 253–56, 274–78, 340; Jensen, *Founding of a Nation,* 74–76. On Otis, see Waters, *The Otis Family,* and Shaw, *American Patriots,* 77–108.
8. Shaw, *American Patriots,* 87–100.
9. John C. Miller, *Sam Adams: Pioneer in Propaganda* (Stanford, 1936), 3–47; Pauline Maier, *The Old Revolutionaries: Political Lives in the Age of Samuel Adams* (New York, 1980), 5–11, 17–21; Edmund S. Morgan, "The Puritan Ethic and

the American Revolution," *WMQ,* 3d ser., 24 (1967): 3–43; JA to William Tudor, June 5, 1817, JAPM, reel 123.

10. Patterson, *Political Parties,* 45–46, 52–62.
11. [Joseph Galloway], *Historical and Political Reflections on the Rise and Progress of the American Rebellion* (London, 1780), 67–68; *ADA* 1:271; AA to Mary Cranch, July 15, 1766, *AFC* 1:54.
12. Pauline Maier, *From Resistance to Revolution: Colonial Radicals and the Development of American Opposition to Britain, 1765–1776* (New York, 1972), 4–7; Dirk Hoerder, "Boston Leaders and Boston Crowds, 1765–1776," in Alfred F. Young, ed., *The American Revolution: Explorations in the History of American Radicalism* (DeKalb, Ill., 1976), 237–38; James Henretta, "Economic Development and Social Structure in Colonial Boston," *WMQ,* 3d ser., 22 (1965): 75–92; Patterson, *Political Parties,* 57–62; Marc Egnal and Joseph A. Ernst, "An Economic Interpretation of the American Revolution," *WMQ,* 3d ser., 29 (1972): 15, 29; Nash, *Urban Crucible,* 247–63, 292–300.
13. Hoerder, "Boston Leaders," *American Revolution,* 241–46.
14. *ADA* 1: 263, 271; 3:276; JA to Hezekiah Niles, Feb. 13, 1818, Adams, *Works* 10:282; JA to MOW, July 20, 1807, "Adams-Warren Letters," 340; JA to Rev. Dr. Moore, March 9, 1809, JAPM, reel, 118; JA to Jedidiah Morse, Nov. 29, 1815, ibid., reel 122; JA to Tudor, March 22, 1817, ibid., reel 123. On JA and the writs of assistance case, see Kinvin Wroth and Hiller B. Zobel, eds., *Legal Papers of John Adams.* 3 vols. (Cambridge, Mass., 1965), 2:106–47.
15. "Instructions to Boston's Representatives Concerning the Stamp Act," Sept.–Oct. 1765, *PJA* 1:132–43; for Adams's newspaper essays, see 1:103–28, 155–69.
16. *ADA* 1:265–67, 273, 275.
17. Adams, *Works,* 259–61; Miller, *Sam Adams,* 99; *ADA* 1:274; W. T. Baxter, *The House of Hancock: Business in Boston, 1724–1775* (Reprint, New York, 1965), 258.
18. *ADA* 1:271, 274, 352; 2:74; Wroth and Zobel, *Legal Papers of JA,* 1:lviii–lix; [JA], "Draft of 'A Dissertation on the Canon and the Feudal Law,'" *PJA* 1:125; Miller, *Sam Adams,* 59, 98–99.
19. Wroth and Zobel, *Legal Papers of JA* 1:lviii; Morgan and Morgan, *Stamp Act,* 138–39.
20. Withey, *Dearest Friend,* 11, 24–26, 28.
21. *ADA* 1:273–314, 318–19; Akers, *AA,* 20, Smith, *JA,* 1:86–87; Withey, *Dearest Friend,* 24–25; AA to Hannah Green, [post July 14, 1765], *AFC* 1:51–52; AA to Mary Cranch, July 15, Oct. 6 and 13, 1766, *ibid.,* 53–57; Andrew Oliver, *Portraits of John and Abigail Adams* (Cambridge, Mass., 1967), 8.
22. JA to Tudor, March 22, 1817, JAPM, reel 123; AA to Mary Cranch, Oct. 6, 1766, *AFC,* 1:56.
23. *ADA,* 1:272, 312–13.
24. Ibid., 312, 312–13n.
25. Ibid., 69, 71, 86, 130, 189, 193, 312–13n.
26. Ibid., 301–05.
27. Ibid., 337, 331.
28. Sewall's articles appeared in the *Boston Evening Post,* Dec. 1, 15, 22, 29, 1766, Jan. 5, 12, 26, Feb. 9, Mar. 2, July 27, and Aug. 3, 10, 1767. An excellent

summary of his views can be found in Carol Berkin, *Jonathan Sewall: Odyssey on an American Loyalist* (New York, 1974), 37–42.

29. [JA], "Replies to Philanthrop, Defender of Governor Bernard," Dec. 9, 1766–Feb. 16, 1767, in *PJA* 1:174–211. For the quotations in the text, see 1:176, 184, 193, and 199.

30. JA to Cranch, June 29, 1766, *AFC* 1:52.

31. AA to March Cranch, Jan. 12, 1767, ibid., 1:57, *ADA* 1:284, 322, 323; 2:41, 48–49.

32. *ADA* 1:316.

33. Mary Cranch to AA, Jan. 15, 1767, *AFC* 1:59; AA to Mary Cranch, Jan. 31, 1767, ibid., 60; AA to JA, Sept. 13, 1767, ibid., 62; *ADA* 1:337–38.

34. *ADA* 1:299; Withey, *Dearest Friend,* 32.

35. *ADA* 2:68; 1:337; Smith, *JA* 2:95–96; Shaw, *Character of JA,* 57.

36. Jensen, *Founding of a Nation,* 215–28.

37. Ibid., 244–52, 266–70, 279–88.

38. Wroth and Zobel, *Legal Papers of JA* 3:173–84; *ADA* 3:306.

39. Jensen, *Founding of a Nation,* 289–90.

40. Wroth and Zobel, *Legal Papers of JA* 2:103, 183; *ADA* 3:287–89; 1:324, 331.

41. *ADA,* 1:331.

42. *PJA,* 1:211–16.

43. The literature on the turbulent protest against the Townshend duties is vast. A good succinct account can be found in Jensen, *Founding of a Nation,* 239–313. On the idea of a British conspiracy, see Bernard Bailyn, *The Ideological Origins of the American Revolution* (Cambridge, Mass., 1967), 95–98, 100–01, 144–59, and Gordon S. Wood, "Conspiracy and the Paranoid Style: Causality and Deceit in the Eighteenth Century," WMQ, 3d ser., 39 (1982): 401–41.

44. ADA, 3:289–91; 1:52, 331, 337–38, 341–43; *PJA* 1:220–35.

45. *ADA,* 3:290–91; 1:349.

46. Ibid., 1:352.

47. Ibid., 341–42.

48. JA to AA and Isaac Smith, Jr., Jan. 4, 1770, *AFC* 1:69.

49. Ibid.

CHAPTER 4

1. Boston Sons of Liberty to John Wilkes, Nov. 4, 1769, and Oct. 5, 1768, *PJA* 1:233, 220.

2. Hiller B. Zobel, *The Boston Massacre* (New York, 1970), 164–77.

3. *ADA* 1:249–50.

4. Zobel, *Boston Massacre,* 180–205.

5. *ADA* 3:291–92.

6. Zobel, *Boston Massacre,* 206–15; JA to William Tudor, Apr. 15, 1817, Adams, *Works* 10:251–52.

7. Zobel, *Boston Massacre,* 32, 41, 49, 214, 217–21, 231, 296; *ADA,* 3:294.

8. On Samuel Adams and his power, see Maier, *Old Revolutionaries,* 17; Miller, *Sam Adams,* 64–69.

9. Zobel, *Boston Massacre,* 241–66.
10. *ADA* 3:293; Zobel, *Boston Massacre,* 26–94.
11. Richard B. Morris, *Seven Who Shaped Our Destiny: The Founding Fathers as Revolutionaries* (New York, 1973), 89–91; Farrell, "JA's *Autobiography*," *NEQ* 62:512–16; JA to John Lowell, Dec. 15, 1770, *PJA,* 1:249; Zobel, *Boston Massacre,* 299–300.
12. Wroth and Zobel, *Legal Papers of JA* 1:lix–lxxxv; JA to AA, Jan. 29, 1774, *AFC* 1:114. On the movement to establish bar associations within Massachusetts, and on the legal profession in general during this period, see Murrin, "Legal Transformation," in Katz and Murrin, *Colonial America,* 415–49.
13. *ADA* 3:294–95; JA to Lowell, Dec. 15, 1770, *PJA* 1:249; Withey, *Dearest Friend,* 35–36.
14. *ADA* 1:6; 3:296; Smith, *JA* 1:128–29.
15. JA to Isaac Smith, Apr. 11, 1771, *AFC* 1:75; *ADA* 3:294.
16. *ADA* 3:294–95; Bernard Bailyn, *The Ordeal of Thomas Hutchinson* (Cambridge, Mass., 1974), 169–75; Donald C. Lord and Robert M. Calhoun, "The Removal of the Massachusetts General Court from Boston, 1765–1772," *JAH* 55 (1969): 735–55.
17. *ADA* 3:294–95; Boston Sons of Liberty to Wilkes, Nov. 4, 1769, *PJA* 1:233–34.
18. Maier, *Old Revolutionaries,* 21–24. Also see Jensen, *Founding of a Nation,* 292–93.
19. *ADA* 1:260; 3:326; JA to JW, Dec. 17, 1773, and May 15, 1776, *PJA* 2:2; 4:186.
20. *ADA* 3:295; 2:6–9, 35.
21. Shepherd, *Adams Chronicles,* 217; *ADA,* 2:6–7; JA to AA, Sept. 17, 1771, and May 23, 1772, *AFC* 1:81, 83; AA to Isaac Smith, Jr., Apr. 11, 1771, ibid., 74–75; AA to MOW, July 16, 1773, ibid., 84. On the marriage of John and Abigail, see: Adams, *Works* 1: Akers, *AA* 29; Paul C. Nagel, *The Adams Women: Abigail and Louisa Adams, Their Sisters and Daughters* (New York, 1987), 19; Withey, *Dearest Friend,* 26, 32; Levin, *AA* 13, 20–21. On the evolving, often conflicting, images of Abigail Adams, see Edith B. Gelles, "The Abigail Industry," *WMQ,* 3d ser., 45 (1988): 656–83.
22. *ADA* 2:18–43; Carl Bridenbaugh, "Baths and Watering Places in Colonial America," *WMQ,* 3d ser., 3 (1946): 152–58.
23. *ADA* 2:35; JA to Smith, Jr., Apr. 11, 1771, *AFC* 1:74.
24. *ADA* 2:35, 76.
25. Ibid., 44–45, 54–55, 63, 65–66.
26. Ibid., 20, 44–45, 54–55, 63, 66, 74.
27. Ibid., 43, 64, 62, 26, 43–44, 12, 53; JA to AA, May [?], 1772, *AFC* 1:83; Wroth and Zobel, *Legal Papers of JA* 1:lx–lxi, lxvi–lxvii, 48–64, 280, 286; 2:48–52.
28. Shepherd, *Adams Chronicles,* 49; *ADA* 2:6, 69, 63; JA to Isaac Smith, [1771], *AFC* 1:81–82.
29. *ADA* 2:73–74.
30. Ibid., 77–79, 79n; John Adams, "On the Independence of the Judges," Jan. 11–Feb. 22, 1773, *PJA* 1:252–55n, 269–309.
31. *Speeches of His Excellency Governor Hutchinson, to the General Assembly of the Massachusetts Bay . . . With the Answers . . .* (Boston, 1773).

32. Bailyn, *Ordeal of Hutchinson* 208; *ADA* 2:76; 3:305; JA to MOW, July 20, 1807, Adams, "Adams-Warren Letters," 4:346.
33. *ADA* 2:77; Bailyn, *Ordeal of Hutchinson,* 209. On the ministry's reaction to Hutchinson's actions, see Robert W. Tucker and David C. Hendrickson, *The Fall of the First British Empire: Origins of the War of American Independence* (Baltimore, 1982), 304.
34. Miller, *Sam Adams,* 255–72.
35. Bailyn, *Ordeal of Hutchinson,* 211, 218–19, 239; *ADA* 2:39–80; *Journal of the House of Representatives of Massachusetts Bay . . . Begun the Twenty-Sixth Day of May . . . 1773* (Boston, 1773); [Anon.], *Copy of Letters Sent to Great Britain, by his Excellency Thomas Hutchinson* (Boston, 1773).
36. Bailyn, *Ordeal of Hutchinson,* 226–53; Miller, *Sam Adams,* 278–82; Shaw, *Character of JA,* 73.
37. Adams, *Works* 1:115, 144; John W. Ellsworth, "John Adams: The American Revolution as a Change of Heart?" *HLQ* 28 (1965): 293–300; Smith, *JA* 1:86, 115; Edmund S. Morgan, *The Meaning of Independence: John Adams, George Washington, and Thomas Jefferson* (New York, 1978) 12–15; Gilbert Chinard, *Honest JA,* 56; Shaw, *Character of JA,* 73–74.
38. JA to Hezekiah Niles, Feb. 13, 1818, Adams, *Works* 10:285–86; JA to William Tudor, June 1, 1817, and July 9, 1818, ibid., 259, 327; JA to AA, Apr. 19, 1794, JAPM, reel 377; JA to Tudor, Nov. 16, 25, and Dec. 7, 1816, ibid., reel 123; JA to Skelton Jones, March 11, 1809, ibid., reel 118; Adams, *Thoughts on Government,* in *PJA* 4:87; JA to MOW, July 20, 1807, Adams, "Adams-Warren Letters," 4:3–44; Bailyn, *Ideological Origins,* 26; John Howe, *The Changing Political Thought of John Adams* (Princeton, 1966), 43; JA to Benjamin Rush, Feb. 27, 1805, May 1 and 21, 1807, in John A. Schutz and Douglass Adair, eds., *The Spur of Fame: Dialogues of John Adams and Benjamin Rush, 1805–1813* (San Marino, Calif., 1966), 35, 36, 80, 88.
39. See Nathan O. Hatch, *The Sacred Cause of Liberty: Republican Thought and the Millennium in Revolutionary New England* (New Haven, 1977), 14, 51–52, 55–96. See also Edmund S. Morgan, "The Puritan Ethic and the Coming of the American Revolution," *WMQ,* 3d ser., 24 (1967), 3–18.
40. *ADA* 1:260; 2:63, 67, 69, 76, 82, 84–85, 86; JA to Catherine Macaulay, Dec. 3, 1772, ibid., 2:75; JA to Warren, Dec. 22, 1773, *PJA* 2:3; [JA], "Letters of Novanglus," ibid., 266; JA to JW, July 17, 1774, ibid., 110; [JA], "Motion on Nonexportation and Defense," [Sept. 30, 1774], ibid., 157; [JA], "Reply to A Friendly Address to All Reasonable Americans," ibid., 196; Howe; *Changing Political Thought of JA,* 28–41; David F. Musto, "The Adams Family," MHS, *Proceedings* 93 (1981): 46, 51–52.
41. John Ferling, *The First of Men: A Life of George Washington* (Knoxville, 1988), 90–91. The Franklin quotation is in Esmond Wright, *Franklin of Philadelphia* (Cambridge, Mass., 1986), 185.
42. *ADA* 2:82–83.
43. Ibid., 87.
44. AA to MOW, Dec. 5, 1773, *AFC* 1:89.

CHAPTER 5

1. Wesley S. Griswold, *The Night the Revolution Began: The Boston Tea Party, 1773* (Brattleboro, Vt., 1972), 14–15, 59–60; Benjamin W. Labaree, *The Boston Tea Party* (New York, 1964), 128; "Extracts of the Journal of the ship *Dartmouth* from London to Boston, 1773," in [Benjamin B. Thacher, ed.], *Traits of the Tea Party; Being a Narrative of George R. T. Hewes* (New York, 1835), 259–60.

2. Labaree, *Boston Tea Party*, 58–79. On the monopoly aspects of the Tea Act, see John W. Tyler, *Smugglers & Patriots: Boston Merchants and the Advent of the American Revolution* (Boston, 1986), 192–205.

3. Ibid., 89–96; Jensen, *Founding of a Nation*, 444–47. On the upheaval in New York, also see Bernard Mason, *The Road to Independence: The Revolutionary Movement in New York, 1773–1777* (Lexington, Ky., 1966).

4. Labaree, *Boston Tea Party*, 89–99; Jensen, *Founding of a Nation*, 443–47; Charles S. Olton, *Artisans for Independence: Philadelphia Mechanics and the American Revolution* (Syracuse, 1975), 34, 37–38, 50–51; Richard Alan Ryerson, *The Revolution Is Now Begun: The Radical Committees of Philadelphia, 1765–1776* (Philadelphia, 1978), 28–38.

5. Labaree, *Boston Tea Party*, 104–6.

6. John Cary, *Joseph Warren: Physician, Politician, Patriot* (Urbana, Ill., 1961), 19–33, 124; David F. Hawke, "Dr. Thomas Young—'Eternal Fisher in Troubled Waters'; Notes for a Biography," *The New-York Historical Society Quarterly* 54 (1970): 6–29; Maier, *Old Revolutionaries*, 101–11; Nash, *Urban Crucible*, 273–82, 296–300. On the role of the merchants in the protest, see Baxter, *The House of Hancock*; G. B. Warden, *Boston, 1689–1776* (Boston, 1970); and Tyler, *Smugglers & Patriots*.

7. Benjamin Rush to JA, Aug. 14, 1809, Lyman H. Butterfield, ed., *Letters of Benjamin Rush.* 2 vols. (Philadelphia, 1951), 2:1013–14; *ADA* 3:297–306.

8. Labaree, *Boston Tea Party*, 108–25.

9. AA to MOW, Dec. 5, 1773, *AFC* 1:88–89; *ADA* 2:86–87, 93; Wroth and Zobel, *Legal Papers of JA* 2:105.

10. Griswold, *Night the Revolution Began*, 21, 65–106; Labaree, *Boston Tea Party*, 126–47; Bailyn, *Ordeal of Hutchinson*, 259–63; Richard D. Brown, *Revolutionary Politics in Massachusetts: The Boston Committee of Correspondence and the Towns, 1772–1774* (Cambridge, Mass., 1970), 149–77.

11. *ADA* 2:85–87.

12. JA to JW, Dec. 17, 1773, *PJA* 2:1–2; *ADA* 2:85–87.

13. *ADA* 2:85–87; JA to JW, Dec. 17, 1773, *PJA* 2:1.

14. Jack Sosin, "The Massachusetts Acts of 1774: Coercive or Preventive?" *HLQ* 26 (1963): 236; Labaree, *Boston Tea Party*, 170–93; Allan J. McCurry, "The North Government and the Outbreak of the American Revolution," *HLQ* 34 (1971): 141–57.

15. Akers, *AA*, 26–28; AA to MOW, July 16, 1773, *AFC* 1:84–85; *ADA* 2:94–95.

16. *ADA* 2:87–88; 3:307.

17. JA to AA, May 12, 1774, *AFC* 1:107; Labaree, *Boston Tea Party*, 219, 224.

18. JA to AA, June 29, 1774, *AFC* 1:110; Labaree, *Boston Tea Party,* 219–26; Jensen, *Founding of a Nation,* 467–69; Patterson, *Political Parties in Revolutionary Massachusetts,* 71–88; Dirk Hoerder, *Crowd Action in Revolutionary Massachusetts, 1765–1780* (New York, 1977), 71–88; Miller, *Sam Adams,* 301–2.
19. *ADA* 2:86, 3:276.
20. Ibid., 2:86, 89, 90–91, 93, 96, 97.
21. Ibid., 96–97; JA to AA, July 7, 1774, *AFC* 1:130; JA to JW, June 25 and July 17, 1774, *PJA* 2:100, 109.
22. JA to AA, June 23, 29, 30, July 1, 2, 3, 4, 5, 6, 7, and 9, 1774, *AFC* 1:108–35.

CHAPTER 6

1. JA to AA July 7 and 9, 1774, *AFC* 1:131–34.
2. Berkin, *Sewall,* 1–104.
3. *AFC* 1:136–37n.
4. JA to JW, July 25, 1774, *PJA* 2:116.
5. *ADA* 2:97–111.
6. Ibid., 111–13; JA to AA, Aug. 28, 1774, *AFC,* 1:144–46; AA to JA, Aug. 15, 19, and Sept. 2, 1774, ibid., 140–43, 146–48.
7. *ADA* 2:114–15, 182.
8. Carl and Jessica Bridenbaugh, *Rebels and Gentlemen: Philadelphia in the Age of Franklin* (New York, 1965), 1–28; Sam Bass Warner, Jr., *The Private City: Philadelphia in Three Periods of its Growth* (Philadelphia, 1968), 3–21.
9. *ADA* 2:115–17.
10. Ibid., 119, 121; [Joseph Galloway], *A Candid Examination of the Mutual Claims of Great Britain, and the Colonies: With a Plan of Accommodation, on Constitutional Principles* (New York, 1775), 40–44.
11. *ADA* 2:117–19, 121; JA to AA, Sept. 14, 1774, *AFC* 1:155; JA to William Tudor, Sept. 29, 1774, *PJA* 2:177.
12. JA to Timothy Pickering, Aug. 6, 1822, Adams, *Works,* 2:512n; *ADA* 2:106; JA to Tudor, Sept. 29, 1774, *PJA* 2:176–77; Jack N. Rakove, *The Beginnings of National Politics: An Interpretive History of the Continental Congress* (New York, 1979), 45; Jerrilyn G. Marston, *King and Congress: The Transfer of Political Legitimacy* (Princeton, 1987), 79.
13. *ADA* 2:115, 122; JA to Jedidiah Morse, Dec. 5, 1815, Adams, *Works* 10:190; Maier, *Old Revolutionaries,* 19; Silas Deane to Elizabeth Deane, [Aug. 31–Sept. 5, 1774], in Smith, *LDC* 1:20–23; Joseph Galloway to William Franklin, Sept. 5, 1774, ibid., 27.
14. Samuel Adams to JW, Sept. 9, 1774, Smith, *LDC* 1:55; Deane to Elizabeth Deane, Sept. 7, 1774, ibid., 1:34; *ADA* 2:124, 127; JA to AA, Sept. 8 and 18, 1774, *AFC* 1:150, 159.
15. *JCC* 1:27–28; *ADA* 2:124–26, 128–31, 156; "James Duane's Propositions" and "James Duane's Speech," [Sept. 7–22], and Sept. 8, 1774, Smith, *LDC* 1:38, 51–54.

16. Samuel Adams to Boston Comm. of Corres., Sept. 14, 1774, Smith, *LDC* 1:71–72; *JCC* 1:31–39.
17. *ADA* 2:131; JA to Tudor, Sept. 29, 1774, *PJA* 2:177; JA to William Cranch, Sept. 18, 1774, *AFC* 1:160; [Galloway], *Historical and Political Reflections on the Rise and Progress of the American Rebellion* (London, 1780), 67–68.
18. *JCC* 1:75–81; *ADA* 2:137–40, 145, 147–49; 155; "Samuel Adams's Notes," [Sept. 27?], 1774], Smith, LDC, 1:107–8; Diary of Deane, Oct. 5–6, 1774, ibid., 143–49, 153–54; David Ammerman, *In the Common Cause: American Response to the Coercive Acts of 1774* (New York, 1874), 73–87.
19. *ADA* 2:141–44; Galloway, *Candid Examination*, 8–36.
20. Ammerman, *In the Common Cause*, 58; John E. Ferling, *The Loyalist Mind: Joseph Galloway and the American Revolution* (University Park, Pa., 1977), 26–31.
21. *JCC* 1:63–73; *ADA* 2:119, 3:309–10; Edmund C. Burnett, *The Continental Congress* (New York, 1941), 52–53; Jensen, *Founding of a Nation*, 505. Congress subsequently accepted less harsh demands as the condition for lifting the boycott, specifying that five acts of Parliament must be repealed. See Ammerman, *In the Common Cause*, 67.
22. JA to Josiah Quincy, Sept. 18, 1774, *PJA* 2:168; JA to Tudor, Sept. 29, 1774, ibid., 176; JA to AA, Sept. 8, 14, and Oct. 9, 1774, *AFC* 1:150, 155, 166; *ADA* 2:127, 132, 134, 136, 140.
23. JA to AA, Oct. 9, 1774, *AFC* 1:166–67; *ADA* 2:131, 132–33, 135, 137, 150, 152, 155, 156; JA to Tudor, Oct. 7, 1774, *PJA* 2:188.
24. JA to Tudor, Sept. 29, 1774, *PJA* 2:176; JA to AA, Sept. 8, 1774, *AFC* 1:150; *ADA* 2:121, 133, 135, 140, 147, 150; 3:308.
25. "JA's Proposed Resolution," Sept. 30, 1774, Smith, *LDC*, 1:131–32.
26. *JCC* 1:60–61; Diary of Deane, Smith, *LDC* 1:138–39; Marston, *King and Congress*, 86–88; *ADA* 3:313. In its response to Gage, Congress ignored a draft letter prepared by Adams; the position Congress ultimately took more closely resembled the stance taken by Samuel Adams in a draft letter that he had prepared. See "JA's Draft Letter," [Oct. 7–8, 1774], Smith, *LDC* 1:158; "Samuel Adams's Draft Letter," [Oct. 7–8, 1774], ibid., 158–60.
27. *JCC* 1:90–101, 105–13, 115–21; JA to TJ, Cappon, *A-J Letters* 2:393.
28. *ADA* 2:150; JA to Tudor, Oct. 7, 1774, *PJA* 2:184.
29. JA to Cranch, Sept. 18, 1774, *AFC* 1:160; JA to Tudor, Oct. 7, 1774, *PJA* 2:188.
30. *ADA* 2:157.

CHAPTER 7

1. *ADA* 2:157–60.
2. AA to JA, Sept. 14, 16, 22, and Oct. 16, 1774, *AFC* 1:151–54, 161–62, 172.
3. AA to JA, Oct. 16, 1774, ibid., 172.
4. *PJA* 2:197–99n.
5. JA to JW, Mar. 15, 1775, ibid., 405; "Report of the Braintree Committee on the Continental Association" and "Report of the Braintree Committee Respecting Minute Men," Mar. 15, 1775, ibid., 391, 396–403.

6. On Loyalist thought, see Ferling, *Loyalist Mind,* 112–27, and Janice Potter, *The Liberty We Seek: Loyalist Ideology in Colonial New York and Massachusetts* (Cambridge, Mass., 1983).

7. JA to Samuel Morse, Dec. 22, 1815, JAPM, reel 122; Arthur M. Schlesinger, *Prelude to Independence: The Newspaper War on Britain, 1764–1776* (New York, 1957), 132, 188; John Langdon Sibley and Clifford K. Shipton, eds., *Biographical Sketches of Harvard University* (Cambridge, Mass., 1873–), 14:643–44.

8. The Novanglus essays can be found, together with a thoughtful introductory essay, in *PJA* 2:216–382. The specific quotations alluded to in this biography are found in ibid., 242–43, 244–45, 255, 297, 358, 362. For an excellent discussion of the Novanglus-Massachusettensis battle, see Albert Furtwangler, *American Silhouettes: Rhetorical Identities of the Founders* (New Haven, 1988), 40–63.

9. AA to MOW, Feb. 3, 1775, *AFC* 1:183; Maier, *From Resistance to Revolution,* 249–52.

10. Robert W. Tucker and David C. Hendrickson, *The Fall of the First British Empire: Origins of the War of American Independence* (Baltimore, 1982), 320–21, 355–78; McCurry, "North Government," *HLQ* 34:141–47.

11. Dartmouth to Gage, Jan. 27 and March 3, 1775, in Clarence E. Carter, ed., *The Correspondence of General Thomas Gage.* 2 vols. (New Haven, 1931), 2:179–83, 186.

12. Allen French, *The Day of Concord and Lexington* (Boston, 1925), 60–99; Arthur B. Tourtellot, *William Diamond's Drum: The Beginnings of the War of the American Revolution* (New York, 1959), 16–127; Robert A. Gross, *The Minutemen and their World* (New York, 1976), 109–32.

13. *ADA* 3:314.

14. Ibid., 314 and 2:163–64; JA to AA, Apr. 30 and May 8, 1775, *AFC* 1:188–89, 195.

15. JA to AA, Apr. 30 and May 8, 1775, *AFC* 1:189, 191–92; Diary of Paine, May 10, 1775, Smith, *LDC* 1:339; Stewart Beach, *Samuel Adams: The Fateful Years, 1764–1776* (New York, 1965), 286.

16. *ADA* 2:117, 133, 157, 173, 385–86. On Dickinson, see Milton E. Flower, *John Dickinson: Conservative Revolutionary* (Charlottesville Va., 1983).

17. JA to AA, May 29, 1775, *AFC* 1:207.

18. *JCC* 2:73–75.

19. JA to JW, May 21, 1775, *PJA* 3:11; Marston, *King and Congress,* 210–13.

20. *ADA* 3:314, 318–19, 321; JA to JW, July 24, 1775, *PJA* 3:89; "John Dickinson's Notes for a Speech," May 23–25, 1775, Smith, *LDC* 1:373.

21. JA to JW, May 21, 1775, *PJA* 3:11; JA to Moses Gill, June 10, 1775, ibid., 21; *ADA* 3:315; JA to AA, June 11 and 18, 1775, *AFC* 1:216, 225; Marsten, *King and Congress,* 213; James Henderson, *Party Politics in the Continental Congress* (New York, 1974), 49. The Olive Branch Petition can be found in *JCC* 2:158–62.

22. Jensen, *Founding of a Nation,* 594–98.

23. *JCC* 2:76–79, 89–91; JA to AA, June 17, 1775, *AFC* 1:216.

24. *ADA* 3:322–23; JA to AA, June 11, 1775, *AFC* 1:215; JA to Elbridge Gerry, June 18, 1775, *PJA* 3:26. The profile of Washington is based upon Ferling, *First of Men.*

25. *ADA* 3:322–23; Eliphalet Dyer to Joseph Trumbull, June 17, 1775, Smith, *LDC*

1:499; Samuel Adams to JW, Sept. 25, 1774, in Harry Alonzo Cushing, ed., *The Writings of Samuel Adams.* 4 vols. (New York, 1904), 3:158; JA to JW, [July] 6, 1775, *PJA* 3:63–64.

26. *ADA* 3:322–23; JA to AA, June 18, 1775, *AFC* 1:225.
27. *JCC* 2:93, 97, 99, 103; JA to Gerry, June 18, 1775, *PJA* 3:25–26; Jonathan G. Rossie, *The Politics of Command in the American Revolution* (Syracuse, 1975), 17–30.
28. Shaw, *Character of JA,* 95; George W. Conner, ed., *The Autobiography of Benjamin Rush: His "Travels Through Life" together with his Commonplace Book for 1789–1813* (Philadelphia, 1948), 140.
29. JA to AA, Sept. 14, 1774, *AFC* 1:155.
30. *ADA* 2:119.
31. Douglas Southall Freeman, *George Washington: A Biography,* completed by J. A. Carroll and Mary W. Ashworth. 7 vols. (New York, 1948–1957), 460.
32. JA to AA, June 23, 1775, *AFC* 1:226–27.

CHAPTER 8

1. JA to AA, May 29, June 2, 6, 10, 23, July 12, and Sept. 26, 1775, *AFC* 1:207, 208, 212, 213, 226, 243, 285; JA to JA, July 23, 1775, *PJA* 3:87.
2. Shaw, *Character of JA,* 80.
3. JA to AA, May 2, July 17, Sept. 26, Oct. 1, 7, 1775, *AFC* 1:192, 252, 286, 289–90, 295; AA to JA, June 22 and Aug. 10, 1775, ibid., 225–26, 272; Shaw, *Character of JA,* 91.
4. JA to AA, June 17, July 7 and 23, 1775, *AFC* 1:216, 242, 253; Conner, *Autobiography of Rush,* 142; Shaw, *Character of JA,* 95.
5. JA to AA, May 2, 26, July 7, 24, 1775, and March 16, 1776, *AFC* 1:192, 206, 241, 255; 2:176; JA, "Letters of Novanglus," *PJA* 2:232, 242, 255, 267, 284; JA, "To a Friend in London," Jan. 21, 1775, ibid., 2:216; JA to James Burgh, Dec. 28, 1774, ibid., 206; JA to JW, March 15, 1775, ibid., 405; *ADA* 3:324.
6. P. C. Kuiper, *The Neuroses: A Psychoanalytic Survey* (New York, 1972), 95–124, 143–63.
7. JA to JW, March 15, 1775, *PJA* 2:405; *ADA* 3:320; JA to AA, May 2, June 10, 23, and July 7, 1775, *AFC* 1:192, 213, 226, 242. Adams had marshaled this defense once before. See "U" to *Boston Gazette,* Aug. 1 and Sept. 5, 1763, *PJA* 1:75, 85, 87; [John Adams], "An Essay on Man's Lust for Power. . . . ," ibid., 82–83; "Humphrey Ploughjogger to the *Boston Evening Post,*" June 20, 1763, ibid., 65.
8. JA to Charles Lee, Oct. 13, 1775, *PJA* 3:302.
9. JA to MOW, Jan. 3, 1775, ibid., 210; JA to AA, May 2, 29, June 10 and 23, 1775, *AFC* 1:191, 207, 213, 226; JA to AA, May 7, 1775, Adams, *FLJA,* 53–54; John Ferling, *A Wilderness of Miseries: War and Warriors in Early America* (Greenwood, Conn., 1981), 57–92.
10. AA to JA, Aug. 10, 1775, *AFC* 1:272; *ADA* 3:326.
11. AA to MOW, Ap. 27, 1776, *AFC* 1:398.
12. AA to MOW, Nov. [5], 1775, ibid., 323.

13. *ADA* 3:325; AA to MOW, Aug. 27, 1775, *AFC* 1:276; JA to MOW, Aug. 26, 1775, *PJA* 3:126.

14. Beach, *Samuel Adams,* 291; AA to JA, Sept. 8, 10, 16, and 25, 1775, *AFC* 1:276–79, 284.

15. AA to JA, Sept. 29, Oct. 1 and 9, 1775, *AFC* 1:287–89, 296. Emphasis added.

16. JA to AA, Oct. 1, 2, 7, 10, and 13, 1775, ibid., 289–91, 294–95, 299, 300–301; JA to JW, Oct. 1 and 12, 1775, *PJA* 3:177, 196; Josiah Quincy to JA, Sept. 22, 1775, ibid., 167; JA to Jos. Quincy, Oct. 6, 1775, ibid., 187.

17. Washington to President of Congress, Sept. 21, 1775, John C. Fitzpatrick, ed., *The Writings of George Washington.* 39 vols. (1931–44), 3:505–13; Ward to Washington, Sept. 17, 1775, Smith, *LDC* 2:27.

18. AA to JA, July 16, Oct. 28, Nov. 12, and Dec. 10, 1775, *AFC* 1:246–47, 314, 325, 335–36.

19. JA to AA, Feb. 18, 1776, ibid., 348; Franklin to David Hartley, Oct. 3, 1775, Albert H. Smyth, ed., *The Writings of Benjamin Franklin.* 8 vols. (New York, 1905–07), 2:103.

20. Henderson, *Party Politics,* 55; *ADA* 3:351–52, 355.

21. *ADA* 3:327–30, 355; JA to JA, Oct. 20 and 28, 1775, *PJA* 3:217, 254–55; Henderson, *Party Politics,* 56–61.

22. Frederick H. Hayes, "John Adams and American Sea Power," *American Neptune* 25 (1965): 35–45. The two JA quotations can be found in William G. Anderson, "John Adams, the Navy, and the Quasi-War with France," ibid., 30 (1970): 118–19.

23. Nathan Miller, *Sea of Glory: The Continental Navy Fights for Independence, 1775–1783* (New York, 1974), 36–69; Gardner W. Allen, *A Naval History of the American Revolution.* 2 vols. (New York, 1973), 1:59–89; Christopher Ward, *The War of the Revolution.* 2 vols. (New York, 1952), 1:114. On the naval articles, see *ADA* 3:350 and *PJA* 3:xx, 147–56.

24. JA to AA, Dec. 3, 1775, *AFC* 1:332; *ADA* 3:350.

25. Perez Morton to JA, Oct. 28, 1775, *PJA* 3:257–58; JA to Morton, Nov. 24, 1775, ibid., 314–15; JA to JW, Oct. 20, 1775, ibid., 218–19; JA, *Dissertation on Canon and Feudal Law,* in ibid., 1:127; JA to MOW, Jan. 8, 1776, ibid., 3:398; JA to Henry, June 3, 1776, ibid., 4:235; JA to Samuel Osgood, Nov. 15, 1775, ibid., 3:309; JA to AA, Nov. 18, 1775, *AFC* 1:328.

26. On the political divisions in Massachusetts, see Patterson, *Political Parties in Revolutionary Massachusetts,* 91–133. The AA quotation is from AA to MOW, July 24, 1775, cited in ibid., 133. Also see Gerry to JA, Nov. 11, 1775, *PJA* 3:288; JA to JW, Apr. 16, 1776, ibid., 4:122; JA to Lovell, June 12, 1776, ibid., 4:250.

27. AA to JA, Nov. 12 and Sept. 16, 1775, *AFC* 1:325, 279.

28. "JA's Service on the Council," Dec. 26, 1775–Jan. 26, 1776, *PJA* 3:377–78.

29. Ibid.

30. *ADA* 2:226–28; JA to AA, Jan. 24, 1776, *AFC* 1:343.

31. Lee to Landon Carter, Jan. 22, 1776, Smith, *LDC* 3:130.

32. Washington to President of Congress, Jan. 4, 1776, Fitzpatrick, *Writings of Washington,* 4:209–10; Ward to ["his daughter"], Jan. 8, 1776, Smith, *LDC* 3:61.

33. On the background of Thomas Paine, see David Freeman Hawke, *Paine* (New York, 1974). *Common Sense,* together with Paine's other published works, can be

found in Philip S. Foner, ed., *The Complete Writings of Thomas Paine.* 2 vols. (New York, 1945).

34. JA to AA, Feb. 18, 1776, *AFC* 1:348; JA to Tudor, Apr. 12, 1776, *PJA* 4:118; JA to JW, May 12, 1776, ibid., 182; Joseph Palmer to JA, Feb. 29, 1776, ibid., 41.

35. JA to Gates, Mar. 23, 1776, *PJA* 4:59; Jensen, *Founding of a Nation,* 649–50, 655.

36. JA to AA, Apr. 15, 1776, *AFC* 1:383; JA to Horatio Gates, Mar. 23, 1776, *PJA* 4:59; JA to Tudor, Apr. 12, 1776, ibid., 118; JA to JW, Apr. 16 and 22, 1776, ibid., 122, 135.

37. [Thomas Paine], "The Forester's Letters," Foner, *Writings of Paine,* 2:81.

38. JA to Palmer, Apr. 2, 1776, *PJA* 4:102; JA to JW, Apr. 20, 1776, ibid., 132; JA to AA, Apr. 12, 1776, *AFC* 1:377.

CHAPTER 9

1. AA to JA, May 7, 1776, *AFC* 1:402.

2. JA to AA, May 17 and 27, 1776, ibid., 410, 420.

3. On the struggle for independence in Pennsylvania, see Ryerson, *Revolution Is Now Begun;* Theodore Thayer, *Pennsylvania Politics and the Growth of Decocracy, 1740–1776* (Harrisburg, Pa., 1953); and David F. Hawke, *In the Midst of a Revolution* (Philadelphia, 1961).

4. JA to Gates, Mar. 23, 1776, *PJA* 4:59; JA to JW, Apr. 16, 20, and May 15, 1776, ibid., 122, 132, 187; JA to Henry, June 3, 1776, ibid., 234.

5. JA to JW, Mar. 21 and May 20, 1776, ibid., 56, 195; Ryerson, *Revolution Is Now Begun,* 166–75.

6. *JCC* 4:342–58; JA to JW, May 15, 1776, *PJA* 4:186.

7. JA to JW, May 20, 1776, *PJA* 4:195; JA to R. H. Lee, June 4, 1776, ibid., 239; Ryerson, *Revolution Is Now Begun,* 219–26; Hawke, *In the Midst of a Revolution,* 140.

8. *JCC* 5:424–25, 427–29; *ADA* 3:392–93; JA to John Lowell, June 12, 1776, *PJA* 4:250; Jensen, *Founding of a Nation,* 688–91.

9. *ADA* 3:335–37; JA to AA, June 26, 1776, *AFC* 2:23–24; Dumas Malone, *Jefferson and His Time.* 6 vols. (New York, 1948–81), 1:220–22; Conner, *Autobiography of Rush,* 140. Also see the notes on Adams's committee activities in *PJA* 4:1–4, 252–65, 341–45.

10. *Pennsylvania Archives.* 9 series (Harrisburg, 1852–1935), 2d ser., 3:658; Ryerson, *Revolution Is Now Begun,* 228–38; JA to JW, May 20, 1776, *PJA* 4:196; JA to Samuel Chase, June 14, 1776, ibid., 313.

11. Gerry to JW, June 25, 1776, Smith, *LDC* 4:316–17; Joseph Reed to Charles Pettit, June 26, 1776, in William B. Reed, *The Life and Correspondence of Joseph Reed.* 2 vols. (Philadelphia, 1847), 1:192.

12. Julian P. Boyd et al., eds., *The Papers of Thomas Jefferson* (Princeton, 1950–), 1:299–308, 413–28; *PJA* 4:341–51; Carl Becker, *The Declaration of Independence: A Study in the History of Political Ideas* (New York, 1942), 194–223; Wilbur Samuel Howell, "The Declaration of Independence and Eighteenth Century Logic," *WMQ* 18 (1961): 463–84.

13. JA to Archibald Bulloch, July 1, 1776, *PJA* 4:352.
14. "Dickinson's Notes for a Speech in Congress," July 1, 1776, Smith, *LDC* 4:351–58; *ADA* 3:396.
15. *ADA* 3:396; John M. Head, *A Time to Rend: An Essay on the Decision for American Independence* (Madison, Wis., 1968), 34, 61–62. On the notion of partition, see James H. Hutson, "The Partition Treaty and the Declaration of Independence, *JAH* 58 (1972): 351–58.
16. *ADA* 3:396; Shaw, *Character of JA,* 98: Farrell, "JA," *NEQ* 62:526–27.
17. John H. Hazelton, *The Declaration of Independence: Its History* (New York, 1906), 161–62.
18. Jensen, *Founding of a Nation,* 700.
19. JA to AA, July 3, 1776, *AFC* 2:27–30.
20. Ibid., 30.
21. [Thomas Jefferson], "Composition Draft" and "Original Rough Draft of the Declaration of Independence," Boyd, *Papers of Jefferson,* 1:413–28; Smith, *LDC* 4:386.
22. JA to AA, July 3, 1776, *AFC* 2:28; JA to George Otis, Feb. 9, 1821, *New England Historical and Geneological Register* 30 (1876): 329–30; JA to MOW, July 20 and 27, 1807, *Adams-Warren Letters* 4:339–40, 355; JA to Skelton Jones, Mar. 11, 1809, Adams, *Works* 9:611; JA to Rush, Aug. 23, 1805, and May 1, 1807, Schutz and Adair, *Spur of Fame,* 34–35, 82; JA to Jefferson, Aug. 24, 1815, Cappon, *A-J Letters* 2:455. The "Child Independence" quotation is from Richard B. Morris, *The American Revolution Reconsidered* (New York, 1967), 17. Adams's recollection of Britain's treatment of the colonial soldiers appears to have had a basis in fact. See Fred Anderson, *A People's Army: Massachusetts Soldiers and Society in the Seven Years' War,* 111–15. In his later years, Adams took great pride in having predicted as early as 1755—years before anyone had heard of Thomas Paine, he liked to say—that the removal of the French would inevitably result in America independence. Indeed, as an old man he came to see himself as embracing independence even before Samuel Adams came to such a determination. With much delight, he recalled having suggested a year before the French and Indian War was declared that, if the colonists could "remove the turbulent Gallicks" from Canada, the process of "setting up for ourselves"—establishing independent governments—could be begun. See JA to Rush, May 21, 1807, Adams, *Works* 9:596; JA to Nathan Webb, Oct. 12, 1755, *PJA* 1:5.
    On the various factors that led others to chose independence, see Wright, *Franklin of Philadelphia,* 250, on Benjamin Franklin; Ferling, *First of Men,* 92, on George Washington; Noble E. Cunningham, Jr., *In Pursuit of Reason: The Life of Thomas Jefferson* (Baton Rouge, 1987), 45, on Thomas Jefferson. The Bernard Bailyn quotation can be found in Bailyn, "*Common Sense:* The Most Uncommon Pamphlet of the Revolution," *American Heritage* 25 (Dec. 1973): 92.
23. JA to MOW, Apr. 6, 1776, *W-A Letters* 72:221–23; JA to Reed, *PJA* 4:364; JA to AA, July 3, 1776, *AFC* 2:28; JA to Hezekiah Niles, Jan. 14 and Feb. 13, 1818, Adams, *Works* 10:276, 282; JA to William Wirt, Jan. 5, 1818, ibid., 272; JA to Jedediah Morse, Nov. 29, 1818, ibid., Nov. 29, 1818, ibid., 182. Also see Howe, *Changing Political Thought of JA,* 32–36, 46–49. On the eighteenth-century

theory of the rise and decline of states, see Drew R. McCoy, *The Elusive Republic: Political Economy in Jeffersonian America* (Chapel Hill, 1980), 13–47.

24. JA to Tudor, June 5, 1817, and Mar. 11, 1818, JAPM, reel 123; JA to Wirt, June 5, 1818, ibid., reel 123; JA to Rush, May 21, 1807, Schutz and Adair, *Spur of Fame,* 88.

25. Shaw, *Character of JA,* 75, 87–88, 103–4; Chinard, *Honest JA,* 71, 98; Smith, *JA* 1:237–43, 257; Morris, *Seven Who Shaped Our Destiny,* 102; Morgan, *Meaning of Independence,* 15–17; Adams, *Works* 1:172.

26. JA to Patrick Henry, June 3, 1776, *PJA* 4:235.

27. Washington to John A. Washington, May 31, 1776, Fitzpatrick, *Writings of Washington,* 5:92; JA to MOW, Apr. 16, 1776, *PJA* 4:124.

28. *ADA* 3:351–52, 355–57, 360; JA to AA, Mar. 19, 1776, *AFC* 1:363; JA to Tudor, Apr. 12, 1776, *PJA* 4:118; JA to JA, May 12, 1776, ibid., 182.

29. *ADA* 3:351–52, 354–55; *PJA* 4:65–86.

30. [John Adams], *Thoughts on Government,* in *PJA* 4:86–93.

31. JA to James Sullivan, May 26, 1776, ibid., 208–11; JA to Henry, June 3, 1776, ibid., 235; Howe, *Changing Political Thought of JA,* 84–88.

32. JA to Gates, Mar. 23, 1776, *PJA* 4:59–60; JA to Samuel Osgood, Nov. 15, 1775, ibid., 3:309; JA to Joseph Hawley, Nov. 25, 1775, ibid., 316–17; JA to Francis Dana, Aug. 16, 1776, ibid., 4:466; Shaw, *Character of JA,* 92–94; Howe, *Changing Political Thought of JA,* 59–101.

33. Jackson Turner Main, *The Sovereign States, 1775–1783* (New York, 1973), 186–221.

34. JA to AA, Oct. 4, 1776, *AFC* 2:138; Flower, *Dickinson,* 168–85.

35. For example, see JW to JA, Mar. 30, 1776, *PJA* 4:96–97.

36. Patterson, *Political Parties in Revolutionary Massachusetts,* 139–66; Lowell to JA, Aug. 14, 1776, *PJA* 4:460.

37. JA to Dana, June 12, 1776, *PJA* 4:248; JA to Lowell, June 12, 1776, ibid., 250; JA to Winthrop, June 23, 1776, ibid., 332; JA to JW, Apr. 16, 1776, ibid., 122; JA to MOW, Apr. 16, 1776, ibid., 125.

38. JA to JW, Apr. 20, 1776, *PJA* 4:132; JA to AA, Feb. 13, May 22, and June 26, 1776, *AFC* 1:349, 412; 2:23–24.

39. JA to AA, May 29, 1775, Feb. 13 and Aug. 25, 1776, *AFC* 1:207, 347; 2:108–9; JA to JW, July 27, 1776, *PJA* 4:413; JA to Cooper, May 30, 1776, ibid., 221; JA to Parsons, Aug. 19, 1776, *ADA* 3:448.

40. JA to AA, Feb. 18, 1776, *AFC* 1:349.

41. JA to AA, Mar. 19 and Aug. 18, 1776, ibid., 1:363; 2:100.

42. JA to AA, May 22, 1776, ibid., 1:412–13.

43. JA to AA, Mar. 19, May 22, Apr. 28, July 11 and 16, 1776, ibid., 363, 399, 413; 2:44, 50.

44. *JCC* 5:434; JA to AA, Oct. 1, 1776, *AFC* 2:131; "John Adams and the Board of War," *PJA* 4:252–59; Shaw, *Character of JA,* 95.

45. Smith, *JA* 1:289; Shaw, *Character of JA,* 101; Gilbert Chinard, *Honest JA,* 109–10; JA to JW, June 25, 1774, Sept. 26, 1775, and July 27, 1776, *PJA* 2:100; 3:170; 4:414; JA to MOW, Nov. 25, 1775, ibid., 3:318; JA to Gen. Daniel Roberdeau, Dec. 24, 1777, JAPM, reel 89; JA to James Lovell, Dec. 24, 1777,

ibid.; JA to Rush, Feb. 8, 1778, ibid.; JA to AA, June 23, July 24, 1775, Mar. 19, Apr. 28, May 22, July 11, 1776, Feb. 17, July 26, Sept. 2, 1777, and May 12, 1780, *AFC* 1:226, 255, 363, 399, 412–13; 2:44, 131, 163, 289, 336; 3:342.

46. JA to AA, July 16, 1776, *AFC* 2:50.

47. AA to JA, July 13, 29, Aug. 1, 5, 12, 14, 17, 18, and 20, 1776, ibid., 45, 55, 65, 69, 72, 79, 86–87, 93, 98, 101; JA to AA, Aug. 27, 28, and 30, 1776, ibid., 110, 111, 115.

48. Edith B. Gelles, "Abigail Adams: Domesticity and the American Revolution," *NEQ* 52 (Sept. 1979): 500–521; AA to JA, May 14 and 27, 1776, *AFC* 1:408, 415–16.

49. JA to AA, May 15, 1777, *AFC* 2:238; AA to JA, May 14, 1776, ibid., 408.

50. AA to JA, Apr. 7, 18, and May 7, 1776, *AFC* 1:375, 387; 2:13–16.

51. JA to AA, July 15 and 16, 1776, ibid., 50–51; JA to JW, July 27, 1776, *PJA* 4:414.

52. For Adams's views on the failure of American arms in Canada, see: JA to Cooper [?], June 9, 1776, *PJA* 4:242–44; JA to Sullivan, June 23, 1776, ibid., 330; JA to Bulloch, July 1, 1776, ibid., 352–53. Good general accounts of the war in 1776 can be found in John Alden, *The American Revolution. 1775–1783* (New York, 1954), 90–111; James Kirby Martin and Mark E. Lender, *A Respectable Army: The Military Origins of the Republic, 1763–1789* (Arlington Heights, Ill., 1982), 48–78; Don Higginbotham, *The War of American Independence: Military Attitudes, Policies, and Practice, 1763–1789* (New York, 1971), 148–71, and Robert Middlekauf, *The Glorious Cause: The American Revolution, 1763–1789* (New York, 1982), 333–62.

53. JA to AA, July 11, 15, and 20, 1776, *AFC* 2:43, 49, 52; JA to Zabdiel Adams, June 21, 1776, ibid., 1:20; JA to Reed, July 7, 1776, *PJA* 4:362; JA to JW, July 15 and 24, 1776, ibid., 4:382, 408; JA to Gen. William Heath, Aug. 3, 1776, Aug. 3, 1776, ibid., 426.

54. JA to AA, Sept. 6, 1776, *AFC,* 2:120–21; JA to JW, Sept. 8, 1776, Sept. 8, 1776, *PJA* 5:220–21.

55. *ADA* 3:417–19.

56. Ibid., 419–20.

57. JA to AA, Sept. 6, 1776, *AFC* 121; JA to Samuel Adams, Sept. 14, 1776, *ADA* 3:426–29; Edward Tatum, ed., *The American Journal of Ambrose Serle* (New York, 1969), 101.

58. JA to AA, Oct. 8, 1776, *AFC* 2:140; JA to JW, Oct. 5, 1776, *PJA* 5:46; JA to Tudor, Sept. 26 and [?], 1776, *ADA* 3:437–41; JA to Knox, Sept. 29, 1776, ibid., 441–42; JA to Col. Hitchcock, Oct. 1, 1776, ibid., 442–44; JA to Parsons, Oct. 2, 1776, ibid., 444–46.

59. JA to Parsons, June 22, 1776, *PJA* 4:328; JA to JW, Sept. 25, 1776, ibid., 5:38; *ADA* 3:434; *JCC* 5:762–63, 788–807.

60. *ADA* 3:423; JA to AA, Oct. 8, 1776, *AFC* 2:140; JA to Cooper, Sept. 4, 1776, *PJA* 5:11; JA to Knox, Sept. 29, 1776, *ADA* 3:441–42; JA to Hitchcock, Oct. 1, 1776, ibid., 442–44.

61. JA to AA, Oct. 4, 8, and 11, 1776, *AFC* 2:137, 139, 141.

62. *ADA* 2:251; JA to [?], Nov. 5, 1776, *PJA* 5:52.

63. JW to JA, Sept. 19., 1776, *PJA* 5:33; JA to JW, Oct. 5, 1776, ibid., 46–47.

64. AA to JA, May 14, 1776, *AFC* 1:407–8; JA to Hawley, Aug. 25, 1776, *PJA* 4:495.
65. *ADA* 4:1; JA to JW, Oct. 5, 1776, *PJA* 5:46–47.
66. JA to AA, Oct. 8, 1776, *AFC* 2:140.

CHAPTER 10

1. AA to MOW, Jan. [?], 1777, *AFC* 2:150.
2. Akers, *AA,* 19; Withey, *Dearest Friend,* 86–87.
3. AA to MOW, Jan. [?], 1777, *AFC* 2:150; JA to AA, Jan. 9 and [17 or 18], 1777, ibid., 144, 146.
4. JA to AA, Aug. 4, 1777, ibid., 299; AA to MOW, Jan. [?] and Aug. 14, 1777, ibid., 150, 314; Musto, "The Adams Family," MHS 93: 49–50.
5. Conner, *Autobiography of Rush,* 140–41; David F. Hawke, *Benjamin Rush: Revolutionary Gadfly* (Indianapolis, 1971), 164–65; G. S. Rowe, *Thomas McKean: The Shaping of an Republican* (Boulder, Colo., 1978), 164–65; Hawley to JA, July 25, 1774, *PJA* 2:117; JW to JA, Dec. 3, 1775, ibid., 3:348; John Avery to JA, Mar. 7, 1777, ibid., 5:101; William Gordon to JA, Mar. 27, 1777, ibid., 133; Greene to JA, May 7, 1777, ibid., 181–82; Nathan Rice to JA, Dec. 10, 1777, ibid., 354–55; *ADA* 2:76; JA to Skelton Jones, Mar. 11, 1809, Adams, *Works* 9:612.
6. JA to Jones, Mar. 11, 1809, Adams, *Works* 9:612; JA to Tudor, Mar. 29, 1817, ibid., 10:245. On the height of Franklin and Jefferson, see Carl Van Doren, *Benjamin Franklin* (New York, 1938), 91; David Freeman Hawke, *Franklin* (New York, 1976), 8; Malone, *Jefferson,* 1:48; Robert M. Johnstone, Jr., "The Presidency," in Merrill D. Peterson, ed., *Thomas Jefferson: A Reference Biography* (New York, 1986), 353. Also see Kenneth L. Sokoloff and George C. Villaflor, "The Early Achievement of Modern Stature in America," *Social Science History* 6 (1982): 435–81.
7. *ADA* 2:362–63.
8. Merrill Peterson, *Thomas Jefferson and the New Nation: A Biography* (New York, 1970), 298; John C. Miller, *Alexander Hamilton: Portrait in Paradox* (New York, 1959), 519–20; *ADA* 1:51, 54, 67–68, 74, 79, 83, 86, 95, 100, 109, 113, 118; 4:164n; JA to AA, Aug. 4 and 18, 1776, *AFC* 2:75, 100; AS to JA, Apr. 30, 1764, ibid., 1:42; JA to MOW, Nov. 25, 1775, *PJA* 3:318; Adams, *Works* 1:57–58n.
9. JA to AA, Aug. 18, 1776, *AFC* 2:100; JA to Josiah Quincy, Feb. 9, 1811, JAPM, reel 118; JA to Rush, July 7, 1805, ibid., reel 118; Conner, *Autobiography of Rush,* 110, 140.
10. William Shaw to JA, Jan. 21, 1799, JAPM, reel 393; JA to AA, Feb. 9, 1799, ibid., reel 393; JA to Francis Vanderkemp, Apr. 18, 1815, ibid., reel 122. AA confirmed that her husband was ill at ease with most women, although she added that some women whom he had known for years could entice a pleasant conversation from him. See AA to Wm. Shaw, Feb. 2, 1799, Shaw Papers, LC.
11. JA to AA, Aug. 25, 1776, Aug. 11, 1777, Apr. 25, 1778, and Feb. 13, 1779, *AFC* 2:109–10, 306; 3:17, 170.
12. AA to JA, Mar. 16, 1776, ibid., 1:359; JA to AA, Apr. 14, 1776, ibid., 381–82.

AA's famous admonition to her husband to "Remember the Ladies" should not be taken as a call for either political or social equality for women. She accepted—and valued—the domestic role assigned to women in her era. Instead, she was concerned with the sexual oppression of women, as well as with the subordinate legal status of married women. AA's statement has triggered an avalanche of recent studies. A good survey of the findings can be found in Edith B. Gelles, "The Abigail Industry," *WMQ* 45: 666.

13. JA to Robert Evans, June 8, 1819, Adams, *Works* 10:380; AA to JA, Sept. 22, 1774, and Mar. 3, 1776, *AFC* 1:162, 369; Withey, *Dearest Friend,* 80; *PJA* 3:xvi; JA to JW, July 7, 1777, ibid., 5:242; JA to Jonathan Dickinson Sergeant, Aug. 17, 1776, ibid., 4:469.

14. AA to JA, Mar. 17, 1797, JAPM, reel 383; Akers, *AA,* 141–42; AA to Lucy Cranch, Apr. 2, 1786, Charles F. Adams, ed., *Letters of Mrs. Adams. The Wife of John Adams.* 2 vols. (Boston, 1841), 2:129–30; AA to Elizabeth Shaw, Mar. 4, 1786, ibid., 125; JA to Evans, June 8, 1819, Adams, *Works* 10: 380; JA to Vanderkemp, Feb. 16, 1809, ibid., 9:609–10.

15. JA to AA, Aug. 18, 1776, *AFC* 2:100

16. Zoltan Haraszti, *John Adams and the Prophets of Progress* (Cambridge, Mass., 1952), 14–48; John Adams, "Literary Commonplace Book," *PJA* 1:7–10n; JA to JW, July 25, 1774, ibid., 2:116–17.

17. *ADA* 2:103, 116; JA to AA, Aug. 4, 1776, and May 12, 1780, *AFC* 2:75; 3:342; Edmund S. Morgan, *The Meaning of Independence: John Adams, George Washington, Thomas Jefferson* (Charlottesville, Va., 1976), 8. Emphasis added to the Adams quotation.

18. JA to Tufts, Apr. 9, 1764, *AFC* 1:20; JA to AA, July 1, 1774, and May [?], 1772, ibid., 118, 83.

19. Ibid., 144n.

20. Ibid.; JA to AA, Feb. 2, 1777, ibid., 2:151.

21. JA to AA, Feb. 2, 1777, ibid., 2:151.

22. "JA's Service in the Continental Congress, 2 Jan.–6 Nov., 1777," *PJA* 5:58n

23. JA to AA, Feb. 18, 21, Mar. 16, Apr. 24, 26, and May 18, 1777, *AFC* 2:163, 166, 176, 177n, 224, 243, 327.

24. JA to AA, Feb. 21, May 15, 17, 21, 22, July 18, Aug. 2, Sept. 2, and Oct. 15, 1777, ibid., 165, 238, 239, 244, 246, 285, 298, 336, 353.

25. JA to AA, Apr. 13, 19, May 15, 21, 24, Aug. 11, and Sept. 8, 1777, ibid., 207–8, 213–14, 239, 243, 246, 306, 337.

26. JA to JW, Mar. 18, 1777, *PJA* 5:115; JA to AA, Apr. 2 and 3, 1777, *AFC* 2:196, 198.

27. JA to Greene, May 9, 1777, *PJA* 5:185; JA to AA, Apr. 16 and Mr. 7, 1777, *AFC* 2:211, 170.

28. JA to AA, Feb. 21, Sept. 1, and Aug. 19, 1777, *AFC* 2:165, 320, 335; JA to Greene, Mar. 1777, *PJA* 5:108; JA to Tudor, Feb. 25, 1777, ibid., 93.

29. JA to AA, Apr. 16, May 21, 24, June 2, and Aug. 23, 1777, *AFC* 2:211, 243, 246, 253, 325.

30. JA to AA, Mar. 16 and 7, 1777, ibid., 176, 170.

31. JA to JQA, Mar. 30, 1777, ibid., 190–91; JA to AA, June 8, Mar. 31, and Apr.

13, 1777, ibid., 259–60, 192, 209; JA to Nabby Adams, July 5, 1777, ibid., 274–75.

32. JA to AA, Aug. 8, July 18, and 10, 1777, ibid., 303, 284, 278.

33. AA to JA, Feb. 8, Mar. 9, Apr. 7, 17, and June 1, 1777, ibid., 157, 173, 202, 212, 250.

34. AA to JA, June 1, 1777, ibid., 250; JA to AA, Apr. 29, 2:227–28.

35. JA to AA, Jan. 9 and June 21, 1777, ibid., 143, 268; AA to JA, July 10, ibid., 278.

36. AA to JA, June 8, 23, and July 2, 1777, ibid., 258, 269–70, 272.

37. AA to JA, July 9, 10, and 16, 1777, ibid., 277, 278–79, 282–83.

38. JA to AA, July 28 and 30, 1777, ibid., 292, 296–97.

39. JA to AA, July 26 and Aug. 23, 1777, ibid., 289, 325.

40. JA to AA, Aug. 24, Sept. 1, 8, 14, and Aug. 19, 1777, ibid., 327–28, 335, 337, 342, 318–19.

41. *ADA* 2:264–67; JA to AA, Sept. 30, *AFC* 2:344–50; JA to Speaker of the Massachusetts House of Representatives, Jan. 15, 1778, Emmett Collection, NYPL.

42. *ADA* 2:263; JA to AA, Oct. 26, 1777, *AFC* 2:361.

43. JA to AA, Oct. 28 and 26, 1777, *AFC* 2:362, 361; Rush to JA, Oct. 13 and 21, 1777, *PJA* 5:315, 316–18; JA to Rush, Feb. 8, 1778, ibid., 403.

44. JA to AA, July 8 and Nov. 3, 1777, *AFC* 2:276, 365; JA to JW, May 15, 1776, *PJA* 4:187; Howe, *Changing Political Thought of JA*, 59–67; *ADA* 2:243–50, 267; *JCC* 9:880.

45. James H. Hutson, *John Adams and the Diplomacy of the American Revolution* (Lexington, Ky., 1980), 33; *ADA* 4:3; MOW to JA, Mar. 10, 1776, *PJA* 4:51.

CHAPTER 11

1. *ADA* 4:1

2. JA to Gerry, Dec. 6, 1777, *PJA* 5:345; JA to Lovell, Dec. 6, 1777, ibid., 347; JA to Daniel Roberdeau, Dec. 9, 1777, ibid., 353–54; *ADA* 4:2; Smith, *JA* 1:348–49.

3. "Commission for Benjamin Franklin, Arthur Lee, and John Adams," Nov. 27, 1777, *PJA* 5:333–34; Lovell to JA, Nov. 28, 1777, ibid., 337–38.

4. *ADA* 4:1.

5. AA to Lovell, Dec. 15 [?], 1777, *AFC* 2:370–71; AA to Roberdeau, Dec. 15 [?], 1777, ibid., 372–73; MOW to AA, Jan. 8, 1778, ibid., 379; Akers, *AA*, 114.

6. MOW to AA, Jan. 2 and 8, 1778, ibid., 376–77, 379–80.

7. JA to Gerry, Dec. 23, 1777, *PJA* 5:366.

8. AA to John Thaxter, Feb. 15, 1778, *AFC* 2:390.

9. Jonathan R. Dull, *A Diplomatic History of the American Revolution* (New Haven, 1985), 51–55; John R. Alden, *A History of the American Revolution* (New York, 1969), 333–37. On this and other matters relating to diplomatic concerns, also see the classic study of Samuel Flagg Bemis, *The Diplomacy of the American Revolution* (Bloomington, Ind., 1957).

10. On Deane's activities, see Thomas P. Abernathy, "Commercial Activities of Silas Deane in France," *AHR* 39 (1934): 477–85.
11. JA to Charles Lee, Oct. 13, 1775, *PJA* 3:203; JA to John Winthrop, May 12 and June 23, 1776, ibid., 4:184, 331–32; JA to Henry, June 3, 1776, ibid., 234–35; *ADA* 2:236; 3:337. An excellent summary of Adams's views and activities can be found in "Editor's Note," *PJA*, 4:260–65.
12. JA to Winthrop, June 23, 1776, *PJA* 4:331–32.
13. *JCC* 5:428–29, 431, 433, 575, 768, 813.
14. *PJA* 4:262–63; *ADA* 2:236. On the works he used as guides, see *PJA* 4: 262n. JA's draft, as well as both the committee report and the final Model Treaty, can be found in ibid., 265–302. In addition, see William C. Stinchcombe, "JA and the Model Treaty," in Lawrence S. Kaplan, ed., *The American Revolution and "A Candid World"* (Kent, Ohio, 1977), 69–84; James H. Hutson, "Early American Diplomacy: A Reappraisal," in ibid., 40–68; Felix Gilbert, *To the Farewell Address: Ideas of Early American Foreign Policy* (Princeton, 1961), 44–54. The Model Treaty was revised in December 1776 to permit greater territorial concessions to France. See *JCC* 6:1055–56.
15. Stinchcombe, "JA and Model Treaty," 70.
16. *ADA* 2:269; 4:6.
17. Ibid. 2:272–73.
18. Ibid., 274–75.
19. Ibid., 275–93; 4:7–34.
20. Ibid., 292.
21. Ibid., 292–95; 4:36–37.
22. Ibid., 295–96; John Bondfield to JA, Apr. 4, 1778, *AFC* 3:10–11n.
23. *ADA* 2:296–97.
24. This discussion of Franklin in based primarily on Wright, *Franklin of Philadelphia*, and the quotations and specific references to this volume can be found on pp. 15, 23–25, 45–46, 249–50, 262–63. The various editions of *Poor Richard* published between 1731 and 1758 can be found in L. W. Labaree and Whitfield Bell et al., eds., *The Papers of Benjamin Franklin* (New Haven, 1959–), volumes 1–7; for Franklin's memoirs, see Benjamin Franklin, *The Autobiography of Benjamin Franklin*, L. W. Labaree, ed. (New Haven, 1964). For the JA quotations in this section, see JA to Jenings, July 20, 1782, JAPM, reel 357; Adams, *Works* 1:663.
25. The literature on the Franco-American treaties is vast. For an excellent summary, see Dull, *Diplomatic History*, 75–96. The fruit of much recent scholarship on the treaties can be found in Ronald Hoffman and Peter J. Albert, eds., *Diplomacy and Revolution: The Franco-American Alliance of 1778* (Charlottesville Va., 1981).
26. *ADA* 4:48.
27. Ibid., 43; Hutson, *JA and Diplomacy*, 38.
28. *ADA* 4:109–10.
29. JA to Samuel Adams, May 21, 1778, ibid., 106–8: JA to Commercial Committee of Congress, May 24, 1778, ibid., 111–12.
30. Ibid., 108, 67–68; 2:301.
31. Ibid., 92–93.
32. *PJA* 5:xxiv; Hutson, *JA and Diplomacy*, 37.

33. Wright, *Franklin of Philadelphia,* 291.
34. *ADA* 2:346; 4:70; Franklin to Arthur Lee, Apr. 3, 1778, Smyth, *Writings of Franklin,* 7:130; Franklin to Reed, Mar. 19, 1780, ibid., 8:44. Adams was careful not to attack Lee in public. See Samuel Adams to Elizabeth Adams, Mar. 7, 1779, Smith, *LDC* 12:158–59; Richard Henry Lee to A. Lee, Mar. 21, 1779, ibid., 219; and Lovell to Lee, Sept. 17, 1779, ibid., 13:506.
35. *ADA* 4:87, 106. On the Vandalia Company bribe, see *PJA* 6:14n.
36. JA to Lovell, Feb. 20, 1779, *PJA* 7:419; Shaw, *Character of JA,* 115. On the working relationship between Franklin and JA, see *PJA* 7:xvi–xvii.
37. *ADA* 2:367, 369; 4:59–60, 69, 118–19; JA to AA, Apr. 25, 1778, *AFC* 3:17, 17n; Wright, *Franklin of Philadelphia,* 265–66; Carl Van Doren, *Benjamin Franklin* (New York, 1938), 636–37; JA to Samuel Adams, Dec. 7, 1778, Emmett Collection, NYPL.
38. JA to Roger Sherman, Dec. 6, 1778, *PJA* 7:254; JA to Samuel Adams, Feb. 14, 1779, ibid., 412–13; JA to President of Congress, Aug. 4, 1779, ibid., 8:111. For Franklin's views and his remarks that have been cited, see William C. Stinchcombe, *The American Revolution and the French Alliance* (Syracuse, 1969), 206, and Gerald Stourzh, *Benjamin Franklin and American Foreign Policy* (Chicago, 1954), 157. Stourzh describes Franklin's approach toward France as a "diplomacy of gratitude." Also see Dull, "France and the American Revolution as Tragedy," in Hoffman and Albert, *Diplomacy and Revolution,* 81–85.
39. *ADA* 2:347, 351; JA to Samuel Adams, May 21, 1778, ibid., 4:106–8.
40. Ibid. 2:298–318; Bailyn, "Butterfield's Adams," *WMQ* 19:251; Adams, *Works* 1:58n.
41. *ADA* 4:118.
42. On Franklin's keen understanding of the French, see Alfred O. Aldridge, *Franklin and His French Contemporaries* (New York, 1957).
43. JA to President of Congress, Aug. 25, Sept. 7 and 20, 1778, *PJA* 6:52; 7:8, 58; JA to JW, Aug. 4, 1778, ibid., 6:346, 349; JA to R. H. Lee, Aug. 5, 1778, ibid., 351; The Commissioners to President of Congress, Sept. 17, 1778, ibid., 7:42; The Commissioners to C. W. F. Dumas, Sept. 9, 1778, ibid., 16; JA to Samuel Adams, May 21, 1778, *ADA* 4:106–8.
44. Commissioners to Antoine de Sartine, Sept. 10 and 17, 1778, *PJA* 22:46–48; Vergennes to Commissioners, Sept. 27, 1778, ibid., 7:83–84; Commissioners to John Lloyd and Others, Jan. 26, 1779, ibid., 380–81.
45. Commissioners to Sartine, May 14, 1778, *ADA* 4:99–100; Commissioners to John Paul Jones, May 25, 1778, ibid., 112–14; Commissioners to Vergennes, Aug. 28, 1778, *PJA* 7:402.
46. Roberdeau to JA, Jan. 21, 1778, *PJA* 5:392; Greene to JA, Mar. 3, 1777, ibid., 97; JA to Greene, Mar. 9, 1777, ibid., 108.
47. Commissioners to North, June 4, 1778, *ADA,* 4:128.
48. Commissioners to Prisoners of War, Sept. 17, 1778, *PJA* 7:45; JA to Thomas Greenleaf, Sept. 8, 1778, ibid., 12–13; Commissioners to J. D. Schwighauser, Sept. 13, 1778, ibid., 29; Jonathan Williams to Franklin and JA, Jan. 31, 1779, ibid., 386–88; JA to Franklin, Apr. 29, 1779, ibid., 8:50; JA to Jenings, May 4, 1779, ibid., 55; Franklin to JA, Apr. 21, 1779, Adams, *Works* 7:92.

49. Commissioners to Vergennes, Apr. 19, 1778, *PJA* 6:42; Commissioners to Sartine, May 16, 1778, ibid., 123; Sartine to Commissioners, Nov. 16, 1778, ibid., 7:221; *ADA* 2:357.

50. Franklin and JA to Sartine, Oct. 30, 1778, *PJA* 7:177–78; Commissioners to President of Congress, Nov. 7, 1778, ibid., 197–98.

51. JA to JW, [May 3], 1777 and Aug. 4, 1778, ibid., 5:174; 6:346, 348; Commissioners to Sartine, Nov. 12, 1778, ibid., 7:206; JA to Samuel Adams, Nov. 27 and Dec. 7, 1778, ibid., 234, 256; JA to Elbridge Gerry, Nov. 27, 1778, ibid., 236; JA to Lovell, Nov. 27, 1778, ibid., 236; JA to President of Congress, Dec. 3, 1778, ibid., 249; JA to Henry, Dec. 8, 1778, ibid., 266; JA to Jenings, Apr. 13, 1779, ibid., 8:35.

52. JA to Ralph Izard, Sept. 25, 1778, ibid., 7:73; JA and Commissioners to Vergennes, [Dec. 20–Jan. 9], 1778–79, ibid., 294–309.

53. Hutson, *JA and Diplomacy,* 42.

54. JA to Lovell, Sept. 26, 1778, *PJA* 7:77.

55. *ADA* 3:188n; JA to Lovell, July 26, 1778, Feb. 20 and Aug. 13, 1779, *PJA* 7:318, 419; 8:121; JA to Cushing, Feb. 24, 1779, ibid., 7:424–25; JA to Cooper, Feb. 28, 1779, ibid., 432–33; *AFC* 3:188n; JA to AA, Dec. 3, 1778, and Feb. 20, 1779, ibid., 129, 175.

56. *ADA* 2:345, 353; JA to Samuel Cooper, Feb. 28, 1779, *PJA* 7:433.

57. JA to Vergennes, Feb. 11 and 16, 1779, *PJA* 7:401–3, 416–17.

58. JA to AA, Dec. 30, 1778, Jan. 18, Feb. 13, 20, and 28, 1779, *AFC* 3:142, 149, 169, 175, 181.

59. JA to AA, Feb. 20, 1779, ibid., 3:175.

60. JA to AA, Feb. 21 and 28, 1779, ibid., 177, 182.

61. Ibid., xxviii; JA to AA, Dec. 3, 18, 1778, Feb. 13, 19, and 20, 1779, ibid., 128, 138, 169, 173–74.

62. Lovell to AA, Feb. 22, 1778, *AFC* 2:393; 3:44n; Akers, *AA,* 64; Edith B. Gelles, "A Virtuous Affair: The Correspondence Between Abigail Adams and James Lovell", *AQ* 39 (1987): 254–55.

63. Lovell to AA, Apr. 1 and June 13, 1778, ibid., 3:1–2, 43.

64. AA to Lovell, June 24, Aug. 19, 1778, and July 28, 1779, ibid., 48–49, 76, 215.

65. Lovell to AA, Sept. 1, 1778, ibid., 2:83–84. The most complete study made of the Adams-Lovell relationship is that of Gelles, "A Virtuous Affair," *AQ* 39:252–69. She concludes that Abigail Adams "continued to endure James Lovell for over five years because he helped her." In my estimation, she more than merely endured Lovell, although I agree that the relationship remained a "virtuous" one.

66. Thaxter to AA, Sept. 2, 1778, ibid., 3:88; *ADA* 2:402n.

67. *ADA* 2:357–59.

68. Ibid., 363–75; Samuel E. Morison, *John Paul Jones* (Boston, 1959), 187–89.

69. *ADA* 2:379.

70. *ADA* 2:381; AA to Lovell, June 18–26, 1779, *AFC* 3:206; AA to JA, June 8, 1779, ibid., 199.

71. *ADA* 2:381–400. See Hutson, *JA and Diplomacy,* 50, for the allegation that JA suspected that Franklin plotted his death or capture. This reads far too much into a remark made by JA, who, like any traveler crossing the Atlantic in wartime, feared for his safety. See JA to Jenings, June 8, 1779, *PJA* 8:79–80.

72. AA to Lovell, July 28, 1779, *AFC* 3:214.
73. Samuel Adams to AA, July 31, 1779, ibid., 217.
74. Edith B. Gelles, "Abigail Adams: Domesticity and the American Revolution," *NEQ* 52 (1979): 505.
75. JA to Samuel Freeman, Ap. 27, 1779, *PJA* 5:161; Patterson, *Political Parties in Revolutionary Massachusetts,* 171–96.
76. Smith, *JA* 1:439.
77. JA to Gerry, Oct. 18, 1779, *PJA* 8:205–6; JA to MOW, Aug. 3, 1779, ibid., 108; *ADA* 4:145; Patterson, *Political Parties in Revolutionary Massachusetts,* 197–217.
78. JA to MOW, Aug. 3, 1779, *PJA* 8:108; JA to Jenings, Feb. 25, 1780, ibid., 364; JA, *Thoughts on Government,* ibid., 4:75; Ronald P. Formisano, *The Transformation of Political Culture: Massachusetts Parties, 1790s–1840s* (New York, 1983), 25–33.
79. On JA's draft and an excellent essay on his role in the preparation of the Constitution of 1780, see: "The Massachusetts Constitution, ca. 28–31 October 1779," *PJA* 8:228–71. See also: Robert J. Taylor, "Construction of the Massachusetts Constitution," Am. Antiq. Soc., *Proceedings* 90 (1980): 317–46; Howe, *Changing Political Thought of JA,* 67, 83, 85, 88, 90, 94–96; Patterson, *Political Parties in Revolutionary Massachusetts,* 218–47; and William M. Fowler, Jr., *The Baron of Beacon Hill: A Biography of John Hancock* (Boston, 1980), 243–72.
80. Laurens to JA, Oct. 4, 1779, Smith, *LDC* 14:17–19.
81. JA to AA, Nov. 13, 1779, *AFC* 3:224; AA to JA, Nov. 14, 1779, ibid., 233–34; AA to Lovell, Nov. 29, 1779, ibid., 240; Gelles, "AA: Domesticity," *NEQ* 52:515.
82. AA to Lovell, Nov. 18, 1779, *AFC* 3:236.

CHAPTER 12

1. *AFC* 3:224n.
2. *ADA* 4:191; 2:400; JA to AA, Nov. 14, 1779, *AFC,* 3:234, 235n.
3. *ADA* 2:403–4; 4:191–203; *AFC* 3:238n; Thaxter to John Thaxter, Sr., Nov. 20 and Dec. 15, 1779, Thaxter MSS, MHS.
4. Thaxter to AA, Dec. 15, 1779, *AFC* 3:251; JA to AA, Feb. 12, 1779, ibid., 3:271; *ADA* 2:404–34; 4:193–240; Thaxter to Thaxter, Sr., Jan. 15 and Feb. 14, 1780, Thaxter MSS, MHS.
5. *ADA* 4:241; JA to Vergennes, Feb. 19, 1780, *RDC* 3:503–04; *Boston Patriot,* May 18, 1811; Hutson, *JA and Diplomacy,* 170n.
6. On the course of the war, see: Higginbotham, *War of American Independence,* 145–313; Piers Mackesy, *The War for America, 1775–1783* (Cambridge, Mass., 1975), 279–80; Dull, *Diplomatic History,* 97–113; Jonathan Dull, *The French Navy and American Independence: A Study of Arms and Diplomacy, 1774–1787* (Princeton, 1975), 122–24.
7. JA to President of Congress, Feb. 7, 1781, JAPM, reel 101.
8. William Stinchcombe, *The American Revolution and the French Alliance,* 62–76.
9. JA to Lafayette, Feb. 21, 1779, *PJA* 7:421; JA to Jay, Feb. 22, 1780, ibid., 8:349; JA to Samuel Adams, Feb. 23, 1780, ibid., 353; JA to Cooper, Feb. 23, 1780, ibid., 355; JA to Tristram Dalton, Feb. 23, 1780, ibid., 8:356; JA to JW, Feb. 23,

1780, ibid., 8:359; JA to Jenings, Feb. 25, 1780, ibid., 364. On conditions in America in 1780, see Robert Gross, *The Minutemen and their World* (New York, 1976), 140–43; and Rakov, *Beginnings of National Politics,* 243–74. On the Franco-Spanish failure to invade England, see Richard B. Morris, *The Peace-makers: The Great Powers and American Independence* (New York, 1965), 27–42.

10. Franklin to Polly Stevenson, Sept. 14, 1767, in L. W. Labaree et al., eds., *The Papers of Benjamin Franklin* (New Haven, 1959–), 14:253.

11. Morris, *Peacemakers,* 112; JA to Vergennes, Feb. 12, 1780, *RDC* 3:492–93.

12. Vergennes to JA, Feb. 15 and 24, 1780, *RDC* 3:496, 518–19; [Comte de Vergennes], "Observations on Mr. Adams' Letter," July 17, 1780, ibid., 4:3–6; JA to Vergennes, Feb. 25, 1780, ibid., 3:519–20.

13. "Notation," JA Letterbook, Mar. 8–12 [?], 1780, JAPM, reel 96; *AFC,* 4:272n; JA to AA, Mar. 15, 16, Apr.–May [?], May 5, 12, and June 3, 1780, ibid., 3:302, 305, 333, 337, 341–42, 360.

14. JA to JQA, Mar. 17 and 22, 1780, *AFC* 3:308, 315, 316; JA to M. Pechigny, May 16, 1780, ibid., 347.

15. JA to James Moylan, Mar. 6, 1780, JAPM, reel 96; JA to Capt. Lewis, Feb. 22, 1780, ibid., reel 96; JA to AA, Feb. 28, 1780, *AFC* 3:290; Cranch to JA, Apr. 26, 1780, ibid., 3:327; Withey, *Dearest Friend,* 121.

16. JA to Edmund and Charles Dilly, *PJA* 8:342; JA to President of Congress, Feb. 20, 1780, ibid., 346; JA to Genet, May 15, 1780, *RDC* 3:679–80; Genet to JA, May 17, 1780, ibid., 685; Shaw, *Character of JA,* 138. For JA's essays in the British press, together with a convenient introduction and an enlightening essay on Edmund Jenings, see James H. Hutson, ed., *Letters from a Distinguished American: Twelve Essays on American Foreign Policy, 1780* (Washington, 1978).

17. JA to President of Congress, Mar. 3, 12, June 16, and June 23, 1780, *RDC* 3:528–29, 542–45, 790–91, 877–78; JA to Vergennes, July 13, 1780, ibid., 3:848–55.

18. JA to Cooper, Feb. 28, 1780, *PJA* 8:374–75.

19. JA to Jenings, July 18, 1781, JAPM, reel 352; AA to Lovell, July 20–Aug. 6, 1781, *AFC* 4:184; Hutson, *JA and Diplomacy,* 71; JA to President of Congress, May 9 and June 2, 1780, *RDC* 3:668, 758–61.

20. JA to Livingston, Sept. 6, 1782, Adams, *Works,* 7:628; JA to Livingston, May 25, 1783, JAPM, reel 108; Franklin to President of Congress, Aug. 9, 1780, Smyth, *Writings of Franklin,* 8:126–28; Hutson, *Diplomacy of JA,* 71–72; Gerald Stourzh, *Benjamin Franklin and American Foreign Policy* (Chicago, 1954), 154–55.

21. Hutson, *JA and Diplomacy,* 58–63.

22. JA to Vergennes, June 22, July 13, 17, and 26, 1780, *RDC* 3:811–15, 848–55, 861–63; 4:7–11.

23. Shaw, *Character of JA,* 131–63; Hutson, *JA and Diplomacy,* 51–74. Historian Edward S. Corwin has depicted JA as naive and "obsessed" with the notion of moving hurriedly out of a mistaken notion that the British public was ready for peace. See Corwin, *French Policy and the American Alliance* (New York, 1916), 274. On JA's "John Yankee" remark, see JA to JW, Aug. 4, 1778, *PJA* 6:348

24. Hutson, *JA and Diplomacy,* 71–73; Vergennes to Franklin, July 31, 1780, *RDC*

4:18–19. JA's key letters to Vergennes are those of July 13 (which argued for a greater French naval commitment in America), July 17 (which argued for a direct approach to the British), and July 26 (which sought to refute Vergennes's refutation. They can be found in *RDC* 3:848–55, 861–63; 4:7–11.

25. JA to Knox, Mar. 18, 1780, JAPM, reel 96; JA to Lovell, Mr. 29, 1780, ibid., reel 96; Bemis, *Diplomacy of American Revolution,* 120, 155–59; Dull, *Diplomatic History,* 20.

26. Middlekauf, *Glorious Cause,* 571.

27. Hutson, *JA and Diplomacy,* 66, 72–73, 99; Franklin to JA, Oct. 2, 1780, Smyth, *Writings of Franklin,* 7:262; *Boston Patriot,* May 18, 1811; JA to Samuel Huntington, July 23, 1780, Adams, *Works* 7:233–35.

28. JA to Gerry, June 29, 1780, JAPM, reel 96; JA to President of Congress, Aug. 14, 1780, Adams, *Works* 7:245; Hutson, *JA and Diplomacy,* 75.

29. JA to William T. Franklin, Dec. 7, 1780, JAPM, reel 96; Thaxter to AA, Mar. 7, 1782, *AFC* 4:288; JA to AA, Mar. 22, 1782, ibid., 301.

30. *JCC* 17:535; JA to President of Congress, Aug. 14, 23, Sept. 19, 24, 25, and Nov. 17, 1780, *RDC* 4:29–32, 41–42, 60–61, 66–69, 155–56; JA to A. Lee, Dec. 6, 1780, JAPM, reel 102.

31. *Boston Patriot,* Sept. 12, 1780; JA to Dumas, Jan. 25, 1781, JAPM, reel 102; JA to Jenings, Dec. 6, 1780, ibid., reel 102; JA to Lovell, Dec. 7, 1780, ibid., reel 102; JA to Franklin, Feb. 20, 1781, *RDC* 4:260–61; JA to President of Congress, Mar. 18, 1781, ibid., 4:306–13.

32. JA to Carmichael, Apr. 8–10 [?], 1780, JAPM, reel 96; JA to Jenings, Apr. 15, 1780, ibid., reel 96; JA to Dumas, Jan. 25, 1781, ibid., reel 102; JA to Dana, Mar. 15, 1781, ibid, reel 102.

33. *JCC* 18:1205; JA to President of Congress, Mar. 19, 1781, *RDC* 4:313–15; Hutson, *JA and Diplomacy,* 87–94.

34. JA to Livingston, Feb. 21, 1782, Adams, *Works* 7:528. Also see ibid., 405–06n.

35. JA, "Memorial to the States General," Apr. 19, 1781, *RDC* 4:370–76; JA, "Memorial to the Prince of Orange," Apr. 19, 1781, ibid., 376–77.

36. JA to AA, Apr. 28, 1781, *AFC* 4:108, JA to Franklin, Apr. 27, 1781, *RDC* 3:390; JA to MOW, July 30, 1807, "Adams-Warren Letters", 4:377; JA to Sigourney, Ingraham, and Bromfield, Apr. 9, 11, and 13, 1781, JAPM, reel 102; JA to Dumas, Feb. 2, 1781, ibid., reel 102.

37. JA to [?], May 26, 1780, JAPM, reel 96; AA to JA, Sept. 29, 1781, *AFC* 4:220, 222n.

38. AA to JA, Dec. 10, 1779, Dec. 25, 1780, and Apr. 23, 1781, *AFC* 3:242; 4:50, 103; AA to JA, May 21, 1778 and Mar. 1780, AA MSS, Boston Public Library; Gelles, "AA" Domesticity," *NEQ* 52:515.

39. Withey, *Dearest Friend,* 118–23; JA to AA, Oct. 18, 1782, JAPM, Reel, 358; JA to JW, June 17, 1782, Adams, *Works* 9:513; Gelles, "AA: Domesticity, *NEQ,* 52:508.

40. AA to JA, May 3, June 13, Oct. 15, 1780, and May 25, 1781, *AFC* 3:336, 364; 4:7, 130.

41. AA to JA, July 16, Oct. 8, 1780, and June 28, 1781, ibid., 3:377; 4:3, 70; AA to Lovell, Feb. 13, 1780, ibid., 3:274; Elizabeth Dana to AA, Apr. 26, 1780, ibid.,

327; AA to MOW, Sept. 1, 1780, ibid., 402; AA to JQA and Charles Adams, Feb. 8, 1781, ibid., 4:78, xi; MOW to AA, Oct. 20, 1780, ibid., 10–11; Gelles, "AA: Domesticity," *NEQ,* 52:515.

42. Withey, *Dearest Friend,* 123; AA to Thaxter, July 23, 1778, AA MSS, Boston Public Library.

43. AA to Lovell, Sept. 20 [?], 1781, and Jan. 6, 1780, *AFC* 4:215; 3:256. Also see ibid., 241n.

44. Lovell to AA, Jan. 6, 13, July 14, 1780, and Jan. 8, 1781, ibid., 256, 257, 374; 4:61.

45. AA to Lovell, June 11, Sept. 3, 17, 1780, Jan. 3, Mar. 17, May 10, and June 23, 1781, ibid., 3:363–64, 407–8, 414; 4:57, 91–92, 111, 160.

46. AA to Lovell, Sept. 20 [?], 1781, and Nov. 29, 1779, ibid., 215: 3:240.

47. AA to Lovell, Nov. 29, 1779, and Jan. 23, 1781, ibid., 3:240; 4:161; AA to JA, Nov. 13, 1780, ibid., 13–14.

48. AA to JA, Nov. 13, 1780, ibid., 13.

49. JA to Franklin, Oct. 31, 1780, Jared Sparks, ed., *The Diplomatic Correspondence of the American Revolution.* 12 vols. (Boston, 1829–30), 5:370; JA to President of Congress, June 23, 26, July 11, and Aug. 6, 1781, *RDC* 4:514–15, 517–19, 560–61, 623; JA to Franklin, Aug. 25, 1781, Adams, *Works* 7:465.

50. Beranger to JA, Jan. 5, 1781, Adams, *Works* 7:423–24; JA to Beranger, Jan. 8, 1781, ibid., 426; JA to President of Congress, July 11, 1781, *RDC* 4:560–61; JA to Vergennes, July 13, 16, and 19, 1781, ibid., 4:571–73, 576–77, 591–94; Bemis, *Diplomacy of the American Revolution,* 172–86. For the terms of the mediation proposal, see *RDC* 4:560.

51. JA to Joseph Ward, Apr. 15, 1809, JAPM, reel 118; Morris, *Peacemakers,* 210; Bemis, *Diplomacy of the American Revolution,* 186.

52. Hutson, *JA and Diplomacy,* 98; Shaw, *Character of JA,* 151.

53. JA to Dumas, Oct. 4, 1780, JAPM, reel 102; Adams, *Works,* 7:450n; JA to President of Congress, July 11, 1781, *RDC* 4:517–19; Morris, *Peacemakers,* 179–83, 204–05, 207; Bemis, *Diplomacy of the American Revolution,* 181–82.

54. Franklin to JA, Aug. 6, 1781, Adams, *Works* 7:456; JA to Franklin, Aug. 25, 1781, ibid., 459–60; JA to Franklin, Oct. 4 [26], 1781, JAPM, reel 104; JA to A. Lee, Oct. 10, 1782, ibid., reel 107; *ADA* 2:369; Hutson, *JA and Diplomacy,* 52–55, 131–40; Shaw, *Character of JA,* 148.

55. "Instructions from [President of Congress] to Adams, Franklin, Jay, Laurens, and Jefferson," June 15, 1781, *RDC* 4:257; Hutson, *JA and Diplomacy,* 97.

56. Benjamin Watherhouse to Levi Woodbury, Feb. 20, 1835, *ADA* 4:110n; JA to AA, July 11 and Oct. 9, 1781, *AFC* 4:170, 224; Hutson, JA and Diplomacy, 77–78; JA to MOW, July 30, 1807, Adams, "Adams-Warren Letters," 4:388; JA to Livingston, Feb. 21, 1782, Adams, *Works* 7:523.

57. Darrett B. and Anita H. Rutman, "Of Agues and Fevers: Malaria in the Early Chesapeake, *WMQ* 33 (1976); 33–34. For an excellent guide to the scientific literature on malaria, see ibid, 33n.

58. JA to AA, Oct. 9, 1781, and Aug. 17, 1782, *AFC* 4:224, 364; JA to Cranch, July 2, 1782, ibid., 340; JA to AA, Aug. 14, 1783, L. H. Butterfield, ed., *The Book of Abigail and John: Selected Letters of the Adams Family, 1762–1784* (Cambridge, Mass., 1975), 361–62; JA to Dana, Apr. 28, 1782, JAPM, reel 107; JA to

President of Congress, Oct. 15, 1781, *RDC* 4:779–80; JA to Franklin, Aug. 25, 1781, Adams, *Works* 7:465; JA to Dana, Dec. 14, 1781, ibid., 493.

59. JA to President of Congress, Oct. 15, 1781, *RDC* 4:779–80; JA to Ambrose Serle, Dec. 6, 1781, JAPM, reel 102; JA to Jenings, Oct. 9, 1781, ibid., reel 102; JA to AA, Dec. 2, 1781, *AFC* 4:250–51; JA to Franklin, Aug. 25, 1781, Adams, *Works* 7:465.

60. *ADA* 4:225n; JA to AA, Dec. 18. 1781, and Jan. 4, 1782, *AFC* 4:265, 272; JA to Jenings, Dec. 26, 1781, JAPM, reel 102; JA to Dana, Mar. 18, 1782, ibid., reel 102; JA to AA, Aug. 14, 1783, Butterfield, *Book of Abigail and John,* 361–62.

61. JA to AA, Dec. 2 and July 11, 1781, *AFC* 4:249, 170; Marie B. Hecht, *John Quincy Adams: A Personal History of an Independent Man* (New York, 1972), 31.

62. Thaxter to JA, Apr. 5, 1781, *AFC* 4:97; JA to AA, Apr. 28, Oct. 9, Dec. 2, 1781, and Mar. 25, 1782, ibid., 108, 224, 249, 294; Levin, *AA,* 118, 133.

63. JA to President of Congress, Feb. 19, 1780, *PJA* 8:336; JA to Lafayette, Feb. 21, 1779, ibid., 7:422. On JA's receipt of the news of the Battle of Yorktown, see JA to Jay, Nov. 26, 1781, Adams, *Works* 7:484. On the battle, see Higginbotham, *War of American Independence,* 376–83.

64. JA to Vauguyon, May 1, 1781, *RDC* 4:397; JA to President of Congress, May 7, 1781, ibid., 313–15, 463–64; JA to Franklin, Apr. 13, 1781, ibid., 390. For the best survey of events in Holland in 1782, see Hutson, *JA and Diplomacy,* 104–16.

65. JA to AA, Mar. 22, May 14, July 1, Aug. 15 [?], 1782, *AFC* 4:300, 323, 338, 361; Hutson, *JA and Diplomacy,* 108; Smith, *JA* 1:489.

66. JA to Dana, Mar. 18, 1782, JAPM, reel 102; JA to William T. Franklin, Dec. 7, 1781, ibid., reel 102; Thaxter to AA, Mar. 7, 1782, *AFC,* 4:288; JA to AA, Dec. 2, 1781, June 16, and July 1, 1782, ibid., 249, 324, 337; Smith, *JA* 1:512–13, 517.

67. JA to AA, May 14, 1782, *AFC* 4:323; JA to Dana, Feb. [?], and Mar. 18, 1782, JAPM, reel 102; JA to Jenings, Apr. 3, 1782, ibid., reel 102.

68. JA to Jay, Aug. 10, 1782, JAPM, reel 107.

69. Jay to JA, Sept. 28, 1782, Adams, *Works* 7:641; *ADA* 3:17n.

CHAPTER 13

1. Alan Valentine, *Lord North,* 2 vols. (Norman, Okla., 1967), 1:473; 2:274; Bemis, *Diplomacy,* 191–92.

2. Esmond Wright, "The British Objectives, 1780–1783: 'If Not Dominion then Trade,'" in Ronald Hoffman and Peter J. Albert, eds., *Peace and the Peacemakers: The Treaty of 1783* (Charlottesville, 1986), 3–29.

3. Van Doren, *Franklin,* 669.

4. JA to Jenings, July 20, 1782, JAPM, reel 107; JA to Laurens, Feb. 11, 1784, ibid., reel 107; James H. Hutson, "The American Negotiators: The Diplomacy of Jealousy," Hoffman and Albert, *Peace and the Peacemakers,* 59–61; Morris, *Peacemakers,* 267.

5. JA to AA, June 16, July 1, Aug. 15, 17, and Sept. 24, 1782, *AFC,* 4:324, 338, 360, 366, 382; JA to Cranch, June 17, 1782, ibid., 331; JA to Dana, Sept. 17, 1782, JAPM, reel 107; JA to Jay, Aug. 13, 1782, ibid., reel 107.

6. Bemis, *Diplomacy,* 207–8.
7. Ibid., 210–11; Morris, *Peacemakers,* 303; JA to Jay, Aug. 13, 1782, JAPM, reel 107.
8. Bemis, *Diplomacy,* 215–27; W. J. Eccles, "The French Alliance and the American Victory," in John Ferling, ed., *The World Turned Upside Down: The American Victory in the War of Independence* (Westport, Conn., 1988), 149–53.
9. Shaw, *Character of JA,* 164–65.
10. JA to Jay, Oct. 7, 1782, Adams, *Works* 7:646; *ADA* 3:16, 29–37, 142n; Shaw, *Character of JA,* 164.
11. *ADA* 3:37; Herbert E. Klingelhofer, "Mathew Ridley's Diary During the Peace Negotiations of 1782," *WMQ,* 3d ser., 20 (1963): 95–99.
12. *ADA* 3:37–38.
13. *Boston Patriot,* July 27, 1811; *ADA* 3:40n, 47, 82; Klingelhofer, "Ridley's Diary," *WMQ* 20:123; Frank Monaghan, ed., *The Diary of John Jay during the Peace Negotiations of 1782* (New Haven, 1934), 14; JA to Livingston, Nov. 8, 1782, Adams, *Works* 8:5.
14. JA to MOW, Aug. 8, 1807, Adams, "Adams-Warren Letters," 4:427; JA to A. Lee, Oct. 10, 1782, JAPM, reel 107; JA to Jonathan Jackson, Nov. 17, 1782, ibid., reel 110; JA to Livingston, Oct. 31, 1782, Adams, *Works* 7:653; Hutson, *JA and Diplomacy,* 123. The Congressional instructions to adhere to French advice had been communicated to Adams in August 1781, but he was quite ill when the message arrived and may simply have missed this important directive. He later gave some indication that he was unaware of the order because of a problem in deciphering the instructions. See Shaw, *Character of JA,* 170–72.
15. JA to Jackson, Nov. 17, 1782, JAPM, reel 110; JA to Livingston, Nov. 8, 1782, *RDC* 5:864–66.
16. Quoted in Schutz and Adair, *Spur of Fame,* 39.
17. JA to Samuel Chase, July 1, 1776, *PJA* 4:354; JA to Genet, May 17, 1780, Adams, *Works,* 7:174–75; JA to President of Congress, Dec. 28, 1780, *RDC* 4:213; Hutson, *Letters,* 27.
18. JA to Vergennes, Mar. 30, May 9 and 17, 1780, *RDC* 3:581–82, 664–66, 685–88.
19. JA to Franklin, Oct. 31, 1780, Sparks *Diplomatic Correspondence of American Revolution,* 5:370; JA to Franklin, Aug. 17, 1780, Adams, *Works* 7:247–48; JA to President of Congress, Aug. 6, 1781, *RDC* 4:623.
20. JA to John Luzac, Sept. 15, 1780, Adams, *Works* 7:25–56; JA to Vergennes, July 26, 1780, *RDC* 4:7–11; Hutson, *Letters,* 4–6, 15–16, 26, 36.
21. JA to Izard, Sept. 25, 1778, *PJA* 7:73–74.
22. *ADA* 3:47; JA to Robert Livingston, Nov. 8, 1782, Adams, *Works* 8:5.
23. *ADA* 3:40; Morris, *Peacemakers,* 291, 351, 357; Charles Ritcheson, "Britain's Peacemakers 1782–1783: 'To an Astonishing Degree Unfit for the Task?'" in Hoffman and Albert, *Peace and the Peacemakers,* 70–100.
24. *ADA* 3:46–72.
25. Ibid., 65–66, 82; 4:5; Smith, *JA* 1:545.
26. *ADA* 3:72–85; Bemis, *Diplomacy,* 238.
27. *ADA,* 3:43–44, 50n; Hutson, *JA and Diplomacy,* 126–127.

28. JA to Jackson, Nov. 17, 1782, JAPM, reel 110; JA to JQA, Feb. 25, 1815, ibid., reel 122; JA to James Lloyd, Mar. 12, 1815, ibid., reel 122.
29. *ADA* 3:81n; 1:265.
30. Morris, *Peacemakers,* 380–83; Wright, *Franklin,* 317.
31. *ADA* 3:82; JA to AA, Jan. 22, 1783, Butterfield, *Book of Abigail and John,* 337; JA to Benjamin Rush II, June 25, 1815, JAPM, reel 122.
32. Bemis, *Diplomacy,* 255; JA to Jenings, Aug. 12, 1782, JAPM, reel 107.
33. *ADA* 3:52, 61, 85; Hutson, "American Negotiators," Hoffman and Albert, *Peace and Peacemakers,* 52–69; JA to A. Lee, Apr. 12, 1783, JAPM, reel 360; JA to Wm. Lee, Apr. 6, 1783, ibid., reel 108.
34. Elkanah Watson, *Men and Times of the Revolution* (New York, 1857), 203–5; William Cobbett, ed., *The Parliamentary History of England.* 36 vols. (London, 1802–20), 23:203–7.
35. *ADA* 3:103, 108; JA to JW, Apr. 9, 1783, *W-A Letters* 2:205–6; JA to AA, Dec. 2, 1781, *AFC* 4:251; JA to AA, Feb. 27, 1783, in Charles Francis Adams, ed., *Letters of John Adams, Addressed to his Wife.* 2 vols. (Boston, 1841), 2:92; Smith, *JA* 1:549.
36. JA to Dumas, Mr. 28, 1783.
37. JAPM, reel 108; JA to JW, Apr. 9, 1783, *W-A Letters* 2:205–6; JA to AA, Feb. 18 and 27, JAPM, reel, 108; JA to Jenings, Apr. 18, 1783, ibid., reel 108; JA to Livingston, Jan. 23 and Feb. 5, 1783, *RDC* 6:227–28, 242–47; Madison to Jefferson, May 6, 1783, Boyd, *Papers of Jefferson* 6:265.
38. JA to AA, Feb. 18, 1783, JAPM, reel 108; JA to Livingston, Apr. 14, 1783, *RDC* 6:373–74.
39. Dull, *Diplomatic History,* 159; Bemis, *Diplomacy,* 249–50; JA to AA, May 20, 1783, JAPM, reel 360; *ADA* 3:112, 123–24, 131–33; *Boston Patriot,* Feb. 1, 1812.
40. JA to AA, May 30, 1783, JAPM, reel 360; Hutson, *JA and Diplomacy,* 130; JA to Livingston, Feb. 5, 1783, *RDC* 6:242–43; JA to JW, Mar. 21 and Apr. 13, 1783, *W-A Letters* 2:197, 210.
41. *ADA* 3:100; JA to JW, Apr. 9 and 13, 1783, *W-A Letters* 2:197, 209–11; JA to Livingston, May 25, 1783, JAPM, reel 108; JA to Wm. Lee, Apr. 6, 1783, ibid., reel 108; JA to Osgood, Apr. 12, 1783, ibid., reel 108; JA to Jenings, ibid., reel 108; Hutson, *JA and Diplomacy,* 127; Franklin to Livingston, July 22, 1783, Smyth, *Writings of Franklin,* 8:62; JA to Livingston, Jan. 23, 1783, *RDC* 6:227–28; *ADA* 3:104–5, 107, 117; Smith, *JA* 1:569.
42. JA to Livingston, July 9, 1783, *RDC* 6:529; JA to AA, Mar. 28 and May 10, 1783, JAPM, reels 360, 361.
43. JA to Livingston, July 14, 23, 28, and Aug. 1, 1783, *RDC* 6:543, 591–95, 607–9, 626–28; *ADA* 3:141.
44. *ADA* 3:141–42, 142n.
45. JA to President of Congress, Sept. 5 and 8, 1783, *RDC* 6:674–76, 681–82, 683–84; JA to AA, Sept. 7, 1783, JAPM, reel 107; JA to AA, Mar. 28, 1783, Butterfield, *Book of Abigail and John,* 343.
46. *ADA* 3:143; *Boston Patriot,* Apr. 29 and May 2, 1812; Morris, *Peacemakers,* 525, n25; JA to MOW, Sept. 10, 1783, JAPM, reel 107. Peter Shaw sees this illness as

still another nervous breakdown, a collapse brought on by overwork, inadequate recognition, and persistent contention with Franklin. See Shaw, *Character of JA,* 188–89.

47. *ADA* 3:145–47; JA to AA, Nov. 8, 1783, Adams, *Letters of JA* 2:104–5.

48. AA to Lovell, June 30, 1781, *AFC* 4:166; AA to JA, Aug. 1, Sept. 29 and Oct. 21, 1781, ibid., 190, 220, 230.

49. AA to JA, Dec. 23, 1781, and Apr. 10, 1782, ibid., 271, 305; AA to Elizabeth Shaw, Feb.–Mar., 1782, ibid., 284.

50. AA to JA, Apr. 10 and Aug. 5, 1782, ibid., 306–7, 358.

51. AA to Isaac Smith, Jr., Apr. 20, 1771, ibid., 1:76; AA to JA, Aug. 5, Sept. 3 and 5, 1782, ibid., 4:358, 372, 377.

52. JA to AA, May 14, 1782, ibid., 323; JA to AA, Feb. 18, 27, Apr. 7, 11, May 18, 20, and June 6, 1783, JAPM, reels 108 and 360.

53. JA to AA, Jan. 29, 1783, Butterfield, *Book of Abigail and John,* 339; Levin, *AA,* 148.

54. JA to AA, Sept. 7, 1783, JAPM, reel 107; JA to Dumas, May 16, 1783, ibid., reel 108.

55. *ADA* 3:144–49, 144n, 150n, 156n.

56. *Boston Patriot,* May 9, 13, and 16, 1812; *ADA* 3:149–54n; Smith, *JA* 1:583.

57. *Boston Patriot,* May 9, 13, and 16, 1812; *ADA* 3:152–54n.

58. Smith, *JA* 1:584–85.

59. AA to JA, Feb. 11, 1784, Butterfield, *Book of Abigail and John,* 375.

60. AA to JA, Oct. 8 and Dec. 23, 1782, ibid., 330, 334–35; JA to AA, Jan. 22, 29, and Feb. 4, 1783, ibid., 336–40; Withey, *Dearest Friend,* 144–47; Levin, *AA,* 155–63. For the best history of this episode, see Edith B. Gelles, "Gossip: An Eighteenth-Century Case," *Journal of Social History* 22 (1989): 668–71.

61. Withey, *Dearest Friend,* 146–47; JA to Tyler, Apr. 3, 1784, JAPM, reel 362.

62. *ADA* 3:154–66; AA to Elizabeth Shaw, July 10 [?], 1784, Butterfield, *Book of Abigail and John,* 382; AA to Mary Cranch, July 20, 1784, ibid., 385.

63. *ADA* 3:166.

64. Ibid., 166–67n; AA to JA, July 23, 1784, Butterfield, *Book of Abigail and John,* 388–90; AA to Mary Cranch, July 25, 1784, AA Papers, AAS.

65. *ADA* 3:170, 170n; JA to AA, Aug. 1, 1784, Butterfield, *Book of Abigail and John,* 397; JA to Dumas, Aug. 25, 1784, JAPM, reel 107.

66. AA to Mary Cranch, [Dec. 12, 1784], Butterfield, *Book of Abigail and John,* 397n.

CHAPTER 14

1. Caroline Smith De Windt [Abigail Adams Smith], ed., *Journal and Correspondence of Miss Adams* (New York, 1841), 8–10; Withey, *Dearest Friend,* 162.

2. AA to M. Cranch, Sept. 5, 1784, Abigail Adams, *Letters of Mrs. Adams.* 2 vols. (Boston, 1841), 2:49–50; De Windt, *Journal and Correspondence of Miss Adams,* 16, 18, 20, 40, 53; Lavin, *AA,* 174, 176; Withey, *Dearest Friend,* 167; AA to Isaac Smith, May 9, 1785, Smith-Townsend Collection, MHS.

3. De Windt, *Journal and Correspondence of Miss Adams,* 34, 59, 68–69; Lavin, *AA,* 180; Withey, *Dearest Friend,* 165–66.

4. JA to Gerry, Nov. 4, 1784, JAPM, reel 107; JA to A. Lee, Jan. 31, 1785, ibid., reel 107; JA to Waterhouse, Feb. 2, 1807, ibid., reel 118; AA to M. Cranch, Dec. 9, 1784, AA, *Letters of Mrs. Adams* 2:60–62; De Windt, *Journal and Correspondence of Miss Adams,* 64–65; Withey, *Dearest Friend,* 167.

5. The literature on Jefferson is voluminous. This sketch is based primarily on Merrill Petterson, *Thomas Jefferson and the New Nation* (New York, 1970); Fawn Brodie, *Thomas Jefferson: An Intimate History* (New York, 1974); Alf J. Mapp, Jr., *Thomas Jefferson: A Strange Case of Mistaken Identity* (New York, 1987), and Malone, *Jefferson.* For the most comprehensive bibliography on Jefferson, together with excellent essays on various aspects of his life, one should see: Merrill D. Peterson, *Thomas Jefferson: A Reference Biography* (New York, 1986).

6. Malone, *Jefferson* 2:3–13; Mapp, *Jefferson,* 211; AA to M. Cranch, May 8, 1785, AA, *Letters of Mrs. Adams* 2:94; JA to Gerry, Nov. 4, 1784, JAPM, reel 107; JA to Knox, Dec. 15, 1784, ibid., reel 107; JA to A. Lee, Jan. 31, 1785, ibid., reel 107; JA to Rush, Oct. 25, 1809, Schutz and Adair, *Spur of Fame,* 159.

7. Merrill Jensen, *The New Nation: A History of the United States during the Confederation, 1781–1789* (New York, 1950), 158–62.

8. JA to Gen. Palmer, Aug. 26, 1784, JAPM, reel 107; JA to Gerry, Nov. 4, 1784, and Mar. 11, 17185, ibid., reel 107; JA to Livingston, June 23 and July 18, 1783, Emmet Collection, NYPL. For the reports of the commissioners of Nov. 11 and Dec. 15, 1784, and Feb. [9], 1784, see Boyd, *Papers of Jefferson* 7:493–500, 573–74, 646–47.

9. *ADA* 3:177n; JA to R. H. Lee, Apr. 29, 1785, JAPM, reel 107; Smith, *JA* 2:619–20.

10. *ADA* 3:176; Levin, *AA,* 188–89; De Windt, *Journal and Correspondence of Miss Adams,* 71; Withey, *Dearest Friend,* 171.

11. Levin, *AA,* 170; Smith, *JA* 2:643.

12. JA to AA, Aug. 15, 1782, *AFC* 4:361.

13. Smith, *JA* 2:643; Oliver, *Portraits of JA and AA,* 27–47.

14. *ADA* 3:180–81n; Smith, *JA* 2:627; Withey, *Dearest Friend,* 176; AA to M. Cranch, Aug. 15, 1785, AA Papers, AAS.

15. JA to Jay, June 2, 1785, Adams, *Works* 8:255–59. The London newspapers are quoted in Levin, *AA,* 195–96.

16. AA to JQA, Nov. 22, 1786, JAPM, reel 369; JA to AA, June 6, 1789, ibid., reel 372.

17. Levin, *AA,* 223–24; *ADA* 3:178–96.

18. *ADA* 2:355–56n; JA to Jefferson, July 16, 1785, Cappon, *A-J Letters* 1:41; AA to M. Cranch, Apr. 24, 1786, AA Papers, AAS.

19. Mary Beth Norton, *The British Americans: The Loyalist Exiles in England, 1774–1789* (Boston, 1972), 8–9, 31–32; AA to Isaac Smith, June 30, 1785, Smith-Carter Collection, MHS.

20. Berkin, *Sewall,* 142.

21. Their correspondence can be found in Cappon, *A-J Letters.*

22. Jefferson to JA, July 7, 1785, ibid., 1:38; JA to Jefferson, July 18 and Aug. 4, 1785, ibid., 42, 48; *ADA* 3:184–86.

23. Malone, *Jefferson* 2:50–51; AA to Jefferson, June 26, July 6 and 10, 1787,

Cappon, *A-J Letters* 1:178, 183–84, 185; JA to Jefferson, July 10, 1787, ibid., 187.

24. *ADA* 3:196–200, 203–8, 201–2n; AA to Jefferson, Feb. 26, 1788, Cappon, *A-J Letters* 1:227; AA to Lucy Tufts, Sept. 3, 1785, JAPM, reel 365; AA to M. Cranch, June 26, 1785, Adams, *Letters of Mrs. Adams* 2:102–5; Smith, *JA* 2:708, 728.

25. AA to JA, Dec. 23, 1781, *AFC* 4:271; Levin, *AA,* 239.

26. AA to MOW, May 14, 1787, *W-A Letters* 2:290; AA to Jefferson, June 6, Oct. 7, 1785, Feb. 11, 1786, and Feb. 26, 1788, Cappon, *A-J Letters* 1:29, 79, 119, 288; Smith, *JA* 2:638; Levin, *AA,* 237; Withey, *Dearest Friend,* 162, 175; AA to Wm. Smith, May 8, 1785, Smith-Carter Collection, MHS; AA to Elizabeth Shaw, Mar. 4, 1786, ibid.; AA to AAS, Jan. 9, 1791, Adams, *Letters of Mrs. Adams* 2:214.

27. Levin, *AA,* 210–11, 216–23; Withey, *Dearest Friend,* 185–86; Nagel, *The Adams Women,* 106–8, 112–17; Gelles, "Gossip," *Journal of Social History* 22:671; AA to M. Cranch, Aug. 15, 1785, Feb. 26, Mar. 21, June 13, 1786, and Apr. 26, 1787, AA Papers, Am. Antiq. Soc.

28. JA to Jay, Apr. 13, 1785, Adams, *Works* 8:235.

29. JA to Jay, Feb. 14, 1788, June 26, July 19, 29, Oct. 21, and Nov. 1, 1785, ibid., 8:476, 274–75, 282, 289, 331, 336; JA to S. Adams, Jan. 26, 1786, JAPM, reel 113.

30. JA to Gen. Palmer, Aug. 26, 1784, JAPM, reel 107; JA to Gerry, Jan. 31, 1785, and May 24, 1786, ibid., reels 107 and 113; JA to Ezra Stiles, Apr. 27, 1785, ibid., reel 107; JA to Stephen Higginson, Oct. 4, 1785, and Feb. 18, 1786, ibid., reel 107; JA to Rufus King, Feb. 14, 1786, ibid., reel 107; JA to Jay, June 10, 1785, Adams, *Works* 8:242, 265–66; Gerard Clarfield, "John Adams: The Marketplace and American Foreign Policy," *NEQ* 52 (1979): 345–57. A good study of the British side in these years is: Charles R. Ritcheson, *Aftermath of Revolution: British Policy toward the United States, 1783–1795* (New York, 1971), 33–87.

31. JA to Jay, June 17 and Nov. 1, 1785, Adams, *Works* 8:268–73, 336; JA to Thaxter, June 2, 1786, JAPM, reel 113; JA to Tufts, July 4, 1786, ibid., reel 113.

32. JA to Jay, Apr. 13, Oct. 21, 1785, Sept. 23 and Nov. 15, 1787, Adams, *Works* 8:234–35, 331, 453–54, 460–61; JA to S. Adams, Jan. 26 and June 2, 1786, JAPM, reel 113; JA to Lafayette, June 26, 1786, ibid., reel 113.

33. *ADA* 3:182–83n, 201n; Smith, *JA* 2:618–19, 652, 654, 671–72, 674; JA to Isaac Smith, Sept. 2, 1785, and Mar. 12, 1786, Smith-Carter Collection, MHS; JA to Wm. Smith, July 4, 1786, ibid. AA also dispatched business tips to relatives. See AA to Isaac Smith, June 20, 1786, ibid.

34. JA to Jay Jay, Feb. 3, 1787, Adams, *Works* 8:429; *ADA* 1:123; 3:13.

35. AA to Jefferson, Jan. 29, 1787, Cappon, *A-J Letters* 1:168–69; AA to John Cranch, Mar. 7, 1787, AA MSS, Boston Public Library; AA to Isaac Smith, Mar. 12, 1787, Smith-Carter Collection, MHS. Historian Joyce Appleby has argued persuasively that Adams did not write his *Defence* in response to Shays's Rebellion. See Joyce Appleby, "The New Republican Synthesis and the Changing Political Ideas of John Adams," *AQ* 25 (1978): 578–95. I think he was more troubled by the tumult in Massachusetts than she concedes, however. Unable to learn precisely what had occurred at home, Adams's initial letters on the Shaysites were contradic-

tory. His characterization of the upheaval as "extremely pernicious" was made in 1789, after he was in possession of considerable information regarding the rebellion. For JA's responses, see JA to Jefferson, Nov. 30, 1786, Cappon, *A-J Letters* 1:156; JA to JW, Jan. 9, 1787, *W-A Letters* 2:280; JA to MOW, May 7, 1789, JAPM, reel 115.

36. Howe, *Changing Political Thought of JA,* 171; Smith, *JA* 2:690.
37. Appleby, "New Republican Synthesis," *AQ* 25:580–81, 584.
38. JA to John Boylston, Mr. 5, 1779, *PJA* 8:3; JA to Tudor, Feb. 25, 1777, ibid., 5:94; JA to John Avery, Mar. 21, 1777, ibid., 118; JA to William Gordon, Apr. 8, 1777, ibid., 149; JA to Unknown, Apr. 27, 1777, ibid., 163; JA to Gerry, Dec. 3, 1777, ibid., 346.
39. John Adams, *A Defence of the Constitutions of Government of the United States of America Against the Attack of M. Turgot, in His Letter to Dr. Price,* in Adams, *Works* 4:359, 391, 427–28.
40. Ibid., 289–91; 6:73, 97–99.
41. Ibid., 4:285–90, 354–55, 379, 381, 585–88.
42. JA to Jefferson, Mar. 1, 1787, Cappon, *A-J Letters* 1:176.
43. For an excellent essay contrasting JA's ideas with the prevalent thinking in the United States in the late 1780s, see Wood, *Creation of the American Republic,* 567–92.
44. Paul C. Nagel, *Descent from Glory: Four Generations of the John Adams Family* (New York, 1983), 46.
45. AA to Jefferson, Feb. 26, 1788, Cappon, *A-J Letters* 1:227. Also see the editor's comments, ibid., 205–7.

CHAPTER 15

1. *ADA* 3:216–17n; Levin, *AA,* Shaw, *Character of JA,* 225.
2. *ADA* 3:217n; L. H. Butterfield, "Adams," [National Park Service], NP.
3. AA to AAS, July 7 and 16, 1788, De Windt, *Journal and Correspondence of Miss Adams* 2:84–86, 88–89; *ADA* 3:247.
4. AA to AAS, July 16, 1788, ibid., 2:87; *ADA* 3:216–17n; Hecht, *JQA,* 49.
5. JA to AAS, Nov. 11, 1788, De Windt, *Journal and Correspondence of Miss Adams* 2:106–7; AA to AAS, July 16, 1788, ibid., 89; Smith, *JA* 2:739; JA to Trumbull, Nov. [?], 1805, JAPM, reel 118.
6. Alexander Hamilton to Theodore Sedgwick, Oct. 9 and Nov. 9, 1788, *PAH* 5:225, 231; Hamilton to Madison, Nov. 23, 1788, ibid., 235–36; Sedgwick to Hamilton, Oct. 16 and Nov. 2, 1788, ibid., 226, 228; Benjamin Lincoln to Washington, Sept. 24 and Dec. 21, 1788, Dorothy Twohig et al., eds., *The Papers of George Washington: Presidential Series* (Charlottesville Va., 1987–), 1:7, 196; Madison to Washington, Nov. 5, 1788, ibid., 96.
7. Hamilton to Madison, Nov. 23, 1788, *PAH* 5:236; Hamilton to James Wilson, Jan. 25, 1789, ibid., 247–48; JA to MOW, May 29, 1789, *W-A Letters* 2:312–13; JA to Rush, May 17, 1789, JAPM, reel 115; Jacob E. Cooke, *Alexander Hamilton* (New York, 1982), 67.

8. AAS to JA, July 27, 1788, De Windt, *Journal and Correspondence of Miss Adams* 2:90–92; JA to AAS, Nov. 11, 1788, ibid., 105.
9. Smith, *JA* 2:743–44; George W. Harris, ed., William Maclay, *Sketches of Debates in the First Congress of the United States* (Harrisburg, 1880), 79.
10. Ferling, *First of Men,* 371–72.
11. JA to Jefferson, Nov. 10, 1787, Cappon, A-J Letters 1:210; JA to Jay, Dec. 16, 1787, JAPM, reel 112; JA to Roger Sherman, July 17, 18, and 20, 1789, ibid., reel 115.
12. Smith, *JA* 2:762–63.
13. On President Washington's struggle with office seekers, see the first two volumes of Twohig, *Papers of Washington.*
14. MOW to JA, May 7, 1789, *W-A Letters* 2:310–12; JA to MOW, May 29, 1789, ibid., 312–14; JA to Cotton Tufts, Sept. 16, 1789, Adams Papers, NYHS; Lester H. Cohen, "Explaining the Revolution: Ideology and Ethics in Mercy Otis Warren's Historical Theory," *WMQ* (1981): 202–03.
15. Washington to JA, May 10, 1789, Twohig, *Papers of Washington* 2:245–47; JA to Washington, ibid., 312–14.
16. JA to Trumbull, Mar. 12, 1790, JAPM, reel 115.
17. JA to Rush, June 9 and July 5, 1789, Alexander Biddle, ed., *Old Family Letters, Copied from the Original for Alexander Biddle.* 2 vols. (Philadelphia, 1892), 1:38, 40; JA to Tudor, June 14, 1789, JAPM, reel 115; *ADA* 1:355.
18. Jefferson to Madison, July 29, 1789, Boyd, *Papers of Jefferson* 15:315–16; Smith, *JA* 2:758–59; Shaw, *Character of JA,* 230.
19. JA to Rush, June 9, 1789, Biddle, *Old Family Letters* 1:37–38; JA to Rush, July 24, 1789, JAPM, reel 115; JA to Franklin, Jan. 27, 1787, John Bigelow, ed., *The Works of Benjamin Franklin,* 12 vols. (New York, 1904), 11:299; Howe, *Changing Political Thought of JA,* 182; JA to Vanderkemp, May 20, 1787, Feb. 27, Mar. 27, 1790, Mar. 19, 1793, and Mar. 9, 1806, HSP.
20. Bailyn, *Ideological Origins,* 282–83n; JA to J. H. Tiffany, Apr. 30, 1819, Adams, *Works* 10:378; JA to Vanderkemp, Feb. 20, 1806, HSP.
21. Washington to Jay, Aug. 1, 1786, Fitzpatrick, *Writings of Washington,* 28:503; Washington to David Stuart, July 26, 1789, Twohig, *Papers of Washington* 3:323; Howe, *Changing Political Thought of JA,* 171.
22. [Thomas Jefferson], *Anas,* in Ford, *Writings of Jefferson* 1:159–60.
23. [John Adams], "Discourses on Davila, A Series of Papers on Political History," can be found in Adams, *Works* 6:223–404. See especially 6:232, 236–42, 251–56. The final "Davila" essay does not appear in this source, however. It was published in the *Gazette of the United States* (Philadelphia), Apr. 27, 1791. See also Zoltan Haraszti, *John Adams and the Prophets of Progress* (Cambridge, Mass., 1952), 30, 165–79.
24. JA to Niles, Feb. 13, 1818, Adams, *Works* 10:282; *ADA* 3:326; JA to MOW, Apr. 16, 1776, *W-A Letters* 1:222.
25. Isaack Kramnick, "The 'Great National Discussion': The Discourse of Politics in 1787," *WMQ* 45 (1988): 7; Washington to Jay, Aug. 1, 1786, Fitzpatrick, *Writings of Washington,* 28:502; Washington to Humphreys, Oct. 22, 1786, ibid., 29:27; Washington to H. Lee, Oct. 31, 1786, ibid., 29:34. Also see Ferling, *First of Men,* 350–52.

26. Eugene P. Link, *Democratic-Republican Societies, 1790–1800* (New York, 1942), 47–48; JA to Trumbull, Apr. 2, 1790, JAPM, reel 115; Adams, *Defence,* Adams, *Works* 6:25; JA to Rush, July 9, 1787, Biddle, *Old Family Letters* 1:37–38; Madison to Jefferson, June 27, 1791, in William T. Hutchinson et al., eds.,*The Papers of James Madison* (Chicago, 1962–), 14:37; Madison to Rush, Oct. 1, 1792, ibid., 14:373; James Madison, "Memorandum on a Discussion of the President's Retirement," May 5, 1792, ibid., 302–3. That Adams occupied common ground with those who led the movement for a new United States constitution can be seen in his initial reaction to the document produced by the Philadelphia Convention. He grieved that a "Declaration of Rights" had not been included in the proposed constitution, and he wished for "a more complete Separation of the Executive from the Legislative." Otherwise, he applauded the work of the convention; he counseled for immediate ratification and against a second convention to make alterations to the original document. See: JA to Cotton Tufts, Feb. 12, 1788, Adams Papers, NYHS.

27. JA to Rush, Apr. 4, 1790, Biddle, *Old Family Letters* 1:168–70; JA to Gerry, Feb. 20, 1797, JAPM, reel 117; JA to AA, Dec. 27, 1796, ibid., reel 382.

28. Linda Dudik Guerrero, *John Adams's Vice Presidency, 1789–1797: The Neglected Man in the Forgotten Office* (New York, 1982), 14; JA to AA, [ND], 1789, Mar. 8 and Nov. 14, 1794, JAPM, reels 373, 377, 378; Donald Jackson and Dorothy Twohig, eds., *The Diaries of George Washington.* 6 vols. (Charlottesville Va., 1976–79), 5:460–73.

29. JA to J. B. Varnum, Dec. 26, 1808, Adams, *Works* 9:606; Ferling, *First of Men,* 385–88, 394–95; Cooke, *Hamilton,* 73–108. On JA and the trade restriction issue, see Drew R. McCoy, *The Elusive Republic: Political Economy in Jeffersonian America* (New York, 1980), 141–44; Drew R. McCoy, "An Unfinished Revolution: The Quest for Economic Independence in the Early Republic," in Jack P. Greene, ed., *The American Revolution: Its Character and Limits* (New York, 1987), 141–46; Robert A. Rutland, *James Madison: The Founding Father* (New York, 1987), 101–2.

30. Guerrero, *JA's Vice Presidency,* 128; JA to AA, Nov. 15, 1794, JAPM, reel 378; JA to JQA, Dec. 2, 1794, ibid., reel 378. For JA's views on the Hamiltonian economic program, see Charles A. Beard, *Economic Origins of Jeffersonian Democracy* (New York, 1915), 318. Also see JA to Rush, Sept. 27, 1808, and Aug. 28, 1811, Adams, *Works,* 9:602–3, 638–39; JA to Rush, June 20, 1808, Schutz and Adair, *Spur of Fame,* 110–11; Adams, *Thoughts on Government, PJA* 4:91; Tufts to JA, Apr. 26, 1776, *AFC* 1:395.

31. Guerrero, *JA's Vice Presidency,* 173–78; JA to Washington, Aug. 29, 1790, Adams, *Works* 8:496–97; JA to AA, Jan. 9, 1794, Adams, *Letters of JA* 2:137.

32. Ferling, *First of Men,* 403–11, 448–52; JA to Knox, June 19, 1791, JAPM, reel 375.

33. JA to AA, Mar. 25, 1796, JAPM, reel 381.

34. JA to Trumbull, Mar. 31, 1791, ibid., reel 115; Guerrero, *JA's Vice Presidency,* 214–18.

35. Jefferson to JA, Apr. 20, 1790, and Nov. 25, 1791, Cappon, *A-J Letters* 1:244, 252; Jefferson to Washington, May 8, 1791, Boyd, *Papers of Jefferson* 20:291, 284–87n.

36. My summary of the rival parties draws heavily on Forrest McDonald, *The Presidency of Thomas Jefferson* (Lawrence, Kansas, 1976), 17–22. It was also influenced by the spirited battle among scholars over the meaning of the Republican opposition. For those who see the Jeffersonians drawing largely on the past, see Lance Banning, *The Jeffersonian Persuasion: Evolution of a Party Ideology* (Ithaca, 1978); Lance Banning, "Jeffersonian Ideology Revisited: Liberal and Classical Ideas in the New American Republic," *WMQ* 43 (1986): 3–19; and John M. Murrin, "The Great Inversion, or Court versus Country: A Comparison of the Revolution Settlements in England (1688–1721) and America (1776–1816)," in J. G. A. Pocock, ed., *Three British Revolutions: 1641, 1688, 1776* (Princeton, 1980), 368–453. For works treating the Jeffersonians as modernists, see Joyce Appleby, *Capitalism and a New Social Order: The Republican Vision of the 1790s* (New York, 1984); Joyce Appleby, "Commercial Farming and the 'Agrarian Myth' in the Early Republic," *JAH* 68 (1982): 833–49; Joyce Appleby, "What is Still American in the Political Philosophy of Thomas Jefferson?" *WMQ* 39 (1982): 287–309; and Joyce Appleby, "Republicanism in Old and New Contexts," *WMQ* 43 (1986): 20–34. Especially useful treatments of the subject can also be found in John C. Miller, *The Federalist Era, 1789–1801* (New York, 1960), 99–125; Joseph Charles, *The Origins of the American Party System* (Williamsburg, 1956); James M. Banner, Jr., *To the Hartford Convention: The Federalists and the Origins of Party Politics in Massachusetts, 1789–1815* (New York, 1970); Noble E. Cunningham, *The Jeffersonian Republicans: The Formation of a Party Organization, 1789–1801* (Chapel Hill, 1957); Robert Kelley, *The Cultural Pattern in American Politics: The First Century* (New York, 1979); Buel, *Securing the Revolution,* 1–90. For a good view of JA and the issues of his day, see Steven Watts, *The Republic Reborn: War and the Making of Liberal America, 1790–1820* (Baltimore, 1987), 28–42.

37. Washington to Hamilton, Jefferson, and Knox, Apr. 4, 1791, *PAH* 8:243.

38. JA to AA, Mar. 13, 1789, JAPM, reel 372; AA to M. Cranch, Jan. 5, 1790, and Jan. 9, 1791, Stewart Mitchell, ed., *New Letters of Abigail Adams* (Boston, 1947), 35, 67; AA to AAS, Nov. 21, 1790, Adams, *Letters of Mrs. Adams* 2:207; AA to T. Brand-Hollis, Sept. 6, 1790, ibid., 205; Levin, *AA,* 257, 261; Withey, *Dearest Friend,* 208.

39. AA to AAS, Nov. 21 and Dec. 26, 1790, Adams, *Letters of Mrs. Adams* 2:207, 212; AA to Elizabeth Shaw, Mar. 20, 1791, ibid., 222.

40. AA to M. Cranch, Dec. 18, 1791, Feb. 5, Mar. 20, Apr. 20, 1792, Mitchell, *New Letters of AA,* 75, 77, 78–79, 81–82.

41. JA to AA, Jan. 23, 1795, JAPM, reel 379; Smith, *JA* 2:864.

42. JA to Tufts, June 12, 1789, JAPM, reel 115; JA to AA. Nov. 24, 1783, Jan. 2, Nov. 18 and 23, 1794, ibid., reels 376, 377, 378; JA to Tudor, June 14, 1789, ibid., reel 115; JA to Trumbull, Mar. 9, 1790, ibid., reel 115; JA to AA, Nov. 19, 1794, and Apr. 6, 1796, ibid., reels 378, 381. In retirement, JA looked back on this period as "a nauseous fog." See JA to Rush, Jan. 4, 1812, Schutz and Adair, *Spur of Fame,* 263.

43. JA to JQA, May 19, 1794, JAPM, reel 377; JA to AA, Feb. 10 and Dec. 9, 1795, ibid., reels 379, 380; JA to Trumbull, Apr. 2, 1790, ibid., reel 115.

44. JA to AA, Feb. 17, Dec. 22 and 30, 1793, Jan. 21, 1794, and Jan. 26 and Feb. 8, 1796, ibid., reels 376, 377, 381; JA to JQA, Dec. 13, 1790, ibid., reel 374; Charles Mee, *The Genius of the People* (New York, 1987), 11.

45. JA to AA, June 6, 1789, Dec. 16, 1795, Feb. 1, 8, and Mar. 11, 1796, JAPM, reels 372, 380, 381; Smith, *JA* 2:829.

46. JA to AA, May 14, June 6 and 7, 1789, JAPM, reel 372.

47. JA to AA, Jan. 24, 1793, Dec. 5 and 16, 1794, Jan. 5, 1795, and Apr. 1, 1796, ibid., reels 376, 378, 379, 381.

48. Erikson, "Identity and the Life Cycle," *Psychological Issues* 1:56–61, 95; Roger L. Gould, "Transformation during Early and Middle Adult Years," in Neil J. Smelser and Erik H. Erikson, eds., *Themes of Work and Love in Adulthood* (Cambridge, Mass., 1980), 235–36; Daniel J. Levinson, "Toward a Conception of the Adult Life Course," in ibid., 284, 286–87; Roger L. Gould, *Transformation: Growth and Change in Adult Life* (New York, 1978), 309–19; Daniel Gutman, "An Exploration of Ego Configurations in Middle and Late Life," in Bernice L. Neugarten, et al., eds., *Personality in Middle and Later Life: Empirical Studies* (New York, 1964), 119–30.

49. JA to AA, Mar. 15, 1796, JAPM, reel 381; AA to JA, Jan. 7, 1793, ibid., reel 376.

50. Hecht, *JQA,* 58–64, 75–76; David F. Musto, "The Youth of John Quincy Adams," American Philosophical Society, *Proceedings* 113 (1969): 275; Nagle, *Descent from Glory,* 53.

51. Nagel, *Descent from Glory,* 52; Levin, *AA,* 273.

52. Nagel, *Descent from Glory,* 51, 78; AAS to JQA, Oct. 26–Nov. 14, 1795, JAPM, reel 380; Charles Adams to AA, June 24, Oct. 8, 1792, Jan. 31, 1793, Sept. 22, 1794, and Feb. [?], 1795, ibid., reels 375, 376, 378, 379; Charles Adams to JA, Dec. 19, 1793, and May 9, 1794, ibid., reels 376, 377; AAS to JQA, Oct. 26, 1795, ibid., reel 380. Allegations of Steuben's "profligacy" were made by his contemporary and initial biographer. See Friedrich Kapp, *Life of Frederick William von Steuben* (New York, 1859). The standard biography of Steuben sidesteps the issue. Nevertheless, on the character of Steuben, see John F. Palmer, *General von Steuben* (New Haven, 1937), 321, 364–66. Steuben acknowledged having been forced out of the Prussian army for a mysterious "inconsiderate step." See ibid., 44.

53. JA to AAS, July 16, 1788, De Windt, *Journal and Correspondence of Miss Adams* 2:87–89; Levin, *AA,* 281; Nagel, *Descent from Glory,* 58–59; JA to Washington, June 20, 1789, Twohig, *Papers of Washington* 2:287–88n; Samuel Webb to Catherine Hogeboom, June 7, 1789, ibid., 277n; Gelles, "Gossip," *Journal of Social History* 22:677.

54. JA to AA, Jan. 5, 1796, JAPM, reel 381.

55. JA to AA, Jan. 7, 20, Feb. 1, Mar. 9 and 13, 1796, ibid., reel 381; JA to Trumbull, Mar. 12, 1790, ibid., reel 115.

56. JA to AA, Jan. 7, Feb. 8, 10, and 15, 1796, ibid., reel 381.

57. AA to JA, Jan. 21 and Feb. 20, 1796, ibid., reel 381; JA to AA, Mar. 15 and 19, 1796, ibid., reel 381.

58. JA to AA, Feb. 1, 8, 10, Mar. 1 and 15, 1796, ibid., reel 381.

59. JA to AA, Apr. 9, 17196, ibid., reel 381.

CHAPTER 16

1. JA to JQA, May 5, 1796, JAPM, reel 381.
2. *ADA* 3:226–50; JA to AA, Feb. 10, 1796, JAPM, reel 381.
3. Jefferson to Monroe, July 10, 1796, in Paul L. Ford, ed., *Writings of Thomas Jefferson*. 10 vols. (New York, 1892–1899), 7:90; Hamilton to Rufus King, May 4, 1796, *PAH* 20:158; Robert G. Harper to Hamilton, Nov. 4, 1796, ibid., 372.
4. Milton Lomask, *Aaron Burr.* 2 vols. (New York, 1979–1982), 1:187; AA to TBA, Nov. 8, 1796, Adams, *Letters of Mrs. Adams* 2:231; Malone, *Jefferson* 3:280, 283.
5. The discussion of Hamilton is based primarily on Cooke, *Hamilton;* John C. Miller, *Alexander Hamilton: Portrait in Paradox* (New York, 1959); Morris, *Seven Who Shaped Our Destiny,* 221–58; and Adrienne Koch, *Power, Morals, and the Founding Fathers: Essays in the Interpretation of the American Enlightenment* (Ithaca, N. Y., 1961), 50–80. On Hamilton and Washington, see Ferling, *First of Men,* 256–57. For the quotations by and about Hamilton, see Hamilton to Edward Stevens, Nov. 11, 1769, *PAH* 1:512; Jefferson to Rush, Jan. 16, 1811, A. A. Lipscomb and A. E. Burgh, eds., *The Writings of Thomas Jefferson.* 20 vols. (New York, 1903), 13:4. The Jefferson quotation on Hamilton's machinations can be found in Mapp, *Jefferson,* 1–2. Washington defended Hamilton. His secretary of the Treasury was ambitious, he said, but his ambition was "of that laudable kind, which prompts a man to excel in whatever he takes in hand." See Washington to JA, Sept. 25, 1798, Fitzpatrick, *Writings of Washington* 35:460–61.
6. [Alexander Hamilton], "Letter . . . Concerning the Public Conduct and Character of John Adams, Esquire, President of the United States," Oct. 24, 1800, *PAH* 25:194–95; Hamilton to Jeremiah Wadsworth, Dec. 1, 1796, ibid., 20:418; Cooke, *Hamilton,* 172–73; JA to [?], Mar. 12, 1797, JAPM, reel 117. For a different view of Hamilton's role in this election, see Stephen G. Kurtz, *The Presidency of John Adams: The Collapse of Federalism, 1795–1800* (Philadelphia, 1957), 96–113, 192–206.
7. *PAH* 25:193–94n; Hamilton, "Letter," Oct. 24, 1800, ibid., 193, 194, 196.
8. *ADA* 3:228–29; JA to AA, Dec. 12, 1796, Adams, *Works* 1:495–96; Gerry to JA, Feb. 3, 1797, ibid., 8:521–22.
9. JA to AA, Apr. 9, 1796, Dec. 8 and 12, 1796, JAPM, reels 381, 382; JA to Knox, Mar. 30, 1797, ibid., reel 117.
10. JA to AA, Dec. 20 and 30, 1796, JAPM, reel 382.
11. Kurtz, *Presidency of JA,* 4112–13; Hamilton to [?], Nov. 8, 1796, *PAH* 20:377.
12. JA to AA, Dec. 6 and 16, 1796, JAPM, reel 382; Hamilton to Washington, Nov. 4 and 11, 1796, *PAH,* 20:372–73, 389–90; Kurtz, *Presidency of JA,* 132, 160, 167; Malone, *Jefferson* 3:288; Edward Stanwood, *A History of the Presidency.* 2 vols. (New York, 1898), 1:51.
13. JA to AA, Dec. 30, 1796, JAPM, reel 382; JA to Gerry, Feb. 20, 1797, ibid., reel 117; AA to Gerry, Dec. 31, 1796, MHS, *Proceedings* 57:499; JA to Tristram Dalton, Jan. 19, 1797, Emmet Collection, NYPL; Malone, *Jefferson* 3:294.
14. JA to Rush, Aug. 23, 1805, Jan. 6, 1806, and Apr. 22, 1812, Schutz and Adair, *Spur of Fame,* 36, 46, 214; Jefferson to Gerry, May 13, 1797, Ford, *Writings of Jefferson* 7:120. The JA quotation concerning his political ineptness is from Ber-

nard Bailyn, "Butterfield's Adams: Notes for a Sketch," *WMQ,* 3d ser., 19 (1962): 251.

15. On Pickering, see Gerald H. Clarfield, *Timothy Pickering and the American Republic* (Pittsburgh, 1980).

16. Kurtz, *Presidency of JA,* 22.

17. See Bernard C. Steiner, *The Life and Career of James McHenry* (Cleveland, 1907); Mee, *Genius of the People,* 38, Washington to Hamilton, Fitzpatrick, *Writings of Washington,* 36:394.

18. In the absence of a modern biography of Wolcott, see George Gibbs, ed., *Memoirs of the Administrations of Washington and John Adams, Edited from the Papers of Oliver Wolcott, Secretary of Treasury.* 2 vols. (New York, 1846), and James D. Wettereau, "Oliver Wolcott," in *Dictionary of American Biography.* 21 vols. (New York, 1928–1937), 20: 443–45; Washington to Hamilton, Aug. 9, 1798, Fitzpatrick, *Writings of Washington,* 36:394.

19. JA to AA, Mar. 17, 1797, JAPM, reel 383; Ferling, *First of Men,* 484; Malone, *Jefferson* 3:297; Shepherd, *Adams Chronicles,* 184.

20. JA to AA, Mar. 9, 1797, JAPM, reel 383.

21. James D. Richardson, ed., *A Compilation of the Messages and Papers of the Presidents.* 20 vols. (New York, 1897–1917), 1:218–22; Malone, *Jefferson,* 3:297.

22. JA to AA, Mar. 5 and 9, 1797, JAPM, reel 383; Eliza Powel to Washington, Feb. 6 and 8, 1797, Mount Vernon Library; Washington to Dandridge, Apr. 3, 1797, Fitzpatrick, *Writings of Washington,* 35:428–29; Washington to Mary White Morris, May 1, 1797, ibid., 35:441–42; [George Washington], "Household Furniture [Memorandum]," Feb. [?], 1797, Washington Papers, University of Virginia; Freeman, *Washington,* 7:438–44.

23. JA to AA, Mar. 22 and Apr. 7, 1797, JAPM, reels 383, 384; AA to JA, Apr. 12, 1797, ibid., reel 384; Ferling, *First of Men,* 383; Mee, *Genius of the People,* 43; Shepherd, *Adams Chronicles,* 184.

24. JA to AA, Dec. 8 and 20, 1796, JAPM, reel 382.

25. See Hamilton's "No Jacobin" essays in *PAH* 15:145–51, 184–91, 203–7, 224–28, 243–46, 249–50, 268–70, 281–84, 304–6; Madison's rejoinders are in Gaillard Hunt, ed., *The Writings of James Madison.* 9 vols. (New York, 1900–1910), 7:133–88. Also see Charles D. Hazen, *Contemporary Opinion of the French Revolution* (Baltimore, 1897), 164–73; Harry Ammon, *The Genet Mission* (New York, 1973), 44–53; Link William A. Williams, *America Confronts a Revolutionary World, 1776–1796* (New York, 1976), 49–50; Eugene Perry Link, *The Democratic-Republican Societies, 1790–1800* (New York, 1942), 125–55.

26. Washington to Jefferson, Apr. 12, 1793, Fitzpatrick, *Writings of Washington,* 32:415; Alexander DeConde, *Entangling Alliance: Politics and Diplomacy under George Washington* (Durham, N.C., 1958), 157–61, 197–99; Freeman, *Washington* 7:27–28, 80–81; JA to Jefferson, June 30, 1813, Adams, *Works* 10:47; JA to William Cunningham, Oct. 15, 1813, in E. M. Cunningham, ed., *Correspondence Between the Honorable John Adams . . . and . . . William Cunningham, Esquire* (Boston, 1823), 103.

27. Anna C. Clauder, *American Commerce as Affected by the Wars of the French Revolution and Napoleon, 1793–1812* (Philadelphia, 1932), 37–36; Forrest McDonald, *The Presidency of George Washington* (Lawrence, Kans. 1974), 134.

28. Ferling, *First of Men,* 438.
29. Samuel Flagg Bemis, *The Jay Treaty: A Study in Commerce and Diplomacy* (New Haven, 1926), 252–71.
30. JA to AA, June 11 and 14, JAPM, reel 379.
31. De Conde, *Entangling Alliance,* 438.
32. Washington to Hamilton, May 8, 1796, Fitzpatrick, *Writings of Washington,* 35:41.
33. Alexander DeConde, *The Quasi-War: The Politics and Diplomacy of the Undeclared War with France, 1797–1801* (New York, 1966), 9, 11; Hamilton to Sedgwick, Jan. 20, 1797, *PAH* 20:474; Hamilton to Washington, Jan. 25–31, 1797, ibid., 480–81; Albert Hall Bowman, *The Struggle for Neutrality: Franco-American Diplomacy During the Federalist Era* (Knoxville, 1974), 290.
34. William A. Williams, *The Contours of American History* (Cleveland and New York, 1961), 139–40, 157, 167–74; JA to Jefferson, May 11, 1794, Cappon, *A-J Letters* 1:255.
35. JA to AA, Nov. 27, 1796, JAPM, reel 382; JA to JQA, July 15, 1797, ibid., reel 385; Richardson, *Messages and Papers* 1:218–22.
36. [Thomas Jefferson], *Anas,* Mar. 2–6, 1797, Ford, *Writings of Jefferson* 1:272–73.
37. Ibid., Mar. 2, 1797, 1:272; [John Adams], "Correspondence Originally Published in the *Boston Patriot,*" Adams, *Works* 9:285; JA to Knox, Mar. 30, 1797, JAPM, reel 117; JA to Rush, Aug. 23, 1805, Biddle, *Old Family Letters* 1:76–77; Wolcott to Hamilton, Mar. 31, 1797, *PAH* 20:571; Bowman, *Struggle for Neutrality,* 280; William Stinchcombe, *The XYZ Affair* (Westport, Conn., 1980), 13.
38. Paul Varg, *Foreign Policies of the Founding Fathers* (East Lansing, Mich., 1963), 118, 125; R. R. Palmer, *The World and the French Revolution* (New York, 1967), 228; Jefferson to Mazzai, Apr. 24, 1796, Ford, *Writings of Jefferson* 7:72–78; Malone, *Jefferson* 3:267.
39. JA to Knox, Mar. 30, 1797, JAPM, reel 117; JA to JAQ, Mar. 31, 1797, ibid., reel 117; JA to Gerry, Feb. 13, 1797, ibid., reel 117; JA to Cranch, Mar. 25, 1797, ibid., reel 117.
40. Pickering to Hamilton, Mar. 30, 1797, *PAH* 20:559; Wolcott to Hamilton, Mar. 31, 1797, ibid., 571–73; Hamilton to McHenry, Mr. [?], 1797, ibid., 574–75; Hamilton to Pickering, May 11, 1797, ibid., 21:81–84; Hamilton to Wolcott, Mar. 30, 1797, ibid., 20:568.
41. JA to Joseph Ward, Nov. 14, 1809, JAPM, reel 118; JA to Heads of Department, Apr. 14, 1797, Adams, *Works* 8:540–41; Winfred E. A. Bernhard, *Fisher Ames: Federalist and Statesman, 1758–1808* (Chapel Hill, 1965), 292–93.
42. JA to AA, Dec. 18, 1796, JAPM, reel 382; Bowman, *Struggle for Neutrality,* 279–80, 289; Kurtz, *Presidency of JA,* 284–85; DeConde, *Quasi-War,* 188; Stinchcombe, *XYZ Affair,* 36–37, 39, 44; William Stinchcombe, "Talleyrand and the American Negotiations of 1797–1798," *JAH* 62 (1975): 575–90.
43. McHenry to Hamilton, Apr. 14, 1797, *PAH* 21:48; Hamilton to McHenry, Apr. 29 and Apr. [?], 1797, ibid., 61–68, 72–75; Hamilton to Pickering, May 11, 1797, ibid., 81–84; Pickering to JA, May 1, 1797, in Charles W. Upham, *The Life of Timothy Pickering.* 4 vols. (Boston, 1873), 3:369.
44. Ralph Adams Brown, *The Presidency of John Adams* (Lawrence, Kans., 1975), 39–40.

45. Richardson, *Messages of the Presidents,* 1:223–29.
46. Madison to Jefferson, Feb. [?], 1798, Hunt, *Writings of Madison* 6:309–10; De Conde, *Quasi-War,* 28–29; Smith, *JA* 2:927; Gerry to JA, July 3, 1797, JAPM, Reel 385; JA to Walsh, Mr. 10, 1797, ibid., reel 117; JA, "Correspondence . . . *Boston Patriot,*" Adams, *Works* 9:286–87; Samuel E. Morison, "Elbridge Gerry, "Gentleman-Democrat," *NEQ* 2 (1929): 6–33; George A. Billias, *Elbridge Gerry: Founding Father and Republican Statesman* (New York, 1976), 245, 253; JA to JQA, Adams, *Works* 8:545; Gibbs, *Memoirs of Wolcott,* 1:471.
47. *ASP* 2:153–57.
48. JA to Charles Adams, Oct. 28, 1798, JAPM, reel 119; Paul Varg, *New England and Foreign Relations, 1789–1850* (Hanover, N.H., 1983), 33; Manning J. Dauer, *The Adams Federalists* (Baltimore, 1953), 135.
49. Harrison G. Otis to Sally Otis, Nov. 20, 1798, Otis Papers, MHS; AA to JA, Apr. 6, 1797, JAPM, reel 384; JA to AA; Mar. 13, 22, Apr. 6, 7, and 11, 1797, ibid., reels 383, 384; AA to JQA, July 14, 1797, ibid., reel 385; AA to Mary Cranch, May 5, 16, 24, 1797, Mitchell, *New Letters of AA,* 88, 89–90, 91, 96, 98, 104; Levin, *AA,* 332; Nagel, *Adams Women,* 125–26; AA to Wm. Smith, July 9 and 11, 1797, Smith-Carter Collection, MHS; AA to Wm. Smith, Nov. 19, 1799, and Mar. 3, 1800, Smith-Townsend Collection, MHS; AA to Elizabeth Smith, Jan. 17, 1800, Smith-Carter Collection, MHS. Worried about her husband's health, Abigail continually sought to induce the president to spend long periods away from the capital. He "will have vacations enough I am sure," she said. See AA to Wm. Shaw, Dec. 14, 1798, Shaw Papers, LC.
50. Withey, *Dearest Friend,* 250; AA to Mary Cranch, July 6, 1797, Mitchell, *New Letters of AA,* 101.

CHAPTER 17

1. Smith, *JA* 2:941–42.
2. Nagle, *Adams Women,* 160–67.
3. Ibid., 167, 199–200; Levin, *AA,* 322–27, 330–31; AA to TBA, June 10, 1796, JAPM, reel 381; Hecht, *JQA,* 100–17; Jack Shepherd, *Cannibals of the Heart: A Personal Biography of Louisa Catherine and John Quincy Adams* (New York, 1980), 64–65, 72–77. JQA spoke of his pending marriage as a "duty." See Illick, "JQA," *Journal of Psychohistory,* 4:194.
4. Pickering to JA, Aug. 24 and Sept. 5, 1797, JAPM, reel 385; McHenry to JA, Sept. 7 and 24, 1797, ibid., reel 385; Wolcott to JA, Sept. 26 and Sept. [?], 1797, ibid., reel 385; JA to McHenry, Oct. 20, 1797, ibid., reel 119; AA to Wm. Smith, Oct. 23, 1797, Smith-Carter Collection, MHS.
5. DeConde, *Quasi-War,* 59; AA to Wm. Smith, Oct. 23, 1797, Smith-Carter Collection, MHS.
6. Adams, *Presidency of JA,* 47; JQA to JA, Sept. 21, 1797, JAPM, reel 385; JA to Dalton, July 1, 1797, quoted in Varg, *Foreign Policies,* 130; DeConde, *Quasi-War,* 36–38.
7. JQA to JA, Sept. 21, 1797, JAPM, reel 385.

8. JA, "Speech to Congress," Nov. 23, 1797, Adams, *Works* 9:121–25; DeConde, *Quasi-War,* 62.
9. McHenry to Hamilton, Jan. 26, 1798, *PAH* 21:339; Hamilton to McHenry, Jan. 27–Feb. 11, 1798, ibid., 341–46.
10. McHenry to JA, Feb. 15, 1798, JAPM, reel 387; DeConde, *Quasi-War,* 65.
11. Richardson, *Messages of the Presidents* 1:253–54. For excellent accounts of this episode, see Stinchcombe, *XYZ Affair,* 54–58, and Gerald H. Clarfield, *Timothy Pickering and American Diplomacy, 1795–1800* (Columbia, Mo., 1969), 144.
12. Smith, *JA* 2:953–54; Hamilton to Pickering, Mar. 17, 1798, *PAH* 21:364–66; Clarfield, *Pickering and American Diplomacy,* 146.
13. Shaw, *Character of JA,* 255–56; Adams, "Message," ND, JAPM, 387.
14. Ibid., JA, "Speech to Congress," Mar. 5, 1798, Adams, *Works* 9:156–57.
15. Jefferson to Madison, Mar. 21, 1798, Ford, *Writings of Jefferson* 7:219; Pickering to Hamilton, Mar. 25, 1798, *PAH* 21:370–72; Hamilton to Pickering, Mar. 23, 1798, ibid., 368; *Annals of Congress.* 42 vols., (Washington, 1834–56), 7:525, 535–36; 8:1374–75; DeConde, *Quasi-War,* 70–73.
16. AA to JQA, Apr. 21, 1798, JAPM, reel 388; AA to Louisa Catherine Adams, May [?], 1798, ibid., reel 388; AA to Wm. Smith, Nov. 21, 1797, Smith-Townsend Collection, MHS; DeConde, *Quasi-War,* 76–77; Jefferson to Madison, Mar. 21, 1798, Ford, *Writings of Jefferson* 7:219; Malone, *Jefferson* 3:371–73; Donald H. Stewart, *The Opposition Press of the Federalist Period* (Albany, 1969), 296–97. Few in the capital were more bellicose than the First Lady. She thought France the anti-Christ and depicted the Directory as bent on seizing Louisiana, Florida, and, of course, Canada. For all his belligerence, the president's tone was considerably more restrained than that of his wife. See AA to Wm. Shaw, Apr. 9 and June 2, 1798, Shaw Papers, LC.
17. [Alexander Hamilton], "The Stand," Mar. 30–Apr. 21, 1798, *PAH* 21:381–87, 390–96, 402–08, 412–18, 418–32, 434–40, 441–47. The source of the Hamilton quotation is *PAH* 21:403.
18. John Adams, "Special Message," May 16, 1797, Richardson, *Messages of the Presidents* 1:237–38; JA to the Students of Dartmouth College, June 12, 1798, JAPM, reel 389; JA to Jefferson, May 11, 1794, Cappon, *A-J Letters* 1:255; JA to Rush, Aug. 23, 1805, Schutz and Adair, *Spur of Fame,* 36.
19. DeConde, *Quasi-War,* 77, 80; Hamilton, "The Stand," no. 6, Apr. 19, 1798, *PAH* 21:439–40; Levin, *AA,* 338–39; Richard H. Kohn, *Eagle and Sword: The Federalists and the Creation of the Military Establishment in America, 1783–1802* (New York, 1975), 205–6; Sedgwick to Henry Van Shaack, Dec. 14, 1797, Sedgwick Papers, MHS; Sedgwick to Ephraim Williams, Jan. 29, 1798, ibid. Perhaps reflecting her husband's outlook, AA concluded in these weeks that war could not be avoided. She began to stockpile supplies for the family that might be difficult to procure during wartime, and she announced that "I see not but War is inevitable." See: AA to Wm. Smith, Mar. 5, 1798, Smith-Carter Collection, MHS; AA to Elizabeth Peabody, June 22, 1798, Shaw Papers, LC.
20. JA to Plymouth and Kingston, Mass., June 8, 1798, JAPM, reel 389; JA to N.Y. Society of Cincinnati, July 9, 1798, Myers Collection, NYPL.
21. DeConde, *Quasi-War,* 84, 91, 96; Smith, *JA* 2:965; Kohn, *Eagle and Sword,* 219–29; William J. Murphy, Jr., "John Adams: The Politics of the Additional Army,

1798–1800," *NEQ* 52 (1975): 234–49; James R. Jacobs, *The Beginnings of the United States Army, 1783–1812* (Princeton, 1947), 207–8; AA to AAS, Apr. 11, 1798, De Windt, *Journal and Correspondence of Miss Adams* 2:151; AA to Tufts, Apr. 14, 1798, JAPM., reel 388; Otis to Sally Otis, Apr. 21, 1798, Otis Papers, MHS.

22. JA to Cannonsburg, Pa., July 5, 1798, JAPM, reel 390; JA to Wilmington, N.C., May 31, 1798, ibid., reel 388; JA to Talbot County, Md., June 8, 1798, ibid., reel 389; JA to Accomack, Va., June 9, 1798, ibid., reel 389; JA to McPherson's Blues, Philadelphia, June 18, 1798, ibid., 389; JA to Berkeley County [Va.] Militia, June 20, 1798, ibid., reel 389; JA to N.Y. Society of Cincinnati, July 9, 1798, Myers Collection, NYPL; Richard Buel, Jr., *Securing the Revolution: Ideology in American Politics, 1789–1815* (Ithaca, 1972), 166.

23. William G. Anderson, "John Adams, the Navy, and the Quasi-War with France," *American Neptune* 30 (1970): 117–32.

24. Hamilton to Washington, May 19, 1798, *PAH* 21:466–68; Washington to Hamilton, May 27, 1798, ibid., 470–74; AA to Wm. Smith, July 7, 1798, Smith-Carter Collection, MHS.

25. JA to Washington, June 22, 1798, Adams, *Works* 8:573; McHenry to Washington, June 26, 1798, Washington Papers, Univ. of Virginia.

26. Washington to Adams, July 4, 1798, Fitzpatrick, 36:312–15; Washington to McHenry, July 4, 1798, ibid., 36:304–12.

27. Ibid., 36:326n.

28. JA to Washington, July 7, 1798, Adams, *Works* 8:575; Hamilton to Washington, July 8, 1798, *PAH* 21:534–35.

29. JA to McHenry, July 6, 1798, Adams, *Works* 8:574; JA to John A. Smith, Feb. 1, 1813, JAPM, reel 121; JA to James Lloyd, Feb. 14, 1815, ibid., reel 122.

30. James T. Flexner, *Washington: The Indispensable Man* (Boston, 1969), 373–74; Washington to Pickering, July 11, 1798, Fitzpatrick, *Writings of Washington* 36:323–27; Pickering to Washington, June 6, 1798, ibid., 324n; Washington to JA, July 13, 1798, ibid., 329; Washington to McHenry, July 5, 1798, ibid., 331–32; Washington to Hamilton, July 14, 1798, ibid., 331–32; Hamilton to Washington, June 2, 1798, *PAH* 21:479; Smith, *JA* 2:974, 978. Pickering soon learned that Hamilton was willing to serve under Knox, but he did not report that information to either the president or General Washington. See Hamilton to Pickering, July 17, 1798, *PAH* 22:24; Brown, *Presidency of JA,* 221n.

31. On the psychological portrayal of JA as submissive to his betrayers, see Shaw, *Character of JA,* 252–53. For the paragraphs concerning JA and the army appointments imbroglio, see *Executive Journal* 1:292; McHenry to Hamilton, July 25, 1798, *PAH* 22:29–30; AA to Wm. Smith, July 23, 1798, Smith-Townsend Collection, MHS; AA to Wm. Smith, July 7, 1798, Smith-Carter Collection, MHS; Joseph Charles, "Adams and Jefferson: The Origins of the American Party System," *WMQ* 12 (1955): 416; JA to AA, Jan. 9, 1797, JAPM, reel 383; JA to Lloyd, Feb. 17, 1815, ibid., reel 122; Adams, *Works* 8:618n.

32. Knox to Washington, July 29, 1798, Fitzpatrick, *Writings of Washington* 36:347–49n; Knox to JA, Aug. 5, 1798, JAPM, reel 390. For JA's relationship with Knox, see Bernhard Knollenberg, "John Adams, Knox, and Washington," Am. Antiq. Soc., *Proceedings* 56 (1946): 207–38.

33. JA to McHenry, Sept. 24, 1798, JAPM, reel 391.
34. JA to McHenry, Aug. 29, 1798, *PAH,* 22:8n.
35. Wolcott to JA, Sept. 17, 1798, ibid., 10–14n; Washington to Adams, Sept. 25, 1798, Fitzpatrick, *Writings of Washington,* 36:453–62; JA to McHenry, Sept. 30, 1798, *PAH* 22:16n.
36. JA to Rush, Nov. 11, 1807, Schutz and Adair, *Spur of Fame,* 99; JA to Washington, Oct. 9, 1798, JAPM, reel 119; JA to Wolcott, Sept. 24 and Oct. 22, 1798, ibid., 391 and 119; JA to McHenry, Sept. 30, 1798, *PAH* 22:16n.
37. Dauer, *Adams Federalists,* 170; John C. Miller, *Crisis in Freedom: The Alien and Sedition Act* (Boston, 1951), 74.
38. JA to the Inhabitants of Harrison Country, Va., Aug. 13, 1798, Adams, *Works* 9:215–17; Jefferson to Madison, Apr. 9, 1798, Ford, *Writings of Jefferson* 7:235–38; AA to JA, Jan. 12, 1799, JAPM, reel 393. On Gallatin, see Raymond Walters, Jr., *Albert Gallatin: Jeffersonian Financier and Diplomat* (Pittsburgh, 1957).
39. Walters, *Gallatin,* 108–9; *Philadelphia Aurora,* June 16, 1798, in Steward, *Opposition Press,* 305; AA to Mary Cranch, Apr. 28, 1798, Mitchell, *New Letters of AA,* 167.
40. Miller, *Crisis in Freedom,* 11, 23; Dauer, *Adams Federalists,* 153; JA to Jefferson, June 30, 1813, Cappon, *A-J Letters* 2:346–47. For an excellent summary of the exaggerated Federalist notions of a Republican conspiracy, see Kohn, *Eagle and Sword,* 202–4. Also see Sedgwick to Williams, Jan. 11, 1797, Sedgwick Papers, MHS; Sedgwick to van Shaack, May 4, 1797, ibid.
41. JA to the Boston Marine Society, Sept. 5, 1798, JAPM, reel 119; JA to Judge Sewall, Nov. 4, ibid., reel 122; JA to the Young Men of Boston, May 22, 1798, Adams, *Works* 9:194; JA to Rush, Sept. 30, 1805, Schutz and Adair, *Spur of Fame,* 40; JA to Dalton, Jan. 19, 1797, Emmet Collection, NYPL; Howe, *Changing Political Thought of JA,* 171–72, 198; Jefferson to Madison, Apr. 26, 1798, Ford, *Writings of Jefferson* 7:247; Stephen B. Kurtz, "The French Mission of 1799–1800: Concluding Chapter in the Statecraft of John Adams," *Political Science Quarterly* 80 (1965): 549.
42. Jefferson to Madison, Apr. 26, 1798, Ford, Writings of Jefferson, 7:244.
43. Dauer, *Adams Federalists,* 135; Miller, *Crisis in Freedom,* 59, 61, 67–70.
44. JA, "Correspondence . . . in *Boston Patriot,*" Adams, *Works* 9:290–91; Hamilton to Pickering, June 7, 1798, *PAH* 21:495; Hamilton to Wolcott, June 29, 1798, ibid., 522.
45. See Smith, *JA,* 2:977 on the Alien and Sedition acts. Also see: JA to the Grand Jury of Dutchess, N.Y., Sept. 22, 1798, Adams, *Works* 9:223; Wm. Shaw to AA, Jan. 2, 1799, JAPM, reel 393; AA to MOW, Apr. 25, 1798, *W-A Letters* 73:338; AA to Mary Cranch, Apr. 26, 1798, Mitchell, *New Letters of AA,* 165; AA to Wm. Smith, July 7, 1798, Smith-Carter Collection, MHS.
46. Miller, *Crisis in Freedom,* 89–90, 99, 106–9; James Morton Smith, *Freedom's Fetters: The Alien and Sedition Laws and American Civil Liberties* (Ithaca, 1956), 181–82, 200–203.
47. Smith, *Freedom's Fetters,* 181.
48. JA to Jefferson, June 14, 1813, Cappon, *A-J Letters* 2:329; Brown, *Presidency of JA,* 125; Miller, *Crisis in Freedom,* 188–90. Adams signed warrants for the deportation of three individuals. See: Brown, *Presidency of JA,* 125.

49. AA to Mary Cranch, Feb. 6, Mar. 5, Apr. 22, 26, and 28, 1798, Mitchell, *New Letters of AA,* 130, 141, 163, 166, 167; Levin, *AA,* 353–54.
50. AAS to JQA, Sept. 28, 1798, JAPM, reel 391; AA to Catherine Johnson, June 26, 1798, Abigail Adams Papers, Houghton Library, Harvard Univ.; AA to Elizabeth Peabody, June 11, 1798, Shaw Papers, LC.
51. JA to JQA, Oct. 16, 1798, JAPM, reel 119; Levin, *AA,* 354.
52. JA to Pickering, Aug. 25 and Oct. 15, 1798, JAPM, reel 119; JA to McHenry, Aug. 29, Oct. 22 and 28, 1798, ibid., reel 119; JA to Washington, Oct. 9, 1798, ibid., reel 119.
53. AAS to JQA, Sept. 28, 1798, ibid., reel 391.
54. JA to Pickering, Oct. 20, 1798, ibid., reel 119; JA to McHenry, Oct. 22, 1798, ibid., 191.
55. JA to AA, Nov. 13, 1798, ibid., reel 382; JA to Samuel Malcolm, Aug. 28, 1798, ibid., reel 119.
56. JA to AA, Nov. 15, 1798, ibid., reel 392; Shaw to AA, Nov. 25, 1798, ibid., reel 392.
57. Wolcott to JA, Nov. 26, 1798, ibid., reel 392; McHenry to JA, Nov. 25, 1798, ibid., reel 392; Pickering to JA, Nov. 27, 1798, ibid., reel 392; Stoddert to JA, Nov. 25, 1798, ibid., reel 392; Jacob E. Cooke, "Country Above Party: John Adams and the 1799 Mission to France," in Edward P. Willis, ed., *Fame and the Founding Fathers* (Bethlehem, Pa., 1967), 58n; Adams, *Works* 1:536–37; *Debates and Proceedings of the Congress of the United States . . . all Laws of a Public Nature.* 42 vols. (Washington, 1834–49), 9:2420.
58. Richardson, *Messages of the Presidents* 1:261–65. On Adams's physical appearance at this period of his presidency, see AA to Elizabeth Peabody, June 22, 1798, Shaw Papers, LC.
59. JA to AA, Dec. 13 and 17, 1798, JAPM, reel 392.

CHAPTER 18

1. JA to AA, Dec. 25, 1798, JAPM, reel 392.
2. Sedgwick to Hamilton, Feb. 7, 1799, *PAH* 22:471; Hamilton to Otis, Dec. 27, 1798 and Jan. 26, 1799, ibid., 22:394, 440; Jefferson to Edmund Pendleton, Apr. 22, 1799, Ford, *Writings of Jefferson* 7:375–76.
3. JA to David Sewall, Dec. 22, 1802, JAPM, reel 118; DeConde, *Quasi-War,* 191.
4. McHenry to JA, May 31, 1800, *PAH* 24:564; Sedgwick to Hamilton, Feb. 25, 1799, ibid., 22:503; JA to Massachusetts Militia, 1st Brigade, Oct. 11, 1798, JAPM, reel 119; JA to Trumbull, July 27, 1805, ibid., reel 118; JA to Joseph Ward, Apr. 15, 1809, ibid., reel 118; JA to Stoddert, Nov. 16, 1811, quoted in Mapp, *Jefferson,* 369; Kohn, *Eagle and Sword,* 253; Malone, *Jefferson* 3:395–405.
5. JA to Dana, Nov. 7, 1798, JAPM, reel 119; Kurtz, *Presidency of JA,* 341; JA to Gerry, Dec. 15, 1798, Adams, *Works* 8:617.
6. *Correspondence of the Late President Adams, Originally Published in the Boston Patriot* (Boston, 1809), 10.
7. Hecht, *JQA,* 16.
8. Murray to JA, July 1, 17, 22, Aug. 3, 20, and Oct. 7, 1798, Adams, *Works* 8:677–

91; DeConde, *Quasi-War,* 147–48, 162; Samuel Flagg Bemis, *John Quincy Adams an the Foundations of American Foreign Policy* (New York, 1956), 100–101.

9. JA to Smith, Nov. 26, 1815, JAPM, reel 122.
10. JA to AA, Jan. 10 and 16, 1799, ibid., reel 393; Levin, *AA,* 361.
11. Bemis, *JQA,* 99; Murray's key correspondence can be found in Worthington C. Ford, ed., "Letters of William Vans Murray to John Quincy Adams, 1797–1803," *Annual Report of the American Historical Association* (1912), 347–715.
12. Murray to JA, Oct. 7, 1798, Adams, *Works* 8:688–90; DeConde, Quasi-War, 174, 177; JA to AA, Jan. 1, 1799, JAPM, reel 393; Kurtz, *Presidency of JA,* 347. Talleyrand's letter can be found in the *Executive Journal* 1:313–14. For an extended discussion of relations between Great Britain and the United States during the Quasi-War, see Bradford Perkins, *The First Rapprochement: England and the United States, 1795–1805* (Philadelphia, 1955).
13. Barlow to Washington, Oct. 2, 1798, Jared Sparks, ed., *The Writings of Washington.* 12 vols. (Boston, 1834–37), 11:560; JA to Washington, Feb. 19, 1799, Adams, *Works* 8:625; Malone, *Jefferson* 3:431; Smith, *JA* 2:669.
14. Washington to JA, Feb. 1, 1799, Fitzpatrick, *Writings of Washington* 37:119–20.
15. JA to Washington, Feb. 19, 1799, Adams, *Works* 8:626.
16. JA to Trumbull, Nov. [?], 1805, JAPM, reel 118; DeConde, *Quasi-War,* 170, 179–80; JA to Washington, Feb. 19, 1799, Adams, *Works* 8:626.
17. Bemis, *JQA,* 100; Cook, "Country above Party," in Willis, *Fame and the Founding Fathers,* 64.
18. Jefferson to Madison, Feb. 19 and 26, 1800, Ford, *Writings of Jefferson* 7:361–67, 370; Richardson, *Messages of the Presidents* 1:272–73.
19. Samuel E. Morison, *Harrison Gray Otis, 1765–1848: The Urbane Federalist* (Boston, 1969), 159; Jefferson to Madison, Feb. 26, 1799, Ford, *Writings of Jefferson* 7:370.
20. JA to AA, Feb. 22, 1799, JAPM, reel 393; Sedgwick to Hamilton, Feb. 19, 22, and 25, 1799, *PAH* 22:487–88, 494–95, 503; Sedgwick to [?], Feb. 9, 1800, Sedgwick Papers, MHS; *Correspondence of the Late President Adams,*" 22–25; Brown, *Presidency of JA,* 97; DeConde, *Quasi-War,* 182–83; Arthur B. Darling, *Our Rising Empire, 1763–1801* (New Haven, 1940), 343; Howe, *Changing Political Thought of JA,* 201.
21. Hamilton to Sedgwick, Feb. 21, 1799, *PAH* 22:493; Talleyrand to Pichon, 7 Vendemaire [Sept. 29], 1799, *ASP* 2:240; DeConde, *Quasi-War,* 185; Clarfield, *Pickering and American Diplomacy,* 202–3.
22. JA to Forrest, May 13, 1799, JAPM, reel 119; AA to Sally Otis, Ap. 1, 1799, ibid., reel 394; TBA to JQA, June 3, 1799, ibid., reel 395; Smith, *JA* 2:1005; AA to Wm. Shaw, Feb. 18 and 21, 1799, Shaw Papers, LC.
23. Smith, *JA* 2:1014, 1006; AA to TBA, Apr. 2, 1799, JAPM, reel 395.
24. JA to AA, Feb. 22, 1799, JAPM, reel 393; AA to JQA, Dec. 30, 1799, ibid., reel 396; AA to [?], Nov. 13, 1799, ibid., reel 396; AA to TBA, July 15, 1799, ibid., reel 395; Smith, *JA* 2:1006, 1010; Shaw, *Character of JA,* 257–58.
25. Sedgwick to Hamilton, Feb. 7, 1799, *PAH* 22:471; Cabot to Christopher Gore, May 2, 1799, in Henry Cabot Lodge, *Life and Letters of George Cabot* (Boston,

1877), 231; JA to Charles Lee, Mar. 29, 1799, Adams, *Works* 8:629; AA to TBA, Sept. 4, 1799, JAPM, reel 396.

26. Hamilton, "Letter from Hamilton," Oct. 24, 1800, *PAH* 25:190, 192–93, 214, 222; Fisher Ames to Rufus King, Sept. 24, 1800, in Charles R. King, *The Life and Correspondence of Rufus King*. 6 vols. (New York, 1895), 3:304; Miller, *Hamilton*, 493–94.

27. AA to Mary Cranch, Mar. 27, 1798, Mitchell, *New Letters of AA*, 148; Arthur B. Darling, *Our Rising Empire, 1763–1801* (New Haven, 1940), 319–28; Gerald Stourzh, *Alexander Hamilton and the Idea of Republican Government* (Stanford, 1970), 194–95; Hamilton to James Gunn, Dec. 22, 1798, *PAH* 22:389.

28. JA to Pickering, Aug. 6, 1799, JAPM, reel 120.

29. Pickering to JA, Sept. 11, 1799, ibid., reel 396; Clarfield, *Pickering and the American Republic,* 208; Gibbs, *Memoirs of Wolcott* 2:357–61.

30. JA to Pickering, Sept. 14, 1799, JAPM, reel 120; Kurtz, "French Mission," *Political Science Quarterly,* 80:556.

31. AA to TBA, Apr. 2, 1799, JAPM, reel 395; AA to JQA, June 12, 1799, ibid., reel 395.

32. Stoddert to JA, Aug. 29 and Sept. 13, 1799, Adams, *Works* 9:18–19, 26–29; JA to Stoddert, Sept. 21, 1799, ibid., 33–34.

33. JA to AA, Oct. 12, 1799, JAPM, reel 396; JA to Stoddert, Sept. 21, 1799, Adams, *Works* 9:34; Shepherd, *Adams Chronicles,* 204.

34. JA to AA, Oct. 24, 1799, JAPM, reel 396; Shaw to AA, Oct. 12, 1799, ibid., reel 396.

35. JA to Pickering, Sept. 21, 1799, Adams, *Works* 9:33.

36. "Draft Instructions," Sept. 10, 1799, JAPM, reel 396; Pickering to Ellsworth and Davies, Oct. 22, 1799, *ASP* 2:301–6; DeConde, *Quasi-War,* 220.

37. *Correspondence of the Late President Adams,* 29–30; AA to Mary Cranch, Dec. 30, 1799, Mitchell, *New Letters,* 224–25; Hamilton to Washington, Oct. 21, 1799, *PAH* 23:545.

38. Miller, *Hamilton,* 503.

39. JA to AA, Oct. 12, 1799, JAPM, reel 396; Akers, *AA,* 165.

40. AA to TBA, Jan. 23 and June 30, 1799, JAPM, reels 393, 395; AA to JQA, June 12, 1799, ibid., 395; AA to Mary Cranch, Oct. 20 and 31, 1799, Mitchell, *New Letters of AA,* 209–11.

41. JA to AA, Dec. 17 and 31, 1798 and Feb. 14, 1799, JAPM, reels 392, 393; AA to JA, Jan. 12, 1799, ibid., reel 393.

42. Nagel, *Adams Women,* 123, 126; JA to AA, Dec. 31, 1798, and Jan. 5, 1799, JAPM, reel 392, 393; JA to Smith, Dec. 19, 1798, Adams, *Works* 8:617–18; AA to Wm. Smith, Oct. 23, 1797, Smith-Carter Collection, MHS.

43. AA to JA, Feb. 20, 1799, JAPM, reel 393; AA to TBA, Aug. 4, 1799, ibid., reel 396; TBA to AA, Jan. 22, 1799, ibid., reel 393; TBA to JA, Sept. 26, Oct. 15, 1799, and Aug. 18, 1800, ibid., reels 396, 398; JA to TBA, Oct. 19, 1799, ibid., reel 396; AA to E. Peabody, July 18, 1800, Shaw Papers, LC.

44. Nagel, *Descent from Glory,* 137; Musto, "Youth of JQA," American Philosophical Society, *Proceedings,* 103:270; AA to JQA, Feb. 1, 1799, JAPM, reel 393.

45. Hecht, *JQA,* 120, 129–30; Nagel, *Adams Women,* 171; Shepherd, *Adams Chronicles,* 191.

46. Smith, *JA* 2:1018.
47. Ferling, *First of Men,* 506; AA to Mary Cranch, Dec. 30, 1799, Mitchell, *New Letters,* 225.
48. AA to JQA, Dec. 30, 1799, JAPM, reel 396; AA to [?], Jan.–Feb. [?], 1800, ibid., reel 397; AA to Mary Cranch, Dec. 22, 1799, Mitchell, *New Letters of AA,* 22.
49. Shaw, *Character of JA,* 254, 265; AA to Mary Cranch, Dec. 11, 1799, Mitchell, *New Letters of AA,* 221; AA to TBA, June 23 and Sept. 8, 1799, JAPM, reels 395, 396; JA to Gerry, June 12, 1797, ibid., reel 384; [Anon.] to JA, Mar. 11 and 19, 1800, ibid., reel 397; Sedgwick to Hamilton, Feb. 7, 1799, *PAH* 22:471; JA to Cunningham, Oct. 15 and Nov. 25, 1808, *Correspondence between Adams and Cunningham,* 39, 40, 45, 50, 57–58.
50. TBA to AA, Aug. 8, 1799, JAPM, reel 396; AA to Mary Cranch, Dec. 11, 1799, Mitchell, *New Letters of AA,* 221; McHenry to John McHenry, Jr., May 20, 1799, *PAH* 24:509; Kurtz, *Presidency of JA,* 367–73, 384–93.
51. AA to Mary Cranch, Feb. 3, 1800, JAPM, reel 397; AA to JA, Mar. 3, 1799, ibid., reel 393; Kohn, *Eagle and Sword,* 258, 263–64; Sedgwick to Hamilton, May 13, 1800, *PAH* 24:482.
52. Hamilton to Sedgwick, May 4, 1800, *PAH* 24:453; AA to JA, Mar. 3, 1799, JAPM, reel 393; Jefferson to Madison, May 12, 1800, Ford, *Writings of Jefferson* 7:446; Miller, *Hamilton,* 512–13.
53. McHenry's recollection of the confrontation can be found in McHenry to Hamilton, May 31, 1800, *PAH* 24:552–65.
54. JA to Pickering, May 10 and 12, 1800, JAPM, reel 120; Pickering to JA, May 12, 1800, ibid., reel 397; AA to Mary Cranch, Dec. 11, 1799, Mitchell, *New Letters of AA,* 221.
55. McHenry to JA, May 6, 1800, Adams, *Works* 9:51–52; McHenry to JA, May 31, 1800, *PAH* 24:557; Hamilton to McHenry, June 6, 1800, ibid., 573; JA to Pickering, May 11 and 12, 1800, ibid., 9:53–55; DeConde, *Quasi-War,* 272; Clarfield, *Pickering and American Diplomacy,* 213–14; Pickering to Timothy Williams, May 19, 1800, Pickering Papers, MHS; Pickering to Christopher Gore, June 10 and 16, 1800, ibid., Kohn, *Eagle and Sword,* 266–67; Murphy, "Politics of the Additional Army," *NEQ* 52:237–38.
56. For Adams's views on the Fries Affair, see JA to Lloyd, Mr. 31, 1815, JAPM, reel 122. Numerous contemporary documents on the clash between the president and his cabinet on the question of clemency for Fries and his compatriots can be bound in ibid., reel 397.
57. JA to AA, June 13, 1800, ibid., reel 398; Shaw to AA, June 5 and 8, 1800, ibid., 398.
58. JA to AA, June 13, 1800, ibid., reel 398.

CHAPTER 19

1. AA to TBA, July 12, 1800, JAPM, reel 398; AA to JQA, Sept. 1, 1800, ibid., reel 398.
2. AA to Mary Cranch, May 3, 1800, Mitchell, *New Letters of AA,* 250.

3. H. G. Otis to [?], Dec. 3, 1800, Otis Papers, MHS; AA to TBA, July 12, 1800, JAPM, reel 398; Sedgwick to Sedgwick II, Dec. 5, 1800, Sedgwick Papers, MHS.

4. Hamilton to Charles Carroll, July 1 and Aug. 7, 1800, *PAH* 25:2, 60.

5. AA to TBA, July 12, 1800, JAPM, reel 398; "Introductory Note," *PAH* 24:574–85. The Adamses probably overestimated the power of the Essex Junto. See David H. Fischer, "The Myth of the Essex Junto," *WMQ* 21 (1964): 191–253.

6. Wolcott to Hamilton, Sept. 3 and Oct. 2, 1800, *PAH* 25:107–8, 140–46.

7. The letter and a useful introduction to Hamilton's desperate ploy can be found in *PAH* 25:173–234. The quotations used in this study can be found in 25:190, 192, and 222.

8. JA to Tudor, Nov. 14, 1819, JAPM, reel 399; JA to Uzal Ogden, Dec. 3, 1800, ibid., reel 399; "Introductory Note," *PAH* 25:178–80; Malone, *Jefferson* 3:489.

9. JA to Pinckney, Oct. 27, 1800, JAPM, reel 399; Smith, *JA* 2:1046–47; Buel,*Securing the Revolution,* 230.

10. Noble E. Cunningham, "Election of 1800," in Arthur M. Schlesinger, Jr. et al., eds., *The Coming to Power: Critical Presidential Elections in American History* (New York, 1971), 46–47, 52–53; Malone, *Jefferson* 3:480. Also see Noble E. Cunningham, *In Pursuit of Reason: The Life of Thomas Jefferson* (Baton Rouge, 1987), 221–37; JA to Ward, Jan. 8, 1810, JAPM, reel 118; Ames to King, July 15, 1800, King, *Life of King* 3:275.

11. Cunningham, "Election of 1800," in Schlesinger, *Coming to Power,* 51–52.

12. AA to Catherine Johnson, Aug. 20 and Oct. 10, 1800, JAPM, reels 398, 399.

13. AA to Mary Cranch, Nov. 10 and 16, 1800, Mitchell, *New Letters of AA,* 255, 256.

14. AA to Mary Cranch, Nov. 21, 1800, ibid., 257.

15. Ferling, *First of Men,* 396–98, 422; Marcus Cunliffe, *American Presidents and the Presidency* (New York, 1972), 46; AA to Tufts, Nov. 28, 1800, JAPM, reel 399; AA to Mary Cranch, Nov. 21, 1800, Mitchell,*New Letters of AA,* 257, 259; AA to AAS, Nov. 21, 1800, Adams, *Letters of Mrs. Adams* 2:242; Malone, *Jefferson* 3:491.

16. Richardson, *Messages of the Presidents* 1:305–8.

17. H. G. Otis to [?], 1800, Otis Papers, MHS. As early as mid-November Adams knew from unofficial returns that he had lost South Carolina, rendering his election unlikely. See AA to TBA, Nov. 13, 1800, Adams, *Letters of Mrs. Adams* 2:237–39.

18. Sedgwick to Sedgwick II, Dec. 10, 1800, Sedgwick Papers, MHS; James Gunn to Hamilton, Dec. 13, 1800, *PAH* 25:254.

19. Cunningham, "Election of 1800," in Schlesinger, *Coming to Power,* 41; John C. Miller, *The Federalist Era, 1789–1801* (New York, 1960), 267; AA to Mary Cranch, May 5, 1800, Mitchell, *New Letters of AA,* 251.

20. JA to MOW, July 20, 1807, JAPM, reel 118; AA to TBA, Nov. 13, 1800, Adams, *Letters of Mrs. Adams* 2:238; JA to Lloyd, Feb. 6, 1815, Adams, *Works* 10:15.

21. Cunningham, "Election of 1800," in Schlesinger, *Coming to Power,* 61–63; Brown,*Presidency of JA,* 193; Miller,*Hamilton,* 510; AA to TBA; Nov. 13, 1800, Adams, *Letters of Mrs. Adams* 2:238. Jefferson to Rush, Jan. 16, 1811, Ford,

Writings of Jefferson 9:926–97. The Republican victory in New York hinged on carrying New York City, a feat accomplished by a mere 250 votes. See Miller, *Federalist Era,* 268n.

22. TBA to JQA, Dec. 6, 1800, JAPM, reel 399; JA to TBA, Dec. 17, 1800, ibid., reel 399; AA to Mary Cranch, Dec. 8, 1800, Mitchell, *New Letters of AA,* 261–62; JA to Jefferson, Cappon, *A-J Letters* 1:264.

23. AA to JQA, Jan. 29, 1801, JAPM, reel 400; AA to TBA, Dec. 27, 1801, ibid., reel 401; JA to Jefferson, June 19, 1815, Cappon, *A-J Letters* 2:443.

24. TBA to JA, Dec. 14, 1800, JAPM, reel 399.

25. AA to Mary Cranch, Nov. 21, 1800, Mitchell, *New Letters of AA,* 258; AA to TBA, Nov. 13, 1800, Jan. 15 and 26, 1801, JAPM, reels 399, 400.

26. JA to Tudor, Jan. 20, 1801, ibid., reel 400; JA to Jay, Dec. 19, 1800, Adams, *Works* 9:91–92; JA to Boudinot, Jan. 26, 1801, ibid., 9:93.

27. JA to Boudinot, Jan. 26, 1801, Adams, *Works* 9:94; JA to Tudor, Jan. 20, 1801, JAPM, reel 400.

28. AA to Mary Cranch, Jan. 15 and Feb. 7, 1801, Mitchell, *New Letters of AA,* 263, 265–66.

29. DeConde, *Quasi-War,* 223–58.

30. Ibid., 279, 283, 288; Gunn to Hamilton, Dec. 13, 1800, *PAH* 25:254.

31. H. G. Otis, Dec. 17, 1800, *PAH* 25:260; JA to the Senate, Jan. 21, 1801, *ASP* 2:295.

32. Morris to Hamilton, Jan. 5, 1801, *PAH* 25:298; Hamilton to Morris, Jan. 10, 1801, ibid., 25:307.

33. JA to TBA, Jan. 24 and 16, 1801, JAPM, reel 400.

34. AA to TBA, Dec. 25, 1800, Feb. 2 and Apr. 22, 1801, ibid., reels 399, 400; AA to Mary Cranch, Jan. 15 and Feb. 7, 1801, Mitchell, *New Letters of AA,* 264, 266.

35. Smith, *JA* 2:1065; Nagel, *Adams Women,* 128, 132–34. Adams had recommended a restructuring of the federal judiciary eighteen months before the Federalist party, in the aftermath of its stunning defeat in the elections of 1800, rammed the Judiciary Act of 1801 through Congress. See Brown, *Presidency of JA,* 199–200.

36. Ferling, *First of Men,* 483–84.

37. JA to Vanderkemp, Aug. 23, 1806, JAPM, reel 118; JA to Rush, Aug. 12, 1809, Schutz and Adair, *Spur of Fame,* 143.

38. JA to Rush, Aug. 23, 1805, and Nov. 11, 1807, Schutz and Adair, *Spur of Fame,* 36, 99; JA to Trumbull, Nov. [?], 1805, JAPM, reel 118; JA to William Cunningham, *Correspondence between the Hon. John Adams, Late President of the United States, and the Late William Cunningham* (Boston, 1823), 44; JA to MOW, July 20, 1807, *Adams-Warren Letters* 4:332.

39. JA, *Defence,* in Adams, *Works* 6:516; JA to Rush, Apr. 18, 1808, and Aug. 21, 1812, Schutz and Adair, *Spur of Fame,* 108, 243; JA to MOW, July 20, 1807, *Adams-Warren Letters* 4:332.

40. JA to Rush, Aug. 28, 1811, Schutz and Adair, *Spur of Fame,* 191; JA, "*Boston Patriot* Letters," in Adams, *Works* 9:241–48, 268.

41. The "Schlesinger Polls" can be found in *Life* 25 (November 1, 1948), 65–66, and the *New York Times Magazine,* July 29, 1962. Also see Charles A. Beard, *Economic Origins of Jeffersonian Democracy* (New York, 1915), 353; Kurtz, *Presiden-*

cy of JA, 407; Marshall Smelser, "The Jacobin Phrenzy: Federalism and the Menace of Liberty, Equality and Fraternity," *The Review of Politics* 13 (1951): 482; Dauer, *Adams Federalists,* 264–65; Brown, *Presidency of JA,* 215; Smith, *JA* 2:1058.

42. JA to AA, Mar. 17, 1797, JAPM, reel 383; Haraszti, *JA and the Prophets of Progress,* 57.

43. JA to JW, June 17, 1782, quoted in Adrienne Koch, ed., *The American Enlightenment: The Shaping of the American Experiment and a Free Society* (New York, 1965), 89. The *Philadelphia Aurora* quotation can be found in Stephen G. Kurtz, "John Adams," in Morton Borden, ed., *America's Ten Greatest Presidents* (Chicago, 1961), 36.

44. Malone, *Jefferson* 3:3–4; Lomask, *Burr* 1:297.

CHAPTER 20

1. JA to TBA, Dec. 17, 1800, JAPM, reel 399; JA to Jefferson, July 16, 1814, Cappon, *A-J Letters* 2:435.

2. AA to TBA, Jan. 15, Apr. 22, and June 12, 1801, JAPM, reels 400, 401; AA to JQA, Jan. 29, 1801, ibid., reel 400.

3. JA to Dexter, Mar. 23, 1801, ibid., reel 118; JA to Stoddert, Mr. 31, 1801, ibid., reel 118; JA to Charles Gadsden, Apr. 16, 1801, ibid., reel 118.

4. AA to JQA, Jan. 29, 1801, ibid., reel 400; JA to TBA, Sept. 4, 1801, and Feb. 1, 1802, ibid., reels 118, 401; JA to Cranch, May 23, 1801, ibid., reel 118.

5. Adams, *Works* 1:601; JA to Vanderkemp, Nov. 5, 1804 and Feb. 5, 1805, JAPM, reel 118; JA to Trumbull, July 8, 1805, ibid., reel 118. To compare Adams's life in retirement with that of Washington at Mount Vernon, see Ferling, *First of Men,* 324–46, 485–507.

6. JA to Vanderkemp, Sept. 29, 1802, JAPM, reel 118; Shaw, *Character of JA,* 273; JA to Waterhouse, Dec. 3, 1811, in Worthington Chauncey Ford, ed., *Statesman and Friend: Correspondence of John Adams with Benjamin Waterhouse, 1784–1822* (Boston, 1927), 71.

7. AA to JQA, Sept. 1, 1800, JAPM, reel 398.

8. Nagel, *Adams Women,* 172–73. For an example of AA's intrusiveness, see her advice to Louisa Catherine concerning the proper conduct to insure JQA's political success, found in AA to JQA, Sept. 13, 1801, JAPM, reel 401. For a different view of AA, see Gelles, "Abigail Industry," *WMQ* 45:667–69, 674–80; Shepherd, *Cannibals of the Heart,* 103.

9. Louisa Catherine Adams, *The Adventures of a Nobody,* JAPM, reel 269; Levin, *AA,* 397–99; Nagel, *Adams Women,* 173, 175; Shepherd, *Cannibals of the Heart,* 107.

10. Nagel, *Descent from Glory,* 82, 84–85; JQA to TBA, Nov. 28, 1801, JAPM, reel 401; AA to TBA, Feb. 7, 1802, reel 401.

11. AA to JQA, Oct. 22, 1803, JAPM, reel 402; TBA to AA, Mar. 20, 1802, ibid., reel 401; AA to TBA, Dec. 27, 1801, Nov. 7, 1802, and May 8, 1803, ibid., reels 401, 402.

12. Nagel, *Descent from Glory,* 82, 86–88; Levin, *AA,* 404; AA to TBA, Dec. 13, 1802, JAPM, reel 401.
13. Smith, *JA* 2:1107; Shaw, *Character of JA,* 285–86; Nagel, *Descent from Glory,* 95; AA to AAS, Dec. 8, 1808, De Windt Collection, MHS.
14. *ADA* 1:lxvii; 3:253.
15. Ibid., lxix. For JA's responses regarding the writing of an autobiography, see JA to JQA, Nov. 30, Dec. 6 and 22, 1804, JAPM, reel 401.
16. *ADA* 1:lxxx–lxxi; JA to Vanderkemp, Apr. 30, 1806, HSP.
17. Ibid., 3:335–36; Shaw, *Character of JA,* 280.
18. JA to Cranch, June 29, 1801, JAPM, reel 118; JA to JQA, Feb. 25, 1804, ibid., reel 118; JA to Smith, Dec. 5, 1812, ibid., reel 121; JA to Joseph Varnum, Dec. 7, 1812, ibid., reel 121; JA to Rush, Dec. 28, 1807, Schutz and Adair, *Spur of Fame,* 99.
19. JA to Rush, Apr. 18, 1808, Schutz and Adair, *Spur of Fame,* 107; JA to Cranch, May 23, 1801, JAPM, reel 118.
20. JA to Waterhouse, Oct. 29, 1805, Ford, *Statesman and Friend,* 31; JA to Robert Evans, Feb. 4, 1820, JAPM, reel 124; JA to Jefferson, July 13 and 15, 1813, and Nov. 13, 1815, Cappon, *A-J Letters* 2:357–58, 456; JA to Dalton, Jan. 19, 1797, Emmet Collection, NYPL.
21. JA to JQA, Dec. 6, 1804, and Jan. 9, 1805, JAPM, reels 403, 404.
22. JA to Trumbull, July 27 and Nov. [?], 1805, ibid., reel 118; JA to Vanderkemp, Aug. 23, 1806, Apr. 23, 1807, and Apr. 3, 1815, HSP; JA to Rush, Aug. 23, Sept. 30, 1805, Sept. 2, Nov. 11, 1807, and Apr. 18, 1808, Schutz and Adair, *Spur of Fame,* 35, 42, 94–95, 98–99, 113; JA to Waterhouse, July 12, 1811, Ford, *Statesman and Friend,* 65; Howe, *Changing Political Thought of JA,* 230–32.
23. JA to Vanderkemp, Feb. 5, 1805, JAPM, reel 118; JA to Rush, July 25, 1808, and May [?], 1812, ibid., reel 118; JA to Cunningham, Feb. 24, 1804, *Correspondence between the Hon. John Adams, Late President of the United States, and the Late Wm. Cunningham, Esq. . . . .* (Boston, 1823), 14.
24. Howe, *Changing Political Thought of JA,* 228, 237–38; JA to Noah Webster, Feb. 6, 1816, JAPM, reel 122; JA to Alexander Johnson, Nov. [?], 1814, ibid., reel 122.
25. JA to Rush, ND, 1812, JAPM, reel 112; JA to King, July 29, 1818, ibid., reel 123.
26. JA to Rush, Feb. 6, 1805, Schutz and Adair, *Spur of Fame,* 20.
27. JA to Everett, Aug. 24, 1811, JAPM, reel 118; JA to Plummer, Nov. 4, 1809, ibid., reel 118; JA to Vanderkemp, Aug. 9, 1813, HSP.
28. JA to Vanderkemp, Nov. 13, 1815, ibid., Reel 122; Levin, *AA,* 442; Nagel, *Descent from Glory,* 94–95; JA to Jefferson, Jan. 1, 1812, Cappon, *A-J Letters* 2:290.
29. JA to Jefferson, Feb. 3, 1812, Cappon, *A-J Letters* 2:296; JA to Vanderkemp, Dec. 15, 1809, JAPM, reel 118; AA to TBA, June 29, 1803, ibid. reel 402; AA to TBA, July 12, 1801, Adams, *Letters of Mrs. Adams* 2:246; AA to Elizabeth Shaw, June 5, 1809, ibid., 263–64; JA to Rush, Feb. 27, 1805 Schutz and Adair, *Spur of Fame,* 24; Levin, *AA,* 423, 427, 432, 450; AA to Wm. Shaw, Feb. 11, 1811, Shaw Papers, LC; AA to Abigail Adams Shaw, Aug. 13, 1815, and Mar. 30, 1816, ibid.;

AA to AAS, Mar. 18 and Oct. 3, 1808, De Windt Collection, MHS; JA to Vanderkemp, July 5, 1814, HSP.

30. JA to Vanderkemp, Feb. 5, 1805, and Aug. 23, 1806, JAPM, reel 118; JA to MOW, Jan. 8, 1776, *W-A Letters* 1:201; MOW to AA, Dec. 11, 1775, and July 3, 1776, *AFC* 1:338–39; 2:33.

31. Mercy Otis Warren, *History of the Rise, Progress and Termination of the American Revolution. Interspersed with Biographical, Political and Moral Observations*. 3 vols. (Boston, 1806), 3:303–9, 333, 335, 337, 392–93, 396; MOW to Catherine Macaulay, n.d., 1787, Dec. 18, 1787, July [?], 1789, and May 31, 1791, MOW Letterbook, MHS; MOW to Samuel Otis, n.d., 1787, ibid.

32. JA to MOW, July 20, 26, 30, Aug. 3 and 19, 1807, *Adams-Warren Letters* 4:332, 335, 408, 471–75.

33. MOW to JA, Aug. 27, 1807, ibid., 490–91.

34. *PAH* 15:183. Many of Adams's letters to the *Boston Patriot* were published in *Correspondence of the Late President Adams. Originally Published in the Boston Patriot* (Boston, 1809 [–1810]).

35. JA to Jefferson, June 25, 1813, Cappon, *A-J Letters* 2:333; JA to Rush, May 14, 1812, Schutz and Adair, *Spur of Fame,* 216; Shaw, *Character of JA,* 299.

36. AA to Wm. Cranch, Oct. 17, 1811, Adams, *Letters of Mrs. Adams,* 2:268–69; 269–71; Levin, *AA,* 453; Nagel, *Adams Women,* 141–42; JA to Stoddert, Oct. 15, 1811, JAPM, reel 118; AA to Col. Smith, July 23, Aug. 28 and Sept. 27, 1811, De Windt Collection, MHS; AA to Elizabeth Peabody, Aug. 24 and Oct. 22, 1811, Shaw Papers, LC.

37. Nagel, *Adams Women,* 144–45; JA to Vanderkemp, Aug. 9, 1813, HSP.

38. JA to Rush, Jan. 4, 1812, Schutz and Adair, *Spur of Fame,* 263. He later expressed similar sentiments on ambition in a letter to Jefferson. See JA to Jefferson, May 29, 1818, Cappon, *A-J Letters* 2:526.

39. JA to Jefferson, Mar. 24, 1801, Cappon, *A-J Letters* 1:264; AA to Jefferson, May 20, July 1, and Oct. 25, 1804, ibid., 269, 272, 280–81; Jefferson to AA, June 13, 1804, ibid., 270.

40. Jefferson to Rush, Dec. 5, 1811, Ford, *Writings of Jefferson* 9:300n; Rush to JA, Dec. 16, 1811, Butterfield, *Letters of Rush* 2:1110; L. H. Butterfield, "The Dream of Benjamin Rush: The Reconciliation of John Adams and Thomas Jefferson," *Yale Review* 40 (1950): 297–319; Cappon, *A-J Letters* 2:283–86; Malone, *Jefferson,* 6:94n, 95; Cunningham, *In Pursuit of Reason,* 329–31. For an excellent overview of the exchange, see Rush Welter, "The Adams-Jefferson Correspondence, 1812–1826," *AQ* 2 (1950): 234–50.

41. JA to Jefferson, May 1, 1812, June 30, July 3 and 15, 1813, Cappon, *A-J Letters* 2:30, 346–47, 350, 357.

42. JA to Rush, Oct. 25, 1809, Schutz and Adair, *Spur of Fame,* 158–59; Shaw, *Character of JA,* 312.

43. JA to Jefferson, Jan. 1, 1812, Aug. 15, 1823, and Feb. 25, 1825, Cappon, *A-J Letters* 2:290, 596, 609.

44. John M. Coleman, *Thomas McKean: Forgotten Leader of the Revolution* (Rockaway, N.J., 1975), 62–63; L. H. Butterfield, "John Adams's Correspondence with Hezekiah Niles: Some Notes and a Query," *Maryland Historical Magazine* 57 (1962): 150–54.

45. JA to Rush, July 19, 1812, Schutz and Adair, *Spur of Fame,* 239.
46. Rush to JA, Apr. 10, 1813, ibid., 279; JA to Julia Rush, Apr. 24, 1813, ibid., 281.
47. JA to AA, Jan. 28, 1799, JAPM, reel 393; JA to JQA, Nov. 13, 1816, ibid., reel 123; JA to Rush, Apr. 18, 1808, Schutz and Adair, *Spur of Fame,* 106; JA to Jefferson, May 3, 1816, Apr. 19, 1817, Oct. 20, 1818, Cappon, *A-J Letters* 2:471, 509, 529–30; JA to Vanderkemp, July 13, 1815, Adams, *Works* 10:170; JA to Tudor, Nov. 16, 1816, ibid., 10:231. Howard Ioan Fielding, "John Adams: Puritan, Deist, Humanist," *The Journal of Religion* 20 (1940); 33–46.
48. Adams, *Works,* 1:623. For Adams's lengthy correspondence with Morse, see JAPM, reels 122 and 123.
49. Smith, *JA* 2:1101; Shepherd, *Adams Chronicles,* 220; Nagel, *Descent from Glory,* 103, 132; Levin, *AA,* 406, 443.
50. Nagel, *Descent from Glory,* 92–93.
51. Shepherd, *Cannibals of the Heart,* 117.
52. AA to Vanderkemp, Feb. 23, 1814, JAPM, reel 417; JA to Vanderkemp, Dec. 14, 1819, ibid., reel 118; JA to Sewall, Nov. 4, 1815, ibid., reel 122; JA to Niles, Sept. 12, 1817, ibid., reel 123; JA to Rush II, Nov. 13, 1816, ibid., reel 123; JA to Jefferson, May 21, 1819, Cappon, *A-J Letters* 2:541; Levin, *AA,* 461; JA to Rush, Jan. 4, 1812, Schutz and Adair, *Spur of Fame,* 263; AA to Wm. Smith, Jr., Feb. 20, 1816, De Windt Collection, MHS; JA to Vanderkemp, June 23, 1817, HSP.
53. Withey, *Dearest Friend,* 312.
54. JA to Jefferson, Oct. 17, 1817, and Mar. 29, 1818, Cappon, *A-J Letters* 2:521, 526; JA to JQA, Sept. 5, 1816, JAPM, reel 122; Withey, *Dearest Friend,* 312; Levin, *AA,* 464, 484.
55. JA to Stoddert, Oct. 15, 1811, JAPM, reel 118; JA to Plummer, Nov. 4, 1809, ibid., reel 118; JA to Rush, Jan. 4, 1812, Schutz and Adair, *Spur of Fame,* 263.
56. Adams, *Works* 1:623; Nagel, *Adams Women,* 156–57; Levin, *AA,* 487; AA to Harriet Welsh, [Jan.–Feb.], 1818, Smith-Townsend Collection, MHS.
57. JA to Jefferson, Dec. 8, 1818, Cappon, *A-J Letters* 2:530.
58. Peter Whitney, *A Sermon Delivered on the Lord's Day Succeeding the Internment of Madam Abigail Adams . . . November 1, 1818* (Boston, 1819), n.p.; Nagel, *Adams Women,* 157.

CHAPTER 21

1. JA to JQA, Feb. 2, 1819, JAPM, reel 123; Nagel, *Descent from Glory,* 131; Josiah Quincy, *Figures of the Past, from the Leaves of Old Journals* (Boston, 1883), 64–65.
2. Nagel, *Descent from Glory,* 132.
3. JA to Jefferson, May 21, 1819, Cappon, *A-J Letters* 2:540; Jefferson to JA, Nov. 13, 1818, ibid., 2:529.
4. Smith, *JA,* 2:1123; JA to Morse, Dec. 2, 1815, JAPM, reel 122; JA to Jefferson, May 29, 1818, Feb. 13, May 2, 1819, Jan. 20, 1820, and Sept. 18, 1823, Cappon, *A-J Letters* 2:525, 533, 535, 559, 598; Adams, *Works* 1:633; JA to McKean, June 21, 1812, ibid. 10:16.
5. JA to Susanna Clark, June 22, 1819, JAPM, reel 123; JA to Ward Boylston,

Sept. 16, 1820, ibid., reel 124; JA to Louisa C. Adams, Oct. 21, 1820, ibid., 124; JA to Henry Channing, Nov. 3, 1820, ibid., reel 124; JA to Jefferson, Dec. 18, 1818, Cappon, *A-J Letters* 2:530; Adams, *Works* 1:627.

6. JA to the Artillery Co. of Boston, June 1, 1819, JAPM, reel 123; JA to Caroline De Windt, July 13 and Oct. 11, 1820, ibid., reel 124; Smith, *JA* 2:1130–31.

7. JA to George W. Adams, May 12 and 30, 1822, JAPM, reel 124; JA to Boylston, June 23, 1823, ibid., reel 124; JA to Jefferson, June 11, 1822, Cappon, *A-J Letters* 2:579; Quincy, *Figures of the Past,* 73; Adams, *Works* 1:639–40.

8. JA to Jefferson, May 29, 1818, Cappon, *A-J Letters* 2:526; Oliver, *Portraits of John and Abigail Adams,* 179–80.

9. Adams, *Works* 1:639; Cappon, *A-J Letters* 2:viii; JA to JQA, [?], 1824, JAPM, reel 124.

10. Jefferson to JA, Feb. 15, 1825, Cappon, *A-J Letters* 2:609; Quincy, *Figures of the Past,* 73–74.

11. JA to Louisa C. Adams, Apr. 27 and May 8, 1820, JAPM, reel 124; JA to Susanna Clark, Sept. 9, 1820, ibid., reel 124; JA to John Farmer, Jan. 16, 1823, ibid., reel 124.

12. JA to Jefferson, June 11, 1822, Cappon, *A-J Letters* 2:579; JA to Lafayette, Aug. 22, 1824, JAPM, reel 124.

13. Stewart and Clark, "Misanthrope or Humanitarian?" *NEQ* 28:234; Hecht, *JQA,* 436.

14. Malone, *Jefferson,* 6:447–48, 459–60, 468, 471, 496–98; Cunningham, *In Pursuit of Reason,* 348–49.

15. Adams, *Works* 1:634–35.

16. Ibid. 1:636.

AFTERWORD

1. Stewart and Clark, "Misanthrope or Humanitarian?" *NEQ* 28:234–35.

2. JA to King, Dec. 2, 1814, JAPM, reel 122; Merrill D. Peterson, *The Jefferson Image in the American Mind* (New York, 1960), 6.

3. L. H. Butterfield, "The Jubilee of Independence, July 4, 1826," *Virginia Magazine of History and Biography* 61 (1953): 12, 134; Peterson, *Jefferson Image,* 3–6. Many of the eulogies were soon reprinted in *A Selection of Eulogies, pronounced in the Several States, in Honor of those Illustrious Patriots and Statesmen, John Adams and Thomas Jefferson* (Hartford, 1826).

4. The JQA quotation is in Peterson, *Jefferson Image,* 4.

5. On Franklin's reputation, see Wright, *Franklin of Philadelphia,* 349–60, and John G. Cawelti, *Apostles of the Self-Made Man* (Chicago, 1965), 9–36, 191–92. On the shifting popular image of Jefferson, see Peterson, *Jefferson Image.*

6. JA to Rush, Apr. 4, 1790, Biddle, *Old Family Letters* 1:55; JA to Rush, July 23, 1806, Mar. 23 and Apr. 12, 1809, Schutz and Adair, *Spur of Fame,* 61, 137, 143; JA to Vanderkemp, Feb. 5, 1805, and Jan. 29, 1807, JAPM, reel 118; JA to Pickering, Aug. 6, 1822, ibid., reel 124; Morgan, *Meaning of Independence,* 9.

7. Julian Symons, ed., *Carlyle: Selected Works, Reminiscences and Letters* (Cam-

bridge, Mass., 1970), 297, 304, 326; John Stuart Mill, *Essay on Liberty* (New York, 1937), 195–209; Sidney Hook, *The Hero in History: A Study in Limitation and Possibility* (Boston, 1943), 152–53.

8. Arthur M. Schlesinger, Jr., "The Decline of Heroes," in Richard Thruelson and John Kobler, eds., *Adventures of the Mind: From the Saturday Evening Post* (New York, 1958), 105, 113; James MacGregor Burns, *Leadership* (New York, 1978), 3–4, 425–43; Thomas Bailey, *Presidential Greatness: The Image and the Man from George Washington to the Present* (New York, 1966), 170–82.

9. T. H. Breen, *The Character of the Good Ruler: A Study of Puritan Political Ideas in New England, 1630–1730* (New Haven, 1970), 55, 247, 249, 275.

10. *ADA* 1:8, 33, 37.

11. JA to Tudor, Nov. 25, 1816, JAPM, reel 123; JA to Robert Evans, Feb. 4 and Mar. 8, 1820, ibid., reel 124; JA to Rush II, July 22, 1816, ibid., reel 122; JA to Tudor, Nov. 16, 1816, Adams, *Works* 10:231.

12. JA to Robert Woln, Nov. 19, 1822, JAPM, reel 124; JA to Lloyd, Ap. 24, 1815, reel 122; JA to Rush II, July 22, 1816, ibid., reel 122; JA to Vanderkemp, Aug. 23, 1806, ibid., reel 118; JA to Tudor, June 1, 1817, ibid., reel 123; JA to Niles, Feb. 13, 1818, Adams, *Works* 10:285–86; JA to Wirt, Jan. 23, 1818, ibid., 10:277–79; *ADA* 2:119.

13. JA to Rush, Nov. 11, 1807, Nov. 11, 1807, Schutz and Adair, *Spur of Fame,* 97–98; JA to Wirt, Jan. 5, 1818, JAPM, reel 123; JA to Vanderkemp, Apr. 23, 1807, ibid., reel 118; JA to Morse, Nov. 29, 1815, ibid., reel 122; JA to Tudor, Feb. 9, 1819, Adams, *Works* 10:364–65; JA to Morse, Dec. 5, 1815, ibid., 190.

14. JA to Vanderkemp, May 29, 1814, JAPM, reel 122; JA to Lloyd, Feb. 6, 1815, Adams, *Works* 10:115.

15. JA to Evans, June 8, 1819, Adams, *Works* 10:380.

16. Adams, *Works* 1:58n.

17. JA to AA, July 3, 1776, *AFC* 2:28; JA to Jefferson, June 22, 1819, Cappon, *A-J Letters* 2:542; Paine, *Common Sense,* in Foner, *Complete Writings of Paine* 1:45; Jensen, *American Revolution Within America,* 109–26.

18. JA to Jefferson, Dec. 6, 1787, Cappon, *A-J Letters* 1:212.

19. Quoted in Cunningham, *In Pursuit of Reason,* xiii.

20. JA to AA, July 3, 1776, *AFC* 2:31.

Select Bibliography

John Adams did not begin to systematically preserve his papers until he entered the Continental Congress in 1774, but as he lived for more than fifty years thereafter, serving in a public capacity for about half those years and often engaging in protracted and extensive written communications with numerous acquaintances, his correspondence and other works eventually grew to mountainous proportions. For scholars, however, the greatest godsend with regard to Adams's papers was that they were preserved following his death. Unlike the case of George Washington, whose widow, Martha, destroyed his family letters and whose heir, Bushrod Washington, gave away or made irretrievable loans of some of his papers, John Quincy Adams inherited and carefully protected the materials that had belonged to John and Abigail Adams.

This remarkable collection of materials was not available to scholars until more than a century after John Adams's death. Beginning in 1954 and continuing in installments during the next five years, the Massachusetts Historical Society issued the Adams letters and papers in a microfilm edition, a vast undertaking that ultimately ran to 608 reels of film. The collection principally included materials left by John, Abigail, their children, Louisa Catherine Adams, the wife of John Quincy, Ann Harrod Adams, the wife of Thomas Boylston Adams, Col. Stephen Smith, Abigail Adams Smith's husband, and George Washington Adams and Charles Francis Adams, the sons of John Quincy and Louisa.

Nor is this the only collection of papers that relate to John and Abigail Adams. Letters of John Adams can be found in the Historical Society of Pennsylvania, the New-York Historical Society, and in several collections in the New York Public Library. Abigail's letters are more scattered. They can be found in the American Antiquarian Society, Boston Public Library, Houghton Library at Harvard University, Library of Congress, Massachusetts Historical Society, New-York Historical Society, and the Historical Society of Pennsylvania; virtually all her letters to her husband and children are within the Adams Papers at the Massachusetts Historical Society.

A considerable portion of this vast body of documentary material has been published. What will become the definitive edition of Adams papers commenced publication soon after the completion of the microfilm series. L. H. Butterfield, ed., *Diary and Autobiography of John Adams,* 4 vols. (Cambridge, Mass., 1961), came first, followed by L. H. Butterfield et al., eds., *Adams Family Correspondence* (Cambridge, Mass., 1963–); Kinvin Wroth and Hiller Zobel, eds., *Legal Papers of John Adams,* 3 vols. (Cambridge, Mass., 1965); L. H. Butterfield, ed., *The Earliest Diary of John Adams* (Cambridge, Mass., 1966); and Robert J. Taylor et al., eds., *Papers of John Adams* (Cambridge, Mass., 1977–).

This massive endeavor will ultimately supplant all previous publications of Adams papers, but as its completion in the near future is unlikely, several older editions remain useful. Charles Francis Adams, ed., *The Works of John Adams, Second President of the United States: With a Life of the Author,* 10 vols. (Boston, 1850–56), contains several volumes of letters written by Adams in the period following the War of Independence, an era yet untouched by the above cited *Papers of John Adams.* Some of the correspondence between John and Abigail can be found in Charles F. Adams, ed., *Letters of John Adams, Addressed to his Wife,* 2 vols. (Boston, 1841). The postwar correspondence between Adams and Benjamin Rush can be found in John A. Schutz and Douglass Adair, eds., *The Spur of Fame: Dialogues of John Adams and Benjamin Rush, 1805–1813* (San Marino, Calif., 1966). Additional letters between these two, most of it written after the war, appears in Alexander Biddle, ed., *Old Family Letters: Copied from the Originals for Alexander Biddle,* 2 vols., (Philadelphia, 1892). For letters exchanged between the Adamses and Thomas Jefferson, see Lester J. Cappon, ed., *The Adams-Jefferson Letters: The Complete Correspondence Between Thomas Jefferson and Abigail and John Adams,* 2 vols. (Chapel Hill, N.C., 1959). Other Adams letters appear in Worthington C. Ford, ed., *Statesman and Friend: Correspondence of John Adams with Benjamin Waterhouse, 1784–1822* (Boston, 1927) and [Anon.], *Correspondence between the Hon. John Adams, Late President of the United States, and the late William Cunningham, Esq.* (Boston, 1823). Communications between Adams and James and Mercy Warren can be found in two publications. One should see *Warren-Adams Letters: Being Chiefly a Correspondence among John Adams, Samuel Adams, and James Warren,* Massachusetts Historical Society, *Collections,* 2 vols., 72–73 (Boston, 1917, 1925), and Charles F. Adams, ed., "Correspondence between John Adams and Mercy Warren Relating to Her History of the American Revolution," Massachusetts Historical Society, *Collections,* 5th ser., vol. 4 (Boston, 1878).

Essays published by Adams during his wartime embassy to Europe have been gathered in James H. Hutson, ed., *Letters from a Distinguished American: Twelve Essays by John Adams on American Foreign Policy* (Washington, 1978). His official diplomatic correspondence during this period is available in Francis Wharton, ed., *The Revolutionary Diplomatic Correspondence of the United*

States, 6 vols. (Washington, 1899). President Adams's formal speeches are contained in James D. Richardson, ed., *A Compilation of the Messages and Papers of the Presidents,* 20 vols. (New York, 1897–1917). Selections from Adams's published writings are available in George A. Peek, Jr., ed., *The Political Writings of John Adams: Representative Selections* (Indianapolis, 1954).

Numerous collections of Abigail Adams's letters have been issued. Several missives exchanged between her and her husband are available in L. H. Butterfield et al., eds., *The Book of Abigail and John: Selected Letters of the Adams Family, 1762–1784* (Cambridge, Mass., 1975). Additional letters can be found in the several editions of Charles F. Adams, ed., *Letters of Mrs. Adams, the Wife of John Adams. With an Introductory Memoir,* 2 vols. (Boston, 1841); Charles F. Adams, ed., *Familiar Letters of John Adams and His Wife Abigail Adams, during the Revolution* (Boston, 1876); and Stewart Mitchell, ed., *New Letters of Abigail Adams* (Boston, 1947). A few family letters can also be found in Caroline Smith De Windt, ed., *Journal and Correspondence of Miss Adams, Daughter of John Adams,* 2 vols. (New York, 1841), and Caroline Smith De Windt, ed., *Correspondence of Miss Adams, Daughter of John Adams* (Boston, 1842).

Aside from the above cited editions of Abigail Adams Smith materials, the best published primary sources concerning a child of the Adamses are Charles F. Adams, ed., *Memoirs of John Quincy Adams,* 2 vols. (Philadelphia, 1874–77), and Allan Nevins, ed., *The Diary of John Quincy Adams* (New York, 1929).

Numerous editions of primary materials that relate to Adams and his times are available. Worthington C. Ford et al., eds., *The Journals of the Continental Congress,* 34 vols. (Washington, 1904–37), provide a record of that body during Adams's service, while Paul H. Smith et al., eds., *Letters of Delegates to Congress, 1774–1789* (Washington, 1976–), sheds light on Congress and its members' activities. To discover the thoughts of the most important figures during Adams's long public service, one should consult John C. Fitzpatrick, ed., *The Writings of Washington,* 39 vols. (Washington, 1931–44); W. W. Abbot et al., eds., *The Papers of George Washington* (Charlottesville, Va., 1983–); L. W. Labaree et al., eds., *The Papers of Benjamin Franklin* (New Haven, Conn., 1959–); Albert H. Smyth, ed., *The Writings of Benjamin Franklin,* 10 vols. (New York, 1905–1907); Harold C. Syrett and Jacob E. Cooke, eds., *Papers of Alexander Hamilton,* 26 vols. (New York, 1961–79); Julian P. Boyd et al., eds., *The Papers of Thomas Jefferson* (Princeton, 1950–); and A. A. Lipscomb and A. E. Bergh, *The Writings of Thomas Jefferson,* 20 vols. (New York, 1903).

Several important secondary works on John Adams and members of his family are available. The first biographer to draw on Adams's unpublished papers at the Massachusetts Historical Society was Page Smith. His acclaimed study, *John Adams,* 2 vols. (New York, 1962), remains a necessary work for anyone interested in Adams and his times. His biography supplanted Gilbert Chinard, *Honest John Adams* (Boston, 1933). Peter Shaw's *The Character of John Adams* (New York, 1976) is a fascinating portrait of Adams's personality. For a brief narrative overview of Adams's life, see Robert A. East, *John Adams* (Boston, 1978). Adams has even been the subject of a fictional biography. The interested reader should see Catherine Drinker Bowen, *John Adams and the American Revolution* (Boston, 1950).

Adams's political thought is treated in John Howe, *The Changing Political Thought of John Adams* (Princeton, N.J., 1966); Correa Moylan Walsh, *The Political Science of John Adams* (New York, 1915); Zoltan Haraszti, *John Adams and the Prophets of Progress* (Cambridge, Mass., 1952); Helen Saltzberg Saltman, "John Adams' Earliest Essays: The Humphrey Ploughjogger Letters," *WMQ* 3d ser., 37 (1980), 125–35; and Timothy Breen, "John Adams' Fight Against Innovation in the New England Constitution: 1776," *NEQ* 40 (1967): 501–20. For an excellent essay on the often paradoxical and enigmatic qualities of Adams's thought, see Edward Ryerson, "On John Adams," *AQ* 6 (1954): 253–58. Two important essays on Adams's thought during his last years are Joyce Appleby, "The New Republican Synthesis and the Changing Political Ideas of John Adams," *AQ* 25 (1973): 578–95, and Gordon S. Wood, *The Creation of the American Republic, 1776–1787* (Chapel Hill, N.C., 1969), especially chapter 14, "The Relevance and Irrelevance of John Adams."

Adams's religious outlook is scrutinized in Howard Ioan Fielding, "John Adams: Puritan, Deist, Humanist," *Journal of Religion* 20 (1940): 33–46. On Adams and early American warfare, see John Ferling, "'Oh that I was a Soldier': John Adams and the Anguish of War," *AQ* 36 (1984): 258–75. On Adams as a lawyer, and specifically his role in the Boston Massacre trials, see Hiller Zobel, *The Boston Massacre* (New York, 1970). For Adams and the coming of Independence, the following should be consulted: John W. Ellsworth, "John Adams: The American Revolution as a Change of Heart?" *HLQ* 28 (1965): 293–300; Albert Furtwangler, *American Silhouettes: Rhetorical Identities of the Founders* (New Haven, Conn., 1988), 40–63; Richard M. Gummere, "The Classical Politics of John Adams," *Boston Public Library Quarterly* 9 (1957): 167–82; and John M. Head, *A Time to Rend: An Essay on the Decision for American Independence* (Madison, Wis., 1968).

Surprisingly little has been written about Adams's congressional activities, save for his efforts to promote Independence. However, on his role in the creation of the revolutionary navy, see Frederick H. Hayes, "John Adams and American Sea Power," *American Neptune* 25 (1965): 35–45. Adams's wartime diplomatic missions are the subject of James H. Hutson, *John Adams and the Diplomacy of the American Revolution* (Lexington, Ky., 1980). His vicepresidential years are ably treated in Linda Dudik Guerrero, *John Adams' Vice*

Presidency, 1789–1797: The Neglected Man in the Forgotten Office (New York, 1982). On Adams's role in the titles controversy during the Washington presidency, see James H. Hutson, "John Adams' Titles Campaign," *NEQ* 41 (1968): 34–41.

The best general treatments of the Adams presidency include Ralph Adams Brown, *The Presidency of John Adams* (Lawrence, Kans., 1975); Stephen G. Kurtz, *The Presidency of John Adams: The Collapse of Federalism, 1795–1800* (Philadelphia, 1957); and John C. Miller, *The Federalist Era, 1789–1801* (New York, 1960). A good account that places the Adams administration in the context of the times can be found in Richard Buel, Jr., *Securing the Revolution: Ideology in America Politics, 1789–1815* (Ithaca, N.Y., 1972).

The politics of the era are traced in Manning J. Dauer, *The Adams Federalists* (Baltimore, 1953), but important works that should also be consulted include William Chambers, *Political Parties in a New Nation: The American Experience, 1776–1809* (New York, 1963); Joseph Charles, *The Origins of the American Party System: Three Essays* (Williamsburg, Va., 1956); and John F. Hoadley, *Origins of American Political Parties, 1789–1803* (Lexington, Ky., 1986).

Adams and the Quasi-War are appraised in Jacob E. Cooke, "Country Above Party: John Adams and the 1799 Mission to France," in Edward P. Willis, ed., *Fame and the Founding Fathers* (Bethlehem, Pa., 1967); William G. Anderson, "John Adams, the Navy, and the Quasi-War with France," *American Neptune* 30 (1970): 117–32; William J. Murphy, Jr., "John Adams: The Politics of the Additional Army, 1798–1800," *NEQ* 52: (1979), 234–49; Bernhard Knollenberg, "John Adams, Knox and Washington," American Antiquarian Society, *Proceedings* 55 (1946): 207–38; Alexander De Conde, *The Quasi-War; The Politics and Diplomacy of the Undeclared War With France, 1797–1801* (New York, 1966); E. F. Kramer, "John Adams, Elbridge Gerry and the Origins of the XYZ Affair," *Essex Institute Historical Collections* 94 (1968): 37–58; and Albert Hall Bowman, *The Struggle for Neutrality: Franco-American Diplomacy During the Federalist Era* (Knoxville, Tenn., 1974).

A specialized assessment of Federalist governance is provided by Leonard D. White, *The Federalists: A Study in Administrative History* (New York, 1948). Adams's role in the passage and enforcement of the Alien and Sedition acts is covered in John C. Miller, *Crisis in Freedom: The Alien and Sedition Acts* (Boston, 1951), and James Morton Smith, *Freedom's Fetters: The Alien and Sedition Laws and American Civil Liberties* (Ithaca, N. Y., 1966). On Adams's defeat in the Election of 1800, see Noble E. Cunningham, "Election of 1800," in Arthur M. Schlesinger, Jr. et al., eds., *The Coming to Power: Critical Presidential Elections in American History* (New York, 1971).

Aspects of Adams's long retirement years are treated in Donald H. Stewart and George P. Clark, "Misanthrope or Humanitarian?: John Adams in Retirement," *NEQ* 28 (1955): 216–36, and L. H. Butterfield, "John Adams' Correspondence with Hezekiah Niles: Some Notes and a Query," *Maryland Historical Magazine* 57 (1962): 150–54.

Several excellent interpretive essays on Adams are available. An essential starting point for understanding Adams's passion for recognition is the essay by Douglass Adair, "Fame and the Founding Fathers," in Trevor Colbourn, ed., *Fame and the Founding Fathers: Essays by Douglass Adair* (New York, 1974). One should also see Edmund S. Morgan, *The Meaning of Independence: John Adams, George Washington, and Thomas Jefferson* (New York, 1976), 3–25; "John Adams: The Puritan as Revolutionary," in Richard B. Morris, *Seven Who Shaped Our Destiny: The Founding Fathers as Revolutionaries* (New York, 1973), 72–114; and "Adams and the Taming of Power," in Adrienne Koch, *Power, Morals, and the Founding Fathers: Essays in the Interpretation of the American Enlightenment* (Ithaca, N. Y., 1961), 81–102. For a stimulating article, see Robert A. East, "The Strange Pause in John Adams' Diary," in Hans L. Trefousse, ed., *Toward a New View of America: Essays in Honor of Arthur C. Cole* (New York, 1977). Good for understanding how Adams saw himself is Earl N. Harbert, "John Adams' Private Voice: The Diary and Autobiography," *Tulane Studies in English* 15 (1967): 89–105. A provocative essay on Adams can be found in Bernard Bailyn, *Faces of Revolution: Personalities and Themes in the Struggle for American Independence* (New York, 1990).

Before plunging into the literature on Abigail Adams, it would be advisable to read Edith B. Gelles, "The Abigail Industry," *WMQ,* 3d ser., 45 (1988): 656–83. Three fine biographies of Abigail Adams have appeared in recent years. One should see Charles W. Akers, *Abigail Adams: An American Woman* (Boston, 1980); Lynne Withey, *Dearest Friend: A Life of Abigail Adams* (New York, 1981); and Phyllis Lee Levin, *Abigail Adams: A Biography* (New York, 1987). In addition, Edith B. Gelles is the author of three important pieces that focus on different aspects of Abigail's life. Her essays are as follows: "Abigail Adams: Domesticity and the American Revolution," *NEQ* 52 (1979): 500–21; "A Virtuous Affair: The Correspondence between Abigail Adams and James Lovell," *AQ* 39 (1987): 252–69; and "Gossip: An Eighteenth-Century Case," *Journal of Social History* 22 (1989): 667–83. The most negative view of Abigail Adams can be found in two works by Paul C. Nagel, *Descent from Glory: Four Generations of the John Adams Family* (New York, 1983), and *The Adams Women: Abigail and Louisa Adams, Their Sisters and Daughters* (New York, 1987).

The sons of John and Abigail are treated by Nagel in the former study, Abigail Adams Smith in the latter. Not surprisingly, John Quincy Adams has received more scholarly attention than any of the Adams children. For psychohistorical works on John Quincy that also touch on his parents, see David F. Musto, "The Youth of John Quincy Adams," American Philosophical Society, *Proceedings* 113 (1969): 269–82, and Joseph E. Illick, "John Quincy Adams:

The Maternal Influence," *Journal of Psychohistory* 4 (1976): 185–95. Good treatments of his early years can be found in Marie B. Hecht, *John Quincy Adams: A Personal History of an Independent Man* (New York, 1972); Robert A. East, *John Quincy Adams, the Critical Years: 1758–1794* (New York, 1962); Samuel F. Bemis, *John Quincy Adams and the Foundations of American Foreign Policy* (New York, 1949), and Jack Shepherd, *Cannibals of the Heart: A Personal Biography of Louisa Catherine and John Quincy Adams* (New York, 1980). In addition to the works previously cited, the best available treatments of Abigail Adams Smith can be found in Katherine Metcalf Roof, *Colonel William Smith and Lady* (Boston, 1929), and in the more popular Lida Mayo, "Miss Adams in Love," *American Heritage* 16 (1965): 36–39, 80–89.

The Adamses sat for many artists. Details on these paintings are available in Andrew Oliver, *Portraits of John and Abigail Adams* (Cambridge, Mass., 1967), and Andrew Oliver, *Portraits of John Quincy Adams and His Wife* (Cambridge, Mass., 1970).

The Massachusetts Historical Society has published numerous "picture books" on early America. Two of these pamphlets deal with the Adamses and are of interest. See Howard C. Rice, Jr., ed., *The Adams Family in Auteuil, 1784–1785, As Told in the Letters of Abigail Adams* (Boston, 1956) and *John Adams & a "Signal Tryumph"* (Boston, 1982).

For additional secondary and primary works that pertain to the great events of John Adams's lifetime, see the notes that accompany this study. Full citation of a particular work may be found in the list of abbreviations that precede the notes or in its first appearance in the notes.

Index

About the Author

JOHN FERLING is a professor of history at West Georgia College and has written extensively on the Revolutionary War period. He is the author of *The First of Men: A Life of George Washington; A Wilderness of Miseries: War and Warriors in Early America; The Loyalist Mind;* and *Struggle for a Continent: The Wars of Early America.* He is the editor of *The World Turned Upside Down: The American Victory in the War of Independence;* and *The Homefront in the American Revolution.*